INDIAN AFFAIRS ANNUAL 2008

INDIAN AFFAIRS ANNUAL 2008

(In 9 Vols.)

Vol. 3

Chronology of Events

(18-06-2007 to 30-08-2007)

Shailendra Sengar

KALPAZ PUBLICATIONS

KALPAZ PUBLICATIONS

DELHI - 110052

Indian Affairs Annual 2008

Rs. 6300 (Set)

ISBN: 81-7835-693-7 (Set)
ISBN: 81-7835-696-1 (Vol. 3)

Published in 2008 in India by
Kalpaz Publications
C-30, Satyawati Nagar,
Delhi-110052
E-mail: kalpaz@hotmail.com
Phone : 9212729499

Laser Type Setting by: Quick Media, Delhi
Printed at : Singhal Print Media, Delhi

INDIAN AFFAIRS ANNUAL 2008

Chronology of Events

(18-06-2007 to 30-08-2007)

1563. (18-6-2007) NEW DELHI : An official meeting of the NDA was held today under the Chairmanship of Shri A.B. Vajpayee, and the Convenor Shri George Fernandes. The NDA at this official meeting today took a formal, duly authorized decision about the forthcoming elections to the office of the President of India. It is our unanimous view that the most qualified and suitable candidate for this high office is only Shri Bhairon Singh Shekhawat. He combines a life time's experience of dedicated public service with rare qualities of head and heart. A public figure of eminence, high repute, unmatched credentials, Shri Bhairon Singh Shekhawat has discharged his latest responsibilities as the country's Vice President and Chairman of Rajya Sabha, entirely beyond party affiliations and with impeccable secular credentials. Convinced of this the NDA is unanimously of the view that Shri Bhairon Singh Shekhawat, as a non party and an independent candidate would be the most appropriate choice. In light of all this the NDA wholeheartedly supports Shri Bhairon Singh Shekhawat as an independent candidate for the high office of the President of India. Shri Bhairon Singh Shekhawat's victory is definite.

1564. (18-6-2007) NEW DELHI : Financial Intelligence Unit-India (FIU-IND) has been admitted as the member of the Egmont Group at its recent Plenary Session at Hamilton, Bermuda. The Egmont Group is the international organization for stimulating cooperation amongst FIUs across the globe and has FIUs of more than 100 countries as its members. Membership has been granted to FIU-IND after verification of its operational status by the Egmont Group and on being satisfied with legal position and ability of FIU-IND to share information with foreign FIUs. Membership of the Egmont Group, apart from meeting an important requirement of the Financial Action Task Force (FATF), will facilitate and enhance exchange of information by FIU-IND with its counterpart FIUs. Admission of FIU-IND as a member of the Egmont Group is a major step forward in India joining the international community in its fight against money laundering and terrorism financing. Indian Government continues to remain committed to fight the menace of money laundering and financing of terrorism with its full might. The global community is united in its fight against money laundering and financing of terrorism. On its part, India has enacted the Prevention of Money Laundering Act, 2002 (PMLA) which has been brought into force from 1st July, 2005. Financial Intelligence Unit-India has also been set up to receive information relating to large cash and suspicious transactions under PMLA from various entities in financial sector and disseminate information in appropriate cases to relevant intelligence/ law enforcement agencies. FIU-IND has, till now, received more than 27 lakh Cash Transaction Reports and more than 1100 Suspicious Transaction Reports from various entities in financial sector. FIU-IND is also authorized to share information relating to suspect financial transactions with its counterpart FIUs.

1565. (18-6-2007) NEW DELHI : The services in the Iron Ore Mining Industry will continue as a public utility service under the Industrial Dispute Act, 1947 for another six months with effect from today, i.e., June 18, 2007. In a notification issued here, the Labour Ministry said that this is being done in the public interest. Earlier, the services in the industry were declared a public utility for six months from June 18, 2006 and subsequently for another six months from December 18, 2006. The employees in the said industry would, among other things, be required to give notice to their employers six weeks in advance of proceeding on strike so that conciliatory proceedings could be started. During the conciliatory proceedings and seven days after their completion, the employees cannot go on strike.

1566. (18-6-2007) NEW DELHI : The Defence Minister, Shri AK Antony has asked the top brass of the Armed Forces to draw up a roadmap for the transformation of the Forces to meet varied security challenges. Inaugurating the two-day Unified Commanders'-in-Chief Conference here today, Shri Antony said the transformation plan must be developed under the overarching principle of 'jointness' for highest efficacy. He expressed confidence that the central idea of the transformation will be given the required shape so that our future perspective plans are not only efficient and cost effective but also keep pace with the changing times. Shri Antony said, terrorism and the role of non-state players are the major challenges facing us. The Minister stressed the need for developing a 'security paradigm' that is relevant to the emerging multi-polar world order. "The new paradigm ideally should be a mix of security cooperation, developing strategic partnerships and deterrence-in consonance with our security and strategic interests. Our strategic policy must reorient our relations with major powers, developing economies and our neighbours"' he said. Shri Antony lamented that while Globalisation has been accompanied by widely accepted international rules to cope with its economic and commercial dimensions, similar mechanisms 'are either absent or are still in the process of evolution' when it comes to dealing with terrorism and the emergence of non-state players. He said, often these mechanisms are affected by vested interests and that we should articulate the terms which serve the interests of the nations most effectively. He called upon the Commanders to factor the 'changing security architecture' while evolving our long-term strategic thought because the global war on terror has shifted the focus of major powers to the Asian region leading to realignments. He informed the gathering that the Eleventh Army Plan document has been finalized and is expected to be approved soon. "This will help in planned development, modernization and upgradation of the Army, by ensuring timely actions for acquisition of requisite weapons and equipment. It should also help in enhancing efficiency in planned expenditure of the budget allotted to the Armed Forces," he said. Shri Antony delved on the security scenario in our immediate neighbourhood and beyond. He said, the most crucial challenge facing us in the near future is the growing instability in our neighbourhood. The Minister said, the rising tide of religious fundamentalism and cross-border terrorism continues unabated and this has affected our regional security environment too. Referring to Afghanistan, Shri Antony said the situation there has deteriorated recently due to the resurgence of Taliban. "Certain vested interests are trying to scuttle our role in rebuilding Afghanistan. We are committed to support this process and help Afghanistan to emerge as a stable, democratic state", he said. The Defence Minister expressed concern at the continuing cases of suicide and fratricide in the Forces and asked the top Commanders to address the issue most urgently. "I once again urge you all to take all possible steps to reduce the stress on our Jawans. I wish to emphasize the urgent need to lay adequate emphasis on the humanitarian side through a more humane man management. There must be more opportunities for enhanced interaction between senior and junior officers-both qualitatively and quantitatively. The officers and commanders have to become more accessible to Jawans and promptly attend to their grievances". Shri Antony said the Government is committed to achieve absolute transparency and fairness in our defence deals. He said, the Offset Policy seeks to provide equal opportunity to medium and small-scale entrepreneurs. "This will assist smaller players in upgrading their engineering and manufacturing skills", the Minister said.

1567. (18-6-2007) NEW DELHI : Shri Ashwani Kumar, Minister of State for Industry, has said that India's economic growth story was unique in as much as overall economic growth had been achieved in the country consistent with the Government's commitment to social justice and inclusive agenda. The Minister while delivering the keynote address at a session on "Rapid emergence of India and China as global economic powers and their impact on the developed world" at an UBS CEO Forum in Florence, Italy, yesterday said that growth in the emerging economies has positively impacted on consolidation of the developed economies themselves by spurring demand and supply, ensuring economies of scale, increasing the global labour force and ensuring a coherence in the global development agenda. The Minister stated that the embrace of the market economies by India and China will make possible emergence of an international treaty based regime towards a fully integrated global economy. He appealed to the investors to consider the resilience of India's democratic institutions as the nation's strength and rejected the debate between democracy and freedom as spurious exercise. Infrastructure development in India requires an estimated expenditure of 550 billion dollars in the medium term, and at least one third of the resources can be obtained through FDI. "The manufacturing sector in India was likely to grow by 12 percent per annum by 2010 which could generate additional 1.6 million jobs every year. The UPA Government under Prime Minister Manmohan Singh was committed to ensuring distributive equities by enlarging opportunities for wealth generation and without compromising human dignity and moral integrity. Further, the SEZ policy in the country was being fine tuned to ensure transparency and employment opportunities for those who were displaced from the land for developmental projects", he said. Later, answering questions from the participants, Shri Kumar stated that the National Rural Guarantee Programme, the Bharat Nirman Programme and the Urban Renewable Programme in addition to a host of other initiatives were intended to generate large-scale employment for the unemployed youth of India. Other key participants in the Session included Shri Mukesh Ambani, CMD, Reliance Industries, Shri Sanjay Chandra, MD, Unitech Limited, Dr. Fu Yuning, Director & President, China Merchants Group, Eddie Wang, President, China Minsheng Banking Corporation.

1568. (19-6-2007) NEW DELHI : In a bid to bring major simplifications of service tax related issues, Government proposes to issue two comprehensive circulars-one on technical issues and the other on procedural issues in lieu of all the existing clarifications issued so far. For this purpose, two draft circulars were placed here today on the CBEC website (www.cbec.gov.in). These circulars have taken into account the report submitted by Shri T.R. Rustagi, views and suggestions received from the trade and industry associations, departmental officers and others. Central Board of Excise & Customs has solicited views, comments and suggestions on the draft circulars, particularly suggestion for inclusion of any additional issues in the proposed circulars, from the trade and industry associations, departmental officers and others. The views, comments and suggestions may be sent so as to reach CBEC.

1569. (19-6-2007) NEW DELHI : There have been reports in a section of press wherein the delimitation exercise being undertaken by the Delimitation Commission of India has been criticized. The Delimitation Commission has in its purview all the Lok Sabha constituencies and all the Assembly constituencies in India. The Commission has completed its work in respect of 20 States, viz. Goa, Pondicherry, Tripura, Mizoram, Kerala, Rajasthan, West Bengal, Punjab, Chhatisgarh, Maharashtra, Sikkim, Delhi, Gujarat, Orissa, Uttar Pradesh, Himachal Pradesh, Haryana, Madhya Pradesh, Uttaranchal and Andhra Pradesh. Karnataka, Tamil Nadu and Meghalaya are likely to be notified shortly. In Manipur, the High Court has struck down the 2001 census figures and the matter is pending in the Supreme Court of India. The Commission is at the final stage of its work so far as the States of Assam and Jharkhand are concerned. The public sittings in the State of Jharkhand were scheduled on 31st May and 1st June 2007 whereas in Assam the public sittings were to commence on 16th June 2007 but due to agitations in these States and after considering the prevailing situation in Assam and Jharkhand, the Commission, by reasoned orders, have unanimously decided not to hold the public sittings and instead invite further suggestions and objections from the public by giving fresh notice in the newspapers. The updating of National Register of Citizens (NRC) in accordance with "Assam Accord" is the primary issue in the State of Assam. The demand is that the delimitation process be deferred till the time the NRC is updated. In Jharkhand, the only grievance is that the number of Scheduled Tribe seats in Lok Sabha and State Legislative Assembly should not be reduced. The problems in both the States are outside the purview of the Commission. The process of delimitation of the assembly and parliamentary constituencies in terms of the Delimitation Act 2002 is mandatory and is followed by the Commission meticulously. The statutory provisions regarding consulting the Associate Members, inviting suggestions and objections from the public and holding public sittings are being followed. Large number of meetings are held with the Associate Members before preparing the draft proposals. For example, 11 meetings were held with the Associate Members from Assam before preparing the draft proposals. Consultations with the Associate Members are done strictly in accordance with law. Every constituency in the working paper is discussed with them and their views are given due importance. Reservation for Scheduled Castes and Scheduled Tribes is done strictly in accordance with law. Only those seats are reserved where the population of Scheduled Castes/Scheduled Tribes is comparatively large. Where there is a cluster of Scheduled Caste seats, the Commission makes an effort to distribute them, however, in the process a constituency with a small scheduled caste population cannot be reserved leaving the one with large scheduled castes population. There is total transparency in the Commission's working. The Commission cannot and would not permit gerrymandering which is anathema to the delimitation process. So far as the administrative units are concerned, the Delimitation Act and the Commission's guidelines are very clear. Within a State, district is the largest administrative unit thereafter either the revenue units or the development units are adopted, in consultation with the Associate Members. The administrative units within a district are only broken if it is necessary to adjust the population. By and large the administrative units are kept intact. The final notification in respect of Rajasthan was published more than a year back. Dausa Parliamentary constituency has been reserved for the Schedule Tribes on the basis of the tribe population in the constituency. Mr. Sachin Pilot, the Congress Member of Parliament has been in touch with the Commission at all relevant stages. He met the Chairman a number of times. The Press report that Commission's proceedings were not transparent is wholly unjustified. The Commission is at the fag end of its work. 90% work has been completed. All the constituencies have been formed in accordance with the Delimitation Act and the guidelines.

1570. (19-6-2007) NEW DELHI : The first meeting of the National Board for Micro, Small and Medium Enterprises will be held here tomorrow under the

Chairmanship of Shri Mahabir Prasad, Union Minister for Micro, Small and Medium Enterprises. The Board has been constituted as per the provisions of the Micro, Small and Medium Enterprises Development Act, 2006 for playing pro-active role in facilitating and coordinating the inter institutional linkages among the organizations of Central/State Governments for the growth and development of Micro, Small and Medium Enterprises (MSME).

1571. (19-6-2007) NEW DELHI : The following is the full text of External Affairs Minister Shri Pranab Mukherjee's address at a function yesterday jointly organised by the Embassy of India in Jakarata and the Indonesian Council on World Affairs on "India's Growing Engagement with East Asia": Dr. Arifin M. Siregar, Chairman of the Governing Body of the Indonesian Council on World Affairs and Distinguished Guests, It gives me great pleasure to be here today to address this distinguished and knowledgeable gathering on the topical subject of India's growing engagement with East Asia. I have chosen to speak on this topic for a number of reasons. As many of you would be aware, India has undergone significant changes over the last decade and a half. During the same period, the international order has seen a profound structural transformation. Consequently, the foreign policy of India has had to re-formulate its priorities. Among the major changes, the economic story is well known. India has achieved an average growth rate of 9% in the last three years and hopes to push it even further. Driven so significantly by domestic consumption, we have had to create our own model of growth. There is perhaps no precedent for change taking place on such a scale within a democratic framework. An era of 10% growth, which appears within sight, clearly calls for a different approach, given that closer integration with the global economy is a sine qua non for most developing countries. Expanding foreign trade and attracting greater foreign investment flows requires recalibration and reallocation of our energies. We have also taken note of the shift in the economic centre of gravity of the global economy towards the Asia Pacific region. Amidst this scenario, energy cooperation, with particular emphasis on supply and distribution in the long term, is among the subjects acquiring greater salience in our thinking. In this context, East and South-East Asia have come to assume an important place in our policy priorities. Talking about this region, one of its unique, yet universally recognized features is the importance we attach to mutual respect and peaceful coexistence between nations. Within the nations themselves, the importance given to family values, culture and traditions needs no elaboration. When we talk about a family or comity of nations, it is understood in the right perspective. The freedom of expression which we espouse finds reflection in the strong democratic system that prevails in our countries. An inclusive government, responsive to the concerns of our peoples, gives us the needed energy to deal with the diverse and pluralistic societies our countries represent. Our shared historical traditions give us yet another reason for working together. India's policy towards ASEAN nations and the nations of the Pacific was conceived in the context of various factors, including national interest, security concerns and economic imperatives. This policy was prompted by significant changes in the global political and economic scenario and by our own adoption of economic reforms and liberalization. ASEAN's economic, political and strategic importance in the Asia Pacific region and its potential to become a major partner of India in trade and investment were significant elements in our approach to the region. India's "Look East" policy can thus be described as the search for political and economic convergence with this most dynamic region of Asia which, through its emergence as an economic powerhouse of the world economy, provided India with a model worthy of emulation. India has pursued its "Look East" policy and developed multi-faceted relationships with countries of the ASEAN region and the South Pacific within a multilateral as well as a bilateral context. We have been actively engaged with the ARF and as a Full Dialogue Partner of the ASEAN since 1996 and have been having annual summits since 2002. India also participated in the East Asia Summits held in Kuala Lumpur and Cebu in December, 2005 and January, 2007 respectively. We signed the "India-ASEAN Partnership for Peace, Progress and Shared Prosperity" at the 3rd India-ASEAN Summit in Vientiane in November, 2004. The Agreement envisages strengthening cooperation in the UN and the multilateral fora, including the WTO, combating international terrorism, transnational crimes, human trafficking, cyber and economic crimes, sea piracy and cooperation in capacity building.

1572. (19-6-2007) NEW DELHI : The third India-Indonesia Joint Commission meeting was held yesterday in Jakarta. A Joint Press Statement was issued after the meeting. The following is the full text of the Joint Press Statement: On this day, Monday, 18th of June 2007, the meeting of the Third Joint Commission between Indonesia and India was held in Jakarta and Co-Chaired by the Minister of Foreign Affairs of Indonesia HE Dr. N. Hassan Wirajuda and the Minister of External Affairs of India HE Mr. Pranab Mukherjee. The first two meetings were conducted in Yogyakarta in 2003 and in New Delhi in 2005 respectively. Today's meeting assumes great significance since it is the first meeting after the forging of a "New Strategic Partnership" by President Susilo Bambang Yudhoyono and Prime Minister Manmohan Singh during the State Visit of the former to India in November 2005. The meeting of the Joint Commission was convened in a warm and friendly atmosphere. The Delegations from both countries discussed and exchanged views on the various sectors of cooperation to explore and expand cooperation in a range of fields, including political, defense and security, transportation, economy and investment, health, education and training, science and technology, tourism and culture, technical cooperation and legal cooperation. The Agreed Minutes were signed by both Heads of Delegation to signify their intention to strengthen and deepen bilateral cooperation bearing in mind the challenges facing Asia's two largest and pluralistic democracies. With an intention to implement the New Strategic Partnership, both countries have agreed upon a Plan of Action to implement this partnership in a clear and measurable manner. Some of the highlights of bilateral relations discussed during the Joint Commission Meeting include the following: The appreciation of both countries on the convening of the First Joint Defense Cooperation Committee between Indonesia and India on 12-14 June 2007 in Jakarta, after the ratification of the Defense Cooperation Agreement between Indonesia and India in December 2006; The significant increase in the exchange of visits between members of parliament, government and military officials, trade missions, academicians, and "people to people" exchanges from both countries over the past few years; Enhancing economic, investment and trade relations through the diversification of the trade basket and addressing the impediments to the expansion of trade and investment, with the aim of reaching the two-way trade volume target of US$ 10 billion by 2010, as mentioned in the Joint Declaration of 2005; The meeting identified new fields of cooperation, such as Special Economic Zone cooperation, development of alternative energy sources, the conclusion of a Mutual Legal Assistance Treaty (MLAT) in Criminal Matters and Extradition Treaty, cooperation in health and pharmaceuticals, oil and gas, and mining, biotechnology and women's empowerment. The Indian delegation expressed appreciation at the extension of Visa on Arrival facilities to Indian nationals by Indonesia and also take note to simplify of Indian visa grants for Indonesian nationals; The meeting discussed the strengthening of cooperation in information technology, nuclear technology, biotechnology, tele-education, tele-health, and strengthening cooperation in space technology, especially after the successful establishment of the Second Telemetry Tracking and Command Centre in Biak by ISRO and the recent piggy back launch of the LAPAN TUBSAT Micro Satellite by India in January 2007; The Indonesian side welcomed the Indian Prime Minister's offer to assist in the restoration work at the Prambanan Temple Complex through the Archaeological Survey of India; both sides agreed to cooperate closely in the hospitality and tourism sector as well. Both sides have also agreed to enhance technical cooperation and cooperation in education through the granting of scholarships to students of both countrievs. As a symbol of India's contribution to the recovery of Aceh, a Memorandum of Understanding concerning the Setting Up of a Vocational Training Centre for the Construction Sector in Aceh was signed by the Minister of Public Works of Indonesia Mr. Djoko Kirmanto and the Minister of External Affairs of India. The Ministers emphasized the unique characteristics of the relations between India and Indonesia as Asia's two largest and pluralistic democracies and recalled that the two countries have had contacts in history for more than of 2000 years. They expressed their confidence that the outcome of the Joint Commission Meeting would build a strong foundation for Indonesia and India to continue cooperation for the mutual benefit of their peoples.

1573. (19-6-2007) NEW DELHI : 59 candidates have qualified for interview/ Personality Test on the basis of results of the written part of the Indian Economic Service/Indian Statistical Service Examination, 2006 held by Union Public Service Commission from 18th to 20th November 2006. Out of these 59 candidates, 21 are for the Indian Economic Service and 38 for the Indian Statistical Service. The candidature of these candidates is provisional. In accordance with the Rules of the Examination, all these candidates have to fill up the Detailed Application Form (DAF), which will be supplied to them by the Commission before being called for Interview/Personality Test.

1574. (19-6-2007) NEW DELHI : A Memorandum of Understanding was signed between the Indira Gandhi Rashtriya Uran Academy (IGRUA) and Canadian Aviation Electronics (CAE) Inc. a Canadian Company, for the purpose of management contract regarding IGRUA's flight school operations. The MoU was signed in the presence of the Minister of Civil Aviation Shri Praful Patel and other Senior officials of the Ministry of Civil Aviation in Paris today.

1575. (19-6-2007) NEW DELHI : A Memorandum of Understanding between the Airport Authority of India (AAI) and Canadian Aviation Electronics (CAE) Inc. of Canada was signed in Paris today to form a Joint Venture between the AAI and CAE to establish the National Flying Training Institute (NFTI) at Gondia in Maharashtra. The MoU was signed in the presence of the Minister of Civil Aviation Shri Praful Patel and other senior officials of the Ministry of Civil Aviation. The purpose of the MoU is to establish business principles for collaboration between AAI and CAE for the establishment of NFTI.

1576. (19-6-2007) NEW DELHI : The telecom sector further expanded with the net addition of 6.3 million in the number of telecom subscribers during the month of May 2007. While the addition in the GSM and CDMA segments was 5 million and 1.5 million respectively, the fixed line segment declined by 0.2 million. Maharashtra, Tamil Nadu and Andhra Pradesh circles have added more than 4.5 lakh subscribers each. As a result, the total number of telephones in the country is now more than 218.06 million registering a growth of 46.9 per cent between June 2006 and May 2007. The overall teledensity improved further to 19.25% in May 2007. In the GSM segment, Tamil Nadu telecom circle added more than 4.1 lakh subscribers. While in the CDMA segment, Maharashtra telecom circle added 1.49 lakh subscribers during the period. The growth of broadband connections improved further and at the end of April 2007, about 2.38 million broadband connections were provided and coverage of broadband connectivity by public sector service providers has reached 1039 cities. The total number of existing ISP licencees is now 377.

1577. (19-6-2007) NEW DELHI : Mrs. Anupama Singh, President Army Wives Welfare Association (AWWA), inaugurated a Courier Collection Centre, for empowering persons with disabilities, here today. Shri Subhashish Chackraborty, the Managing Director of D.T.D.C Courier & Cargo Ltd. was also present. The Army has a large number of soldiers who suffer injuries and disabilities due to a variety of reasons while in service to include injuries sustained in anti militancy operations. Ventures such as this aim at their economic rehabilitation as well as that of the kin of army personnel so challenged. DTDC Couriers & Cargo Ltd. with a large national and international network & AWWA, which enjoys the support of the Indian Army, has an edge over the others in providing the much needed logistics & man-management support to such ventures. Such ventures also aim to Reach the Unreached and establish a link between rehabilitation professionals with those in need.

1578. (19-6-2007) NEW DELHI : A National Manufacturing Portal-the first of its kind in the country-was launched at a function in New Delhi this morning 19th June, 2007 by Dr. V. Krishnamurthy, Chairman, National Manufacturing Competitiveness Council (NMCC) as a major new initiative which will enhance the competitiveness of India's manufacturing sector especially the small and medium enterprises (SMEs) through the use of information technology and enable them to compete more effectively in today's globalised environment. The Portal (www.nmcc-vikas.gov.in or www.nmcc-vikas.in) has been created by NMCC with active support from the Microsoft Corporation (India) Pvt Limited as a part of the " Project Vikas" which is aimed at making the Indian SME sector competitive and to help establish "Made in India" as a global brand. Highlighting the importance of the Portal, Dr. Krishnamurthy said: "Through an ICT based intervention model, Project Vikas will empower India's SME sector and give it a competitive edge in the global market. NMCC is delighted to partner with Microsoft in this Public Private Partnership endeavour to improve the overall competitiveness of Indian manufacturing through skill enhancement. Project Vikas aims to develop knowledge networks through the creation of R & D linkages, capacity building with regional training institutes, sharing of best practices and enable linkage with the SME cluster ecosystem. We at NMCC are convinced that with suitable inputs of information technology, the competitiveness of Indian SMEs will significantly improve". Elaborating on Project Vikas and partnership with NMCC as a model of Public-Private Partnership, Mr. Ravi Venkatesan, Chairman/Microsoft Corporation (India) Pvt Ltd. said: "In today's extremely competitive global environment, it is imperative that the Indian manufacturing sector gears up and draws out a winning strategy for making a global footprint while achieving domestic successes. ICT can be a critical enabler for bringing about this leap into the next phase of growth. Driven by this sentiment, we have worked with the NMCC to deliver on our Project Vikas programme, which entails a holistic and scalable five year action plan to enhance the competitiveness of India's SME sector by leveraging ICT". Project Vikas fits in perfectly with the Microsoft Unlimited Potential-its global commitment to close the digital divide by creating new products and programmes that would help bring social and economic opportunity to an estimated 5 billion people across the globe who are currently not realising the benefits of technology, he added. Highlights of the National Manufacturing Portal include: Knowledge base on different manufacturing sectors/ sub-sectors; Resources on Indian and international clusters; intellectual property rights (IPR) information to achieve niche competitiveness; Know the Micro Small and Medium Enterprises (MSMEs) through MSME Data Bank; Latest articles and publications in the area of competitiveness; Market information to improve market access; Credit and finance related areas for SMEs including various policies, schemes etc.; Empowering SMEs through ICT-such as how to analyse ICT needs at firm and cluster levels-A to Z. IT and VAT handbooks on hardware and software, important forms for taxes etc.; Database of different clusters, updated directory information and applications to find companies and clusters on India map; Central and state government Industrial Acts, policies, schemes, incentives etc. for the manufacturing sector; and related useful links. In his special address, Mr. V. Govindarajan, Member Secretary/NMCC, stated that the National Strategy for Manufacturing drawn by the NMCC has been accepted by the Government for implementation and that enabling SMEs to achieve competitiveness through ICT was one of the key elements of this strategy. He further indicated that the NMCC has been engaging with all the Ministries as well as with state governments concerned in firming up the programme of action and implementing the strategy. The industry associations are also involved in the implementation of their side of the programme. Specific issues requiring immediate action have been taken up through the institutional mechanism of the High Level Committee on Manufacturing set up under the Chairmanship of the Hon'ble Prime Minister through the Empowered Sub-Committee of the HLCM for resolution of the policy issues etc.

1579. (19-6-2007) NEW DELHI : The total approximate earnings of Indian Railways on originating basis during the period 1st June-10th June 2007 were Rs. 1726.79 crore compared to Rs. 1590.43 crore during the same period last year, registering an increase of 8.57 per cent. The total goods earnings have gone up from Rs. 1064.05 crore during 1st June-10th June 2006 to Rs. 1137.91 crore during 1st June-10th June 2007, showing an increase of 6.94 per cent. The total passenger revenue earnings during the period 1-10 June 2007 were Rs. 513.58 crore compared to Rs. 465.45 crore during the same period last year, an increase of 10.34 per cent. The revenue earnings from other coaching amounted to Rs. 54.21 crore during this period compared to Rs. 43.97 crore during the same period last year, an increase of 23.29 per cent. The total sundry earnings have gone up from Rs. 16.96 crore during 1-10 June 2006 to Rs. 21.09 crore during 1-10 June 2007, showing an increase of 24.35 per cent. The total approximate number of passengers booked during the period 1-10 June 2007 were 179.51 million compared to 177.11 million during the same period last year, showing an increase of 1.36 per cent. In the suburban and non-suburban sectors, the number of passengers booked during 1-10 June 2007 were 99.25 million and 80.26 million compared to 98.77 million and 78.34 million during the same period last year, registering an increase of 0.49 per cent and 2.45 per cent respectively.

1580. (19-6-2007) NEW DELHI : The Income Tax department is today conducting search on a commodity exchange and its associates in Mumbai. Surveys are also being conducted on its branches in Ahmedabad, Bangalore, Chennai, Delhi and Kolkata. There is no search in the case of any share broker connected with a stock exchange per se.

1581. (19-6-2007) NEW DELHI : The Prime Minister, Dr. Manmohan Singh called on the President, Dr. A.P.J. Abdul Kalam at Rashtrapati Bhavan today. The meeting lasted 25 minutes. The Prime Minister briefed the President on his discussions with leaders of various counties during his recent visit to Heiligendamm in Germany from June 7 to 9, where he attended the Summit Meeting of the G8 Countries and Outreach Countries (Brazil, China, India, Mexico and South Africa). The two leaders also discussed issues of national importance. The meeting was part of the regular interactions between the two leaders.

1582. (20-6-2007) NEW DELHI : The Union Minister of Shipping, Road Transport & Highways, Thiru. T.R. Baalu has said that the work on the Sethusamudram Ship Channel Project (SSCP) would be completed before December, 2008. The Minister today reviewed the progress of the Project with the officials of the Sethusamudram Corporation Limited (SCL) and Dredging Corporation of India (DCI) besides other concerned agencies. The DCI, which has been awarded the contract for carrying out the dredging works, informed that a total of five dredgers are deployed for the dredging work-four at Adam's Bridge area and one at Palk Bay/Pak Strait. As on date, a total of 18.74 Million Cubic Metres of dredging has been carried out. The Minister directed the officials to re-work the inspection schedule of the dredging work to ensure that the progress of work on the Project is continuously monitored and problem areas are addressed to immediately. DCI had also, pursuant to the direction of the Minister, prepared weekly targets for the dredging to be carried out, which are being monitored on regular basis. A meeting has also been held with the Chairman, M/s. Kojimagumi Company Limited, a Japanese company, who are in possession of the world's largest Grab dredger and wish to offer it for SSCP. Thiru. Baalu directed the officials to finalise the negotiations with this company at the earliest. Thiru. Baalu also reviewed the progress of the repair of dredger Aquarius and expressed his satisfaction that the work is progressing as per schedule. The dry docking would be completed by October, 2007 onwards, which is the next working season after the South-West Monsoon. The procurement of Barge Handling System for dredger Aquarius, which would greatly improve its productivity is also being finalised. This Barge Handling System is targeted to be installed on dredger Aquarius by November, 2007.

1583. (20-6-2007) NEW DELHI : India should engage with many more developing countries & sectors for Development Cooperation Assistance (DCA) to enhance her strategic & commercial interests and to help poorer nations in their development efforts. This was stated by the Finance Minister Shri P. Chidambaram while addressing the Parliamentary Consultative Committee attached to his Ministry here today. In this process people of Indian origin living in the donee countries also get the benefit of DCA, he added. The Finance Minister stated that in view of India's growing stature in international affairs there is a need to increase aid to poor countries. He said that in the budget for 2007-08, he had proposed the establishment of India International Development Cooperation Agency in which Ministries of External Affairs and Commerce, apart from Finance would be represented. The Finance Minister said that DCA is an emerging, developing and evolving programme which is very attractive because of interest subsidy provided by the Government to lines of credit extended by Exim bank of India. Shri Chidambaram said India provides lines of credit to friendly developing foreign countries & this helps the Indian companies in promoting the export of goods including project exports to these countries and also secures goodwill of beneficiary countries. More importantly Indian companies participate in executing many projects *e.g.* those in Railways, Information Technology, Power generation and transmission, buses, sugar mills and also agricultural projects. Thus India is fast emerging as the promoter of economic growth of many developing countries, he added. He said that DCA is divided into two categories *i.e.* Government to Government LOC and the Lines of credit through Exim Bank. Shri Chidambaram informed the members that till now 67 GOI supported LOCs through Exim Bank of India for US$ 2772 million approx. have been approved. The countries which have benefited are-Afghanistan, Angola, Djibouti, Burkina Faso, Cambodia, Chad, Congo, Cote d' Ivoire, Ethiopia, Equatorial Guinea, Fiji, Gambia, Ghana, Guyana, Guinea Bissau, Honduras, Jamaica, Lao PDR, Mali, Mauritius, Mozambique, Myanmar, Nepal, Niger, Senegal, Sri Lanka, Sudan, Suriname, Vietnam and Zambia. These LOCs include special initiatives like New Partnership of African Development (NEPAD) of Africa, TEAM-9 initiative of India and ASEAN initiative. Besides this, a technical cooperation agreement was drawn up between Government of India and African Development for giving grant to utilize for financing consultancy services, training and other techno economic activities. The Finance Minister said that NEPAD is a special international initiative which seeks long term economic development of the region. India has pledged US$ 200 million for this initiative. So far, 6 proposals of lines of credit involving a total amount of US$ 122.77 million to various African countries have already been approved under the NEPAD initiative. 8 proposals collectively amounting to US$ 261.77 million for funding various projects in the member countries of TEAM-9 by way of Exim Bank of India lines of credit have been approved. Under the ASEAN initiative, 5 proposals amounting to US$ 152.34 million to 3 countries (Myanmar: US$ 10 mn + US$ 60 mn. + US$ 20 mn; Vietnam : US$ 45 mn.; and also Lao PDR: US$ 17.34 mn.) were approved in 2006-07.

1584. (20-6-2007) NEW DELHI : Prof. Saifuddin Soz, the Union Minister for Water Resources has said that the activities identified under Hydrology Project are very important for the water sector as these will help in developing reliable data for addressing various planning and management issues related to water. He was addressing the meeting of the Members of Consultative Committee of the Ministry of Water Resources to discuss "Hydrology Project" here today. The Minister informed the Members that first phase of Hydrology Project was taken up during 1995-2003. The project cost of Phase_I was Rs. 605.28 crores. The implementing bodies of the first Phase were 9 States and 6 central agencies. The States are Madhya Pradesh, Orissa, Maharashtra, Andhra Pradesh, Tamil Nadu,

Kerala, Karnataka, Chhattisgarh and Gujarat and 6 central agencies are Ministry of Water Resources, Central Water Commission, India Meteorological Department, National Institute of Hydrology, Central Ground Water Board and Central Water and Power Research Station. It helped in creating improved hydrological information system facilities by way of establishing standardized procedures for data collection, collation, processing and exchange and in creating a sound basis for water resources planning and management. Prof. Soz further informed that Phase-II of Hydrology Project has been taken up in April, 2006 and is being implemented in 13 states and 8 central agencies. The cost of Phase-II is Rs. 631.83 crores. The Project is being assisted by the World Bank. Hydrology Project Phase-II will take forward the progress made in HP-I and promote sustained effective use of HIS by potential users. The data will be further strengthened by the development of decision support system for surface water planning, ground water planning, reservoir operations, irrigation management, drought monitoring management and conjunctive use of surface water and ground water. Addressing the meeting Minister of State for Water Resources Shri Jai Prakash Narayan Yadav said that water is very important factor in life. In compare to other countries, in proportion to available land and population only four per cent water is available in India, out of which the amount of pure water is very less. Climate changes, pollution and other factors are creating serious problems all over the world. In this situation, the Ministry is working on various projects to make maximum water available. A power point presentation on "Hydrology Project" was made on the occasion.

1585. (20-6-2007) NEW DELHI : India and Canada have agreed to further strengthen cooperation in the field of agriculture. The visiting Indian Minister of State for Agriculture, Shri Kanti Lal Bhuria held discussions with Mr. Chuck Strahl, Canadian Minister of Agriculture and Agribusiness at Montreal last evening. They will have further, detailed, discussions today on exchange of technology, trade and investment in the field of agriculture. In the morning today, Shri Kanti Lal Bhuria participated in the 13th International Economic Forum of the Americas. He addressed the Innovation and International Trade session of the Economic Forum.

1586. (20-6-2007) NEW DELHI : Admiral Sureesh Mehta, Chief of the Naval Staff is undertaking a visit of UK from 18 to 23 Jun. 2007. The visit is aimed at enhancing IN-RN relations and to further areas of cooperation, further the scope of content in combined exercises and cross attachment of personnel. Whilst at UK, Admiral Mehta is scheduled to meet the First Sea Lord (Chief of the Naval Staff) of the Royal Navy, the Chief of Defence Staff and the Permanent Under Secretary of Defence. He will also be visiting a naval shipyard, Permanent Joint Headquarters and Royal Naval Training Establishments. Discussions on the security situation in the Indian Ocean Region, West and South East Asia and about the experiences of the UK Armed Forces in the recent past are also on the agenda. The modalities for sharing of information in the maritime domain are likely to figure prominently.

1587. (20-6-2007) NEW DELHI : Congress Spokesperson Smt. Jayanti Natarajan said that it is unfortunate that the Third Front which gives the impression of being the second front of the NDA, has brought the name and the high office of our President, Dr. APJ Abdul Kalam into unnecessary controversy by making him the object of speculation and controversy. Had there been any serious intention on their part to propose the candidature of Dr. Kalam, they should have done so at the outset well before positions had been taken by the two major groupings, the UPA and the NDA and the candidates announced. In the present context, specially in view of the clear majority in terms of the committed votes enjoyed by the UPA–Left candidate Smt Pratibha Patil . It is very obvious that the announcement made by the Third Front is only a ploy to muddy the waters and create confusion. It is also possible that certain components of the Third Front wish to indirectly support the NDA candidate. The NDA as always is a picture of confusion and disunity. Even the members of the NDA are unclear about who their candidate is. Hours after declaring their support for the independent candidature of Shri Bhairon Singh Sekhawat we witnessed the bizarre spectacle of the BJP president and other leaders declaring NDA support for Dr. Kalam instead .This inspite of the fact and more than a month ago Shri Atal Behari Vajpayee went to President Kalam and expressed the inability of the NDA to support him for a second time due to lack of consensus. We wish to point out that when we had asked for consensus with regard to a second term for Shri KR Narayanan who was not only an extremely distinguished President and citizen but also the first Dalit President of India, at that time the BJP and NDA said that it was a matter of convention that a second term would not be given to a President. It is very clear that at the same time when the NDA in government sought for consensus for the name of Dr. Abdul Kalam. The Congress, sitting then in Opposition, came forward to agree upon the name and cooperated with the election of Dr. Abdul Kalam. Therefore, the same kind of request for consensus made by the Congress, the BJP is not willing to come forward to support the consensus giving us to imagine that the only consensus that is possible is a consensus on their terms. All attempts by the NDA and the Third Front to speak now about the consensus are nothing more than attempts to create confusion and do not represent a genuine desire for consensus. We call upon all political parties to come together to vote for the UPA-Left candidate, Smt Pratibha Patil and become part of the historic occasion when she becomes the first women President of India. To a question as to why Dr. Kalam was not given second term in office, Smt Natarajan said that we had our own candidate and there is no question of any reservations. We had discussions within the UPA and decided that our candidate would be Smt Pratibha Patil and in the fullness of time, in the 60th year of India's independence it would be historic initiative to have a first women President. To a question that why was Dr. Kalam not considered for second term, Smt. Natarajan said that first of all, our candidate had already been decided. Secondly, when the NDA went to President Kalam, Shri. Vajpayee himself informed President Kalam that it is not possible to consider him for a second term because there is no precedent and also because of the lack of consensus. This was the result of the NDA's meeting with President Kalam. Therefore, the question of a consensus or a discussion on President Kalam did not and does not arise. Our candidate has been announced and therefore attempts to drag the high office of such a successful and popular President is very unfortunate. To a question as to why President Kalam could not make a cut, what are his shortcomings, Smt Natarajan said that our candidate is Smt. Pratibha Patil. We have utmost respect and regard for Dr. Kalam who has had a very distinguished and popular tenure. To a question that Jayalalithaa did not attend the Third Front meeting, what is your reaction, Smt. Natarajan said that I think that whether or not Ms. Jayalalithaa attended the meeting, the Third Front is already divided over the issue of who the President be and this reflects their own internal contradictions. We would only call upon all political parties to support the candidature of Smt. Pratibha Patil. To a question that is President Kalam not dragging himself into speculation controversy, Smt. Natarajan said that it is the NDA and the Third Front who have unnecessarily dragged him into speculation.

1588. (20-6-2007) NEW DELHI : Satellite Based Distance Learning in the Vocational System has been launched by the Directorate General of Employment and Training (DGET) in the Ministry of Labour and Employment on a pilot basis. The DGET-EDUSAT Pilot Programme was launched recently from the Vishveswaraiah Technological University (VTU) Studio in Bangalore. It is transmitted to 12 Industrial Training Institutes (ITIs) being covered under the Centres of Excellence (COE) scheme of DGET in Karnataka. The Pilot Programme is also being received in a number of other locations in the southern states. During the Pilot Programme the lectures are being telecast from the VTU Studio for 2 hours every day during June, 2007 in subjects like life skills and engineering drawing. The Government of India is the nodal agency for monitoring, supervision and coordination of vocational training in the country. The Secretary, Labour and Employment Smt. Sudha Pillai said while inaugurating the Pilot Programme that it will help the ITIs especially those located in remote areas with quality teaching faculty. Highlighting the importance of introducing distance-learning programme in the Vocational Training System in the country Smt. Pillai said that through the Satellite Based Distance Learning system, widely disbursed locations could be covered in shortest possible time. She emphasized that this system can ensure uniformity of content, control on the quality, repeatability of the lecture content and sharing of the network by other user groups. This system can lead to substantial reduction in cost on account of travel, logistics and other infrastructural facilities, she added. The Director General of Employment and Training Shri. Sharda Prasad said that the Pilot Programme has been launched to test the technology in the Vocational Training System and subsequently DGET proposes to introduce it in all the ITIs of the country by setting up a National Studio at the Apex Hitech Institute in Bangalore and Regional Studios in different parts of the country in a phased manner.

1589. (20-6-2007) NEW DELHI : Union Minister for Petroleum and Natural Gas Shri Murli Deora laid the foundation stone of "OIDB Bhawan" at NOIDA today. Union Minister of State for Petroleum and Natural Gas Shri Dinsh Patel, Shri Ashok Pradhan, Member of Parliament, Shri Satyaveer Singh Gurjar, Member of Legislative Assembly (Uttar Pradesh) and Shri M. S. Srinivasan, Secretary, Ministry of Petroleum and Natural Gas were present on the occasion. Speaking about the important role being played by Oil Industry Development Board (OIDB) in the oil and gas sector, Shri Deora informed that an amount of Rs. 2400 crore would be spent on construction of strategic crude oil reserve storages which will be funded by OIDB. The Government of India had earlier decided to construct a 5 million metric tonne strategic crude oil reserves to meet the emergent demands of oil sector. For this purpose, a Special Purpose Vehicle by the name of "Indian Strategic Petroleum Reserves Limited" (ISPRL) has been created as a wholly owned subsidiary of OIDB. The ISPRL will construct crude storages at three locations namely, Visakhapatnam, Mangalore and Padura. He also informed that the Government of India is proposing to set up an Educational Institute of national importance for the petroleum sector *i.e.* the Rajiv Gandhi Institute of Petroleum Technology in UP. This institute will serve the needs of the Petroleum Sector both in India and abroad and will be partially funded by OIDB. To encourage research and development activities, Shri Deora called upon OIDB to lay special emphasis on funding R&D activities in the oil and gas sector including development of alternate sources of energy. He said "In fact, these activities should remain the first charge on OIDB funds". Shri Deora also informed that OIDB has so far given loan assistance of about Rs.21,600 crore for various important projects like Mumbai High of ONGC, Numaligarh Refinery in Assam, City Gas Distribution & CNG projects in Delhi and Mumbai, projects for improving quality of petrol and diesel and gas pipeline projects of GAIL etc. Apart from giving grants to its five grantee institutions like DGH, CHT, OISD, PPAC & PCRA and participating in ISPRL's equity, OIDB has so far given overwhelming support to the Research & Development activities of Oil & Natural Gas Corporation, Oil India Limited, National Geophysical Research Institute Hyderabad, Indian Institute of Petroleum Dehradun, Indian Institute of Technology Delhi, Regional Research Laboratory Jorhat, Central Institute of Plastics Engineering and Technology Chennai and Indian School of Mines Dhanbad etc. He also said that OIDB has so far given grants to the tune of Rs.1070 crore for its grantee institutions as well as for research and development in the oil industry. Minister of State for Petroleum Shri Dinsha Patel described the decision on the part of OIDB and the ministry as timely to make a modern and green building to house the OIDB secretariat along with all its grantee organizations under one roof so that there is coordination between them. He advised that this project should be completed on time. Oil Industry Development Board (OIDB) is an autonomous and statutory organization under the Ministry of Petroleum and Natural Gas established in 1975 under an act of Parliament, to provide financial assistance for the development of oil and gas industry. OIDB is constructing its own building at NOIDA to house not only its own Secretariat but also its grantee institutions like Directorate General of Hydrocarbons (DGH), Centre for High Technology (CHT), Oil Industry Safety Directorate (OISD), Petroleum Planning and Analysis Cell (PPAC) and Indian Strategic Petroleum Reserves Ltd. (ISPRL) under one roof. At present, these organizations are housed in different buildings in Delhi. Bringing them all together would not only result in savings by way of rentals but would also ensure proper coordination and synergy between these institutions. The OIDB Bhawan would be a 10 storied building comprising two blocks. The total built up area would be about 24020 sq.mtr. with additional provision for parking areas and utilities. The OIDB Bhawan will be an environmental friendly and Green building which will use state-of-the-art technology to meet the lighting, air-conditioning and other needs of the building. The building will maximize the use of solar energy and rainwater harvesting and will have an Auditorium, Boardroom, Conference Hall, several meeting rooms, a medical centre and library, besides adequate office space. Estimated to cost about Rs. 135 crore, this building would become a landmark for the area and would be ready for occupation by September 2008.

1590. (20-6-2007) NEW DELHI : India and China have signed a Cultural Exchange Programme (CEP) for the years 2007-09 here today. The CEP was signed by the Minister of Tourism and Culture Smt. Ambika Soni and visiting Chinese Minister of Culture Mr. Sun Jiazheng. According to the CEP both the countries will Exchange one Government/ Official delegations, of five members, for a period upto seven days. Both the countries shall encourage to hold performances, exhibitions and cultural festivals in respective countries. Both the countries will exchange one delegation of ten writers for a period of ten days, to two three archivists for a period of one week. Both the countries will encourage the China Dunhuang Research Institutions and the Indira Gandhi National Centre for Arts to have a long-term academic collaboration. Both sides will encourage the Chinese Federation of Literary and Art Circles and the Sangeet Natak Akademi and Lilit Kala Akademi of India, to exchange musicians, dancers, artists and critics for attachment upto 3 months at appropriate institutions for lectures and workshops. Both sides will exchange a delegation of anthropologists to study the status of bio-cultural research in the respective countries. Both sides will encourage their respective Radio and TV organizations to exchange Radio and Television programmers reflecting cultural life in both countries. Both the countries will exchange one media delegation of upto eight members for a period of two weeks.

1591. (20-6-2007) NEW DELHI : Canadian Aviation Electronics (CAE) has signed a memorandum of understanding for a joint venture with the Airport Authority of India (AAI) to develop the National Flying Training Institute (NFTI). CAE has also signed a memorandum of understanding to become the managing partner of the Indian government's flight training academy: Indira Gandhi Rashtriya Uran Akademi (IGRUA). More than 400 pilots would be licensed annually through these new schools. The total output would grow to over 600 pilots with Multi Pilot Licence (MPL) stream of licensing. "The selection of CAE by the government of India for these schools is a significant milestone for flight training in India," said Jeff Roberts, CAE's Group President, Innovation and Civil Training & Services. "Given our extensive experience in building world-class flight-training organizations, we intend to provide India with the expertise and support they need to develop a solid infrastructure and implement the most modern standards in flight training. With these new schools, which would complement our upcoming training centre in Bangalore, we will be able to address the need for pilots in India." "Creating these world-class institutions in-country with CAE as our partner is a major government initiative targeted at tackling both the acute shortage of Indian pilots while improving the overall quality of the cadet supply within India," said Praful Patel, India's Minister of Civil Aviation. "Today there are approximately 2,500 active pilots in India and we estimate that we will need up to an additional 5,000 pilots over the next 5 years to meet the needs of the industry. These initiatives will go a long way to help remedy our pilot shortage." Over the next decade, the rapid growth in air travel will generate an enormous demand for pilots, cabin crew, maintenance staff and infrastructure to support this growth. The Air Passengers Association of India estimates that the annual air traffic growth rate in the country has been around 26% over the past two years, causing the Indian airline industry to order approximately 400 new aircraft, to be delivered by 2010. Once final agreements are signed, CAE will offer these schools the possibility of becoming members of the CAE Global Academy. The CAE Global Academy is a worldwide network of flight training organizations that offers pilot candidates an optimized programme with standard operating procedures. CAE currently has six member schools in its Global Academy and can license annually 1,000 pilots. Once they have graduated from the Academy, the new first officers are able to proceed for type-rating in one of CAE's training centres, including CAE's upcoming training centre in Bangalore. CAE has contracts with several airlines to supply them with pilots. CAE has recruited, trained and supplied more than 800 pilots for commercial airlines over the last year.

1592. (20-6-2007) NEW DELHI : The news about China building a metalled road to the Mount Everest base camp is not only an ecological disaster but is yet another attempt by China to assert across the border. The construction of the 108-km road to the height of 5,200 meters will begin within a week. This road will endanger ecosystem, which is fragile and already threatened. What is worse is that Government of India seems to be clueless about the whole development. Recently, India's Defence Minister A.K. Antony had spoken with concern about China rapidly building infrastructure on its side of the border. All these developments are not isolated incidents. In the recent past China denied visa to Arunachal officials stating that they don't require visa as it is part of China. Even direct claims were made on Arunachal by various authorities in China. The settled principle of boundary dispute to be restricted to non-populated areas has also been challenged by the Foreign Minister of China, threatening the bilateral talks between the two countries. Report about Chinese efforts to divert the Brahmaputra river flow away from India is also news of serious ramification. The project envisages a series of 11 dams around the Brahmaputra loop. It includes a tunnel through the mountains bringing water to a powerhouse, which has a capacity to produce 48,000 MW of electricity. For South Asia and more particularly for India the enormity of the scheme and its closeness to the Indian border cannot be ignored. It will have ominous consequences for millions of people downstream. Surprisingly, Government of India has kept mum on majority of all these issues. Bharatiya Janata Party holds that these developments are of great significance for bilateral relations and interests of India. Nation does not know whether India has conveyed its anguish over these developments to China or not. Bharatiya Janata Party demands that UPA Government should take up these issues of national importance with China and sort them out immediately.

1593. (20-6-2007) NEW DELHI : Stressing the need to address the challenge on the energy front on a war-footing, the Prime Minister, Dr. Manmohan Singh emphasized that the complacency of the past, be it with respect to conventional or non-conventional sources of power, or indeed nuclear power, must end. He pointed out that the availability of quality power at affordable cost has emerged as the most important constraint on the pace of our development. Dedicating the East-North Tala Power Transmission System to the Nation, here today, he observed that the people of our country are not going to wait endlessly for us to sort out our administrative, political and theological problems. Expressing gratitude to His Majesty, the King of Bhutan and the people of Bhutan for their role in the project, the Prime Minister pointed out that the Tala hydro-electric project and the Tala transmission system symbolize our resolve to find new pathways of regional cooperation for sustainable development. Dr. Singh expressed the hope that we can replicate our highly successful, win-win model of bilateral cooperation with Bhutan in the power sector with Nepal too. "Hydro power is clean and renewable. We must tap the energy in our river systems in this region more effectively and efficiently. This can be done to the benefit of all countries in the region. It is a win-win model of cooperation", he added. Stating that the potential for regional cooperation in South Asia is immense and we have not even scratched the surface, Dr. Singh said, "I believe that the best is yet to come and we must all work towards realizing this." The Prime Minister expressed the hope that special courts for speedy disposal of power theft cases will be operationalised soon. The Union Minister for Power, Shri Sushilkumar Shinde, the Minister of State in PMO, Shri Prithviraj Chavan, the Secretary, Power, Shri Anil Razdan, senior officials of the Power Grid Corporation of India and other dignitaries were present on the occasion.

1594. (20-6-2007) NEW DELHI : The Rig Veda manuscripts from Bhandarkar Oriental Research Institute, Pune, have been selected for inscription in UNESCO's "Memory of the World" Register 2007. The programme for the Memory of the

World was started in UNESCO fifteen years back to honour significant landmarks in the documentary heritage and record them in its "Memory of the World Register" as world's inheritance. The Memory of the World programme seeks to guard against collective amnesia, calling upon the preservation of the valuable archival holdings and library collections all over the world, ensuring their wide dissemination. The National Mission for Manuscripts of the Ministry of Culture submitted the nomination on behalf of the Bhandarkar Oriental Research Institute. The documentary heritage reflects the diversity of languages, peoples and cultures. So far, India has had three other nominations inscribed on the Register i) The I.A.S. Tamil Medic Manuscript Collection (1997) ii) Archives of the Dutch East India Company (2003) _ Dutch nomination iii) Saiva Manuscripts in Pondicherry (2005) The Vedas are the first literary documents in the history of humankind, they transcend far beyond their identity as scriptures. The Rigveda, the oldest among the four Vedas, is the fountain source of the so-called Aryan culture in all its manifestations that spread beyond the Indian subcontinent to large parts of South and South East Asia, as well as parts of Central Asia. This valuable treasure of the ancient world has been preserved in the form of manuscripts in India, and handed down over centuries from generation to generation. Out of the total number of 28,000 Manuscripts housed at the Bhandarkar Oriental Research Institute, Pune, the 30 manuscripts of the Rigveda form a valuable part of the collection. These manuscripts evince several unique features in terms of scripts, accentuation marks and support material used, among others. Even the pioneering Indologist, Prof. F. Max Müller, used one of the Rigveda manuscripts currently at the Institute to prepare his famous critical edition of the Rigveda, complete with a translation of one of the earliest known commentaries-that of Sayana. The material in this collection of Rigveda manuscripts was also used to prepare the well known Critical Edition of the Rigveda by the Vaidika Samshodhana Mandala, a premier institute in Pune for Vedic Studies. These manuscripts are of a high value as unique examples of the intellectual and cultural heritage not only of India, but of the world. The Minister of Tourism and Culture Smt. Ambika Soni has welcomed the development and said whenever the items related to cultural heritage of India get recognition by the world, it brings happiness to all the countrymen.

1595. (21-6-2007) NEW DELHI : Government has permitted induction of M/s. Mittal Energy Investments Pte Ltd. (MEI), 100% subsidiary of M/s. Mittal Investments (MI), as JV partner in Bhatinda Refinery Project being executed by Guru Gobind Singh Refinery Ltd., presently a 100% subsidiary of HPCL. The investment by MI of Rs. 3506 crore (or about 5% of total FDI in 2006-07) is the first and the largest Foreign Direct Investment (FDI) brought into the petroleum refining sector in collaboration with a PSU. The project itself has been approved by CCEA earlier with permission to induct JV partner if so required subsequently. It consists of a 9 million metric tonne per annum (MMTPA) refinery, 1000 KM crude oil pipeline from Mundra to Bhatinda and Single Point Mooring (SPM) & crude oil terminal at Mundra. The 'As built' cost assessed by SBI Caps is Rs.

18,919 crore. Each partner, HPCL and MI (through MEI), will contribute 49% equity individually of Rs. 3506 crore each and balance 2% equity of Rs. 143 crore will be taken by Indian financial institutions. MI investment will put the project on a fast track. It will create a lot of jobs directly and indirectly in the state of Punjab. There will be industrialization and development of support industries. It will also improve the level of oil security in the area. For HPCL, the investment by MI will allow HPCL to use its capital for other planned expenditure. Also, HPCL will leverage the strength of MI in globalizing its operations as well as seeking equity oil abroad.

1596. (21-6-2007) NEW DELHI : In a landmark development in the defence history of the country, the President and the Supreme Commander of the Armed Forces Dr. A P J Abdul Kalam handed over a replica of the mobile autonomous launchers of the BrahMos land system to the Chief of Army Staff Gen J J Singh, symbolizing the commencement of delivery of the supersonic cruise missiles to the Indian Army, at a function here today. The missile is launched from a Transport Launch Canister (TLC) which also acts as storage and transport container. The Government had approved induction of three regiments of BrahMos Missile system in the Indian Army out of which the Army had initially placed the requirement for one regiment. The delivery of this system was to start from July 2008. However, for early operationalisation of the missile system, the delivery of one Mobile Command Post and two Mobile Autonomous Launchers has been advanced by one year. The function was attended among others by the Defence Minister Shri A K Antony, the Minister of State for Defence Shri M M Pallam Raju, Scientific Advisor to Raksha Mantri Shri M Natrajan, the Ambassador of Russia to India Mr. Vyacheslav Trubnikov and the Chief Executive Officer and Managing Director of BrahMos Aerospace Dr. A Sivathanu Pillai. Speaking on the occasion, the President Dr. A P J Abdul Kalam said we have to aggressively market this world-class product which will have a market shelf life of not more than 5 years. He said there will be competitors who would be developing contemporary products which will be detrimental to the market leadership. 'No smart developer can afford to lose the competitive edge which he has generated and hence increasing the orders and continuously improving the products have to be aggressively pursued', he said. The President said, time has come for BrahMos Aerospace to work on Mark-II version of BrahMos so that it will still be the market leader in hypersonic cruise missiles. 'In the emerging network centric warfare scenario, the fast deployment of hypersonic missile systems will be necessary to maintain our force level supremacy. I visualize long range hypersonic cruise missiles not only delivering pay loads but also returning to the base after the mission, leading to re-usable class of cruise missiles within the next decade. It is time that the three services work with the team of BrahMos Aerospace to evolve the QR for such a system in a time bound manner', he said. Describing the BrahMos joint venture programme between Indian and Russia as a 'great template' for international cooperation, the President said it combined the core competence of the two countries for realizing a high-technology product in an extremely competitive global defence market with minimum investment from each side. The President also handed over 61 documents relating to operation and maintenance of each system of BrahMos to Gen. J J Singh. The Prime Minister Dr. Manmohan Singh in a message on the occasion described the BrahMos system as one of the most advanced supersonic cruise missiles comparable to the best in the world and said, it is an excellent model of high technology cooperation between India and Russian Federation. The Defence Minister Shri A K Antony said that the induction of BrahMos weapon system will catapult India with the most powerful supersonic cruise missile which can precisely hit the target. He said the capabilities of the missile system which have been proved through a series of successful flight trials, will bolster the Indian Army and enhance the defence preparedness of the nation. 'In the changing face of the war theatre, induction of BrahMos and similar high-technology systems will play a commanding role in protecting the nation's interests'. Shri Antony however said that production orders to the required quantity must be made to make the joint venture economically viable. In order to cater to the growing demands of the Indian and Russian Armed Forces and export market the production activities have to be geared up to meet the growing demands, he said. The Chief of Army Staff Gen J J Singh said that he had witnessed two launches of the BrahMos system in the desert and was confident that the missile system will be a force multiplier in our strategic armoury. Speaking on the occasion Dr. Pillai said, when all four versions of BrahMos-Ship, Mobile Complex, Air and Submarine launched missiles are used in a seamless integration among the various services, it will effectively destroy any kind of threat. 'BrahMos will be a war winner and will play a crucial role in the future warfare', he said. Dr. Pillai said that DRDO has played a very important role in the development of a number of systems for the missile and ground complex and continues to work on many developmental efforts including INS + Glonass integration, seeker, improved operational software in the network centric warfare, in close coordination with the Services.

1597. (21-6-2007) NEW DELHI : Shri Kanti Lal Bhuria, Minister of State for Agriculture held discussions with the Canadian Agriculture Minister at Montreal last evening to explore the possibilities of strengthening cooperation in the field of agriculture. After the discussions the Minister said that both the sides realise that there are immense possibilities for Indo-Canada cooperation in the areas of trade and exchange of technologies. Shri Bhuria also addressed the International Economic Forum meeting being held at Montreal. Speaking on Innovation and Economic Development, the Minister stated that this issue is high on the agenda of the Indian Government. In view of limited scope for expansion of area under agriculture, any development in agriculture would have to be guided by innovation and relevant research, Shri Bhuria added.

1598. (21-6-2007) NEW DELHI : The Prime Minister, Dr. Manmohan Singh reviewed the progress of the implementation of the National Rural Employment Guarantee Programme at a special review meeting on 20th June, 2007. The

Minister for Rural Development apprised the Prime Minister of the successful implementation of the programme in 330 districts. It was reported that so far over 2.1 crore persons had been provided employment under NREGA. This included 1.2 crore SC & ST and 0.8 crore women. Under NREGA employment generation has been linked to rural asset creation and infrastructure development. The majority of the works undertaken related to water conservation, water harvesting, flood control, irrigation and renovation of traditional water bodies, and construction of rural roads. The review noted that as a result of introduction of NREGA there is a decline in distress migration, improvement in land productivity, increased awareness among rural poor regarding minimum wages. There has also been an increase in wage earnings as well as improvement in participation of women in the rural work force. It was also noted that wage earners have been able to open savings bank account, take up insurance and improve literacy. Taking note of the successful implementation of the NREGA, the Prime Minister called for independent professional evaluation of the programme and its impact on employment generation, rural wages, gender disparity, agricultural productivity and rural infrastructure development. The Prime Minister urged State Governments that were lagging behind in the implementation of the programme to learn from the experience of the States that were actively implementing the programme. The Prime Minister has called for the preparation of district-wise District Employment Report, giving information on NREGA, to be presented on Labour Day, 1st May, 2008.

1599. (21-6-2007) NEW DELHI : Farm commodity prices monitored by the Department of Consumer Affairs have generally remained steady or have shown mixed trend in different centres across the country in the week ending 15.06.2007. Wheat prices remained steady at majority of reporting centres and declined at Bhopal and Bangalore. Sugar prices remained steady across majority of the centres; declined at Bhopal and increased at Hyderabad. Gram prices remained steady over the week across most of the centres; declined at Agartala and Kolkata; and increased at Mumbai. Tur dal prices were also steady across most of the centres; declined at Agartala and increased at Bhopal and Kolkata. At Delhi, prices of wheat, atta, tea, salt and groundnut oil remained steady over one week; those of gram and tur dal, sugar, rice, milk and mustard oil remained steady over one month; and prices of vanspati remained steady for six months. Prices of the following commodities have increased at Delhi in the week ending 15th June potato and onion. As on 20th June, public sector agencies have contracted import of 6.725 lakh tonne pulses of which 1.86 lakh tonnes has already reached Indian ports. The imported pulses include urad, moong, dunpeas, masoor, chana, yellow peas and tur.

1600. (21-6-2007) NEW DELHI : The Cabinet Committee on Economic Affairs (CCEA) today gave its approval to create an additional buffer stock of 30 lakh tonnes for a period of one year to give relief to sugar industry and sugarcane farmers.

1601. (21-6-2007) NEW DELHI : The Cabinet Committee on Economic Affairs today approved the revision of Royalty rates on coal and lignite effecting amendment to the Second Schedule of the Mines and Minerals (Development and Regulation) Act, 1957 through a Gazette Notification in terms of Section 9 of the said Act. The weighted average royalty payable after revision excluding West Bengal as a percentage of weighted coal price (based on 2004-05 production level) works out to about 14%. This will give the coal producing States a reasonable share of the income earned by production and selling of a non-renewable mineral resources like coal. The earnings of coal producing States will increase as a result of revision in the coal and lignite royalty rates.

1602. (21-6-2007) NEW DELHI : The Cabinet Committee on Economic Affairs today gave its approval for a centrally sponsored scheme of Merit Cum Means Based Scholarship to students belong to Minority Communities to be implemented by the State Governments/Union Territories. The scheme will be launched during the financial year 2007-08 targeting 20,000 scholarships per annum. Students from the minority communities fulfilling the merit-cum-means criteria and pursuing professional/technical courses at undergraduate and postgraduate levels in institutes recognized by the appropriate authorities will be eligible for this scholarship. The scheme has the potential to lift the economic condition of minority communities, which in turn, will contribute to the economic development of the country. The CCEA also gave its approval for incurring recurring expenditure pf Rs.761.69 crore during the XIth Five Year Plan for the scheme.

1603. (21-6-2007) NEW DELHI : The Cabinet Committee on Economic Affairs today gave its approval for the extension of the Centrally sponsored Swayamsidha scheme for one year upto March 31, 2008. The CCEA also gave the permission to utilize the funds to the tune of Rs.27.81 crore available under the Scheme as on 31.3.2007 during the extended period. The extension of time would ensure the completion of unfinished tasks in order to sustain outcomes of the project.

1604. (21-6-2007) NEW DELHI : The Union Cabinet today approved the formation of the Joint Venture as envisaged under the JV agreement and addendum with the induction of M/s. Mittal Energy Investment Pte. Ltd., 100% subsidiary of Mittal Investments, S.a.r.l., Luxembourg in Guru Gobind Singh Refineries Ltd. with 49% equity. The Cabinet has also given its approval for authorising Hindustan Petroleum Corporation Ltd. (HPCL) to make its investment of 49% in JV. This will enhance the availability of petroleum products in the north. This JV will be the largest FDI in PSU in refining sector. This decision will result in industrialisation and creation of jobs in Punjab. It will also help in globalization of HPCL.

1605. (21-6-2007) NEW DELHI : The Union Cabinet today gave its approval to amend the Merchant Shipping (Amendment) Bill, 2004 pending in Lok Sabha on the basis of the recommendations of Parliamentary Standing Committee. This Bill aims to amend the Merchant Shipping Act, 1958 and Indian ports Act, 1908 so that it takes care of recent international developments in the International Maritime Organisation and UN instruments. The provisions of security in general are based on amendments to the Chapter V and XI of Safety of Life and Sea Convention, 1974 concerning special measures to enhance maritime safety and security. The implementation of the special measures will make important contribution towards safe and secure operation of ships and for the safety and security of those on board and ashore in Indian context.

1606. (21-6-2007) NEW DELHI : The reported response of Government of India that China's effort to build a metalled road to Mount Everest is not a serious security concern, clearly connotes its unwillingness to face the situation in the right perspective. The road to Everest is not an isolated incident but part of a series of China's assertive actions across the border. Over the last one month, China's denial of visa to an IAS officer from Arunachal, further assertive claims on Arunachal, diversion of the Brahmaputra river via a tunnel, and trying to redefine the settled principle on the boundary dispute are all cases that confirm serious connotations. The BJP expects the government to give an unambiguous and comprehensive response on all these issues with more seriousness and taking long term national interests into consideration. The news about China building a metalled road to the Mount Everest base camp is not only an ecological disaster but is yet another attempt by China to assert itself from across the border. The construction of the 108-km road to the height of 5,200 meters will begin within a week. This road will certainly endanger an already fragile and threatened ecosystem. Recently, India's Defence Minister A.K. Antony had spoken with concern about China rapidly building infrastructure on its side of the border. In the recent past, China denied visa to Arunachal officials stating that they don't require visa as the area is considered a part of China. Even direct claims have been made on Arunachal by various authorities in China. The settled principle of boundary dispute to be restricted to non-populated areas has also been challenged by the Foreign Minister of China, threatening the bilateral talks between the two countries. The BJP does not view these developments as isolated incidents. Reports about Chinese efforts to divert the Brahmaputra river flow away from India is also news of serious ramifications. The project envisages a series of 11 dams around the Brahmaputra loop. It includes a tunnel through the mountains bringing water to a powerhouse, which has a capacity to produce 48,000 MW of electricity. For South Asia and more particularly for India the enormity of the scheme and its closeness to the Indian border cannot be ignored. It will have ominous consequences for millions of people downstream. The Bharatiya Janata Party demands that the UPA Government should take up these issues of national importance with China, sort them out immediately in the national interest.

1607. (21-6-2007) NEW DELHI : Shri Jairam Ramesh, Minister of State for Commerce, launched here today, a new web-based software "GrapeNet" that will provide traceability regarding the table grapes exported from India to European

Union (EU). The software developed by APEDA will help in raising the confidence of the importers by enabling monitoring of pesticide residue and by achieving product standardization and thus boost grape exports to EU. The software works on the regulations of tracing back to the origin of the produce in the reverse order from shelf to farm at the click of a mouse at one's computer. "Now, the importers, export regulation authorities abroad and in the country, in fact, anyone who will be using this software will be able to access the information at one's convenience at their tables about any grape export transaction", Shri Ramesh said. By clicking the phytosanitary No. or Agmark No. one can reach directly to the certificate issuing authorities thereafter one can reach at the inspection reports to laboratory analysis, certificate of residue analysis and the pack house details, which are available in detail instantly. The software is designed to reach at the root of any grape export transaction. Traceability has helped 40,000 grape farmers to come together and apply uniform farming practices. There is complete accountability in the system and farmers have earned 40% more value for their grapes. Export value has grown from 8 Euro to 11.5 Euro for a pack of 5 kg in 06-07. The success achieved in implementing the residue monitoring system and IT based traceability procedure has enabled all stakeholders in India and importers & supermarkets in the EU to develop considerable confidence in Indian grapes with a result that export of table grapes from India has doubled during the last three years. The present level of exports (2005-06) is of the order of about 40 million Euros. About 55,000 MT of grapes were exported in 2005-06 out of a total production of around 1.5 million tones. 80% of exports were from Maharashtra alone.

1608. (21-6-2007) NEW DELHI : The Ministry of New and Renewable Energy plans to celebrate 'Rajiv Gandhi Akshay Urja Diwas' by spreading the message of new and renewable energy technologies and systems through out the country this year. Ministry celebrates late Prime Minister's birthday *i.e.* 20th August every year as Akshay Urja Diwas. The national function will be organized at Hyderabad in Andhra Pradesh. National Marathon (21 km) for men and women, 'Run For Run' for senior citizens and others, 3 day Renewable Energy Exhibition and administering Renewable energy pledge to 30,000 school children and other participants will be main events. Winners of the Marathon will be given handsome prizes.

1609. (21-6-2007) NEW DELHI : First meeting of the India Japan Joint Working group on urban development took place in Tokyo on 19 June 2007. The meeting was co-chaired by the Urban Development Secretary, Shri M Ramachandran and the Japanese Vice minister for Engineering affairs, Ministry of Land, Infrastructure and Transport Shri Taniguchi. The Group was constituted after Prime Minister, Dr. Manmohan Singh's visit to Japan recently. The issues on urban development, water environment and urban transport were deliberated during the visit. Areas identified for mutual cooperation include water management, trenchless technology, urban planning, metropolitan planning and management, intelligent transport system for urban transport, metro for big cities, roof top gardening and others. Speaking on the occasion, Shri Ramachandran said the way greenery is maintained in such a large city like Tokyo is worth studying. He expressed keenness to carry forward the beginning made by organizing the first ever urban joint initiative by continuing the dialogue with counterparts, visits by experts to India and further focusing on specific areas identified. Shri Taniguchi remarked at the end of the meeting that this first such effort has been very successful. He said that both sides have been able to understand a lot about India's urban sector and its problems. The Indian delegation was shown among other things the waste disposal site which included land reclamation by filling waste, odor less incinerator facility, top class underground parking facility at Asakusa, quake proof building technology, new transport systems, underground drainage river and Tokyo metro It is expected that this new beginning will not only encourage interest in Japanese technology assisting India's construction sector but will also lead to more investment in the urban sector as a corollary to the massive urban Jawaharlal Nehru National Urban Renewal Mission programme launched by the UPA government for India's large cities.

1610. (21-6-2007) NEW DELHI : The Union Minister of Shipping, Road Transport and Highways, Thiru. T.R. Baalu has approved a sum of Rs.31.50 crore for road improvement works under Central Road Fund Scheme in the state of Tamil Nadu. The amount will be used for widening and strengthening 14 road stretches of State Highways, Major Districts Roads and other District Roads in Tamil Nadu. Following are the stretches where the road improvement work will be carried out in the state: Improvements to Krishnagiri Varatannapalli-Kandhakuppam Road km 1/0-18/5, 18/9-23/0 including minor bridge at 9/6 at a cost of Rs.475 lakh and improvements to Bargur-Jegadevi Road km 0/0-8/2 at a cost of Rs.150 lakh in Krishnagiri. Widening and strengthening of Cuddalore-Chittor road to Arpakkam via Kovoor Km 0/0-11/0 at a cost of Rs.200 lakh and widening and strengthening of Perumanam road Km 0/0-8/6 at a cost of Rs.160 lakh in Thirupattur. Raising the road level in Mettur-Palakkanuthu-Oddanchatram-Dharapuram-Kangeyam-Erode road km 16/0-20/0 at a cost of Rs.405 lakh in Dindigul. Widening and improving the Thandalam-Perambakkam Road km 5/0-10/0 at a cost of Rs.350 lakhs in Sriperumpudur. Widening and improvements to Palani-Dharapuram Road (via) Alangiam km 27/250-32/680 at a cost of Rs.275 lakh in Coimbatore. Widening and strengthening of Alwarthirunagari-Nazereth-Sathankulam-Ittamozhi-Valliyur Road km 37/0-41/0 at a cost of Rs.250 lakh in Thiruchendur. Construction of High level bridge at km 69/2 of Salem-Thiruppathur-Vaniyambadi Road across Thenpennai river at a cost of Rs.250 lakhs in Dharmapuri. Widening and Strengthening of Ammanpuram-Arumuganeri Road km 0/0-4/8 at a cost of Rs.200 lakh in Tuticorin. Widening and improvements to Karaikudi-C. Siruvayal Road km 0/0-7/4 at a cost of Rs.200 lakh and widening and improvements to Aathanigudi-Konappattu Road km 0/0-1/6 at a cost of Rs.50 lakh in Sivaganga. Strengthening Arcot Villupuram Road km 110/0-114/4 at a cost of Rs.150 lakh in Thiruvannamalai.

Widening and strengthening of Grivalam road in Palani town at a cost of Rs.40 lakh. It may be recalled that an amount or Rs. 77.70 crore was sanctioned in March this year for carrying out Road Improvement Works in 26 Road Stretches in the State of Tamil Nadu.

1611. (22-6-2007) NEW DELHI : A delegation of the United National Progressive Alliance (UNPA) met the President, Dr. A.P.J. Abdul Kalam at Rashtrapati Bhavan today. After discussions on the Presidential election, the President told the delegation that after considering their request and reviewing the situation carefully from all angles, he has decided that in the current scenario he will not be interested in running for the second term as he does not want Rashtrapati Bhavan to become involved in any political process. Dr. Kalam also thanked the UNPA for its initiative. Dr. Kalam also told them that his mission in life is to work for development of the country which he will continue to do wherever he will be. The President also thanks the people of India for the overwhelming love and affection towards him.

1612. (22-6-2007) NEW DELHI: After three-and-half hours of confabulations between the National Democratic Alliance and the United Nationalist Progressive Alliance here on Thursday, the common strategy that emerged was that the NDA would support A.P.J. Abdul Kalam for a second term as President if he were to contest. However, the UNPA failed to give any assurance to the NDA on supporting the candidature of Vice-President Bhairon Singh Shekhawat in the event of Mr. Kalam not contesting. To a question, Telugu Desam Party president N. Chandrababu Naidu said: "We are hopeful some good will come out of our efforts [in favour of Kalam], so the question [of supporting Shekhawat] does not arise ... our mission is only Kalam." The UNPA leaders expressed the hope that AIADMK chief Jayalalithaa would join them on Friday, when they plan to call on Mr. Kalam to discuss with him the issue of "certainty" in the outcome of the poll he raised. Senior Bharatiya Janata Party leader Jaswant Singh made it clear to reporters that the discussions in the evening — first it was a meeting of NDA leaders sans the Shiv Sena, and then it was a session of the UNPA and the NDA at the residence of the former Prime Minister, Atal Bihari Vajpayee — centred around a strategy to make Mr. Kalam a winnable candidate for ensuring a big defeat to the Congress and the United Progressive Alliance.

1613. (22-6-2007) NEW DELHI : The Chief Minister of Punjab Shri Prakash Singh Badal called on the Union Minister of Shipping, Road Transport and Highways, Thiru T.R. Baalu here today to discuss issues relating to road development in the State of Punjab. On the State Government's request to reduce the land acquisition on a particular stretch of 500 meters on NH-22 in Zirakpur Town from 45 meters to 40 metres, Thiru Baalu assured the Chief Minister that a team of NHAI officials would be sent to visit the site very soon to sort out this issue.

Regarding Patiala-Bhatinda stretch of NH-64, Thiru Baalu informed the Chief Minister that the Inception report has already been submitted to the Government of India. The proposal for consultancy services has been included in the Annual Plan 2007-08, he said and the execution of work will be taken on BOT basis. Regarding Amritsar-Pathankot stretch of NH-15, Thiru Baalu directed the Ministry officials to expedite sanction of the estimate submitted by the State PWD for the improvement of the 23 kms of the dilapidated stretch. In the meantime, the State PWD can go ahead with the bidding process. However, the award of the work should be done only after the sanction. Thiru Baalu also assured the Punjab Chief Minister that the State Government's request to extend the Ludhiana-Talwandi Bhai stretch upto Firozpur under NHDP-III, would be considered and a decision would be taken soon in this regard by NHAI.

1614. (22-6-2007) NEW DELHI : The Annual Plan outlay for Uttarakhand for the year 2007-08 was finalized at a meeting, here today, between the Deputy Chairman Planning Commission, Shri Montek Singh Ahluwalia and Chief Minister of Uttaranchal Shri B.C. Khanduri. The Annual Plan size was agreed at Rs.4378.63 crores. This includes additional Central assistance of Rs.275 crores of which Rs.175 crores would be for projects of special interest to the State and Rs.50 crores each for infrastructure related to Kumbh Mela at Haridwar and South Asian Winter Games respectively. Deputy Chairman, Planning Commission, complemented the State for performance during the Tenth Plan period and said that economic growth was higher than the all India average. He pointed out that against approved outlay of Rs.7630 crores, expenditure during the plan was Rs.9784.35 crores. He said the State government should give more emphasis to infrastructure development for sustaining high growth achieved in industrial development. Public private partnership in development of infrastructure should be encouraged. He said the State should integrate science & technology in development programmes and initiate action plan at improving tourism. Institutional framework should be strengthened and private sector participation enhanced in infrastructure development. Rural health institutions should be strengthened and efforts made to reduced gender gap in literacy. Attention was also drawn to high poverty levels. The State was advised to encourage participatory irrigation management and have more emphasis on sanitation. Attention was also drawn to health indicators. Briefing the Commission on the development strategy, Mr. Khanduri said that a strict financial discipline in public expenses was being imposed as the State was against becoming a debt ridden State. He said focus will be on optimum utilization of land resources and adherence to FRBM. Key drivers would be tourism, horticulture, medicinal plants, hydro-energy and biotechnology. He said employment generation would be the thrust of planning as local people have only marginally benefited from the new industries that have come in the State. To make growth more inclusive the State government will work towards addressing problem of regional imbalance. Infrastructure development will get highest priority with special emphasis on improving connectivity of remote and inaccessible areas.

1615. (22-6-2007) NEW DELHI : The Finance Minister, Shri P. Chidambaram conferred Navratna status on three Central Public Sector Enterprises (CPSEs), viz (i) Bharat Electronics Limited, (ii) Hindustan Aeronautics Limited and (iii) Power Finance Corporation Limited and released the "Guidelines on Corporate Governance for CPSEs", here today. Conferring the Navratna status on three CPSEs, the Finance Minister said, "we need to reassess the role of CPSEs in the context of growing economy." He said more and more CPSEs should list on the Stock Exchange. Shri Chidambaram said, he was confident that the Heavy Industries and Public Enterprises Minister, Shri Sontosh Mohan Dev would continue to take firm, bold and decisive steps in revitalizing the CPSEs. Navratna status would empower Boards of Directors of these CPSEs to exercise greater autonomy and powers and thereby substantially improve their performance. Besides, these CPSEs can improve their activities to become global giants. In August, 2005, the Government had substantially enhanced the powers delegated to the Boards of Directors of Navratna, Miniratna and other profit making CPSEs. The Government also approved the Guidelines on Corporate Governance for CPSEs. These guidelines have been formulated through a consultation process with various stakeholders and keeping in view the relevant laws, rules and instructions. These guidelines cover issues like composition of Board of Directors, setting up of Audit Committees, role and powers of Audit Committees, issues relating to subsidiary companies, disclosures, accounting standards, risk management, compliance and schedule of implementation, etc. These guidelines will be for an experimental phase of one year and suitable adjustments would thereafter be made in these guidelines in the light of experience gained. Proper implementation of these guidelines would facilitate protection of interests of shareholders and other stakeholders. Earlier, in his speech, Union Minister for Heavy Industries and Public Enterprise, Shri Sontosh Mohan Dev said, "the CPSEs have a glorious history. From a modest beginning in April 1951 with 5 enterprises, their number has now gone up to 245. The investment in CPSEs has gone up from Rs.29 crore in 1951 to about Rs.4 lakh crore in 2006. In 2005-06, the Public Enterprises with a total turnover of about Rs.8.3 lakh crore accounted for 11 per cent of GDP." He said that the Government under NCMP had taken a number of steps to create favourable business environment for CPSEs. Government supported revival of 26 CPSEs with cash and non-cash assistance of Rs.8,450.00 crore, he added. Shri Dev said, four more companies *i.e.* National Aluminium Company Limited, National Mineral Development Corporation of India Limited, Power Grid Corporation of India Limited and Rural Electrification Corporation Limited would also be conferred Navratna status as soon as they fulfilled the condition of requisite number of non-official Directors on their Boards. Earlier, the Navratna Companies consisted of nine CPSEs : BHEL, BPCL, GAIL, HPCL, IOC, MTNL, NTPC, ONGC and SAIL. The Minister of State for Heavy Industries and Public Enterprises, Smt. Kanti Singh and Secretary, Ministry of Heavy Industries and Public Enterprises, Dr. R.C. Panda also spoke on the occasion.

1616. (22-6-2007) NEW DELHI : A delegation of the United National Progressive Alliance (UNPA) met the President, Dr. A.P.J. Abdul Kalam at Rashtrapati Bhavan today. After discussions on the Presidential election, the President told the delegation that after considering their request and reviewing the situation carefully from all angles, he has decided that in the current scenario he will not be interested in running for the second term as he does not want Rashtrapati Bhavan to become involved in any political process. Dr. Kalam also thanked the UNPA for its initiative. Dr. Kalam also told them that his mission in life is to work for development of the country which he will continue to do wherever he will be. The President also thanks the people of India for the overwhelming love and affection towards him.

1617. (22-6-2007) NEW DELHI : Following is the text of the Prime Minister, Dr. Manmohan Singh's address at the 150th Anniversary of University of Mumbai: "For me it is always a pleasure to be at a University and among students. Today, it gives me added pleasure to be here at the 150th anniversary celebrations of this great University. I wish you all well on this very happy and auspicious occasion. May your University continue to light the lamp of education and serve the cause of national development. Set up originally as the University of Bombay, Mumbai University is one of our oldest and greatest Universities of the modern era. Like the great universities of ancient India, Nalanda, Takshasila and Nagarjuna, the Mumbai University has played an exceedingly important role in the spread of knowledge and learning in our country. It has been the alma mater of some of our greatest national leaders-like Shri Gopala Krishna Gokhale, Justice Ranade, Dr. B.R. Ambedkar, Lokmanya Bal Gangadhar Tilak, Dadabai Nauroji, Shri Badaruddin Tyabji, Smt. Usha Mehta and Sir Chintamani Deshmukh to mention only a few. This galaxy of eminent scholars, scientists, industrialists, administrators and professionals in all walks of life have received their education at this great University. No wonder it is rated among the top-500 universities in the world and I venture to suggest that this is not good enough. This University should have the ambition to be among the top of atleast 100 Universities in the world. My young friends, you have much to be proud of about the 150-year-old legacy of your University. When you leave the portals of this University, you must always remember that you have been the beneficiaries of a unique opportunity-an opportunity of studying at the University of Mumbai. I am happy to say that in my own academic life I came in contact with many distinguished scholars from this University. In my own discipline of economics, the Mumbai University has left a lasting imprint through the work of such great Indian economists as Prof. C.N. Vakil, Prof. P.R. Brahmananda, Prof. D.T. Lakdawala and Prof. M.L. Dantwala. They gave leadership to what came to be called the "Bombay School of Economics". They had a different worldview and contested the ideas of other great thinkers such as Prof. P.C. Mahalanobis, Prof. K.N. Raj and other teachers at the Delhi School of Economics. In other disciplines too, Mumbai University has made a mark for itself. In the popular imagination the City of Mumbai has come to represent the world of finance, business and cinema. However, let us not forget that Mumbai is also a great intellectual centre and home to some of our most important research institutions in the fields of science, technology and the social sciences. Some of our most distinguished scientists have worked here at the Tata Institute of Fundamental Research and the Bhabha Atomic Research Centre. I therefore salute the great contribution Mumbai has made to the world of knowledge, academia and the cause of research in our country.

1618. (22-6-2007) NEW DELHI : With the advancement of Southwest monsoon sowing of Kharif crops has picked up in various states. Transplanting of rice is in progress in the states of Andhra Pradesh, Assam, Haryana, J&K, Karnataka, Kerala, Orissa, Punjab, Tamil Nadu, Uttarkhand and West Bengal. The total coverage has been 23.140 lakh hectare, the weekly crop weather watch group meeting of the Ministry of Agriculture was informed here today. Total coarse cereals covers an area of 8.306 lakh hectare, with jowar in 1.780 lakh hectare, bajra in 0.686 lakh hectare and maize in 4.781 lakh hectare. Cotton has been sown in 15.290 lakh hectare in the States of Haryana, Maharashtra, Punjab, Rajasthan and Tamil Nadu. Out of this 8.68 lakh hectare is under BT cotton. Sugarcane coverage is reported to be 44.020 lakh hectare and jute 7.864 lakh hectare. As for oilseeds, the total coverage so far has been 4.52 lakh hectare with the break up of groundnut in 2.53 lakh hectare, soyabean in 0.24 lakh hectare, sunflower 0.81 lakh hectare, sesamum in 0.77 lakh hectare and castor in 0.17 lakh hectare.

1619. (22-6-2007) NEW DELHI : Shri Kamal Nath, Minister of Commerce and Industry said today that the talks among the G-4 Ministers broke down in Potsdam (Germany) on 21 June, 2007 because of the failure of the developed countries to accept effective reductions in their agricultural subsidies and at the same time, seeking additional market access in the developing countries for their agricultural products, including for their highly subsidized ones. "Agreeing to this would have not only been against the mandate of the Doha Development Round, it would have seriously jeopardized the livelihoods of the farmers of the developing and least developed countries and threatened the food security of many poorer nations", Shri Kamal Nath said, emphasising that there was no question of any compromise on agricultural market access issues which would have affected our farmers. The Trade Ministers of G-4 (India, Brazil, the EC and the US) met in Potsdam 19-21 June 2007. This was the second meeting of the G-4 Trade Ministers since April 2007, when they had charted out a road map in New Delhi for meetings among themselves to engage intensively on all the important issues relating to the stalled Doha Round negotiations of the World Trade Organisation (WTO). The Ministers had resolved then to try to seek convergence on as many issues as possible by the third week of June, so as to facilitate a consensus in the larger multilateral process in the WTO. On the issue of market access in non-agricultural products or industrial tariffs, the developed countries had proposed Swiss coefficients of 10 and 15 for themselves and developing countries respectively, which would have led to the former taking average tariff cuts in their industrial products of just over 30%, while the developing countries would have had to reduce their tariffs by more than 60% on an average. This could only have helped the developed countries to make heavy inroads into the markets of developing countries while offering negligible reciprocal gains to the latter. It also held out the specter of deindustrialization of the developing countries along with a reduction of foreign direct investment flows into them. This was totally unacceptable to the developing countries, as it would have led to increasing unemployment among their workforce. The developed countries also expressed reluctance in allowing the reform of the current regime of trade defence measures including anti-dumping and countervailing duties, which have often been used unfairly by them against the developing countries, in order to curb their export growth. The other major issue was the unwillingness of the developed countries to accept the discipline of the International Convention on Bio-Diversity in the arena of patents and trademarks so as to allow untrammeled exploitation of traditional knowledge and natural genetic resources, without prior consent or benefit sharing with the community. While expressing his disappointment at the failure of the G-4 talks, Shri Kamal Nath stated that the Doha Round had been announced as a Development Round and had raised the expectations of the developing world that it would help them tackle their problems of unemployment and poverty through increased trade opportunities. However, the current aspirations of many of the developed countries were totally oblivious to the development content of the Round and were instead focused mainly on seeking greater market access for their own products. The Minister expressed hope that India, which was a firm believer in a rule based, fair and transparent multilateral system of trade, would work with other like minded countries-both developing as well as developed, to bring about a successful conclusion of the Doha Round, which was truly reflective of the development objectives of the Round. It may be recalled that prior to the Potsdam meeting, Shri Kamal Nath had participated in the meetings of the G-20, G-33 and NAMA-11 Ministers in Geneva on 11th June, 2007.

1620. (22-6-2007) NEW DELHI : The High Level Committee on Manufacturing chaired by the Prime Minister has decided that the apparel & garments sector which is a high employment generating sector will be given high priority. The Committee at meeting yesterday decided that specific policies to encourage the sector would be put in place with high priority in plan allocations for this sector. It highlighted that adequate supply of fibre is essential for the long term growth of the textiles and garment industry. And for this purpose, an expert committee would be constituted to prepare a comprehensive long term fibre policy covering both cotton and manmade fibres. The industry is expected to grow at an average rate of 16%. Already there are signs of shortage of skilled manpower. It was decided that a major skill training programme be taken up immediately to meet the short fall. The textile Industry is expected to grow substantially over the next few decades. It would require large-scale textile machinery. Currently there is a shortage in supply of textile machinery which is also impeding the growth of textile & garments sector. Therefore, it has been decided to set up a working group to look into the issues relating to the development of textile machinery and make recommendations. Technical textiles which includes Agrotech, Geotech, Autotech, Buildtech, etc., is an important area with high growth potential and also for exports. India has been lagging behind in this area. The HLCM decided that the recommendations of the expert committee report which is already available would be implemented on a priority basis with in six months. The two important schemes viz-Technology Upgradation Fund Scheme (TUFS) and the Scheme for Integrated Textile Parks (SITP) would be continued and provided with adequate funds in the 11th Plan to ensure robust growth of the textile and Garments sector.

1621. (22-6-2007) NEW DELHI : The Government has sold about 19.62 lakh Handloom Mark labels and till now 1303 units have been registered to avail the benefits of the Handloom Mark Scheme. The handloom Mark was launched by the Prime Minister on 28th June, 2006 on the same lines as the Wool Mark and Silk Mark so as to give a distinctive identity to handloom products. Handloom Mark will not only serve as a guarantee to the buyer that the product, consumer is purchasing, is genuine hand woven product but also be able to give better remuneration to the weaver for his hard work and skill. It will help in distinguishing a handloom product from the power loom and mill products and help in increasing sales. The Textile Committee in the Ministry of Textiles is the implementing agency. Individual weavers, master weavers, cooperatives, handloom corporations, retailers and exporters are the intended beneficiaries.

1622. (22-6-2007) NEW DELHI : Till date 80 houses were inspected in Delhi, out of which 67 have been recommended for approval under the 'Incredible India Bed & Breakfast Scheme'. These 67 approved houses provide a total of 187 rooms, out of which 71 rooms are in Gold category and 116 rooms are in Silver category. In addition, 41 other applications were received in Delhi, which were incomplete and the applicants have been asked to complete the applications and send it to the Regional Director (North), New Delhi. At present, only 16 applications are pending in Delhi, which are complete and out of these, 10 applicants would be inspected in the next week. The accredition fees for Gold category is Rs. 5,000 per unit and Rs. 3,000 per unit for Silver category.

1623. (22-6-2007) NEW DELHI : A list of 90 Minority Concentration Districts (MCDs) in the country has been prepared by the Ministry of Minority Affairs, Government of India on the basis of the 2001 census data on population, socio-economic indicators and basic amenities indicators. These districts are backward with unacceptably low levels of either socio-economic or amenities indicators or both and they are in urgent need of focused attention. In 1987, a list of 41 Minority Concentration Districts was prepared based on the data of census 1971. A single criterion of minority population in a district was applied for an identification of such districts. It has been decided to prepare and implement area/problem specific special development plans for these 90 districts. It has also been decided to ensure that the benefit of programmes of poverty alleviation, education, health and provision of basic amenities etc., reach these districts in a focused manner. All Ministries/Departments concerned with such programmes are being advised suitably.

1624. (22-6-2007) NEW DELHI : The Board of Approval (BOA) of the Special Economic Zones (SEZs) met here today to consider proposals for setting up of Special Economic Zones and also approve other miscellaneous requests pertaining to SEZs. In this meeting, 53 applications for setting up SEZs were considered and 36 Formal approvals and 9 In-principle approvals were granted. Prominent among the Formal approvals are: Electronic Hardware SEZ by Foxconn India Developers Private Limited in Tamil Nadu; Aviation Sector SEZ by GMR Hyderabad International Airport Limited in Andhra Pradesh; One IT/ITES SEZ and one Gem and Jewellery SEZ by Omnibus Industrial Development Corporation of Daman & Diu and Dadra & Nagar Haveli; Three SEZs for Biotechnology, Light Engineering and Pharmaceuticals by Navi Mumbai SEZ Private Limited in Maharashtra; IT/ITES SEZ by Reliance Infocom Infrastructure Private Limited in Maharashtra and six IT/ITES SEZs by Electronic Corporation of Tamil Nadu in various Districts of Tamil Nadu and MAS Fabrics Textile SEZ in Andhra Pradesh which is being developed with 100% FDI. Prominent In principle approvals granted are : Electronics and Electrical SEZ, Engineering Equipment & Components SEZ and a Multi Product SEZ by TIDCO in Tamil Nadu; Multi product SEZ by DLF Limited in Rajasthan; Aerospace related industries SEZ by KIADB in Karnataka. With this set of approvals, the total number of SEZs granted formal approval is 339 *i.e.* 339 SEZs are there with land and of these 126 have so far been notified. Investment of 35145 Crores has taken place so far and current employment in new SEZs is about 33000 persons. It is expected that by end of the year additional employment in the new SEZs would cross 100,000. The Chairman of BOA Shri G.K.Pillai, apprised the Members of the Board that the Central Government has issued certain instructions with regard to approval of SEZs and the land acquisition for SEZs and the Chief Secretaries of all the State Governments have been informed that the State Governments would undertake acquisition of land for SEZs only when 100% of the owners give consent. The State Government representatives were informed that if any proposal for compulsorily acquired land comes up, the same would not be notified as SEZ. It was also advised that to the extent possible, double crop and multiple crop lands should not be acquired.

1625. (22-6-2007) NEW DELHI : Rapid urbanisation is a global phenomenon. It is happening in India at a greater pace as well. As a result, there are multifarious challenges to meet the basic civic and other infrastructure requirements effectively, keeping in tune with the changing dynamics of the country's urbanscape. It is heartening to state that the UPA government at the Centre has put in place a comprehensive action-plan to respond to the growing urban needs. A case in point is the roadmap of Union Ministry of Urban Development for the 11th Five-Year Plan. The ministry has not only been able to visualize the emerging needs in years to come, but has worked the blueprint to meet them adequately.

1626. (22-6-2007) NEW DELHI : Congress Spokesperson Smt Jayanti Natarajan said that the Congress president, Smt Sonia Gandhi, strongly condemns the appearance of a poster in Moradabad depicting her as a Goddess. She has directed the Pradesh Congress Committee to enquire into the matter and identify the person or persons responsible for this and take immediate action to expel them from the party if they are Congressmen. In case the person or persons involved do not belong to the Indian National Congress, steps should be taken to initiate legal proceedings against the perpetrators. Following this, the DCC president of Moradabad Shri Ajay Saraswat Soni has been relieved from his post with immediate effect. To a question whether Smt Gandhi would apologise as the Congress Party had earlier sought apology from Smt Vasundhra Raje when a similar poster had appeared in Rajasthan, Smt Natarajan said that an inquiry has been ordered to find out how this has happened. And unless the inquiry comes out with details it is not possible for me to say anything further. Regarding the Rajasthan issue, the top BJP leadership till today have absolutely done nothing about those posters. They did not even file an FIR and the Congress leadership, in fact, has reacted within 24 hours and this is the difference between the Congress and the BJP. To a question on allegations made against Pratibha Patil, Smt Natarajan said this is absolutely scandalous allegation and I deny them as being totally baseless without any foundation and is politically motivated It is very clear that the opposition and certain people, since they are not able to find a proper candidate to match the stature of Smt Pratibha Patil, are attempting to create some controversy against her. I feel that this should be strongly condemned and the decorum of the presidential election should be maintained at all costs. It is possible for anybody to make allegations like this. To a question that is the incumbent President playing politics? Smt Natarajan said that we have already made our statement that the high office of President should not be dragged into controversy. This is what is being sought to be done by the leaders of the Third Front. Our candidate is Smt Pratibha Patil and we are very confident that she will win the election and become the next President of India.

1627. (22-6-2007) NEW DELHI : Maj Gen AC Soneja, VSM**, Provost Marshal at the Adjutant General's Branch, Integrated HQ of MoD (Army), DHQ Post, New Delhi-110 011 has been appointed as the new appellate authority under Right to Information (RTI) Act 2005 for the Army HQ. Earlier this was vested with DG (DC & W) at the Army HQ. Henceforth Maj Gen AC Soneja will receive all appeals relating to the Army under RTI 2005.

1628. (22-6-2007) NEW DELHI : The President of India has accepted the resignation of Smt. Pratibha Patil as Governor of Rajasthan and has appointed Dr. A.R. Kidwai, Governor of Haryana to discharge the functions of the Governor of Rajasthan in addition to his own duties.

1629. (22-6-2007) NEW DELHI : Following is the text of the Prime Minister, Dr. Manmohan Singh's address at the CNBC-TV18 Emerging India Awards, 2007 for Small and Medium Enterprises in Mumbai today: "The emergence of a new generation of Indian enterprise is one of the great success stories of modern India. Indeed, there are few parallels in the developing world for this phenomenon. The values of an open economy and an open society enshrined in our Constitution have enabled lakhs of first generation entrepreneurs to flower impressively in the course of a generation. This is a matter of great pride for us. It shows that as new opportunities emerge, Indians are ready to make full use of them. We are second to none when it comes to entrepreneurship. I salute the spirit of enterprise of our people. There is a commonly held but not fully accurate notion that, in the post-independence period, the Indian economy was essentially a government dominated public sector economy. It is true that in the early years, the public sector had to step in to create the foundations for the growth of private enterprise. It is also true that private enterprise was constrained by a plethora of controls and regulations. However, that is the story whose time has gone by. Private enterprise did grow wherever opportunities presented themselves. This has been more in evidence in the past 15 years since we launched the programme of liberalization. On an occasion like this much has been said and done to celebrate the growth of modern Indian enterprise in recent years. However, much of this celebration has been confined to the success of big business houses. I do not deny this success. But, the profile of top business houses has seen a sea-change since late 50's and today. Large private business groups have overtaken public sector firms and more interestingly, first generation entrepreneurs have overtaken more established business houses. And many of them began as SMEs. This does point to the dynamism in the corporate sector. It also provides hope and confidence that many of you here today will smoothly transform yourselves into large industrial houses in the future in years to come. It is this animal spirit of enterprise and creativity, nurtured in SMEs, that we have unleashed and which is going to be the vehicle for our sustained growth. The growth and spread of small and medium enterprises in the last six decades is impressive. They have contributed both to the growth of new industries as well as of new industrial centres. Cities and towns like Surat, Rajkot, Tiruppur, Coimbatore, Hosur, Faridabad, Ludhiana, Visakhapatnam and scores of others have come up because of the growth of small and medium enterprises. We must acknowledge the role which corporate entities, both in the public and private sector, have played in nurturing SMEs through sub-contracting and ancillarisation. This has been particularly true in industries like automobiles and auto accessories, steel products, machine tools, textiles and apparels, chemicals and pharmaceuticals. The growth of SMEs has also been facilitated by the rejuvenation of artisanal skills and traditional crafts. SMEs have also benefited from the winds of change blowing across our economy as a result of our increasing openness. They have today greater access to global markets and have become part of evolving global supply chains. Consequently, they have also upgraded their own skills, capabilities and technology levels. I will suggest that we must also recognize the role that public policy has played in enabling the growth of the SME sector. The policy of encouraging small industry, the support given by public financial institutions and particularly by banks whose shining example is shown by ICICI and the infrastructure provided by states have all contributed to the growth of SMEs. Economists sometimes criticize some of the policies on the grounds that they have discouraged efficiency, employment growth and have contributed to high capital intensity, even in the SME sector. Some of the criticism is probably valid. However, one should not take a narrow economics-oriented view of our SME policy. I believe we must take a wider sociological view. SMEs have proved to be the largest creators of employment opportunities. They account for more than a third of our manufacturing output and exports. They will be the best bet for the future in creating more and more employment opportunities that we need if we have to reduce the proportion of our population dependent on agriculture. SMEs have also contributed to creativity, innovation and dynamism in the industrial sector. They have led to the spread of industrial development across the country and have strengthened the foundations of industrial capitalism. The spread of wealth and its wider dispersal of managerial and technical competence, and of learning-by-doing knowledge are considerable. This should not be under estimated. A large part of the process of urbanization in India is based on the growth and spread of small and medium enterprises. The time has come for a new leap forward for our SME sector. You must become more globally competitive. You must reduce costs and improve productivity. You must pay greater attention to quality and to the welfare of your employees and workers. International experience shows that it is possible for SMEs to remain globally competitive even in an increasingly integrated global market. In fact, the increasing need for greater customer choice and the move away from mass production of uniform products to small batch production of differentiated products have made SMEs more relevant to the spirit of our times.

1630. (23-6-2007) NEW DELHI : The Prime Minister, Dr. Manmohan Singh spoke to the Chief Minister of Assam regarding the bomb blasts and the flood situation. The Prime Minister conveyed his condolences to families of dead and also condemned the attack. He expressed his sympathies for flood-affected people. The Central Government has offered to extend all help.

1631. (23-6-2007) NEW DELHI : The Prime Minister, Dr. Manmohan Singh was briefed by the Chief Ministers of Andhra Pradesh and Kerala on the flood situation in both States. The Prime Minister offered central assistance and conveyed condolences to families of dead and his sympathies and help to affected people.

1632. (23-6-2007) NEW DELHI : Glaring facts have appeared in public domain regarding the alleged attempt by Smt. Pratibha Patil, UPA's Presidential candidate, to protect her brother who has been accused of conspiring the murder of the president of the Jalagaon District Congress Committee. These are all stark, important and disturbing facts much in existence even before she was considered as a candidate for the highest Constitutional office of the country. Therefore, consistent with the norms of dignity, transparency and Constitutional propriety relating to such high office, the BJP would like Smt. Pratibha Patil herself to satisfactorily reply to some of the most disturbing questions that have emerged from Smt. Rajani Patil's revelations yesterday: 1) Shri V.G. Patil, President of District Congress Committee, Jalagaon was murdered on Sep 21, 2005 and his widow Prof. Rajani Patil has been repeatedly alleging since then that the murder was the outcome of a political conspiracy in which Dr. G.N. Patil, brother of Smt. Pratibha Patil, and one Dr. Ulhas Patil, were the key conspirators. The conspirators were allegedly angry with V.G. Patil because he had defeated Dr. G.N. Patil in election to the office of Jalagaon District President, just a few months before the murder. Did Smt. Pratibha Patil, who also hails from Jalagaon, ever offer a word of sympathy to the widow of a slain Congress leader? 2) Is it not a fact that, on September 27, 2005, Smt. Rajani Patil named Dr. G.N. Patil and Dr. Ulahas Patil as the principal conspirators and demanded action against them in her letter to the Police Chief, Jalagaon? Why is it that, even 21 months after the murder, neither of the alleged conspirators has even been summoned for preliminary questioning, leave aside being arrested? Could this have happened if Dr. G.N. Patil had no high connections? 3) Is it not a fact that Raju Mali and Raju Sonawane; the two alleged assassins who went on an indefinite fast inside the jail, told in the programme 'Hatyara Kaun?' on Aaj Tak in Oct 2006 that they have been made sacrificial lambs in this case and that the real conspirators, named by Smt. Rajani Patil, have been allowed to go scot-free? In spite of this, why did the police not question Dr. G.N.Patil and Dr. Ulhas Patil? 4) When Smt. Rajani Patil did not get any justice for a fair investigation by the state CID, she filed Criminal Writ Petition No. 646 of 2005 in the Aurangabad Bench of Bomay High Court where she, in paragraph 3 and 4 of the writ petition made specific complaints against Dr. G.N. Patil and Dr. Ulhas Patil. She also mentioned that he late husband had complained to the Congress high command about the misdeeds of these two leaders. In fact, in paragraph 4 of the Writ Petition it was also mentioned that Dr. G. N. Patil happens to be the bother of the Governor of Rajasthan. The High Court vide its order dated 23/02/2007, having regard to the importance of issue involved, took cognisance of the alleged complicity of the influential political leaders, and found the case to be fit to be investigated by the CBI. Smt. Pratibha Patil should explain who are the influential political leaders whose complicity the High Court suspected. 5) As per the High Court ruling, the CBI team visited Jalagaon on April 4, 2007. On April 7, the CBI interrogated Smt. Rajani Patil. Very curiously, on the same day, Raju Mali, the principal assassin, who was in Police custody, died in mysterious circumstances. Is just a coincidence? Or, rather, doesn't it reinforce the charge of conspiracy and suppression of evidence? 6) From the chronology of these facts it obvious that there has been a persistent attempt to prevent any fair investigation into such a high profile murder. The surrounding circumstances are not only very suspicious but clearly point out to the interplay of highly influential forces because the widow, Smt. Rajani Patil, had personally met Smt. Sonia Gandhi in her quest of justice. She had also, in a detailed letter to Smt. Sonia Gandhi on 5 March 2007, stated that Dr. G.N. Patil, the brother of Smt. Pratibha Patil, had given a 'supari' (contract to kill) to kill her husband. This allegation has been made by the widow of a Congress leader to the Congress president. Therefore, Smt. Pratibha Patil should come clean if she also clarified her position to the Congress president. 7) Therefore, it is important that Smt. Pratibha Patil must herself respond to these disturbing questions because these facts are related to her and the resultant questions are also related to her. The Congress spokespersons cannot speak on her behalf and dismiss Smt. Rajani Patil's revelations as a "smear campaign" by the opponents of the UPA. The BJP does not have the slightest doubt that the Congress leadership knew about all these facts. Yet, Smt. Pratibha Patil was chosen to be the UPA candidate for the presidential election. Is it because, apart from loyalty to the 'Gandhi Family', she was also vulnerable, so that she would sign on the dotted line?

1633. (23-6-2007) NEW DELHI : The first Meeting of the National Committee for Commemoration of Tri centenary of Guru-ta-Gaddi of Shri Guru Granth Sahib was held today on 23.6.2007. The commemoration is scheduled to be held in September-October, 2008. Shri Shivraj V. Patil, Hon'ble Home Minister of India chaired the meeting. Shri Vilasrao Deshmukh, Hon'ble Chief Minister of Maharashtra co-chaired. Smt. Ambika Soni, Hon'ble Minister of Culture, Government of India, Shri S.S. Barnala, Governor, Tamil Nadu, Shri R.L. Bhatia, Governor, Kerala, Shri Prakash Singh Badal, Chief Minister, Punjab, Shri Buta Singh, Chairman, Commission for Scheduled Castes, Smt. Surya Kanta Patil, Union Minister of State for Rural Development and Parliamentary Affairs, Shri Ashok S. Chavan, Minister of Industry and Culture, Govt. of Maharashtra, Shri Avtar Singh, President, S.G.P.C., Smt. Rajinder Kaur Bhattal, Leader, Congress Legislative Party, Punjab, Paramjit Singh Sarna, President, Delhi Gurdwara Prabandhak Committee (DGPC), amongst others attended the meeting. All the members unanimously congratulated the Central Govt. and Govt. of Maharashtra for commemorating Tri centenary of Guru-ta-Gaddi of Guru Granth Sahib. Collector, Nanded, made a detailed presentation regarding the progress of development works being undertaken at Nanded at a total cost of Rs.817 crores approximately. These development works are mainly being funded by the Central Government under the Jawaharlal Nehru Urban Renewal Mission and the State Government.

1634. (23-6-2007) NEW DELHI : The Minister for Steel, Chemicals and Fertilisers Shri Ram Vilas Paswan is leaving New Delhi today for Australia. The high level delegation will explore opportunities in Australia for meeting growing demand for coking coal in India. The delegation includes the Chairman of Steel Authority of India Shri S.K.Roongta, Joint Secretary in the Ministry of Steel Shri George Elias and senior officials from the Rashtriya Ispat Nigam Limited and National

Mineral Development Corporation.. The two public sector companies, SAIL and RINL, together import over 15 million tones of coking coal in a year, nearly 90 percent of which comes from Australia. With the two companies set to double their installed capacity in the next few years and private steel companies also adding to their capacity the issue of raw material security remains the strategic issue for the Indian steel sector. The delegation will see first hand the opportunities available there for wider and deeper cooperation for ensuring steady supply of coking coal. Shri Paswan will have discussions with the federal Minister for Industries of Australia Mr.Ian McFarlane and ministers in the provincial governments of Western Australia. Western Australia is one of the key outsourcing points for coking coal. During his stay in Australia the Minister will have meeting with Chamber of Minerals and Energy at Perth and will also be given presentations by some leading companies like Rio Tinto and BHP Billiton. Shri Paswan will visit Illawarra coking coalmines at Wollongong. The delegation will visit Port Kembla to witness high speed handling of cargo.

1635. (24-6-2007) NEW DELHI : Shri Murli Deora, Union Minister of Petroleum and Natural Gas today laid the Foundation Stone of BPCL's Kochi Refinery Expansion-Cum-Modernisation Project at Cochin. On this occasion Shri. V.S. Achuthanandan, Chief Minister of Kerala and Shri. Vayalar Ravi, Union Minister for Overseas Indian Affairs among others were present. Shri M.S.Srinivasan, Secretary Ministry of Petroleum & Natural Gas and Shri Ashok Sinha, Chairman & Managing Director of Bharat Petroleum Corporation Ltd. also attended the ceremony. Speaking on the occasion, Shri Deora informed that Kochi refinery is being expanded to 9.5 million metric tonne per annum (MMTPA) from the existing 7.5 MMPA at a cost of about Rs.2,600 crore. In addition, Kochi Refinery is also implementing a single point mooring project which will enable import of crude through VLCCs. This project will be commissioned over the next 3 months at an estimated cost of over Rs.800 crore. Thus, Kochi Refinery will invest about Rs.3,500 crore in next two to three years. Petroleum Minister further emphasized that Investment by Kochi Refinery will not only lead to creation of direct and indirect jobs but also boost industrial activity in the State. There will be development of support industries leading to economic and social development. After the expansion, Kochi Refinery will supply green fuels conforming to Euro III/IV specifications. Shri Deora also informed that Oil Industry now is largest merchandise exporter of the country with exports of over $17.5 billion during last year. It is expected that the oil sector will become a much larger exporter during the 11th plan. BPCL's refineries including Kochi Refinery will participate in making the country an export hub of petroleum products. Referring to the oil Ministry's efforts to improve the oil security of the nation, he said that another initiative in this direction has been to introduce bio-fuels, particularly Ethanol Blended Petrol (EBP), across the country. With a notification effective November, 2006, whole country except a few identified areas will be covered under the 5% EBP programme with the aim of enhancing energy security. Pointing out that EBP not only benefits the environment but also the farmers, Shri Deora sought full cooperation of the State Governments of three southern States namely Kerala, Tamil Nadu and Karnataka. He took a meeting yesterday evening at Cochin to review the progress of implementation of EBP Programme in these States. Shri asked the State Government of Kerala to issue the necessary notification on levy of applicable taxes/duties on ethanol meant for blending with petrol at an early date. The State Government assured to soon take appropriate action. In respect of Tamil Nadu, the State Government was requested to allow supply of ethanol for EBP Programme as the resumption of supplies for the EBP Programme in the State will ultimately benefit the farmers besides reducing import dependence for hydrocarbons. Tamil Nadu also assured to consider the issue. Shri Deora expressed happiness that State Government of Karnataka responded favourably to his suggestion for appropriately reducing VAT on ethanol meant for EBP. Karnataka issued a notification yesterday reducing VAT from 20% to 4%. The meeting was attended by Shri Thomas Issac, Finance Minister of Kerala, Secretary, Food and Consumer Affairs of Kerala and Transport Secretary of Tamil Nadu besides Union Petroleum Secretary Shri M S Srinivasan and senior officers of the Ministry of Petroleum and Natural Gas and the Oil Marketing Companies. Shri Murli Deora further said that the UPA Government has undertaken strong measures to protect the consumers from the impact of soaring global oil prices and to keep the economy on the track. The Government and the oil companies are together sharing 87% of the burden of under-recoveries caused by the high oil prices this year. To keep the home fires burning, the prices of the common man's fuels, domestic LPG and PDS Kerosene, have been kept unchanged despite the global oil prices touching record highs. Later responding to the questions of media persons, Shri Deora informed that the Kochi LNG Terminal of Petronet LNG Ltd. is expected to be completed in February 2011. This LNG terminal is planned to have a capacity to receive 2.5 MMTPA LNG and would involve an investment of about Rs 3,000 crore. He clarified that there was no shortage of LPG in the State or in the country. However some difficulties were caused factors like strike.

1636. (24-6-2007) NEW DELHI : Shri Mani Shankar Aiyar, Union Minister for DoNER has stated that time has now come for an Indian delegation from the North-East to visit Thailand to attract Thai investment and to create business opportunities in the region. He urged the business persons from North-East to make presentations to the Thai side when they visit Thailand. The visit could be arranged under the aegis of the North-East Council (NEC) and the Indian Chamber of Commerce. The Minister hoped that the year 2008 will be the year of cooperation between the NE states and Thailand. He was speaking at the Special Session on 'Investment Opportunities in the North East' held at Shillong today. Shri Aiyar hoped that the Thai side would provide arrangements for holding sectors specific business meetings between the Indian delegation and the Thai side. The special session was organized as part of the visit of the Thai delegation to the North-East to study investment prospects in the region. Commenting on India's 'Look East

Policy' Shri Aiyar said that the policy should primarily benefit the NE Region, which is the gateway to South East Asia. The NE Region has cultural, historical relationship with Thailand, as well as contiguity which could facilitate cooperation between them. The Thailand Commerce Minister Shri Krirk-Krai Jirapet said that Thailand has identified various sectors to invest in NE, such as, tourism, hydropower, minerals, horticulture etc. and urged the investors from the NE to visit Thailand. He said that there was a need to give a greater thrust to cooperation between India and Thailand, both having common contacts and relationships. Giving the welcome address at the function, the Meghalaya Chief Minister, Dr. D.D. Lapang, hoped that investments will rise in NE Region with the keen interest shown by the Thai delegation. Meghalaya has rich natural resources like limestone, coal etc., which can be tapped for investment. Various North Eastern States like Meghalaya, Nagaland, Arunachal Pradesh and Sikkim gave presentations on various sectors for investment like tourism, horticulture, mineral resources, floriculture, hydel power, post harvest management, packaging industries in food processing, etc. The function was also attended by Ministers and senior officials from the NE states, NEC and DoNER.

1637. (24-6-2007) NEW DELHI : The newly – elected BJP National Discipline Committee held its first meeting in party's Central Office today. The Committee president Shri Ram Naik threw light on discipline sections enshrined in party's constitution. These sections determine the rights and responsibilities of the Discipline Committee. The president of the Discipline Committee Shri Ram Naik along with the members —S/Shri O. Rajagopal (Kerala), Indramani Bora (Assam) and Smt. Mridula Sinha called on the party president Shri Rajnath Singh. Party's national president gave vent to his expectations from the Discipline Committee. He desired special focus in future on organisational matters and added that indiscipline at any level will not be tolerated. He observed that one way of strengthening the organisation is to trim discipline machinery. Emphasising the importance of the Discipline Committee, the Party President expressed desire to talk to all state presidents to constitute Discipline Committees soon in their states. He also desired early constituting of Discipline Committees in Parliament and State Assemblies. He further suggested to hold meeting of presidents of all state Discipline Committees so that party men in entire country may get message that no leniency will be made in the cases indiscipline. Smt. Mridula Sinha was nominated Secretary of the Discipline Committee. All party units will be requested to correspond with her and in her name. Former M.P Shri Ramnath Kovind could not attend the meeting of this five member committee due to his train being late. Shri Ram Naik declared the meeting concluded with vote of thanks to the party president.

1638. (24-6-2007) NEW DELHI : Shri Jairam Ramesh, Minister of State for Commerce, today launched a new initiative of the Spices Board in the Karbi Anglong district of Assam, one of the most backward regions of the state populated by the indigenous people belonging to the Karbi Tribe. This initiative intends to start the organic cultivation of turmeric (haldi), ginger (adrak) and chilli (mirchi) in the district on a large-scale and to promote its processing and export as well. The Chief Minister of Assam, Shri Tarun Gogoi was also present on the occasion of the launch in Karbi Anglong. Two companies have been set up as producers' companies under Section 581 of the Companies Act, 1956—Coinonya Farms Producers Company Limited for turmeric and Karbi Farms Producer Company Limited for ginger and chilli. Producers' Companies is a new provision in the Companies Act which give primary producers' the flexibility to organize themselves as a normal company but on the basis of a one man-one vote principle which is the essence of a cooperative institution. Producers' Company combines the economic advantage of a corporate entity with the social benefits of a cooperative. Section 581 was introduced into the Companies Act, 1956 in the year 2003. The two companies are located in Paroli and Rongmanpi in the Hamren sub-division of Karbi Anglong district. Each company has a full-time chairman and managing director. The Spices Board owns 49% of each company and its equity stake is Rs 1 crore in each company. Local tribal farmers, mostly small and marginal, traditionally practicing jhum cultivation own 51% in each company. Land owned by these farmers have been transferred to these two companies as their contribution to equity. 600 farmers own 51% of Coinonya Farms Producer Company Limited and 400 farmers own 51% of Karbi Farms Producer Company Limited. Each company will initially have a plantation area of 500 hectares which will be cultivated over a five year period, with 175 hectares being taken up in the first year itself. MOUs are being signed with private companies for processing and marketing. The first such MOU has already been signed by Coinonya Farms with Arjuna Natural Extracts for extraction and marketing of turmeric products. Speaking on the occasion, Shri Jairam Ramesh highlighted the social and economic significance of the project. He reiterated his commitment to giving a special and vastly expanded Northeast focus to the Kochi-based Spices Board, particularly in the area of organic spices which command a premium in world markets and in which the northeastern states have a natural competitive advantage. These include ginger where the Northeast already accounts for over 50% of the country's production, turmeric, chilli, black pepper, chilli and large cardamom. He stressed the need for value-addition and the need for organizations like the producer companies established in Karbi Anglong so that the benefits of export growth flow directly to tribal families. He said that at present, the contribution of the Northeast to India's spice exports of about $ 800 million (in 2006/07) is very small but there is great scope for increasing this contribution. For this, the Union Ministry of Commerce is establishing cold storage facilities at Guwahati, Aizawl, Imphal, Agartala and Dimapur airports and has announced a subsidy scheme by which 90% of air freight to Kolkata airport and 50% of air freight to New Delhi and Mumbai airports from Northeast airports for all horticulture products destined for exports is subsidized by the Union government. Shri Ramesh expressed the hope that the Karbi Anglong initiative will be replicated in other parts of the northeast.

He congratulated Shri Donald Ingty, Commissioner of Customs in Kochi who spearheaded this project for the benefit of the community to which he belongs and who sought out the support of the Spices Board in this venture. He appealed to the state government to improve road connectivity to and within Karbi Anglong district and also improve the supply of electricity for the processing units. He promised to take up the issue of improved telecom connectivity with BSNL soon.

1639. (24-6-2007) NEW DELHI : Shri Jairam Ramesh, Minister of State for Commerce, today launched a new initiative of the Spices Board in the Karbi Anglong district of Assam, one of the most backward regions of the state populated by the indigenous people belonging to the Karbi Tribe. This initiative intends to start the organic cultivation of turmeric (haldi), ginger (adrak) and chilli (mirchi) in the district on a large-scale and to promote its processing and export as well. The Chief Minister of Assam, Shri Tarun Gogoi was also present on the occasion of the launch in Karbi Anglong. Two companies have been set up as producers' companies under Section 581 of the Companies Act, 1956—Coinonya Farms Producers Company Limited for turmeric and Karbi Farms Producer Company Limited for ginger and chilli. Producers' Companies is a new provision in the Companies Act which give primary producers' the flexibility to organize themselves as a normal company but on the basis of a one man-one vote principle which is the essence of a cooperative institution. Producers' Company combines the economic advantage of a corporate entity with the social benefits of a cooperative. Section 581 was introduced into the Companies Act, 1956 in the year 2003. The two companies are located in Paroli and Rongmanpi in the Hamren sub-division of Karbi Anglong district. Each company has a full-time chairman and managing director. The Spices Board owns 49% of each company and its equity stake is Rs 1 crore in each company. Local tribal farmers, mostly small and marginal, traditionally practicing jhum cultivation own 51% in each company. Land owned by these farmers have been transferred to these two companies as their contribution to equity. 600 farmers own 51% of Coinonya Farms Producer Company Limited and 400 farmers own 51% of Karbi Farms Producer Company Limited. Each company will initially have a plantation area of 500 hectares which will be cultivated over a five year period, with 175 hectares being taken up in the first year itself. MOUs are being signed with private companies for processing and marketing. The first such MOU has already been signed by Coinonya Farms with Arjuna Natural Extracts for extraction and marketing of turmeric products. Speaking on the occasion, Shri Jairam Ramesh highlighted the social and economic significance of the project. He reiterated his commitment to giving a special and vastly expanded Northeast focus to the Kochi-based Spices Board, particularly in the area of organic spices which command a premium in world markets and in which the northeastern states have a natural competitive advantage. These include ginger where the Northeast already accounts for over 50% of the country's production, turmeric, chilli, black pepper, chilli and large cardamom. He stressed the need for value-addition and the need for organizations like the producer companies established in Karbi Anglong so that the benefits of export growth flow directly to tribal families. He said that at present, the contribution of the Northeast to India's spice exports of about $ 800 million (in 2006/07) is very small but there is great scope for increasing this contribution. For this, the Union Ministry of Commerce is establishing cold storage facilities at Guwahati, Aizawl, Imphal, Agartala and Dimapur airports and has announced a subsidy scheme by which 90% of air freight to Kolkata airport and 50% of air freight to New Delhi and Mumbai airports from Northeast airports for all horticulture products destined for exports is subsidized by the Union government. Shri Ramesh expressed the hope that the Karbi Anglong initiative will be replicated in other parts of the northeast. He congratulated Shri Donald Ingty, Commissioner of Customs in Kochi who spearheaded this project for the benefit of the community to which he belongs and who sought out the support of the Spices Board in this venture. He appealed to the state government to improve road connectivity to and within Karbi Anglong district and also improve the supply of electricity for the processing units. He promised to take up the issue of improved telecom connectivity with BSNL soon.

1640. (25-6-2007) NEW DELHI : Trade between India and Thailand has touched US $ 2 billion in the first 8 months of the financial year 2006-07 (for which data is available), indicating strong growth in bilateral trade relations between the two countries. At a meeting here today between Shri Kamal Nath, Minister of Commerce & Industry and the Commerce Minister of Thailand, Shri Krirk-Krai Jirapaet, both the Ministers expressed satisfaction over the growth in bilateral trade and reiterated their commitment to further intensification of trade and economic relations between the two countries. Bilateral trade between India and Thailand has shown phenomenal growth over the last 5 years, both the Ministers noted. Noting that Thailand has emerged as an important investor in India and now ranks as the third largest investor in India from the ASEAN region after Singapore and Malaysia, Shri Kamal Nath also expressed satisfaction over the growth in Thai investment in India and invited Thailand to explore more opportunities for joint ventures between the two countries. Referring to the India-Thailand FTA, Shri Kamal Nath reiterated the need to simultaneously conclude negotiations so that the Agreement could cover not only Trade in Goods but also Trade in Services and Investment.

1641. (25-6-2007) NEW DELHI : In a fierce firefight with militants in Kupwara Sector of J&K, a Junior Commissioned Officer (JCO) decorated twice earlier for gallantry, was martyred yesterday in Kupwara Sector of Jammu and Kashmir. As per reports reaching here, troops of a Jammu & Kashmir Light Infantry (JAK LI) battalion observed some suspicious move near the line of control (LC) during the intervening night of 23/24 June in Keran sector of Kupwara district. Due to low clouds and poor visibility the movement of terrorists could not be tracked very effectively at night. A search party led by Naib Subear Chunni Lal was launched in the morning hours of Sunday to ascertain facts. The JCO led his troops from the front, though with caution. The troops were fired upon by a group of terrorists hiding near LC. The JCO retaliated immediately with heavy volume of fire. The young JCO putting his acumen into act maneuvered his troops to block all escape routes of the terrorists. This led to elimination of two fleeing terrorists at the outset, the remaining terrorists finding themselves surrounded and out maneuvered made a suicidal bid to escape, injuring two soldiers. Sensing the criticality of the situation and threat to life of his fellow soldiers Naib Subedar Chunni Lal, with total disregard to personal safety not witnessed very often, charged at the terrorists. This act of daredevilry took the remaining three terrorists by total surprise. The JCO though wounded and profusely bleeding, continued to fire at the terrorists till all the remaining three terrorists were killed. This act of great bravery, leadership and supreme sacrifice by a Naib Subear Chunni Lal not only resulted in elimination of five Pak trained terrorists but also saved the lives of his fellow soldiers under his command. Late Naib Subedar Chunni Lal was born in the year 1968 in Baderwah. He joined the JAK LI in 1984. During the course of training he excelled in military subjects, displayed courage and camaraderie, displaying the potentials of making of a great soldier from the very beginning. On joining his unit, young Chunni Lal lived up to the promise of an ideal soldier when in the year 1987, he volunteered and played an important role in capturing the now famous 'BANA Post' located at 21153 feet in the Siachen Glacier, the highest battle filed in the world. For this act of Gallantry he was awarded the SENA MEDAL. Not letting past glories and laurels dull his basic soldierly instincts, zeal and determination to excel, he set for him even higher goals and continued to display a high degree of devotion to duty. He became an example to emulate when in the year 1999 while serving with his unit in the Poonch Sector in 'OPERATION RAKSHAK' he fought an attempted intrusion by Pakistan Army and was instrumental in beating back the Pakistan attack on the post. For this act of gallantry he was awarded the VIR CHAKRA. An asset to Indian Army and the nation, Naib Subedar Chunni Lal, VIR CHAKRA, SENA MEDAL yet again displayed his utility and unflinching devotion to duty when serving in the difficult operating situation of Sudan as a peacekeeper with the United Nations. Here too he was at the forefront in the operations at Malakal. For this action, the Battalion received the United Nations Citation for valour. The valiant JCO belongs to Village Bhaar, Malothi of Bhadarwah tehsil in Doda District of J&K. He will be cremated with full military honours on Wednesday. He is survived by his wife, Mrs. Chinta Devi and two children- a 16 year old son and a eight years old daughter.

1642. (25-6-2007) NEW DELHI : The Defence Minister Shri AK Antony has called for optimal utilization of resources for revenue and capital spending for Defence to ensure the best value for money. Speaking at the foundation laying ceremony of the office of the Controller General of Accounts in New Delhi today the Minister said to achieve this goal, we must make cost effective investments and purchase decisions and make timely and correct payments for stores and services. He said as Internal Financial Advisers to the services, the Defence Accounts Department must undertake greater responsibilities and set an example for others in the services to follow. Shri Antony said "You must ensure that every paisa is spent judiciously". Emphasizing the role of internal audit, the Defence Minister said the best international practices of internal audit must be studied, analysed and imbibed by the Department. He said "A major challenge for you all is to explore auditing through computers and to the maximum extent possible, not rely on paperwork." The Minister was of the view that the Department should achieve cent percent computer literacy within a fixed timeframe. Shri Antony said "your mandate to render transparent, prompt and efficient pensionary services to nearly 21.59 lakh ex-servicemen and other retired defence personnel is a major challenge facing you." The Defence Minister asked the Defence Accounts Department that it must exhibit a high degree of responsiveness for the prompt redressal of grievances of its customers and ensure that the complaint redressal mechanism functions optimally. Shri Antony said "Though financial resources are no doubt important in a department like yours, in the ultimate analysis the quality of human resource is the most crucial factor." The Defence Minister called for adequate attention to optimise human resource development to enhance all-round performance. In his welcome address the Controller General of Defence Accounts Shri Jnan Prakash said that the proposed complex for the office of the Controller General of Defence Accounts, spread over 6.00 acre area has been designed as a state-of-the-art building with perfect blend of aesthetics and architectural features. The proposed disable friendly building conforms to the latest BS codes, environment regulations and is compliant to the seismic zone IV requirement. The project is to be carried out through DRDO with a completion period of 24 months. Secretary Defence Finance Shri VK Mishra also spoke on the occasion.

1643. (25-6-2007) NEW DELHI : Consortium of RITES Ltd. (India)-PCI (Japan)-PBI (USA)-SYSTRA (France) has been awarded the work of providing "General Consultancy Services" for implementation of "Bangalore Metro Project Phase 1" by Bangalore Metro Rail Corporation Ltd. RITES is leader of the Consortium of the International consultants who are renowned and world leaders in the field of Urban Transport. The Consortium has won this contract under very stiff competition from other International companies. The total value of the consultancy services is about Rs. 215 crores out of which the RITES's share is Rs. 126.50 crores (58.8%). In terms of the manmonths, RITES's share is 8795 manmonths (94% of the total technical manmonths). Consultants will provide advise on system design to commissioning of the project including its integration with the other modes of transport in Bangalore. The project consists of 33 Km of the Metro network in two corridors, namely East-West corridor (18Km) and North-South Corridor (15km). It includes 7 Km of the underground portion and balance as elevated. The project is scheduled to be commissioned by 31st December 2011. The project is partly being funded by JBIC, Japan. The present assignment is of much significance and prestige to RITES in view of the fact that RITES is the Leader of the Consortium. RITES was also involved as consortium member in providing the General Consultancy Services for Delhi Metro Project Phase-1 which has been successfully accomplished. RITES is also providing the consultancy services as member of the Consortium for Delhi Metro Phase-2 as well as for the Airport Metro Line.

1644. (25-6-2007) NEW DELHI : Congress Spokesperson Shri Devender Dwivedi said that the election of the President is an important event in the nation's constitutional process and certain sanctity attaches to the election and to the electoral process. Consistent with the nature of the high office of presidency which was described by Nehru as on of "great authority and dignity" the election campaigns in the past have been marked by a certain decorum and dignity. Unfortunately from the day one, the BIP and the NDA have taken a resort, over and covert, to mudslinging, smear campaign and encouraging totally malicious, false and unfounded allegations against UP A Left candidate. This is seeking to destroy the sanctity of the constitutional process and trivialize the electoral campaign. The BJP is setting a very bad precedent. The dubious and controversial nature of the BJP's electoral strategy has also marked the candidature of Shri Shekhawat. The rise and fall and again rise of his candidature have been marked by gross constitutional and political improprieties. Mr. Shekhawat is the first constitutional functionary who has indulged, in a most brazen manner, in politicking while occupying the second highest constitutional post. He as Vice-President attended a BJP-cum-NDA meeting and has been participating in designing his campaign strategy through means which are a common knowledge. The decision of Vice-President Shekhawat to contest the presidential election, however, raises another very important question which has grave implications for our constitutional values. The scheme of our Constitution provides for disqualification of members on the ground of defection and under the Xth Schedule, the Chairman of Rajya Sabha, which the Vice-president is, has been designated as the competent authority to decide any question that may arise as to whether a member has become subject to disqualification on the ground of defection and his decision is final. one same presiding officer of Rajya Sabha has decided to contest presidential election on the sole premise and solitary ground that he would be able to engineer defections on a mass scale from the UPA, Left, BSP combine. Such a piquant situation has no precedent in our parliamentary history. Those who are committed to constitutional values should ponder over the blatant constitutional immorality and gross impropriety of a situation in which the basic plank of the NDA's 'independent' candidate is victory through defections. To a question whether the Congress Party is asking Shri Shekhawat to resign, Shri Dwivedi said that in all fairness there are two kinds of precedents .There have been as many as five Vice-Presidents who have be been elected Presidents, who contested the elections and who did not resign. There has been one case who took on the establishment and he fought the election against the establishment. Therefore, in his wisdom, chose to resign and that was Shri V.V. Giri. Shri Shekhawat will be contesting the elections and the way the office is used or misused is something which we will see and whatever the political parties say should have an element of legitimacy and public perception. To a question that Shri Natwar Singh has signed Shri Shekhawat's nomination, what has Congress Party to say? Shri Dwivedi said that there is no objection to it. He is as much a member of the electoral collage like anybody else To a question on the fresh revelations made against Smt Prathibha Patil, Shri Dwivedi said that my answer is very simple. We have had revelations and you will have many many revelations and people are working at that. There are two central facts which stand out as impertinent and germane to the entire issue and that is the nature of Prathibha Patil's association with the bank, her role in any irregularity, any impropriety or anything which can be remotely regarded as misconduct. Secondly, whether she herself has been attributed to any impropriety. The latest revelation which has come today tells only one side of the story. Smt Prathibha Patil resigned as the chairman of that bank in 1994 and the bank became sick much thereafter. All the allegations and all the irregularities pointed out by the Reserve Bank of India and I have not read the report but from newspapers, what I gather is the fact that all the incidents which the report is talking about is of that period when Smt Prathibha Patil had no legal responsibility as an office-bearer. There is nothing, even remotely, has any bearing on her moral integrity.

1645. (25-6-2007) NEW DELHI : The percentage of indebtedness among the rural labour households has come down from about 60 per cent to around 25 per cent during the last three and half decades. According to the latest Rural Labour Enquiry (1999-2000), conducted by the Labour Bureau, the average debt indebted per household, however, has gone up from around Rs. 250/-(in 1963-65) to about Rs. 6000/-. Money lenders continued to be the biggest source of debt followed by banks and cooperatives. Household consumption accounts for the major purpose of debt followed by marriage and other ceremonies and purchase of land and construction of buildings.

1646. (25-6-2007) NEW DELHI : The Ministry of Rural Development has released Rs. 34.50 crore as balance payment of first instalment of Phase-V for 67 road works valued at Rs.149.00 crore, as Grants-in-aid to the SIKKIM RURAL ROADS DEVELOPMENT AGENCY (SRRDA), which is the Autonomous Agency for receiving the funds for the programme under Pradhan Mantri Gram Sadak Yojana (PMGSY). The grant is towards the Plan expenditure and will be subject to the conditions laid down from time to time in the guidelines of the PMGSY and supplementary directions. PMGSY was launched in December 2000 as a 100 per cent Centrally Sponsored Scheme with a target of connecting every habitation that has a population of more than 1000 within the next three years and every habitation with a population of more than 500 by the year 2007 *i.e.* by the end of the 10th Five Year Plan through good all-weather road. A sum of Rs.20,400.70 crore has been released to the States/UTs towards the programme and up to December 2006, 35,868 roadworks covering a length of 1,07,569.08 Kms. have been completed.

1647. (25-6-2007) NEW DELHI : The Bharatiya Janata Party expresses its grave concern over the total insensitivity and obduracy on the part of the UPA Government and in particular of the Shipping and Transport Minister Shri T.R. Balu in unabashedly proceeding with the implementation of the controversial alignment of the Setu Samudram Canal Project (SSCP) by completely ignoring the opinions of internationally recognized experts, rejecting the appeals from all sections of the society including signatures by 3.6 million people submitted to the President of India demanding a change in the present alignment of the SSCP which is bound to destroy the bridge which is revered by millions of people Hindus, Muslims and Christians as Setu Mandir, Rama Setu, Adi Setu, Adam's Bridge etc., and is considered as the most ancient heritage of our country. Delegations of Acharya Sabha and representatives of Shankaracharyas had waited upon the President and the Prime Minister to apprise them of the strong resentment in the people because they apprehended imminent destruction of the Setu if the proposed alignment was implemented. The Acharyas impressed upon both of them the religious and cultural importance of Ram-Setu and the deep sentiments of the people associated with the Setu. The Prime Minister asked them to meet the Shipping Minister. The Acharya Sabha delegation met Shri Balu, and categorically told him that the opposition was not to the Project but to the alignment and for selecting it arbitrarily which has hurt the sentiments of the people. They also requested to suspend the dredging and to explore the possibility of selecting an alternative alignment which was feasible and would also save the Setu. During the talks Shri Balu invited the Acharyas to visit the site before further discussions. Despite repeated requests from the Acharya Sabha the Minister has been avoiding their visit to the site on one pretext or the other. Obviously he and the government have something to hide. What is even more reprehensible is his statement that those who are opposing the Project are antinational. Infact the Minister, through his various statements, was trying to misguide the public by denying even the existence of a Setu constructed between India and Srilanka in the hoary past. The government has also turned a blind eye to the representations of thousands of fishermen who will lose their only source of livelihood. In the month of March 2007 reports were received about wide spread opposition, particularly in the districts of Madurai and Ramnathpuram and the Rameshwaram region, to the dredging which was about to hit the Setu. Considering the gravity of the situation and importance of the Ram Setu for crores of people who believed the bridge to have been constructed at the command of Shri Ram, the BJP appointed a fact finding Committee with Dr. M.M. Joshi, Sarvashri Yashwant Sinha, Vedprakash Goyal, Shreegopal Vyas, Su Thirunavukkarasar, all M.Ps. and Shri La Ganeshan President Tamil Nadu State B.J.P. The committee visited Chennai, Ramnathpuram, Rameshwaram region and Dhanushkodi between 19th to 22nd March. The Committee also visited the Project Office at Rameshwaram and had a discussion with the officers. The Committee has during and subsequent to their visit interacted with scholars, journalists, scientists, retired navy officers, fishermen, lawyers, local leaders, activists working for environmental concerns, and also religious leaders.

1648. (26-6-2007) NEW DELHI : The 'Toll Free National Drug Helpline' was launched by the Minister for Social Justice Empowerment, Smt. Meira Kumar here today on occasion of International Day Against Drug Abuse and Illicit Trafficking. She said that this helpline would come handy to all of us particularly to youth to combat this menace of drugs. She informed that the Ministry of Social Justice is undertaking a national survey through National Sample Survey Organisation to gather authentic data on nature and extent of the problem of drugs in our country. Initially NSSO will be conducting pilot study in selected districts all over the country, which will be followed by National Household Survey. This survey would provide much needed information for a holistic planning for drug abuse prevention. Smt Meira Kumar said that the Ministry has also set up a National Centre for Drug Abuse Prevention in the National Institute of Social Defence for capacity building of service providing NGOs. NISD has built partnerships with Nehru Yuva Kendra Sangathan, the largest youth network in the country and field communicators of Directorate of Field Publicity. She also said that the issue of drugs needs to be addressed frontally and comprehensively. The Ministry has initiated a number of programmes to contain the menace of drugs. We are supporting over 350 de-addiction centres and over 40 counselling centres all over the country. Capacity of 200 centres have been augmented with support from NACO to effectively deal with drug-driven HIV and AIDS. However, a complex societal problem that drug abuse has become today, it requires a larger partnership, She added. The Minister further said that the serious concern is the linkage of drug abuse with HIV and AIDS. Injecting Drug Use is a very efficient mode of HIV transmission. Though it does not contribute more than 2.4% to the pandemic pool, South Asia has the largest IDU population in absolute numbers. Instances of injecting drug use are reported to be on rise in India too. She also informed that every year a theme is selected to mark the occasion. This year, the theme is "Do drugs control your life? Your life. Your community. No place for drugs". The Ministry of Social Justice and Empowerment has also taken up a national level awareness programme under the slogan 'I decide, I won't take drugs'. The campaign basically targets young people explaining the consequences of drug abuse and how the individual is responsible ultimately for his drug behaviour. It also deals with stigma and discrimination issues and why it is important to openly talk about Drugs. She said we must realize that the problem of Drugs is a global one. Drugs are linked with peace. If there is peace, then alone could you expect development that takes care of the weak and the marginalized. Drugs have connections with social-justice. A society plagued with the virus of drugs can have no opportunity appropriate enough to think about the welfare of the poor and the needy. Thus, drug is not just a psycho-social-medical issue alone. It is a more fundamental issue.

1649. (26-6-2007) NEW DELHI : The Chief Minister of Orissa, Shri Naveen Patnaik, called on Dr. Raghuvansh Prasad Singh, Minister of Rural Development to pursue the issues pertaining to implementation of Rural Development Schemes in the State. The State Government of Orissa has requested that selection of IAY beneficiaries for 2007-08 may be allowed from the permanent IAY wait list prepared by the State Government on the basis of BPL Census 1997 as the 2002 Census has not yet been completed. Dr. Raghuvansh Prasad Singh has agreed to the proposal and has allowed the selection of beneficiaries out of permanent wait list based on 1997 BPL Census for the current financial year. It was also requested by the state Government that component of 1.87 lakh MT of foodgrains which has been allotted under SGRY for special SGRY for taking employment creation opportunities in the natural calamity affected areas of the State should be allowed to be utilized for works in all districts of the State. The Minister has assured to look into the matter and informed that as the NREGA has also been notified, the need for additional requirement of employment generation should not be there. However, any request should be met out of the NREGA normal programme activities. The Minister of Rural Development also agreed to look into the matter regarding the issue of a road from Vijayawada to Ranchi via areas of Orissa.

1650. (26-6-2007) NEW DELHI : The Union Minister of Shipping, Road Transport & Highways, Thiru T.R. Baalu has asked all Major Port Authorities to ensure that vessels leaving or entering Ports are safely maneuverable till they are well clear of the vicinity of the Ports and their approaches. The Minister took a meeting here today in the wake of five incidents of merchant ships being disabled or grounded in the Indian coastal waters due to very rough weather conditions during the last few days leading to loss of four vessels and four lives. These incidents have taken place off Andaman Islands, New Mangalore Port Trust, Vadakara near Calicut, Khanderi Island near Mumbai and Porbandar. The high-level meeting, attended by senior officers from Coast Guard, Indian Navy, Ministry of Defence, DG Shipping and Shipping Corporation of India, was convened to review the situation and identify immediate steps for improving emergency response and preparedness to mitigate such incidents in future. Based on the initial reports available on these incidents, several remedial measures were considered during the meeting. The Minister asked the participants to further strengthen the existing coordination amongst various agencies dealing with maritime control, safety and emergencies. Thiru Baalu directed the Port Authorities to ensure that Masters of all vessels leaving Port are adequately cautioned about the prevailing weather conditions outside the port area. The Ports were also directed to ensure that during deteriorating weather conditions, vessels at anchor should keep their engines on standby and sea-worthy. The Mercantile Marine Department has been instructed to undertake mandatory rigorous Port State Control inspection in respect of vessels older than twenty years to ensure their safety and accident-free voyages.

1651. (26-6-2007) NEW DELHI : The Indian agriculture is facing multi-dimensional challenges both from within and outside. The agrarian crisis is spreading and the farmers' indebtedness is rising thus posing a grave challenge to the nations' food security. The farmers across the country are depressed and are angry, as they feel let down by the government. Unfortunately, the UPA government seems to be either unaware of the gravity of the situation or has no concern for the country's food security and safety of the farmers. The government had declared the year 2006 as 'Farmers Year'. But the farmers were the worst sufferers that year and the sufferings continue even now. The so-called package to stop farmers from committing suicides proved to be of no use. The prices of most agricultural products have risen nominally or remained stagnant, while the prices of the inputs are spiraling day by day. Due to decline in farm incomes, rising cost of production, lack of reasonable timely credit, lack of remunerative prices and frequent crop failures on account of natural calamities, indebtedness is growing which is driving thousands of farmers to commit suicide. In spite of making the farmers problems big issue in the last elections, the UPA failed to make any meaningful assistance in securing returns for the farm produces, bank loans at cheaper rates, adequate timely credit, higher price for the produce, assured irrigation facility, availability of seed, pesticide and fertilizers at reasonable rates. The farmers were left to their fate and are given only lip service. On one hand the industrial growth has picked up and on the other the agriculture growth is almost stagnant. Farmers' per capita incomes rose by a measly 0.28% as compared to 4 % in other sectors. This is not an ideal situation for the country where more than 60 per cent of population is dependent on agriculture. It is also shocking to note that the draft of the Approach Paper for the Eleventh Plan, which has been prepared by the UPA government, fails to address the food and nutrition security, which is required urgently. The country needs to take seriously the warning given by the eminent agriculture scientist Prof. MS Swaminathan that "the situation is deteriorating rapidly and the entire farming sector is heading for a total collapse, if no rapid remedial measures are taken." It is also pertinent to note that both the Prime Minister and the Agriculture Minister are lamenting that farming has become increasingly unviable but are silent on correctives - a great disservice done to the nation by the UPA government. The UPA government has practically abandoned the Farm Income Insurance Scheme and desired attention is not being paid to the Crop Insurance Scheme, which was initiated by the NDA government. It has also put the most popular and useful scheme of river linking in cold storage. Even important projects like rural godowns, cold storage chain, drip irrigation, horticulture that were all given top priority during the NDA government are now getting raw deal. The BJP feels that there is urgent need for the government and the country to understand the seriousness of the situation and move forward to take urgent steps to set right the same. The BJP is also of the opinion that there is need to evolve a long-term strategy to achieve self-sufficiency in food production. The budgetary provision for agriculture has come down significantly and 60 per cent of the population, which is dependant on agriculture, is getting less than 2 per cent of the total budget allocations. The BJP strongly condemns the government's inaction in not acting upon the constructive recommendations made by the National Farmer's Commission, which has in fact covered various challenges on the agriculture front and the responses required. There is urgent need for mustering of political will to address these challenges. Protecting the interest and welfare of the farmer whose contribution to the nation's wealth is enormous and particularly in production of food grains, pulses, sugar cane etc., cannot be ignored. There were surplus food stocks during the NDA regime. On account of wrong policies of the UPA including laxity in procurement and inadequate support price, the surplus has been converted in to shortages thus pushing the country to the corner of importing food grains, which in long term will adversely affect the interest of the farmers and destroy the basic domestic output. The Government of India's decision to import 50 lakh MT of food grains is ill conceived, ill timed and adversely affecting wheat producing farmers in the country. Wheat procurement is getting reduced every year during UPA government's regime. It has come down from 206 lakh MT in 2002 to just 92 lakh MT in 2006. The farmers commission's recommendation that India should have home-grown food security based on adequate, affordable, nutritious and balanced food for every Indian citizen. This is possible only when the farmers are able to increase production by increased agricultural productivity and remunerative prices for agriculture produce.

1652. (26-6-2007) NEW DELHI : The Ministry of Rural Development has sanctioned Grants-in-aid amounting to Rs. 142.46 crore towards balance of first instalment of funds to 31 Districts of Uttar Pradesh as Central assistance for the implementation of the Sampoorna Grameen Rozgar Yojana (SGRY) during the current financial year (2007-08) as per details given in Annexure. The grant is towards plan expenditure and will be utilized for approved items of works subject to the conditions laid down in the SGRY Guidelines. No deviation from the provisions of the Guidelines is permissible. The expenditure on implementation of the programme with regard to cash component is to be shared on 75:25 basis between the Central and the State Government, respectively.

1653. (26-6-2007) NEW DELHI : The Ministry of Rural Development has released Rs. 276.51 crore as balance payment of first instalment of grants-in-aid for Phase VI of Pradhan Mantri Gram Sadak Yojana (PMGSY) to Rajasthan Rural Road Development Authority (RRRDA), which is the autonomous agency for receiving funds under the programme. Funds amounting to Rs.640 crore have already been released as part payment of first instalment to the RRRDA under the scheme from Jan., 2007 to April, 2007. The grant is towards the Plan expenditure and will be subject to the conditions laid down from time to time in the guidelines of the PMGSY and supplementary directions. The Pradhan Mantri Gram Sadak Yojana (PMGSY) is a 100% Centrally sponsored Scheme, with the target of connecting, through good all-weather roads, every habitation that has a population of more than 1000 within 3 years and every habitation with a population of more than 500 by the end of the Tenth Plan. In respect of the Hill States (Himachal Pradesh, Jammu & Kashmir, Uttranchal), North-East, Sikkim, Desert Areas and Tribal (Schedule-V) areas, the objective is to connect habitations with a population of 250 persons and above. According to latest figures made available by the State

Governments under a survey to identify Core Network as part of the PMGSY programme, about 1.72 lakh Unconnected Habitations are eligible for coverage. Rural Roads have been identified as one of the six components of Bharat Nirman and a total of 66,802 habitations is proposed to be covered under the programme involving construction of 1,46,185 Kms. of rural roads and upgradation of 1,94,130 Kms. of rural roads.

1654. (26-6-2007) NEW DELHI: Congress Spokesperson Shri Abhishek Singhvi said that those who swear by the dignity and decorum of the President's office are plumbing new depths of unethical conduct. It is unfortunate that gross conflict of interest is ignored when the nomination forms for the election of Shri Shekhawat are filed. The principal proposer for Mr. Shekhawat's nomination is Shri Natwar Singh – someone who has been the subject of detailed discussion by Justice Pathak in the Volker Report and is currently a person in search of a party. But more importantly, Mr. Natwar Singh actively campaigned for the Samajwadi Party and has been repeatedly captured on the electronic media sharing electoral platform with the office bearers of the SP. Everybody knows that the member of one party if campaigning for another party directly incurs the disqualification under the 10th Schedule, whose sole judge is Vice President Shekhawat and also the Chairman of the Upper House. A petition seeking disqualification of Shri Natwar Singh was in fact presented by the Congress Chief Whip Shri Narayanswamy to the office of the Vice President through the Secretary General in the May Session of Parliament. After discussing the same with the SG, the Chief Whip Shri Narayanswamy also discussed the matter for over half an hour with the Vice-President, emphasizing the Congress demand for disqualification of Shri Natwar Singh. The Vice-President was thus fully aware of the impending disqualification petition. Earlier, during the Indo-US nuclear debate, the Vice-president had been intimated of the Congress decision to seek disqualification of Shri Natwar Singh. Indeed, Shri Natwar Singh had sought permission to speak during the Indo-US Nuclear debate and this permission had been denied by the Party on the basis of its disqualification demand. On this basis, the Vice-President had refused to give the party's time to Shri Natwar Singh to speak in the debate. Knowing all this, the office of the Vice-president had returned the initial petition presented by the Chief Whip for completion of procedural formalities. A formal petition seeking his disqualification has been filed today. The delay in formal consideration of this petition has also been thus occasioned by the Vice-President's office. It is unfortunate that knowing of the impending disqualification petition, Shri Natwar Singh has been made the principal proposer of the Vice-President's Presidential nomination. In a sense, it amounts to the Chief Judge and Adjudicator (*i.e.* Shri Sekhawat), with prior knowledge of the impending complaint against the principal accused (*i.e.* Shri Natwar Singh), making that accused his principal proposer. This is unprecedented and completely unethical, improper and immoral. We are not surprised-the NDA is fully aware of the clear, unambiguous and unequivocal arithmetic, made even more clear by yesterday's developments. Those who do not learn the lessons of arithmetic are condemned to repeat their errors. Their only object is to insult, embarrass, vilify and denigrate the Presidency. We have seen it in the Press Conference held at a former Cabinet Minister's residence and organised by a former PM's personal aide and a sitting Rajya Sabha Member of the NDA. The country is waiting for an answer about this unheard of conflict of interest knowingly indulged in by the NDA and the Presidential Candidate who is also a sitting Constitutional functionary. To a question that during the last Presidential elections, Congress party filed nomination for their presidential candidate knowing fully well that the arithmetic was against it, Shri Singhvi said that your question is completely hypothetical, speculative and we will cross such speculative visions when we come to it. Standing for election is not unethical, it is a democratic right of everyone. To a question regarding the statement made by Shri Advani, Shri Singhvi said that everybody is entitled to his own opinion and I think Mr. Advani's opinion is nothing but echoing the views of the presidential candidate from the party which Mr. Advani represents. To a question on Shiv Sena endorsing Smt. Pratibha Patil's nomination, Shri Singhvi said that they are welcome to do and certainly I think the same grace which the Congress president, Smt Sonia Gandhi showed by personally telephoning several persons including personally telephoning Shri Vajpayee, Shri Advani and others because the post of president is a national post and should not be compartmentalized or politicized. The same grace was shown by the Prime Minister this country who telephoned Shri Bal Thakare and I think those who are here to denigrate the topic will not understand such graces.

1655. (26-6-2007) NEW DELHI : The Government had decided to give the following non-cash incentives to sugar factories undertaking export of sugar: (i) The sugar meant for export would be exempted from the levy obligation; (ii) The quantity of sugar released for export would be treated as advance non-levy (free sale) releases to be adjusted in the free sale stocks of the sugar factories after a period of 12 months. The above incentives were not applicable to exports under preferential quota. Further, the incentives were to be given on export of sugar made during the period 03.1.2007 to 02.7.2007 under Advance Authorization Scheme and 23.01.2007 to 22.07.2007 for exports under Open General License. Now, the Government has decided to extend the period of above incentives by another six months or till further orders, whichever is earlier. Accordingly, the period of incentive stands extended from 03.07.2007 to 02.01.2008 for exports under Advance Authorization Scheme and 23.07.2007 to 22.01.2008 under Open General License Scheme or till further orders whichever is earlier. Further, these incentives would not be available to preferential quota exports.

1656. (27-6-2007) NEW DELHI : The Minister of State for Coal Dr. Dasari Narayana Rao has said that while augmenting coal production the companies should adopt the concept of 'zero harm' which would ensure implementation of good safety systems and practices for the coal miners. While chairing the 30th meeting of the Standing Committee on Safety in Coal Mines here today Dr. Rao said that for such an approach, periodical review of safety of miners is a must and our efforts in doing so through this forum will go a long way in protecting the interest of work persons in mines and increasing coal production and productivity. The Minister called upon coal companies to adopt the concept of risk assessment and management of mines and putting efforts in making workings safe. Dr. Rao advised the Directorate General of Mines Safety (DGMS) to evolve fresh guidelines within 3 months for risk assessment of all 560 mines of Coal India Ltd. (CIL). He further asked all coal companies both in private and public sector to ensure that the short-fall in all categories of statutory personnel is filled up by December 2007. This will greatly improve safe operations in coal mining. Presently there is a short-fall in coal India of 2500 in executive category and 1600 in non executive category. The personnel is non-executive category include surveyors, mining sirdars, overman while executive category personnel are, IInd class mining engineers, electrical & mechanical engineers and welfar officers, etc. It was decided that replacement of manual drilling by mechanical drilling in underground coal mines should be done within one year. This will not only make mining safer but also improve efficiency in mining. Referring to the disturbing trend of rising accidents in opencast mines due to dumper movements, Dr. Rao stressed that this should not be tolerated as the same is totally avoidable. He asked Managements of coal companies to devise appropriate traffic movement systems and totally avoid recurrence of such accidents. The meeting was attended by Secretary (Coal) Shri H.C. Gupta, DG, DGMS, senior officers of the Ministry of Coal and Ministry of Labour, CEOs of Private/Public Sector Coal Companies, representatives of major Trade Unions, other professionals, etc.

1657. (27-6-2007) NEW DELHI : USS Nimitz will be anchoring off Chennai during its scheduled port call from 01 to 05 JuIy 2007. This is not the first visit by a nuclear powered ship to an Indian port. In fact, The Indian navy has operated INS Chakra, a nuclear powered submarine, from 1988 to 1991. Additionally, nuclear powered ships and submarines from France, United Kingdom and United States have visited Indian ports. Notable amongst them was the French Aircraft Carrier 'Charles De Gaulle' that had called at Goa in April 2004 and again in April 2006. In fact, the process of clearing a harbour for berthing of nuclear vessels evolved when INS Chakra was inducted into the Indian Navy on 05 Jan 1988 This included survey by an Environmental Survey Committee (ESC) constituted by the Scientific Advisor to Defence Minister. A Radiation Safety Contingency Plan was also drawn up and implemented prior to berthing of INS Chakra. In 2001, the Indian Navy conducted the 'International Fleet Review' during which the French Nuclear Submarine Perle berthed in Mumbai harbour from 15 to 20 February. For this purpose the Environmental Safety Committee, as per 'Standard Operating Procedure' carried out a complete survey and examination of Mumbai harbour.

1658. (27-6-2007) NEW DELHI : Grants-in-aid amounting to Rs. 1.63 crore as balance of first instalment, out of the allocation of Rs. 3.76 crore has been released by the Ministry of Rural Development to West Khasi Hills of Meghalaya State, as Central assistance for the implementation of the SGRY during the current financial year (2007-2008). Rs. 62.72 lakhs has already been released as part of the first instalment. The grant is towards plan expenditure and will be utilized for approved items of works subject to the conditions laid down in the SGRY Guidelines. No deviation from the provisions of the Guidelines is permissible. The expenditure on implementation of the programme with regard to cash component is to be shared on 75:25 basis between the Central and the State Government, respectively.

1659. (27-6-2007) NEW DELHI : The Minister of Rural Development, Dr. Raghuvansh Prasad Singh, while addressing the 44th Executive Committee Meeting of the CAPART in New Delhi today has informed that the new projects formulated by CAPART on Rural Young Professional Training Scheme, Rain Water Harvesting, Village Knowledge Centre, Sanitation, Fruit & Vegetable Processing have been well received and substantial progress has been made both in terms of the quality of proposals received and expenditure during the last financial year and also during first part of the current year. The system of on-line monitoring and submission of projects has been introduced and financial & administrative systems at the national and regional level have also been streamlined, the Minister informed. 312 NGOs have been blacklisted during the year 2006-07. The Minister further said that there has been steady progress in the Grameen Vikas Aandolan Programme and Nirmal Gram Abhiyan. CAPART has taken several new initiatives, such as selection of Nodal NGOs in a focused manner on need based and location specific approach, Scheme of Financial assistance for preparing Young Professionals in rural areas, Standardised Costing for Water Harvesting and Sanitation and the Scheme of developing Village Knowledge Centre. A module for Training of NGOs for Training Rural Young Professionals, Grameen Vikas Andolan, Stabilized Mud Blocks (SMB) Technology-an alternative of Bricks, Model Scheme on food Processing, Model Scheme on Village Gasifier Technology and Training of NGOs for training Rural Young Professionals have also been developed.

1660. (27-6-2007) NEW DELHI : Following is the text of Keynote address made by the Finance Ministry Shri P. Chidambaram at the India Europe Investment Forum in London today: "I thank you for the opportunity to address the India-Europe Investment forum. The linkages between Europe and India go back a long way. In recent years-to be more exact, since 1991-India has embarked on a voyage of self-discovery and, in the process, has reached out to the other countries of the world in order to explore opportunities for trade and investment. Our engagement has produced splendid results. We have strengthened old linkages and established new connections. The time is now ripe to renew and reinforce these linkages and take our partnership to a new and higher level. Let me begin by congratulating the representatives of the countries of the European Union on the historic treaty that the 27 nations concluded at the Brussels summit three days ago. Your leaders have shown great courage, wisdom and foresight. The European Union is poised to become a stronger economic union and a major driver of global growth. India's relations with Europe have expanded over the years to cover many areas of mutual interest, including trade, investment and development cooperation. Let me take trade first: Trade with the European Union has grown impressively over the years. India's exports to the EU stood at US$23.8 billion in the eleven months from April 2006 to February 2007 and accounted for 21 per cent of our total exports. India's imports from the EU during the same period stood at US$24 billion and accounted for 15 per cent of our total imports. Among the major commodities exported to the EU were textiles and related products, engineering goods, chemicals and gems and jewellery. The major commodities imported from the EU were pearls, precious and semi-precious stones, non-electrical machinery, electronic goods, iron and steel and chemicals. Now, let us look at investment: The European Union is India's largest source of foreign direct investment (FDI). EU has accounted for 25.3 per cent of total FDI inflows between August 1991 and December 2006. The investment has mostly been in the power, telecommunications and transport sectors. However, I should also note that in the list of EU's preferred FDI destinations India's rank is an unsatisfactory 18, and India receives only 0.3 per cent of the EU's worldwide investments. As a country that actively seeks foreign investment, I acknowledge that the onus is upon India, and its political and business leaders, to communicate the 'India opportunity' to the rest of the world. My presence here, along with Indian business leaders, is part of a determined effort to convey to you the India growth story and win more support for that story. I believe that there is a large scope for expanding the flow of FDI from Europe to India. The institutional arrangements for promoting investment flows are already in place. India is a signatory to the Multilateral Investment Guarantee Agreement (MIGA). We have also signed bilateral investment promotion and protection agreements with 19 of the 27 EU countries. With such intense trade interaction and considerable interest in investment opportunities, there is no reason why FDI flows should not be much higher than present levels between the EU and India. FDI is not simply investing capital or making profits or capturing markets.

1661. (27-6-2007) NEW DELHI : Government has released 36 lakh tonnes of non-levy (free sale) sugar for the quarter July to September, 2007. For the month of July 2007, the non-levy sugar quota released is 10 lakh tonnes. In addition, 1.89 lakh tonnes is released under levy for distribution in Public Distribution System. Further, the non-levy sugar quota of June 2007 has already been allowed to be sold up to July 15, 2007. Thus, with the expected carry over of 3 lakh tonnes of non levy sugar of June 2007 quota, the total availability of sugar for consumption in the month of July comes to 14.89 lakh tonnes. The July-September, 2007 quota of non-levy sugar of 36 lakh tonnes as well as the July quota of 10 lakh tonnes and the carry over of 3 lakh tonnes from the previous month, is expected to maintain the retail prices of sugar at reasonable levels. However if sugar prices show any abnormal increasing trend in any State, additional releases shall be made to sugar mills of that State so as to bring down the sugar prices.

1662. (27-6-2007) NEW DELHI : Tamil Nadu, Maharashtra and Karnataka together account for 54 per cent of the total average daily employment in Motor Transport Undertakings in the country. According to the information made available by various State governments and Union Territories to the Labour Bureau for the year 2004, Tamil Nadu accounted for the highest percentage of motor transport workers at 24.63 per cent followed by 21.31 per cent in Maharashtra and 8.26 per cent in Karnataka. Of the total registered Motor Transport Undertakings, Andhra Pradesh has the distinction of reporting highest percentage of registered Motor Transport Undertakings under the Motor Transport Workers Act, 1961. The state accounted for 28.4 per cent of the total registered Motor Transport Undertakings followed by 24.1 per cent in Assam, 9.7 per cent in Kerala, 8.77 per cent in Bihar and 7.7 per cent in Rajasthan. The data on state-wise distribution of Motor Transport Undertakings reveals that smaller units employing less than 10 workers constitute the bulk of 98 per cent of the total number of undertakings in all the states and union territories. The bigger units employing 1000 or more workers are reported to be only 0.2 per cent. The data also reveals that smaller Undertakings (employing less than 50 workers) accounting for 98.8 per cent of total undertakings employed only 17.3 per cent of workers, while the bigger undertakings accounted for 70.9 per cent of the total employment.

1663. (27-6-2007) NEW DELHI : The Prime Minister, Dr. Manmohan Singh released a book titled 'The New Asian Power Dynamic' edited by Shri M.K. Rasgotra, here today. Following are excerpts from the Prime Minister's address on the occasion: "I am delighted to release this book put together by my good friend Maharaj Krishna Rasgotra. I compliment all the contributors to this volume and also the Observer Research Foundation. I have always believed that we have not invested enough in a systematic study of the world, especially of countries and regions that matter more to us. So I compliment the institutions and the individuals associated with the production of this volume. Rasgotraji is one of our most distinguished diplomats. I have had the good fortune of working with him for nearly three decades. More recently I have had the benefit of his sage advice and his vast experience in matters relating to our foreign and strategic policy. He has a deep understanding of world affairs and of our rich history and heritage. I hope that his wisdom, knowledge and vast experience will continue to guide us for many, many years to come. I wish him a long life and good health. This volume is a collection of essays on the changing dynamics of power and prosperity in Asia and their implications for India. As I have said before, on many occasions, the most important development of the 21st century will be the rise of Asia. India's independence from colonial rule and the gradual evolution of a strong, stable, dynamic and democratic India has also contributed to Asia's resurgence. There is no doubt that the rise of Asian economies will alter the global balance of wealth and power. This need not worry the West. A dynamic and prosperous Asia can power global growth and provide new opportunities for growth for the world economy, as indeed it is already doing. But, power comes with responsibility. We in Asia must learn to deal with this new opportunity. We need cooperative and consultative institutions and mechanisms to deal with the changing dynamics. We need a better understanding of each other both at the level of States and of civil society. The first step towards the orderly progress of Asia should, therefore, be an informed understanding of each other. We need more energetic institutions to facilitate this outcome. We also need a new attitude towards each other to enable mutual comprehension of each others' concerns and priorities. We Asians often look at each other through borrowed eyes. Through tinted glasses and distorted mirrors. This must change. In particular, we in India, need to devote more time and resources in studying the strongest economies of Asia-China, Japan and South Korea. Our Government has re-activated the Indian Council of World Affairs and has offered support to other think tanks to invest in the study of Asia, Africa and our neighbourhood. I have asked the Ministry of External Affairs to be more pro-active in funding research and in seeking professional inputs into our foreign policy. I hope efforts like these will help in our formulating a more informed policy towards our Asian neighbours. We also need global institutions and new global "rules of the game" that can facilitate the peaceful rise of new nations in Asia. It also means that existing global institutions and frameworks of cooperation must evolve and change to accommodate this new reality. This is as true for the reform and revitalization of the United Nations and the restructuring of the United Nations Security Council, as it is true for the management of multilateral trading system, or for the protection of global environment or for the security of world energy supplies. We need new pathways of cooperation to deal with the scourge of international terrorism.

1664. (28-6-2007) NEW DELHI: Prime Minister Manmohan Singh on Wednesday defended the United Progressive Alliance-Left candidate for President, Pratibha Patil, accusing her detractors of indulging in "mudslinging." Speaking to reporters on the sidelines of a book release function at his residence here, Dr. Singh said that in the case of her sugar mill — which was served a notice by a bank for failure to repay a loan — nobody levelled any charge of wrongdoing against Ms. Patil. "This is only mudslinging," he said. The Prime Minister said there were "environmental reasons" behind the failure of sugar mills in Maharashtra and noted that the Jansatta newspaper just published a list of 72 such mills, which defaulted as a result. Asked about the propriety of the comments made by two senior ministers in his Cabinet about President A.P.J. Abdul Kalam, Dr. Singh said those remarks had to be seen in context. Earlier, President Kalam spoke about a second term if there was "consensus" but then raised the issue of "certainty." It was in the context of this change that the ministers commented on his candidature, the Prime Minister added. On the Indo-U.S. nuclear deal, Dr. Singh said there were "one or two" difficult areas and efforts were under way to resolve them. He expressed his hope that these would be settled and said he had every intention of taking Parliament into confidence on the final shape of the agreement. Though he had been invited by President George W. Bush to visit the presidential ranch in Crawford, Texas, in August, he had a very busy domestic schedule that month and it was not yet clear whether he would be able to travel then, Dr. Singh said. He would go to the U.S. for the U.N. General Assembly in September. Earlier, releasing the book, The New Asia Power Dynamic, edited by veteran diplomat M.K. Rasgotra, the Prime Minister said a rising Asia was altering the global balance of wealth and power, and the continent "must learn to de al with this opportunity." Asian countries needed to improve their understanding of one another by conducting their own research and studies and not relying on perspectives developed in Europe and the U.S.

1665. (28-6-2007) NEW DELHI : The Central allocation for the State is Rs. 614.40 crore under major allocation based schemes during the year 2007-08. So far, Rs. 445.63 crore has already been released. Statement of financial progress is given in the Annexure. For the year 2006-07, the Central allocation for Orissa for allocation-based programmes of the Ministry of Rural Development was Rs. 685.29 crore and against this allocation Rs. 1076.00 crore was released. The higher releases are mainly due to about Rs.373 crore additional funds released under Pradhan Mantri Gram Sadak Yojana (PMGSY). However, the total release including the demand-based programmes National Rural Employment Guarantee Act (NREGA) from the Centre was Rs. 1346.83 crore and an amount of Rs. 1393.77 crore was reported to have been spent.

1666. (28-6-2007) NEW DELHI : The Home Minister, Shri Shivraj Patil will visit Jammu and Kashmir from Saturday. During the two-day visit, he will discuss with the Chief Minister and senior officers of the State Government the security situation in the State. He will also review the security arrangements made for the Amarnath Yatra. The Home Minister will be accompanied, among others, by the Directors General of CRPF and BSF and Special Secretary (Internal Security) in the Ministry of Home Affairs.

1667. (28-6-2007) NEW DELHI : In exercise of the power conferred by clause (1) of article 224 of the Constitution of India, the President is pleased to appoint Shri Hareswar Baruah, to be an Additional Judge of the Gauhati High Court, for a period of two years with effect from the date he assumes charge of his office.

1668. (28-6-2007) NEW DELHI : Much as the myriad pattern of VIBGYOR colours blend to form a rainbow after the rains recede, none emerged as the dark and looming clouds beseeched the sky in and around Royal Air Force (RAF) Waddington, located 3 miles south of Lincoln Town in Eastern England, for over a week. "Its quite unlike the usual downpour during this part of the year", says RAF Sergeant Ashwin 'Azzy' Rana of the No. 8 Fighter Squadron from the RAF Waddington airbase who is the liaison person for the visiting IAF contingent at UK. With rains abating following the unprecedented rainfall that led to flooding in certain areas in Lincoln, a rainbow pattern is now set to emerge and loom over UK airspace as the ten-day joint Indo-UK air exercise-'Indra Dhanush-07' (meaning 'rainbow'), gets underway from July 2 to 12, here. The first of the two IL-76's ferrying 50 IAF air warriors, comprising ground crew and technicians from India yesterday arrived at the RAF airbase around midday (1630 hrs IST) via Doha in Qatar and Tanagra in Greece. "This is the first time-ever that an IL-76 has landed at any RAF airbase", informed Wing Commander PS Arora, the Leader of the first IL-76 that landed at RAF Waddington yesterday. The six Su-30 MKI's and two IL-78 MKI fuel-tankers, together with the second IL-76 ferrying the remaining complement of the IAF personnel is slated to arrive today. Excitement and anticipation of the much-touted Su-30 MKI's has brought-in most aviation aficionados and 'spotters', camping near the fencing around the airbase with cameras, awaiting first glimpse of the IAF aircraft arriving for the first-time in the history of the airbase. RAF Waddington is a fully operational unit of No. 2 Group within RAF Air Command and is home to the RAF's airborne Intelligence, Surveillance, Target Acquisition and Reconnaissance (ISTAR) aircraft. The aircraft that are operated from the airbase include Boeing E-3D Sentry and Nimrod R1. The former constitutes the UK Component of the NATO Early Warning Force. But apart from the excitement that the arrival of Indian aircraft have generated, activities on a grand scale are afoot within the airbase in preparation for the Waddington International Air Show, the largest of the RAF's official air shows. Three Su-30 MKI's are expected to draw large crowds at the air show when they are put up for static display on June 30 and July 1, preceding the exercise. A fly-past by one IL-78 MKI Fuel-Tanker flanked by two Su-30 MKI's in patrol formation on either side will also enthrall the onlookers at the airshow. The venue has acquired a hard-earned reputation amongst visiting pilots and aircrew for its excellent hospitality, and is consequently always very well supported by aircraft from around the western world-many not often seen in the UK.

1669. (28-6-2007) NEW DELHI : Vice Chief of Army Staff, Lt. General Deepak Kapoor, has called upon the NCC cadets to inculcate the spirit of adventure and discipline to tackle challenges in life. Flagging-in the successful NCC Boys mountaineering expedition to Kalanag peak in the Garhwal Himalayas here today, General Kapoor said this sort of activity would go a long way to promote adventurism in the youth and nurture qualities of character, courage, leadership and comradeship. He also complemented the 20-member team of NCC cadets and officers for scaling the 20,956 ft high peak, considered very difficult and treacherous. Earlier, the Director-General, NCC, Lt. General Prakash S. Chaudhary, in his welcome address, highlighted the prorgammes and activities of the NCC. He said this was the 59th mountaineering expedition launched by the NCC and another NCC Girls mountaineering expedition would be launched in August. The team, led by Lt. Colonel Amrek Singh, conquered the peak on June 13th. During their trekking, the NCC cadets cleared the route of plastic and other non-biodegradable garbage. Doctors and paramedics accompanying the expedition held free medical camps for benefit of local people residing in remote and inaccessible areas.

1670. (28-6-2007) NEW DELHI : During the month of April 2007, the Ministry of Micro Small and Medium Enterprises continued to implement its various schemes, programmes, etc. to assist the promotion and growth of small enterprises. NSIC conducted 12 Intensive Campaigns and 9 Marketing Promotion Seminars at various places in the country. The National Institute of Small Industries Extension Training (NISIET), Hyderabad conducted 50 training programmes for 1074 participants. The Indian Institute of Entrepreneurship (IIE), Guwahati conducted 15 training programmes for 452 participants. The National Institute for Entrepreneurship and Small Business Development (NIESBUD), NOIDA conducted 5 training programmes for 70 participants. Under ISO-9000/14001 Reimbursement Scheme, an amount of Rs.0.88 crore was reimbursed to 190 SSI units.

1671. (28-6-2007) NEW DELHI : The comment of the Prime Minister that the allegations against Smt. Pratibha Patil are mere mudslinging is not only ironical but comical. Mr. Prime Minister please face the fact which are stark, disturbing and unfortunate concerning Smt. Pratibha Patil and her family members which are out into public domain without any allegation by the BJP or other opposition parties. These facts antedate even her nomination as the presidential candidate by the UPA. Therefore, in the context of the unabashed defence of Smt. Patil by Dr. Manmohan Singh the BJP would like to pose certain question to the Prime Minister. i) Is it not a fact that the RBI in its inspection report year 2003 has severely condemned the entire working of Pratibha Mahila Sahakari Bank (of which Smt. Pratibha Patil was the founder chairperson). The report found that the bank deposit of small depositors was squandered away in giving irregular loans to various family members of Smt. Patil in utter disregard of banking norms. The RBI subsequently recommended for closer of bank. Dr. Manmohan Singh has been a former Governor of the RBI. Should a legitimate question emanating from such report be called mudslinging? ii) Based upon the said report, the Finance Ministry cancelled the banking licence of the said bank. Dr. Manmohan Singh has been the Finance Minister of India in the past and should a very legitimate question arising from such a decision be called mudslinging? iii) In the another family controlled Muktabai Cooperative Sugar Factory, large funds were diverted from the above bank which was found to be grossly irregular by the administrative officer in his show cause notice to the bank after liquidation. The sugar factory closed much before coming in steam and the bank played with the hard earned money of small depositors. Questions concerning such irregularity relating to public money are quite legitimate when they are linked to a person as a possible future President of India, the highest constitutional post. iv) The employees of the said bank had complained that their one day salary, deducted for Kargil fund was never deposited in the said fund. If such a gross complain is made from a bank employees, which is established and controlled by Smt. Pratibha Patil and her family members, how can the nation have an assurance about her as the Supreme Commander of armed forces in event she becomes the President. v) Is it not a fact that after liquidation the Chief Administrator appointed by the Government of Maharashtra in the Cooperative Department had sent a show cause notice to one Mr. P.D. Patil, the Manager of the bank in which a part from other things it was alleged that in disregards of constitutional requirements posts meant for SC, ST and OBC were also filled up with the close relations of Smt. Pratibha Patil and other Board Members. vi) Mr. Prime Minister being an experienced administrator you are very much aware that even in the case of a minor appointment proper information are collected including IB clearance. This is called due diligence. Glaring and unfortunate allegations about Smt. Pratibha Patil and her family members are coming into public domain with alarming irregularity. Mr. Prime Minister did you or, the Congress President undertake any due diligence about a person projected as a candidate to the highest constitutional office in the Country. Your belated and comical defence only shows that you all knew it yet she is there because may be the UPA indeed wants not only a pliant but also a vulnerable President.

1672. (28-6-2007) NEW DELHI : The total approximate earnings of Indian Railways on originating basis during the period 11th June-20th June 2007 were Rs. 1807.65 crore compared to Rs. 1617.20 crore during the same period last year, registering an increase of 11.78 per cent. The total goods earnings have gone up from Rs. 1085.81 crore during 11-20 June 2006 to Rs. 1206.73 crore during 11-20 June 2007, showing an increase of 11.14 per cent. The total passenger revenue earnings during the period 11-20 June 2007 were Rs. 536.11 crore compared to Rs. 469.44 crore during the same period last year, an increase of 14.20 per cent. The revenue earnings from other coaching amounted to Rs. 44.33 crore during this period compared to Rs. 42.57 crore during the same period last year, an increase of 4.13 per cent. The total sundry earnings have gone up from Rs. 19.38 crore during 11-20 June 2006 to Rs. 20.48 crore during 11-20 June 2007, showing an increase of 5.68 per cent. The total approximate number of passengers booked during the period 11-20 June 2007 were 199.73 million compared to 185.32 million during the same period last year, showing an increase of 7.78 per cent. In the suburban and non-suburban sectors, the number of passengers booked during 11-20 June 2007 were 115.31 million and 84.42 million compared to 105.69 million and 79.63 million during the same period last year, registering an increase of 9.10 per cent and 6.02 per cent respectively.

1673. (28-6-2007) NEW DELHI : Farm commodity prices monitored by the Department of Consumer Affairs have generally remained steady or have shown mixed trend in different centres across the country in the week ending 22.06.2007. Wheat prices remained steady at all centres. Sugar prices remained steady across majority of the centres; declined at Bhubaneshwar, Shillong and Hyderabad and increased at Lucknow. Gram prices remained steady over the week across most of the centres; declined at Bhubaneshwar and increased at Lucknow. Tur dal prices were also steady across most of the centres; and increased at Lucknow, Bhubaneshwar, Shillong and Hyderabad. At Delhi, prices of wheat, atta, salt, potato, mustard oil and groundnut oil remained steady over one week; those of gram and tur dal, sugar, rice, milk and vanaspati remained steady over one month; and prices of onion increased during the week. As on 25th June, public sector agencies have contracted import of 10.38 lakh tonne pulses of which 1.87 lakh tonnes has already reached Indian ports. The imported pulses include urad, moong, dunpeas, masoor, chana, yellow peas and tur.

1674. (28-6-2007) NEW DELHI : The Government of India has declared 29th June of each year as Statistics Day to be celebrated as a special day at the national level. Statistics Day is meant to give recognition to the contribution of Statistics and of Indian statisticians to the development of the country. It is being held on 29th June, the birth anniversary of Professor P.C. Mahalanobis, the doyen of Indian statistics, to pay tribute to the multi-faceted contributions of Professor Mahalanobis; as a scholar and academician, as an institution builder, and as a pioneer in the application of statistics to development issues. Dr. Manmohan Singh, Prime Minister of India, will inaugurate the first Statistics Day on 29th June, 2007 at Vigyan Bhawan, New Delhi. On this occasion he will also release a commemorative brochure dedicated to the memory of Professor Mahalanobis. In the Technical Session following the Inaugural Session, Professor Suresh Tendulkar, Chairman, National Statistical Commission, will deliver a memorial address, which will be followed by a documentary film on Professor Mahalanobis prepared by the Indian Statistical Institute. The key-note address will be delivered by Dr. I.P. David, an internationally reputed statistician from the Philippines, who is this years winner of the international Professor Mahalanobis Award. Dr. David is well-known as an expert on issues of poverty measurement, among his other qualifications. Shri G.K. Vasan, MOS, Ministry of Statistics & Programme Implementation, will confer the National Award in Statistics for Young Statisticians in honour of Professor C.R. Rao for the year 2006-07 on Dr. Ayanendranath Basu of ISI, Kolkata. Dr. Basu is not only a well-known theoretical statistician, he has also done fundamental work on measuring the spread of HIV. Dr. Basu will deliver a lecture on this occasion. Shri Vasan will also distribute prizes to eleven post-graduate students who have won the Essay Competition organized in memory of Professor Mahalanobis by CSO.

1675. (28-6-2007) NEW DELHI : The Ministry of Rural Development has released Rs. 5.82 crore to Central Public Works Department-the nominated Central Agency for implementation of Pradhan Mantri Gram Sadak Yojana (PMGSY) for the year 2007-08 in Begusarai, Darbhanga, Madhubani and Samastipur Districts of Bihar. The grant is towards the Plan expenditure and will be subject to the conditions laid down from time to time in the guidelines of the PMGSY. PMGSY was launched in December 2000 as a 100 per cent Centrally Sponsored Scheme with a target of connecting every habitation that has a population of more than 1000 within the next three years and every habitation with a population of more than 500 by the year 2007 *i.e.* by the end of the 10th Five Year Plan through good all-weather road. A sum of Rs.20,400.70 crore has been released to the States/ UTs towards the programme and up to December 2006, 35,868 roadworks covering a length of 1,07,569.08 Kms. have been completed.

1676. (28-6-2007) NEW DELHI : The Union Cabinet today gave its approval for introduction of the 'Clinical Establishments (Registration and Regulation) Bill, 2007' in Parliament. The proposal would provide a legislative framework for the registration and regulation of clinical establishments. It would improve the quality of health services by prescribing minimum standards for facilities and services with a view to standardising health care services. It would also initiate the process for the creation of a national registry of clinical establishments. The Bill will be introduced in the next session of Parliament.

1677. (28-6-2007) NEW DELHI : BJP President Shri Rajnath Singh has announced the formation of various committees to prepare a time bound roadmap and implementation strategy in identified priority areas of the party. This was disclosed by party spokesman Shri Ravi Shankar Prasad at a press briefing today. Shri Prasad said that keeping in mind the Lok Sabha and various assembly elections, Shri Rajnath Singh announced a Booth Management programme with a view to strengthen the organizational reach and efficacy of the party at the booth level all over the country. Shri Prasad added that a three month programme would begin on 6th July 2007, the birth anniversary of Dr. Shyama Prasad Mukherjee and culminate on 25th September 2007, the birth anniversary of Pt. Deendayal Upadhaya. During this period, the national, state and local leadership of the party would vigorously campaign to consolidate the booth level management and working of the party from the Panchayat to the Lok Sabha levels. Shri Rajnath Singh also appointed a committee headed by Smt. Sushma Swaraj for preparing a roadmap on the decision of providing 33% reservation for women in the party organizational structure. The committee, which is expected to submit its report in the next meeting of the BJP National Executive Meeting, includes the following members: Smt Sushma Swaraj (Convenor), Smt. Sumitra Mahajan, Smt. Kiran Maheshwari, Smt. Najma Heptulla, Prof. Bal Apte, Shri Kiran Rijju and Shri Kishan Reddy. With a view to study the problems of the farmers and agricultural sector in detail and also to formulate a comprehensive agriculture policy for the protection of agriculture and the welfare of the farmers, Shri Rajnath Singh has announced the formation of a Committee on Agriculture to be headed by Shri M. Venkaiah Naidu. The other members of the committee include Shri Kalyan Singh, Shri Sahib Singh Verma, Shri Nitin Gadkari, Shri Vinod Pandey and Smt Jaskaur Meena. With a view to conduct an detailed study about the common problems related to border management and other relevant issues such as security, cross border infiltration, etc., the BJP President announced the formation of the Border Management Inquiry Committee headed by Shri Kharvel Swain, MP. The other members of the Committee are Shri Kiran Rijju, MP (Arunachal Pradesh), Shri Nikhil Choudhary, MP (Bihar), Shri Dharmendra Pradhan, MP (Orrisa), Shri Narayan Chandra Borkataky, MP (Assam) and Shri Harendra Pratap. To plan the celebrations of the 150th year of the country's first war of independence of 1857, the BJP President has formed a Committee for the Celebration of 150 Years of 1857. The committee will plan various programmes across the country and also bring to light the contributions of the known and unknown heroes of the 1857 war of independence. The committee will be headed by Shri Ananth Kumar.

1678. (28-6-2007) NEW DELHI : Shri Kamal Nath, Minister of Commerce & Industry, has said that there is immense scope to have greater trade, investment and technology cooperation between India and USA. "The US is India's largest trading partner and foremost export destination accounting for 16.83% of India's export and around 6.34% of India's imports in 2005-06", he noted. While speaking at the Plenary Session on "Listening to one another-The importance of a deeper trade relationship" of the Indo-US Business Council at Washington last evening, the Minister called for a partnership between the two countries and hoped that US investors would avail the growing opportunities available in India's agriculture, energy, tourism, civil aviation and other sectors. Shri Kamal Nath informed that a majority of US firms in India have been reporting double-digit year on year growth and highlighted the success of companies like Coke, US based banks viz., Bank of America and Citibank, GE etc., in India. The Minister also quoted a Goldman Sachs report predicting that productivity growth will help India sustain an over 8% growth for India until 2020 and become the world's second largest economy by 2050. During the period April 2006-February 2007, India's exports to US was US $ 16.9 billion while imports were valued at US $ 9.2 billion. The US is also the most important destination of Indian investments abroad. Major items of Indian exports to US are gems & jewellery ($ 4.2 billion), RMG cotton including accessories ($ 2 billion), machinery & instruments ($ 1.1 billion). Major import items from US are electronic items ($ 1.4 billion), machinery except electric & electronics ($ 1.3 billion) and fertilisers ($ 0.7 billion).

1679. (28-6-2007) NEW DELHI : Australia has supported the proposal from Indian steel companies to acquire equity stake in coking coal companies there and to acquire coking coal properties. The Australian Federal Minister of Industry, Tourism and Resources, Mr. McFarlane gave this assurance when the Minister for Steel, Chemicals and Fertilisers Shri Ram Vilas Paswan met him in Brisbane today. Mr. McFarlane assured the Minister of all possible help in fast-tracking these ventures of Indian Steel companies, which are absolutely critical for India's proposed expansion of steel sector capacity. Despite the worldwide demand for Australian coking coal, Mr. McFarlane assured that there was good potential for Indian companies to invest in Australia. Mr. McFarlane also assured Australia's assistance for Indian fertilizer companies to commence operation in Australia when LNG supply becomes available in near future. Shri Paswan and Mr. McFarlane were very optimistic about enhanced economic and commercial cooperation between both countries in the context of India's accelerating economic growth and the Asian commodities and resources boom. The proposal for SAIL, RINL, CIL, NMDC and NTPC to jointly acquire interest in coking coal property in Australia has received a fillip with this visit and this proposal has been warmly welcomed by the Australian Government. Both sides also agreed to explore possibility of sourcing key materials like Nickel, Ferro Manganese and Silico manganese from Australia. During discussions, it was also decided that teams of officials would be constituted to carry forward this dialogue and to concretize the decision taken during the delegation of shri Paswan to Australia. Shri Paswan also held talks with Mr. Eric Ripper, Deputy Premier of the State of Western Australia at Perth; senior officials and Chambers of Mines and Minerals. The delegation also visited key Australian states like Western Australia, New South Wales, and Queensland which are rich in raw materials required for the steel sector. The delegation also visited the Port Kembla in New South Wales State, which is a key port for dispatching coal to India. Both the State Governments of Australia as well as leading Australian mineral companies such as BHP Biliton and Rio Tinto expressed their keen desire to the Minister to invest in the mineral sector in India. Minister Paswan assured the Australian Government and the Companies of requisite assistance within the boundaries of India's investment policies and our mineral exploration policy. Shri Ram Vilas Paswan is leading a high level delegation to Australia to ensure supply of strategic raw materials like coking coal, nickel, ferro manganese and silico manganese, for meeting India's enhanced steel production requirements in the context of India's ambitious plans to double steel production capacity over the 11th five year plan period. The delegation includes the Chairman of Steel Authority of India Shri S.K.Roongta, Joint Secretary in the Ministry of Steel Shri George Elias and senior officials from the Rashtriya Ispat Nigam Limited and National Mineral Development Corporation.

1680. (29-6-2007) NEW DELHI : Government of India have announced the sale of a new 10-year Government stock for a notified amount of Rs. 6,000 crore (nominal) through a yield based auction using multiple price method. Government of India have also announced the sale (re-issue) of "8.33 per cent Government Stock, 2036" for a notified amount of Rs. 4,000 crore (nominal) through a price based auction using multiple price method. The auction will be conducted by the Reserve Bank of India, Mumbai Office, Fort, Mumbai on July 6, 2007 (Friday).

Up to 5% of the notified amount of the sale of both the stocks will be allotted to eligible individuals and Institutions as per the Scheme for Non-Competitive Bidding Facility in the Auction of Government Securities. Bids in the prescribed form obtainable from the Regional Director, Reserve Bank of India, Mumbai Office (Public Debt Office), Fort, Mumbai-400 001 and RBI website www.rbi.org.in should be submitted to that Office on July 6, 2007. The NDS members should submit competitive as well as non-competitive bids in electronic format using Primary Market Operation (PMO) module of NDS. All bids should be submitted by 12.30 P.M. The result of the auctions will be announced on July 6, 2007 and payment by successful bidders will be during banking hours on July 9, 2007 (Monday). Both the Stocks will be eligible for "When Issued" trading in accordance with the guidelines issued by the Reserve Bank.

1681. (29-6-2007) NEW DELHI: India and Pakistan on Thursday reached an in-principle agreement on transportation charges that New Delhi would pay Islamabad for the Iran-Pakistan-India $7.4-billion gas pipeline, even as Iran sought the last-minute inclusion of a clause for a revision in the price of natural gas every three years. Both India and Pakistan are opposed to this demand. On the first day of the tripartite Secretary-level talks here, Iran sought revision every three years based on international fuel prices and the energy mix. The talks will continue on Friday and a declaration is expected. A Ministerial-level meeting will be held next month to sort out the issue before a formal agreement is signed. India and Pakistan had agreed on the Iranian formula, according to which gas would be priced at $4.93 per million British thermal unit (mBtu), and wanted it to remain the basis of pricing for the entire 25-year duration of the contract. Sources said India and Pakistan reached an agreement on the formula for computing the charges payable to Islamabad for transporting gas through the 1,050-km section of the pipeline in that country. However, the issue of transit fee for allowing passage of the pipeline to India could not be resolved, and it was left to be decided at the Ministerial-level talks. The Indian side was led by Petroleum Secretary M.S. Srinivasan and Pakistan by his counterpart, Ahmad Waqar. They were joined in the post-lunch session by Hajjatollah Ghanimifard, special envoy of the Iranian Oil Minister. The discussions were centred on the delivery point and schedules, framework agreement, legal and financial provisions in the contract and safeguards. The proposed pipeline will initially carry 60 million cubic metres of gas, split equally between Pakistan and India. The delivery point will be at the Iran-Pakistan border.

1682. (29-6-2007) NEW DELHI : Lt. Gen Narayan Mohanty took over as the first Director General of Remount Veterinary Services (RVC) here today. Lt. Gen Mohanty is an alumni of the Orissa Veterinary College, Bhubaneshwar and graduated in 1969. He did his post graduation in Vet Surgery in 1986 from the same college. Lt. Gen Mohanty has a distinguished career in Army spanning 37 years. He has commanded the Military Veterinary Hospital at the President Body Guard (PBG). Besides, he has had the distinction of commanding Remount Training School &

Depot, Hempur and Equine Breeding Stud Farm, Babugarh-the two leading, bastions of the Remount Veterinary Corps. A sportsman of repute, he has promoted the equestrian sports in the country and was actively associated in selection and training of Indian team for ASIAD-2006 which won a Bronze Medal for the country. Currently he is associated with the development of Equestrian sports and was instrumental in creating world class infrastructure in the country. A qualified International Judge, he has participated in the 1982 Asian Games, Delhi as Judge and as Manager-cum-Coach of the Indian Equestrian Contingent for the Doha Asian Games 2006. He has been conferred with the prestigious "Fellow of National Academy of Veterinary Sciences (India)" by National Academy of Veterinary Sciences, India. As Director General Remount Veterinary Services, he is the custodian of the largest organized Equine & Canine Breeding, rearing, training and health care operations in the country. He has been awarded Vishisht and Ati Vishist Sewa Medals for his distinguished Services.

1683. (29-6-2007) NEW DELHI : With further advancement of Southwest monsoon sowing of Kharif crops has picked up in different States. Transplanting of rice is in progress in the States of Andhra Pradesh, Assam, Haryana, J&K, Karnataka, Kerala, Maharashtra, Orissa, Punjab, Rajasthan, Tamil Nadu, Uttarkhand and West Bengal. The total coverage of rice has been 31.64 lakh hectare, the weekly Crop Weather Watch Group meeting of the Ministry of Agriculture was informed here today. Total coarse cereals cover an area of 20.781lakh hectare, with jowar in 2.864 lakh hectare, bajra in 6.474 lakh hectare and maize in 8.764 lakh hectare. Cotton has been sown in 15.29 lakh hectare in the States of Haryana, Maharashtra, Punjab, Rajasthan and Tamil Nadu. Out of this 8.68 lakh hectare is under BT cotton. Sugarcane coverage is reported to be 44.72 lakh hectare and jute 7.864 lakh hectare. As for oilseeds, the total coverage so far has been 13.04 lakh hectare with groundnut in 5.95 lakh hectare, soyabean in 2.91 lakh hectare, sunflower 2.04 lakh hectare, sesamum in 1.49 lakh hectare and castor in 0.63 lakh hectare.

1684. (29-6-2007) NEW DELHI : The All India Consumer Price Index Number for Industrial Workers (CPI-IW) (base 2001-100) during May 2007 increased by one point to stand at 129 (one hundred and twenty nine) points. The Rise/Fall in index varied from centre to centre. The index recorded an increase of 4 points each in Jalpaiguri and Rourkela centres and 3 points each in Madurai, Bhilai and Belgaum centres. The index also witnessed an increase by 2 points each in 8 centres and by one point in 25 centres. The index during May 2007 decreased by 3 points in Siliguri centre, 2 points each in Jharia, Mungher Jamalpur and Agra centres. It decreased by one point in 12 centres, while in the remaining 23 centres the index remained stationary. The increase of 4 points in Jalpaiguri centre was mainly on account of increase in the prices of Rice, Wheat/Wheat Atta, Fish Fresh, Vegetable & Fruit Items etc. while in Rourkela centre this increase was the outcome of increase in the prices of Rice, Goat Meat, Vegetable & Fruit Items, Snack Saltish, Firewood etc. The decrease of 3 points in Siliguri centre was mainly on account of the fall in the prices of Wheat Atta, Vegetable & Fruit Items etc.

1685. (29-6-2007) NEW DELHI : In exercise of the powers conferred by clause (1) of article 224 of the Constitution of India, the President is pleased to appoint (i) Shri Amblikal Narayana Gowda Venugopala Gowda, (ii) Shri Ravindra Basavaraj Naik, (iii) Shri Lingappa Narayana Swamy, (iv) Shri Arali Nagaraj Amarappa, and (v) Shri Arvind Shiwagouda Pachhapure, to be Additional Judges of the Karnataka High Court, in that order of seniority, for a period of two years with effect from the dates they assume charge of their respective offices.

1686. (29-6-2007) NEW DELHI : All India meeting of field directors from all the tiger States resolve to strengthen field production in tiger reserves in protected areas. This will form agenda for the forthcoming meeting of National Board for Wild Life. Two days deliberations under National Tiger Conservation Authority at Ranthambhor, Rajasthan, adopted resolutions to consolidate and strengthen the resource populations of tiger in tiger reserves and protected areas. Government of concerned states of all tiger bearing states will immediately take up special recruitment drives for filling up of all front line vacant posts. In cases where there is major gap between sanctioned posts and actual requirements of posts, like the namdapha tiger reserve; the sanctioned strength should be increased accordingly without loss of time. Eco-tourism with involvement of local people to be given priority. Large number of tourists will generate considerable revenue. In few States, such tourism receipts are recycled back for the benefit of local communities and ecotourism. However, in most of the States such funds are not available to protected areas. A portion of such funds may also be used for providing ecologically sustainable livelihood options to local people to reduce their dependency on the protected area resources. The recent amendments to the Wildlife (Protection) Act in 2006 has made enabling provision for creating 'Tiger Conservation Foundation' in tiger reserves, which would facilitate the process. Source populations of tiger will be consolidated and management of source-sink dynamics will be taken up. All the staff members and others who are deployed in front line areas will be given proper facilities and special provision for free ration, medical facilities and insurance cover. Relocation of villagers from crucial habitats in tiger reserves will be concluded within two years with settlement of rights. The compensation pattern and the simplified procedure will be followed as being practiced in the States like of Maharashtra, Madhya Pradesh and West Bengal. Villagers also will be compensated for crop damage caused due to recurrent depredations by wide herbivores. Corridor beyond buffer between two source tiger population will be managed. A site specific redressal strategy will be developed for the Tiger Reserves which are affected by extremists' activities. A Committee will formed to advice a solution for this problem. Wherever relocation of human population is proposed on forest lands outside protected areas, the provision of modification /acquisition of rights on such forest lands will be made. Relocation can be done either on forest land, or on revenue land or a cash compensation may be given.

1687. (29-6-2007) NEW DELHI : The process of electing the next President of India has begun. Tomorrow is the last date for filing nominations. July 4 is the last date for withdrawal of nominations. I would like to make yet another appeal to the leaders of the UPA to avail this last opportunity to withdraw the nomination of Smt. Pratibha Patil and replace her with any other suitable candidate of their choice. In the past few days, the print and electronic media have carried a spate of highly incriminating revelations about Smt. Patil and close members of her family. The list of scandals and controversies with which her name is associated keeps growing by the day. Each of these is a serious revelation that tars the reputation of any person in public life, whose norms of probity demand that he or she comes clean. But taken together, these revelations are of such grave nature that they completely and incontestably render the person unfit to occupy the highest Constitutional office in the country. I am therefore saddened by Prime Minister Dr. Manmohan Singh's defence of Smt. Patil and calling all the media revelations "mudslinging" by the opposition. He should know that none of these is cooked-up by the opposition. All these antedate her selection as the UPA's candidate and can be sourced to verifiable records of the RBI, other government agencies and memoranda submitted by the people affected by the scandals. I would like to ask the Prime Minister: "You have been the Governor of the RBI. Would you have turned a blind eye to the loot of the Pratibha Mahila Sahakari Bank by the promoter's family, none of whose members is punished so far? You have been the Finance Minister of India. Would you have brushed aside the loan default of crores of rupees by a sugar factory, which hardly produced any sugar but gobbled up people's money? You are now the Prime Minister of India. Would you be unconcerned by the anguished cry of the widow of a murdered Congress leader, if the person accused of being the conspirator were someone other than the brother of Smt. Patil? Frankly, Dr. Manmohan Singhji, I did not expect this of you. Everybody knows that you do not wield real power in the Government of India. But many are today disappointed that you have lent the prime ministerial voice to defend the indefensible." "Indeed, if all the facts about all the scandals and controversies are placed before members of your own Council of Ministers, and if they were to give their true personal opinion, I am sure that most of them would favour withdrawal of Smt. Patil's nomination even at this late stage. I appeal to you, therefore, to once again consult your ministerial colleagues and leaders of the allies of your party and nominate any other suitable person for the Presidential election." Dr. Manmohan Singh, as also all the leaders of the constituent parties of the UPA, should realize that an attitude of arrogance and inflexibility at this crucial moment could prove costly for India's democracy. Privately, most leaders of the Congress and its allies have been already admitting that "a terrible mistake has been committed". The Prime Minister and his senior colleagues, and all the other responsible leaders of the UPA, should summon the courage to rise above partisan considerations and correct the mistake when there is still time to do so.

1688. (29-6-2007) NEW DELHI : In its biggest ever cash purchase, Government today acquired entire Reserve Bank of India (RBI) shareholding in State Bank of India (SBI) consisting of 31,43,39,200 equity shares with face value of Rs. 10/- each @ Rs. 1130.35 per share at a total amount of Rs. 35,531,33,14,720 (Rupees Thirty five thousand five hundred thirty one crore, thirty three lakhs, fourteen thousand seven hundred twenty). Though, SEBI (Substantial Acquisition of Shares and Takeovers) Regulations, 1997, known as Takeover Regulations, per se were not applicable in this transaction, for sake of greater transparency, the valuation of RBI stake in SBI was worked out as per SEBI guidelines taking 28th February, 2007, as the "reference date", the day on which the decision of the Government to acquire RBI stake in SBI was announced by Finance Minister in his Budget Speech and the intention of the Government to acquire SBI was made public. Government has also decided to acquire RBI shareholding in NABARD and NHB by June, 2008. The Committee on Banking Sector Reforms (Narasimham Committee II), inter-alia, observed that it is inconsistent with the principles of effective supervision that the regulator is also an owner of a bank and this would require the Reserve Bank of India (RBI) to divest its holding in banks and financial institutions. In its Monetary and Credit Policy for the year 2001-02, RBI announced its intention to transfer the ownership of shares in State Bank of India (SBI), National Housing Bank (NHB) and National Bank for Agriculture and Rural Development (NABARD) in favour of the Government of India. Accordingly, RBI sent a proposal to transfer its shares in these entities to the Government of India. RBI holds 59.73% stake in SBI, 72.50% in NABARD and 100% in NHB. Finance Minister, in his Budget Speech for the year 2007-08, announced the proposal of the Government to acquire entire stake of RBI in SBI, and provided a sum of Rs. 40,000 crore for transfer of RBI shareholding in SBI to the Government of India. An Ordinance was promulgated to provide requisite statutory provisions in State Bank of India Act, 1955 to facilitate this transaction, and Government appointed 29th June, 2007 the date for transfer of stake.

1689. (29-6-2007) NEW DELHI : The Minister of Petroleum and Natural Gas Shri Murli Deora has said that the Government is committed to protect the interest of the common man by ensuring equitable burden sharing of the impact of rising global oil prices. Chairing the Parliamentary Consultative Committee (PCC) meeting here late last evening the Minister said that the oil prices in the international market continue to be volatile. Referring to the Indian basket of crude oil touching $ 69.63 per barrel on 19.6.2007, Shri Deora pointed out that the UPA Government has undertaken strong measures to protect the consumers from the impact of soaring global oil prices and keeping our economy on track. He recalled that in view of the softening of global oil prices post August, 2006 Government reduced the prices of petrol and diesel on 30.11.2006 and on 16.2.2007. The Minister added "though the international prices have increased, thereafter there has been no revision in the domestic prices of these products". He informed that the estimated under recoveries of Oil Marketing Companies (OMCs) will be about Rs.50,000 crore during 2007-08. The members of the PCC complemented the Government in general and Shri Deora in particular for taking timely & effective steps to protect commonman. Elaborating the latest developments and initiatives in the oil and gas sector, Shri Murli Deora informed that notifications inviting Expressions of Interest (EOI) have been issued for laying a number of pipelines for transportation of natural gas across the country to meet the energy requirements of various sectors such as fertilizers, power, etc. GAIL proposes to lay the Jagdishpur-Haldia pipeline, Kochi-Kanjirrkkod-Mangalore/Bangalore pipeline, Dabhol-Bangalore pipeline, Dadri-Bawana-Nangal pipeline and Chainsa-Gurgaon-Jhajjar-Hissar pipeline. Notifications have also been issued inviting EOIs for Reliance Gas Transportation Infrastructure Limited (RGTIL) laying Chennai-Tuticorin pipeline and Chennai-Mangalore-Bangalore pipeline. Letters of authorization for construction of the Vijaywada-Nellore-Chennai pipeline and Kakinada-Basudebpur-Howrah pipeline by RGTIL have also been issued. Members praised Shri Deora for paving way for expediting the refinery project at Bhatinda in Punjab, with the Union Government approving a proposal for the formation of Joint Venture with the induction of M/s. Mittal Energy Investments(MEI) Pvt. Ltd., a 100% subsidiary of Mittal Investments S.a.r.l., Luxembourg in Guru Govind Singh Refineries Limited (GGSRL) promoted by HPCL. The investment of Rs. 3506 crore by MEI is the largest Foreign Direct Investment (FDI) brought into the petroleum refining sector in collaboration with a Public Sector Undertaking and second largest FDI in energy sector besides being third largest ever in the country. Shri Murli Deora informed that he has planned Region-wise meetings with Chief Ministers of the concerned States to resolve the issues relating to Ethanol Blended Petrol (EBP) programme throughout the country. The first meeting in this series was held in Srinagar on 19th June, 2007 to resolve the issues of hilly States of Uttarakhand and Himachal Pradesh. The second meeting was held on 23rd June, 2007 at Kochi in respect of the States of Kerala, Karnataka and Tamil Nadu. As a result of these efforts Karnataka Government issued the notification on 23rd June 2007 reducing the VAT on ethanol from 20% to 4%.

1690. (29-6-2007) NEW DELHI : In exercise of the power conferred by clause (1) of article 224 of the Constitution of India, the President is pleased to appoint Shri Sudershan Kumar Misra to be an Additional Judge of the Delhi High Court for a period of two years with effect from the date he assumes charge of his office.

1691. (29-6-2007) NEW DELHI : The Defence Acquisition Council (DAC) headed by the Defence Minister Shri AK Antony has cleared the process for the procurement of 126 Medium Multi Role Combat Aircraft (MMRCA) for the Indian Air Force. During its meeting here today, the DAC debated various issues related to the initial purchase, transfer of technology, licensed production and life time maintenance support for the 126 MMRCA and gave the final go-ahead for the project. In pursuant to the recent assurance given by the Defence Minister for an early issue of the much awaited Request for Proposal (RFP) for the 126 fighter jets, the Ministry of Defence and Indian Air Force officers have been working overtime to scrutinize all aspects of the RFP. In view of the size and operational importance of the likely purchase, the criteria for selecting the final MMRCA contender from amongst some of the best combat aircraft offered by American, Russian and European companies, has been fine tuned. The RFP would contain a selection model that would involve an exhaustive evaluation process as detailed in the Defence Procurement Procedures-2006. The proposals from the likely contenders would first be technically evaluated by a professional team to check for compliance with IAF's operational requirements and other RFP conditions. Extensive field trials would be carried out to evaluate the performance. Finally, the commercial proposal of the vendors, short-listed after technical and field evaluations, would be examined and compared. The aircraft are likely to be in service for over 40 years. The vendors are required to provide a life time support and performance based warranty for the aircraft. MoD officials have confirmed that great care has been taken to ensure that only determinable factors, which do not lend themselves to any subjectivity, are included in the commercial selection model. The selection would be transparent and fair. The DAC has approved that a majority of the MMRCA would be produced in India under transfer of technology. The vendor finally selected would also b e required to undertake offset obligations in India. It is expected that the ToT and offset contracts would provide a great technological and economic boost to the indigenous defence industries, which would include DPSUs, RURs and other eligible private sector industries. Foreign vendors would be provided great flexibility in effecting tie-up with Indian partners, for this purpose. There are three guiding principles for this procurement scheme. First, the operational requirements of IAF should be fully met. Second, the selection process should be competitive, fair and transparent, so that best value for money is realized. Lastly, Indian defence industries should get an opportunity to grow to global scales. With the decks finally cleared, the RFP is planned to be issued in the near future.

1692. (29-6-2007) NEW DELHI : The Defence Acquisition Council (DAC) headed by the Defence Minister Shri AK Antony has cleared the process for the procurement of 126 Medium Multi Role Combat Aircraft (MMRCA) for the Indian Air Force. During its meeting here today, the DAC debated various issues related to the initial purchase, transfer of technology, licensed production and life time maintenance support for the 126 MMRCA and gave the final go-ahead for the project. In pursuant to the recent assurance given by the Defence Minister for an early issue of the much awaited Request for Proposal (RFP) for the 126 fighter jets, the Ministry of Defence and Indian Air Force officers have been working overtime to scrutinize all aspects of the RFP. In view of the size and operational importance of the likely purchase, the criteria for selecting the final MMRCA contender from amongst some of the best combat aircraft offered by American,

Russian and European companies, has been fine tuned. The RFP would contain a selection model that would involve an exhaustive evaluation process as detailed in the Defence Procurement Procedures-2006. The proposals from the likely contenders would first be technically evaluated by a professional team to check for compliance with IAF's operational requirements and other RFP conditions. Extensive field trials would be carried out to evaluate the performance. Finally, the commercial proposal of the vendors, short-listed after technical and field evaluations, would be examined and compared. The aircraft are likely to be in service for over 40 years. The vendors are required to provide a life time support and performance based warranty for the aircraft. MoD officials have confirmed that great care has been taken to ensure that only determinable factors, which do not lend themselves to any subjectivity, are included in the commercial selection model. The selection would be transparent and fair. The DAC has approved that a majority of the MMRCA would be produced in India under transfer of technology. The vendor finally selected would also b e required to undertake offset obligations in India. It is expected that the ToT and offset contracts would provide a great technological and economic boost to the indigenous defence industries, which would include DPSUs, RURs and other eligible private sector industries. Foreign vendors would be provided great flexibility in effecting tie-up with Indian partners, for this purpose. There are three guiding principles for this procurement scheme. First, the operational requirements of IAF should be fully met. Second, the selection process should be competitive, fair and transparent, so that best value for money is realized. Lastly, Indian defence industries should get an opportunity to grow to global scales. With the decks finally cleared, the RFP is planned to be issued in the near future.

1693. (29-6-2007) NEW DELHI : Since 2003, India Meteorological Department (IMD) has been following a two-stage forecast strategy for the southwest monsoon rainfall over the country as a whole, in which the first forecast is issued in April with the data up to March and the forecast update is issued by end of June with the data up to May. This year, IMD introduced the following new statistical forecast models for operational long range forecast of southwest monsoon rainfall over the country as a whole. A new 5-parameter statistical forecasting system requiring data up to March, for the first forecast in April. A new 6-parameter statistical forecasting system requiring data up to May for the forecast update in June. The most important aspect of the new forecast system is the introduction of the concept of ensemble forecasts. For developing the models, two different statistical techniques namely, Multiple Regression (Mr.) and Projection Pursuit Regression (PPR) were considered.. Using the new 5-parameter statistical model, on19 April, IMD issued the following forecast for the 2007 southwest monsoon rainfall over the country as a whole. "IMD's long range forecast for the 2007 southwest monsoon season (June to September) rainfall is that the rainfall over the country as a whole is likely to be 95% of the long period average with a model error of ± 5%."

1694. (29-6-2007) NEW DELHI : The Prime Minister, Dr. Manmohan Singh has stressed the role of statistics as the country progresses in the path of development towards becoming a knowledge economy, and as we integrate with the international economic order. In his address after inaugurating the Statistics Day celebrations, here today, he pointed out that in such a situation, the hallmark of a country's reputation will be the credibility and transparency of its statistical system. Referring to the National Statistical Commission set up by the Government last year towards this end, Dr. Singh observed that two aspects of its mandate are of particular importance. "The first is to evolve and lay down national quality standards in different areas of statistics; and the second is to exercise statistical coordination between Ministries, Departments and State Governments", he added. The Prime Minister appealed to all concerned to extend full cooperation to the National Statistical Commission and to actively seek its assistance in improving our statistical data bases. Stating that we should all be proud of our collective heritage in the field of statistics and resolve to take our country to the pinnacle of this discipline, Dr. Singh expressed hope that young statisticians from India will continue to lead the world in theoretical and applied statistics, and bring a further sense of pride and accomplishment to our Nation. The Prime Minister paid glorious tribute to Late Prof. P.C. Mahalonobis for his pioneering contributions in a wide range of areas including anthropology, educational testing, statistical quality control, agriculture, flood control, meteorology and for institution building. Paying homage to the memory of Professor Mahalanobis, the Minister for Statistics Shri G.K. Vasan said Professor Mahalanobis is the builder of modern statistical system in India. His contributions to the development of statistics as a science are fundamental and well recognised all over the world. The Government of India has declared 29th June of each year as Statistics Day to be celebrated as a special day at the national level. Statistics Day is meant to give recognition to the contribution of Statistics and of Indian statisticians to the development of the country. It is being held on 29th June, the birth anniversary of Professor P.C. Mahalanobis, the doyen of Indian statistics, to pay tribute to the multi-faceted contributions of Professor Mahalanobis; as a scholar and academician, as an institution builder, and as a pioneer in the application of statistics to development issues. In the Technical Session following the Inaugural Session, Professor Suresh Tendulkar, Chairman, National Statistical Commission, will deliver a memorial address, which was followed by a documentary film on Professor Mahalanobis prepared by the Indian Statistical Institute. The key-note address was delivered by Dr. I.P. David, an internationally reputed statistician from the Philippines, who is this years winner of the international Professor Mahalanobis Award. Dr. David is well-known as an expert on issues of poverty measurement, among his other qualifications. Shri G.K. Vasan, MOS, Ministry of Statistics & Programme Implementation, conferred the National Award in Statistics for Young Statisticians in honour of Professor C.R. Rao for the year 2006-07 on Dr. Ayanendranath Basu of ISI, Kolkata. Dr. Basu is not only a well-known theoretical statistician, he has also done fundamental work on measuring the spread of HIV. Dr. Basu will deliver a lecture on this occasion. Shri Vasan will also distribute prizes to eleven post-graduate students who have won the Essay Competition organized in memory of Professor Mahalanobis by CSO.

1695. (29-6-2007) NEW DELHI : Shri Kamal Nath, Minister of Commerce & Industry, has said that there is immense scope to have greater trade, investment and technology cooperation between India and USA. While speaking at the Plenary Session on "Listening to one another-The importance of a deeper trade relationship" of the US-India Business Council (USIBC) at Washington on June 27, the Minister called for a partnership between the two countries and hoped that US investors would avail the growing opportunities available in India's agriculture, energy, tourism, civil aviation and other sectors. Shri Kamal Nath informed that a majority of US firms in India have been reporting double-digit year on year growth and highlighted the success of companies like Coke, US based banks viz., Bank of America and Citibank, GE etc., in India. The Minister also quoted a Goldman Sachs report predicting that productivity growth will help India sustain an over 8% growth for India until 2020 and become the world's second largest economy by 2050. During the 2-day visit (27-28 June, 2007), Shri Kamal Nath had three meetings with the US Trade Representative, Susan Schwab. He also met the US Secretary of Agriculture, Mike Johanns, US Treasury Secretary, Henry Paulson, US Commerce Secretary Carlos M. Gutierrez and had a luncheon meeting with former USTR and World Bank President-designate, Robert Zoellick. Shri Kamal Nath had also met the US Secretary of State Condoleezza Rice on the margins of the USIBC meeting. Shri Kamal Nath also spoke at the Carnegie Endowment for International Peace on "The Doha Agenda-Delivering on Development", yesterday. The 250-strong audience included members of government, think tanks, the diplomatic community and the media.

1696. (29-6-2007) NEW DELHI : India and European Union (EU) formally launched negotiations on a broad based Bilateral Trade and Investment Agreement in Brussels, yesterday. The Indian delegation was led by Commerce Secretary Shri G.K. Pillai and the EU delegation was led by Mr. Davis O'Sullivan, Director General, European Commission. The following is the joint statement issued at the launch of negotiations: "On 28th June 2007, the EU and India began negotiations on a broad-based bilateral trade and investment agreement in Brussels, Belgium. These negotiations are pursuant to the commitment made by political leaders at the EU-India Summit held in Helsinki on 13 October 2006 to move towards negotiations of a broad-based trade and investment agreement. There has already been significant preparatory work. The EU-India High Level Trade Group has been preparing the ground for these negotiations since October 2005 and its report will form the basis for further deliberation. The EU and India expect to promote bilateral trade by removing barriers to trade in goods and services and investment across all sectors of the economy. Both parties believe that a comprehensive and ambitious agreement that is consistent with WTO rules and principles would open new markets and would expand opportunities for EU and Indian businesses. The EU and India are important trading partners and committed proponents of the multilateral system. Both reiterated their belief in the primacy of the multilateral trading system and reaffirmed their commitment to the DDA round of negotiations".

1697. (29-6-2007) NEW DELHI : The Engineering Units of Central Public Sector Enterprises (CPSEs) achieved a turnover of Rs.1319.63 crore against a target of Rs.1294.73 crore during May 2007. The turnover of non-Engineering Units for the month was Rs.114.67 crore, while the turnover of Consultancy/ Contract Units was Rs.112.90 crore. The CPSEs that achieved or exceeded their targets were Bharat Heavy Electricals Ltd., Bharat Heavy Plates & Vessels Ltd., Bharat Pumps & Compressors Ltd., Rasjasthan Elecronics & Instruments Ltd., Sambar Salt Ltd., Nepa Ltd., Tyre Corporation of India Ltd., Engineering Projects (India) Ltd., Braithwaite Burn & Jessop Construction Company Ltd., Bridge & Roof Company Ltd. and HMT (International) Ltd.

1698. (29-6-2007) NEW DELHI : Rural Development Ministry has released grants-in-aid amounting to Rs. 3.77 crore as balance of first instalment, out of the allocation of Rs.8.70 crore to North Tripura District of Tripura State, as Central assistance for the implementation of the Sampoorna Grameen Rozgar Yojana (SGRY) during the current financial year (2007-2008). Rs.1.45 crore has already been released as part of first instalment. The grant is towards plan expenditure and will be utilized for approved items of works subject to the conditions laid down in the SGRY Guidelines. No deviation from the provisions of the Guidelines is permissible. The expenditure on implementation of the programme with regard to cash component is to be shared on 75:25 basis between the Central and the State Government, respectively.

1699. (30-6-2007) NEW DELHI : The Minister of State (Independent Charge) for Labour and Employment, Shri Oscar Fernandes has condoled the death of former Union Labour Minister and BJP Leader Dr. Sahib Singh Verma. Regretting his untimely death in a tragic road accident today, Shri Fernandes said that Sahib Singh Verma's contribution as Union Labour Minster from 2002 to 2004 for the welfare of workers would be long remembered. He said that Sahib Singh Verma always had the welfare of the downtrodden close to his heart.

1700. (30-6-2007) NEW DELHI : The Prime Minister, Dr. Manmohan Singh has expressed deep grief at the demise of Shri Sahib Singh Verma in a road accident today. In a letter to his wife, Smt. Sahib Kaur, Dr. Singh said, "I was deeply grieved to learn of the sad and untimely demise of Shri Sahib Singh Verma in a road accident in Rajasthan today. I had the privilege of knowing him for many years and working with him in Parliament. In his untimely and unfortunate passing away, the country and his constituents have lost a prominent leader. Please accept my heart-felt condolences and sympathy on this sad occasion. His absence will be deeply felt by his wide circle of friends and admirers and followers."

1701. (30-6-2007) NEW DELHI : The Minister of State for Heavy Industries & Public Enterprises, Smt. Kanti Singh has expressed great shock and sorrow over the tragic and untimely death of Dr. Sahib Singh Verma, former Chief Minister of Delhi and Union Minister as well. She recalled Dr. Verma as a soft spoken, popular and cheerful personality. In his death, she said, has lost a good neighbour. In her condolence message Smt. Singh has said: "I am very much shocked to learn about the tragic death of Shri Sahib Singh Verma in a fatal road accident today. It is unbelievable to me that Shri Sahib Singh Verma is no more. He was a stalwart of the Bharatiya Janta Party and very well established in the fields of politics and education. He was soft spoken, very popular, cheerful and a mass-based leader. He believed in struggle. He represented Outer Delhi Parliamentary Constituency so many times in the Lok Sabha and was also the Chief Minister of Delhi State in the recent times. With his death, there has been a void in the political arena and I have lost a good Neighbour. I pray to God to give peace to the departed soul and courage to the aggrieved family"

1702. (30-6-2007) NEW DELHI : Vice President, Shri Bhairon Singh Shekhawat has expressed profound grief over the tragic and untimely death of Dr. Sahib Singh Verma in a road accident. In a condolence message sent to Dr. Verma's wife, he said that Dr. Verma was truly a leader of the masses whom he served with boundless zeal and commitment. Dr. Verma shall always be remembered for his administrative acumen, organizational ability besides his selfless service to the people. In his death, the country has lost a promising leader and a fine human being.

1703. (30-6-2007) NEW DELHI : In line with the Government's "Look East Policy" that requires strengthening of rail linkages in the region especially with our South East Asian neighbours, the Government of India has signed the Inter-Governmental Agreement on Trans-Asian Railway. The Agreement was signed by Shri J.P.Batra, Chairman Railway Board, Indian Railways, on behalf of Government of India on 29th June 2007 at UN Headquarters, New York. Earlier, 18 countries had signed the agreement at Busan, Republic of Korea in November 2006. Now with India and Bangladesh signing the agreement, a total number of 20 countries have become signatories of this agreement. The total Trans-Asian Railway Network as finalised by the agreement has 80,900 Kms. of Railway line in 28 countries including 22,600 Kms. in South Asia, Islamic Republic of Iran and Turkey. The Southern Corridor of the network as decided in an expert group meeting held in Dhaka in 1999, commences from Kunming in China and Bangkok in Thailand and ends in Kapikule in Bulgaria. The total length of this route between Bangkok and Kapikule is 11,460 Kms. and it provides trans continental rail connectivity to the countries of China, Thailand, Myanmar, Bangladesh, Pakistan, India, Iran and Turkey. The route as proposed will enter India at Tamu, bordering Myanmar, entering Bangladesh at Mahisasan/Shabajpur and again enter India from Bangladesh at Gede. On the west side, the route is proposed to enter Pakistan at Attari. This route has a missing link of 315 Kms. between India and Myanmar of which 180 Kms alone is in India between Jiribam and Tamu in Manipur state. Trans-Asian Railway Network will improve transport linkages between Asia and Europe facilitating movement of goods and containers among SAARC and ASEAN countries resulting in enhanced trade. It will also provide a unique opportunity for the Government to strengthen our ties with South East Asia. The Tran-Asian Railway Network will also strengthen rail linkages in North Eastern part of the country. Indian Railways has the largest and most developed rail network in the region. A multi-lateral agreement in the region will harmonize different standards and technologies adopted by different countries benefiting Indian Railways. Tran-Asian Railways Project of UN-ESCAP aims for promoting infrastructure development in the ESCAP region. An Inter-Governmental agreement to formalize the Trans-Asian Railway Network was negotiated under UN-ESCAP and was adopted by the ESCAP at its 62nd session at Jakarta in April 2006.

1704. (30-6-2007) NEW DELHI : The President, Dr. A.P.J. Abdul Kalam has condoled the passing away of the former Union Minister and former Chief Minister of Delhi, Dr. Sahib Singh Verma. In a condolence message, the President has said that he is saddened to learn about the passing away of Dr. Verma. Dr. Kalam said he had closely known Dr. Sahib Singh Verma when he was a Union Minister and had the occasion to have personal interactions with him, during this period. He served with distinction in various important assignments in public life, including those in the State and Central Governments. The President said he also admired him, because of his interest in library science and because he had worked as a librarian for a long time.

1705. (1-7-2007) NEW DELHI : Delegations representing the Governments of India and Kuwait met in Kuwait on 28-30 June 2007 to address issues of mutual interest in the field of Civil Aviation. The Indian delegation was led by Mr. R. K. Singh, Joint Secretary, Ministry of Civil Aviation. The Kuwait delegation was led by Mr. Fawaz Al-Farah, President, Civil Aviation. The Indian Ambassador in Kuwait, Mr. M. Ganapathi, also participated in the discussions as a member of the Indian delegation. Both sides reaffirmed their commitment to the Air Services Agreement which governs the civil aviation relations between India and Kuwait. Air services between the two countries would continue unhindered and without interruption. They also reached a common understanding that increases in future traffic rights and capacity entitlements would be to serve only the direct India-Kuwait market and not indirect markets to/from third countries. Both delegations agreed to increase capacity entitlements of each side from 8,320 to 12,000 seats per week. The Kuwaiti carriers were granted access to 3 additional points of call in India-Hyderabad and Kolkata with immediate effect and Bangalore with effect from Winter 2008. The two delegations emphasized the historic and friendly relations between India and Kuwait and agreed to continue the dialogue on cooperation in the field of civil aviation.

1706. (1-7-2007) NEW DELHI : The first international Tax Conference-co-hosted by the Ministry of Finance, Asian Development Bank (ADB) and Organization of Economic Cooperation and Development (OECD) will be held from 2nd July, 2007 in New Delhi. The two-day Conference will bring together, on a common platform, experts from the various countries and India as well as tax officials of the Government of India to discuss tax reforms in different countries. The Conference provides to the international participants, a unique opportunity of understanding Indian tax reforms as well as to contribute to the process. Changes in the policies in India will have a large overall impact since one sixth of the humanity lives in the country. In early 1990's India chose to move to an alternative form of development which relied much more on the market economy and private sector while lessening reliance on the public sector's control of 'commanding heights of the economy'. Increasing the size of the cake, has been recognized, is as important as dividing it equitably. This shift in the Government's policy entailed several structural adjustments. Rupee was made convertible, imports and exports were liberalized, and manufacturing was freed from 'license permit raj'. Fiscal reforms-an important element of these adjustments-followed a consistent pattern of moderating rates of taxes, minimizing exemptions, broadening the tax base, easing the procedures and removing the discretionary powers of officers. The result has been a growth in tax revenues, transparency in procedures and a healthy growth of the economy. After over 16 years of consistent reforms, it is felt necessary to take stock of the fiscal reforms and learn from experts from other countries about experiences in their countries as well as how they see Indian reforms. Such a reflection, would give us a better insight into what India has been doing so far as well as what should be done in future. This Conference would be a success if it achieves this objective. The two Plenary Sessions at the beginning set the tone for the proceedings of the Conference. The six parallel sessions that follow, focus on a specific topic each. The third Plenary Session gives everyone an opportunity to learn about the conclusions of the Parallel Sessions while the last Plenary Session seeks to chalk out the future course of action. Apart from the formal methods of interaction, the Conference provides an excellent opportunity for the participants to develop informal contacts and exchange views and information which may also develop some longtime associations.

1707. (2-7-2007) NEW DELHI : Addressing a high powered business delegation, including chairmen of major Japanese companies, led by Japan's minister of economy, trade and industry, Mr. Akira Amari, Prime Minister Manmohan Singh said: "A very warm welcome awaits Prime Minister Shinzo Abe next month." Prime Minister Singh described his visit to Japan in December 2006 as a "historic and landmark visit" that had contributed to "widening and deepening" India-Japan economic and business cooperation. He also said "India and Japan are united by shared and common values-our commitment to democracy, to the rule of law and respect for fundamental human freedoms." Welcoming the renewed interest in investing in India among Japanese companies, the Prime Minister expressed

India's gratitude for Japan's official development assistance (ODA) and hoped that Japan would invest in more projects like the Delhi Metro and the Dedicated Rail Freight Corridor (DFC). Mr. Taizo Nishimuro, Chairman of the Board of Tokyo Stock Exchange informed the Prime Minister that Japanese companies could use Japanese Deposit Receipts (JDRs) to tap nearly $13 trillion of Japanese household savings for investment in India. Prime Minister welcomed this new initiative and hoped JDRs would help finance projects in the Delhi-Mumbai Industrial Corridor (DMIC). He said Government of India is working closely with concerned State Governments to ensure early and speedy implementation of the DFC and the DMIC projects. He said "India hopes Japanese capital, technology and enterprise will play an important role in helping us realize our growth potential." Both Prime Minister Singh and Mr. Amari expressed satisfaction with the on-going dialogue on cooperation in energy, especially in developing clean coal and energy efficient technologies. The Prime Minister also welcomed Prime Minister Abe's initiative on climate change which recognized the development aspirations of poor countries. He said that strategies to manage global warming must ensure "sustainable development and sustainable globalization." The Prime Minister requested JETRO to encourage small and medium enterprises from Japan to also invest in India. He also welcomed Japan's proposal to set up a high powered economic research institute focused on East Asian economies. Chairman of Suzuki, Mr. Osama Suzuki said India was also emerging as an attractive "gateway to Europe for Japanese companies."

1708. (2-7-2007) NEW DELHI : Central Water Commission is monitoring storage position of 77 important reservoirs spread all over the country, of which as many as 32 reservoirs have significant hydro-power benefits with installed capacity of more than 60 MW each. The combined live storage in these 77 reservoirs at the beginning of monsoon *i.e.* June 1, 2007 was 25% of their designed capacity and stood at 26% of the designed capacity as on June 28, 2007. The present storage is 118% of last year's storage and 161% of last 10 years average storage during the same period. Out of these 77 reservoirs, there are presently 18 reservoirs where this year's storage is 80% or less than the average of previous 10 years and in the remaining 59 reservoirs the storage is more than 80 % of the average of previous 10 years. In order to derive the best possible benefits from the available water, Central Water Commission is keeping in touch with the Department of Agriculture and Cooperation and providing information of the weekly storage position to the Crop Weather Watch Group for evolving suitable crop strategies and also apprising the situation to various Departments and Ministries involved in Water Resources Planning. Basinwise storage position as on June 28, 2007: The storage position in nine basins namely Ganga, Indus, Narmada, Mahi, Sabarmati, Krishna, Godavari, Cauvery and Neighbouring East Flowing Rivers and West Flowing Rivers of South is better than average of previous 10 years. Whereas, it is close to normal in Tapi and Mahanadi & Neighbouring East Flowing Rivers. It is deficient in Rivers of Kutch. Out of 32 reservoirs with significant hydro potential, 12 reservoirs have storage build up less than the average of last 10 years capacity and two reservoirs namely Kangsabati in West Bengal and Sriramsagar in Andhra Pradesh have negative storage *i.e.* less than MDDL.

1709. (2-7-2007) NEW DELHI : The Indian Army today agreed to take all the 14 Main Battle Tanks (MBT) Arjun for trial by September 30, 2007. The decision was taken after successful demonstration of all modifications including medium fording (*i.e.* going underwater) to the Defence Minister Shri AK Antony and other senior officials from the Ministry of Defence including the Secretary Defence Production Shri KP Singh and senior Army officials. Shri Antony who was on a day's visit to the Combat Vehicle Research and Development Establishment (CVRDE) and the Heavy Vehicles Factory (HVF) at Avadi, was apprised of the various capabilities of MBT Arjun Tank. He was shown the various production capabilities at HVF. The Defence Minister congratulated all the stake holders for jointly solving the problems relating to the tank to the satisfaction of the Armed Forces.

1710. (2-7-2007) NEW DELHI : The Home Secretary level talks between India and Pakistan on terrorism and drug trafficking are being held here on July 3-4, 2007. These are a part of the on-going composite dialogue process between the two countries. The last Home Secretary level talks were held in May last year in Islamabad. During the talks, the Indian side will raise security concerns and urge the Pakistani side to widen cooperation in combating the menace of terrorism in deference to the objectives set out by the leaders of both countries in the joint statements issued from time to time in this regard. An understanding is expected to be reached on early finalisation and signing of the MOU between the drug control agencies of the two countries to set up a regular institutional mechanism for cooperation on drug-related matters. The issues of release of fishermen and their boats and also of prisoners and strengthening of mutual cooperation between CBI and FIA would also come up for discussion. The Union Home Secretary, Shri Madhukar Gupta has welcomed the visit of the Interior Secretary of Pakistan, Syed Kamal Shah. He is hopeful that the talks would be both positive and fruitful and further contribute to the process of confidence building and improving people to people contact between the two countries.

1711. (2-7-2007) NEW DELHI : Congress Spokesperson Shri Abhishekh Singhvi said that as the UPA –Left presidential candidate marches to certain victory, it is very clear that the arithmetic of the nomination papers themselves, which were found fully valid today, makes victory a forgone conclusion for the UPA-Left candidate. As some of you know all the four nomination papers or set of papers were found valid as the number there itself, 70 proposers and 66 seconders in the first one for example; 71 proposers and 71 seconders in the other one for example; 52 and 56 in the third one and so on and so forth. This itself makes it clear that Smt. Pratibha Patil, the UPA-Left candidate is supported from across the length and breadth of this large country, from every nook and corner, from every state and Union Territory, indeed with the exception of the Lakshwadeep, every possible area had been covered in the detailed nomination papers, all of which were approved. But it is not a question of arithmetic and numbers alone, knowing fully well the facts, the proposers, seconders, the arithmetic, it is most unfortunate that the Opposition has tried to demean and denigrate the dignity of this high office by uncalled for, baseless, frivolous allegation time and again. It is important for the Opposition to introspect and to see whether their conduct is that of a responsible Opposition. Take for example the Leader of the Opposition, Shri Advani, himself, clearly a tainted former deputy Prime Minister, clearly a person against whom charges were framed under the section of the IPC, know as 153, which carries a maximum sentence of seven years, and is that kind of a person, the person who will question the credentials of the UPA-Left candidate. Is it because of the BJP's consistent anti-women stand? Is it because of Shri Advani's party attitude towards the vulnerability of a female candidate and here is the BJP talking of conscience? Their conscience, off course, was not touched with the goings on in Modi's Gujarat. Their conscience was not touched during Mr. Advani's rath yatra where hundreds lost their lives. And does a call for a so-called conscience vote and remember there is no whip in this election, there is a secret ballot, so the vote has to be as per everybody's conscience. But does that conscience vote mean an invitation for cross-voting? Or for violation of the constitutional anti-defection law by the presiding deity supposed to adjudicate that law itself. Or does a so-called conscience vote refer to antics and tricks like the cash for query MPs who were caught or candid camera? What it means, the BJP alone knows. The BJP alone knows because it always believes in creating chaos and confusion. Alongwith the NDA it has scant regard and respect for institutions. We have seen how they have repeatedly demeaned and denigrated institutions which have taken decades to build up, like the Election Commission and we have on record the BJP's comments about that kind of institutions.

1712. (2-7-2007) NEW DELHI : The Central Government today notified the coming into force the Sikkim University Act, 2006 (10 of 2007). Prof. Mahendra P. Lama of the School of International Studies, JNU, at the Centre for South, Central, South East Asian & South West Pacific Studies, has assumed the office of the first Vice Chancellor of Sikkim University w.e.f. the 2nd July, 2007. Sikkim University would be the 23rd Central University established by an Act of Parliament. With the coming into force of the Sikkim University Act, the North Eastern region of the country now has at least one Central University in each State, thereby delivering on the commitment of the Central Government to remove disparities in access to higher education and addresses the issue of regional imbalances thereto. While the university being autonomous, would chalk out its own plan of action and developmental design in respect of faculties and disciplines, it is expected that the university would also reflect the unique ambience of Sikkim. Prof. Mahendra P. Lama is an authority on political economy and has been associated with policy research in the specific context of South Asia. Many of his research publications have been major policy inputs for the South Asian Association for Regional Cooperation (SAARC). He has a large number of publications to his credit and has been an active researcher at the JNU. Prof. Lama is also one of the few authorities on Sikkim having piloted the publication of the first ever Human Development Report of the State in 2001 and was also instrumental in completing the first ever Economic Survey of the State recently.

1713. (2-7-2007) NEW DELHI : Council for Advancement of People's Action and Rural Technology, CAPART is an autonomous society under the Ministry of Rural Development established in 1986. CAPART is involved in catalyzing and co-coordinating the partnership between Voluntary Organizations and the Government of India for sustainable development of rural areas. It acts as a catalyst for development of technologies appropriate for the rural areas and implementation of projects for the enhancement of rural prosperity. CAPART's initiatives are not channelised through State Departments/District Administration. Monitoring, evaluation and selection of NGOs is done directly by CAPART Headquarters in New Delhi and its regional offices based at nine places all over India at Jaipur, Lucknow, Ahmedabad, Bhubaneshwar, Patna, Chandigarh, Hyderabad, Guwahati and Dharwad. Regional Centre of CAPART at Dharwad was established in 1999. Its area of operation consists of the states of Goa, Karnataka and Kerala as well as the Union Territory of Lakshadweep. Over the years, the centre has assisted a large number of NGOs for implementation of variegated projects. Between 1999-2000 to 2003-04, about 400 Voluntary Organisations (VO) of Karnataka and 150 VOs of Kerala have been sanctioned projects worth approximately Rs. 900 Lakhs and Rs. 700 Lakhs respectively. From 2004-05 to 2006-07, 249 projects worth approximately Rs.1020 lakhs have been sanctioned in Kerala and Karnataka. As the Mission of CAPART mandates it to listen to the voice of the people and strengthen their hands by harnessing the resources, the regional centre of CAPART at Dharwad undertook a unique project to provide drinking water facility to a village with no source of water in Dharwad Taluk. Lakhmapur is a village of 750 houses with a population of around 3000. There is no lake or a tank/pond near the village. Nor any river flows nearby Lakhmapur. The villagers had access to one borewell from the private farm land nearly 2 kms away from their cluster of houses. They depended on that borewell for all their needs. Since it was the only borewell which fulfilled the farming needs of the farmer owning the land and also provided water to the village, the water was rationed to each and every house. Realising the scarcity and also the necessity of drinking water facility in Lakhmapur, CAPART along with Siddeshwara Grameeena Abhivridhi Sanga based in Yadhwad initiated a project to provide drinking water facility to the village. A bore well was dug just outside the village and a water pipe was linked to the borewell. A tank was constructed with a tap and a common place for villagers to wash their clothes was provided near by. The tank was further connected with the Community taps inside the village, which to a large extent has helped to solve the problem of drinking water. The project was completed in 2 years. Inside the village there are now 22 community taps. Once the project was completed, it was handed over to the Yadhwad gram panchayat under which Lakhmapur village comes. The gram panchayat has the responsibility of maintenance of the borewells and the tanks. It is a classic example of Built Operate Transfer (BOT) happening at the grassroot level.

1714. (2-7-2007) NEW DELHI : The Delhi Mumbai Industrial Corridor (DMIC) will pass through Madhya Pradesh as well, Shri Kamal Nath, Minister of Commerce and Industry, announced at a joint press conference with the visiting Japanese Minister of Economy, Trade and Industry, here this afternoon. The massive project, with an investment requirement of US $ 90 billion spread over seven years is expected to transform the industrial landscape of over half a dozen states through which it will pass, including Madhya Pradesh, Shri Kamal Nath said. The project will see major expansion of infrastructure and industry-including industrial clusters and rail, road, port, air connectivity-in the states along the route of the Corridor. Conceived to be developed as a Global Manufacturing and Trading Hub, the project is expected to double employment potential, triple industrial output and quadruple exports from the region in 5 years. The total employment to be generated from the project-to be launched in January 2008-is 3 million, the bulk of which will be in the manufacturing/processing sectors. The first phase of the project is scheduled to be completed by 2012, the Minister said.

1715. (2-7-2007) NEW DELHI : The Goa Shipyard Limited (GSL) will build a 105 meter Advanced Offshore Patrol Vessel (AOPV) for the Indian Coast Guard (ICG). Launched by Dr. (Smt) Sushmita Dutt, wife of Defence Secretary Shekhar Dutt, in Goa today, the AOPV, named ICGS Samrat is the biggest vessel designed and being constructed by the GSL. The AOPV, which will have berthing facility for an Advanced Light Helicopter, is totally indigenous and will be built by GSL using state-of-the-art technology. The vessel will have a range of 6,500 nautical miles and reach a speed up to 24 knots. It will be armed with a 30 mm gun, maneuvered by a fire control system. The Defence Secretary Shri Shekhar Dutt was the Chief Guest at the launching ceremony. The function was attended by Vice Admiral RF Contractor, Director General, Coast Guard and Rear Admiral AK Handa, Chairman and Managing Director, GSL among others.

1716. (2-7-2007) NEW DELHI : In exercise of the powers conferred by clause (1) of article 224 of the Constitution of India, the President is pleased to appoint (i) Shri Raghuvendra Singh Rathore, (ii) Shri Mahesh Chandra Sharma, (iii) Shri Sangeet Raj Lodha and (iv) Shri Munishwar Nath Bhandari, to be Additional Judges of the Rajasthan High Court, in that order of seniority, for a period of two years with effect from the dates they assume charge of their respective offices.

1717. (2-7-2007) NEW DELHI : In exercise of the powers conferred by Section 95 of the Constitution of Jammu & Kashmir, the President is pleased to appoint Shri Mansoor Ahmad Mir, Additional Judge of the Jammu & Kashmir High Court to be the Judge of the Jammu & Kashmir High Court with effect from the date he assumes charge of his office.

1718. (2-7-2007) NEW DELHI : The Ministry of Labour and Employment has condoled the death of former Chief Minister of Delhi and former Union Labour Minister, Shri Sahib Singh Verma. At a condolence meeting held here today, the Minister of State (Independent Charge), labour and Employment, Shri Oscar Fernandes and various staff members of the Ministry expressed their deep grief and sorrow at the passing away of Shri Sahib Singh Verma in a car accident on Saturday. The meeting adopted a condolence resolution which described Shri Sahib Singh Verma as an extremely energetic and vocal political leader who was wedded to the land and nurtured human values. The resolution said that Shri Verma has left a lasting impression on the Labour Ministry's working. It said that he worked tirelessly for social and economic empowerment of marginalised sections of society. The resolution added that the entire staff of the Labour and Employment Ministry expressed deep condolences to the bereaved family and prays to God to give its members enough strength to bear this loss. The meeting observed 2-minutes silence as mark of respect to the departed soul. Later, Shri Oscar Fernandes accompanied by senior officials and other staff members of the Ministry visited the residence of Shri Sahib Singh Verma to offer condolences to the bereaved family members. Floral tributes were also offered at the potrait of the late leader.

1719. (2-7-2007) NEW DELHI : The Delhi-Mumbai Industrial Corridor (DMIC) project, with an estimated investment of US $ 90 billion, is at an advance stage of finalisation. This was indicated by Shri Kamal Nath, Minister of Commerce and Industry, at the Indo-Japan CEO Luncheon Meeting here today, which he attended along with Mr. Akira Amari, Minister of Economy, Trade and Industry, and members of the Japanese business delegation. Stating that DMIC will become yet another fine example of Indo-Japanese collaboration, Shri Kamal Nath referred to India's successful experience with Japan in the development of the Delhi metro and said he was confident that the DMIC would add another successful chapter to the saga of Indo-Japan partnership in India. "Stakeholders have taken a decision to set up 5 investment regions and 5 industrial regions, one in each state in the Phase I. The first phase is scheduled to be completed by 2012, in synchronization with the Dedicated Rail Freight Corridor. Later on, more such investment regions will be identified in consultation with the states. The approach in DMIC project is to work within the present system of policies and incentives and provide global quality infrastructure to spur the industrial growth further. Feasibility of infrastructure development will come by coverage of a large impact area and the excellent rail, road and port connectivity. We have set ourselves a project goal of doubling employment potential and tripling the industrial output", the Minister said, adding that the investment of US $ 90 billion would be spread over a 7-year period. The project is expected to transform the industrial landscape across half-a-dozen Indian states leading to the rapid development of industrial as well as physical infrastructure along the route of the corridor. Given the importance of this massive project and its positive economic fallout, especially in terms of employment, Shri Kamal Nath said: "I am of the view that though DMIC is a North-Western India specific project, such initiatives should not be restricted to a particular area, but replicated all over India. Other Indian states like West Bengal have already expressed their willingness to replicate this model and I expect initial studies on the proposed eastern India corridor to begin early next year. With India stepping up the pace of infrastructure development, I invite Japanese companies to utilise the investment opportunities arising out of India's thrust on infrastructure. This is your chance to convert your investments into productive business opportunities". Today's interaction as well as the visit of the Japanese delegation in connection with the DMIC has been organised by the Department of Industrial Policy & Promotion (DIPP) Ministry of Commerce and Industry; Ministry of Economy, Trade & Industry (METI) of Japan in association with the Confederation of Indian Industry (CII) and the Japan External Trade Organisation (JETRO). Mr. Amari, accompanied by a delegation of Japanese business executives of around 15 leading Japanese companies headed by Mr. Osama Suzuki, Chairman of Suzuki Motor Corporation/Japan, is currently on a visit to India to participate in discussions relating to the "Delhi Mumbai Industrial Corridor" and the meeting of the "Second Japan-India Energy Dialogue" between the two countries. Mr. Amari had a bilateral interaction with Shri Kamal Nath this evening. Mr. Shigeyuki Tomita, Senior Vice Minister of Finance of Japan, also called on Shri Kamal Nath later today.

1720. (2-7-2007) NEW DELHI : Cumulative value of India's merchandise exports for the period April-May, 2007 was US $ 22436.39 million ($ 22.4 billion) or Rs.92944.16 Crore as against US $ 18639.50 million ($ 18.6 billion) or Rs.84243.20 Crore during the same period last year, registering an increase of 20.37%. Merchandise exports during May, 2007 were valued at US $ 11861.28 million which was 18.07 % higher than the level of US $ 10045.99 million during May, 2006. In rupee terms, exports touched Rs.48371.98 crore, which was 6.04% higher than the value of exports during May, 2006. India's Imports during May, 2007 were valued at US $ 18077.81 million representing an increase of 26.36 % over the level of imports valued at US $ 14306.76 million in May, 2006. In Rupee terms, imports increased by 13.49 %. Cumulative value of imports for the period April-May, 2007 was US$ 35713.14 million (Rs.148053.58 Crore) as against US$ 26841.29 million (Rs.121304.73 Crore) during the same period last year Oil imports during May, 2007 were valued at US $ 4740.29 million which was 2.99% lower than oil imports valued at US $ 4886.44 million in the corresponding period last year. Oil imports during April-May, 2007 were valued at US $ 9165.20 million which was 1.01% higher than the oil imports of US $ 9073.62 million in the corresponding period last year. Non-oil imports during May, 2007 were estimated at US $ 13337.52 million which was 41.58 % higher than growth on non oil imports of US$ 9420.32 million in May, 2006. Non-oil imports during April-May, 2007 were valued at US$ 26547.94 million which was 49.42% higher than the level of such imports valued at US$ 17767.67 million in April-May, 2006. The trade deficit for April-May, 2007 was estimated at US $ 13276.75 million which was higher than the deficit at US $ 8201.79 million during April-May, 2006.

1721. (2-7-2007) NEW DELHI : The Government has constituted the Group of Ministers (GOM) to whom the Civil Aviation Policy has been referred. The Group of Ministers will be headed by Shri Pranab Mukherjee Minister for External Affairs. The others Members of the group are: Shri Sharad Pawar, Minister for Agriculture and Minister of Consumer Affairs, Food & Public Distribution, Shri Lalu Prasad Yadav, Minister for Railways, Shri A.K. Antony, Minister for Defence, Shri Shivraj V. Patil, Minister for Home Affairs, Shri Jaipal Reddy, Minister for Urban Development, Shri P.Chidambaram, Minister for Finance, Shri T.R. Baalu, Minister for Shipping, Road Transport & Highways, Shri H.R. Bhardwaj, Minister for Law Justice, Smt. Ambika Soni, Minister for Tourism and Minister for Culture, Shri Praful Patel, Minister for Civil Aviation, and Shri Montek Singh Ahluwalia, Dy. Chairman of Planning Commission. The Civil Aviation Policy was referred to a Group of Ministers on 15th June 2007 for further consultation.

1722. (2-7-2007) NEW DELHI : The two-day Royal Air Force (RAF) Waddington International Air Show 2007, that began over the weekend on Saturday, June 30, had an eclectic mix of flying machines-military and civil, both vintage and modern. Yet none could take the sheen and glory away from the formidable Sukhoi-30 MKIs of the Indian Air Force (IAF) that pronounced their thunderous presence at this annual pilgrimage of aircraft in UK. And as if maintaining a studied silence at the ongoing, an IL-78 MKI fuel-tanker of the IAF stood majestic, towering over all the other aircraft put together at the static display. The visitors just could not have enough of the two Su-30 MKIs of the IAF's No. 30 Squadron ('Rhinos') and the giant IL-78 MKI that were put-up for display. Aircrew and aviation enthusiasts were seen busy, persuading IAF air warriors to part with their squadron and aircraft badges for keepsake, and most willingly obliged. Clearly IAF was winning hearts all the way. Lieutenants Elden and Nordtun, F-16 pilots from the No. 331 'Sniper' Squadron, based in Bodoe, Norway who were here at the air show with their jets, interacting with IAF pilots queried if the IAF Su-30 MKIs could also visit Norway. "Wish you could come to Norway. They (Su-30 MKIs) are big and intimidating! Never seen them before" shared the duo, visibly impressed. On learning of the Aero-India shows held at Bangalore, Elden chuckled, "It would be really nice if we were invited to participate. Maybe the IAF could provide us the mid-air refuel support". The statement just summed up the camaraderie of the inter-mingling aircrew that was clearly evident at the venue. The static display by the IAF was declared the 'best static display', confirmed Group Captain Girish Saini, the IAF contingent leader here at Waddington. The honour is a 'matter of pride' indeed considering the maiden participation at an International Air Show by IAF abroad. There were nearly 100 aircraft of various types at the static display. An estimated gathering of over 40-thousand visitors was at the air show when IAF fighter aircraft's air display flight took place at the UK air show. The weather that played truant here for long spells this season, continued to be a spoilsport, denying sunshine and clear blue skies on both days. The air show scheduled on Sunday had to be called off due to bad weather. "Due to the recent heavy rain and the forecast of more to come, it is with regret that we have decided to cancel the Air Show today (Sunday, 1st July) for reasons of public safety", the organizers of the air show announced. But clouds, rains or the overcast sky could hardly dampen the festive atmosphere and high-spirits of the aviation enthusiasts and airmen at the air show. "But for the weather, the numbers could have been much higher as they usually do", informed Flight Lieutenant Sarah Dickson, the Media Communications Officer (MCO) of RAF Waddington airbase. Even as several participating aircraft carried out aerobatics and other displays, nearly all waited with bated breath for the IAF Su-30 MKI's maiden fly past in the UK. The 'Rhinos', with their motto-'Boundless Valour', did not disappoint. Doubts, if any, were laid to rest as three Su-30 MKIs lined-up on the runway for a staggered 'minute apart' stream take-off, roaring away into the sky shortly after midday on the first day of the air show. Arriving a bit later, the formation having joined-up in right echelon formation flew over the runway at about 500 feet and at a speed of 750 kmph. While two of the air superiority fighters landed off after a 'peel-off' manouevre, a single Su-30 MKI carried out an overshoot before executing a gentle touchdown. The RAF Waddington International Air Show that began in 1995 has grown to be one of the largest Military air shows and one of the largest events of its type in the UK. The show is famed for it's spectacular flying displays and exhibits. Opening the show, a trio of Britain's most advanced reconnaissance aircraft, the Sentinel R1, the Nimrod R1 and E-3D Sentry that were to fly in a formation carried out individual fly pasts.

1723. (3-7-2007) NEW DELHI : The following is the text of opening remarks of Shri K.Mohandas, Addl. Secretary (Revenue) Ministry of Finance on the outcome of two-day International Tax Conference here today: "An International Tax Conference was organized in New Delhi on 2nd-3rd July, 2007. Co-hosted by the Ministry of Finance-Government of India, ADB and OECD, the conference focused primarily on 'Tax Reforms in India-Achievements and Challenges.' The first such international conference to be held in India brings together, on a common platform, experts from nine countries (USA, UK, Canada, South Africa, China, Japan, Malaysia, Thailand, South Korea), international bodies like ADB, OECD, IMF, tax experts from international consultancy firms *i.e.* KPMG, E&Y, Delloit Haskins & Sells, and officials of the Government of India to discuss and learn from tax reforms in different countries. After over 16 years of reforms, it was felt that there isn't adequate international understanding of the reforms undertaken by India. It was also felt necessary to take stock of the fiscal reforms and learn from experts from other countries about experiences in their countries as well as how they see Indian reforms. Such a reflection would give us a better insight into what India has been doing so far as well as what should be done in future. With these objectives in view, the Conference was organized. The first plenary session, designed to discuss cross-country experiences in tax reforms, was initiated with opening remarks from the Chairperson, Mr. P. V. Bhide, Revenue Secretary. The Chairperson welcomed delegates from various countries and gave a brief background of policy changes brought bout in the last 15 years in India. He stated that we have to go on from here towards a regime of an integrated GST by the year 2010 and for that he emphasized upon the need for States to cooperate in this endeavour. Subsequently, a brief presentation by Mr. K. Mohandas, Additional Secretary (Revenue) highlighted the concept of 'fiscal federalism' in India and emphasized that reforms in taxation were aimed at improving Tax/GDP ratio & reducing Tax Deficit. This was intended to be done through (i) moderating rates of taxes; (ii) minimizing exemptions; (iii) widening of tax base; (iv) simplification of procedures; and (v) removing the discretionary powers of officers.

1724. (3-7-2007) NEW DELHI : The Prime Minister, Dr. Manmohan Singh called the Chief Minister of Gujarat, Shri Narendra Modi to enquire about the flood situation in the State. The Prime Minister has assured Central assistance for flood relief and rehabilitation.

1725. (3-7-2007) NEW DELHI : Government of India have not stopped circulation of any coin of any denomination and coins of all denomination including 25 paise are acceptable in all parts of the country by all and sundry. This clarification is issued in response to some complaints received from General Public about non-acceptance of coins of lower denominations such as 25 paise by certain organization/ agencies.

1726. (3-7-2007) NEW DELHI : The Election Commission, on receipt of a communication dated 30th June, 2007, from Sh.P.R.Dasmunsi, Minister for Parliamentary Affairs on the issues relating to the expenditure on certain items during the campaign/meeting of the candidate with the electorates and use of government machinery by the political functionaries accompanying such candidate, issued the following clarifications:—1) The candidate irrespective of the office held by him /her in the past or at present has to undertake his/her election campaign in his/her individual capacity. The expenditure on this account has to be borne by him/her or by any political party that supports his/her candidature. The provisions of section 171H of the Indian Penal Code will be applicable in this regard. Besides, it is clarified that the candidate cannot use any government machinery including government vehicle/ aircraft for the purpose of election campaign. 2) Any Minister of Union Government or State Government who accompanies the candidate during election campaign will be doing so in his or her individual capacity. Hence, he /she has to use the private vehicle only. 3) There is no objection to the candidate meeting the members of the Electoral College in any reception, breakfast/dinner or in any other get-together organized by any Chief Minister/Union or State Minister or any political party. However, no expenditure can be incurred out of State exchequer in organizing any such reception, breakfast, dinner or get-together for promoting the candidature of any candidate. The expenditure can be incurred by any Chief Minister or Union/ State Ministers in their individual capacities or by any political party that supports the candidature of the said candidate and organizes such reception subject to the fulfilment of the provision of section 171H of the I.P.C

1727. (3-7-2007) NEW DELHI : Following is the text of valedictory address delivered by Minister of State for Finance (Revenue), Shri S.S. Palanimanickam at the two-day International Tax Conference here today: "Vice President, Asian Development Bank; Deputy Secretary General, OECD; Chairman, CBEC; Chairman, CBDT; participant experts, speakers; and dear friends It gives me great pleasure to be here and address this distinguished gathering of tax experts and officials, both from within the country and abroad, at the concluding session of the International Tax Conference hosted by the Asian Development Bank. Tax Reform has been a very prominent theme in the New Economic Policy adopted by India way back in 1991 when we made a fresh `tryst with destiny' in a bid to give to our people faster economic growth and a better quality of life. The reasons for this are not far to seek. To begin with, tax departments are the public face of Government and their conduct often determines the degree of trust and confidence that the latter inspires in public eye. From the development perspective, the efficiency of the tax collection machinery not only affects the quantum of resources available to Government but also the quantum of private investment in new businesses-whether domestic or overseas. And finally, unlike many of its other functions, the Government cannot exercise the 'fashionable' option of `outsourcing' this sovereign function! It has been a long journey for tax reforms in India. They have been fairly broad in their sweep covering all the taxes levied and collected by the Centre, namely-Central Excise (or CENVAT), Service Tax, Customs, corporate tax and personal income tax. In fact, in the realm of commodity taxation, they have even touched upon taxes levied and collected by the States. The introduction of State VAT (to replace the outmoded Sales tax) has been a very significant achievement of this process resulting in harmonization across States and taking us closer to the goal of a common market. The improved revenue buoyancy as a result of this measure has encouraged and emboldened us to announce that we intend to adopt a Goods and Services Tax (GST) by the year 2010. Apart from their expanse, the depth of our tax reforms has also been quite remarkable. They have been evenly poised in addressing tax policy and administration issues. The broad thrust of policy changes has been to simplify and moderate the rate structure; rationalize exemptions and remove anomalies. It has also been their concern to expand the tax base so that the tax burden is shared more evenly and equitably and the level of voluntary compliance improves. On the administration side, the cornerstone has been procedural simplification. The objective is to make it easier for the taxpayer to quantify and discharge his tax liability and comply with the processes of registration, filing, and timely remittance. For achieving this, emphasis has been placed in a big way on the use of Information

Technology solutions and computerization. It is common knowledge that these provide the tools for making governance non-intrusive and hassle-free. The interface with the taxpayer has been substantially converted to the electronic mode with facilities for e-filing, e-payment and web-based status verification being available for a variety of purposes. For these changes to be meaningful, it is obviously not enough to change the facade alone. Work processes at the back-end need to be in sync. As a precursor to this process, the business processes in CENVAT and Service Tax have already been re-engineered and a state-of-art workflow application is on the verge of implementation. On the income tax side, a BPR exercise is currently underway. The list of initiatives that constitute the reform package is long. I am sure a very wholesome and detailed account has already been provided to you during the deliberations over the last two days. In this era of globalization it would be naive to even imagine, far less claim, that these reforms are entirely homegrown or an exclusive product of Indian genius. While they may have a predominantly Indian flavour, they have been inspired by various success stories all over the world. It would be equally naive to presume that they would endure and succeed in the true sense unless there is wholehearted conviction among tax officials, who provide flesh and blood to policy, that they are needed. For these officials, conferences such as this one provide an opportunity to interact and brainstorm with their counterparts from other administrations as well as experts and to learn first-hand from their experiences. To the extent their experiences resonate with those of other countries, their belief in the reform process and its content is strengthened.

1728. (3-7-2007) NEW DELHI : The Minister for Yourth Affairs & Sports, Panchayati Raj and DoNER Shri Mani Shankar Aiyar has condoled the death of former cricketer Dilip Sardesai. In a message, Shri Aiyar said: "I am deeply saddened at the passing away of legendary Cricketer, Shri Dilip Sardesai, in Mumbai yesterday. His death is a great loss to the cricketing world and to the nation. The cricketing fraternity and his fans will fondly remember his exploits on the cricket field which brought him and his country glory. I pray to the Almighty to grant peace to the departed soul and courage to his family to bear this great loss."

1729. (3-7-2007) NEW DELHI : The Ministry of Defence today gave clear indications that it has taken seriously the alleged suicide by a lady Army Officer, Captain Megha Razdan in Jammu on Sunday when the Defence Minister Shri A K Antony chaired a special meeting here to discuss the issue. The meeting was attended among others by the Defence Secretary Shri Shekhar Dutt, senior officials of Army, Defence Institute of Psychological Research (DIPR) and the Director General, Armed Forces Medical Services. The Defence Minister asked the Army to expedite its probe into the case. He also directed the Ministry officials to send a request to the Jammu and Kashmir state government to speed up the police enquiry into the case to arrive at the truth. Shri Antony directed the Ministry of

Defence, Army and DIPR officials to follow up on remedial measures as evolved in the last few months after he took over as the Defence Minister.

1730. (3-7-2007) NEW DELHI : The Prime Minister of Vietnam, Mr. Nguyen Tan Dung will pay a State Visit to India from July 4-6, 2007. During his visit, he will hold bilateral talks with Prime Minister Dr. Manmohan Singh and call on the President on July 6, 2007. The Minister of State for External Affairs, Shri Anand Sharma, the Speaker of Lok Sabha, Shri Somnath Chatterjee and the Leader of the Opposition, Lok Sabha, Shri L.K. Advani will call on the visiting dignitary. Prime Minister Dr. Manmohan Singh will host a banquet in honour of the visiting dignitary on July 6, 2007. The Vietnamese Prime Minister will visit Kolkata, Jamshedpur and Mumbai apart from New Delhi during his State Visit to India. On his visit to India, Prime Minister Mr. Nguyen Tan Dung will be accompanied by the Minister of Trade, Mr. Truong Dinh Tuyen, Minister of Science and Technology, Mr. Hoang Van Phong and Minister of Fishery, Mr. Ta Quang Ngoc and senior officials from the Vietnamese Government. During the State Visit of the Vietnamese Prime Minister, an MoU on Cooperation in the Field of Fisheries and Aquaculture, the Cultural Exchange Programme between India and Vietnam for the period 2007-09 and a Work Plan in the Field of Agriculture for the period 2007-09 will be signed in the presence of the two Prime Ministers after the conclusion of the bilateral talks on July 6, 2007. India's relations with Vietnam are warm and cordial. The two countries have had a long history of close political, economic and societal ties and are committed to working together for a broad based expansion of relations in the political, security, economic, cultural and science and technological spheres. Both countries also seek an expansion of societal linkages and people to people contacts. India assists Vietnam through grants and soft loans for development projects and through technical assistance and training provided under India's ITEC programme. Vietnamese nationals are also recipients of ICCR scholarships for undergraduate and post graduate education in India. The visit of the Vietnamese Prime Minister takes place during the 35th Anniversary year of the Establishment of Full Diplomatic Relations between India and Vietnam. The two countries are working together in the organization of a series of cultural events to celebrate this important anniversary in a befitting manner. Bilateral trade between India and Vietnam reached a volume of US $ 1 billion in 2006. Both countries have set a target of doubling trade and reaching a volume of US $ 2 billion by 2010. Indian companies including Essar and Tata Steel have entered into Agreements to make major investments in the steel sector in Vietnam.

1731. (3-7-2007) NEW DELHI : Shri S.K. Vasishta, IRSSE has assumed charge of the post of Managing Director, RailTel Corporation of India Ltd., a Public Sector Undertaking of the Ministry of Railways, here today. He has taken charge from his predecessor Mr. KK Bajpeyee who superannuated on June 30, 2007 after putting in more than 36 years of service. Shri Vasishta is an officer of the Indian Railways Service of Signal Engineers (IRSSE) of 1972 batch. He started his carrier in January 1974 and has put in more than 33 years of service. He has headed various signalling and telecommunication departments of several Zonal Railways including Eastern Railway, Northern Railway and North Western Railway.

1732. (3-7-2007) NEW DELHI : Under the Sampoorna Grameen Rozgar Yojana (SGRY) scheme, the Ministry of Rural Development has approved the release of 2341 MTs of Common Rice during the year 2007-08 to Howrah District of West Bengal State through Food Corporation of India depots in the State. The release is towards plan expenditure and will be utilized for approved items of works subject to the conditions laid down in the SGRY Guidelines. The State Government must ensure timely payment of wages and timely and adequate supply of food grains. If the food grains are not available, wages should be paid in cash.

1733. (3-7-2007) NEW DELHI : Grants-in-aid amounting to Rs. 78.82 lakh as balance of first instalment, out of the allocation of Rs.181.88 lakh has been released by the Ministry of Rural Development to West District of Sikkim State, as Central assistance for the implementation of the Sampoorna Grameen Rozgar Yojana (SGRY) during the current financial year (2007-2008). An amount of Rs.30.31 lakh has already been released as part payment of the first instalment. The grant is towards plan expenditure and will be utilized for approved items of works subject to the conditions laid down in the SGRY Guidelines. No deviation from the provisions of the Guidelines is permissible. The expenditure on implementation of the programme with regard to cash component is to be shared on 75:25 basis between the Central and the State Government, respectively.

1734. (3-7-2007) NEW DELHI : Grants-in-aid amounting to Rs. 256.91 crore has been released by the Ministry of Rural Development as first instalment of Phase II of Pradhan Mantri Gram Sadak Yojana (PMGSY) to Orissa State Rural Road Agency (OSRRA), which is the autonomous agency for receiving funds under the programme. The grant is towards the Plan expenditure and will be subject to the conditions laid down from time to time in the guidelines of the PMGSY and supplementary directions. The Pradhan Mantri Gram Sadak Yojana (PMGSY) is a 100% Centrally sponsored Scheme, with the target of connecting, through good all-weather roads, every habitation that has a population of more than 1000 within 3 years and every habitation with a population of more than 500 by the end of the Tenth Plan. In respect of the Hill States (Himachal Pradesh, Jammu & Kashmir, Uttarakhand), North-East, Sikkim, Desert Areas and Tribal (Schedule-V) areas, the objective is to connect habitations with a population of 250 persons and above. According to latest figures made available by the State Governments under a survey to identify Core Network as part of the PMGSY programme, about 1.72 lakh Unconnected Habitations are eligible for coverage. Rural Roads have been identified as one of the six components of Bharat Nirman and a total of 66,802 habitations is proposed to be covered under the programme involving construction of 1,46,185 Kms. of rural roads and upgradation of 1,94,130 Kms. of rural roads.

1735. (3-7-2007) NEW DELHI : The Union Minister of Shipping, Road Transport & Highways, Thiru T.R. Baalu has said that there is a greater need to give special attention to the safety aspects relating to the interchanges and flyovers being constructed by NHAI within the cities and on stretches approaching the major cities. He said this while chairing a review meeting relating to the National Highway Projects being executed in and around Chennai here today. The Minister directed that the high mast lighting should be provided on all important flyovers and interchanges at the National Highways being developed by NHAI in the country. On the issue of high energy tariff for the operation of these lighting arrangements, the Minister stated that he would take up the issue of energy tariff with the Chief Ministers of all the States and Union Territories for making tariff rates for this purpose at par with the tariff being charged for installation supplies to the local bodies. With regard to the Chennai projects, the Minister directed the NHAI officials for additional deployment of labour and machines for the early execution of these projects. With a view to achieve accelerated implementation of the projects of interchange at Kathipara and Padi and improvement at Koyambedu, Airport approaches, NH-4 and Chennai by-pass, Thiru Baalu directed the Secretary (Road Transport & Highways) Shri Vijay Singh and the Chairman, NHAI Shri Pradeep Kumar to undertake a joint inspection of the project areas with the top management officials of the contracting firm, Supervision Consultant and the State Government officials to resolve the issues relating to the execution of projects and pending problems responsible for the delay. The Minister directed NHAI authorities to have more frequent reviews of the NHAI to ensure that slippages if any could be plugged in time and projects are executed within the given schedule.

1736. (3-7-2007) NEW DELHI : The Prime Minister, Dr. Manmohan Singh, has condemned the killing of Food Corporation of India Executive Director, Shri Phulchand Ram and conveyed his condolences to the bereaved family. The Prime Minister in his message to the family of Shri Phulchand Ram, said he was greatly distressed to hear of the killing of the Officer who was kidnapped by militants in April. Dr. Manmohan Singh described the killing as a dastardly and shameful act which has shocked the country. He said it needs to be condemned in the strongest terms. The Prime Minister said the country was with the family members in their moment of grief.

1737. (3-7-2007) NEW DELHI : Shri Kamal Nath, Minister of Commerce & Industry, has warned that the decision of the US Government to end the GSP (Generalised System of Preferences) for gold jewellery and brass lamps from India could lead to a number of jobs being lost in the jewellery sector in India. In reply to a question after his recent speech at the Carnegie Endowment meet in Washington asking about India's reaction to the US decision, Shri Kamal Nath said that "GSP is a unilateral programme of the US government and is not a result of negotiations with GSP beneficiaries. Hence, it is upto US government to decide on how it wishes to administer the programme. However, the decision is likely to lead to a number of jobs being lost in the jewellery sector in India, specially among vulnerable groups of society". On 28th June, 2007, the US Administration decided not to renew the Competitive Needs Limitation (CNL) Waiver for gold jewellery and brass lamps from India, thereby ending the GSP preference. The Federal Register Notice is expected to be published soon and the changes will be effective within seven days of publication. GSP has been withdrawn from 8 out of 9 products for which the review was carried out under the new regulations. The only country for which it has been continued is Columbia for mini carnations.

1738. (3-7-2007) NEW DELHI : Shri Kamal Nath, Minister of Commerce & Industry, and Mr. Akira Amari, Minister of Economy, Trade and Industry of Japan, has directed the Task Force to finalise a concept paper on Delhi-Mumbai Industrial Corridor (DMIC) Project before Prime Minister of Japan Shinzo Abe's visit to India scheduled for August 2007. The two Ministers welcomed the announcement of Tokyo Stock Exchange (TSE) to introduce the Japanese Depository receipt (JDR) scheme. India can become a first destination for such scheme that can be also utilised as one of the financial resources for the development of the DMIC project. This is indicated in the Joint Statement signed by the two Ministers here last night following the conclusion of their discussions on DMIC project. Mr. Akira Amari and Shri Kamal Nath co-chaired the first meeting of the Japan-India Policy Dialogue (JIPD) between the two Ministers on the occasion of Minister Amari's visit to India from June 30 to July 3, 2007. Minister Amari was accompanied by the Japanese business delegation headed by Mr. Osamu Suzuki, Chairman and CEO of Suzuki Motor Corporation. At the meeting, the Ministers had extensive discussions to advance the relevant elements of the agenda of the "Japan-India Special Economic Partnership (SEPI)", which was announced by the leaders of the two countries on December 15, 2006 in Tokyo. The Ministers also discussed relevant global and regional economic issues such as Doha Development Agenda (DDA), Comprehensive Economic Partnership in East Asia (CEPEA) and Economic Research Institute for ASEAN and East Asia (ERIA). The Ministers decided to cooperate towards the successful conclusion of the DDA by the end of 2007. During the course of the meeting, the Ministers exchanged views on the DMIC project, which is a flagship cooperation project between the two countries, based on the discussion at the Task Force for the DMIC project, co-chaired by Secretary, Department of Industrial Policy & Promotion (DIPP), Ministry of Commerce & Industry of India and Vice Minister, Ministry of Economy, Trade & Industry of Japan. The Ministers welcomed the inputs made and interests shown by the business leaders from both countries. The Ministers reaffirmed the importance of facilitating the business and technology match making between the two countries in a range of sectors that include food processing and other manufacturing industries. The Ministers welcomed the MOU between the Confederation of Indian Industries (CII) and the Japan External Trade Organisation (JETRO) signed on July 2, 2007 which aims to facilitate closer business interaction between enterprises in India and Japan. The Ministers reviewed the status of India-Japan Economic Partnership Agreement (EPA) / Comprehensive Economic Partnership Agreement (CEPA) negotiations and directed the negotiators to expedite the conclusion of negotiations within the agreed timeframe. The Ministers discussed some of the outstanding trade-related issues between India and Japan and decided that the relevant authorities on both sides need to continue the dialogue for satisfactory resolution of these issues.

1739. (3-7-2007) NEW DELHI : The total import of sensitive items for the period April 07 has been Rs.1118 crores as compared to Rs.1328 crores during the corresponding period last year thereby showing a decrease of 15.8%. The gross import of all commodities during same period of current year was Rs.17635 crores as compared to Rs.12535 crores during the same period of last year. Thus import of sensitive items constitute 10.6% and 6.3% of the gross imports during last year and current year respectively. Imports of edible oil, cotton & silk, fruits & vegetables (including nuts), products of SSI, spices and marble & Granite have shown a decline at broad group level during the period. Imports of items viz. automobiles, rubber, Alcoholic beverages and milk & milk products have shown increase during the period under reference. In the edible oil segment, the import has decreased from Rs.810 crores last year to Rs.625 crores for the corresponding period of this year. The import of both crude oil as well as refined oil have gone down by 23% and 21.1% respectively. The fall in edible oil import is mainly due to significant decrease in import of Soya-bean oil and its fractions (Crude), which has gone down by 62%. Imports of sensitive items from Indonesia, Thailand, Germany, Japan, Pakistan IR, Bhutan, United Arab Emirates etc. have gone up while those from Argentina, China P RP, United States of America, Malaysia, Egypt A RP, Sri Lanka DSR etc. have shown a decrease.

1740. (3-7-2007) NEW DELHI : The term of the Liberhan Ayodhya Commission of Inquiry has been extended by two months up to 31st August 2007. The Commission is inquiring into the destruction of the Ram Janma Bhoomi-Babri Masjid structure at Ayodhya on 6th December, 1992.

1741. (3-7-2007) NEW DELHI : A two-day Conference of Ministers in-Charge of rural drinking water supply and rural sanitation in States and Union Territories is commencing from tomorrow in New Delhi. The Conference will focus on ensuring "Sustainability in Drinking Water Supply projects and Sanitation for All" in the rural areas of the country by 2012. The Prime Minister, Dr. Manmohan Singh is inaugurating the Conference and releasing the document on Water Sustainability. Minister for Rural Development, Dr. Raghuvansh Prasad Singh, Minister of Water Resources Shri Saifuddin Soz, and Ministers of State for Rural Development Shri Chandra Sekhar Sahu and Smt. Suryakanta Patil will attend the Conference. "Sustainability of water sources" has emerged as a major challenge in the rural drinking water sector in recent times. The challenge lies in working out strategies to make water supply systems sustainable in terms of quantity and quality and ensuring that the fully covered habitations do not fall back to status of non-covered and partially covered etc. The Conference will broadly focus on the issues, such as, progress under Bharat Nirman, issues of sustainability and convergence; Water Quality Surveillance Programme, Data Management & use of technology for Planning and Sanitation for all by 2012 with focus on aged, specially abled and children and Solid & Liquid Waste Management. Effective implementation of the Drinking Water component in Bharat Nirman, the flagship programme of the Government of India, and State-specific Action Plans under Accelerated Rural Water Supply Programme (ARWSP), ARWSP (DDP), Sub Mission on Quality Control and the National Quality and Surveillance Programme will also be reviewed. The Total Sanitation Campaign, the Nirmal Gram Puraskar and Sanitation for All by 2012 will be taken up for discussion and review under Rural Sanitation. The usage of Web Based Integrated Management Information Systems developed by the Department of Drinking Water Supply for all future programmes/ expenditure will be key to the Review process.

1742. (4-7-2007) NEW DELHI : The second bilateral Indo-UK air exercise- 'Indradhanush-2007', involving the Indian Air Force (IAF) and the Royal Air Force (RAF), got underway here at the Royal Air Force (RAF) base, Waddington, on Monday. The inaugural day, primarily for familiarization of the participating IAF Su-30 MKI aircrew with the flying environment in UK, saw them flying alongside RAF F3 Tornadoes of the XXV Squadron that are based at RAF Leeming, but are operating from Waddington alongside IAF Su-30 MKIs for the duration of the exercise. Also airborne were a Eurofighter Typhoon from No. 17 Squadron from RAF Conningsby, and a Hawk aircraft. "It will be a mutual learning experience for both", said Wing Commander AK Bharti, talking of the learning values in terms of inter-operability between the two air forces after returning from a sortie, of a four-aircraft formation comprising a Su-30 MKI, F3 Tornado, Typhoon and a Hawk. The 'airborne warning and control' (AWAC) system experience, a veritable electronic 'eye-in-the-sky' platform was also observed by few IAF personnel onboard an E3-D Sentry AWAC aircraft belonging to RAF's No. 8 Fighter Squadron, based here in Waddington. The E3-D Sentry and the F3 Tornadoes also participated in the first series of Exercise Indradhanush-2006, held at Gwalior in India, last year. The exercise between two simulated air elements, the "Red Air" (aggressors) and the "Blue Air" (defenders) forces will have the training element for the latter. Missions comprising multiple aircraft will form some of the intrinsic training missions, some of them highly advanced and complex missions. Mediating between the two will be the "White" force, who remain neutral and whose decisions will be the last word, to mitigate differences, if any. They comprise 'observers' from both sides, and include members from the IAF's 'Tactics and Combat Development Establishment' (TACDE) and the RAF's 'Air Warfare Centre' (AWC), the premiere institutions of the two air forces, constituting the 'best-amongst-the-best' aircrew and personnel on both sides.

1743. (4-7-2007) NEW DELHI : The Petroleum Minister Shri Murli Deora has said that his priority is to see the completion/commissioning of this project rather than laying its foundation stone. Addressing a delegation of the Members of Legislative Assembly of Punjab led by Ms. Rajinder Kaur Bhattal, Leader of Opposition in Punjab Legislative Assembly, here today, he said that the way forward for implementation of Bhatinda Project has been found with steadfast commitment of UPA chairperson Smt. Sonia Gandhi and the Prime Minister Dr. Manmohan Singh to the project for development of Punjab. He asked the promoters of Bhatinda refinery to expedite setting up this project on fast track. The delegation had called on Shri Deora to convey their appreciation for his efforts to encourage participation of M/s. Mittal Investment as joint venture (JV) partner in Bhatinda Refinery Project. Government on 21st June 2007 approved the proposal of Mittal Energy Investments Pvt. Limited (MEI), a 100% subsidiary of M/s. Mittal Investments (MI) to own 49% equity as Joint Venture (JV) partner in M/s. Guru Govind Singh Refinery Ltd. (GGSRL) which was earlier incorporated as 100% subsidiary of Hindustan Petroleum Corporation Limited (HPCL) for setting up Bhatinda Refinery. HPCL will hold 49% and Indian financial institutions (IFIs) will hold balance 2% equity. Equity investment by HPCL and MI (through MEI) comes to Rs.3506 crore each and by IFIs Rs. 143 crore. With Government's nod for participation of Mittals, Shri Deora said, decks have been cleared for implementation of this important project. He also took stock of the steps contemplated by the promoters to put implementation of refinery on a fast track. Shri Deora recalled the significant contribution of the Government of Punjab which signed a Deed of Assurance in August 2005 extending tax concessions for Guru Gobind Singh Refinery. This is a critical input for viability of the Rs.19,000 crore refinery project. Shri Arun Balakrishnan, CMD HPCL and Shri B.S. Sant, MD GGSRL made a detailed presentation on the steps planned to be taken to put the project on fast track. The project did not make the desired progress in the past for various reasons, even though its foundation stone was laid way back in 1988. Previous efforts to solicit participation of corporate entities did not bear fruit despite HPCL approaching several Multi National Companies (MNCs) during last ten years. In one case the company had even signed an MoU with British Petroleum to join as JV partner. The investment by MI of Rs. 3506 crore (or about 5% of total FDI in 2006-07) is the first and the largest Foreign Direct Investment (FDI) brought into the petroleum refining sector in collaboration with a PSU. The investment is the second largest FDI in the energy sector and the third largest ever that the country has received. The project itself was earlier approved by CCEA with permission to induct JV partner if so required subsequently. It consists of a 9 million metric tonne per annum (MMTPA) refinery, 1000 KM crude oil pipeline from Mundra (Gujarat) to Bhatinda and Single Point Mooring (SPM) & crude oil terminal at Mundra. The 'As built' cost assessed by SBI Caps is Rs. 18,919 crore. The project will create a lot of jobs directly and indirectly in the

State of Punjab. This will give a boost to industrialization and development of ancillary industries. It will also improve the distribution efficiency of petroleum products in the North West region. Further, it will enhance the national capabilities of providing latest quality/environment friendly products.

1744. (4-7-2007) NEW DELHI : Union Power Minister Shri Sushilkumar Shinde has said that in order to bridge the existing gap between demand and supply and to meet the future requirement, there is a need to increase the existing installed capacity of 1,34,000 MW to about 2,10,000 MW by 2012. He was speaking after inaugurating the International Conclave on "Key Inputs for Accelerated Development of Indian Power Sector for 11th Plan and Beyond" organized by the Ministry of Power and Central Electricity Authority in New Delhi. He said capacity addition of 78,500 MW has been planned for the 11th Plan and the capacity addition target for 12th Plan is likely to be about 82,000 MW. Commensurate Transmission and distribution system has also to be provided from the generating stations to the ultimate consumers of electricity. The two-day Conclave is being attended by equipment manufacturers, contractors entrepreneurs, power utilities, financial institutions and training institutes. It will focus on the key inputs, including Human Resource Development measures required for implementing various generation, transmission and distribution projects targeted for completion during the 11th Plan (2007-2012) and beyond. The capacity addition programme for the 11th Plan is more than thrice of what could be actually achieved during the 10th Plan. However the preparedness at the beginning of the 11th Plan is much better than what it was at the beginning of 10th Plan. At the beginning of the 11th Plan, projects with an aggregated capacity of about 49,000 MW are under execution (out of which 1580 MW capacity has already been commissioned) as against about 21,000 MW at the beginning of the 10th Plan. MOP and CEA are pursuing with the projects developers to expedite placement of order for balance about 29,000 MW by the end of December, 2007. Thus a major milestone of placement of orders for the 11th Plan projects is likely to be achieved during the first year of 11th five year plan. Having achieved the first major milestone of project execution, it is necessary to provide necessary inputs like timely supply of equipment, wide base of construction companies, deployment of adequate construction machinery, manpower and finances to ensure timely commissioning of the units. Shri Shinde stated that BHEL which is the largest supplier of equipment will not be able to meet the entire additional demand of power sector and stressed for augmentation of production capacities and increase of vendor base including project executing agencies. He informed that in pursuance of the decision taken in Chief Minister's Conference held on 28th May, 2007, a professionally managed National Power Project Management Board for monitoring the timely commissioning of the unprecedented capacity addition and associated transmission projects will be formed shortly. The States are also expected to set up similar dedicated apparatus for state projects. He informed that 8 to 10 lakh strong workforce is required to be built up for construction and O&M of the additional capacity in generation, transmission and distribution. He appealed to the project developers, CPSUs and industries to take up apprentice training programme to build up the required trained manpower. They could also adopt ITIs around the project areas and provide the necessary infrastructure for training of the technicians in the required trades. The main aim of the Conclave is to discuss and apprise the equipment manufacturers, contractors, power utilities and industry associations about the capacity addition and transmission/distribution expansion programme during the 11th Plan and beyond and to discuss their preparedness with respect to meeting these targets. Working Group on Power for 11th Plan has identified some of the constraints relating to key inputs likely to be faced. The Conclave will discuss these issues to draw a road map for overcoming the bottlenecks in implementation of the capacity addition plan as also the corresponding transmission and distribution programmes. The conclave will focus on very important topics related to key inputs required for future power development programmes in the country including manufacturing capabilities for plant and equipments for thermal and hydro plants. This also includes auxiliaries, capacity building for transmission and distribution systems, opportunities for employment generation and training requirement for skilled manpower and financial requirement. It is expected that after conclusion of the Conclave both the Government and private industries would collectively gear up to face the forthcoming challenges.

1745. (4-7-2007) NEW DELHI : The Ministry of Railways has offered jobs to two unemployed daughters of unprivileged Shri Vinayak Rao Tope, the descendents of Martyr Tatya Tope, the hero of India's first war of independence (1857). The Minister for Railways, Shri Lalu Prasad handed over the appointment letters to the daughters namely Tripiti and Pragati for their appointment as Commercial Assistant at Kanpur Terminal of Container Corporation of India Ltd., a Public Sector Undertaking of Minister of Railways at a function here today. Also present on the occasion among others were the Union Minister for Corporate Affairs, Shri Prem Chand Gupta and family of Shri Vinayak Rao Tope. Speaking on the occasion, Shri Lalu Prasad said that the Ministry of Railways has decided to connect Bithore with the broad gauge network as its tribute to Martyr Tatya Tope. For this, the narrow gauge line running between Mandhana to Brahmavarta which connects to the famous city of Bithore will now be converted to broad gauge at an estimated cost of Rs. 15 crore. This work has been approved as a supplementary work of the Kanpur-Farrukhabad main line. The gauge conversion work will be completed and the section will be opened for passenger service during the current financial year. The Minister also said that Railways will continue to extend all possible assistance to similar noble cause. Shri Prem Chand Gupta, Minister for Corporate Affairs has announced that all possible efforts will be made to build the statue of Martyr Tatya Tope in Kanpur.

1746. (4-7-2007) NEW DELHI : Shri Priyaranjan Dasmunsi said that the nomination process for the Presidential election was over on 30th June. The scrutiny was over on 2nd July. The withdrawal of nominations was over by 3pm today and now it is very clear that we have two candidates, yet I must say that after 3pm today, our candidate Smt. Pratibha Patil issued her appeal from her office to the media. Shri Dasmunsi said that the BJP has created a new history by not agreeing to support the first woman candidate having full prospects of a thumping victory in the presidency of the country in our 60th year of independence. Our tour plan has been conveyed upto July 8 and the tour programme beyond that is taking time because of unpredictable weather in various parts of the country, specially the North-East and few other parts also. On the electoral scenario, Shri Dasmunsi said that it is not unknown to you. According to my estimation on behalf of the candidate and I can only tell you in advance today after the withdrawal that we definitely shall go beyond five lakh, seventy five thousand-first preference votes. We are also hopeful that by another two or three days the picture will improve. However, the statement that has been issued by our candidate today is as follows:- "My nomination papers having been found valid after scrutiny, I am now formally a candidate for the highest office of the nation. To be a candidate to occupy the highest office of the world's largest democracy, is a distinct honour. I shall seek the votes of the electoral college in a spirit of humility. Under no circumstances should the campaign, directly or indirectly, demean the dignity of the highest office. In my over five decades of public life, I have always endeavoured to be true to my conscience. All the allegations against me are motivated and have already been answered. If I am elected, I shall discharge my duties and responsibilities consistent with the Constitutional scheme and conventions established by my illustrious and distinguished predecessors. Shri Dasmunsi said that we do hope from the UPA side and the side of the supporting parties, BSP, Left that everywhere while approaching our electorate those who have assured and committed and beyond that we shall not use any kind of material which will only lead to disinformation, misinformation because this is a limited electorate, matured with about 4,800 odd numbers. However, we strongly feel that the election of this 13th presidency shall bring back the tradition that we maintained in this highest office of election but in the last few days what had happened I do not blame any individual nor the electronic channel or the print media and that whatever is placed before them, they have a right to edit or unedit and give it to the nation for the viewers and the readers. But those who provide this feedback, it is for them to understand the importance of this office and how it means in public life and most of us by being in the legislature, in the Parliament, in various other capacities may have a different position as per their political parties, as per their ideological commitment. But this is an election which is glorifying highest office of the country, when one reaches, be it the office of the President or the Vice-president, one of the top-key official in the Constitution who also put his or her seal an every matter of the country's final decision and that is the most important thing we have to bear in mind and I am thankful to my candidate for having issued this appeal today. To a question, that Pratibha Patil made this statement under pressure from the Left and as to who has answered her questions, Shri Dasmunsi said that I cannot consider that you join in the Politburo discussion of a certain party. It could be a presumption or assumption, there is no pressure from any quarter to our candidate to issue this statement. She is competent enough in her own conscience as to what is to be done. I had made it quite clear to the media before that she will first speak before the Tamil Nadu Legislature party; that UPA will make their collective declaration once again on July 3rd and that her statement will come on July 4th, so, therefore the question of pressure could be a very articulated point of your side and I thank you for your wisdom but this is not the case. Secondly, yes, we answered all the questions, not once but twice. To a question that now when the nomination process is over, will Pratibha Patil answer the queries of the media, Shri Dasmunsi said that never ever any candidate for the President of India has ever addressed a press conference before or during the tenure of the election. To a question that the name of Pratibha Patil has been tarnished, Shri Dasmunshi said that I can only say that they are irresponsible. Those who are depending on this, I should say, they are not serious about their own responsibilities and their commitment to their own profession and the concept. Those who are insisting on this, I think, they all will be frustrated.

1747. (4-7-2007) NEW DELHI : Finance Minister, Shri P. Chidambaram received, here today a final dividend cheque of Rs. 56 crore from Union Bank of India which was handed over by its Chairman & Managing Director, Shri M.V. Nair. The Government's holding in the Bank is 55.43%. Shri Chidambaram also received a dividend cheque of Rs. 23.35 crore from Vijaya Bank which was presented by its Chairman & Managing Director, Shri Prakash P. Mallya. With the Interim Dividend of 10% paid earlier, the Bank has rewarded its shareholders with a total Dividend of 20% for the financial year 2006-07.

1748. (4-7-2007) NEW DELHI : The Ministry of Civil Aviation has received a techno-feasibility study and project report from the Government of Uttar Pradesh (UP) for setting up an airport at Greater Noida. The Ministry has considered the report and has assured the State Government of Uttar Pradesh that it would require approximately three months to get an 'in-principle' approval for the airport from the Government of India under the prevailing circumstances. The proposal for setting up an airport at Grater Noida was first received by the Ministry of Civil Aviation from the Uttar Pradesh Government in 2001 and the technical approval for the selected site, was conveyed to the Ministry in 2003. The proposed site, identified for the construction of the Taj International Aviation Hub by the UP Government is nearly 72 kms. from Delhi and 120 kms. from Agra. Approximately 1500 hectares of land had been identified for the construction of the project. As per the feasibility report of the Uttar Pradesh Government the site has been selected keeping in mind all other strategic points in the nearby areas and so as to have the least environmental impact. The project cost is estimated at Rs. 35050 million. The Taj Expressway Authority will be nominated as the Sponsor of the project and the land acquisition will be done in accordance with the policy of the UP Government. The project Sponsor will acquire the land. The structure to be adopted will be that of a Special Purpose Vehicle (SPV) as Joint Venture with a private party selected through a competitive bidding process; wherein the equity composition will be-private party: 74%, Government of UP through Sponsor: 13% and other Government agencies such as AAI :13%.

1749. (4-7-2007) NEW DELHI : The Union Minister for Shipping, Road Transport and Highways Thiru T.R. Baalu today announced the constitution of an inter-ministerial group of experts comprising representatives from Navy, Coast Guard and Ports under the Chairmanship of Director General Shipping to look into the existing response mechanism and formulate a blue print for strengthening the response system in view of the recent spate of marine accidents on the Indian Coast. The group would look into the information-sharing, search and rescue and salvage operations, the availability of equipment and vessels etc. and submit its report within a fortnight. Thiru Baalu convened a meeting of Chairmen of all the Major Ports and senior officers from the Ministry of Defence, Navy, Coast Guard, Directorate General of Shipping, Directorate General of Lighthouses & Lightships and Shipping Corporation of India to take stock of the situation and to further review the measures to be taken in view of the recent spate of marine accidents. This was a follow up of the review held by the Minister recently. It may be recalled that there have been 13 weather related marine casualties during the last fortnight, since the onset of monsoon resulting in the rough weather conditions in the Indian coastal areas. Prima facie the cause of these casualties is the incapacitation of very old vessels due to the inclement weather. The Minister directed that immediate measures should be taken to restrict the operation of old vessels especially during the monsoon. He also directed the concerned agencies to alert their local units so that they can immediately respond in a coordinated manner to such exigencies. Thiru Baalu also reviewed the progress of Plan Schemes and Projects in the Major Ports. Some of the important projects reviewed were the iron ore and coal terminals at Paradip, container teminal projects at Tuticorin and JNPT, multipurpose berths at Kandla, dredging projects at JNPT and Ennore etc. The traffic handled at the Major Ports in the first quarter in 2007-08 is 123.09 Million Tonnes, an increase by 14.3% over the traffic handled in the corresponding period last year.

1750. (4-7-2007) NEW DELHI : The Micro, Small and Medium Enterprises Minister Shri Mahabir Prasad has urged the banks to come forward in providing loans to the unemployed youth of the country without collateral. He said since the Government in the Ministry of Micro, Small and Medium Enterprises vouches for the entrepreneur, there should not be any problem on the part of the banks to provide loans to these entrepreneurs. He was speaking at the Parliamentary Consultative Committee meeting attached to the Ministry of Micro, Small & Medium Enterprises here today. The Minister said the Credit Guarantee Fund

Scheme for Small Industries (CGFSI) was launched by the Government to make available collateral-free credit to the micro and small enterprise sector. Both the existing and the new enterprises are eligible to be covered under the scheme. The Ministry of Micro, Small & Medium Enterprises and Small Industries Development Bank of India (SIDBI), established a Trust named Credit Guarantee Fund Trust for Small Industries (CGTSI) to implement the Credit Guarantee Fund Scheme for Small Industries. The scheme was formally launched on August 30, 2000 and is in operation with effect from 1st January 2000. The corpus of CGTSI is being contributed by the Government and SIDBI in the proportion of 4:1 respectively and have contributed Rs.1346.54 crore to the corpus of the Trust up to May 31, 2007. Based on the future requirement, the corpus is likely to be raised to Rs.2500 crore. The Minister explained various achievements of the Coir Board to the Members. He said development of "Pithplus", for composting coir pith, "Coirret", for speeding up the retting process, coir plywood, "Anugraha", the compact metallic loom for weaving coir geotextiles, Anupam loom with inbuilt provision for providing training in weaving to woman artisans are a few of the achievements of the Board. The Minister said in the 11th Plan a new scheme has been announced for modernization and technological upgradation of coir industries. The aim of the scheme is to create additional employment of 1.76 lakh at a cost of Rs.1654 crore. Shri A.C.Jose, Chairman Coir Board said that the Board had been implementing the Coir Board Coir Workers' Group Personal Accident Insurance Scheme for the benefit of coir workers in the country. The scheme came into effect on 1st December 1998. The scheme provides for compensation up to a maximum amount of Rs.50,000/-. Some of the Members congratulated the Minister for the research and development work undertaken by the Coir Board. They however felt that the research findings need to be popularized among the masses and all the stakeholders should benefit from it. They also hailed the Minister for the new upgradation and rejuvenation programme for the coir industry in the 11th Plan.

1751. (4-7-2007) NEW DELHI : India is providing a Line of Credit for US$ 14.5 million for housing project in Gabon and on a request from Government of Gabon, the Finance Minister, Shri P. Chidambaram has approved India's concurrence to liberalise the LoC further. This was conveyed in a letter from Shri P. Chidambaram addressed to the Finance Minister of Gabon, Mr. Paul TOUNGUI. This letter was delivered by the Minister of State for Finance, Shri Pawan Kumar Bansal to Ms. Gisele Laure Eyang Ntoutoume, Deputy Minister for Housing & Urban Development, Gabon at a bilateral meeting held here today. Ms. Gisele is heading the Gabon delegation which had meetings with officials of the Ministry of Finance at New Delhi and with Exim Bank of India at Mumbai. This LoC will be used to construct houses in Libreville, the capital of Gabon. Shri Bansal expressed his fond hope that the housing project would be a standing testimony of excellent bilateral relations between India and Gabon. He explained that India has a good expertise in housing construction and Gabon can further take its benefit through coordination with National Housing Bank. The State Minister said that there is a tremendous potential to increase the bilateral trade between the two countries. India and the Gabon Republic have a close relationship covering areas of mutual interest, including political relations, trade and investment, economic and development cooperation, civil society and cultural exchanges, Shri Bansal added. The Gabon delegation leader stated that housing is one of the difficult and costly projects in their country and the LoC would greatly help in this field. She said her country would look forward for more cooperation from India especially in the health, housing and agriculture sector.

1752. (4-7-2007) NEW DELHI : Dr. Duvvuri Subbarao assumed the charge of Finance Secretary in the Ministry of Finance today. He has been holding the post of Secretary, Economic Affairs in the same Ministry from May 1, 2007. He belongs to IAS (AP cadre) and topped the Civil Services Exam 1972. Dr. Subbarao has wide experience on issues in public finance and has held important posts in this area. He was lead Economist in the World Bank during 1999-2004 and worked on issues of public finance in countries of Africa and East Asia. Dr. Subbarao studied at IIT Kanpur and was one of the first IIT products to join the civil services.

1753. (4-7-2007) NEW DELHI : The Prime Minister, Dr. Manmohan Singh, while inaugurating in New Delhi today a two-day Conference of Ministers in-charge of rural drinking water supply and rural sanitation in States & UTs, expressed concern over the shortage of water during the coming decades and called for a move towards forging a genuine partnership between the Government and citizens for conserving water and said that Government agencies must create a framework for collective action with NGOs and civil society. He also urged the State Governments to consider empowering district level institutional structures to handle water supply. This is also a Constitutional obligation as water supply is one of the basic functions to be carried out by rural and urban local bodies as per the Eleventh Schedule of the Constitution, the Prime Minister said. He said that there is urgent need for effective action to ensure the sustainability of water sources in view of increase in the number of "slipped-back" habitations on account of the failure of sources. We need proper institutional arrangements to ensure that both scientific expertise for location of sources as well as collective action for water recharge are effectively mobilized, he underlined. He further said that the Ministry of Rural Development should consider, where resources are difficult to find, to fund water recharge activities at the district level through the NREGP and district-based plans of the Departments of Agriculture & Irrigation. While speaking on the technical capacity of Managers of drinking water supply system, he said that there has to be planned capacity building for the staff of public health engineering department in geo-hydrology so that they are able to appreciate issues of environmental sustainability. Access to safe and adequate drinking water and sanitation are key to the well being of out people and drinking water is one of the key components of the `Bharat Nirman' programme for building efficient and modern rural infrastructure. The Prime Minister said that accordingly sufficient resources have been allocated for this important sector with substantial enhancement in allocation from Rs.4,560 crore during 2006-07 to Rs.6,500 crore during the current year for rural drinking water supply and the onus is now on the States to ensure that these resources get translated in to actual entitlements of safe drinking water and improve services for the common man. The Prime Minister also released documents on water sustainability on the occasion. The documents provide a road map to achieve sustainability in drinking water supply in rural areas and incorporate ranges of technical options from traditional water harvesting practices to use of modern day state of art technologies and have been prepared with the help of water experts and experiences from many States. The Minister for Rural Development, Dr. Raghuvansh Prasad Singh, while welcoming the gathering said that water is essential to life and Drinking Water Supply programme is thus a flagship programme under `Bharat Nirman' to ensure supply of safe drinking water to every habitation in the country in a time bound manner. He further said that the progress of programmes under `Bharat Nirman' coming under his Ministry is satisfactory and expected to fulfil the set targets by 2009. Ensuring availability, sustainability and quality of drinking water are the three priority areas under the programme of Drinking Water Supply, the Minister informed. Prof. Saifuddin Soz, Minister for Water Resources underscored the urgent need for adoption of better management practices for ensuring optimum utilization of water resources for meeting the ever-growing requirements of water for various purposes. He further informed that the Department of Drinking Water supply and Ministry of Water Resources have now embarked upon the programme of working together in the area of assessment of the ground water resources.

1754. (4-7-2007) NEW DELHI : Union Minister for Human Resource Development (HRD), Shri Arjun Singh has launched online Admission 2007-Project (Ni-On) of National Institute of Open Learning here today. National Institute of Open Schooling (NIOS) has initiated Online Admissions under its NIOS Online (Ni-On) Project from this year onwards. This unique facility, available for the first time in any Open Learning System in India, will facilitate the learners in directly accessing NIOS. It will lead to a rapid increase in the numbers of learner enrolment with NIOS and thereby assist the Government's effort of Universalisation of Secondary Education. Under Ni-On Project, NIOS has tailor-made '3' Streams of Online admissions for meeting the requirements of different groups of its potential learners. Under Stream-1 all the learners can access NIOS directly Online through its website (www.nos.org) for the purpose of seeking admission. The choice of Study Centres will be purely that of the learners and they will not be forced to go to any particular Study Centre. Stream-2 has been designed to save one year of all those who have been unsuccessful in CBSE/ ICSE/Other recognized State Education Boards. These learners can seek Online Admissions in the Stream '2' and also appear in the Public Examinations of October-November 2007, whose results will be declared by December 2007 itself, thereby saving almost one year for such learners. Stream-3 of Online Admissions also caters to the learners covered by Stream '2' but allows them an additional advantage of appearing in On Demand Examination (ODE) at Secondary level only based on his or her state of academic preparation. Last two Streams have been designed to provide "Safety Net" to all such unsuccessful learners of the Formal School System, who would like to save their precious time and carry on further with higher studies or enter the job market through Vocational Stream of NIOS, if they want. Based upon the design of Online Admissions, it is expected that annual enrolment of NIOS will increase by more than a lakh. Under Ni-On Project, learners of NIOS will be able to access Study Material Online. There will be a direct linkage in between NIOS and its learners for the first time, thereby removing a large number of "Student Support Services" related problems. It will improve academic intervention and delivery mechanism of NIOS substantially for the learners, thereby improving the quality of teaching-learning process of NIOS and overcome the digital divide that NIOS learners are facing so far. By harnessing ICT, NIOS will establish a direct linkage with the learners and provide them a bouquet of choices for entering and leaving the Open Learning System according to their requirements, thereby improving educational access at school level, at minimal cost.

1755. (4-7-2007) NEW DELHI : 133 settlements were arrived at between various Managements and Workers' Union in the Central sphere during the quarter ending March 31, 2007. According to the information received at the Labour Bureau, most of these settlements were arrived through conciliation proceedings by the Central Industrial Relations Machinery (CIRM) under the Industrial Disputes Act. Some of the settlements were also arrived at through bi-partite negotiations. About 43 per cent of these settlements involved service matters, 41 per cent included wages, Dearness Allowance and Bonus while house rent allowance, health, conveyance, leave and liveries were common issues in the large number of these settlements. Issues like compensation, shift allowance and retrenchment compensation were also the issues that comprised most of the remaining settlements. The major settlements pertained to four disputes involving about 9000 workers pertaining to Cochin Port Trust, Defence Electronic Laboratory, Hyderabad and Orissa Mineral Development Company Limited, Thakuran.

1756. (4-7-2007) NEW DELHI : The Ministry of Women and Child Development released financial support of Rs. 10.16 crores for the welfare of street children during 2006-07. The Ministry is implementing a scheme 'An Integrated Programme for Street Children' with the aim of preventing destitution and withdrawal of children from a life on the street and their placement into the national mainstream. Number of beneficiary street children during the period was 32,931. The goal of the Scheme is to achieve full and wholesome development of children without homes and family ties. The programme components include: Establishment of 24 hours drop-in shelters with facilities for night stay, safe drinking water, bathing, latrines, first-aid and recreation. Non-formal education programmes providing facilities for training in meaningful vocations, trades and skills to earning capacity

Programmes for reintegration of children with their families and placement of destitute and children in foster care homes/hostels and residential schools and their maintenance. Grant-in-aid is released to NGOs who are running street children and childline projects.

1757. (4-7-2007) NEW DELHI : The Prime Minister, Dr. Manmohan Singh has stressed the need to provide affordable and safe drinking water and clean and low cost sanitation facilities to all sections of our people. Inaugurating the Conference of Ministers of State Governments in charge of rural drinking water supply and sanitation, here today, Dr. Singh urged all State Governments to empower district level institutional structures to handle water supply, fund water recharge activities through NREGA and capacity building for the staff of public health engineering departments in geo-hydrology so that they are able to appreciate issues of environmental sustainability. Expressing serious concern over the increase in water borne diseases and also referring to linkages between drinking water and health, the Prime Minister directed the Department of Drinking Water to take proactive action to sensitise the community on safe water and its use. Stating that our planet will encounter in the next few decades severe shortages of water if we are not careful in conserving and preserving precious water resources, Dr. Singh called for forging a partnership between the government and citizens for conserving water. Expressing concern over the increase in numbers of "slipped-back" habitations each year on account of the failure of sources, the Prime Minister stressed the urgent need for effective action to ensure the sustainability of sources. "We need proper institutional arrangements to ensure that both scientific expertise for location of sources as well as collective action for water recharge are effectively mobilized", he added. Three booklets on drinking water and sanitation were released by the Prime Minister. The Union Minister of Rural Development, Dr. Raghuvansh Prasad Singh, Minister of Water Resources, Shri Saifuddin Soz, Ministers of State in the Ministry of Rural Development, Shri Chandrasekhar Sahu and Smt. Suryakanta Patil and Ministers from various States and Union Territories dealing with Drinking Water and Sanitation were among dignitaries present on the occasion. Following is the text of the address of the Prime Minister on the occasion: "I am very happy to be present at the inauguration of this very important Conference of Ministers of State Governments in charge of rural drinking water supply and sanitation. I compliment my colleague, Minister of Rural Development, Dr. Raghuvansh Prasad Singh, and his Ministry for organizing this Conference to address an issue of vital national importance for a country of India's size and India's diversity. The Conference has rightly decided to focus on the issue of sustainability of water supply systems and sound water management. Our efforts to provide drinking water supply to all our citizens would depend critically on environmental sustainability, with which our water security is intimately connected. Access to safe and adequate drinking water and sanitation are key to the well being of our people. Drinking water is one of the key components of the Bharat Nirman programme for building efficient, modern rural infrastructure. Accordingly, sufficient resources have been allocated for this important sector. There has been a substantial enhancement in the allocation from Rs.4,560 crore during 2006-07 to Rs.6,500 crores during the current financial year for rural drinking water supply schemes. The onus now is on the State Government to ensure that these resources get translated into actual entitlement of safe drinking water and improved services for the benefit of common man. Since the Accelerated Rural Water Supply Programme was introduced in 1972-73, there has been considerable progress in providing safe water to habitations. But the numbers of "slipped-back" habitations increases each year on account of the failure of sources and this is a major lacunae in the programme as it has been implemented thus far and this points to the urgent need for effective action to ensure the sustainability of water sources. We need proper institutional arrangements to ensure that both scientific expertise for location of sources as well as collective action for water recharge are effectively mobilized.

1758. (4-7-2007) NEW DELHI : In an emergency meeting called by Prime Minister's Office, Principal Secretary to Prime Minister, Shri T.K.A Nair took stock of the position of essential supplies in the Northeastern states. The meeting was held following damage of a railway bridge on the main arterial route to Lumding-Badarpur on the North Frontier Railway. Shri Santosh Mohan Dev, Minister for Heavy Industries & Public Enterprises had met the Prime Minister to apprise him of the incident of damage to the bridge and the need to take immediate action to avoid any disruption in the flow of essential commodities to Assam and other Northeastern States. Prime Minister had directed for an immediate meeting to be taken by Principal Secretary to PM and attended by the Ministries of Railways, Food & Public Distribution, Petroleum, Road Transport, Home, and the Government of Assam. In the meeting, the State Government apprised that there are sufficient stocks of essential commodities, including foodgrains, petroleum products and other items that are available in the Northeastern States, and there is no cause for any alarm. Both FCI and IOC assured the State Government that the flow of foodgrains and petroleum products would be maintained. Principal Secretary to PM directed that the alternate routes identified for movement of goods would be maintained open round the clock, for which purpose BRO and NHAI would set up control centres on the identified Highways. The Railways have also been instructed to put in place necessary transshipment both for freight and passenger movement in consultation with the State Government of Assam. Assam Police and BRO have also been instructed to ensure that adequate checks are conducted to rule out over loading by transporters so that potential damage to bridges is avoided. The meeting in Prime Minister's office was also attended by Shri Santosh Mohan Dev, Minister of Heavy Industries and Public Enterprises, and Shri Bhumidhar Barman, Revenue Minister, Assam. PMO has also directed that Chief Secretary, Assam, while taking necessary action to ensure unhindered flow of essential commodities, would also hold weekly meetings with all concerned agencies to take continuous stock of the situation and keep the PMO apprised.

1759. (4-7-2007) NEW DELHI : A section of the media has carried some reports ostensibly on the basis of the Union Home Minister's interview with a TV Channel at Gulmarg, Jammu & Kashmir on July 01, 2007 regarding infiltration and violence in Jammu and Kashmir. The Home Minister has been wrongly quoted in the reports. The highly distorted reports have created totally avoidable confusion and controversy.

1760. (5-7-2007) NEW DELHI : The Ministers in-charge of Rural Development from North-Eastern States called on Dr. Raghuvansh Prasad Singh, Union Minister of Rural Development here today. They submitted a Memorandum requesting for changing the present formula of Centre-State sharing of funds of schemes from 75:25 to 90:10 as the North-Eastern States finds it difficult to raise funds to the present ratio due to availability of meager resources. The State Ministers also urged Dr. Singh to help them in tackling the drinking water problem in particular as most of the NE States are all hilly terrains and their geographical situation is different from the rest of the country. Dr. Raghuvansh Prasad Singh, assured the Ministers visiting him of all cooperation from his Ministry and informed them that the matter has already been taken up with the Planning Commission and is likely to get resolved shortly.

1761. (5-7-2007) NEW DELHI : The Union Cabinet today approved the proposal of the Ministry of Overseas Indian Affairs to sign an additional protocol to the existing labour agreement between India and Qatar. This additional protocol, which is an initiative of Shri Vayalar Ravi, Minister of Overseas Indian Affairs, was finalized and initiated at the official level in September 2006 after two rounds of negotiations between the two countries. The existing Agreement on the regulations of the employment of Indian Manpower was signed on 11th April 1985. The Additional protocol contains several new bilateral initiatives for the benefit of Indian workers in Qatar. Article (2) enlarges the mandate of the Joint Committee in terms of promotion of emigration to Qatar from India and protection/welfare of Indian workers. Article (4) stipulates that the Joint Committee would meet twice a year alternatively in India and Qatar. This will ensure regular engagement between the two Governments on issues relating to Indian workers. Articles (5) and (6) provides that if the State of Qatar decides to repatriate Indian workers pre-maturely before expiry of their contracted period, it will ensure that full wages and other entitlements accruing to them under the contracts of employment and under the Labour Laws of the State of Qatar are paid to the workers for the entire un-availed period of the contracts before their repatriation. The additional protocol provides for the welfare of Indians working in the unorganized sector in Qatar by making a specific provision under Article (7) as well as in the Preamble. In addition, the Government of Qatar intends to promulgate a new law for the unorganized sector as reflected in the agreed minutes. This is an important breakthrough since a large number of Indian workers in Qatar do not have any protection under their protection/welfare. The Ministry is concerned about the malpractices by intermediaries and unscrupulous employers. To address this issue, Article (8) provides for appropriate steps to be taken to curb practices detrimental to the welfare of the Indian workers working in or seeking work in the State of Qatar. Qatar has drawn up huge development plans in view of its economic growth and need for infrastructure development. As a result, substantial investment for development is expected in Qatar in the years to come. This, in turn, will create significant additional demand for workers from overseas Indian workers can be positioned as well trained and highly skilled make use of these emerging opportunities in Qatar. The additional protocol will facilitate deployment of Indian workers against emerging employment opportunities. The size of the Indian diasporas is estimated at about 25 million, of which the Indian workers in the Gulf constitute about 5 million. A large number of unskilled, semi-skilled and skilled categories of workers have been migrating from India to Qatar. The strength of Indian community is about 1,72,000. The number of workers is estimated at 1,40,000, out of which some 70% are unskilled, semi-skilled and skilled workers, 20% white collar workers, and 10% professionals and managerial cadres. Over the years the Indian emigrant population in Qatar has been growing. Shri Vayalar Ravi will shortly be visiting Qatar to sign the additional protocol.

1762. (5-7-2007) NEW DELHI : The Minister of Rural Development, Dr. Raghuvansh Prasad Singh in his concluding remarks, here today, assured the State Ministers In-charge of Rural Water supply & Sanitation participating in the two-day Conference on 'Sustainable Drinking Water Supply, Sanitation for all-2012' that there will be no resource crunch in the implementation of schemes under Drinking Water Supply and Sanitation. He urged them to monitor the implementation of schemes at all levels, State, District and Block to review the performance of each and every Panchayat and formulate District specific programmes. He felt that there is need for dovetailing and convergence of different schemes run at the District level. For instance, the States should seek effective convergence of govt programmes like NREGA, soil and water conservation programmes under Agriculture, Central Ground Water Board (CGWB), Forest Deptt., etc. for protecting and strengthening the existing water sources and creation of new water bodies. He asked the States to focus on problems of arsenic and fluoride affected habitations on priority basis. The Minister requested the States to explore possibilities of use of non-conventional energy to cut down costs of water supply systems. He emphasized the need for timely completion of all projects under Bharat Nirman. While speaking on 'Sanitation for all', the Minister emphasized that all the Anganwadis and schools should be covered on priority basis and community toilets should be made where community is willing to manage and maintain the assets created. The inclusion of solid and liquid waste management is recent initiatives and the States need to promote the same, he said. The Minister assured that the demand for enhancing norms for construction cost of toilets will be duly considered. He further emphasized the need of strict vigilance and monitoring systems especially where the work has not started at village, block and district level The NGOs and Self-Helf Groups can be involved in the programmes of rural sanitation for awareness creation and for better water management, Dr. Singh opined. "Sustainability of water sources" and "Sanitation for All" were the main focus of the Conference. The progress of all States under Bharat Nirman programme was reviewed for 2006-07. An action plan for coverage of all uncovered rural habitations till 2009, to tackle the problem of quality affected habitations and to restore the status of habitations that have slipped back to fully covered status was discussed during the two-day Conference. State-wise review was conducted on the progress of Sub Mission on Water Quality projects and the National Rural Drinking Water Quality Monitoring & Surveillance programme. The usage of Web Based Integrated Management Information Systems developed by the Department of Drinking Water Supply for all future programmes / expenditure was impressed upon the participants. Indian Institute of Remote Sensing (NRSA) made a Presentation on the use of geo-informatics for locating water sources. CGWB has provided the expertise regarding the preparation of hydro-geo-morphological maps for better planning and the States have been requested to coordinate with the State Level centres of CGWB in this regard. The Ministry of Rural Development, Deptt. of Drinking Water Supply, will shortly be sponsoring a course for PHED engineers to be conducted by Indian Institute of Remote Sensing for enhancing their skills for scientific planning. The participating Ministers in-charge of water and sanitation raised various state specific issues during the Conference. The demand for revising the funding pattern for special category States like the North East and the hilly regions was also highlighted. The Conference was attended by representatives of various Ministries/Departments like Ministry of Water Resources, CGWB, Agriculture, New and Renewable Energy, Planning Commission as well as representatives of external support agencies like WSP, WHO, UNICEF.

1763. (5-7-2007) NEW DELHI : Locust migration from Africa to the Indian sub-continent is not likely to be a threat to India. So far only scattered and localized presence of locust has been reported from Gujarat. No reports of locust spotting have been received from Rajasthan. Ministry of Agriculture and the Locust Unit of Directorate of Plant Protection & Quarantine are in constant touch with the State Government of Gujarat and Rajasthan and Punjab. The Food and Agriculture Organisation (FAO) issued a locust warning on 27th June 2007 stating that locust swarms were seen in the North-Eastern Somalia and the swarms could arrive in Pakistan and Rajasthan in the next 7 to 10 days. On receiving this high alert from FAO, the Central Government advised the State Governments to keep constant vigil and to keep themselves prepared to combat any locust infestation. On 28th June, Agriculture Secretary, Dr. P.K. Mishra spoke to the Gujarat Chief Secretary and Principal Secretary of Agriculture on this issue. The field units of Locust Warning Organisation of India (LHO) located in Gujarat and Rajasthan, and the State Governments have been alerted and instructed to intensify the survey to detect any locust movement in the costal areas of Gujarat and the scheduled desert areas of Rajasthan. Considering the probability of landing in Gujarat, the Collectors of Kutch, Rajkot, Jamnagar and other District authorities have been alerted. Control Rooms have been set up at the Office of District Collector, Bhuj and at LWO, Bhuj. The BSF authorities have also been alerted. Four teams from LWO and four teams from the State Government are in the field for survey and control. Till 3rd July 2007, Joint Survey Teams surveyed a total 125 villages in Kutch District. The surveillance teams initially found small population of locust in about 100 ha. in Lakhpat Taluk of Kutch district, which is about 1.5 k.m. inside from the coastline. On further survey, they located locust population over a strip of area, extending approximately 10 km X 0.5-1 km covering the villages of Nanicher, Shilpar and Angarpura villages of Lakhpat Taluk of Kutch district of Gujarat. There is adequate stock of pesticides and equipment for the control operations if such a need arises in future.

1764. (5-7-2007) NEW DELHI : BJP National Vice President Shri Mukhtar Abbas Naqvi today said that with view of effectively preparing for the forthcoming elections, the BJP is launching a nation-wide campaign starting from 6th July, 2007 to form a team of dedicated and active workers on the 15 lakh booths throughout the country. Shri Naqvi added that the BJP National President Shri Rajnath Singh will inaugurate the "BJP ON EACH BOOTH" campaign from Madhya Pradesh. The Madhya Pradesh Chief Minister Shri Shivraj Singh Chauhan, General Secretary Shri Ananth Kumar and National Secretary Shri Prabhat Jha will join the National President in this inaugural ceremony. Shri Naqvi further added that all prominent leaders of the party will tour various states during the next three months period of the "BJP ON EACH BOOTH" campaign which is being undertaken with a view to strengthen and streamline a comprehensive strategy for the forthcoming assembly elections in eleven states to be held in 2007-08 and for the Lok Sabha elections to be held in 2009. Shri Naqvi observed that on the occasion of the inauguration of the "BJP ON EACH BOOTH" campaign on July 6, Dr. Murli Manohar Joshi will participate in the programme in Delhi, Shri M. Venkaiah Naidu in Haryana, Shri Kalyan Singh in U.P. Prof. Vijay Kumar Malhotra in Delhi, Prof. Bal Apte in Kerala, Shri M.A. Naqvi in Uttar Pradesh, Sh. Yashwant Sinha in Delhi, Sh. Gopinath Munde in Maharshtra, Sh. Om Mathur and Sh. Narendra Modi in Gujarat, Sh. Ram Lal and Sh. Vinay Katiyar in Orissa. Shri Naqvi added that the Chief Ministers and Presidents of all states will also individually take part in various programmes to be held in their respective states. Shri Naqvi further added that apart from these leaders, the other prominent leaders who will also participate in the "BJP ON EACH BOOTH" campaign in various states include Sh Kalraj Mishra in Bihar, Sh Ravi Shankar Prasad in Uttarakhand, Sh Prakash Javadekar in West Bengal, Sh Kaptan Singh Solanki in Maharastra, Sh Balbir Punj in Kerala, Sh Rajiv Pratap Rudi in Bihar, Sh Manohar Parikar in Goa, Sh Arjun Monda in Jharkhand, Sh Jual Oram in Arunachal Pradesh, Sh Sidharth Nath Singh in Nagaland, Sh Vijay Goel in Andhra Pradesh, Dr. Anil Jain in Uttrakhand, Sh Satyapal Jain in Himachal Pradesh, Sh Shyam Jaju in Maharastra and Sh Syed Sahanawaz Hussain in Bihar. Shri Naqvi asserted that the BJP is making ground level preparations keeping in view the ensuing elections during 2007-08 to state assemblies in Gujarat, Himachal Pradesh, Madhya Pradesh, Rajasthan, Chhattisgarh, Delhi, J & K, Tripura Nagaland, Meghalaya, Mizorum and in 2009 to Lok Sabha. Sh. Naqvi said that the 1 st phase of "BJP ON EACH BOOTH" campaign will start on July 6th the birth anniversary of Dr. Shyama Prasad Mukerjee and will continue till September 25th the birth anniversary of Pt. Deendayal Upadhyay. During these three months, teams of BJP workers will be formed for each booth and these teams will tour from village to village to strengthen the party organization. Sh. Naqvi disclosed that state level and district level committees have been set up in all states and districts and their working will be monitored by the central party from time to time. Sh. Naqvi expressed a view that it is desirable that the Election Commission should expedite the delimitation proceedings of the Lok Sabha and assembly constituencies and should clarify by the end of the year whether the coming Lok Sabha elections will be held according to the new delimitation or not. Sh. Naqvi added that slow pace of the Election Commission's delimitation proceedings have put political parties and potential candidates under a cloud of uncertainty due to which the main political parties are not being able to finalize the selection of their candidates for the forthcoming Lok Sabha elections. Sh. Naqvi demanded from the Election Commission should accelerate the proceeding of delimitation of seals so that it could be finalized by the end of the year.

1765. (5-7-2007) NEW DELHI : The Prime Minister Dr. Manmohan Singh has approved the extension of term of the National Commission for Enterprises in the Unorganised Sector (NCEUS) for a further period of one year *i.e.* up to September 2008. It may be recalled that in line with the commitment made by the United Progressive Alliance (UPA) Government in the National Common Minimum Programme, the NCEUS was set up in September 2004 under the chairmanship of Dr. Arjun K. Sengupta as an advisory body and as a watchdog for the unorganized sector. The Commission has the mandate to examine the problems of the unorganized sector (also referred to as informal sector) and suggest measures to overcome them. The term of the Commission, which was initially fixed at one year, had been extended to three years. Now the term has again been extended to one more year. The Commission has been assigned wide-ranging terms of reference. Being an advisory body, the Commission has to submit its recommendations to the Government of India. An Advisory Board has also been constituted to enable the Commission to have the benefit of the advice of experienced persons in the relevant areas. The Commission has been focusing on a few significant programmatic interventions, which could be adopted in the immediate term. These interventions are aimed at bringing about improvement in the productivity of enterprises in the unorganized/Informal Sector, generation of large-scale employment opportunities on a sustainable basis and enhancing the welfare of the workers in the unorganized sector.

1766. (5-7-2007) NEW DELHI: An all-party delegation of legislators and Parliamentarians from Kerala on Wednesday urged Prime Minister Manmohan Singh to convene a meeting of the Chief Ministers of Tamil Nadu and Kerala at the earliest to resolve the differences over the formation of the Salem Division by hiving off portions of the existing Palakkad Division of the Indian Railways. Reminding the Prime Minister about his own earlier assurance that the Salem Division would be set up only after discussions between the two Chief Ministers, the delegation pointed out that work was progressing on this front despite apprehensions expressed by all sections of people from Kerala. Led by Chief Minister V.S. Achuthanandan, the delegation also drew the Prime Minister's attention to the unanimous resolution passed by the Kerala Legislative Assembly on June 28 about the step-motherly treatment meted out to the State by the Railways. As a case in point, the delegation brought up the shifting of the office of the Chief Engineer (Construction) from Thiruvananthapuram to Chennai. Besides, the delegation also demanded a separate Railway Zone headquartered in Kerala. The delegation included Leader of the Opposition in Kerala Assembly, Oommen Chandy, several members of the State Cabinet and members of Parliament. However, the Opposition did not attend the press conference convened immediately afterwards. Briefing mediapersons, the Chief Minister said the Prime Minister was receptive to Kerala's contention not just on the Railways issue but also on immediate relief for people affected by the torrential rains that lashed the State last month. The State has sought immediate relief of Rs. 100 crore from the Central Government. And, keeping in mind the long-drawn out process of the Centre sending a team to the State to assess the damage and make an estimate about the actual requirement, Mr. Achuthanandan said he told the Prime Minister that precious time should not be lost in this bureaucratic exercise. The Chief Minister said his Government was planning a legislation to regulate the entry of corporates in retail trade. "If need be, we will consider a ban to protect the small retailers," he said; insisting that there was no contradiction between what the Left Democratic Front Government was proposing to do in Kerala and the position taken by the LDF in West Bengal.

1767. (5-7-2007) NEW DELHI : The Government has today approved setting up of Rajiv Gandhi Institute of Petroleum Technology at Jias, Rai Bareli District, Uttar Pradesh as 'Institute of National Importance' under an Act of Parliament. The Rajiv Gandhi Institute of Petroleum Technology (RGIPT) is envisaged to serve as the fountainhead for the nurturing of world class technical human resources capable of serving as the leaders and innovators of tomorrow in the field of Petroleum Technology. To start with the Institute will commence its academic operations by admitting students in basic undergraduate courses from the academic year 2008-09, from a rented campus. The institute will become fully operational in 2015-16. On its becoming fully operational the Institute would have 7 B. Tech,

6 Integrated Masters Degrees, 8 M.Tech/MBA and 12 PGD and Ph.D programmes. The total estimated capital cost of the project is Rs.435 crores which would be met partially through budgetary support of Rs. 285 crores and Rs. 150 crores from Oil Industry Development Board. The total estimated recurring expenditure of Rs. 260.58 crores would be met from the accrual of interest on Endowment Fund of Rs. 250.00 crores to be created with the contribution of Oil Public Sector Undertakings (PSUs), student fees, donations and other earnings of the Institute through Research & Development, consultancies, students' placement fees, etc. The Institute is envisaged to be self sufficient and self-reliant by the year 2015-16. It is important to note that Government had come out with the New Exploration Licensing Policy in 1999 and with the passage of time this policy has been made more and more attractive to foreign companies as well as Indian private and public sector companies. As on date, only 30% of the sedimentary basins in India has been explored and there is still a vast potential in terms of acreages that are to be explored. The Government is committed to increase the exploration coverage to an extent of 100% by the year 2015. In a recent study conducted by consultant Price Waterhouse Coopers for Petrofed, the gap between the availability and requirement of trained manpower in India is projected to be about 36000 by the year 2019 and the existing institutes may not be adequate to meet the increasing requirement of technical manpower in the petroleum sector. The proposed Rajiv Gandhi Institute of Petroleum Technology is expected to meet this shortfall to a significant extent.

1768. (5-7-2007) NEW DELHI : A Loan Agreement for "Third National HIV/AIDS Control Project" was signed between India and the World Bank, here today for US $ 250 million for the purpose of supporting the National AIDS Control Programme (2007-2012) through: (i) Promotion of behaviour change by scaling up prevention efforts in the High Risk Groups and the general population: and (ii) Increased care, support and treatment of people living with HIV/AIDS. The World Bank is supporting this project through its soft IDA window. The agreement was signed by Shri Madhusudan Prasad, Joint Secretary (Fund Bank), Department of Economic Affairs, Ministry of Finance on behalf of Government of India and Ms. Isabel M. Guerrero, Country Director, World Bank, on behalf of the World Bank Besides the World Bank, United Kingdom's Department for International Development (DfID) is also providing a grant in a principal amount of GBP 100 million through a common pool. An agreement to this effect was also signed between DfID and Government of India today. The agreement was signed by Shri Kumar Sanjay Krishna, Joint Secretary (Bilateral Cooperation) on behalf of Government of India, and Mr. Mark Lewis, Acting Head, DfID (India) on behalf of DfID, UK. Other development partners supporting the project include the Global Fund to Fight AIDS, TB and Malaria, USAID and UN system organizations. The closing date of the project is 30th September, 2012.

1769. (5-7-2007) NEW DELHI : The Public Sector, Rashtriya Ispat Nigam

Limited (RINL), has achieved the best ever First Quarter (Q-1) Sales Turnover of Rs. 2026 crore during the period April-June'07. This is 14% rise over the same period last year (Rs. 1774 crores). The Company sold 6.34 lakh tonnes of steel in the domestic market registering a growth of 7% over the same period last year. RINL's focus towards value added steel has resulted in the sale of 2.94 lakh tonnes of value added steel in the Ist quarter, a whopping 43% rise over the same period last year. Another significant feature of marketing performance was sale of 1,45,767 tonnes for Projects segment which recorded a growth of 16% over the same period last year. The sale of 5571 MT to District Level Dealers serving the rural market is also the highest for any quarter, since inception. On the production front, the Value added production of 3, 51,893 tonnes during Q-1 of 2007-08 is the best for any quarter, since inception. Similarly, production of 2,17,810 tonnes of bars is the best Q-1 production, since inception.

1770. (5-7-2007) NEW DELHI : Shri Sis Ram Ola, Minister of Mines informed the Parliamentary Consultative Committee (PCC), here today, that in a major turn around Hindustan Copper Ltd. (HCL), a PSU under his Ministry, has made a record profit of Rs. 331.78 crore during 2006-07. Prior to his taking charge of Ministry of Mines in 2004-05, Shri Ola said that HCL had been incurring losses continuously for the previous eight years. The Minister pointed to the commencement of a turn around in year 2004-05 when the Company posted a profit of Rs. 52 crore and in 2005-06 the profit increased to Rs.100.22 crore before reaching all time high levels in 2006-07. Agenda for today's PCC meeting was "working of HCL". Shri Ola also emphasized that the urgent need of further strengthening the Company and said necessary steps are being taken in that direction. The Company has utilized its capacity appropriately and ore production & copper production of the Company has shown significant growth. During 2006-07 HCL's ore production was 32.70 lakh tones against 26.37 lakh tones in 2005-06. Production of metal in concentrates increased to 30231 tonnes from 22984 tonnes during this period. India has vast reserves of copper. HCL is the only copper producing company in India which has mining operations. Annual copper demand in the country stand at about 4.40 lakh tonne while domestic production was 30,231 tonne during 2006-07. The annual demand growth of about 7% calls for urgently augmenting copper production from domestic resources, in which HCL has a crucial role to play. Members made several important suggestions. These include immediate recruitment of staff in HCL which has been held up for 12 years including the candidates from weaker sections like SCs/STs, enhancing retirement age of the employees to 60 years from 58 years at present in line with other PSUs etc. Members also suggested that efforts should be made to stop exodus of experienced and qualified personnel from mining PSUs. The members who attended the meeting are: S/Shri Jual Oram, K. Virupakshappa, Tushar A. Choudhary, Dr. Prasanna Kumar Patasani, Tukaram Renge Patil and Raghuraj Singh Shakya from Lok Sabha and Shri Rudra Narayan Pany from Rajya Sabha. Shri J.P. Singh, Secretary (Mines) and senior officers of the Ministry of Mines and HCL were also present.

1771. (5-7-2007) NEW DELHI : Grants-in-aid of Rs. 4.68 crore has been released by the Ministry of Rural Development as first instalment being equal to 60% of the total allocation of Rs. 7.80 crore to Howrah District of West Bengal State, as Central assistance for the implementation of the Sampoorna Grameen Rozgar Yojana (SGRY) during the current financial year (2007-2008). The grant is towards plan expenditure and will be utilized for approved items of works subject to the conditions laid down in the SGRY Guidelines. No deviation from the provisions of the Guidelines is permissible. The expenditure on implementation of the programme with regard to cash component is to be shared on 75:25 basis between the Central and the State Government, respectively.

1772. (5-7-2007) NEW DELHI : Grants-in-aid amounting to Rs. 15.00 crore has been released by the Ministry of Rural Development to Central Public Works Department, the nominated Central Agency for the implementation of Pradhan Mantri Gram Sadak Yojana (PMGSY) in Begusarai, Darbhanga, Madhubani and Samastipur District of Bihar for the year 2007-08. The grant is towards the Plan expenditure and will be subject to the conditions laid down from time to time in the guidelines of the PMGSY and supplementary directions. The Pradhan Mantri Gram Sadak Yojana (PMGSY) is a 100% Centrally sponsored Scheme, with the target of connecting, through good all-weather roads, every habitation that has a population of more than 1000 within 3 years and every habitation with a population of more than 500 by the end of the Tenth Plan. In respect of the Hill States (Himachal Pradesh, Jammu & Kashmir, Uttarakhand), North-East, Sikkim, Desert Areas and Tribal (Schedule-V) areas, the objective is to connect habitations with a population of 250 persons and above. According to latest figures made available by the State Governments under a survey to identify Core Network as part of the PMGSY programme, about 1.72 lakh Unconnected Habitations are eligible for coverage. Rural Roads have been identified as one of the six components of Bharat Nirman and a total of 66,802 habitations is proposed to be covered under the programme involving construction of 1,46,185 Kms. of rural roads and upgradation of 1,94,130 Kms. of rural roads.

1773. (5-7-2007) NEW DELHI : The Ministry of Rural Development has sanctioned Rs. 31.98 crore to the State Government of Chhattisgarh towards balance of first instalment of funds against the provisional allocation of Rs.95.95 crore made for the Government of Chhattisgarh under the Centrally sponsored Accelerated Rural Water Supply Programme (Normal) of Rajiv Gandhi National Drinking Water Mission, during the year 2007-08. Up to 15 % of the funds released under this sanction is to be utilized for Operation & Maintenance and up to 5% of funds is to be spent for taking sustainability measures. States are delegated powers for management of Rural Water Supply Schemes through the Panchayati Raj Institutions (PRIs). The release of funds is made for execution/ completion of schemes to provide safe drinking water facilities to rural habitations and schools under the Centrally Sponsored ARWSP.

1774. (5-7-2007) NEW DELHI : The two-day National Workshop on Improvement of Agricultural Statistics began here today with a strong call to the States to ensure accuracy and timeliness in compilation of agricultural data. Inaugurating the Workshop, Agriculture Secretary, Dr. P.K. Mishra emphasized that at present agricultural statistics plays a very crucial role in taking policy decisions ranging from export and import of farm commodities, pricing decisions, crop diversification, payment of drought relief and settling insurance claims. It is, therefore, necessary that data is collected efficiently at village, block and district levels, speedily compiled and validated with other sources of data, he said. Dr. Mishra exhorted the participants, which include economic and statistical experts, officers from various central ministries/organisations and State representatives, to address issues relating to accuracy and consistency in estimation of crop area, yield and production. States must bring their statistical departments to the mainstream of agricultural planning and put systems in place for timely collection of estimates and checking them with data generated by Department of Space, the Meteorological Department, NSSO, trade sources and other agencies, Dr. Mishra advised. Agriculture Secretary highlighted some major areas that need special attention. For example, he said, we do not have reliable and exhaustive database on horticultural crops. A strong statistical base is needed to monitor the progress of various schemes initiated in the recent years to give impetus to this sector, he said. The impact of the latest developments in agriculture also needs to be captured properly so as to make correct inferences for policy decisions. The land-use data needs to be frequently updated to make it useful. Agriculture Census is another area that needs to be paid special attention, the Secretary said. At present it takes 8-10 years to release data of Agriculture Census, which makes the data stale for taking decisions. Ideally, the Agriculture Census should be out within one year of capturing field data, he said. Wide variations observed in crop production estimates provided by different agencies is another major area of concern, Dr. Mishra said and asked the participants to evolve a system for cross-checking and validation of data at different levels.

1775. (5-7-2007) NEW DELHI : The Cabinet Committee on Economic Affairs today gave its approval for continuation of the National Mission on Bamboo Applications till November, 2009 in the Eleventh Plan, with in the approved outlay of Rs.100 crore. The scheme was approved by the CCEA in November 2004, with an outlay of Rs.100 crore. The Mission, which was initially structured as a five year programme, has been operational for 29 months, beginning November, 2004. The Mission has achieved significant successes and in several critical areas, the targets assigned have been exceeded. The Mission has created a base for economic activities with an annual turnover of more than Rs.270 crore, and has generated employment for 25.2 million mandays in extraction, processing and value addition in bamboo growing areas, across the country. The Mission has developed and commercialized technologies and applications in segments of wood substitutes, bamboo based gasification, bamboo based charcoal making, edible bamboo shoot processing, bamboo fibre based hygiene products, bamboo fibre reinforced thermoplastics for critical and non-critical segments. Effective intervention in provision of infrastructure is one of the major and significant achievements of the Mission. Over 8000 bamboo composite based pre-fabricated structures for schools, hospitals, sanitation and housing in the areas where construction is difficult and which are earthquake prone and Tsunami affected, have been installed. These structures have wide acceptability for their being cost effective, fire retardant, disaster proof and easy to install.

1776. (5-7-2007) NEW DELHI : The Union Cabinet today gave its approval for setting up of Rajiv Gandhi Institute of Petroleum Technology at Jias, Rai Bareli District, Uttar Pradesh, commencement of the basic course from the 2008-09 academic session, creation of various posts in the academic and supporting staff and budgetary support of Rs.285 crore to the Institute during 11th Five Year Plan. The institute will serve as the fountain-head for the nurturing of world-class human resources capable of serving as the leaders and innovators of tomorrow in the broad field of Petroleum Technology and Engineering covering the entire hydrocarbon value chain. A Bill will be introduced in the ensuing Session of Parliament, 2007.

1777. (5-7-2007) NEW DELHI : The Union Cabinet today gave its approval for setting up of the Pan-African Network in 53 countries of African Union at a cost of Rs. 542.90 crores. The project will show-case India's capability in IT sector, technology, health care and education. The project only pertains to setting up a demonstration model in each country, and is conceived as a developmental project. Its successful implementation is expected to enhance India's profile in the region and add a fresh dimension to India's partnership with Africa. Pursuant to African Unions' endorsement of the project an India-AU MOU for setting up of the Pan-African e-Network was signed in October 2005. Draft Country Agreement between each African Union Member States participating in the Pan-African e-Network Project and TCIL was also signed. Till date 23 countries have signed the model agreement with TCIL

1778. (5-7-2007) NEW DELHI : The Union Cabinet today gave its approval for the following: i) To the project titled Indian Participation in International Thermonuclear Experimental Reactor, at a base cost of Rs.2500 crore. The FE component calculated at base cost will be Rs.1129 crore. ii) To constitute an Empowered Board by the Governing Council of Institute for Plasma Research with sufficient powers required for effective implementation of the project within the framework of the agreement signed among the parties to the ITER and ITER International Organisation and also within the sanctioned amount for the project of Rs.2500 crore. This shall, inter alia, include: a) Full financial powers, particularly powers in respect of single limited and restricted tendering process and administrative powers to the total extent of the budgetary sanction and resource allocation for the project. b) Full autonomy in laying down the rules, procedures and guidelines for financial, administrative and any other matters related to the execution of the project. c) Full autonomy in deciding the delegation of powers in financial and administrative matters in conformity with the various stipulations and guidelines of the Government and Central Vigilance Commission. d) Power to create posts and lay down suitable recruitment norms depending upon size and nature of activities subject to over all sanctioned manpower requirement. To ensure this the Empowered Board, in turn, shall frame administratively and financially sound policies and put into place procedurally transparent rules, regulations and practices. India's joining ITER is recognition of India's scientific and technical capability in fusion energy. Considering India's large energy needs in future, our gaining technological capability in fusion energy will be of considerable long term benefit. India's participation in ITER will allow India to leapfrog in terms of our national technological capability in fusion energy.

1779. (5-7-2007) NEW DELHI : The Union Cabinet today gave its ex-post facto approval for signing the Memorandum of Understanding on Labour, Employment and Manpower Development between Kuwait and India. The Agreement would benefit the Indian workers especially the un-skilled, semi-skilled and skilled workers.

1780. (5-7-2007) NEW DELHI : The Union Cabinet today gave its approval for signing Additional Protocol to the Agreement on the regulation of the employment of Indian manpower between Qatar and India. The scheme would benefit the Indian workers especially the un-skilled, semi-skilled and skilled workers.

1781. (5-7-2007) NEW DELHI : The bald and mechanical denial by the UPA presidential candidate Smt. Pratibha Patil that all allegations against her are motivated, conceals more than it reveals. There is not even the remotest denial of any specific allegation all of which are based upon documentary evidence including proceedings of the Court, Inspection Report of the Reserve Bank of India as also the Finance Ministry, Government of India. These relate to gross abuse of money of small depositors admittedly squandered away by a bank of which she was not only the founder but also retained effective control till the very last when it went bust because huge amount of depositors money was given as unsecured loans to her relatives in violation of banking norms. There are allegations of a widow of a murdered Congress President, the investigation of which was grossly unfair because one of the principal conspirator happens to be her brother, a charge found prima-facie true by the High Court which referred the investigation to CBI in a writ petition filed by the widow of the said Congress leader. Now, there is the further charge of diversion of her MPLAD funds into a trust of her husband in violation of all the norms, when she was Member of Parliament. Every day new facts emerge about some wrong doing by nearly every institution with which she or her family members are associated. These are disturbing, stark and very specific issues and yet her conspicuous silence on all this only reinforces the highly suspicious circumstances surrounding her. The people of the country need to ask this question, is she, with such a past and a haunting present, at all fit to occupy the highest constitutional office of over one billion people.

1782. (5-7-2007) NEW DELHI : The Union Cabinet today gave its approval for extension of the term of the 2nd Administrative Reforms Commission by a period of seven months, *i.e.* upto 31.03.2008. The ARC has submitted five Reports and proposes to submit 14 Reports on various aspects of Administrative Reforms by 31st March, 2008. The 2nd ARC was set up to prepare a detailed blueprint for revamping the public administration system. Implementation of its Reports after due consideration is bound to improve service delivery etc.

1783. (5-7-2007) NEW DELHI : The Indian Air Force's microlight aircraft presently on 'Round the World' expedition entered into the western hemisphere by crossing the International Date Line (IDL) this morning IST. The microlight aircraft took of from Anader in Russia and landed today at Nome in Alaska after crossing the IDL at about 0915 IST this morning and thereby gaining one day. It may be recalled that an IAF microlight expedition has been undertaken on the occasion of Force's platinum jubilee year and was flagged off on 01 Jun 07 from Air Force Station Hindan near Delhi. The expedition flown by Wg Cdr Rahul Monga and Wg Cdr Anil Kumar also aims to set a new world record by competing in 300 Kg weight category microlight of make CSTW advance. On being asked on telephone how it felt to cross over the IDL, Wg Cdr Monga answered in stoic vein saying "We have got one more day in our expedition to live it fully". The expedition has so far flown and crossed over Myanmar, Thailand, China and Russia and in doing so they have covered the most difficult terrain and successfully negotiated bad weather conditions. The weather over China due monsoons was particularly bad. The terrain of Eastern Russia and freezing Siberia was covered successfully. Though the expedition is a few days behind scheduled due to bad weather, the crew and the team at operations-centre is very confident of catching up and setting the new world record. The expedition is being tracked in its operations-centre at New Delhi by a satellite tracking system called I-Trax with a satellite tracker on board. The progress of the expedition can be seen on satellite picture on website called web sentinel.net or even on IAF's Official website by opening the expedition's link. The microlight would be undergoing scheduled maintenance at Nome in Alaska after having completed in 80 hours of flying.

1784. (5-7-2007) NEW DELHI : The following is the list of Agreements/MoUs signed between the Government of India and the Government of Federal Democratic Republic of Ethiopia during External Affairs Minister's visit to Ethiopia: Agreement between the Government of the Federal Democratic Republic of Ethiopia and the Government of the Republic of India on the Establishment of Joint Ministerial Commission. Protocol for Consultations between the Ministry of Foreign Affairs of the Federal Democratic Republic of Ethiopia and the Ministry of External

Affairs of the Republic of India. Agreement between the Government of the Federal Democratic Republic of Ethiopia and the Government of the Republic of India on Cooperation in the fields of Science and Technology. Agreement between the Republic of India and the Federal Democratic Republic of Ethiopia for the Reciprocal Promotion and Protection of Investments. Exchange Programme between the Government of the Federal Democratic Republic of Ethiopia and the Government of the Republic of India in the field of Education.

1785. (6-7-2007) NEW DELHI : The Indian Army has served the nation with courage and fortitude in difficult circumstances for many years. It has worked upon constructive suggestions and even criticism to improve various facets of its functioning. However some reports as concerning factual details of suicides in the Army need correction. While the Army is deeply concerned for every loss of life due to suicides, it is entirely untrue that the number of suicides in the Army out number deaths due to operations. To elucidate, the approximate ratio for last four years (2003-06) has been approximately one suicide to 3.7 operational deaths. This year too, the suicides are far less in number as compared to the operational casualties. As relating to suicides by women officers, three women officers (including one from AMC) committed suicide in the last three years.

1786. (6-7-2007) NEW DELHI : Mangalore Refinery & Petrochemicals Ltd. (MRPL) a PSU under the Ministry of Petroleum and Natural Gas & a subsidiary of ONGC has entered into a contract with State Trading Corporation (STC) of Mauritius to supply petroleum products to Mauritius. The contract signed here today in presence of Union Minister of Petroleum & Natural Gas Shri Murli Deora and the Mauritian Minister of Industry, SME, Commerce and Cooperatives Dr. Rajesh Jeetah, provides for supplying 1 million tonne petroleum products a year for a period of three years to meet complete petroleum requirements of Mauritius. Speaking on the occasion Shri Deora said that the 3 year product supply agreement is a very important and a major step forward in strengthening the long and friendly relations between India and Mauritius. He assured the Mauritian Minister to meet the trust and faith reposed in India and to cater to all requirements of Mauritius in respect of oil sector. He also informed that the petroleum product exports of 1 MMT by MRPL over three year period is valued at about $ 2 billion (approximately Rs.8000 crore). Shri Deora added that term contract signed today will provide long term assurance and comfort to Mauritius on continued availability of strategic and sensitive petroleum products. The visiting Mauritius Minister Dr. Rajesh Jeetah conveyed greetings of the people of Mauritius to the people of India. He complemented the major role India played in developing institutions and infrastructure in Mauritius. Describing the occasion as historic, Mr. Jeetah pointed to the strong cultural and emotional bonds between India and Mauritius taking a new turn with rapidly growing economic and technical ties. The present one-year contract between MRPL and Mauritius' STC, signed in 2006, expires in July 2007. The new contract for three more years from August 2007 to July 2010 was inked by MRPL's Managing Director Mr. R. Rajamani and STC's General Manager Mr. R.S. Soomarooah. High Commissioner of Mauritius in India Mr. M. Chooni, Additional Secretary MoP&NG Shri S. Sundareshan and CMD of ONGC Mr. R. S. Sharma were also present. In June 2006, for the first time, STC of Mauritius finalized import of its entire petroleum product (Gasoline, Diesel, Jet Fuel, and Furnace Oil) requirement from MRPL, adding to around 1 million tonne. Based on satisfactory experience over the year, the import arrangement has been extended for a further period of three years. The products, imported by STC from MRPL, are sold to the local oil companies in Mauritius, viz. Shell (Mauritius), Total Mauritius Ltd., Caltex Oil (Mauritius) Ltd. and IndianOil (Mauritius) Ltd. Apart from STC of Mauritius, MRPL (accorded Mini Ratna status by the Government now) started exporting to other new markets in 2006-07 like Emirate National Oil Company of Dubai, aggregating to 1.5 million tones of liquid petroleum products. Mangalore Refinery and Petrochemicals Ltd. (MRPL) set up in 1996, has a design capacity of 9.69 million metric tones per annum (mmtpa). In 2006-07, the refinery processed 12.54 mmtpa of crude (129% of design capacity). The capacity is being expanded to 15 mmtpa. The Naphtha generated in the MRPL refinery will be upgraded to Paraxylene in a Petrochemicals (Aromatics) Complex which is coming up, at a cost of Rs. 5000 crore. The refinery is being upgraded to improve distillate yield along with expansion in capacity at a cost of around Rs. 8000 crore.

1787. (6-7-2007) NEW DELHI : As per data received in Agriculture Ministry, sowing of Kharif crops is progressing well across the country. The total coverage of rice has gone up to 46.02 lakh ha as compared to 31.64 lakh hectare last Friday, the weekly Crop Weather Watch Group meeting of the Ministry of Agriculture was informed here today. However, the rice acreage was 47.72 lakh ha at this time last year. Transplanting of rice is in progress in of Andhra Pradesh, Assam, Haryana, J&K, Karnataka, Kerala, Maharashtra, Orissa, Punjab, Rajasthan, Tamil Nadu, Uttarakhand and West Bengal. Total coarse cereals cover an area of 60.78 lakh ha as compared to 20.78 lakh hectare last Friday and 58.48 lakh in the corresponding period last year. Cotton has been sown in 59.6 lakh ha (last Friday: 15.29 lakh ha and last year: 37 lakh ha). Out of this, 23.36 lakh hectare is under BT cotton. Sugarcane coverage is reported to be 45.16 lakh hectare (last Friday: 44.72 lakh ha; last year: 46.13 lakh ha) and jute, 7.88 lakh hectare (last Friday: 7.86 lakh ha; last year: 8.18 lakh ha). The total coverage of oilseeds so far has been 42.27 lakh ha (last Friday: 13.04 lakh hectare; last year: 32.63 lakh ha). Pulses have occupied 26.84 lakh ha land so far as compared to 11.35 lakh ha last Friday and 26.57 lakh ha at this time last year.

1788. (6-7-2007) NEW DELHI : The Minister for Health & Family Welfare, Dr. Anbumani Ramadoss has expressed concern over the increasing trend in the prevalence of life style diseases in India including diabetes, cardiovascular diseases and cancer. Speaking at ICMR Awards function, here today, the Minister said that there is an urgent need to understand the disease process and its etiology in Indian context to assess the disease burden and to evolve practical approaches for the control of these diseases. The Minister further added that one of the most significant developments in the vaccine development in the country has been the development of HIV vaccine against sub type C which is the most common cause of HIV / AIDS. He commended the contribution of ICMR laboratories in identifying and establishing the cause of various outbreaks in different parts of the country. Dr. Ramadoss honoured Prof. Samir Brahmachari and Dr. M.R.S. Rao with the prestigious Dr. B.R. Ambedkar Centenary Award. 31 other biomedical scientists from throughout the country were also awarded for the year 2004 and 2005 for their outstanding contributions in respective fields of medical research. The Minister of State for Health & Family Welfare, Smt. Panabaka Lakshmi complimented the ICMR for taking up several other initiatives towards improving medical research in the country.

1789. (6-7-2007) NEW DELHI : The President, Dr. A.P. J. Abdul Kalam, is launching National e-Courts Project for extensive computerisation of courts in New Delhi on Monday (July 9, 2007). The Chief Justice of India, Justice Shri K.G. Balakrishnan, the Minister for Law and Justice, Shri H.R. Bhardwaj, the Minister for Communication and Information Technology, Shri A. Raja and Judges of the Supreme Court and other senior judicial functionaries would be present at the launching ceremony. The project of computerisation of courts has been devised following the Report submitted by the E-Committee on National Policy and Technology in the Indian Judiciary. The project is to be implemented in three phases spread over a period of five years at a cost of Rs. 854 crore. Under the first phase spread over a period of two years, computer rooms and judicial service centres would be set up in all 2500 court complexes. About 15 thousand judicial officers would be provided with laptops. Digital inter-connectivity would be established between all courts from the Taluka level to the Apex Court. The other major features of the project under the first phase are creation of well structured database of all the stakeholders, Courts and cases with user friendly retrievable facilities as well as digital archiving of the Supreme Court and High Courts. The project also aims at creation of e-filling facility in the Supreme Court and High Courts. The first phase also envisages development of comprehensive and integrated customised software.application for the entire judicial system with regional language support. The outlay for the first phase of the project is Rs. 442 crore. Already the Ministry of Law and Justice has made available Rs. 187.05 crore to NIC upto March 31, 2007 and the remaining amount is being provided during the current financial year. The first phase is scheduled to be completed by the end of the current financial year as a result of which there would be an improvement in capacity building of judges primarily in subordinate courts for delivery of speedy and quality justice. It would also help in creation of National Judicial Data Centre to provide litigational trends in the country for all levels and geographical locations. Digital production of under-trial prisoners and distant examination of victims through video conferencing would be possible. The phase two would also be completed in the next two years following which it would be possible to provide Information and Communication Technology (ICT) coverage of judicial processes from filing to execution level and also of all administrative activities. The third and final phase would be of one year duration. It would lead to the creation of Information Gateways between courts and public agencies and departments. The project is expected to lead to complete demystification of the adjudicatory process thereby ensuring transparency, accountability and cost-effectiveness.

1790. (6-7-2007) NEW DELHI : There is no fresh report of any locust swarm movement, settling and population-development from any locality of district Kutch (Bhuj) except in villages Nanicher, Shilpar and Khangarpur where the locust population was reported earlier on 3rd and 4th July, 2007. Two separate Locust Warning Organisation (LWO) teams have been deployed, one each in Khadoa and Lakhpat area today and one is kept standby at LWO Bhuj for emergency purposes. The State Government teams deployed at village Dayapar of Lakhpat Taluka have also reported no locust activity. One LWO field camp has been set up in Lakhpat area today for intensive locust monitoring and undertaking control operations, if needed. All the resources required for control operations are in readiness to meet any locust emergency.

1791. (6-7-2007) NEW DELHI : Grants-in-aid of Rs. 1.21 crore, out of the Central allocation of 3.64 crore has been released by the Ministry of Rural Development as balance payment of first instalment of central Share of funds to Gopalganj District of Bihar State for the implementation of the 'Swarnjayanti Gram Swarojgar Yojana' (SGSY) during the current financial year (2007-2008). An amount of Rs. 60.79 lakh has already been released as part of first instalment. The amount should be utilized on the Programme as per approved guidelines of SGSY. The funding pattern will be 75:25 by the Centre and the State. The State Government should release its share within one month of the date of release of the Central assistance. Under SGSY, assistance is given to the poor family living below the poverty line for taking up self-employment. It actively promotes group approach by organising the rural poor into Self-Help Groups.

1792. (6-7-2007) NEW DELHI : Under the Sampoorna Grameen Rozgar Yojana (SGRY) scheme, the Ministry of Rural Development has approved the release of 783 MTs of Wheat during the year 2007-08 to Muktsar District of Punjab State through Food Corporation of India depots in the State. The release is towards plan expenditure and will be utilized for approved items of works subject to the conditions laid down in the SGRY Guidelines. During the year 2007-08, food grains will be given to the labourers under SGRY at the rate of 3 Kg. instead of 5 Kg. per manday as part of wages. The State Government must ensure timely payment of wages and timely and adequate supply of food grains. If the food grains are not available, wages should be paid in cash.

1793. (6-7-2007) NEW DELHI : Grants-in-aid amounting to Rs. 17.04 crore as balance of first instalment has been released by the Ministry of Rural Development to Five Districts of Orissa, as Central assistance for the implementation of the Sampoorna Grameen Rozgar Yojana (SGRY) during the current financial year (2007-2008) as per details below. An amount of Rs.4.54 crore has also been released as first instalment being equal to 60% of the total alloction of Rs.7.57 crore to Kendrapara Distt. of Orissa under the scheme.

1794. (6-7-2007) NEW DELHI : Vietnam has requested India to grant market economy status under the WTO mechanism and stated that its economy is well qualified for the same. The request was communicated by Mr. Nguyen Danh Vinh, Deputy Trade Minister of Vietnam during his meeting with Dr. Ashwani Kumar, Minister of State for Industry, here today. Dr. Kumar informed the Vietnamese delegation that a decision on this issue would require a thorough examination and necessary deliberations at various levels. Mr. Vinh also emphasised the need to speedily conclude the Indo-ASEAN Free Trade Agreement and made specific requests for greater market access on certain agricultural products of importance to Vietnam such as coffee, tea and pepper. Dr. Kumar observed that the same products are also important to India both in terms of economic value and employment and any decision on the issue would require a win-win situation for both countries. Vietnam expressed keenness to take bilateral trade with India to a much higher level and hope that greater Indian investment would flow into Vietnam. While Vietnam had bilateral trade in excess of US $ 10 billion each with China and US its trade with India has just touched US $ 1 billion. Dr. Kumar also agreed with the need for greater economic engagement between the two countries and highlighted energy sector as one particular area where Indian companies can invest in Vietnam. "Trade relations with Vietnam are very much a part of India's Look East Policy", he said. The Vietnamese Minister proposed setting up of a Forum for Trade and Investment Policy Exchange which could provide a platform for engagement of officers and businessmen from both countries to engage on trade and investment relations, in the area of investment promotion, tourism, trade facilitation etc. Dr. Kumar agreed with the value of such a Forum and both countries would work towards setting up the same. Major items of export to Vietnam include oilmeals, drugs & pharmaceuticals, primary & semi-finished iron and steel etc., while major import items from Vietnam are spices, coal, coke, organic chemicals etc.

1795. (6-7-2007) NEW DELHI : Farm commodity prices monitored by the Department of Consumer Affairs have generally remained steady or have shown mixed trend in different centres across the country in the week ending 29.06.2007. Wheat prices remained steady at 10 centres. Guwahati and Bangalore saw an increase in wheat prices during the week. Sugar prices remained steady across majority of the centres and increased at Bhubaneshwar. Gram prices remained steady over the week across most of the centres; declined at Ahmedabad and

Guwahati and increased at Shimla, Bhubaneshwar and Bangalore. Tur dal prices were also steady across majority of the centres; and increased at Shimla, Aizwal, Bhubaneshwar, Bangalore and Chennai. At Delhi, prices of gram dal, tea, potato and salt remained steady over one week; those of rice, wheat, atta, tur dal, sugar, groundnut oil, vanaspati and milk remained steady over one month; and prices of mustard oil and onion increased during the week. As on 2.7.07, public sector agencies have contracted import of 10.38 lakh tonne pulses of which 1.88 lakh tonnes has already reached Indian ports. The imported pulses include urad, moong, dunpeas, masoor, chana, yellow peas and tur.

1796. (6-7-2007) NEW DELHI : Congress Spokesperson Shri Abhishek Singhvi said that the UPA-Left candidate for President had a successful tour of Kerala and Pondicherry yesterday. Smt Pratibha Patil is travelling to Karnataka and Andhra Pradesh today and tomorrow she will be travelling to Jammu & Kashmir, Haryana and Punjab. She is meeting different segments of Electoral College and the response is overwhelming. We hope and trust that the weather allows the schedule to progress because the UPA-Left is concerned about the positive aspect of this campaign which is to reach out to the electorate to not only ensure the inevitable victory which the inevitable arithmetic tells us but to see that it is a thumping, a absolutely unconditional and a strong victory to send a signal to persons who have tried to cloud the issues, who have tried to muddy the waters by motivated and ulterior and extraneous considerations. I may also inform you that on the 8th July, everything else permitting, the presidential candidate will address the Electoral College and meet them in Delhi. We believe that this overwhelming response is based on the unique choice, a choice made for the first time in independent India, of a woman who is going to occupy the highest office in the land and we believe that those who try to do only negative campaigning, those who with awareness of the figures persist in mudslinging will be given and will face their true lesson on the day of counting on 21st July. To a question about the misappropriation of MPLAD fund by Smt. Pratibha Patil, Shri Singhvi said that there is a news item which suggests so but that is not correct. As and when full information is available, I am sure, we will have more occasions to share but let me tell you, as always, unless the facts are seen properly, they can be very misleading. The first point is: that a NGO petitions the High Court where the matter was pending for many years in Nagpur. And the basis of this petition was that the 1996 funds should not be given to any other project, should not be diverted till the claim of a particular NGO who filed the petition is decided. That matter was resolved only by the High Court judgment recently and today the picture is this: on account of the 1996 litigation, till today, the money which was or would have been used in the MPLAD scheme of 1996 has not been utilized. The land continues and belongs and is in the possession of the government. And what is most important is that, the MPLAD scheme, if I remember, the MPLAD scheme started in 1991 and this was the first five years of its operation. Under the guidelines no money is disbursed to or by the MP. The ministry receives recommendations and then sends the funds directly to the Collector. And now the most important point. All recommendations all over the country, not only for this, are received by the Collector. It is the Collector whose official duty, job, responsibility, specific, discretion under the guidelines, rules is to decide as to which scheme is eligible and which scheme is not eligible. The Collector is the one who decides, disposes, recommends to the ministry, receives the money and then it is executed. Different MPs send different recommendations but it is the Collector's responsibility to recommend and the Collector takes that decision. In this case it is ultimately the Collector who has decided on a matter which has not been implemented, mind you, since then. And the Collector's decision, to the best of his knowledge of wisdom, is assumed to be within the guidelines. To a question that the govt. leased out that land to Mrs. Patil's husband for constructing sports complex, Shri Singhvi said that the recent decision is irrelevant. The point is, the recommendation, and we are talking of 1996, was for building a sports complex at a land adjacent to a society run by Mrs. Patil's husband. It has nothing to do with that land. Now that adjacent land was the subject matter of legal proceeding in the Nagpur High Court by an NGO which said that in 1996, the term is expiring and this money should not be used for anything else till the matter is decided. That matter has been decided now after eight/nine long years. To a question that with allegations pouring in everyday, is the Congress Party now rethinking about its presidential candidate, Shri Singhvi said that there is no question of rethinking. It may be in your own mind and a figment of your own imagination and all the other imagination are of your own creation. To a question that Pratibha Patil asked not to demean this high office but you are now demeaning it, Shri Singhvi said that who is demeaning? You never use those words. For the last two weeks when there were allegations against Pratibha Patil. Let's get it clear. Did you ever use the word demeaning the office from day one when a Press Conference was held at the residence of Mr. Dhindsa. Who was demeaning the office then? When Mr. Sudendra Kulkarni flew down from Bombay with Rajni Patil, did you think about the word demeaning? At that time you asked me to answer the allegations, now today when I am asking a question based on published reports in newspapers. I didn't say last week, two days ago or four days ago.

1797. (6-7-2007) NEW DELHI : In order to clear extra rush of the passengers, Railways will run Bi-Weekly Rajdhani Special Train No. 2309A/2310A between Rajendra Nagar and New Delhi as per the following programme:- The 2309A Rajendra Nagar-New Delhi Bi-Weekly Rajdhani special train will depart from Rajendra Nagar at 08.30 p.m. from 5.7.07 to 16-08-07 on every Thursday and Sunday to arrive at New Delhi at 09.50 a.m. the next day. In the return direction the 2310A-New Delhi-Rajendra Nagar Bi-Weekly Rajdhani special train will depart from New Delhi at 05.05 p.m. from 07-07-07 to 18-08-07 on every Tuesday and Saturday to arrive at Rajendra Nagar at 6.10 a.m. the next day. Comprising of One First A.C, Four A.C. 2 tier, Five AC. 3 Tier and two brake van coaches the 2309A/2310A New Delhi-Rajendra Nagar Bi-Weekly Rajdhani special train will halt at Kanpur, Allahabad, Mughalsarai and Patna stations enroute in both the directions.

1798. (6-7-2007) NEW DELHI: Prime Minister Manmohan Singh on Thursday described the UPA Presidential nominee Pratibha Patil as "an outstanding candidate" who survived in public life for 25 years because of her competence. Speaking to a group of women journalists at his residence here, the Prime Minister said there were no charges against her. "I have already said the allegations are mud-slinging. We are not apologetic about her choice. Not only the UPA but the entire country is united about her. We have made the right choice. She is deserving of the high office." Dr Singh said Ms. Patil had been in public life since 1962, as a member of the Maharashtra Assembly, State Minister, Deputy Chairperson of the Rajya Sabha, and Governor of Rajasthan for three years. Taking a dig at the Bhartiya Janata Party, he said even though Bhairon Singh Shekhawat was its member, he did not want to contest the Presidential elections under the BJP banner and wanted to be an Independent. Dr Singh began his 45-minute interaction, saying he attached great importance to the meeting as it was taking place in the year India would have its first woman President. "This meeting is a celebration of that year." *Women's Bill.* To a question on the Women's Reservation Bill, Dr. Singh said the UPA Government would place it in Parliament as early as possible. In a coalition government, he could not have a situation in which his own Minister from another party would stand up and oppose the Bill. "Before politicians become statesmen, they have to remain in government longer," he said with a smile. On the relationship with the Left, which extends outside support to the government, Dr Singh said though the Congress was not well-equipped to handle the dynamics of coalition politics, it had not done badly. In the three years the Congress cohabited with the Left parties, there was "cooperative attitude." With the rest of the parties, Cabinet meetings were held every week and these were smooth. Dr. Singh took exception to recent comments by BJP leader L.K. Advani that he was a "handpicked Prime Minister." "The language used by Mr Advani is not healthy. We may differ, but we must learn to respect one another, and that is missing. That kind of situation is not good for the government and the principal Opposition party." On the economic front, Dr. Singh said India was poised to sustain a growth rate of 8-9 per cent. Agriculture was cause for concern and it would be addressed. Already a Rs 25,000-crore package was announced for States which came up with climate and region-specific, district schemes. He, along with Agriculture Minister Sharad Pawar, would visit a few States to assess the progress on the farm front. On the issue of fertile land coming under Special Economic Zones, Dr. Singh admitted that some mistakes were made in the past and said the government was mindful of the side-effects. "There was no developed country in the world that was not industrial. It should be done in a manner that the [urban-rural] gap was not widened and the dispossessed rural families acquired a stake in the new enterprise." The Prime Minister said the progress in various sectors was far from uniform. The priority in the next two years would be for health, education and agriculture. On the recent clashes between Gujjars and Meenas in Rajasthan over reservation under the Scheduled Tribe category, he said there was no proposal to undertake a caste-based census. Dr. Singh played down the arrival of the nuclear-powered American aircraft carrier USS Nimitz to the Chennai coast, saying it was an ordinary development. In the past naval ships from France, the United Kingdom and even China visited the Indian coast. In a lighter vein, he said, "In fact, I came to know about it from the newspapers."

1799. (6-7-2007) NEW DELHI : The Bio-fuel programme in India is to be developed on Public-Private Partnerships which would promote bio-fuel plantations on government, community and private lands. Simultaneously, the industrial sector is also being encouraged to increase ethanol production from non-food feedstocks. Addressing the 'International Bio-fuels Conference' at Brussels today, Shri Vilas Muttemvar, the Minister for New and Renewable Energy said that several Indian corporates and business houses have in collaboration with the Government started to establish Jatropha plantations on waste lands or have begun contract farming on private holdings. Shri Muttemvar said that several state governments have announced policies to encourage Jatropha cultivation, setting up bio-diesel plants and supply chains up in many states. Incidentally, 100% foreign direct investment in new and renewable energy is allowed under the automatic route in India. The Minister said that the Government is in the process of preparing a 'National Policy on Bio-fuels' expected to lay the foundation for the accelerated development of the sector and the areas likely to be covered there in are-R&D, capacity building, purchase policy and registration for enabling bio-fuel use. The policy will aim at a short-term blending proportion of 5% by 2012, medium term of 10% by 2017 and a long-term of above beyond 2017 and the policy would also recommend fixation of minimum support price for Jatropha and other non-edible oilseeds. The Minister said that the focus of our bio-fuel programme is on indigenous development to the extent possible by using science and technology and industrial capabilities. We look forward to working with the European Union and all participating countries for achieving our bio-fuel aims and targets. Our priorities for cooperation include programmes for increasing crop yields, oil content of oilseeds, and reducing the environmental impact of bio-fuel usage. The Government is also looking at cooperation in fuel conversion technologies from waste cellulosic materials and dedicated cellulosic crops. The Minister further emphasized that bio-fuels are an integral component of our 'National Energy Policy'. The effective implementation of the bio-fuel programme would go a long way in reducing India's dependence on oil besides helping to address climate change concerns. The Minister said that India has been among the world leaders in the deployment of new and renewable energy. Over these years, the contribution of renewable energy has increased significantly in India, meeting about 15 per cent of the electricity needs, of which 12 percentage points comes from large hydro. Around 45,000 MW renewable power generating capacity to date or one-third of the total has been installed comprising over 7000 MW from wind, 1200 MW from bio power and over 36,000 MW from hydro power of which 2000 MW is from small hydro power. He further said that India has met with phenomenal success in solar hot water systems area. Already 2 million square meters collector area has been installed so far and the Government is planning to add an additional 10 million square meters during the next five years. Shri Muttemvar informed that a 'National Hydrogen Energy Road Map' for the introduction of a hydrogen economy has been formulated and the preparation of the Road Map entailed detailed discussions among policy makers, scientists and corporates etc. There is a great deal of realism in our projections for a hydrogen future and India is aiming to add one-million hydrogen powered 2/3/4 wheelers by 2020 or so.

1800. (6-7-2007) NEW DELHI : The decision of the Andhra Pradesh Government to grant 4% reservations to Muslims is an exercise of crass political opportunism devoid of justice and principle. The government, after failing in its earlier two attempts to provide religious based reservations to Muslims, has resorted to an even more unethical practice of dividing Muslims on the one hand and denying justice to the deprived sections among Hindus on the other hand. The Bharatiya Janata Party condemns this decision, which has been taken without a holistic vision of the welfare of the entire society and which is based purely on political expediencies. This decision clearly exhibits the divisive agenda of the Congress and UPA. The OBC reservations already includes some sections of the Muslim community like Dudhey Kullah (cotton weavers), Noor Bhasha, Netar (Scavengers) and Pinjari as per the Mandal Commission recommendation. The AP government, in its bid to appease, has unnecessarily attached a religious tag to hitherto included sections under the OBC category. This is a case of divisive politics that goes completely against the principles of secularism and against the spirit of the Constitution. The Andhra Pradesh government has gone beyond the Mandal recommendations by including Sheikh, Siddiki and some other sections of the Muslim community in the list of backwards and in the process has done further injustice with the deprived sections amongst the Hindus. The Backward Commission in Andhra Pradesh has already recommended inclusion of Lodh, Kurmi, Gaur Shetty, Bundili, Balija, Gajla and other 36 backward castes in the OBC reservation category. The government has gone ahead to include some sections of Muslims in the OBC category without including its earlier recommendation on the inclusion of 36 Hindu castes. The state government has not even conducted an enquiry about the status of the Kapu, Telga, Oantari castes for inclusion in OBC list even after the directions of the High Court. The entire exercise shows a total lack of vision on the part of the state government and displays its eagerness and commitment towards furthering politics on purely communal lines.

1801. (6-7-2007) NEW DELHI : The Rehabilitation Package for Closed Tea Gardens is expected to result in revival of 33 closed tea gardens, which employ more than 30,000 workers. The package will allow these tea gardens to avail loans and subsidies under the Special Purpose Tea Fund (SPTF) Scheme for rejuvenation and replantation. Shri Kamal Nath, Minister of Commerce & Industry, has said that: "As a medium and long-term measure, a major stepping up of the rate of replantation and rejuvenation holds the key to competitiveness of the Indian tea industry, given the high age profile of tea bushes throughout the country. Over 2 lakh hectares which fall in the vulnerable category of low yielding areas is to be targeted for replantation and rejuvenation". Referring to the revival of closed tea gardens, the Minister observed that "on revival, the gardens would infuse additional capital in plants and machinery resulting into increasing in the crop yields and total tea production for domestic and export purposes". In order to address the problems of the closed tea gardens, the government had appointed expert committees to make an in-depth study of gardens lying closed in the States of West Bengal, Kerala, Assam and Tripura and suggest a package of measures for their viability and revival. Considering the reports and recommendations of the committees, the government has approved a Rehabilitation Package for Closed Tea Gardens. The package is aimed at reviving the closed tea gardens in the interest of tea garden workers and considering the importance of the industry in the export performance of the country. The Package provides for restructuring of existing outstanding bank loans of closed tea gardens by converting the same into term loans with a moratorium period of 5 years. The recovery of the outstanding converted loans would start from 6th year onwards and upto 10th year. The accumulated penal interest on the loans will be waived. The banks will charge a simple rate of interest of 11% per annum on the restructured loan. There will be a moratorium of one year for payment of the interest. The accumulated simple interest is to be shared equally by the banks, central government and the beneficiaries to the extent of one-third each. The loans advanced by the Tea Board to such gardens would waive. After financial restructuring as given above these gardens will become eligible to obtain loan and subsidy from the Tea Board under Rs.4500 crore SPTF scheme for rejuvenation and replantation. They will also become eligible to get 25% subsidy for upgradation and modernisation of their factories. An interest subsidy at the rate of 3% on the working capital loans would be provided by the government for a period of 5 years on the working capital loans that will be taken by such gardens for resumption of their operation. Chairman, Tea Board, will be the nodal officer for implementing the Rehabilitation package.

1802. (6-7-2007) NEW DELHI : The following is the text of the Statement of External Affairs Minister, Shri Pranab Mukherjee on his departure from Ethiopia: "My delegation and I were extremely happy to be in Ethiopia. We spent three days on Ethiopian soil and have been touched by the warmth of the welcome and the generous hospitality extended to us by the government and people of Ethiopia. Our historical ties go back in history and we have civilisational links. My visit was at the invitation of H.E. Mr. Seyoum Mesfin, Minister of Foreign Affairs of the Federal Democratic Republic of Ethiopia. The main purpose was to deepen and widen our traditionally warm relations. We look forward to regular exchange of such visits. I have invited His Excellency the Foreign Minister of Ethiopia to visit India in 2008. An important result of my meeting with the Foreign Minister was to formalize regular bilateral dialogue focusing on bilateral, regional and global issues among the Foreign Offices and to establish a Joint Commission. I also had productive meetings with Their Excellencies the President, Prime Minister, and the Hon'ble Speaker of Ethiopia, apart from discussions with senior cabinet ministers. In our bilateral discussions, we have drawn up a forward looking agenda of engagement in the political, trade, economic, science and technology, agriculture, culture, education and other sectors. We have agreed to expand the scope of our cooperation in capacity building, cooperation in education, health care etc. The Agreement on Science and Technology and the Education Exchange Programme which we signed will help accelerate the ongoing capacity building efforts including in agriculture and human resource development. Our bilateral relationship is to be further diversified and expanded. It was decided to enhance economic and business linkages in both public and private sectors with a greater participation by Indian entities in the infrastructural development of Ethiopia. We signed the bilateral Investment Promotion and Protection Agreement and decided to speed up the finalisation of the Double Taxation Avoidance Agreement to provide the necessary incentives and institutional framework. We have also discussed regional issues including those pertaining to African integration, Darfur and Somalia and other international issues engaging the attention of the international community such as the fight against terrorism, climate change, trade issues and UN reforms. Today, I inaugurated the pilot projects of tele-education and tele-medicine, which India will be implementing on an Africa wide basis. This is a positive example of South cooperation which uses IT and space technology and generates a multiplier developmental effect. This morning, I had the privilege of addressing the Foreign Affairs, Defence and Security Committee and the Ethiopia-India Parliamentary Friendship Group of the Ethiopian Parliament. I spoke about our commitment to work towards a substantive enhancement of the broad-based bilateral relationship between the two democracies which also share developmental goals. In my meeting with the Hon'ble Speaker of the House of Representatives, we discussed ways and means of developing closer association between the Ethiopian and Indian Parliaments. I reiterated India's support for the development of democratic institutions in Ethiopia. We agreed to enhance parliamentary exchanges and agreed to have an Indian parliamentary delegation visit Ethiopia in the near future.

1803. (6-7-2007) NEW DELHI : The constitution of a task force with the Prime Minister's approval about a month ago to review our existing policy on disarmament, nonproliferation and other security related issues is a matter of serious concern. The ostensible purposes for which the has been set up and its timing arouse apprehensions that it would be used to change our long-held policies on these issues so that they conform to the Hyde Act which is to govern the Indo-US nuclear deal. If the present government was keen to undertake such an exercise, it would have undertaken it immediately after assuming office or at any rate prior to the commencement of negotiations on the nuclear deal with the USA. The setting up of this task force at this juncture is nothing more than a thinly veiled move towards reversing our nuclear related policies with a view to bringing them in conformity with many of the highly objectionable provisions of the Hyde Act; and then to pretend that the changes have been undertaken by us autonomously. The confidence of the U.S. Secretary of State that the Indo-U.S. nuclear deal would be concluded before the end of this year may also be linked to the review of India's policies. Amongst the various measures included in the Hyde Act, designed to stymie the development of India's nuclear weapons capability, the two which will have the greatest adverse impact on our national security are those pertaining to the ban on nuclear tests by India and its "working actively with the United States for the early conclusion" of a "multilateral" Fissile Material Cut Off Treaty (FMCT). While India has long maintained a voluntary moratorium on conducting nuclear weapons tests, it has done so as all other nuclear weapons states as well as Pakistan are also observing a similar moratorium. We are, at present, free at any time to resume testing which may become necessary particularly in response to the actions of other countries. Once the nuclear deal comes into effect, the Hyde Act will ensure that India loses forever its option of conducting a nuclear weapons test, even if any other country tests. It not only makes Indo-US civil nuclear cooperation contingent upon India not testing but also envisages that the US would insist on the right of return of nuclear materials and equipment given to India. To add insult to injury the Hyde Act requires that in the event the US terminates nuclear transfers to India it will "seek to prevent" such transfers to India from all other sources also. Clearly, therefore, operationalisation of the nuclear deal within the framework of the Hyde Act will require a change of our policy on testing. It would be a grave mistake to do so as it will compromise our capability to keep abreast of other countries in nuclear weapons development. In an effort to accelerate the conclusion of an FMCT in line with its own policies, the USA, in May 2006, tabled a draft text in the Conference on Disarmament (CD) proposing the use of 'national technical means'——intelligence— for purposes of ensuring compliance as opposed to an international and effective verification mechanism which had been contemplated by us as well as the international community since the 90's- the sort of mechanism that had been put in place for the Chemical Weapons Convention and the Comprehensive Test Ban Treaty.

1804. (7-7-2007) NEW DELHI : There have been some reports in the media stating that a cheque of the Prime Minister's National Relief Fund for relief to farmers in Vidarbha, has bounced reportedly due to delay in releasing funds and also mentions a state government affidavit filed in the supreme Court. It is clarified that the Prime Minister during his visit to Vidarbha in July 2006 had, in addition to other initiatives, announced financial assistance from Prime Minister's National Relief Fund, to alleviate the suffering of debt stressed farmers of Maharashtra, Andhra Pradesh, Karnataka and Kerala, by placing an amount of Rs.50 lakh at the disposal of 31 districts, 6 of them in Vidarbha. State Govt was to utilize the fund for giving assistance to needy debt stressed farmers and their families, for expenditure in connection with health and education, especially for children. Rs 3 crores was dispersed to 6 districts of Vidarbha in July 2006 itself, and there was no delay in releasing the funds. It was a one time grant of funds of Rs.50 lakh at the disposal of the concerned District Collector. As far as the filing of an affidavit by the State Government before the Supreme Court is concerned, it was acknowledged by the State Government in March 2007, that there was no delay on the part of the PMO to release funds, and an additional Affidavit was filed to clarify the position. The cheque under reference was issued by the local District authorities in Maharashtra, and not honoured because of local issues, and not on account of any delay in release of funds from PMNRF. The District authorities are taking action to disburse relief in cash immediately. In addition to Rs 3 crores for 6 districts of Vidarbha, funds to the remaining 25 districts of Andhra Pradesh, Karnataka and Kerala have also been released without any delay, amounting to Rs 12.5 crores, and the Prime Minister's announcement of this initiative, from Prime Minister's National Relief Fund, has been completed. Further to the Press Release issued earlier today by PMO regarding the alleged bouncing of a cheque issued by District authorities in Yavatmal District, Maharashtra, for disbursement of funds under Prime Minister's National Relief Fund, it is hereby clarified that instead of issuing a cheque from CM's Relief Fund, under which funds were available with District authorities, a cheque was issued under PMNRF by mistake, by district officials, even after the Rs 50 lakhs provided by PMO under PMNRF had been fully disbursed. According to information provided by the District Collector, Yavatmal District, the concerned officer and clerks who issued the wrong cheque have been given show cause notice and necessary administrative action is being taken against them.

1805. (7-7-2007) NEW DELHI : Much was at stake of its reputation, when for the first-time-ever, the Royal Air Force's (RAF) Eurofighter Typhoon, developed by a consortium of European manufacturers and recently inducted into the RAF, was to engage in any kind of an aerial combat with any non-RAF/NATO fighter. The Indian Air Force's (IAF) Sukhoi-30 MKI 'air superiority fighter', which are at Waddington, UK for the bilateral air 'Exercise Indradhanush-2007', had an opponent for the befitting duel. The operational part of the 'Exercise Indradhanush-2007' began with a series of 1 vs 1 air combat sorties. Both variants landed with their much-touted reputations intact as each side tested their potentials with their adversary in the air to their limits. These sorties were premised not entirely on having winners or losers-but more for their evaluator and training values as encapsulated in the objectives. Both sides ended-up sharing an enhanced respect for each other's capabilities-both in terms of training values, and combat potentials of the diverse aerial platforms. While the RAF fielded some of their most-experienced and highly-qualified pilots, some of them being very senior performance evaluators in active service, the IAF pilots were a mix of 'young to middle-level pilots' from the 'Rhinos' squadron. The RAF pilots were candid in their admission of the Su-30 MKI's observed superior manoeuvring in the air, just as they had studied, prepared and anticipated. The IAF pilots on their part were also visibly impressed by the Typhoon's agility in the air. While it does not imply to say that the 1 vs 1 air combat sorties were meant for backslapping each other, it may be understood that in today's aerial combat scenarios of 'beyond visual range' (BVR) capabilities of air platforms, it is highly unlikely that any of the modern-day fighters will ever get into a situation that warrants extreme close air combat, as in the situation simulated in the 1 vs 1 sorties. With a 'kill' criterion of front-gun ranges being mostly under 1000 metres and a visual tracking envelope behind the target for only up to a 60-degree cone mostly for most fighter aircraft of the world, the unlikely scenario gets more exemplified. But the irony also lies in the fact that while there is a number of counter and counter-counter measures to make the modern missiles with claims of inescapable parameters redundant by using 'chaff' and other active/passive measures, a 'gun kill' is invariably a most certain kill. The pilots invariably begin honing their tracking and combat skills under such close combat situations. The exercise that nearly runs into midway by the weekend constitutes mostly mixed missions where RAF F3 Tornados, Hawks and Typhoons are packed together with IAF Su-30 MKIs. The sorties include combat situations of 2 vs 1, 2 vs 2 and upward combinations. The raiders are tasked 'High Value Asset' (HVA) busting on the ground and 'High Value Airborne Asset' (HVAA) busting in the air with the defensive elements designated to counter their ambitions.

1806. (7-7-2007) NEW DELHI : The Prime Minister, Dr. Manmohan Singh urged the Defence Research and Development Organisation [DRDO] to strive for the highest standards of performance and delivery of weapon systems. Addressing a function here today after giving away DRDO Awards for 2006 for path breaking research and technology development, Dr. Singh urged them to avoid long gestation periods in the development of weapon systems. "Delays at the development stage run the risk of obsolescence of the weapon system by the time they are ready for serial production. Causing delays at the stage of production mean that our armed forces are deprived of timely deliveries, which often compel the Government to look for external procurement to fill emerging gaps in our inventories", he added. The Prime Minister asked the DRDO, Indian industry and the armed forces to work jointly to enhance and modernize our country's defence capabilities. He declared the Government's commitment to help the DRDO adapt to the rapidly changing global scenario and to the development of a vibrant defence industry in our country. Reaffirming the Government's desire to seek a neighbourhood of peace and prosperity, Dr. Singh said, "We don't wish to engage in an arms race with any one. As a possessor of advanced technologies, we will continue to maintain the highest standards of non-proliferation controls." Shri A.K. Antony, Raksha Mantri, Shri M.K. Narayanan, National Security Advisor, General J.J. Singh, Chief of Army Staff, Admiral Suresh Mehta, Chief of the Naval Staff, Air Chief Marshal F.H. Major, Chief of the Air Staff, Scientific Advisor to Raksha Mantri, Shri Natarajan, Dr. Pillai, Dr. Selva Murthy were present on the occasion. Following is the text of the Prime Minister's speech on the occasion:- "It is indeed a matter of great happiness to give away the very prestigious Awards to DRDO Scientists for distinguished service. I convey my heartiest congratulations to the Scientists and to the members of their families and to the entire DRDO fraternity. India stands for peace and for the peaceful resolution of all problems between nation states. Our national goal is to foster an external and internal environment of peace and stability, which will allow us adequate space to concentrate on the multiple economic and social challenges facing our people. But the reality is that we live in a world of unequal power relations. We live in an uncertain international security environment. We are therefore obliged to create adequate defence preparedness to manage any potential challenge to our security and vital national interests. A key factor driving the power of nations is their ability to operate on the frontiers of scientific and technological knowledge. This is as important for our national defence as it is for our economic security and strength. Our country looks to the DRDO to fulfil this vital national goal. Today let all those associated with the organization rededicate themselves to the original purpose of the establishment of the DRDO, which is the application of science and technology for the defence of our motherland. I am happy to note some of the significant developments of the DRDO during the past one year. The successful launch of the Agni-III missile has made us all very proud as a nation. The successful launches of the Brahmos supersonic cruise missile from different platforms have validated its performance. With the successful demonstration of anti-ballistic missile technology, India has entered an exclusive club of countries possessing such a capability. These are laudable achievements of the DRDO, which has made the entire nation very proud. The other ongoing programmes of DRDO have also achieved significant milestones. The first of the limited series production block of the Light Combat Aircraft, Tejas, underwent a successful first flight. The production of the MBT- Arjun Tank is in progress. Crucial advances have been made in electronic warfare, radar and communication systems, as well as in naval systems, materials technology and in the application of the life sciences in our defence preparedness.

1807. (8-7-2007) NEW DELHI : As a mark of respect to the departed leader Shri Chandra Shekhar the national flag shall fly at half-mast for 7 days (8.7.2007 to 14.7.2007) to observe the state mourning. The full state funeral shall take place at 5 p.m. at Ekta Sthal tomorrow *i.e.* on 9th July, 2007. The body of the departed leader will lie in state from 9 a.m. onwards tomorrow *i.e.* 9th July, 2007 at his residence. The funeral procession will start at 4 p.m. from the residence of late Shri Chandra Shekhar at 3, South Avenue. The route of the funeral procession will be as follows: South Avenue Lane: T/R South Avenue: T/R Tyagraj Marg R/A Rajaji Marg: K. Kamraj Marg: R/A Sunehari Masjid: Maulana Azad Road Akbar Road: T/L 'C'-Hexagon: T/L Tilak Marg "W" Point: "A" Point: Bahadurshah Zafar Marg: Delhi Gate Crossing: T/R JLN Marg: Rajghat Crossing: T/L Mahatma Gandhi Marg (Ring Road): Shanti Van Chowk: Ring Road against flow of traffic T/R and enter Samadhi area All the Central Government offices/establishment located in Delhi/New Delhi shall remain closed tomorrow *i.e.* July 9, 2007 after 1.30 p.m. to facilitate the mourners to join the funeral.

1808. (8-7-2007) NEW DELHI : All the Central Government Offices located in Delhi/New Delhi will remain closed after 0130 PM on 09th July 2007 to enable the participation of Central Government employees in the funeral of former Prime Minister of India Late Shri Chandrashekhar.

1809. (8-7-2007) NEW DELHI : The Union Cabinet met here today and adopted the following Condolence Resolution condoling the death of former Prime Minister, Shri Chandra Shekhar. "The Cabinet expresses profound sorrow at the demise of Shri Chandra Shekhar, former Prime Minister of India, on 8th July, 2007. Shri Chandra Shekhar was an eminent parliamentarian, social worker and able administrator who has left his imprint on every aspect of our national life. Born on 1st July 1927 in Ibrahimpatti in District Ballia of Uttar Pradesh, Shri Chandra Shekhar received his education in Allahabad University. He entered the Parliament as a Member of the Rajya Sabha in 1962. He first became a member of the Lok Sabha in 1977 where he served for eight terms. Shri Chandra Shekhar steered the nation as Prime Minister from November 1990 to June 1991. Shri Chandra Shekhar was a truly secular nationalist and a man of the people committed to their welfare and well-being. He was known for his conviction, courage and integrity. Throughout his life, he devoted himself to espouse the cause of the downtrodden, ad worked relentlessly for rapid social change. Shri Chandra Shekhar was in many ways a grassroots worker deeply interested in primary education and health services. He undertook a long padyatra across the country in 1983 to establish rapport with the masses and understand their problems. A reflective writer, Shri Chandra Shekhar was also the Founder-Editor and Chairman of the Editorial Advisory Board of 'Young Indian'. In his passing away, the nation has lost an eminent son, a wise national leader and a statesman. The Cabinet deeply mourns the sad demise of Shri Chandra Shekhar, and extends sincere condolences on behalf of the entire nation to the bereaved family."

1810. (8-7-2007) NEW DELHI : The Union Minister for Human Resources Development, Shri Arjun Singh has condoled the death of former Prime Minister Shri Chandra Shekhar. Following is the text of the condolence message: "It was with deep shock and grief that I heard of the sad demise of Shri Chandra Shekhar, former Prime Minister of India, a veteran parliamentarian and a leader of unsurpassed stature. Shri Chandra Shekhar epitomized the dictum of simple life and high thinking through his personal example. He, apart from being a truly secular nationalist, was deeply committed to the welfare of the people. In his death, the nation has become poorer by leaders who had the wisdom, experience and vision of the onerous task of nation building. I am sure that Shri Chandra Shekhar would always be remembered by the nation for his immense contribution in public life. I extend my heartfelt condolences to the grieved family and join his countless admirers and followers in paying homage to the departed soul."

1811. (8-7-2007) NEW DELHI : The Union Home Minister, Shri Shivraj Patil, has condoled the death of former Prime Minister Shri Chandrashekhar and said that it has caused a great loss to the nation. Shri Patil described Shri Chandrashekhar as a friend of people who received his help in their times of need. Recalling his long association with Shri Chandrashekhar, Shri Patil said that he was a very warm hearted human being and was affectionate towards him. Shri Chandrashekhar's qualities endeared him to all sections of the society.

1812. (8-7-2007) NEW DELHI : The Election Commission has already issued instructions vide its letter No.479/9/2007-PLN-III dated 18th June, 2007, to all the Members of the Parliament allowing them to cast their vote, during the Presidential Election, 2007, at any place of poll set up at the State Headquarters for this purpose. Similarly, an instruction vide no.481/2007-PS-III dated 6th July, 2007, has also been issued allowing the MLAs of any State to cast their vote at the place of poll set up at the Parliament House, New Delhi during the Presidential Election 2007. As a normal practice, Commission does not extend the facilities of casting votes by any MLAs at any place of poll, other than his own State or at Parliament House, since it is very difficult to send the ballot paper of all the states to every other state. Needless to mention that the ballot paper in respect of every state is different from each other. But there may be extreme cases where some MLAs may be forced to remain away from their own State on the day of poll due to compelling and justifiable reasons and may not be able to cast their vote either at their own State Headquarter or at Parliament House, New Delhi. In order to enable such MLAs to cast vote during the current Presidential Election, the Commission has decided, in exceptional cases, to allow the MLAs of any State to cast their votes at any State Headquarter other than their own if they apply for the Commission's permission well in advance *i.e.* 96 hours before the commencement of poll, with full justification in order to enable the Commission to send ballot paper of his State to the place where he intends to vote on 19th July, 2007, so that the Presiding Officer is able to issue the same to him during the poll. All the Assistant Returning Officers, who are normally the Secretary of the State Legislative Assemblies, have been requested to intimate the electors of their States in writing about this decision of the Commission for availing this facility by the intending elector.

1813. (8-7-2007) CHENNAI: The Madras High Court has called for particulars relating to individual complaints and allegations of irregularities in the ongoing cooperative election process in Tamil Nadu. When advocates sought urgent hearing of poll-related cases, Justice A. Kulasekaran said the court would not stay the process. At the same time, it would not close its eyes and ears if a prima facie case of large-scale violation of democratic norms and election rules was made out. If need be, the court would invoke its powers under Article 226 of the Constitution, he said. The matter was then adjourned to Wednesday. While some of the petitioners alleged that their nomination papers had been improperly rejected, others said they were prevented even from filing nominations. A petitioner from

Vellore district said his nomination was rejected on the ground that his proposer had not signed the form. He claimed that the paper had been duly signed. Another petitioner said that though he had not withdrawn his nomination, he was informed that his papers were taken as withdrawn. Another petition contended that though a total of 30 persons had filed nomination papers, only 11 were validated during scrutiny. Other papers were rejected because it was sufficient to have 11 members on the Board of the society to which election was being held. Two writ petitioners from Salem district apprehended threat from ruling partymen and sought police protection. To this, the Government side informed the court that all District Collectors and Superintendents of Police had been instructed to give adequate police protection to all cooperative societies in their jurisdiction. Protection could be extended to individuals if they were ready to bear the cost for the facility.

1814. (8-7-2007) NEW DELHI : BJP National President Shri Rajnath Singh expressed his grief over the demise of former Prime Minister Shri Chandra Shekhar. Shri Rajnath Singh said that Shri Chandra Shekhar was not just the former Prime Minister of India but was also a towering personality, who was deeply committed to the principles and political ideology that he was committed towards. He enjoyed respect of leaders across the political spectrum. Shri Singh said that Shri Chandra Shekhar always upheld the parliamentary dignity and was a prolific orator. The country will always remember his contribution in the JP movement and struggle against the oppressions of emergency. He was not one who only chased the politics of power, but instead he struggled for the values in politics. His struggle and firm commitment have become a source of inspiration and outstanding example for Indian polity to emulate. In his demise the country has lost a great and ideal leader. Shri Rajnath Singh expressed his heart felt sympathy with his family members on this sorrowful occasion.

1815. (8-7-2007) NEW DELHI : The Prime Minister Dr. Manmohan Singh has condoled the death of Former Prime Minister, Shri Chandra Shekhar. In a message, he said: “I received the news of the passing away of former Prime Minister Shri Chandrashekharji with profound sadness. I had the privilege and pleasure of working with him when he was Prime Minister and have had the benefit of his sage advice, abiding trust and sincere affection for me over the years. In recent months, I was deeply moved by the courage with which he fought his illness and soldiered on. The Prime Minister Dr. Manmohan Singh has condoled the death of Former Prime Minister, Shri Chandra Shekhar. The Prime Minister Dr. Manmohan Singh has condoled the death of Former Prime Minister, Shri Chandra Shekhar. Shri Chandrashekharji was a truly secular nationalist, a man of the people, committed to their welfare and well-being. He belonged to a generation that felt deeply about the importance of ideals and idealism in politics. During his brief tenure as Prime Minister, he steered the ship of our nation and economy through stormy waters with statesmanship and wisdom. He was not afraid of taking unpopular decisions if these were in the larger national interest and served the nation in the long term. In his passing away, our country has lost a distinguished son and a great patriot who was passionately committed to sustained development and social equity. I convey my heartfelt condolences to his family and millions of his admirers across our country."

1816. (8-7-2007) NEW DELHI : The President, Dr. A.P.J.Abdul Kalam has condoled the passing away of the former Prime Minister, Shri Chandra Shekhar. In a condolence letter addressed to the Late former Prime Minister's son Shri Pankaj Singh, Dr. Kalam has said that he is saddened to learn about passing away of Shri Chandra Shekhar. The President has said, "Shri Chandra Shekharji was a veteran parliamentarian, secularist and socialist known for his conviction to the principles he believed in. His services to the nation as Prime Minister, Member of Parliament and as an administrator will always be remembered. In his passing away the country has lost a personality who contributed to nation building." Dr. Kalam also conveyed his condolences to all the members of Shri Chandra Shekharji's family.

1817. (9-7-2007) NEW DELHI : The National Commission for Enterprises in the Unorganized Sector (NCEUS) under the Ministry of Micro, Small and Medium Enterprises has released a report on "Comprehensive Legislation for Protection of Unorganized Workers". NCEUS has presented two Draft Bills on Conditions of Work and Social Security for Unorganized Workers to the Prime Minister Dr. Manmohan Singh. The Chairman of the Commission, Dr. Arjun Sengupta MP, presented the Bills, along with an explanatory report. The Report is a curtain raiser to the comprehensive landmark report on India's working poor to be presented to the Prime Minister and publicly released before the end of this month. This report is the first of its kind in the country on the unorganized workers covering both agricultural and non-agricultural sectors. The Bills prescribe minimum conditions of work and introduction of a minimum social security for both agricultural and non-agricultural unorganized workers.

1818. (9-7-2007) NEW DELHI : A number of initiatives including use of new technological tools are likely to be used for crop estimation in future. The two-day National Workshop on Improvement of Agricultural Statistics discussed detail the present crop estimation methodology and infrastructure and has come out with a set of recommendations for improving farm statistics. Precise and timely estimates of crop yield, area, production and other farm data will help in taking correct policy decision and monitoring progress of various programmes and schemes. To conduct and complete the agriculture census in time, statistical legislation was recommended on the lines of Population Census and Industrial Statistics. It was felt that statutory powers are needed for the Agricultural Census Commissioner of India and State Agricultural Census Commissioners. For decentralized planning to agricultural growth, district level data is considered important. However, long time lag was noticed in its receipt and compilation. It was agreed that efforts will be made for online transfer of district level data to the States and from the State headquarters to the Centre on production, prices etc. The use of new technological tools was highlighted, especially in view of depleting staff strengthen in the field. During the Conference, State representatives highlighted that they are closely monitoring collection of area and yield estimates and preparing production estimates based on results of Crop Cutting Experiments. However, in the recent past, for implementation of the National Agricultural Insurance Scheme, the number of Crop Cutting Experiments in various States has increased manifold, which they are finding it difficult to cope owing to the limited staff strength. Since the harvest gets completed within about three weeks, the Crop Cutting Experiments are also to be completed within this critical period. The problem is further compounded, as larger numbers of posts are also lying vacant at various levels. Closer coordination between different agencies including Revenue Department, Agriculture Department, State Directorate of Economics & Statistics and Horticulture Directorate will help in more consistency and precision, and also timely compilation of data. Use of space technology with appropriate ground truthing will be of great help in capturing and validating field data. Considering that no proper database is available on horticultural crops and also because a new thrust is being given to this sector, it was decided that a system would be put in place to capture horticulture data exhaustively.

1819. (9-7-2007) NEW DELHI : The Ministry of Rural Development has released the payment of Grants-in-aid amounting to Rs. 1.56 crore out of the Central allocation of Rs.2.60 crore, as first instalment to the Muktsar District of Punjab State as Central assistance for the implementation of the Sampoorna Grameen Rozgar Yojana (SGRY) during the current financial year (2007-08). The grant is towards plan expenditure and will be utilized for approved items of works subject to the conditions laid down in the SGRY Guidelines. No deviations from the guidelines is permissible. The expenditure on implementation of the programme with regard to cash component is to be shared on 75:25 basis between the Central and the State Government respectively.

1820. (10-7-2007) NEW DELHI : The Minister of Railways, Shri Lalu Prasad has ordered an inquiry into the incident of alleged misbehaviour with two lady passengers by an RPF officer during the journey in Patna bound Sampurna Kranti Express yesterday. The inquiry will be conducted by Shri Gopal Gupta, IG, RPSF, Railway Board, New Delhi. He will be assisted by Smt. Jaya Chauhan, Chief Security Commissioner, North East Railway, Gorakhpur.

1821. (10-7-2007) NEW DELHI : A meeting of the Consultative Committee of the Ministry of Home Affairs was held here today to discuss the issue relating to the Draft National Policy on Criminal Justice. The Home Minister, Shri Shivraj Patil presided over the meeting. Today's meeting was in continuation of the meeting of the Consultative Committee held on the same subject on May 4, 2007. Taking part in the deliberations, the members of the Parliamentary Consultative Committee welcomed the Government's attempt to draft the National Policy on Criminal Justice. The members made certain suggestions during their presentations.

Home Minister Shri Patil assured the Members that good points emerging out of the wide consultation process on this issue would be incorporated while formulating the policy. He also emphasized the need to create more awareness among the common people about the existing laws. The members present at today's meeting included S/Shri Debabrata Biswas, Urkho Gwra Brahma, Raj Mohinder Singh, Dr. K. Malaisamy and Jai Prakash Agarwal of the Rajya Sabha and S/Shri Mani Kumar Subba, Mohanbhai Delkar, Sarbananda Sonowal and Mohan Singh of the Lok Sabha. The Ministers of State for Home, Shri Sriprakash Jaiswal, Shri Manikrao Gavit and Smt. V. Radhika Selvi and the Special Secretary in the Union Home Secretary, Shri M.L. Kumawat were among those who participated in the meeting. The deliberations will continue in the next meeting of the Consultative Committee.

1822. (10-7-2007) NEW DELHI : There are reports in some sections of the media that the Tax Return Preparers (TRPs) are awaiting further permission from the government to start their work of helping small and medium taxpayers file their returns of income. This position is not correct. As soon as a certified TRP receives his / her unique identity card from the training partner-NIIT, he / she is entitled to file income tax returns on behalf of the eligible categories of taxpayers. The new tax return forms have already been devised to furnish information about the TRP filing that return. The due date for filing return of income for the assessment year 2007-08 (relating to financial year 2006-07) expires on July 31, 2007 for non-corporate taxpayers, salaried persons, pensioners, professionals / self-employed taxpayers with turnover below the tax audit limits, etc. Such of these categories of taxpayers, who are having difficulty in filing their tax returns, are advised to take necessary help of TRPs in the matter.

1823. (10-7-2007) NEW DELHI : Defence Minister Mr. AK Antony flagged in the Indian Army Mount Everest Expedition, here today. Lt Col IS Thapa, Sena Medal, led the 23-member team of Army's expedition, while Capt NS Chandel was the deputy leader. Both the officers are from Maratha Light Infantry regiment. The team was predominantly composed of officers and men from Maratha Light Infantry. The expedition was flagged off on 20 March 2007. The team moved from Delhi on 28 March 2007 and arrived at Lhasa on 31 Mar 2007. The team left Lhasa on 02 Apr. 2007 for Everest base camp and reached there five days later via Gyantse, Shigatse and New Tingri. The base camp was located on Rongbuk glacier at a height of about 17000 feet. The road from Lhasa terminated at the base camp. Due to bad weather prevailing continuously from 20 April 2007, the first group of six summiteers could scale Mount Everest only on 15 May 2007, with second group, also of six summiteers scaling it the next day. On both days, an equal number of Sherpas also accompanied the army personnel. The President, Dr. APJ Abdul Kalam, Defence Minister Mr. AK Antony and Army Chief Gen. JJ Singh have commended the success of the team.

1824. (10-7-2007) NEW DELHI : The President, Dr. A. P. J. Abdul Kalam, has said that by connecting all the 15,000 courts in the country from the district courts to the High Court through a wide area network will enhance the efficiency of the judicial system. Inaugurating the e-Courts project for computerisation of courts here on Monday evening (9/7/07), the President said that the e-judiciary initiative should help in transforming court service to better system for meeting the needs of the citizens. Sharing his vision for e-judiciary in the country, the President called for setting up of the judicial e-Governance grid from the district courts to the Apex court. He said, "this grid will ensure seamless flow of information and case objects across the inter-departmental barrier." Dr. Kalam said for this purpose, National Identity Card has to be the primary data base linking all the e-governance activities. The objective of the e-governance should be to ensure the seamless flow of information across the various units of Government, judiciary, institutions and citizens crossing the inter-departmental barrier. The President said that e-judiciary will have to be in a position to provide information in the real time on the rights and responsibilities of the citizens. Delivering the key note address, the Chief Justice of India, Shri Justice K. G. Balakrishnan, described the launching of e-Court Project as "a watershed in the judicial delivery system in India." He said the project on its successful completion would greatly strengthen the people's faith in judiciary as 'we contemplate delivery of speedy justice mechanism.' He said that the objective of the project is to make justice cost-effective, expeditious and transparent. Expressing his full support to the e-judiciary programme, the Law and Justice Minister, Shri H. R. Bhardwaj, said that the legal profession should also adopt e-Governance programme so that there could be convergence between the lawyers and the courts. The Minister of Communication and Information Technology, Shri A. Raja also assured his Ministry's full support to the project. He said that it will facilitate deliverance of speedy justice. The President gave away laptops to four judicial officers from each zone in the country as a symbolic presentation. Around 15000 judicial officers would be provided with laptops. He also launched the Indian judiciary's official website portal www.indianjudiciary.in. The project of computerisation of courts is being implemented in three phases over a period of five years. Under the first phase, computer rooms and judicial service centres would be provided in all the 2500 court complexes in the country. State-of the-art video conferencing facility at the Supreme Court, High Courts and all the district courts would be set up and digital inter-connectivity between all the courts from the Taluka level to the Apex Court would be established. Under the second phase complete automation of registry level processes would be adopted. Digital availability of case laws, statute laws and law literature would be available through the website of Indian judiciary. Facilities of e-filling at the subordinate courts would be made available. The third phase is expected to lead to the creation of Information Gateways between courts and public agencies and departments. The purpose of the project is to rejuvenate the Indian judicial system thereby ensuring transparency, accountability and cost effectiveness in the delivery of justice.

1825. (10-7-2007) NEW DELHI : Reacting to a news report regarding the poor upkeep of the INA Memorial, Prime Minister Dr. Manmohan Singh visited the INA Memorial at Salimgarh in the Red Fort complex today. The Prime Minister walked around the campus and visited the rooms in which INA detainees were kept, the museum where photographs and uniforms are in display. The Prime Minister expressed his concern at the poor upkeep of the museum and premises. He was told that the concerned departments are seized of the matter and appropriate action will be taken. The Prime Minister expressed the hope that such places of historical importance are brought alive with a mix of display of historical material and other lively activity of interest to the general public. The Prime Minister's Office has been instructed to direct the concerned ministry to take necessary action.

1826. (10-7-2007) NEW DELHI : Grant-in-aid amounting to Rs. 11.26 crore has been released by the Ministry of Rural Development to 25 District Rural Development Agencies, in Gujarat towards Balance Payment of Ist instalment of Central Share of funds under Swarnjayanti Gram Swarojgar Yojana (SGSY) during the year 2007-2008 as per details given in the Annexure. The amount should be utilized on the Programme as per approved guidelines of SGSY. The funding pattern will be 75:25 by the Centre and the State. The State Government should release its share within one month of the date of release of the Central assistance. Under SGSY, assistance is given to the poor family living below the poverty line for taking up self-employment. It actively promotes group approach by organising the rural poor into Self-Help Groups.

1827. (10-7-2007) NEW DELHI : The Ministry of Rural Development has released balance payment of first instalment of Central share of funds amounting to Rs. 15.81 crore under the 'Swarnjayanti Gram Swarojgar Yojana' (SGSY) during the year 2007-08 to 16 DRDAs of Chhattisgarh. Details of the allocation are as per Annexure. The amount should be utilized on the Programme as per approved guidelines of SGSY. The funding pattern will be 75:25 by the Centre and the State. The State Government should release its share within one month of the date of release of the Central assistance. Under SGSY, assistance is given to the poor family living below the poverty line for taking up self-employment. It actively promotes group approach by organising the rural poor into Self-Help Groups.

1828. (10-7-2007) NEW DELHI : The number of beneficiaries for Supplementary Nutrition under ICDS Scheme has registered 70% increase. About 415.08 lakh children (0-6 years) and lactating mothers were getting the nutritional support under the scheme in 31st March, 04, the number has increased to 705.43 lakh

(70% increase) in 31st March, 07. Similarly, the number of children (3-6 years) attending Anganwadi Centres (AWCs) for pre-school education has increased from 204.38 lakh in March, 04 to 300.81 lakh in March, 07. It also shows an increase of 47%. The number of Anganwadi Centres operational across the country has also increased to 844743 in March, 2007 from 649307 in March, 2004. The ICDS Scheme has been expanded twice in the recent years. During the 1st phase of expansion in 2005-06, the Scheme was expanded to cover 466 additional Projects and 1.88 lakh Anganwadi Centres (AWCs) across the country. In order to extend the coverage further the population norms for setting up AWCs were relaxed. States were requested to submit their requirements of AWCs or Mini-AWCs, based on the revised population norms. Accordingly, 166 additional Projects, 106833 Anganwadi Centres (AWCs) and 25943 Mini-Anganwadi Centres were sanctioned under the 2nd phase of expansion of the Scheme during 2006-07. With these two phases of expansions, the number of sanctioned AWCs has increased from 7.58 lakh in March 2004 to 10.53 lakh in March, 2007. Alongside gradual expansion of the Scheme, there has also been a significant increase in the Budgetary allocation for ICDS during the last three years. The allocation has increased from Rs. 1675.97 crore in 2003-04 to Rs. 5204.00 crore.

1829. (10-7-2007) NEW DELHI : Union Human Resource Development Minister Shri Arjun Singh has said that Urdu is our composite cultural heritage. Shri Singh was speaking in the Annual General Meeting of National Council for Promotion of Urdu Language (NCPUL) here today. It was decided in Annual General Meeting (AGM) of the Council that to promote Urdu language Urdu cultural centres will be opened in all the states. In this regard the State Govts. have been approached to allot land so that such type of cultural centres are established in different state capitals. While commenting on the event of first war of Independence, HRD Minister informed AGM that a mausoleum in memory of heroes of independence will be built in Delhi where all the important documents and records will be stored so that future generation is able to come across the facts. It may also help in doing further research as far as the freedom struggle is concerned. The Council also resolved to hold a national seminar on the occasion of 150 years of 1857 to highlight the glorious role played by Urdu during the period. It was also suggested in the meeting that apart from holding such Seminars in India, an international conference may also be organized in the gulf countries where there is a sizable number of Urdu speaking population. The Minister has also directed the Council to suggest its restructuring so that appropriate action is taken in this regard. Urdu council has been active in organizing the different types of activities like organizing national book fairs, workshops, seminars in important places in India. The Council also provides grant-in-aid to NGOs for holding seminars, workshops, conferences to promote the language. The Council has also decided to provide grant to Orissa Urdu Academy for publication of book of Shri Sitakant Mohapatra a famous poet and Padmabhushan and Gyanpeeth awardee of Oriya Literature for a bilingual edition *i.e.* Oriya and Urdu.

1830. (11-7-2007) NEW DELHI : The Prime Minister, Dr. Manmohan Singh, had a telephonic conversation with the President of United States, Mr. George W. Bush this evening. The two leaders expressed satisfaction at the strong India-US bilateral relationship and spoke about the forthcoming discussions between the National Security Advisers of both countries, scheduled for next week. They were of the view that these discussions will reinforce our strong bilateral relations. The Prime Minister and the US President also said that they both are looking forward to continue their own discussions at their next meeting.

1831. (11-7-2007) NEW DELHI : A postman with a bag full of postal articles still holds a very respectable place among the people especially in the areas which are not easily accessible. India Post, which is committed to fulfilling the Universal Service Obligations in terms of providing basic postal services throughout the country, irrespective of terrain, at an affordable price is very much alive to the postal needs of the people especially in rural areas and far-flung pockets. The Department of Posts (DoP) in the border state of Jammu and Kashmir is doing a commendable job in providing postal services at the door step of the people, be it a remote village in the Ladakh division, a hilly and far flung area in Gurez or Uri sectors of Kashmir valley or a place in the border district of Poonch or Doda district of the Jammu division. In Jammu & Kashmir, the Department is very much alive to its very first objective of ensuring availability of basic postal services in all parts of the State, including tribal, hilly and remote areas.

1832. (11-7-2007) NEW DELHI : The Joint Forum of BSNL Unions & Associations of Non-executives and Executives have proceeded on One-Day Strike today (11.7.2007). In this connection, it is hereby clarified that the proposal for procurement of 45.5 million lines for 2G and 3G expansion of BSNL was perused by Shri A. Raja, Hon'ble Union Minister of Communications & Information Technology. Hon'ble Minister found some discrepancies in processing of GSM tenders and accordingly, advised BSNL to look into those issues in the larger interest of BSNL. Hon'ble Minister had a meeting with the representatives of the Joint Forum on 9th July, 2007 wherein he explained the reasons for such an advice given by him to BSNL and assured them that the interests of the BSNL and its employees will be protected at any cost. He requested them to call off their proposed Strike.

1833. (11-7-2007) NEW DELHI : The UPSC has declared the results of the written part of Geologists' Examination, 2006, held by the commission in December 2006. These candidates have qualified for the Interview/Personality Test. The candidature of all these candidates is provisional subject to their being found eligible in all respects. All the qualified candidates will be sent Detailed Application Forms, which should be returned to the Commission within the closing date indicated in the forwarding letter. In case any of these candidate does not receive a communication in this regard within two weeks of the publication of this result, he/she should immediately contact UPSC on Telephone No.011-23387402 or on Fax No.011-23387310, giving his/her particulars (*i.e.* full name, roll number, date of birth, address etc.) The marks of candidates who have not qualified shall be available on the Commission's website within 30 days from the declaration of the result and would be available on the website for a period of 60 days.

1834. (11-7-2007) NEW DELHI : Inaugurating the World Population Day Celebrations organized by Jansankhya Sthirata Kosh (JSK) in New Delhi today, the Union Minister for Health & Family Welfare, Dr. Anbumani Ramadoss said that stabilizing the population is critical for sustainable development and making reproductive health care and family planning services accessible to all is the route to achieve that. The JSK has organized a two-days sensitization programme for 500 young people from the underserved villages in 8 States to familiarize them with population growth and other health related subjects. Smt. Panabaka Lakshmi, Minister of State for Health & Family Welfare, Shri Naresh Dayal, Secretary, Health & Family Welfare and Smt. Shailaja Chandra, Director, JSK were also present on the occasion. Speaking further, the Minister said that India is the second most populous country in the world, sustaining 16.7 per cent of the world's population. The population of several Indian States can be compared to the population of many countries. The population of India could be a demographic dividend if every child is born healthy and grows up strong and gets educated. India's population growth will be higher than any country in the world by 2050. We have to be prepared for changes in our demographic profile. It is important to consider population projections because 51% of the country's population is in the reproductive age group. More than 150 million people will be added by 2016. The Minister added that out of the total population increase of 371 million between 2001 and 2026, 187 million are likely to be added in the seven States of Bihar, Chhattisgarh, Jharkhand, Madhya Pradesh, Rajasthan, Uttar Pradesh and Uttaranchal *i.e.* nearly 50% of India's demographic growth. 22% of the total population increase is anticipated to occur in Uttar Pradesh alone. In contrast, the contribution of the four southern States, namely Andhra Pradesh, Karnataka, Kerala and Tamil Nadu, to the total increase in population size is expected to be 47 million-13% of total demographic growth of the country. More than 40% of the population increase would be contributed by those who have 3 or more children per family. 188 million couples require contraceptive coverage but out of them little more than 50% are not using contraceptives. Vast numbers of people cannot avail the services even when they are available due to problems of knowledge and access. Dr. Ramadoss said that the education of women has a direct relationship with the total fertility rate and wherever literacy levels are high fertility has been brought down but where literacy levels are low, the fertility rate remains high. We have to make special efforts to improve the situation particularly in the underserved areas from where you have all come at our invitation. Addressing the participants, the Minister said the sensitization programme will enhance their understanding of population and gender issues, importance of age at marriage, health of the mother and child and spacing between births. He wished JSK and other organisations participating in the programme all success in their endeavours.

1835. (11-7-2007) NEW DELHI : The Prime Minister Dr. Manmohan Singh has condoled the death of the eminent industrialist Shri Bharat Ram. In a letter to his son Shri Vinay Bharat Ram, he said : "I was deeply saddened to hear about the demise of your father, Shri Bharat Ram. I had known him for decades and cherish the moments I have spent in his company. Shri Bharat Ram was not only one of the doyens of Indian industry but was also a multi-faceted personality who left a deep impression in many areas. He was a large hearted philanthropist whose contribution to the development of education, culture and sports have left a lasting impression on our landscape. The institutions he helped establish and develop have set standards of excellence which are benchmarks for the future. He was also a deeply humane person who believed in using wealth for noble causes. His contribution to our nation would be remembered for many generations. Gursharan joins me in offering our condolences to you and your family members and all the admirers of Shri Bharat Ram. I pray that his soul rests in peace."

1836. (11-7-2007) NEW DELHI : Report No. 510 on "Public Distribution System and Other Sources of Household Consumption, 2004-05" based on the seventh quinquennial survey on Household Consumer Expenditure carried out during the NSS 61st round (July, 2004-June, 2005) by the National Sample Survey Organization (NSSO) in the Ministry of Statistics and Programme Implementation has been released. This is one of the reports in the series of seven reports to be brought out on the basis of the survey. The report is based on the data collected on type of ration card possessed, benefits received from four selected food assistance schemes of the Government, sources of consumption of various items and consumption of rice, wheat/atta, sugar and kerosene from Public Distribution System (PDS) by the households. All the data are provided separately for rural and urban sectors of each State and Union Territory of India. Like all regular NSS surveys, the present survey covered practically the whole of the Indian Union. All States and Union Territories were covered under the survey except some interior areas of Nagaland, Andaman & Nicobar Islands, and Ladakh and Kargil districts of Jammu & Kashmir. The survey was spread over 7999 villages and 4602 urban blocks covering 79298 rural and 45346 urban households respectively.

1837. (11-7-2007) NEW DELHI : Central Minister Smt. Renuka Chaudhury said that I have outstanding sympathy and pity for the BJP because now they have finally reached the lowest level that can be possible in public life. Of course, it is not a new level for them but for us, we cannot stoop to those standards. They actually have inauguration of websites which have statements unsubstantiated and unfound, but they will promote the myths and fallacy of what they imagine is right. Mr. Arun Shourie talks of one widow. I want to remind Mr. Arun Shourie that in his avatar of Disinvestment Minister, how many of my trade union men, lost jobs when he wrote off and sold profit-making industries also in which thousands of our workforce people were on the roads because there was no future. How come the BJP conscience did not work then? How come the Centaur Hotel sale and resale did not remind them of their moral authority? These are the people who are talking, but I am not surprised. The BJP's attitude towards women has always been the same. It is nothing new and what have they done to the institution of Rashtrapati and what they are doing to the institution of the vice-president. They insult the intelligence of the common man. They say he is an independent candidate but it is announced from the BJP headquarters by Sushma Swaraj. They think the whole country are fools, that they will be fooled like the India Shining campaign. That the people will raise this hype in the media and that they will believe it. They are constantly misleading the media They have constantly repeated lies in their efforts to make it sound like truth. I would like to ask them if they have a soul, and I doubt if they have. Because if they had a soul they would not have stooped so low in their own eyes. They are already low in the eyes of others and therefore the people of this country rejected them. But they do not want to learn from it. And today from this website they are trying to make lies into truth by repeating it hundred times, I feel sorry for the BJP. I want to remind them that did they not have Assembly proceeding to be posted on the website in which there was a reference to someone's son-in-law. The reports are there and the proof is there but they failed to remember it and in psychology we call it selective amnesia. I can seriously recommend mass discount for psychiatric consultation for the BJP and their managers who are doing this. They do not even remember this that when women like me who had donated all their ornaments to fight in the freedom struggle, what were they doing? The BJP, donning the British uniform, were busy praising and serving the Britishers and even fought their own men for the Britishers and they presume that this is patriotism. If you look into the statements made by Advaniji and others, you will find that instead of praising our country they have always found praising other countries and it is unfortunate that the children of this country are unwitting witness to history in the making. The 13th election of the President of this country where history has decided that a woman will come to the top spot, has made up irrespective or recognized by the BJP. It is a direct impact of our fielding Pratibha Patil that today you have the BJP scrambling to constitute committees which Sushma Swaraj is heading to ensure that there is 33% women in the BJP. At last, they are following our footsteps.

1838. (11-7-2007) NEW DELHI : The Ministry of Rural Development has released balance payment of first instalment of Central share of funds amounting to Rs. 22.60 crore under the 'Swarnjayanti Gram Swarojgar Yojana' (SGSY) during the year 2007-08 to 27 DRDAs of Karnataka. Details of the allocation are at Annexure. The amount should be utilized on the Programme as per approved guidelines of SGSY. The funding pattern will be 75:25 by the Centre and the State. The State Government should release its share within one month of the date of release of the Central assistance. Under SGSY, assistance is given to the poor family living below the poverty line for taking up self-employment. It actively promotes group approach by organising the rural poor into Self-Help Groups.

1839. (11-7-2007) NEW DELHI : The ongoing bilateral Indo-UK air exercise-'Indradhanush 2007', at Waddington involves primarily-flying activities. On terra firma overseas, a great deal however involved meticulous logistics, phenomenal administrative, technically flawless and sound operational planning. At the forefront of such planning have been IAF officers at Air HQ, New Delhi, South Western Air Command (SWAC) HQ, Gandhinagar, Central Air Command (CAC) HQ, Allahabad, and at the Air Force Bases at Pune and Agra, for over six months. "Bringing it to fruition was a challenge" says Wing Commander AC Chopra, of the elaborate exercise planning. The Deputy Team Leader who together with the Logistics Officer, Wing Comander Manish Dialani and few more officers from the operational and maintenance side made visits earlier to the UK for coordinating the requirements. "The challenge has just begun," maintains Wing Commander Dialani, of the vast logistical issues that will need winding-up after thorough scrutiny when the team members leave. They were among the core members who arrived at UK ahead of the IAF team and will be amongst the last to leave. "It is good to have a logistics officer accompanying the team"-echoed most IAF members as the nitty-gritty of accommodation, transportation and food have been well taken care of. Wing Commander Chopra-'Choppy'-to mates on either side, who had a year's stint earlier at UK during his Staff course in 2003, was on a familiar ground and that helped matters in administrative tie-ups, locally. "My airmen leave very early in the morning everyday to get the fighters ready in time for the day's exercise. Their requirements of breakfast and vehicles are timely, the going has been smooth" admitted Squadron Leader SBH Reddy, Senior Technical Officer (STO) of the 'Rhinos'. He is at the helm-of-affairs of the technical maintenance of the fighters, and together with his motivated technicians, aims at a '100-percent serviceability' of all the jets during the exercise. Just 3 miles North of the Royal Air Force (RAF) Waddington, the University of Lincoln is normally bustling with student activities. Averaging nearly 17,500 students, the campus now is transformed into a military bastion besieged by the combined strength of Ex-Indradhanush airmen from the two elite Air Forces of the world-IAF and RAF. "It has been possible to accommodate the members from both Air Forces as the students are on vacation," informs the management at the University. With the exercise venue being at RAF Waddington, an arrangement convenient with the University now houses 150-members from IAF and 75 from RAF's No. 25 Squadron. The visitors couldn't have asked for a better location. At just a walking distance from the city centre, and the centuries old historical Lincoln Cathedral and the Lincoln Castle, the University forms an ideal retreat. "We are very happy with the arrangements," says Master Warrant Officer D Arpurtharaj, the senior-most airman from the 'Rhinos', on behalf of his boys. Since it is a first-ever 'out-of-country' assignment for nearly all, the excitement, enthusiasm and joie de vivre is palpable in their day-to-day activities in the flight line. Sickness, another of the worries has been mostly kept at bay. "Primarily there have been only a few cases of loose motions, upper respiratory infections-bronchitis, because of the weather," informs Wing Commander D Chakraborty, the Aviation Medicine specialist accompanying the team who has set-up a small 'medical centre' within the 'daily servicing section' for the ease of his patients. The IAF members arrived at Waddington in the thick of British monsoons after experiencing a simmering hot spell at Doha and Tanagra that led to respiratory problems for a few. That the exercise is truly going on smoothly and on schedule is a result of the efforts of innumerable IAF air warriors at various levels. The IAF contingent has been presenting themselves as a well turned-out and disciplined outfit. "Surely our Air Warriors deserve to be kitted with the best, for they are representing India," said Wing Commander Shyam Sunder proudly, the Senior Logistics Officer at Air Force Station, Race Course, New Delhi before the team's departure from India. The Station is responsible for all the kitting of IAF contingents when going abroad on UN missions and other foreign assignments.

1840. (11-7-2007) NEW DELHI : Central Adoption Resource Agency (CARA), an autonomous body under the Ministry of Women & Child Development has proposed amendments in guidelines on adoption of Indian children without Parental Care. The draft of the amended guidelines was submitted to Smt. Renuka Chowdhury, Minister for Women and Child Development by Shri J.K. Mittal, Chairman, CARA here today. Briefing about the salient feature of the guidelines, the Minister said these would bring more transparency, accountability and streamlined the adoption procedure. According to the proposed amendments, now the State Governments shall register all CCIs (Child Care Institutions) in the State. Cases of all orphan, abandoned and surrendered children shall be processed as per Juvenile Justice Amendment Act, 2006, which will automatically see more adoptions. The Act shall be applicable both in domestic and foreign adoption in case of all children in need of care and protection (orphan, abandoned and surrendered). In the case of inter-country adoption, children leaving with adoption orders and conformity certificate from CARA shall acquire automatic citizenship/nationality and enjoy more safeguards. Single window system will be followed in case of sourcing of children for inter-country adoption. All abandoned and surrendered children will now be committed to adoption agencies and shall be declared legally free for adoption by CWC after following due procedure. Prospective adopters would be able to adopt a child from any part of the country from registered agency. No child adoption agency can deny registration of such Prospective Parents. For example, a couple from Kerala working in North East can adopt without any hassle. All applications for foreign adoptions shall be received at CARA for advance approval. If foreign agencies/Central authorities have given a choice of a particular Indian agency, it will be considered as far as possible, otherwise CARA shall direct foreign agencies/central authorities to transmit their proposal to such placed where more children are available for inter-country adoption. This process will minimize the waiting period of foreign parents and children in the institutions as well. The draft guidelines will be circulated to the all concerned agencies and put on with the website for comments so that it can be given the final shape after a month.

1841. (12-7-2007) NEW DELHI : Shri Kamal Nath, Minister of Commerce & Industry, has announced an export package comprising of enhanced DEPB rates to help Indian exporters who had recently suffered due to a rising rupee. Shri Kamal Nath stated that the new DEPB rates are expected to help sustain the export growth built upon the strength of a booming economy. He expressed hope that the package would neutralize the adverse impact of rising rupee on exports which have been built upon the success of Indian economy achieved through export earnings in recent years. In addition to the reduction in export realisation due to the rupee appreciation, it had been pointed out by the industry that several state taxes / levies *i.e.*, electricity duty, sales tax on petroleum products and CST are presently not rebated. It was also pointed out that due to the rupee appreciation, the value addition prescribed in the DEPB calculation has in fact gone down, which would necessitate upward revision in the DEPB rates. Similarly, the value caps stipulated for various products for DEPB were stated to be unrealistic. Shri Kamal Nath apprised the Prime Minister on this issue and government also held several rounds of discussions. After a series of such wider consultations including export organisations like FIEO and Export Promotion Councils recently, the Minister today informed that the government has announced an export package.

1842. (12-7-2007) NEW DELHI : The Prime Minister, Dr. Manmohan Singh took stock of the state of investigation into the bomb blasts in Mumbai on 11th July 2006. The Prime Minister also reviewed all the steps taken so far for providing compensation to families of victims and those injured in the blasts, including assistance for hospitalization, payment of medical bills and provision of employment for those who have sought such employment. Of the 118 applicants for jobs, approval has been given for 96 so far, according to information provided by the State Government of Maharashtra and the Ministry of Railways. The Railway Ministry has been asked to ensure that the Railway Claims Tribunal expedites the disposal of claims for compensation. It may be noted that the Mumbai Police has so far charge-sheeted 25 persons in this case and the designated Court has issued non-bailable warrants against 15 absconders, and Red Corner Notices have been issued against 2 persons. The case is under trial. The Prime Minister has said that all those against whom cases have already been registered and all those who are wanted in this case will be brought to justice. The Government will not rest till the guilty are punished. The Prime Minister hailed the courage and forbearance of the people of Mumbai and their determination to stand united in the fight against terrorism.

1843. (12-7-2007) NEW DELHI : The following is the text of the opening remarks by Shri P.V. Bhide, Secretary, Revenue, Ministry of Finance at a Press

Conference, here today. "The Ministry of Finance has since worked out the revised All Industry Rates of Duty Drawback for 2007-08 which shall be notified in the Official Gazette shortly. Taking into account the duty incidence on inputs the drawback rates have been increased in most cases. The increased rates of drawback would take effect from 1.4.2007. The Ministry of Finance had constituted a Committee to determine the drawback rates, consisting of Shri Saumitra Chaudhuri, Member, Economic Advisory Council to Prime Minister as Chairman, Shri S.B. Mohapatra, former Secretary, Ministry of Textiles and Shri T.R. Rustagi, former Chief Commissioner of Customs & Central Excise as Members. The Committee held extensive consultations with the various industry and trade associations and other stake holders in various locations and submitted its Report on 6.7.2007. The Government has accepted the drawback rates as suggested by the Committee. Like the previous year, the drawback rates have been determined on the basis of certain broad parameters including, inter alia, the prevailing prices of inputs, standard input/output norms (SION) published by DGFT, share of imports in the total consumption of inputs and the applied rates of duty. As education cess is being collected as duties of excise/customs, the element of education cess has been factored in the drawback rates. The incidence of duty on HSD/Furnace Oil has also been factored in the drawback calculation. Further, the incidence of service tax paid on taxable services which are used as input services in the manufacturing or processing of export goods has been factored. The drawback rates have undergone significant changes in sympathy with the changes in prices of inputs, duties etc. The rates have been revised upwards on most products. In the case of silk, the drawback rate for higher quality silk fabrics is being increased from 8.3% with a drawback cap of Rs.250/kg to 10.8% with a drawback cap of Rs.325/kg. The new drawback rate for grey cotton yarn of less than 60 counts is 5.4% with a cap of Rs.11/kg as against the existing rate of 4% with a cap of Rs.8/kg. The new rate for dyed cotton yarn of less than 60 counts is 6.5% with a cap of Rs.18/kg. In respect of cotton yarn of 60 counts and more, a higher rate of 8.8% / 9.9% with a cap of Rs.26 per kg / Rs.33 per kg is being provided depending upon whether the yarn is grey or dyed. As for cotton fabrics, the new rate is 6.4% (grey) / 7.7% (dyed) with a drawback cap of Rs.19 per kg (grey) / Rs.28 per kg (dyed) as against the existing rate of 4.7% (grey) / 5.7% (dyed) with a cap of Rs.14 per kg (grey) / Rs.20.5 per kg (dyed). The new drawback rate for hand knotted woollen carpets is 12.5% with a cap of Rs.700 per sqm. as against the existing rate of 9.4% with a cap of Rs.565 per sqm. For silk carpets, the new drawback rate is 15.5% with a cap of Rs.2750 per sqm. as against the existing rate of 11.8% with a cap of Rs.1600 per sqm. The drawback rate on cotton durries is fixed at 11.5% with a cap of Rs.26/kg as against the existing rate of 9.4% with a cap of Rs.20/kg.

1844. (12-7-2007) NEW DELHI : Minister for Chemicals, Fertilisers and Steel, Shri Ram Vilas Paswan today reviewed the status of new PCPIR Policy in a meeting with the senior officials. During the discussion it was indicated that several States have shown interest in establishing Petroleum Chemical and

Petrochemical Investment Regions (PCPIRs). Andhra Pradesh has submitted its application proposing to establish the PCPIR in Visakhapatnam-Kakinada-Rajamundhri. Karnataka, Gujarat, Orissa, Tamil Nadu and West Bengal have indicated that they were preparing proposals for submission to the Department of Chemicals & Petrochemicals. The State Governments have given the details of their status of preparation in a meeting taken by Secretary (C&PC) recently. They have also indicated that they would submit their application within the next 3 months. Shri Paswan had released the Policy on PCPIRs on May 8, 2007 in a gathering attended by the State Governments, Industry representatives, representatives from international developers and some prospective investors. Earlier, the CCEA in its meeting held on April 4, 2007 had approved the Policy Resolution for Promotion of Petroleum, Chemicals and Petrochemical Investment Regions. Envisaged to be investment regions with excellent infrastructure, PCPIRs would provide conducive and competitive environment for setting up businesses, specifically for the Petroleum, Chemicals and Petrochemical sectors. This integrated Petroleum, Chemical & Petrochemical complex would reap the benefits of costing, networking and greater efficiency through use of common infrastructure and support services. Such a complex would boost manufacturing, augment exports and generate employment. The states were also informed that there would be a pre-scrutiny mechanism and the department would intimate the date for same to the State Government ordinarily within 15 days of receipt of application. The states have also agreed to share information with each other for possible adoption and guidance.

1845. (12-7-2007) NEW DELHI : The Board of Approval (BOA) of the Special Economic Zones (SEZs) met here today to consider proposals for setting up of Special Economic Zones and also approve other miscellaneous requests pertaining to SEZs. In this meeting, 39 applications for setting up SEZs, including 8 proposals for conversion of in-principle approvals to formal approvals were considered. The Board recommended grant of 21 Formal approvals and 6 In-principle approvals. Prominent among the approvals for conversion from In Principle to Formal approvals are: Multi product SEZ by Navi Mumbai SEZ (NMSEZ) in Dronagiri, Navi Mumbai; Bio-tech SEZ by Parsvnath Developers Limited in Andhra Pradesh; Aluminum and aluminum products SEZ by Hindalco Industries Limited in Orissa; Petro-chemicals and petroleum SEZ by Mangalore SEZ Limited in Karnataka and Leather SEZ by APIIC in Andhra Pradesh. Other prominent formal approvals are: a Multi product SEZ by H.N. Company in Nagaland; IT/ITES SEZ by Unitech Infopark Limited in Tamil Nadu; Electronic hardware and IT/ITES SEZ by True Developers Private Limited in Tamil Nadu and an Engineering SEZ by SIPCOT in Tamil Nadu. Prominent In principle approvals granted are: Bio-tech SEZ by Videocon Realty & Infrastructures Limited in West Bengal; Multi product SEZ by Chhindwara Plus Developers Private Limited in Madhya Pradesh; Automobiles/ auto ancillary SEZ by SIPCOT in Tamil Nadu and Multi product SEZ by Skil Infrastructure Limited in Karnataka. Addressing the BOA members, the Chairman

Shri G.K.Pillai informed that so far formal approvals have been granted for setting up of 341 SEZs out of which 130 have been notified. He informed that over Rs. 43123 crores have been invested in these notified SEZs and that these SEZs are providing direct employment to 35053 persons. He also mentioned that investment of over Rs. 100,000 Crores is expected and 100,000 jobs are also likely to get created in these SEZs by the year-end.

1846. (12-7-2007) NEW DELHI : India has offered assistance to Libya in expanding their infrastructure in the power sector and training human resource. The Union Minister for Heavy Industries and Public Enterprises Shri Sontosh Mohan Dev made this offer while receiving the Libyan Minister for Economy, Trade and Investment Dr. Ali Abdullah Al-Essawi here today. Shri Dev said, "BHEL is our flag ship power equipment manufacturing company. We will be very glad to help you in expanding your infrastructure in power and training human resource so that infrastructure in power sector in Libya can be maintained." Shri Dev also expressed the hope that the Indo-Libyan Joint Venture Company, ECCO formed in 1979 would become the flag ship company for both the countries to promote mutual interest in not only Libya but also in other African countries. It would be a win situation for both the countries, he added.

1847. (12-7-2007) NEW DELHI : The following is the text of the opening remarks by Dr. D. Subbarao, Finance Secretary, Ministry of Finance at a Press Conference, here today. "Reimbursement claims in respect of deemed export benefits are received and payments made by the Ministry of Commerce, subject to monthly and quarterly ceilings on expenditure. Exporters had represented that these monthly and quarterly ceilings restricted their right to receive payments expeditiously. Ministry of Commerce therefore requested relaxation from monthly and quarterly ceilings of expenditure. Accordingly, Ministry of Finance had accorded relaxation from monthly and quarterly ceilings of expenditure to enable the Ministry of Commerce to meet in full the pending reimbursement claims. It is estimated that these claims are in the order of Rs.600 crore. These claims will be examined and fully reimbursed as expeditiously as possible."

1848. (12-7-2007) NEW DELHI : The Quick Estimates of Index of Industrial Production (IIP) with base 1993-94 for the month of May 2007 have been released by the Central Statistical Organisation of the Ministry of Statistics and Programme Implementation. The General Index stands at 264.2, which is 11.1% higher as compared to the level in the month of May 2006. The cumulative growth for the period April-May 2007-08 stands at 11.7% over the corresponding period of the pervious year. 2. The Indices of Industrial Production for the Mining, Manufacturing and Electricity sectors for the month of May 2007 stand at 168.0, 281.9, and 225.6 respectively, with the corresponding growth rates of 3.7%, 11.9% and 9.4% as compared to May 2006. The cumulative growth during April-May, 2007-08 over the corresponding period of 2006-07 in the three sectors have been 3.0%, 12.7%

and 9.0% respectively, which moved the overall growth in the General Index to 11.7% 3. In terms of industries, as many as fourteen (14) out of the seventeen (17) industry groups (as per 2-digit NIC-1987) have shown positive growth during the month of May 2007 as compared to the corresponding month of the previous year. The industry group 'Wood and Wood Products; Furniture and Fixtures' have shown the highest growth of 132.8%, followed by 40.4% in 'Jute and other Vegetable Fibre Textiles (except cotton)' and 24.8% in 'Food Products'. On the other hand, the industry group 'Transport Equipment and Parts' have shown a negative growth of 0.1%, followed by 5.0% in 'Other Manufacturing Industries'. 4. As per Use-based classification, the Sectoral growth rates in May 2007 over May 2006 are 10.2% in Basic goods, 22.9% in Capital goods and 9.1% in Intermediate goods. The Consumer durables and Consumer non-durables have recorded growth of 2.6% and 12.5% respectively, with the overall growth in Consumer goods being 9.8%. 5. Alongwith the Quick Estimates of IIP for May 2007, the indices for April 2007 have undergone the first revision and those for February 2007 have undergone the second (final) revision in the light of the updated data received from the source agencies. There are no significant revisions in the indices for February 2007 and April 2007. 6. Statements giving Quick Estimates of the Index of Industrial Production at Sectoral, 2-digit level of National Industrial Classification (NIC)-1987 and by Use-based classification for the month of May 2007, along with the growth rates over the corresponding month of previous year, including the cumulative indices and growth rates, are enclosed.

1849. (12-7-2007) NEW DELHI : The Prime Minister, Dr. Manmohan Singh reviewed at a meeting yesterday, the recent Tiger conservation measures of the government and was briefed on follow-up measures to be considered to keep up the momentum in the national conservation movement. The Government has put in place a more scientific methodology for counting leading to a more accurate projection of numbers as against the conventional pug mark method liable for double counting. The final report of the Tiger Census it was informed would be ready by October 2007. Further in an effort to revitalize Project Tiger the Government has created an autonomous National Tiger Conservation Authority with effective powers. The Government has also sanctioned the National Wild Life Crime Control Bureau aimed at strengthening anti-poaching activity. The Prime Minister called for time bound action being taken to relocate 270 villages in the critical core areas in sanctuaries based on attractive packages offered to them. The Prime Minister also directed that states be requested fill vacancies of frontline staff urgently. Other follow-up measures discussed include strengthening protection and anti poaching activity through a Tiger Protection Force of Local Residents and Ex-Servicemen. The efforts of the Wild Life Crime Control Bureau and the Forest departments of states can be augmented by local residents working under the supervision of ex-servicemen as a Tiger Protection Force in selected sanctuaries. It would be effective to develop a model where ex-servicemen train and create a tiger protection force using local, mostly tribal residents in nearby villages thereby providing them with income opportunities and create a bond between them and the park. This could be piloted in major tiger sanctuaries. Another measure discussed is the creation of a Park Development Fund and Park Development Committee for each Park. A model for this already exists in Kanha National Park in Madhya Pradesh. The Park Development Fund will be managed by a Park Development Committee. The Park Development Committee could enlist local leadership and wild life activists. This body could direct suitable use of the Park Development Fund. The Minister of State for Forests Shri Regupathy suggested that a Forest Modernization Fund be set up on the lines of the Police Modernization Fund. It was felt that the Ministry of Environment and Forests should develop a career progression plan to attract good forest professionals into the wildlife sector. Further it was felt that wild life sensitization should be made part of the education curriculum. There should be a planned exposure of children and youth to the tiger sanctuaries.

1850. (12-7-2007) NEW DELHI : The Income Tax Department launched the 'Refund Banker Scheme' to issue refunds expeditiously and correctly. Presently the scheme is operative in Delhi and Patna charges. The CBDT plans to extend the scheme to Chennai, Kolkata, Mumbai and Bangalore from 30.09.2007. While implementing the 'Refund Banker Scheme' in Delhi and Patna charges, it has been noticed that a number of refund vouchers are received back due to incorrect address given by the taxpayers. Some of the taxpayers do not give their correct bank account number on the Income Tax return or fail to give correct MICR code of the bank because of which refund cannot be credited to their account. Out of 72,397 refunds dispatched by speed post between February and June 2007, as many as 7,264 have been returned undelivered by the postal authorities. To avoid inconvenience, the taxpayers are suggested to fill up the Tax Return form properly mentioning the correct address at which refund voucher may be delivered, correct bank details *i.e.* account number, name and branch of the bank, and MICR code of the bank. Taxpayers must also intimate the change of address, if any, to the assessing officer immediately.

1851. (12-7-2007) NEW DELHI : Archaeological Survey of India (ASI) is acquiring 228 acres of private land at Hampi at a cost of Rs. 8.31 crores. This proposal originated on account of the World Heritage Site at Hampi being surrounded by private cultivable land, over which the ASI has no ownership. Archaeological remains at Hampi are scattered in an area of 26 Sq.KM. The group of monuments has been inscribed on the world Heritage List considering their outstanding universal value. This land acquisition will help in providing proper access to some of the monuments and facilitate exposing the ancient remains which are in private lands. A part payment of Rs. 1.58 crores was made but this proposal is approved as per the consent award by negotiating the land value with the owners by the State Government. Union Ministry of Culture has accorded sanction to the revised estimate of Rs. 8.31 crores and Union Minister for Tourism and Culture Smt. Ambika Soni has accorded approval to this land acquisition proposal.

1852. (12-7-2007) NEW DELHI : The bungling in the matter of wheat import smacks of a multi-crore scam. The country fails to understand why in the first place government cancelled the tender floated in month of May, 2007 for which the prices quoted were $ 263 per MT. The reason cited was that the prices quoted were higher. Now, how can UPA government justify its decision to accept tenders quoted at much higher prices than the earlier prices, ranging from $ 320 to $ 360 per MT. This dubious decision will cost the nation extra Rs. 400 crore for the purported imports of 5 million MT of wheat. Bharatiya Janata Party demands that Agriculture Minister should resign accepting responsibility for such a grave loss to the country. There are more serious dimensions to the whole scam defrauding the nation. There was curious movement on Chicago Board of Trade (Forward Exchange), where prices rose by as much as 13% since May 2007. This needs a thorough probe. Those in the know of International Trade were upset over the government's unnecessary and untimely announcement of its intention to import 5 million MT of wheat in the month of March, which acted as a catalyst for propping up the prices. It will be worthwhile to mention that government imported wheat at $ 230 last year. The UPA government's bankruptcy has been well exposed as far as the management of the food security is concerned. The food crisis worsened as UPA allowed private corporates to purchase wheat from farmers thus jeoparadising the FCI buffer stocks. What is more curious is the fact that without any real dip in the indigenous wheat production, UPA brought sense of insecurity on the food front. The scene changed from surpluses during NDA regime to shortages under UPA. The UPA converted a stage of complete food security under NDA to a stage of perpetual insecurity. When government is paying Rs. 850 to Indian farmers why it is paying Rs. 1300 to foreign farmers? Last year's experience has established a fact that many farmers hold back the stocks and sold at Rs. 1000-1050 per quintal after the season. Bharatiya Janata Party demands immediate revamp in wheat procurement policy and demands that the Indian farmers should be paid more and a long-term policy of remunerative procurement prices should be announced immediately, so that the question of imports will not arise.

1853. (12-7-2007) NEW DELHI : The 8th World Hindi Conference is being held from 13-15 July 2007 in New York, USA. About 800 delegates are expected to attend the conference including Hindi scholars, literatures, and teachers from across the world. Official delegation comprising eminent Hindi writers, journalists, and representatives of Hindi Organizations including those from non-Hindi speaking regions will attend the Conference. The Minister of State for External Affairs, Shri Anand Sharma will lead the delegation. Official delegations from Mauritius, Nepal and other counties will also participate in the Conference. The Mauritian delegation is being led by Shri D. Gokhool, Minister of Education and Human Resource and the Nepalese Delegation is being led by Shri R. Mahato. The inauguration of the Conference will take placed at the Headquarters of the United Nations followed by the first academic session on 'Hindi in the United Nations' at the same venue. Dr. Girija Vyas, Chair person, National Conference for Woman will chair the session. These will be academic sessions on diverse aspects of Hindi language and literature such as Hindi teaching in India and abroad: problems and solutions; Hindi writing abroad (Pravesi Sahitya), Role of IT in promotion of Hindi; Globalization, Media and Hindi; Role of Hindi films in promotion of Hindi; Hindi, Youth and Science; Hindi language and literature: various dimensions; Role of translation in Literature; Children's Hindi Literature and Devnagari Lipi. Three exhibitions-on ancient Hindi manuscripts, Hindi Books and Hindi and IT-will be held. There will be two parallel academic sessions every day from 10-12.30 PM and 2.30-5.00 PM followed by cultural programme from 8-9.30 PM. The cultural programme will include Kavi Sammelan, Bharat Natyam by Sudha Chandran and group Sitar recital by Shujat Khan and Ghazals by Pankaj Udhas. Forty scholars will be honoured during the Conference in recognition of their valuable contribution. These will include 20 Foreign and 20 Indian scholars. An all India Hindi Essay Competition on 'Hindi Ka Bhavishya' was held for the youth between 10-25 years in the run up to the conference. There were two prizes-one each for Hindi speaking and non-Hindi speaking contestant. The two winners, Ms. Swarnima from Delhi and Ms. Sonia Sonal from Punjab will also be attending the 8th World Hindi Conference.

1854. (12-7-2007) NEW DELHI : Central Minister Smt Renuka Chaudhury said that today the nation woke up to read a statement made by Shri Advaniji where he has said that the PM of the country is appeasing terrorism. I cannot think of a more slanderous and denigrating statement than that. It is a pity that I agree, as Congress Party we are not able to provide terrorist with an aeroplane and organized ministerial escort service for terrorists as the BJP did when they had sent people to Kandhar. And they had so empowered those terrorists that they come back and attacked our Parliament. I agree that we are no match for them. We as Congress Party believe that the Prime Minister has in no way conveyed any kind of appeasement and it is indeed a matter of shame that a hopefully responsible leader of the opposition has made. I salute the Mumbaikers who in the spirit of national unity, who reflected Indian democracy when the Bombay serial blasts took place, that they all stood up and stood by each other in the first tradition of democracy. The nation saluted them and we salute them as a party. To use that platform or rather to misuse that platform and to speak in such a way about the Prime Minister of the country is saddening. It is denigrating the status of our Prime Minister and it is regretful that an opposition can speak in this way. But that does not come as anything new to us because don't forget the BJP has a tradition of denigrating institutions. They spared nobody in the path of their self-service and self-glorification. They have spoken in such tone about the Election Commission, they continued to speak in such denigrating tones about the presidential candidate and now it is the Prime Minister who is the target for them. It is regrettable that these are the examples and these are the people who want to be icons for the youth of our nation. History will not forgive them for the irresponsibility with which they speak. I want to ask BJP one question, where is their conscience? I knew that they didn't have one, it was a genetic bypass, but how is it that they are able to curb and control their tongues where they have no authority to speak on. What happened to Hiren Pandia, who was murdered in broad daylight and now professor Sabbarwals' death which happened in broad daylight and it is on camera that the ABVP people were involved in this murder. Then today the court has struck down on the government ruled by the BJP and the court has condemned what the Madhya Pradesh government has done when a chief minister goes to defend instead of prosecute. Can there be a bigger glaring example of what they have said and what they have done. They have far from preventing, they have encouraged crime such as this. They have told mistruths to the nation and much more than that lying in Parliament. This is the tragedy of our times that they come in the guise of Opposition and erode at the vitals of our nation. For the chief minister to defend an open broad daylight murder and the courts when they are enquiring, you have people going and defending instead of prosecuting is a sad travesty of justice. How then is this moral, mighty Micky Mouse brigade, an authority to speak on anybody else much less the Presidential candidate and even on the Prime Minister of this country. Whether it was the Gujarat's Best Bakery case, whether it is the Election Commission, whether it is what has happened in Madhya Pradesh, this party with an intention of distracting with the intention of diverting, with the intention of diluting, the actual facts and failures of the BJP, that they launched on a canard like this, denigrating every office that comes in the way. I can only extend my heartfelt sympathies for the BJP because they stand exposed in the eyes of the nation and even now they must learn to restrain before they speak so loosely or carelessly about our institutions. They must not forget that they are being watched. The Congress Party needs no lessons in patriotism because we are a party that fought for the freedom of this nation when the freedom took place. We are a party that is extra sensitive to terrorism because we have lost leaders to terrorism. We have lost Smt. Indira Gandhi, we have lost Shri Rajiv Gandhi and we don't need to be taught lessons in patriotism but if the BJP wants to learn then we are willing to teach them because unfortunately they were the Savarkars.

1855. (12-7-2007) NEW DELHI : The Ministry of Rural Development has released balance payment of first instalment of Central share of Rs. 26.46 crore for implementation of Swarnjayanti Gram Swarojgar Yojana (SGSY) during 2007-2008 in 29 DRDAs of Tamil Nadu State. Details of the allocation are as at Annexure. The amount should be utilized on the Programme as per approved guidelines of SGSY. The funding pattern will be 75:25 by the Centre and the State. The State Government should release its share within one month of the date of release of the Central assistance. Under SGSY, assistance is given to the poor family living below the poverty line for taking up self-employment. It actively promotes group approach by organising the rural poor into Self-Help Groups.

1856. (12-7-2007) NEW DELHI : The Union Cabinet today gave its approval to empower the Minister-in-charge of the administrative Ministry/Department concerned to approve the proposals of CPSEs to enhance the age of retirement of its employees from 58 to 60 years, provided that the concerned CPSEs should have made net profits for the last 3 years continuously as per its audited annual accounts and should have positive net worth during the last three years. This benefit will be available to only those CPSEs which have not availed budgetary support for the last 3 years and no budgetary support will be availed by the CPSEs in future. The Government has now decided to clarify the condition relating to budgetary support to the effect that the CPSEs who have not availed budgetary support for the last 3 years for their non-plan expenditure for salary, wages, payment of statutory dues, payment for Voluntary Retirement/Separations Schemes (VRS/VSS) and payment to meet cash losses and no budgetary support for the same will be availed by the CPSEs in future. This move will benefit employees of various profit earning CPSEs who have not availed budgetary support for the last 3 years for their non-plan expenditure and where the retirement age is presently 58 years.

1857. (12-7-2007) NEW DELHI : According to the 2001 Census, there are 127.22 million Women workers in the country. They constitute 25.60 per cent of total female population of 496 million in absolute terms. The majority of women workers are employed in the rural areas. Amongst rural women workers, 87 per cent are employed in agriculture as labourers and cultivators. Amongst the women workers in the urban areas, 80 per cent are employed in unorganized sectors like household industries, petty trades and services, building and construction, etc. The employment of women in the organized sector (both public and private sectors) as on 31.03.2002 was about 4.935 million constituting 17.8 per cent of the total organized sector employment in the country. Majority of women workers in this sector continue to be employed in community, social and personal services sectors. The lowest employment of women has been noticed in electricity, gas and water sectors. In factory and plantation establishments women workers constituted 10% and 5% respectively while in mine establishments they constituted 5% of the total workers in 2000. Although the women workers constitute a significant part of the country's work force, they lag behind men in terms of level and quality of employment. In order to improve their wages and working conditions, to enhance their skills and to open up for them better employment opportunities as well as to strengthen their bargaining capacity, the Government has enacted several legislations. These include the Maternity Benefit Act, 1961, and the Equal Remuneration Act, 1976 to protect and safeguard the interest of women workers at the workplaces. The Equal Remuneration Act, 1976 prohibits any gender discrimination in recruitment, wages and service conditions. Under the Act, a

Central Advisory Committee has been set up at the Centre, to advise the Government at the national level on providing increasing employment opportunities for women and generally reviewing the steps taken for effective implementation of the Act. The State Governments and UT Administrations have also set up similar Committees. The Government has also taken up a number of initiatives to give effect to the guidelines/ norms laid down by the Supreme Court for prevention of sexual harassment of women workers at work places. A separate Women Labour Cell is functioning in the Ministry of Labour and Employment to address these problems. The Women Cell is also administering a Grant-in-Aid Scheme through NGOs for running projects for awareness generation among women workers with a view to educate them about their rights, and also about various women related schemes and programmes run by the central and state governments.

1858. (12-7-2007) NEW DELHI : Inaugurating the two-days State Health Secretaries Conference in New Delhi today, Union Minister for Health & Family Welfare, Dr. Anbumani Ramadoss said all health sector initiatives have to view health as a continuum of preventive, promotive and curative care. The cross linkages with collateral determinants of health including nutrition, drinking water, sanitation, education and women's empowerment etc. also have to be addressed. The Minister of State for Health & Family Welfare, Smt. Panabaka Lakshmi, Secretary (HFW), Shri Naresh Dayal, DGHS, Dr. R.K. Srivastava, senior officials from the Ministry, Health Secretaries and senior officials from the States were also present on the occasion. The following is the text of the Health Minister's speech: "I am happy to be amidst you all today morning at the Conference. I welcome you all to the two day Conference of State Health Secretaries to discuss and deliberate on matters relating to Health sector. In recent past the health sector in the country has seen far reaching changes. We are all fortunate to be part of the process of architectural corrections being carried out in the sector. The States have demonstrated remarkable enthusiasm in accepting the sector wide paradigm change introduced under the National Rural Health Mission (NRHM) and are at various stages of implementation of the strategies. As you would be aware, the NRHM is a flagship programme of my ministry. The aim of NRHM is to provide accessible, affordable, accountable, effective and reliable primary health care facilities. The Mission seeks to rejuvenate the health delivery system through comprehensive upgradation of infrastructure, augmentation of manpower and expansion of capacity for training various stakeholders. The Mission also seeks to hand over the planning, execution and evaluation of the health programmes with the community based organisations. The health facilities are being made responsive to the community through the Rogi Kalyan Samitis and untied funds are being given to all levels of health facilities and we hope to comprehensively rejuvenate the health system in near future. My officers have worked very hard to design a flexible and adaptable road map for rejuvenation of the health delivery system under NRHM. It has taken many days of efforts to crystalise the strategies and design the tool kits and guidelines. I am sure the States would have noticed the immense effort which have gone into the formative years of the NRHM. It is also very heartening to see the enthusiastic participation of State officers in designing of the strategies under NRHM, implementation of the same and the follow up activities. We have noted the active participation of the programme officers relating to various national programmes also in the process. The response from the States has encouraged us and boosted our confidence and morale. The process of change in the health sector is a gradual one and it is necessary to move cautiously, taking the various stakeholders into account. The process is heavily dependent upon the capacities of the stakeholders to maintain focus and persist with the initiative in the wake of daunting challenges of logistics, working conditions and lack of support structures etc. It is therefore, very necessary to have continuous dialogue with all the stakeholders. This Conference is one such initiative and I congratulate all my officers for having organised the same. I also thank all of you for responding to the same so enthusiastically. The era of rigid, vertically designed health programmes, without any horizontal intrasectoral and Intersectoral linkages is over. All health sector initiatives have to view health as a continuum of preventive, promotive and curative care. The cross linkages with collateral determinants of health including nutrition, drinking water, sanitation, education and women's empowerment etc. also have to be addressed. In this process some of the basic features of the health programmes need to be re examined. The range of work of various cadres, the skills required at various levels, reporting channels, budget lines, all need to be rationalized to respond to the sector wide approach. My Ministry has kept a large number of presentations from different divisions over the next two days on these issues. The Financial Management Group in my Ministry has done a lot of hard work to design a format of Administrative and Financial Delegations and I am sure the States would immensely benefit from the presentations which are to be made by them on this matter. The Monitoring Cell of my Ministry has also designed an integrated Health Management Information System (MIS) and I am sure the States would benefit from the presentations. The critical programmes like the Reproductive and Child Health Programme (RCH) Phase-II would also discuss key issues with you. As you would be aware we are committed to the Millennium Development Goals, which include Infant Mortality Rate (IMR), Maternal Mortality Rate (MMR), and Total Fertility Rate (TFR) goals also. The RCH II is the main vehicle for achieving these goals. The disease control programmes of Malaria, Tuberculosis, Leprosy, Blindness and Iodine Deficiency are also integral parts of the NRHM and we seek to strengthen the service delivery under these programmes as part of the rejuvenation of health systems.

1859. (12-7-2007) NEW DELHI : When the Indian Air Force (IAF) Jaguars flew to Alaska during their first overseas joint air exercise "Cope Thunder" in July '04, the newly inducted Ilyushin-78 MKI 'air-to-air' refuellers of the IAF heralded their acquired strategic reach capability. This year, the six Su-30 MKIs that flew from Pune airbase in India to Royal Air Force (RAF) airbase at Waddington (UK), were also accompanied by two IL-78 MKIs of the 'Valorous MARS' (No. 78 Mid-Air-

Refuelling Squadron) from Agra through their long ferry route. Despite the din and the excitement of the first-ever arrival of the formidable Su-30 MKIs at UK, the significant aspect of IAF's continued enhanced strategic reach capability, did not however go unnoticed. "The IL-78 MKIs have been employed in five overseas assignment so far. These include Alaska, South Africa, France, Singapore and now UK," informed Group Captain K Raghavendra, Commanding Officer of the MARS. "We would have loved the experience of tanking RAF fighters during the exercise that would have made inter-operability possible. We look forward to such an experience in the future," he added on RAF Tornadoes not having tanked with them during the exercise. The six IAF Su-30 MKI fighters will have flown nearly 19,000 kms each, tanked eight times and transferred nearly 225 tonnes of fuel mid-air in all, spread over 28 flying hours with stopovers enroute at Doha (Qatar) and Tanagra (Greece), both ways. The Il-78 aircrew also visited RAF Brize Norton, the home to RAF VC-10 Tankers flown by 101 Squadron. Interestingly the RAF squadron is 90 years old. The aircrew had discussions on the procedures and tactics and found lot of common ground in the same. The VC-10 can uplift 70 tonnes of fuel in the air. For a similar route by the IL-78 involving two enroute landings from India to UK, VC-10s would have had to undertake three.

1860. (12-7-2007) NEW DELHI : The first ever-open sea cage has been launched in the near-shore sea of Vishakhapatnam for culturing of Asian Sea Bass. The cage has been designed, fabricated and installed indigenously. The cage net is stocked with about 6000 fingerlings of the highly priced sea bass, which are fed twice daily. A production of two tons of fish is anticipated within 4-5 months of grow out period from the cage. The open sea cage is not only a productive venture to ensure high yields but also an eco-friendly and sustainable mariculture technology which has attracted aqua culturists as well the attention of local public. Further, it is expected that this new activity will attract entrepreneurship development and market and open up a new era in the development of marine fisheries and mariculture in India. Similar cages are being launched at other three centres, Ratnagiri, Diu and Mandapam. These open sea cages are being set up by the Agriculture Ministry under a pilot project implemented through the Central Marine Fisheries Research Institute (CMFRI), Cochin.

1861. (12-7-2007) NEW DELHI : The Cabinet Committee on Economic Affairs today gave its approval on the following: (i) Improvement of Storm Water Drainage System (BRIMSTOWAD) in Mumbai as technically approved by Central Public Health & Environmental Engineering Organization (CPHEEO, technical wing of Ministry of Urban Development) at an estimated cost of Rs.1200.53 crore; (ii) Release of Central Assistance as a grant to the extent of Rs.1200.53 crore only (including 3% contingencies) to the Government of Maharashtra for implementation of the project by Municipal Corporation of Greater Mumbai (MCGM); (iii) Cost escalations, if any, will be borne by Government of Maharashtra / MCGM; (iv) Cost of operations & maintenance and rehabilitation and relief of project affected families shall be borne by State Government itself; (v) The Project shall be jointly monitored by the Centre and State Government to ensure timely completion and that there are no cost over runs. After the completion of the Project, augmentation of the Storm Water Drainage system for higher rainfall intensity with higher runoff coefficient will reduce the incidence of flooding in Mumbai, which in turn will benefit Mumbaikars and save losses of Rs.1550 crore per year. It will also help in enhancing the image of Mumbai as a world class city. The Project will be operationalised within 4 years. Mumbai city has at present Gravity Storm Water system consisting of network of drains below road level in city area and open drains in the both eastern and Western suburbs. Storm Water drainage system in the city is more than 150 years old and is designed for rainfall of 25 mm per hour and a run off coefficient of 0.5. Improvement of the Storm Water Drainage system for higher rainfall intensity reaching up to 100 mm per hour with a higher run-off coefficient of 1, will reduce the incidence of flooding in the Mumbai.

1862. (13-7-2007) NEW DELHI : The Appointments Committee of the Cabinet has approved the appointment of Dr. Arvind Virmani, presently Principal Adviser, Planning Commission, as Chief Economic Adviser, Department of Economic Affairs, Ministry of Finance, on deputation on ad-hoc basis in the post to be vacated by Dr. Ashok Kumar Lahiri, on his, appointment as Executive Director, Asian Development Bank, for a period upto 30th June, 2009 the date of his superannuation or until further orders, whichever is earlier.

1863. (13-7-2007) NEW DELHI : The Prime Minister, Dr. Manmohan Singh chaired the first meeting of the National Council on Climate Change. Following is the text of Prime Minister's Opening Remarks on the occasion: "I am happy to welcome all of you to the first meeting of this Council on Climate Change. We had met in June to discuss the Indian response to Climate Change in the wake of the unequivocal findings of the Inter-Governmental Panel on Climate Change that global warming is a validated fact. At that meeting it was decided that an intersectoral forum should be created as a National Council for Climate Change given our dependence and vulnerability vis-a-vis monsoons, dependence on the Himalayan snow-fed rivers, our large coastline and the growing needs of the economy that puts pressure on natural resources. Even as we forge an international consensus on dealing with climate issues, which are truly beyond geographic boundaries of nation-states, the consensus has been that we need to develop in parallel, a national agenda for adaptation. As decided in our last meeting, most importantly we need to document the work we have done in following a less-energy intensive path to develop. From the First Plan itself, we laid stress on hydro and nuclear energy and decades ago promoted solar, bio-mass and other non-conventional and renewable energy sources which has put us on the pathway to reduction in carbon emissions. We must at the same time explore ways of new and greener ways of development. I suggest that we deliberate on how we can put together a National Programme Document by November 2007 capturing both the efforts that we have made so far and our plans for the future. The first tangible output of our Council must be the production of such a national programme for action. As a prelude to this we must prepare a national report on the Impact of Climate Change. This will help to prepare the public for the steps that may have to be taken and also provide a strong scientific basis for the national programme. It is a matter of satisfaction that India was in the forefront of the development of the Clean Development Mechanism and now we are the largest global player in CDM in terms of number of projects. China is ahead of us in terms of CERs mainly because they have huge HFC (Hydro Fluoro Carbon) projects. The Indian National CDM Authority has accorded host country approval to over 667 projects facilitating an investment of nearly Rs.60,000 crores in sectors such as energy efficiency, fuel, industrial processes, municipal solid waste and renewable energy. Our national CDM authority should work more closely with Chambers of Commerce and Industry, develop competent bundling agencies in the country, as well as work closely with RBI and financial institutions to increase participation of the financial sector. I am given to understand that, of late our PSUs have started developing CDM projects and this trend needs to be accelerated. I would suggest that the Planning Commission should consider in building a mechanism to incorporate CDM strategies in sectoral plans and proposals that it clears. Intensification of adaptation efforts would require coordinated, planning and implementation between State Government and Ministries and, therefore, climate change should be made a critical parameter in plan formulation and investment decisions. Our challenge is both to build on our past track record and to address the global issue of climate change without compromising on the imperatives of poverty alleviation. Our national agenda must focus on understanding and mapping the monsoon at sub-regional levels. Technology development to respond to climate variability in agriculture to ensures food security and economic modelling in Indian circumstances to bring out the cost of adaptation and mitigation should also be central to our agenda. We need to prepare a comprehensive road map for energy efficiency and sustainable development in major sectors like agriculture, forestry, industry, transport, power, housing and environment infrastructure.

1864. (13-7-2007) KOCHI: The Kerala High Court on Thursday directed the State Government to inform it as to which of the 532 pattayams (title deeds) issued by deputy tahsildar Raveendran were proceeded against on the ground that he had not been authorised to issue title deeds. Justice S. Siri Jagan also directed the Government to inform it whether the Government had authorised the officer to issue the title deeds and explain whether the officer had issued title deeds in favour of the two political parties [CPI and CPI(M)] as contended by the petitioner. If so, whether they had been proceeded against, and if not, the reason for the same. The court asked the Government to furnish the information in 10 days. The directions were issued when a petition filed by the Dhanyasree Yatri Nivas, Munnar, challenging the cancellation of the title deeds granted to them came up for hearing. The court said the Government could take possession of the Dhanyasree properties, but the buildings should not be demolished. It ordered that before taking possession, an inventory of the articles in the buildings should be made and the owners be given five days to remove the same. (However, in the afternoon, the Special Task Force initiated action for demolition of the Dhanyasree hotel and stopped it midway.)

1865. (13-7-2007) NEW DELHI : Bharatiya Janata Party demands a CBI probe into Rs. 1200 crore wheat import scam. As more and more details are coming to fore, which confirms our suspicion that earlier cancellation of May 2007 tenders at $263 per MT and placing order in July 2007 @ $320-360 per MT is a big scandal. BJP wants to raise some important questions, which needs categorical explanation by the UPA government. What was the necessity for the government to declare its intention to import 5 million tons of wheat so early in the month of March, when the prices in the world market were high, knowing fully well that this announcement will work as a trigger to price rise ? Why did government feel necessary to import, despite increased production of wheat in the country compared to last year ? Why government did not raise the price of procurement from the farmers to compete with private firms, which would have ensured higher prices to farmers and sufficient buffer stock in FCI godowns at lower price than the import bill ? Why the tenders in May were cancelled when the parties quoted $263 per MT for supplying the required wheat ? Why the UPA government put an order to import wheat at much higher price of $320-360 per MT in the month of July ? And what was the rational for accepting such a high price ? Why government did not wait till August when the world prices are expected to come down as the wheat from Ukraine, Russia and other parts of the wheat-producing world hit the market ? It is clear that the UPA government has bungled badly and many vested interests have played their part in the scam. The scam has put unnecessary burden on the nation and ultimately will work against the farmers and the consumers as well. A CBI inquiry is imperative. If government does not accept our demands of CBI inquiry and resignation, BJP will raise the matter in parliament and agitate against this anti-people decision.

1866. (13-7-2007) NEW DELHI : A tripartite meeting to review the implementation of the Assam Accord was held at Guwahati last Wednesday. It was attended by the Secretary (Border Management), Ministry of Home Affairs, Shri U.N. Panjiar, Chief Secretary, Assam, Shri P.C. Sharma and President, AASU, Shri S.P. Roy among others. It was assured by Secretary (BM) that Government attaches highest importance to the Assam Accord. It was noted in the meeting that 193.68 kms out of 223.81 kms of sanctioned border fence along the Assam-Bangladesh border has already been completed. Chief Secretary, Assam apprised the meeting of the difficulties faced and assured that the remaining stretch of fence would be completed within the current year. The progress would be fortnightly reviewed at the level of the Chief Secretary, Assam. The meeting noted with satisfaction the progress made in regard to the Assam Gas Cracker Project, Bogibeel Rail-cum-Road

Project, improvement of credit deposit ratio in Assam, establishment of 21 additional foreigners tribunals for detection of illegal migrants and steps taken for expansion of the Jyoti Chitraban Film Studio. The meeting also took note of the steps taken by the Government of Assam towards employment generation for youth and the funds earmarked for this purpose and steps taken for flood control measures.

1867. (13-7-2007) NEW DELHI : The area coverage of most of the kharif crops as compared to last week has gone up considerably as per data compiled by Agriculture Ministry. The total coverage of kharif rice has gone up to 54.4 lakh ha as compared to 54.96 lakh hectare at this time last year, the weekly Crop Weather Watch Group meeting of the Ministry of Agriculture was informed here today. The coverage was 46.02 lakh ha last week. Transplanting of rice is in progress in almost all the States. Total coarse cereals have covered an area of 80.361 lakh ha as compared to 86.249 lakh ha the corresponding period last year. 60.78 lakh ha was under coarse cereals on last Friday. Cotton has been sown in 69.05 lakh ha as compared to 58.01 lakh ha last year. The coverage last week was 59.6 lakh ha. Out of this 24.35 lakh hectare is under Bt cotton. Sugarcane coverage is reported to be 44.37 lakh hectare compared to 48.13 lakh ha last year, and jute 7.884 lakh hectare (last year 8.176 lakh ha.). Last week: sugarcane: 45.16 lakh ha, jute: 7.88 lakh ha. The total coverage of oilseeds so far has been 95.19 lakh ha last year 87.42 lakh ha. Last week: 42.27 lakh ha. Pulses cover 40.169 lakh ha land as compared to 47.89 lakh ha at this time last year. Last week: 26.84 lakh ha.

1868. (13-7-2007) NEW DELHI : The Prime Minister, Dr. Manmohan Singh chaired a meeting yesterday, to review two components of Bharat Nirman programme-Rural Telephony and Rural Roads. It was noted the performance of extending telephony to the rural areas was progressing extremely well with the Bharat Nirman target of providing every village with telephone connectivity likely to be achieved by November 2007-about two years ahead of schedule. Out of the 66,822 villages, 48,125 have been covered till May 2007 and the remaining will be covered by November 2007. When completed 14183 villages will be connected through satellite technology the rest through other technologies. And in an effort to increase rural tele-density about 80,000 towers will be installed by May 2008 to facilitate mobile and other wireless services in rural areas. Efforts are also on to provide Broadband services to cover 2 lakh villages in 5000 blocks across the country. The final goal is to create five crore rural connections by 2007 and increase this to 8 crore connections by 2010 and provide broadband connections in every village by 2012. The performance of the Rural Roads has been satisfactory with around 40,000 km of new link roads having been built and 50,000 kms of existing rural roads being upgraded in the first two years (2005-2007) of Bharat Nirman. Against the Bharat Nirman target of connecting 66,802 villages with all-weather roads 13,831 villages have been connected. It was noted that 9 states of Assam, Bihar, Chhattisgarh, Jharkhand, MP, Orissa, Rajasthan, UP and West

Bengal account for 90 per cent of remaining coverage. Among these Rajasthan and MP are well on course while Jharkhand, Bihar, Orissa, Assam, and West Bengal are to gain momentum. The Prime Minister has written to the Chief Ministers of all the states to ensure targets are met and they have assured action.

1869. (13-7-2007) NEW DELHI : Congress Spokesperson Shri Abhishek Singhvi said that as July 19 and 21 draw closer and as the arithmetic of victory seems undeniable, we would call upon the BJP to introspect each of the preceding few weeks, they have shot off arguments, allegations but never substantiated them. They have never denied, for example, that more than 75% of a so-called booklet circulated by them, is nothing but a reproduction of the unsubstantiated allegations of an employee memorandum. They have again, for example never produced the resolution under which they claimed, misleadingly and wrongly to the nation that in 2002, Smt. Pratibha Patil had been authorized to appoint directors to the bank. What are these allegations? They reflect a shoot and scoot policy. A shoot and scoot technique to mislead the nation. I challenge and I call upon the BJP to deny the fact that Shri Shekhawat claimed on the floor of the Assembly in Rajasthan the pendency of a CBI enquiry and let them deny it. Shri Shekhawat claimed the pendency of a CBI enquiry where as the written letter of the central minister denies any such enquiry. Let them categorically, specifically call upon them to deny the very specific facts alleged for example again about Mr. Shekhawat's suspension in a well known magazine which has supported its specific allegations with verbatim interviews with the persons concerned. The point is, the nation is waiting for an answer, the nation is waiting for a response for substantiation. In that sense this is truly the BJP's last chance. This is the last five days to repentance, correction, to join the nation in celebrating women empowerment before the inevitable results are declared. The BJP should search there inner soul and should consider retrieving at least some of the prestige along of course with retrieving the stature of the Presidential post by apologizing to the nation for consistently misleading it for consistently mounting false, untruthful and negative campaigns. The BJP has to ask itself as to what it has got out of this kind of non-substantiated negative campaign apart from polluting, vitiating the environment. We know that the BJP can lecture the nation on Indian tradition and Indian values but we also know that they will never follow that basic Indian sanskar of apology, shamayachana, prayaschit, repentance, paschataap for playing to perfection the role of a irresponsible Opposition. To a question that BJP is making Shekhawat's assets public? Shri Abhisehk Singhvi said that Mr. Shekhawat, his handlers or his supports in any form, direct or indirect, have not got any sense or responsibility. It is actually the playing out of a melodrama which is nothing to do with sudden political sense or responsibility. It is thus playing out a force before the nation. To a question that will Pratibha Patil finally declare her assets, Shri Singhvi said that I am sorry, the Presidential candidate is not obliged to go and do some thing which law does not permit. The Returning Officer is prohibited from receiving and merely because a member of the media want her to do so.

1870. (13-7-2007) NEW DELHI : The Prime Minister, Dr. Manmohan Singh chaired the first meeting of the National Council on Climate Change. The Prime Minister directed the Planning Commission to incorporate clean development strategies into the sectoral plans and proposals for the Eleventh Plan and to make a strategy to deal with climate change an intrinsic part of the Eleventh Plan strategy. The Prime Minister said that the Government would launch a major aforestation programme called "Green India" to convert six million hectares of degraded forest land into green areas. The Prime Minister also called for a long-term strategy to deal with glacial melting of the Himalayas. The meeting decided that a national strategy paper on climate change will be prepared before the end of the year. Participants at the meeting emphasized the need for funding research on impact of climate change including research on management of impact of droughts and floods on crop production and urban planning. Participants emphasized the vital importance of encouraging public transportation in urban areas, reducing dependence on fuel inefficient technologies. Emphasis was placed on collection of reliable data, funding of research for analyzing the data and implementation of practical programmes to improve energy efficiency and reduce wasteful use of natural resources. The National Council on Climate Change has been asked to come forward with a national strategy that protects India's developmental goals and interests while at the same time addressing concerns, both at home and abroad, with respect to global warming and sustainable development.

1871. (13-7-2007) NEW DELHI : Prof. Saifuddin Soz, the Union Minister of Water Resources has written to Chief Ministers drawing their attention to some of the important issues related to water resources, viz. challenges in water sector in the form of declining per capita availability of water, deterioration in quality, over-exploitation of ground water resources leading to lowering of water table in some areas, cost and time overruns in completion of irrigation and multipurpose projects and poor maintenance of the existing system. Further, natural disasters related to water *i.e.* floods and drought are also required to be addressed in proper perspective. In his letter Prof. Soz brought into their notice several reports appearing recently in the media about the impact of climate change on water resources. It remains a fact that climate change and its effects are important issues and necessary studies are required to be taken up on priority with a view to have realistic projections of the impact of climate change and plan appropriate strategies. The Minister informed them that the average annual rainfall in the country is about 1170 mm with an equivalent volume of rainwater of about 4000 billion cubic meter (BCM). After accounting for the losses for evaporation and evapotranspiration, the average annual water availability has been estimated to be about 1869 BCM. However, there is a very high degree of variability both in space and time. Owing to topographical constraints and hydrological features, only about 1123 BCM has been assessed as utilizable which comprises 690 BCM of surface water and about 423 BCM of replenishible ground water. Prof. Soz expressed his concern that due to population growth, industrialization, urbanization and improvement in the living standards, the water requirement for various purposes is increasing year after year. As per the assessment made by the Standing Sub-Committee of the Ministry of Water Resources, the water requirement could be of the order of 1447 BCM by the year 2050 when the population is expected to stabilize. The requirement can be reduced with adoption of better management practices through improvement in efficiency. The National Commission for Integrated Water Resources Development has assessed that with introduction of better management practice the ultimate water requirement would be of the order of 1180 BCM by the year 2050. The Minister suggested the Chief Ministers to take some immediate necessary actions in respect of Improving the efficiency of created facilities for water utilization for various purposes by adopting better management practices; Planning and implementation of various projects / schemes for conservation of water resources to meet the future requirements; and Augmenting the utilizable water. The Minister emphasized that it is necessary to optimally utilize the created facilities in an efficient manner with due emphasis on the sustainability-both physical and financial. We have to (i) take necessary legislative measures, (ii) put in place an appropriate regulatory mechanism, and (iii) encourage participatory management. The Minister appreciated that many States have already taken appropriate action in respect of legislation for ground water management and immediate action is required to be taken by all the States. Further, successful implementation of the measures that would be taken in this behalf should be ensured. He felt that appropriate Water Resources Information System should be put in place at the earliest as this will help considerably in better monitoring. The Minister cautioned the Chief Ministers that the availability of water is highly variable. Therefore, we have to conserve water through a judicious mix of major, medium and minor projects with due emphasis on traditional system of water harvesting. He emphasized that comprehensive and integrated approach to planning is the need of the hour. The Minister said that the National Advisory Council on Recharge to Groundwater, established by Government of India last year, has taken several measures in connection with the management of groundwater. Some of the success stories will be explained to the nation during the Groundwater Congress that will be held in New Delhi on September 11, 2007. We have, however, to be conscious that we are not utilizing our surface water optimally and it is a great disadvantage to us. We have to create facilities for storing water by completing all the on-going projects in a time bound manner and planning for new schemes. Storage sites provided by nature need to be utilized fully and optimally.

1872. (13-7-2007) NEW DELHI : The Karnataka Chief Minister, Shri H. D. Kumaraswamy met the Union Home Minister, Shri Shivraj Patil here today and apprised him of the floods situation in the state. Sh. Kumaraswamy also submitted to the Home Minister a memorandum for central assistance. The Home Minister assured the Chief Minister of all possible central assistance. Shri Patil said that a team would be sent to Karnataka immediately to assess the damage, caused by the floods. He assured the Chief Minister that the second instalment of central share of the Calamity Relief Fund (CRF) amounting to about 47 crore rupees would be released in advance at the request of the state government.

1873. (13-7-2007) NEW DELHI : Ministry of Rural Development has requested all the State Governments to follow the system of joint inspection of Pradhan Mantri Gram Sadak Yojana (PMGSY) Roads Projects by public representatives as has been introduced by the Rajasthan Government since the system adopted by the State is a 'good practice' for enhancing transparency and accountability in execution of projects under the scheme. Rajasthan Government has recently introduced a system of inviting public representatives for joint inspection of road projects undertaken under PMGSY to ensure accountability, transparency and quality control regime. The system provides for fixed periodic joint inspection by public representatives at different tiers. Under the arrangement, the Superintendent Engineer of the concerned Zone or region where a project is executed requests the Member of the Parliament and the Zilla Pramukh representing that zone or the region once in six months to select any PMGSY Project for joint inspection. Similarly, the Executive Engineer in-charge of a division requests the Member of Legislative Assembly and Chairman of the concerned Intermediate Panchayat for joint inspection once in three months of any PMGSY Project of their choice and convenience. The system has also provision for the Assistant Engineer in-charge of the sub-division to request 'Sarpanch' of the Gram Panchayat once in two months to select any project for joint inspection. PMGSY has built-in mechanism for effective quality monitoring as well for ensuring transparency in the execution of projects which includes third party quality audit by independent State Level and National Level Monitors, provision for Citizen Information Boards and placing all the details relating to the projects under execution in the Citizens' Domain of the Online Monitoring System. The measures are expected to further strengthen accountability and transparency in the execution of the rural roads projects under Bharat Nirman.

1874. (13-7-2007) NEW DELHI : Prof. Saifuddin Soz, the Union Minister of Water Resources has written to the Chief Ministers on a couple of suggestions relating to "Conservation of Water". He has requested the Chief Ministers to make a gesture that we should consider water to be a precious gift of nature and we are interested in its conservation in many ways. In his letter Prof. Soz urged the Chief Ministers to consider introduction of small water bottles, say of 200-250 ml at all conferences, meetings, exhibitions etc., wherever drinking water is to be provided. The big bottle has to go as it represents a culture and taste for wastage of this precious resources. He also suggested them to consider to urge people to offer a small glass of water, when required to inculcate a habit of saving water. The guests may take water as much as they like, but they should be offered water in small measures. He urged the CMs to consider issuing instruction prohibiting people from irrigating flower-beds, lawn and kitchen gardens out of the pipes carrying drinking water. He brought to the notice of the Chief Ministers the fact that all the bottled water comes from the ground water which is already under great pressure due to rising demand.

1875. (13-7-2007) NEW DELHI : Speaking at a function on "Against Female Foeticide" organized by the National Federation of Indian Women (NFIW) in New Delhi today, the Union Minister for Health & Family Welfare, Dr. Anbumani Ramadoss said a long-term solution to the problem of female foeticide lies in creating the right socio-economic environment, where sons and daughters are equally valued. This can be achieved by creating awareness about the gender equality through advocacy and communication efforts along with empowering the women suitably. Besides, Mt. Annie Raja, General Secretary of the NFIW and other members of the Federation, Smt. Mohini Giri, Former Chairperson, National Commission for Women were also present at the function. Praising the efforts made by the Federation in creating awareness among the younger generation to the problem of declining sex ratio, the Minister said the answer lies in creating awareness about the true worth of women, the irrelevance-and also the illegality-of sex selection, and the need to question old and outdated rituals and social behaviour. Speaking further he said that legislation like Pre-conception and Pre-Natal Diagnostic Techniques (Prohibition of Sex Selection) Act (PNDT Act) alone cannot solve the problem of sex selection practices and its impact on the adverse sex ratio. It also requires social mobilization. However, if the provisions of the Act are enforced effectively, it can substantially curb such practices and send a loud and clear message to the violators in particular and the society at large that gender-based discrimination shall not be permitted. The Implementation of the Act rests with the States and Union Territories through the Appropriate Authorities appointed under the Act at State, District as well as at Sub-district levels. The violators of the Act are punishable with imprisonment up to 5 years and fine up to Rs.1 lakh, along with cancellation of registration of the license. Under the Act, units using Ultrasound equipment should get themselves registered with the local Appropriate Authorities, failing which they may be sealed and seized. The Minister added that Government of India is taking keen interest to improve the primary health care services in the country. The recently launched National Rural Health Mission would address the problems including the declining sex ratio. Law alone will not be able to solve the problem. Each one within his or her own domain, has to play a role to curb this practice whether as parents, teachers, doctors, lawyers, journalists etc. All of us have to work together to create a gender-balanced society.

1876. (13-7-2007) NEW DELHI : With effect from 15.7.2007, the advance reservation period for booking of rail tickets will be reduced from 90 days to 60 days, and the bookings will be done accordingly. However all the bookings done upto 14.7.2007 under the Advance Reservation Period of 90 days will remain intact. While cancellation of bookings made beyond the period of 60 days will however be permitted. There will be no change in the limit of 360 days for advance booking period for foreign tourists and 30 days for certain day time express trains like Taj Express, Gomti Express, Shane-Punjab Express, etc.

1877. (13-7-2007) NEW DELHI : Ministry of Human Resource Development has conducted a detailed review in a Secretary-level Meeting with the representatives of 16 State governments having a sizeable Urdu speaking population, on the status of implementation of the two Central Government Schemes, *i.e.*, Appointment of Urdu Teachers and the Area Intensive Scheme and Modernization of Madarsas. As a part of the PM's New 15 Point Programme for Welfare of Minorities, Points 3 and 4 concern the Ministry of HRD. Point no 3 says 'Central assistance will be provided for recruitment and posting of Urdu language teachers in primary and upper primary schools that serve a population in which at least one-fourth belong to that language group'. Point no. 4 is 'The Central Plan scheme of Area Intensive and Madrassa Modernisation Programme provides basic educational infrastructure in areas of concentration of educationally backward minorities and resources for the modernisation of Madrassa education'. During the review of Status of Utilisation of funds under the Xth Five Year Plan, it was found that though substantial funds that have been released to various State Governments (Andhra Pradesh, Chhattisgarh, Orissa, Maharashtra, Assam, Delhi, Punjab, Haryana, Tamil Nadu, Uttarakhand, Gujarat, West Bengal etc.) for appointment of Urdu teachers, these were not fully utilized by some of the States and unspent balances are lying with several of them. Similar is the case with funds released under Madrassa Education Programme. The State governments were urged to undertake a survey of Urdu speaking population and availability of schools in these areas so as to come up with concrete proposals and seek assistance from the Central Government under the existing schemes. It was also decided to remove the cap of assistance of Rs. 50,000 per teacher per annum so that the entire salary amount can be reimbursed, and to provide assistance to any area, even if it is smaller than a block, where 25% or more population is Urdu speaking. It has been decided that more Madarsas for girls should be covered by the scheme for Madrassa modernization and the State governments need to pay special attention on the same. The States were requested to forward their comments on the proposed revision of the scheme of modernization of Madrsas during the 11th Plan. States were also requested to give widest possible publicity to the benefits under the Scheme which covers Madarsas volunteering to introduce modern subjects by reimbursing them for expenditure on salaries of two teachers and one time assistance for book banks and teaching aids. It was impressed upon all States that proposals for 2007-08, based on a proper assessment of Urdu speaking population, should be sent within a fortnight. States were urged to stick to this target if funds are to be made available reasonably early so that implementation could commence. It would also be necessary for State Governments and the Department of Higher Education to monitor implementation on a regular and time bound basis. The outlay for the current year under the Scheme of Madrassa Modernization is Rs 55 Cr. The expenditure during Xth Five Year Plan on the combined schemes of Area Intensive and Madrassa Modernization was Rs 142.27 lakhs.

1878. (13-7-2007) NEW DELHI : The Ministry of Rural Development has sanctioned Rs. 37.46 crore to the Government of Arunachal Pradesh towards balance of first instalment of funds against the provisional allocation of Rs.112.41 crore made for the Government of Arunachal Pradesh under the Centrally sponsored Accelerated Rural Water Supply Programme (Normal) of Rajiv Gandhi National Drinking Water Mission, during the year 2007-08. Up to 15 per cent of funds released under this sanction may be utilized for Operation & Maintenance and up to 5 per cent of funds may be spent for taking sustainability measures. States have been requested to delegate powers for management of Rural Water Supply Schemes through the Panchayati Raj Institutions (PRIs) as per the Constitution of India. As such Operation and Maintenance of the completed RWS Scheme should be transferred to the PRIs. No expenditure shall be incurred on taking water quality problems form the present release, as there is a separate allocation for the purpose. This release is being made for execution/completion of schemes to provide safe drinking water facilities to rural habitations and schools under the Centrally Sponsored ARWSP. Priorities set in ARWSP guidelines and through other instructions issued from time to time shall be followed for coverage of rural habitations and rural schools.

1879. (13-7-2007) NEW DELHI : An amount of Rs. 40.80 crore has been sanctioned by the Ministry of Rural Development to the State Government of Orissa towards first instalment of 45% of Central Share of Rs. 90.68 crore for tackling 2,425 water quality affected habitations (46 fluoride, 428 Salinity and 1951 Iron) under Revised Sub Mission programme of Accelerated Rural Water Supply Programme (ARWSP)-(Quality) of Rajiv Gandhi National Drinking Water Mission (RGNDWM) during the year 2007-08. The total cost for tackling these 2,425 water quality affected habitations is Rs.124.29 crore. States have been requested to delegate powers for management of Rural Water Supply Schemes through the Panchayati Raj Institutions (PRIs) as per the Constitution of India. As such Operation and Maintenance of the completed RWS Scheme should be transferred to the PRIs. All terms and conditions indicated in the revised Sub-Mission guidelines are to be strictly followed. Monthly and Quarterly progress report are to be sent urgently.

1880. (13-7-2007) NEW DELHI : Curtains were finally drawn on the second bilateral Indo-UK air exercise-Indradhanush 2007, which concluded on a high note here at Royal Air Force (RAF) Waddington on Thursday. The exercise that began with a series of 1vs1 sorties, reached its crescendo with a highly complex conceivable scenario-a 6vs6 aerial combat involving 4 x Su-30 MKIs, 4 x F3 Tornadoes, 2 x Typhoons and 2 x GR9 Sea Harriers of the Royal Navy. Also airborne were an IL-78 MKI air-to-air refueller and an E3D Sentry AWACS aircraft in the vicinity of the exercise. Air Chief Marshal FH Major, Chief of the

Air Staff (CAS), Indian Air Force (IAF) who is on an official tour to UK currently, was present at RAF Waddington to see the exercise culminate and meet the participating IAF team members. Air Chief Marshal Sir Clive Loader, Commander-in-Chief (CinC) Air Command, RAF accompanied the CAS during the visit. This was the first time that the IAF carried out an exercise anywhere in UK. It was also an exercise where the IAF Su-30 MKI's maiden arrival over the European sky was keenly awaited by thousands of aviation aficionados and spotters, who thronged the perimeter of the airbase unfailingly on a daily basis, all through the exercise duration. This was also an opportunity that provided social and cultural interaction between the two countries. The visit by the IAF team also coincided with the Waddington International Air Show and the Royal International Air Tattoo (RIAT) at Fairford, within a span of two weeks. IAF participation at the two events were a coup of sorts for the organisers. Having been adjudged the 'best static display' at Waddington air show, expectations are already soaring high at the RIAT, the world's biggest air show. The exercise wasn't about winners or losers, yet both sides ended on a winning note. "It was an excellent learning curve for our pilots who will go back with a lot of experience" said the Indian Air Chief. He also thanked the Government and the RAF in England for hosting the IAF. The RAF C-in-C termed the exercise as an 'outstanding success'. Earlier, Station Commander RAF Leeming, Group Captain E Stringer while briefing the visiting CAS stated that the |RAF had adopted a 'building-block' approach to meet future IAF training and coalition aspirations. "The exercise achieved all its aims and objectives"-he further stated. Summing up on the RAF experience he said that a major outcome of the exercise was the appreciation of the fact that the two Air Forces actually "see the world through similar eyes", and that there were many "commonalities" in the tactical procedures of the two air forces, thereby laying a foundation for further RAF-IAF interactions.

1881. (13-7-2007) NEW DELHI : The 23rd Conference of Chief Commissioners and Directors General of Income Tax will be held on 17th and 18th July, 2007 in New Delhi. The Conference will begin with the address of the Finance Minister, Shri P. Chidambaram. The Conference will deliberate upon strengthening the TDS mechanism, strategies for maximizing collection; reduction of arrears and widening of tax base. The progress of computerization and the topic of information collection and monitoring mechanism will also be discussed alongwith the issue of human resource management. Senior officials of the Finance Ministry will also attend the Conference. The Valedictory address will be delivered by Shri S.S. Palanimanickam, Minister of State for Revenue.

1882. (13-7-2007) NEW DELHI : The Government has extended the term of the Delimitation Commission by one year. According to a notification issued by the Legislative Department of the Ministry of Law and Justice, the term of the Commission has been extended up to July 31st 2008. This is the second extension given to the Commission. The Delimitation Commission constituted under the

Delimitation Act 2002, was initially given a term of two years to complete the work of delimiting the Lok Sabha and the Legislative Assembly Constituencies all over the country. The Commission headed by Justice Shri Kuldeep Singh became functional in November/December 2002. As the Commission could not complete its work within the stipulated time period due to many factors such as amendment in Delimitation Act 2002 replacing figures of census 1991 to that of census 2001, dissolution of the 13th Lok Sabha and consequent re-nomination of Associate Members from the 14th Lok Sabha etc., the term of the Commission was extended upto July 31st 2007.

1883. (13-7-2007) NEW DELHI : The Department of Health in the Ministry of Health & Family Welfare, Government of India has issued a draft Prevention of Food Adulteration (Amendment) Rules published vide notification GSR 368 (E) dated 22.05.2007 in the Gazette of India, (Extraordinary) in Part II, section 3, sub-section (i) dated 22.05.2007. The proposed amendments are in respect of irradiation of food products on class basis which have been categorized into 7 classes along with specific purposes of irradiation such as for controlling/inhibiting sprouting, delay in ripening, insect disinfestations, shelf-life extension etc. The details of the notification are available on the Ministry of Health & Family Welfare's website *i.e.* http://www.mohfw.nic.in/pfa.htm. The draft rules are published for inviting public comments for a period of 60 days from the date of availability of the notification to the public. Comments, if any, may be sent to the Secretary, Ministry of Health and Family Welfare, Government of India, Nirman Bhawan, New Delhi within the stipulated time period.

1884. (14-7-2007) NEW DELHI : Progress in promoting affirmative action by Industry reviewed. The second meeting of the Coordination Committee to promote Affirmative Action in the Indian Industry was held today under the Chairmanship of Shri T.K.A.Nair, Principal Secretary to the Prime Minister. Besides Secretaries of the concerned Ministries of Government of India, Presidents of CII and ASSOCHAM, past President, FICCI and other senior representatives of industry attended the meeting. The Committee reviewed the progress made in promoting affirmative action by industry since its last meeting held in October, 2006 and the interaction of senior industry representatives with the Ministry of Industry & Commerce in November, 2006. Since then CII and ASSOCHAM have finalized a Code of Conduct on Affirmative Action being followed by its members and circulated it amongst the members for adopting it. FICCI agreed to soon evolve a similar plan of action for its constituents. There was also agreement that an Ombudsman with regional benches would be set up by each apex chamber to monitor the compliance of the voluntary Code of Conduct by its members. Realising that there is need to enhance their employability, all the Chambers agreed to intensify their efforts in developing the skills sets of SC/ST persons. They are already participating in public-private partnership launched by the Union Ministry of Labour & Employment to adopt 300 ITIs during the current year and develop them as centres of excellence. While noting that stipends are available under the existing government schemes to enable SC/ST candidates to pursue courses in various ITIs, the Chambers agreed to top up, the financial incentives as needed, so as to ensure that the available seats for SC/ST candidates in ITIs do not remain unfilled. In addition, they also agreed that skill development efforts through other mechanisms and institutions are also needed, particularly in those districts where there is heavy concentration of SC/ST population. Another element of affirmative action agreed to by industry was with respect to developing entrepreneurial abilities amongst SC/ST persons. It was noted that all the hambers have taken significant steps during the last few months to promote entrepreneurship through professional agencies. CII mentioned that 345 SC/ST persons selected, after an intensive selection process are currently undergoing training to become entrepreneurs at 7 centres in different parts of the country with the assistance of Entrepreneurial Development Institute, Ahmedabad and during the current financial year it expects to train 500 such persons. FICCI announced the setting up of four such entrepreneurial development centres in each of which it would annually train 600 SC/ST persons. ASSOCHAM indicated that 300 of nearly 1000 candidates trained by it, have already set up their new ventures. There was general agreement that there should be positive discrimination in employment in favour of SC/ST persons, *i.e.*, other things being equal, SC/ST candidates would be given preference in employment. This approach, according to the industry representatives should result in sizeable increase in employment of these persons in the organized industry. In this context, they agreed that they would include reporting of data on the new employment for SC/ST persons created during the year in the Code of Conduct being prescribed for their members. It was further agreed that the Presidents of the Chambers of Industry and Commerce will together deliberate on what further action needs to be initiated by them to make the programme of affirmative action more responsive. This would include evolving measures for encouraging location of industries in areas dominated by SC/ST persons, creating institutional structures within their organizations to carry out activities for skill upgradation and promoting entrepreneurship, and for raising resources from industry to fund their affirmative action programme. The action taken to implement the programme agreed today would be reviewed by the Coordination Committee after a period of two months.

1885. (14-7-2007) NEW DELHI : The Rashtriya Ispat Nigam Limited is thinking of using pellets as inputs on experimental basis to overcome difficulties of processing iron ore with higher levels of alumina content. The chairman and Managing Drector of the Visakhapatnam based plant said this at the quarterly review meeting of its performance chaired by the Minister of Steel, Chemicals and Fertilisers Shri Ram Vilas Paswan here today. He said, the company had tried this earlier two years back with good results. It is also looking at the option to import one ship load of iron ore from Brazil and a long term shipping contract. Making a presentation, the CMD Shri P.K. Bishnoi said, the net profit during the fourth quarter at Rs.

504 Crore was nearly 59 percent higher than the previous quarter profit at Rs. 318 crore. Net profit for the financial year 2006-07 at Rs. 1363 crore was 8.9 percent more than the previous year which was Rs. 1252 crore. This was also 33.4 percent more than the MOU target for the year which was Rs. 1022 crore. Saleable steel production during the fourth quarter was 871,000 tonnes exceeding the MOU target of 837,000 tonnes by 4 percent. Saleable steel production for the year 2006-07 was 3.29 million tonnes against the MOU target of 3.205 million tonnes. The Minister appreciated the good performance of the plant, which has been working consistently at more than 120 percent of the rated capacity and advised them to improve their performance further. The company is expanding its district sales network and will raise its District Level Dealers from 83 to 182 this financial year and further to 576 by 08-09. Shri Paswan reminded the RINL that the expansion plan being implemented is critical and all efforts should be taken to cut short the delays, if any. On the Corporate Social Responsibility front, he advised the company that the model steel villages being developed should be role models for the entire country. He said, all the public sector undertakings of the ministry should coordinate their efforts to realize best results of the expenditure on the CSR. Model guidelines will be formed by the Ministry of Steel to maximize benefits of the scheme. On the issue of recruitment of Scheduled Castes, Scheduled Tribes and OBCs, Shri Paswan asked the company to ensure due representation to them and quickly fill up vacancies, if any, at the earliest. Secretary Ministry of Steel, Shri R.S Pandey said, the company should develop a plan to insulate itself against fluctuations in the price of inputs. Special Secretary, Shri A.K.Rath, senior officials of the Ministry and RINL were present during the review meeting.

1886. (15-7-2007) NEW DELHI : The Prime Minister, Dr. Manmohan Singh has been conferred with a Degree of Letters (Honoris Causa) by the Chancellor of the University of Jammu, Lt. Gen.(Retd.) S. K. Sinha, in Jammu today. Following is the text of the Prime Minister's address on the occasion : "I am honoured and delighted to receive the Degree of Doctor of Letters (Honoris Causa) that has just been conferred on me by His Excellency the Chancellor of the university. I have received similar honours before but your gesture is indeed very special for me. This beautiful state of Jammu and Kashmir has always had a special place in my heart. More recently, its development and well-being have been on top of my agenda in the Government of India. Let me say, at the very outset, that I have been truly impressed by the remarkable strides that the University of Jammu has made in recent years. I compliment you all, particularly, your dynamic Vice-Chancellor, Professor Amitabh Mattoo. The steps taken by your University to establish itself as a centre for excellence are indeed very impressive. This auditorium in which I stand right now is itself a symbol of excellence. I commend the University's achievements in teaching and research, especially in fields like high-energy physics, glaciology, bio-technology and strategic studies. I am also happy that the University has actively participated in extension work, in partnership with civil society, in disaster management, empowerment of rural women and the efforts at strengthening the region's culture of tolerance and peace. It is precisely this blend of academic excellence, social relevance and aesthetic sensibility that our universities must nurture. Our country has a 5,000 year old history of the human quest for knowledge. Ours has always been a knowledge society. The challenge is now to transform it into a knowledge economy. It is clear that our greatest strength, in years to come, will be our human resources. Our huge pool of young women and men, adequately skilled, can become India's greatest force for progress. I have believed that it is this soft power, not just military strength, which will be the real marker of India's greatness. And I am confident that Jammu and Kashmir's young men and women will become a shining example of this soft power. I am, therefore, here to seek your partnership in building Jammu and Kashmir into a robust and vibrant knowledge economy. As a partner, I commit myself and the Central Government to creating institutions of excellence in the State, which can channelise the creativity and energy of the youth of Jammu and Kashmir. We will together build and strengthen a cadre of extraordinarily skilled men and women who are dedicated to a vision of a peaceful and prosperous Jammu and Kashmir. That alone is a guarantee for sustainable peace in the state. Many new and imaginative initiatives have been taken by the state government, including the opening of a large number of degree colleges and the Universities of Jammu and Kashmir have opened off-site campuses in several parts of the state. Campuses are also being proposed for Leh, Poonch, Ramnagar and Reasi. Much more needs to be done, both in terms of access as well as the quest for excellence. The Knowledge Commission, in its recent report, has recommended a vast expansion of our higher education system. I have recently announced that we intend to establish 30 new Central Universities across the country. I would like at least one of them to be in this State. We also need to address the problems of the educated unemployed, especially in Jammu & Kashmir. In the new globally competitive environment, it is essential to keep upgrading skills, build first-rate infrastructure in our institutions of knowledge and ensure top quality of teaching and training. Fortunately, with the latest developments in Information and Communication Technology it is possible as never before to create such facilities quickly, and with relatively little investment.

1887. (16-7-2007) NEW DELHI : The Prime Minister, Dr. Manmohan Singh condemns the militant kidnappings in Assam as an act of cowardice and inhumanity and condoles the death of Cement Corporation of India official Kailash Nath Jha who died of a cardiac arrest on being kidnapped by militants in the State.

1888. (16-7-2007) NEW DELHI : Government of India have announced the sale (re-issue) of "6.65 percent Government Stock, 2009" under Market Stabilization Scheme for a notified amount of Rs. 5,000 crore (nominal). The Government Stock will be sold through price based auction using multiple price method. The auction will be conducted by the Reserve Bank of India, Mumbai Office, Fort, Mumbai on July 18, 2007(Wednesday). Up to 5% of the amount notified for the sale of stock is reserved for allotment to eligible individuals and Institutions on non-competitive basis as per the Scheme for Non-Competitive Bidding Facility in the Auction of Government Securities. Bids in the prescribed form obtainable from the Regional Director, Reserve Bank of India, Mumbai Office (Public Debt Office), Fort, Mumbai-400 001 and RBI website www.rbi.org.in should be submitted to that Office on July 18, 2007. The NDS members should submit competitive as well as non-competitive bids in electronic format using Primary Market Operation (PMO) module of NDS. All bids should be submitted by 12.30 P.M. The result of the auction will be announced on July 18, 2007 and payment by successful bidders will be during banking hours on July 19, 2007 (Thursday).

1889. (16-7-2007) NEW DELHI : The Civil Aviation delegations of India and Malaysia met on 12-13th July, 2007 in Kuala Lumpur to discuss matters relating to air services between the two countries. The Indian delegation was led by Shri Ashok Chawla, Secretary (Civil Aviation). After extensive discussions, both sides reached an agreement culminating into the signing of an MOU. As per this MOU, the provision of "Multiple designation" has been agreed to enabling the aeronautical authorities of both the sides to designate any number of airlines as they wish to operate on the India-Malaysia route. The capacity entitlement for the designated airlines of both sides has been significantly liberalized, which will lead to progressive enhancement of traffic rights over the next two years. It is further decided that the designated airlines of both sides can operate any number of services to/from 18 tourist destinations in India viz. Patna, Lucknow, Guwahati, Gaya, Varanasi, Bhubaneshwar, Khajuraho, Aurangabad, Goa, Jaipur, Port Blair, Kochi, Thiruvananthapuram, Kozhikode, Amritsar, Visakhapatnam, Ahmedabad and Tiruchirapalli. Also the designated airlines of India are now entitled to operate unlimited direct services from any point in India to Johor Bahru in Malaysia. In order to enhance the air services operations and to make the operations commercially viable, provision of a code-share arrangement has been agreed to. Another important outcome of these discussions is reflected in the form of agreement on an Open Sky Policy without any restriction for all cargo services between the two countries. This Agreement will pave way for growth in air operations between India and Malaysia. As a direct outcome of these talks, the operations of Air India Express on India-Malaysia route are likely to commence soon.

1890. (16-7-2007) NEW DELHI : Shri Sontosh Mohan Dev, Union Minister for Heavy Industries & Public Enterprises has expressed great concern regarding the kidnapping of 5 functionaries at Dillai Parbat Mines operated by the Cement Corporation of India (CCI) at Bokajan, Assam. The preliminary report reveals that nearly 20 armed persons entered the mines area of Bokajan at about 8.00 p.m. in the night of 15th July, 2007 and kidnapped Shri K.N. Jha, Manager, Dillai Parbat Mines and Shri S.C. Bora, Security Inspector of CCI. They also took away one Home Guard and two persons of contractor who were local Karbis. It seems that the kidnapping attempt could not be fully successful as the dumper carrying them was stuck. When the kidnappers made them walk, it seems Shri Jha collapsed and others could flee because of the confusion which was created. Shri Bora and the Home Guard have reported back to CCI camp office whereas the other two persons of the contractor have not made any contact as yet. A rescue party found the body of Mr. Jha at the place of incident and he was brought back to the hospital for post mortem. On hearing of the incident, the Minister had called up the DG Police, Assam in the night of 15th July for necessary combing operation which has yielded results. He called on the Prime Minister today to discuss the emerging security related issues with regard to employees of Central PSEs functioning in Assam. Prime Minister has condemned the incident and has directed that necessary security measures should be taken immediately to prevent such incidents from reoccurring. Shri Dev has discussed with the Home Minister and has urged him to immediately review the security arrangements of Central PSEs in Assam. He also has written to the Chief Minister, Assam to strengthen security in the State to safeguard the life and property of Central PSE functionaries in Assam. The Chairman, CCI has gone to the spot for remedial action. In the meanwhile, the body of Shri Jha will be sent to his hometown in Samastipur, Bihar by CCI. CCI will ensure immediate payment of Rs.10 lakh of security insurance which was provided by the company for persons working at the site and in addition, will also pay Rs.2 lakh to the bereaved family as ex-gratia. Minister, HI&PE also spoke to the bereaved family.

1891. (16-7-2007) NEW DELHI : The Government today reiterated the need to implement Pradhan Mantri Rozgar Yojana (PMRY) in letter and spirit and urged the banks to offer collateral-free loans to the unemployed youths of the country. A review meeting on PMRY under the chairmanship of Dr. Chandrapal, Secretary, Ministry of Micro, Small and Medium Enterprises emphasized the need to enhance the target under the PMRY scheme as also various other centrally sponsored schemes being implemented throughout the country. The meeting was attended among others by the representatives of the concerned Departments of various States and Union Territories as also by nationalized banks. Revised guidelines issued for the implementation of PMRY and suggestions/clarifications received from State Governments in respect of different parameters of revised guidelines were discussed in the meeting. Various parameters have been liberalized in the revised guidelines of PMRY. Besides, recovery of loan under PMRY, record maintenance in rural/urban areas, verification of units, utilization certificates were also discussed. Certain operational guidelines have also been included for effective implementation of revised PMRY. Some of them are: (i) No collateral shall be insisted for PMRY loans upto Rs. 5 lakhs. (ii) Of the total target of each State UT, women beneficiaries should constitute at least 30 per cent. (iii) Assistance to SC/ST and Minority beneficiaries should be targeted in such a manner that they are benefited at least in proportion to their population in each District/State; and (iv) preference may be given to develop clusters specializing in specific product at the time of selection of PMRY beneficiaries, etc. Dr. Chandrapal allayed th fears of the banks that the recovery of loan may be difficult as a committe consisting of the District Collector, bank manager etc. will select the entrepreneurs and the viability of the proposed industrial units.

1892. (16-7-2007) NEW DELHI : Agriculture Minister, Shri Sharad Pawar today called upon agricultural scientists to develop linkages of research with the farmer and industry. He was addressing agricultural scientists gathered here from all over the country at the ICAR Foundation Day function, after giving away annual awards for agricultural research. The Minister said that agricultural research has to be geared to address multifarious challenges. Availability of quality seeds, fertiliser and pesticides is of paramount importance. The impact of climate change on agriculture is a major area of concern and therefore, serious attention has to be given to management of natural resources such as water and land. In several major crops, the yield has been stagnating for the last few years, resulting in a lag between the growth in population and the growth in food production. Per capita food availability has shown a declining trend raising concerns about food security. These challenges will have to be addressed and concerted efforts made on various fronts so as to achieve 4% growth in agriculture in the XI Plan, the Minister said. Earlier, the Foundation Day lecture was delivered by Prof. Yash Pal, Chancellor, Jawaharlal Nehru University. Stressing on collaboration of researchers with the farmer, Prof. Yash Pal said that 'the scientists and technologists of ICAR can begin to consider millions of farmers in the country as research collaborators. The whole country can become a laboratory with the world's largest collection of collaborators and innovators.' Minister of State for Agriculture, Shri Kanti Lal Bhuria expressed the hope that India's Agricultural Scientists will soon find solutions to the problems of the farmers. Fifty-four awards under 12 categories were given away to six institutions, 41 scientists, six farmers and one woman journalists. The Best Institution Award has gone to the Central Institute of Fisheries Technology (CIFT), Cochin and Water Technology Centre for Eastern Region, Bhubaneshwar. Rafi Ahmed Kidwal Awards for the Biennium, 2005-2006 have gone to Dr. Nagendra Kumar Singh, Dr. Banawari Mishra, Dr. Thakur Bahadur Singh Rajput, Dr. Vishwa Nath Sharda, Dr. Suman Kumar Pandey, Dr. Devki Nandan Kamara, Dr. Aditya Kumar Misra and Dr. Indrani Karunasagar. Chaudhary Charan Singh Award for Excellence in Journalism in Agricultural Research and Development for 2006 was given away to Mrs. Snehlata Shrivastav for her coverage of problems of cotton growers of Vidarba region of Maharashtra.

1893. (16-7-2007) NEW DELHI : Congress Spokesperson Shri Devendra Dwivedi said that the contentious election for the office of the President has caused severe damage to the institutions of democracy and the Constitutional process. During this period, however, two pillars of our democracy's institutional edifice, the offices of the Vice-President and of the Leader of the Opposition stand specially damaged and denigrated due to the conduct of the present incumbents. Shri Bhairon Singh Shekhawat and Shri L.K. Advani have misconducted themselves in their present offices. Mr. Shekhawat filed his nomination as an independent candidate and continued to hold the office of the Vice-President on the ground that his predecessors who contested and had not resigned. None of them, however, had been a party to a controversial election nor had embarrassing facts about their past had surfaced during the elections. Besides, Mr. Shekhawat cannot dissociate himself from the most outrageous and low level campaign that was launched on his behalf. In retrospect, his independent status looks farcical and his continuance as V.P. has devalued the office. The entire conduct of Mr. L.K. Advani during the campaign has given a body blow to the office of the Leader of the Opposition. The LOP is supposed to be one of the two wheels of parliamentary chariot. Mr. Advani has led and masterminded a highly vicious and malignant campaign based on falsification and distortion of facts and character assassination aimed at devaluation of the electoral process. His letter addressed to the Congress MPs and legislators in which he made disparaging comments about the PM and even dragged the name of the Congress president was a case of rare audacity and political impropriety amounting to political sacrilege. The language used was uncivil, defamatory and devoid of political decency. His letter brought govt-opposition and party-to-party relationship to their lowest ebb. His recent conduct is in tune with his role during the past three years. The responsibility of the leader of the opposition in smooth conduct of the business of Parliament is crucial. During Mr. Advani's leadership of the Opposition, the Lok Sabha proceedings have been regularly obstructed, the Budget deliberations were not permitted and Parliament was even prevented from presenting gracefully an address to the President. He has religiously tried to denigrate the office of the Prime Minister. Mr. Advani has been instrumental in subverting parliamentary system from within and a democratic process from without. Mr. Advani has thus proved his singular unfitness to occupy the post of the LOP. His conduct warrants a condemnation by all concerned. To a question as to when Pratibha Patil will declare her assets, Shri Dwivedi said that my colleagues have earlier responded to this question. Right from the word go we have maintained that we will act according to the Constitution, according to the law of the country and according to the directions of the Election Commission. As a matter of fact, under the law if anybody presents the details of his assets to the Returning Officer or to the Election Commission, legally it is not acceptable. I think what has been done is nothing but gimmickry. From our side whatever will be done, will be done in a responsible way and it will not be a part of competitive populist politics.

1894. (16-7-2007) NEW DELHI : Not without reason it is acclaimed the biggest military air show in the world. With 320 aircraft from 24 countries representing 34 international air arms, and with nearly 2,600 aircrew and ground crew put together converging at the venue with an estimated 17500 visitors, the scenario can hardly be fathomed any bigger. The two-day 'Royal International Air Tattoo' (RIAT), held annually at United States Air Force (USAF) 420 TH Air Base Group at Fairford in Gloucestershire-some 70 miles west of London, concluded over the weekend, on July 14 and 15. The air tattoo is the world's largest military air show and is held annually in support of the Royal Air Force (RAF) Charitable Trust.

The Indian Air Force (IAF), currently celebrating its 75th anniversary, displayed an IL-78 MKI and two Sukhoi-30 MKI fighters at the 'static display'. A single Su-30 MKI flown by Wing Commander H Assudani and Squadron Leader SK Sharma briefly, kept the shutterbugs asking for more. In more ways than one, the continued presence of the IAF at two major military air shows in a row in Europe couldn't have been timed any better, as the IAF is at the threshold of reaching yet another historic milestone this year on October 8. The event also hosted Europe's largest tribute to the USAF on its 60th anniversary, a relationship that was built up between the RAF and USAF when the latter separated from the US Army in 1947. The air tattoo also marked the 65 th anniversary of the US Air Force in Europe (USAFE). Coming close on the heels of IAF's maiden participation at the Waddington International Air Show in which the IAF display was adjudged the best 'static display', the trio of IL-78 MKI flanked by two formidable Su-30 MKIs simply took off from where it left at Waddington, and continued to draw huge fans at their spot. Significantly, a single Hawk aircraft, complete with IAF markings and tricolour roundel, that are set to arrive in India later in September this year, also made a silent static debut at the RIAT. A prize for guessing the right answer as to which Air Force the aircraft belonged, entitled winners to get a RIAT aircraft checklist. Among the guests attending the Air Tattoo were HRH Prince Michael of Kent; HRH Prince Faisal of Jordan; HRH the Duke of Kent; Baroness Margaret Thatcher; Gen. T Michael Moseley, Chief of the US Air Force; Air Chief Marshal Sir Glenn Torpy, Chief of the Air Staff, RAF and Air Chief Marshal FH Major, Chief of the Air Staff, IAF and Mrs Zareen Major. With hundreds of aircraft parked in the vast expanse of the airfield, veteran aviation buffs were taken down the memory lane as some of the old-time favourites such as the Spitfires, Hurricanes and Douglas DC-3 Dakota, also flown once upon a time by the IAF jostled for attention. There was also the legendary P-51D Mustang. It was not easy to pick one from the other given their aviation history in different eras. A Brazilian Embraer R-99A airborne early warning aircraft, which is rarely seen outside South America was also at the display including a Canadian CT-142 navigational training aircraft from the City of Winnipeg Squadron and two Turkish Air Force NF-5Bs. The outstanding aircraft of the modern era also stood out with their uncharacteristic features such as the F-117A Nighthawk Stealth Fighter of the USAF, Eurofighter Typhoons, F-16 Fighting Falcons, F-15E Strike Eagles, F/A-18C Hornets, F-86A Sabre fighters, B1B Lancaster Bomber, Hawks, F3 Tornadoes, Nimrod MRA4, Gulfstream G550, USAF C-130 Hercules and India's formidable Su-30 MKIs and a towering IL-78 MKI to name a few.

1895. (16-7-2007) NEW DELHI : Shri Kapil Sibal, Union Minister for Science and Technology & Earth Sciences, today congratulated the team of 21 Young Indian Scientists/Students who represented India at the 57th Meeting of Nobel Laureates & students in Medicine & Physiology and related subjects at Lindau in June 2007. This was the Seventh team deputed by India. Department of Science and Technology (DST) launched this programme in 2001 for participation of young Indian Scientists in the Annual Meetings of Nobel laureates & Students in Lindau, which is jointly sponsored by the DST from Indian side and the Committee for the Meeting of Nobel laureates & Students and German Research Foundation (DFG) from the German Side. Addressing the young scientists who called on him in New Delhi, Shri Sibal urged them to make best use of the opportunity of the meeting with the best brains in the field by appropriately applying the ideas in their own research. He said the purpose of the programme is to get inspiration from Nobel laureates who are simple persons with great sense of purpose. After listening to the experiences of each young scientist the Minister gave an assurance that his Ministry will facilitate a Lindau like meeting soon in India so that more Indian students get the opportunity to interact with the great minds in Science and students from other parts of the world. The meeting at Lindau lasts for one week, always at the end of June/beginning of July and is aimed at open and informal contact between Laureates and young researchers through round table discussion, lectures and personal small group interactions. This year's meeting was dedicated to medicine and physiology with participation by 18 Nobel Laureates and about 500 young scientists from around the world.

1896. (16-7-2007) NEW DELHI : The services in Industry engaged in manufacture or production of mineral oil (crude oil), motor and aviation spirit, diesel oil, kerosene oil, fuel oil, diverse hydrocarbon oils and their blends including synthetic fuels, lubricating oils and the like have been declared as Public Utility Service for another six months from July 16, 2007. According to a notification issued by the Ministry of Labour and Employment in this regard, this has been done in public interest. The said industry was earlier declared a Public Utility service from January 16, 2007 for six months. The employees in this industry, as a result, would among other things be required to give notice to their employer six weeks in advance of proceeding on strike so that conciliatory proceedings could be started. During the conciliatory proceedings and seven days after their completion, the employees in this industry cannot go on strike.

1897. (16-7-2007) NEW DELHI : Defence Minister Shri A K Antony has called for aggressive Indigenisation in Defence Production. Addressing the Defence Ministry Consultative Committee Meeting on Defence Shipyards in Delhi today, he said this will not only include Defence PSUs but also the private sector. Shri Antony said to achieve this both public and private sector must invest more on research and development. The Minister said the stress on Indigenisation is required because of delay in supplies from foreign vendors which sometimes happens due to change in policy. He said sometimes we find the quality of imported equipment is also not upto the mark. While advocating more and more cooperation between public and private sector Defence industry, the Minister cautioned that this will not be done at the cost of Defence PSUs. The Defence Minister also directed the Defence Ministry officials to explore the possibility of setting up an institution to cater to the design needs of the Armed Forces related to ships, submarines, aircraft and other equipment. He said "I must also state that the design capabilities of Indian Defence Shipyards leave much to be desired. One of the major challenges, facing the shipyards is the lack of design capabilities." Shri Antony said, shipyards and Navy should take immediate measures to upgrade their design house or tie up with well known global majors. The Defence Minister said the Defence shipyards constitute an important element of India's indigenous Defence production capabilities. The Minister informed the members that the total value of production of the three Defence shipyards during the year 2005-06 was Rs. 1430.33 crore, which rose to Rs 2557.51 in 2006-07. He said unlike other DPSUs, the Defence shipyard share a very close relationship with their customer *i.e.* Indian Navy. The Defence Minister said, the Navy has prepared a maritime perspective plan that outlines the total requirement of ships, submarines, etc. upto the year 2022. Shri Antony also informed the members that the three shipyards *i.e.* Mazagon Dock Limited, Garden Reach Shipbuilders and Engineers Ltd. and Goa Shipyard Ltd. are Miniratna category I and have shown consistent profits during the last three years. He said today the 'order-book' position of the three shipyards is comfortable. "The shipyards have embarked on major modernization projects and their focus is on reducing build times and keeping abreast of various technological developments in shipbuilding. Thus, in future a holistic approach on shipbuilding is proposed to be followed by the shipyards", the Minister added. The members while appreciating the performance of the three shipyards made various suggestions to further improve their working. Many members were of the view that the shipyards should seriously look into the problem of time and cost overrun. A member suggested that instead of going for outsourcing the shipyard should try to develop required capabilities, indigenously. A suggestion was also made to send the engineers and technicians from these shipyards to abroad for higher training instead of going for outsourcing. A member suggested the need for benchmarking the products for shipyards so that it could be compared with the best in the world. Another member suggested that salary structure of technicians in the shipyards to prevent them from quitting the job in large numbers. Another member suggested that Government should explore the possibility for securing order for these shipyards from abroad. Earlier, Shri PK Rastogi Addl Secretary Defence Production gave a detailed power point presentation about the three shipyards.

1898. (16-7-2007) NEW DELHI : Grant-in-aid of Rs. 50 lakh has been released by the Ministry of Rural Development to the District Rural Development Agency in Pondicherry towards balance payment of first instalment of funds under 'Swarnjayanti Gram Swarojgar Yojana' (SGSY) during the year 2007-08. Rs. 25.00 lakh has already been released as part of first instalment out of the central allocation of Rs.1.50 crore. The amount should be utilized on the Programme as per approved guidelines of SGSY. The funding pattern will be 75:25 by the Centre and the State. The State Govts/DRDAs/ZPs are also to ensure to submit the report of State and District Levels Vigilance & Monitoring Committee meeting held during current year by March 31, 2007, otherwise Ist instalment during the next year will be held up. The State Government should release its share within one month of the date of release of the Central assistance. Under SGSY, assistance is given to the poor family living below the poverty line for taking up self-employment. It actively promotes group approach by organising the rural poor into Self-Help Groups.

1899. (16-7-2007) NEW DELHI : United Kingdom is one of the most important source markets for India, with over 7 lakh tourists from UK visiting India during 2006. Various promotional activities are being undertaken to further tap the immense potential of this market. Advertising through various media to ensure greater visibility of "Incredible India" Campaign in the market is ensured. With a view to having an effective presence of Incredible India in London, during the "India Now" event, so as to benefit from the reach it would offer amongst visitors at the event, the Ministry of Tourism, Govt. of India is participating in this event, by way of undertaking an extensive Media Campaign in the print and electronic media as well as on buses, taxis and outdoor panels in Central London, during the 3 month period (July to September 2007). As part of the campaign some of the Buses and Taxis plying along the main routes in London will wear a vibrant look with "Incredible India" colours. Outdoor panels will highlight some of London's landmarks through "Incredible India" visuals and the print campaign covering important publications will focus on the close links between India and UK, with the by-line "India is closer than you think". In addition, to the advertising campaign being launched, a series of Road Shows have been planned in UK in August 2007, during the "India Now" event. These Road Shows are being organized in collaboration with the Indian Association of Tour Operators, to facilitate greater interaction of the Indian operators with their counterparts in UK, for promotion of India packages in the UK. 'India Now' is an event being coordinated by the office of the Mayor of London and will be held in London from July to September 2007. This event will comprise a series of India-centric events and activities which will showcase India's contribution to world culture, its rich tradition and more importantly, contemporary India and new Indian trends across art, film, theatre, food, music and fashion. Over 150 cultural organizations from London will participate in this event. It is the biggest festival of India to be staged in the UK, with activities planned across London for the entire season. It is expected that at least one million Londoners and visitors to London will participate in the event and there will be extensive media coverage as well.

1900. (17-7-2007) NEW DELHI : The Prime Minister, Dr. Manmohan Singh, has condoled the death of the Cement Corporation of India official Shri Kailash Nath Jha. In a letter to his wife Mrs. Jha, the Prime Minister said : "Words are inadequate to convey my deep sense of shock and pain at the untimely demise of Shri Jha. His death in Assam due to kidnapping by the militants has caused an irreparable loss to your family and the Cement Corporation of India. In his unfortunate passing away, yet another precious life has been cruelly snatched away from us. The Government of India shares your grief and stand by you and your family at this difficult time. The Government will take all possible measures to extend you the benefits, and all other assistance as permitted by law. This tragic loss has shocked the nation beyond belief. Please accept my heartfelt condolences and convey it to other members of the bereaved family. May the providence give you strength and fortitude to bear this irreparable loss. I pray for peace for the departed soul."

1901. (17-7-2007) NEW DELHI : The Tourism and Culture Minister, Smt. Ambika Soni has said that in acknowledgement of the common heritage between India and its neighbouring countries and promotion of regional solidarity, the visitors from SAARC and BIMSTEC countries will be charged the same rate of entry fees to ASI's ticketed monuments as is charged from Indian citizens. Announcing this in the Consultative Committee meeting of Parliament attached to her Ministries, she further stated that although the debate on charging a uniform entry fee from other foreign visitors is still on, there is a strong point in continuing with the present differential rate of tickets owning to variety of reasons. Giving details of plan expenditure on restoration and maintenance of monuments, Smt. Soni informed the members of the Consultative Committee that the Eleventh Five Year Plan proposals, amounting to Rs. 933 crores, were more than three times the provisions during Tenth Plan Period. A substantial amount of these allocations will be spent on making monuments more attractive by programmes such as Light and Sound Shows at various World Heritage Sites, establishment of tourist facilities and better signage etc. She further stated that additionalities to the budgetary amounts are expected through contributions from business houses and other non-Government agencies to the National Culture Fund (NCF). A need for a more focussed implementation of NCF programmes was also underscored. She invited the members of Parliament to augment this effort by identifying critical projects within their own constituencies and committing some funds under the MPLAD Scheme. Such contributions have now been included under the MPLAD Scheme. Several MPs raised the issue relating to encroachments around national monuments. The issue relating to 100 metres of prohibited area around protected monuments and 200 metres of regulated area beyond that also came up for discussion. The Minister clarified that although ASI was keen to have encroachments removed at all places, it was constrained by its dependence on State Governments for actual removal. Those who attended the meeting are S/Shri Chander Kumar, N.K.S. Chauhan, B. S. Bangawas, Pankaj Chowdhary, N.S. Chauhan, S. Kripalani, Rakesh Singh, Parasnath Yadav, Prasanna Acharya, V. K. Thummar, Shripad Yasso Naik, Sunil Khan, Kunwar Devendra Singh Yadav, Ch. Lal Singh, Ms. Pratibha Singh (all MPs from Lok Sabha), Dr. Chandan Mitra, Dr. Barun Mukherjee and Shri Surendra Motilal Patel (all MPs from Rajya Sabha). Senior officials from the Ministries of Culture, Tourism and ASI including Secretary (Culture), Shri Badal

K. Das, Secretary (Tourism), Dr. Christy Fernandez and DG (ASI), Smt. Anshu Vaish were also present.

1902. (17-7-2007) NEW DELHI : The Prime Minister, Dr. Manmohan Singh called on the President, Dr. A.P.J.Abdul Kalam at Rashtrapati Bhavan today. The meeting lasted 30 minutes. The two leaders discussed matters of national and international importance.

1903. (17-7-2007) NEW DELHI : Dr. Raghuvansh Prasad Singh, Minister for Rural Development today reviewed the ongoing Integrated Wasteland Development Programme (IWDP), Drought Prone Area Programme (DPAP) and Desert Development Programme (DPP) of the 4 States, *i.e.* Madhya Pradesh, Rajasthan, Manipur and Sikkim. The Minister emphasised to streamline and step up the pace of execution of Area Development Programmes under the Hariyali initiative. The Secretary/Principal Secretary, In-charge of these programmes must ensure continuous monitoring & follow up action in execution of these programmes in the respective States. He asked to ensure the online reporting of the progress made so far. The Minister also highlighted the issue relating to capacity building and dedicated machinery for executing the programme, both at the State as well as at National level. He also advised that wherever the NREGA is in progress, necessary convergence between the schemes of Employment Guarantee Programmes and the Area Development Programme be ensured at the ground level. Earlier, Shri Bhaskar Chatterjee, Additional Secretary in the Deptt. of Land Resources, while welcoming the Minister apprised of the progress made by the participating States in the meeting. This meeting was an on-going process of the quarterly progress made by the States under the Hariyali initiative of the Ministry.

1904. (17-7-2007) NEW DELHI : Shri R.C. Jha, CMD, Rashtriya Chemicals and Fertilisers Limited (RCF) today handed over a dividend cheque worth Rs. 51,03,14,900 to Minister for Chemicals & Fertilisers and Steel Shri Ram Vilas Paswan. The Government of India holds 92.5% of the equity in the public sector enterprise. The RCF declared Rs. 55.72 crore at the rate of 10% dividend for 2006-07. Besides Government of India, the financial institutions holding 2.06% equity have earned 1.14 crore rupees while public and corporate bodies holding 5.4% equity got 3 crore. Later, speaking on the occasion Shri Jha said that RCF has become one of the top 10 PSEs on the basis of excellent performance. The Company, crossing Rs. 3500 crore mark for the first time has earned an income of Rs. 3645 crore against Rs. 3187 crore in previous year registering growth of 14.33%. The Company earned a gross profit of Rs. 364 crore as against Rs. 284 crore in previous year. However, the net Profit Before Tax (PBT) at Rs. 241 crore registered an increase of 11.86% over previous year PBT of Rs. 216 crore. He said a DAP Plant is being set up in Rajasthan at Kapasan near Udaipur by a Joint Venture Company Rajasthan Rashtriya Chemicals and Fertilisers Limited (RRCS). RCF is also participating in revival of 2 closed fertilizer units. With the help of

Government, RCF is contemplating to mobilize the necessary resources (Rs. 6500 crore) for these two projects. He further said RCF is coming out with Australian technology to produce load-bearing panels from its waste product Gypsum. These panels will substitute conventional bricks in building houses. These houses will be stronger more economical and less time taking in construction than the conventional houses.

1905. (17-7-2007) NEW DELHI : Certain doubts have arisen in the minds of some of the electors at the current Presidential Election, 2007 and also in the minds of some political parties supporting one or the other candidate at the election, in the wake of a decision stated to have been taken by a group of political parties that the members of Parliament and State Legislative Assemblies belonging to their parties will abstain from voting at the said election. The doubts that have been raised are to the effect whether a member of a political party voting in defiance of the political party's decision would attract the disqualification on the ground of defection under the Tenth Schedule to the Constitution of India or the political party taking such decision would be liable to any penalty for asking their members to vote in a particular manner or not to vote at all. The Commission would like to clarify in this context that the voting at election to the Office of President of India is not compulsory, like the voting at elections to the House of the People and State Legislatures where also there is no compulsion to vote. The 'electoral right' of a voter is defined in section 171A(b) of the Indian Penal Code to 'mean the right of a person to stand, or not to stand as, or to withdraw from being, a candidate or to vote or refrain from voting at election'. Thus, every elector at the Presidential election has the freedom of making a choice to vote for any of the candidates or not to vote at the election, as per his free will and choice. This will equally apply to the political parties and they are free to canvas or seek votes of electors for any candidate or requesting or appealing to them to refrain from voting. However, the political parties cannot issue any direction or whip to their members to vote in a particular manner or not to vote at the election leaving them with no choice, as that would tantamount to the offence of undue influence within the meaning of section 171C of the IPC. The Commission may also like to further clarify that voting at election to the office of President is different from voting by a member of Parliament or State Legislature inside the House and that, as held by the Hon'ble Supreme Court, the provisions of the Tenth Schedule to the Constitution of India may not apply to the voting at the Presidential election. A question arose before the Hon'ble Supreme Court in Kuldip Nayar v Union of India (AIR 2006 SC 3127) whether the provisions of Tenth Schedule to the Constitution would be attracted in the case of the election to the Rajya Sabha if a member of a State Legislative Assembly votes for a candidate in defiance the party's directions, where the votes are now given by the system of open voting. The Hon'ble Supreme Court held that an elector would not attract the penal provisions of the Tenth Schedule for having so voted at the Rajya Sabha election.

Attention may be invited to the following observations of the Hon'ble Supreme Court in that case:-"(183) IT is the contention of the petitioners that the fact that election to fill the seats in the Council of States by the legislative assembly of the State involves 'voting', the principles of Tenth Schedule are attracted. They argue that the application of the Tenth Schedule itself shows that open ballot system tends to frustrate the entire election process, as also its sanctity, besides the provisions of the Constitution and the RP Act. They submit that the open ballot system, coupled with the looming threat of disqualification under the Tenth Schedule reduces the election to a political party issuing a whip and the candidate being elected by a show of strength........ ...... in view of the law laid down in Kihoto Hollohan v. Zachillhu (supra), it is not correct to contend that the open ballot system tends to expose the members of the Legislative Assembly to disqualification under the Tenth Schedule since that part of the Constitution is meant for different purposes." Earlier also, the Hon'ble Supreme Court has observed in Pashupati Nath Sukul v Nem Chandra Jain (AIR 1984 SC 399) that elections to the Rajya Sabha by members of the State Legislative Assemblies are a non-legislative activity and not a proceeding within the State Legislature. The election to the Office of the President is also held by an electoral college which consists of elected members of both House of Parliament and elected members of the State Legislative Assemblies (Article 54 of the Constitution). The electors of this Electoral College vote at the Presidential election as members of the said Electoral College and the voting at such election is outside the House concerned and not a part of the proceeding of the House. Therefore, the above quoted observations of the Hon'ble Supreme Court in the case of Kuldip Nayar (Supra) and Pashupati Nath Sukul (Supra), will apply with equal force at the Presidential election as well. Accordingly, in the Commission's opinion, the voting or not voting as per his/her own free will at the Presidential election will not come within the ambit of disqualification under the Tenth Schedule to the Constitution of India and the electors are at liberty to vote or not to vote at the Presidential election as per their own free will and choice.

1906. (17-7-2007) NEW DELHI : The Central Government (M/o Corporate Affairs), in exercise of powers under section 642 (read with section 605A of the Companies Act, 1956) had prescribed the Companies (Issue of Indian Depository Receipts) Rules, 2004 (IDR Rules), which allowed issue of Indian Depository Receipts by foreign companies. These rules provide, inter alia, for (1) Eligibility for issue of Indian Depository Receipts (IDRs) (2) Procedure for making an issue of IDRs (3) Other conditions for the issue of IDRs (d) Registration of documents (4) Conditions for the issue of prospectus and application (5) Listing of IDRs (6) Procedure for transfer and redemption (7) Continuous Disclosure Requirements (8) Distribution of corporate benefits. SEBI, as capital market regulator, in view of authorization available to it under IDR Rules, has also issued a circular in this regard indicating other eligibility conditions for issuers. Requests were received from SEBI and some stakeholders for review of certain requirements provided in the IDR Rules. These were examined and a draft Notification alongwith an Explanatory Memorandum was placed on the website of the Ministry for comments. Besides, comments of D/o Economic Affairs, SEBI, apex Chambers of Trade & Industry and Professional Institutes (ICAI, ICSI and ICWAI) etc. were obtained.

1907. (17-7-2007) NEW DELHI : The Minister for Sports and Youth Affairs Shri Mani Shankar Aiyar has assured that a mechanism will be put in place to ensure that the sports persons get their reward cheques etc. in a given time frame. Shri Aiyar said that the earlier system of handing over the cheques to the sports person on 29th of August, which is Major Dhayan Chand's Birth Day, will be revived to ensure that no sports person is unnecessarily hassled for collecting the award money. Shri Aiyar was speaking after handing over a cheque of Rs.1.75 lakh to Ms. Chekrovolu Swuro, ace Archer, as an award for her performance in the Asian Archery Championships and the Golden Arrow European Grand Prix. The award was conferred on Ms. Swuro in June 2006. The Minister expressed concern that it took over a year for Ms. Swuro to get a valid cheque from the Ministry of Sports and said that not only in this matter but in all other such matters pending in the Ministry, he will ensure that the money is given to the sports persons at the earliest.

1908. (17-7-2007) NEW DELHI : The Bharatiya Janata Party demands a CBI probe into the multi-crore BSNL tender scam. The nation has a right to know why BSNL approved a much higher rate of US $107 for a GSM connection in a tender amounting to Rs. 20,000 crore than the rate of US $69 that was offered for a similar connection to MTNL recently. Even if the difference between a city connection and rural telephony is factored, the rate approved is evidently phenomenally higher and definitely merits a thorough probe. The UPA regime has become a synonym for corruption. The SEZ scam, wheat import scam, save Quattrocchi scam and now a mobile scam, are all indicative of this. The reported spat on this tender issue between two UPA ministers has proved without doubt that the government is interfering in day-to-day management of BSNL, even after BSNL was corporatised years ago. The present telecom minister Mr. A. Raja has ordered a review on 14th May 2007, even though the purchase order was already in place on 12th May, on the grounds that the order would result in an over payment to the tune of Rs. 10,000 crores. On the other hand, former minister Sh. Dayanidhi Maran has accused a NRI businessman and some other vested interests for trying to stall BSNL's growth. Both these allegations made by the present and former telecom ministers are serious and mandate a CBI probe, for unearthing the truth behind what is emerging to be a scandal of Rs 10,000 crores. The Prime Minister must muster the courage and initiate a tough action on such a vital issue of national importance. The challenge is to unearth corruption on one hand and save BSNL on other hand. The continued interference by the political bosses for narrow vested interests has resulted in BSNL loosing its market share in mobile telephony from 32% in 2006 to 21% in 2007. Inadequate and delayed infrastructure expansion will further erode BSNL's position. The BJP demands that the Prime Minister should immediately order a CBI probe and also divest the present minister of his crucial portfolio as a starting point.

1909. (17-7-2007) NEW DELHI : Shri Arjun Singh, Union Minister for Human Resource Development has said that time has come to make a hard assessment of the Primary Education in India. He said, "this is the last year when we can do something about it and we should have a pragmatic plan after taking into consideration our experience and the suggestions of the members". Shri Arjun Singh was responding to the suggestions offered by Members of the Consultative Committee for the Ministry of Human Resource Development, yesterday. He said that we should take proper stock of things as we, still, have four to five months to go when 11th Plan will be operationalised. Earlier in a power point presentation before the members, the Ministry informed that the number of drop-out rate of primary school children in the age group 6-11 years has decreased from 39 per cent (2001) to 29 per cent (2004) *i.e.* by 11 per cent points. The girls enrolment has increased from 43.7 per cent (2001) to 46.7 per cent (2004) in the age group 6-11 at primary level, and gender gap has reduced from 19 to 6 per cent point in the same period. The Ministry further informed that pupil teacher ratio has improved to 1:41 (2005) at primary level, and many States are in the process of recruiting teachers against the sanctioned posts. The Midday Meal programme reaches out to 10 crore children at the primary stage. The Committee was informed that as per the revised scheme (2006) the cooking cost for conversion of raw grain into a hot cooked meal has been enhanced to Rs. 2/-per child per school day. In the case of NER States Central assistance is provided at Rs. 1.8 per child per school day, while for non NER States, Central assistance of Rs. 1.50 per child is provided. Special attention is being paid to safety specifications, cleanliness and hygiene. The Ministry has also provided funds for construction of 2.21 lakh kitchen sheds as well as procurement of kitchen devices for 5.20 lakh schools. The Ministry has prescribed a comprehensive and elaborate mechanism for monitoring and supervision of the Midday Meal scheme, which includes suo moto declaration of information under the Right to Information Act. The Members were also informed that with the imposition of education cess, resources for elementary education have been significantly augmented. This has resulted in better funding of the two flagship programmes viz SSA and MDM scheme with the objective of attaining the goal of Universal Elementary Education (UEE). In the financial year 2006-07 the proceeds of education cess were released to various States and Union Territories as follows: SSA (5830.67 crores) and Midday Meal (2911 crores). Dr. Harisinh Chavda, Dr. Chinta Mohan, Kumari Bhavana P. Gawali, Shri Asaduddin Owaisi and Shri Ramesh Dube from Lok Sabha and Shri Raashid Alvi, Shri Krishna Lal Balmiki and Dr. Ram Prakash from Rajya Sabha attended the meeting.

1910. (17-7-2007) NEW DELHI : Members of Parliamentary Consultative Committee of Ministry of Steel have said that exports of iron ore should be resorted to only if we have surplus. They said, the demand for iron ore from the domestic producers must be met first. The issue came up during the Parliamentary Consultative Committee Meeting of the Steel Ministry, which met here today to discuss functioning of the Rashtriya Ispat Nigam Limited, Visakhapatnam. Some of the members demanded a complete ban on the export of iron ore while others said, RINL should be given captive iron ore mines on lease. Initiating the discussion Minister for Steel, Chemicals and Fertilisers Shri Ram Vilas Paswan said, production of steel in the country went up by 10.9 percent during 2006-07 and reached 49.39 million tonnes. The revised target for 2010 has been set at 80 million tonnes against the earlier target of 65 million tonnes and the target for 2020 has been set at 200 million tonnes. The two steel majors in the public sector, the Steel Authority of India Limited (SAIL) and the Rashtriya Ispat Nigam Limited (RINL) have initiated a major expansion plans. He said, RINL expansion plan involves a capital outlay of Rs.8692 crore to raise its capacity to 6.3 million tonnes from the current level of 3.4 million tonnes. SAIL is also implementing its expansion plan to raise its capacity to 24 million tonnes from the present 14.6 million tones an investment of over Rs. 40,000 crore. He said, the public sector undertakings under the Ministry of Steel have earned a net profit of Rs. 15,500 crore in FY 07 against Rs. 11,500 crore in the previous year. Expressing satisfaction over the functioning of RINL the Minister said, the company is running at nearly 120 percent of its installed capacity for the last few years. He said, the company, which was referred to BIFR, started earning profit from 2002-03 and has totally wiped out the accumulated losses and is one of the most efficient steel makers in the country today. Shri Paswan said, both SAIL and RINL have been given operational freedom to take investment decisions, which he said should be transparent without compromising with quality. He said, the ministry, which reviews the performance of the companies on quarterly basis, compares their performance on different parameters with private sector companies also. The Minister said, SAIL and RINL have been asked to spend 2 percent of their net profit under Corporate Social Responsibility Scheme for wider benefit of the common people, particularly those living in the peripheral areas of the factory and the mines. RINL, he said, is involved in conducting health melas, distributing artificial limbs and improving educational infrastructure and such other activities. Making a presentation the Chairman and Managing Director of RINL Shri P. K. Bishnoi said, the company which has earned mini-ratna status is focusing on increasing production of value added steel to keep its bottom line rising. He said, the company has excelled in various parameters like asset utilization, energy consumption, and specific water consumption and labour productivity.

1911. (17-7-2007) NEW DELHI : The Civil Aviation delegations of India and Malaysia met on 12-13th July, 2007 in Kuala Lumpur to discuss matters relating to air services between the two countries. The Indian delegation was led by Shri Ashok Chawla, Secretary (Civil Aviation). After extensive discussions, both sides reached an agreement culminating into the signing of an MOU. As per this MOU, the provision of "Multiple designation" has been agreed to enabling the aeronautical authorities of both the sides to designate any number of airlines as they wish to operate on the India-Malaysia route. The capacity entitlement for the designated airlines of both sides has been significantly liberalized, which will lead to progressive enhancement of traffic rights over the next two years. It is further decided that the designated airlines of both sides can operate any number of services to/from 18 tourist destinations in India viz. Patna, Lucknow, Guwahati, Gaya, Varanasi, Bhubaneshwar, Khajuraho, Aurangabad, Goa, Jaipur, Port Blair, Kochi, Thiruvananthapuram, Kozhikode, Amritsar, Visakhapatnam, Ahmedabad and Tiruchirapalli. Also the designated airlines of India are now entitled to operate unlimited direct services from any point in India to Johor Bahru in Malaysia. In order to enhance the air services operations and to make the operations commercially viable, provision of a code-share arrangement has been agreed to. Another important outcome of these discussions is reflected in the form of agreement on an Open Sky Policy without any restriction for all cargo services between the two countries, which will pave the way for the improvement of trade and commerce. This Agreement will pave way for growth in air operations between India and Malaysia. As a direct outcome of these talks, the operations of Air India Express on India-Malaysia route are likely to commence soon.

1912. (17-7-2007) NEW DELHI : In his opening remarks at the Third Meeting of the Mission Steering Group (MSG) of National Rural Health Mission (NRHM) in New Delhi today, the Union Minister for Health & Family Welfare, Dr. Anbumani Ramadoss said the NRHM has now completed two years and during this time the health sector in the country has seen far reaching changes. The process of change is a gradual one and it is necessary to move cautiously, taking the various stakeholders into account. Hon'ble Ministers for Rural Development, Shri Raghuvansh Prasad Singh, Panchayati Raj, Thiru Mani Shankar Aiyar, Minister of State for Health & Family Welfare, Smt Panabaka Lakshmi were present at the meeting. In addition, Shri Naresh Dayal, Secretary (HFW), Secretary, Panchayati Raj, Secretary (AYUSH) and other members of MSG were also present. The following is the text of the Health Minister's speech: "I welcome you all to the third meeting of the Mission Steering Group of NRHM. As you are aware, NRHM has now completed two years. Over the past two years, the health sector in the country has seen far reaching changes. We are all fortunate to be part of the process of architectural corrections being carried out in the sector. The States have demonstrated remarkable enthusiasm in accepting the sector wide paradigm change introduced under NRHM and are at various stages of implementation of the strategies. Over these two years, we have established an unprecedented momentum for change in the health delivery system in the country. We have initiated a series of initiatives, which lead to comprehensive rejuvenation of the health system. The initiatives cover the entire range of activities in the matrix from infrastructure to manpower to logistics & management to decentralization to community participation etc. As you would be aware, the NRHM is a flagship programme of my Ministry. The aim of NRHM is to provide accessible, affordable, accountable, effective and reliable primary health care facilities. The Mission seeks to rejuvenate the health delivery system through comprehensive upgradation of infrastructure, augmentation of manpower and expansion of capacity for training various stakeholders. The Mission seeks to hand over the planning, execution and evaluation of the health programmes with the community based organisations. The health facilities are being made responsive to the community through the Rogi Kalyan Samitis and untied funds are being given to all levels of health facilities and we hope to comprehensively rejuvenate the health system in near future. I would like you to recall the formative stages of NRHM when the strategies were being conceptualized. That was sometime in December of 2004. The officers from my Ministry had a series of consultations with the various stakeholders in the health sector. We talked to the States, public health experts, development partners, medical colleges, industry experts and other departments in the Government of India and then arrived at a vision for the Mission. The related Departments strongly supported the sector wide paradigm of the Mission and we formally launched the mission in April of 2005. Even after that the consultative process continued. All stakeholders have used various platforms provided for under the Mission to add value to the strategies. There have been a large number of review meetings, orientation workshops, discussion sessions with various stakeholders. In fact the states and other stakeholders have been so closely associated with the formulation of the basic strategies under the Mission that the Mission is indeed truly a pan India effort. To that extent it is an unprecedented initiative. In the first two years the States have set-up the basic framework of the Mission including the State Health Mission and the District Health Mission, etc. Simultaneously the orientation programmes for all the participants in the sector have also continued through out the formative years of the Mission. A very large number of training sessions and orientation workshops have been organised at Delhi, in States and also at Mussorie to build capacity amongst the health Departments of all States to carry the Mission forward. The efforts under taken by my Department in such a short time to bring on board such a large number of participants in various States is clearly unprecedented in the history of any programme in the county.

1913. (17-7-2007) NEW DELHI : The Employees State Insurance Corporation (ESIC) has decided to have a comprehensive review of the ESI Act, 1948 in order to improve the quality of medical care to workers as well as to meet their emerging medical needs. This was decided at the 139th meeting of the ESI Corporation here today. Presiding over the meeting the Chairman of the Corporation and the Minister of State (Independent Charge) for Labour and Employment, Shri Oscar Fernandes said that the review would be completed within a time-frame of three months. The meeting was informed that Rs. 168.11 crore were recovered from defaulters as arrears contribution and interest during the last financial year constituting 93.37 per cent of the target. Rs. 100.71 crore were recovered from defaulting units during a special drive launched from November 2006 to March

2007. The meeting was also told that 79 prosecution cases were launched under the ESI Act during the first quarter of the current year. Regarding coverage of new areas the meeting was told that 60 new centres would be covered under the Implementation of the ESI scheme to New Areas as per phased programme during 2007-08 covering over 1.82 lakh employees. The scheme has been implemented in 10 centres up to May 31, 2007 covering more than 10,000 new employees. Shri Chandrakant Khaire, MP and Shri Sharad S. Patil, employees representative, were re-elected as non-official members to the Standing Committee of the ESI corporation.

1914. (17-7-2007) CHENNAI: The Railways is looking for public-private partnership to in introduce ing high-speed trains in select corridors. As such high-speed trains can be operated only on dedicated elevated corridors, costing at least Rs. 70 crore a per kmilometre, private participation has become imperative, according to Southern Railway General Manager Thomas Varghese. There are demands for bullet trains from Chennai to Ernakulam, Bangalore, Coimbatore and Madurai and from Trivandrum to Mangalore. The Railway Board Chairman recently held detailed discussions with Chief Secretaries of Tamil Nadu and Kerala on this issue. As heavy investments are needed to realise these demands, an in-depth market survey on possible clientele who could afford to pay fares on a par with those of airlines would have to be carried out. A bullet train between Chennai and Bangalore would be ideal in view of the increasing passenger patronage between the cities, Mr. Varghese said in an interview on Monday. The Railway Board recently decided to have at least one high-speed corridor in each zone. Chief Minister M. Karunanidhi had written to Railway Minister Lalu Prasad, asking him to consider the possibility of operating bullet trains from Chennai to major cities in the State. Mr.Varghese, who is laying down office on Wednesday after serving in the Indian Railways for over 35 years, said during his two-year stint as General Manager there were no major accidents in the zone. in Southern Railway.

1915. (17-7-2007) NEW DELHI : As a part of its ongoing initiative to launch a countrywide skill upgradation programme for emigrant workers, the Ministry of Overseas Indian Affairs today signed a MOU with the Ministry of Micro, Small and Medium Enterprises. It may be recalled that MOIA had launched a similar project with five State Governments in the year 2006-07. The objective of the MOU is to institute a process to develop and upgrade the skills of Indian workers desirous of emigrating overseas for the purpose of employment. Both the Ministries will work towards developing a framework to benchmark, assess and certify Indian workers seeking employment abroad. This is being done with a view to enhance the image and perception of Indian workers abroad and equip them to be more competitive in an international working environment and promote greater employment opportunities for Indian workers. The programme will also help overseas Indian workers move up the wage chain. While the Ministry of Overseas

Indian Affairs will fund the training programme, the Ministry of Micro, Small and Medium Enterprises will implement the training programme through its training centres across the country. In the year 2007-08, the target will be to train approximately 2,000 emigrant workers in various trades such as electrical, machinist, computers, electronics, welding, plumbing etc. for employment in the Gulf countries. The focus will be on the manufacturing and construction sectors. The duration of the course will vary from 15 days to 3 months. The MOIA proposes to spend upto Rs. 9.00 crores on skill upgradation of workers for overseas employment in partnership with other institutions.

1916. (17-7-2007) NEW DELHI : In a new endeavour, to provide new, modern and improved facilities to the passengers, the Indian Railways today introduced the Train Enquiry call centre, universal telephone number 139. Inaugurating the first phase of the implementation of the Integrated Train Enquiry System (ITES), 'Rail Sampark', the Union Minister of Railways, Shri Lalu Prasad said that introduction of this state of the art facility was announced while presenting the Railway Budget for the year 2007-08 in the Parliament. He said that passengers earlier often complained about railway enquiry telephone lines remaining busy most of the time and now with the introduction of this new computerized train enquiry system, passengers can enquire about arrival and departure of trains, reservation status, fare, concessions etc., by dialing a universal telephone number 139 at local rates. Shri Lalu Prasad further said that initially this facility will be available in eight states and by September this year this facility will be made available throughout the country so that not only urban but rural people are also able to get the desired information instantly by dialing this universal telephone number. The complete network consisting of Interactive Voice Response System and Regional Call Centres is based on state of the art technology and associated processes. This shall enable railways to deliver vastly improved quality of service to our esteemed customer, the Minister added. The Ministers of State for Railways Shri Naranbhai J. Rathwa and Shri R. Velu, Chairman, Railway Board, Shri J.P. Batra and other Board Members will also be present on the occasion. In its first phase Zonal hub for North Region at Delhi and call centre at Noida has been commissioned. Basic Enquiry Services are being made available for general public of Delhi, NCR, Punjab, Haryana Himachal Pradesh, Jammu & Kashmir, Uttar Pradesh, Rajasthan, Uttarakhand state and Chandigarh with MTNL and BSNL as Telecom Service Provider (TSP). The services on other three regions shall be completed by Sep 2007. The services from other TSP shall be made available subsequently. Work of implementation of ITES based on Public Private Partnership model has been assigned to Indian Railways Catering and Tourism Corporation in association with Centre for Railway Informatics System. Execution of Integrated Train Enquiry System is being done by Rail Enquiry Franchisee-M/s Bharat BPO and Bharat Sanchar Nigam Limited. It is consortium firm of Spanco Telesystem & Solution Ltd. and Stracon Backoffice Solution Ltd.

1917. (17-7-2007) NEW DELHI : A meeting of the Consultative Committee of the Ministry of Home Affairs was held here today to discuss the issue relating to the Draft National Policy on Criminal Justice. The Home Minister, Shri Shivraj Patil chaired the meeting. Today's meeting was in continuation of the meeting of the Consultative Committee held on the same subject on May 4, 2007 and July 10, 2007. Taking part in the deliberations, the members welcomed the Government's attempt to draft the National Policy on Criminal Justice. They made certain suggestions during their presentations. These related to issues like admissibility of confessions made to police, control of communal violence, quick disposal of court cases, introduction of the concept of federal crimes, police reforms, victim-orientation to the criminal justice system, etc. The members present at today's meeting included S/Shri Debabrata Biswas, Urkho Gwra Brahma, Lalhmingliana, Raj Mchinder Singh, Dr. K. Malaisamy, Mahmood A. Madani and Jai Prakash Agarwal of the Rajya Sabha and S/Shri Mani Kumar Subba, Nikhil Kumar, Madan Lal Sharma, Manoranjan Bhakta, Raghuvir Singh Kaushal, S.D.Mandlik, Mohan Singh and Dhirendra Agrawal and Smt. B.Susheela of the Lok Sabha. The Ministers of State for Home, Shri Sriprakash Jaiswal and Shri Manikrao Gavit, Minister of State for Rural Development and Parliamentary Affairs, Smt. Suryakanta Patil and the Union Home Secretary, Shri Madhukar Gupta were among those present at the meeting. The deliberations will continue in the next meeting of the Consultative Committee.

1918. (17-7-2007) NEW DELHI : An International Seminar and Exhibition on Naval Armament 'NAVARMS-07' is being jointly organised by the Integrated Headquarters, MOD (Navy) and Confederation of Indian Industry (CII) from 19 Jul 07 to 20 Jul 07 at Hotel Intercontinental, New Delhi. Hon'ble Raksha Mantri will be the Chief Guest for the event. The focus of NAVARMS-07 will primarily be to create awareness about the emerging opportunities for greater participation of Indian and foreign industries in the Indian defence production. The seminar is expected to provide a platform for substantive deliberations towards evolving policies for future selection, sourcing and product support apart from harnessing the potential of public and private partnership for production of Naval Armament. The discussions will also dwell upon evolving maintenance and quality assurance philosophies. The seminar will comprise five plenary sessions. The first session will focus on advances made in armament technology as well as future trends. The second session is structured to appraise the armament manufacturers of the user's concerns and to lay down the basic 'ground rules' for development of a weapon system. The third session on 'Role of Industry-Opportunity and Insight' aims at marketing the possibilities for a manufacturer, be it a small-scale industry or an MNC for armament production. This will be followed by session on "Infrastructure Requirements of the Users and Industry". The synergy that could be brought about by pooling of the technical expertise and resources available with the DRDO and private industry, the infrastructure that would need to be built to promote indigenous production as well as product support are some of the issues that will be deliberated upon. Foreign armament manufacturers from USA, UK, Germany, Italy, Israel and France are also expected to participate in the exhibition and seminar. It is hoped that this maiden attempt would help in bridging the gap between perception of the industry towards armament production and the Navy's expectations from the Industry.

1919. (17-7-2007) NEW DELHI : Shri Kamal Nath, Union Minister of Commerce & Industry, while chairing the Parliamentary Consultative Committee of his Ministry on the subject of "Infrastructure for agro-exports", last evening stated that the agricultural exports have a crucial role to play in the long-term as it has the potential to provide farmers a better price for their produce. "India has a huge potential for organic farming and exports of organic agro-products will be promoted in a big way by the government", he said. The Minister noted that infrastructure remains the major problem confronting Indian agriculture in general and agro-exports in particular. He noted that there was a need to strengthen the cold chain network, transportation, warehousing etc. to ensure that wastage is minimised and the agricultural produce meets high quality standards. Shri Kamal Nath also informed the Members that there was a need to further expand our agro-trade to overseas markets and highlighted the recent success in getting market access for mangoes in Japan and the USA. Australia and New Zealand are yet to open their markets on mangoes while Russia is not allowing import of egg power and meat. There are also other commodities like gherkins and floriculture products that face certain barriers in the EU. "The Ministry is committed to engage with other countries and agencies to remove the current impediments to achieve higher agricultural exports to these markets", he said. Shri Jairam Ramesh, Minister of State for Commerce and Dr. Ashwani Kumar, Minister of State for Industry along with Shri G.K. Pillai, Commerce Secretary and Dr. Ajay Dua, Secretary (DIPP) were also present at the meeting. Members who attended the meeting were: S/ Shri Sharad Joshi, P. Karunakaran, M. Rajasekara Murthi, Naresh Gujral, Abu Asim Azmi, Sudhangshu Seal, Sambasiva Rao, J. M. Aaron Rashid, Ram Singh Kaswan, N.R. Govindarajar, Suresh Prabhu and Rajeev Shukla. Shri Joshi raised the issue of Certification of the quality of agricultural products, noting that there was an urgent need to have recognised laboratories in the country whose certification was valid globally for export purposes. Shri Seal noted that almost 30% of the agricultural produce was wasted due to the lack of cold storage facility and urged the government to take immediate steps to redress the situation. Shri Rajeev Shukla emphasised that lack of infrastructure in the agricultural sector had been a long pending problem and requested the government to ensure better coordination between different ministries viz., Agriculture, Commerce, Finance and Food Processing to ensure that infrastructure development in this area is carried out with priority. The need for better coordination was also reiterated by Shri Suresh Prabhu, who also underlined need for greater public investment in this sector. Shri Kamal Nath also highlighted the need to improve overall agricultural productivity since there was an increasing domestic demand for agricultural products and exports are not possible unless the domestic demand is met. The Minister appreciated the need to set up laboratories for Certification of exports and reiterated the need to develop organic farming. He also noted that the increased competition from different countries such as Vietnam and Sri Lanka in tea necessitated the need to devise a strategy to deal with the increasing competition in this sector. Shri Kamal Nath also hoped that the private sector would supplement the public investment in agro-exports sector pitching in greater investments than ever before. Earlier, Shri K.S. Money, Chairman, APEDA, made a presentation to the members in which he informed that 12 locations have been identified for setting up of centres for handling agro-perishables for exports at Chandigarh, Rai, Muzaffarpur, Agra, Kolkata, Guwahati, Mumbai, Nasik, Pune, Nagpur, Hyderabad and Dharmapuri. The total estimated cost for setting up these centres would be Rs.2500 crore. In another presentation, Shri V.J. Kurien, Chairman, Spices Board, gave an overview of the Indian spices exports and stated that the Indian spices industry has set a target of US $ 10 billion for spices exports by the year 2017. He informed that Regional Quality Control Laboratories are proposed to be set up at Guntur, Mumbai, Chennai and Delhi. This apart, Spices Park are proposed to be set up at Chhindwara (MP) for garlic, chilli and coriander; Idukki (Kerala) for pepper and cardamom; Erode (TN) for turmeric and chilli; Guntur (AP) for chilli and turmeric; Barabanki (UP) for mint and Kota/Jalore (Raj) for coriander, cumin and fennel. Agro exports have grown at a compounded annual growth rate of 9.4% in the Five Year Period from 2000-01 to 2005-06. Total agro exports in 2005-06 were Rs.42,362 crore. Meanwhile, India's spices exports were Rs.3576 crore in 2006-07. The top 3 spices in terms of value of exports are mint products, chilli and oils & oleoresins.

1920. (17-7-2007) NEW DELHI : In the 10th Five year plan Rs.128.47 crore has been sanctioned and Rs.97.42 crore has been released for various projects in Jammu & Kashmir. 12 Tourism Development Authorities at Patnitop, Bhaderwah, Kishtwar, Poonch, Rajouri, Lakhanpur-Sarthal, Pahalgam, Gulmarg, Kokernag, Sonamarg, Leh and Kargil have been identified for specific Tourism Development and an amount of Rs. 118.00 crore has already been sanctioned to the above authorities on the basis of the proposals received from them. Regarding setting up of 50 tourist villages across the State with the allocation of amount Rs.35.00 crore, it was decided in a meeting with Planning Commission that initially 5 pilot villages for development of rural tourism will be taken up. Accordingly, during the Financial Year 2005-06 under the Rural Tourism Scheme of the Union Ministry of Tourism, Govt. of India, 5 projects for development of Rural Tourism infrastructure at Drung in Distt. Baramula, Surinsar in Distt. Jammu, Gagangir, Sonamarg in Distt. Srinagar, Pahalgam in Distt. Anantnag and Jheri in Distt. Jammu received from State Government of J&K have been sanctioned for Rs.50.00 lakh each. In 2006-2007 three more villages Akingaam, Vasaknag, Dori Degair were sanctioned financial assistance of Rs.149.00 lakh under Rural Tourism scheme of the Ministry. Sanction for software work plan for the villages are being provided for development under Capacity Building for Service Providers scheme (CBSP) of the Ministry. The four villages *i.e.* Jhiri, Surinsar and Dori Degair in Distt. Jammu and Akingaam in Distt, Anantnag have already been extended financial assistance under CBSP scheme of the Ministry. Soft loan have been provided to Houseboat owners and Hoteliers/ Guest Houses for their re-establishment. Ministry of Tourism has supported the recommendation on Economic Development on Jammu and Kashmir for upgradation to accelerate renovation and new construction of Houseboat, Hotels and Shikaras by supporting the allocation of Rs.30.00 crores for immediate disbursement as soft loan directly by planning commission. Indian Institute of Skiing & Mountaineering has been upgraded by providing world class ski equipments and snow clearing machines to enable them to run the winter & and water sports in Gulmarg and Srinagar. They have planned 5 water ski courses at Srinagar of 30 students each and all the courses are full. Indian Institute of Hotel Management and Catering is also getting equipped with the new equipment for the coming session. They are also running one year course at the request of State Govt. for Capacity Building. An amount of Rupees three crores have been spent on printing of brochures, CDs, Flyers, bookmarks and advertising Familiarization Tours of Leading Tour Operators/Travel Agents/ Journalist/T.V Teams have been initiated by the Ministry of Tourism to restore the confidence in people about normalcy in J &K. Ministry of Tourism has assisted the Govt. of J&K to successfully organize Singhey Khabab (Sindhu Darshan) and Bhaderwah Festival in the month of June 2007. The Ministry of Tourism is also helping the State Govt. to build up the facilities for devotees to visit Shrine of Amarnath Cave. The inflow of the tourists in the valley has been on the increase during the year 2006. Also the number of pilgrimage going to Mata Vaishno Devi Shrine has shown an increase during the month of January to May in 2007 when compared with the same months of 2006. As a result of the infrastructure development and capacity building for the service providers, considerable amount of employment has been created in Jammu, Kashmir and Ladakh for the youth of the J&K.

1921. (17-7-2007) NEW DELHI : The following is the text of the remarks of External Affairs Minister Shri Pranab Mukherjee at the joint press interaction after the 4th IBSA Trilateral Commission Meeting: "Your Excellency, Mr. Celso Amorim, Minister of External Relations of Brazil, Your Excellency, Dr. Nkosazana Dlamini-Zuma, Minister of Foreign Affairs of South Africa, Distinguished delegates, Ladies and Gentleman, We have just concluded our very fruitful and productive deliberations of the 4th IBSA Trilateral Commission meeting. As you know, IBSA is a unique forum that brings together three large democracies from three different continents facing common challenges. It was just three years ago that the First IBSA Trilateral Commission meeting was held here in Delhi in 2004. In this period, we have identified several areas of cooperation and have been working towards enhancing cooperation in areas such as S&T, education, agriculture, energy, culture, health, social issues, public administration and revenue administration. Several IBSA Working Groups have recently held their meetings. Today we have agreed on a forward looking and substantive agenda of cooperation in the IBSA framework in sectors which are of particular interest to our three countries. We also had a valuable exchange of views on regional and international issues. I am happy to mention that the trade target of US $ 10 billion amongst our three countries by 2007 is expected to be achieved. It will be our endeavour to further increase trade and investment flows amongst us. India has a strategic partnership with both Brazil and South Africa. We value these partnerships and are determined to add significant content to them in the years to come. We are looking at new areas of cooperation and also strengthening existing areas of cooperation keeping in view each other's needs and strengths. As IBSA evolves, I am confident, it will acquire new dimensions. It will be our endeavour to see that IBSA moves to a yet higher level of cooperation, beneficial to our three countries. This will make IBSA an outstanding example of South-South Cooperation. I am happy to announce that the Second IBSA Summit will be held in South Africa later this year. I would like to thank His Excellency Mr. Amorim and Her Excellency Dr. Zuma for attending the 4th IBSA Trilateral Commission meeting."

1922. (18-7-2007) NEW DELHI : The Union Minister of Shipping, Road Transport and Highways, Thiru T. R. Baalu has said that the public sector Shipping Corporation of India (SCI) has prepared an ambitious plan to add over 41 lakh dead weight tonnage (DWT) in the Eleventh Five Year Plan, which would involve an outlay of about Rs.13,135 crores. Addressing the 15th meeting of the Parliamentary Consultative Committee attached to his ministry here today, the Minister said that we need to give shipping, and especially the SCI, all the encouragement and support it requires to maintain its numero uno position in the Indian shipping scene. He said that since inception till date, the SCI has paid Rs.1,487.47 crores to the Government as dividend and it is the only Indian shipping company to have ever crossed the Rs.1000 crores net profit threshold. The Minister informed the Members that the SCI has set up joint ventures with reputed international partners for carrying liquefied natural gas which would give it new business opportunities. The Minister said that the SCI has entered into a joint venture with world renowned partners like MOL & NYK Lines of Japan & 'Q' ships of Qatar for carriage of liquefied natural gas (LNG) for the Petronet project. The SCI also has one of the oldest maritime joint ventures in Iran with an Iranian company, Irano-Hind Shipping Company, which is an India-Iran tie up, the Minister added. The Minister pointed out that the country, today, possesses the largest merchant shipping fleet among the developing countries and is ranked 20th in the world in terms of shipping tonnage. The importance of shipping to our economy may be gauged from the fact that approximately 95 per cent of the country's EXIM trade by volume or 70 per cent by value is moved by sea. Thiru Baalu said that the shipping industry has a multiplier effect on economy by influencing development of ancillary industry and generating employment. He said that in order to give boost to the entire maritime sector, the UPA Government has formulated and is implementing a National Maritime Development Programme that lays emphasis on development of the country's maritime infrastructure. Participating in discussions, the Members suggested that the SCI should prepare a blue-print for next twenty years to meet the growing demands of sea transportation in the liberalized economic scenario. They also expressed concern over the lack of maritime training facilities resulting in shortage of man power in the shipping sector. Members also emphasized that the SCI should make every effort to recover the outstanding dues standing mainly against the Public Sector Companies in a time bound manner and that efforts should be made to fill up all the vacant posts in SCI to make it more efficient. The Members who attended the meeting were S/Shri M. Rajamohan Reddy, Anantha Venkatarami Reddy, Faggan Singh Kulaste, Subhash Maharia, Dr. H.T. Sangliana, G. Karunakara Reddy, Dr. R. Senthil, Laxman Rao Patil, Devendra Prasad Yadav, Hari Kewal Prasad, Brahmananda Panda and Santosh Gangwar (from the Lok Sabha) and S/Shri Silvius Condpan, Mangani Lal Mandal, R. Kamaraj, Jai Prakash Aggarwal, Ms. Mabel Rebello and Ms. Sushila Tiriya (from the Rajya Sabha).

1923. (18-7-2007) NEW DELHI : The first meeting of "India-Japan Strategic Dialogue on Economic Issues" set up recently, was held here today under the co-chairmanship of Finance Secretary, Government of India and Deputy Minister of Foreign Affairs, Government of Japan. During the dialogue the current status of agreed minutes as a follow up of Prime Minister's visit to Japan in December 2006 as reflected in the Joint Statement signed between Prime Ministers of India and Japan on 15th December 2007 and subsequent summit meetings were reviewed. The discussions covered a wide range of topics including Official Development Assistance from Japan, Infrastructure, Trade and Investment, Finance, IT, Science and Technology, Human Resource Development, Energy and Environment etc. The discussions in infrastructure development sector included the Delhi-Mumbai Industrial Corridor and the Dedicated Freight Corridor projects. The status of current negotiations on Economic Partnership Agreement (EPA) between India and Japan was discussed. Both sides agreed to firm up concrete deliverables before the forthcoming visit of the Japanese Prime Minister to India in August, 2007.

1924. (18-7-2007) NEW DELHI : Attention of the Government has been drawn to reports appearing in a section of Press that the Ministry of Human Resource Development is interfering in the process of selection of Directors of the Indian Institutes of Management. These news reports are not based on facts. The practice of selecting Directors through Search-cum-Selection Committees has not been discontinued. As a matter of fact, the present Directors of the various Indian Institutes of Management have been selected on the basis of the existing procedure followed at least since the year 2002. For the selection of forthcoming vacancies, in order to ensure a more broad-based and transparent procedure, the posts have also been widely advertised, as per the present policy in regard to similar posts in autonomous institutions funded by the public exchequer. However, the Search-cum-Selection Committee would be free to go beyond the applications received in response to the advertisements, considering that some eminent academics may not wish to apply in response to advertisements. The Search-cum-Selection Committee would have the representation of the Board of Governors, as per existing practice.

1925. (18-7-2007) NEW DELHI : Fourteen Indian entrepreneurs were today awarded under the Lokheed Martin India Innovation Growth Programme. Giving away the awards in New Delhi, Dr. T. Ramasami, Secretary, Department of Science & Technology said that there is enough scope for innovation in our country and the challenge is to turn these ideas into profit making ideas. Seven awards each were given in gold and silver categories. The Innovations included Waste Plastic Conversion to petroleum fuels, Smart card operated prepaid energy meter with automatic load controller, Apoptopic Proteins that can be used for the treatment of diseases like Allergy and Asthma by fusing them with human proteins, formulation of herbal essential oils extracts and isolates that repels mosquitoes etc. FICCI jointly with the Lockheed Martin Corporation and IC2 Institute, University of Texas at Austin implemented the Lockheed Martin India Innovation Growth Program in India in March 2007. It is a two-year, nationwide project, created to enhance the growth and development of India's entrepreneurial economy.

1926. (18-7-2007) NEW DELHI : Shri Priyaranjan Dasmunsi said that I began the Press Conference on 23rd June immediately after the nomination of Pratibha Patil was over and I am closing the Press Conference on the eve of the poll today. The election of the 13th President should be conducted tomorrow throughout the country by the Election Commission of India fairly and we have high respect for the Election Commission of India for discharging their obligation from time to time in our country. I want to inform you that probably for the first time a large number of Members of either House are voting tomorrow in their respective state capitals and not in Delhi. The MPs voting outside the Delhi are around 58 and many others opted to vote in their state capital. And the party as a whole who have opted to vote in state capital are TRS, TMC and Shiv Sena. Shri Vyalar Ravi, who is not feeling well, has opted to vote in Chennai and National Conference president, Shri Omar Obadullah also opted to vote at Srinagar. Other MPs will be voting in Delhi including 12 MLAs from various parts of India shall be voting in Delhi. We are thankful to the National Conference leadership who decided in their executive committee meeting to strengthen the secular ties and therefore they have decided to support our candidate Smt. Pratibha Patil. I also like to clear one confusion which was prominently carried out in some newspapers that BSP MPs did not attend the dinner hosted for all alliance partner's MPs by UPA Chairperson Smt. Sonia Gandhi. The fact is that three days back the Deputy Chief Minister of Uttar Pradesh, Shri Satish Mishra rang me up on behalf of the Chief Minister Mayawatiji and confirmed that on 17th July they have fixed their dinner alongwith MPs and MLAs in support of our candidate and not only that the BSP Chief had a talk with the UPA Chairperson and she wrote a letter also and that is why they could not come because the dinner was hosted in Lucknow in support of our candidate. So, the confusion about their not attending the dinner hosted by UPA Chairperson has been cleared. All the MPs are arriving by tomorrow morning to vote for Pratibha Patil. There are two parties, JDS, led by Deva Gowdaji, and the other is Trinamool Congress who have yet to make their mind about their voting. Therefore, it appears to me that the real electoral battle will be confined within 9,95,000 votes with around 2,000 less or more and not within 10,97,00 as assessed earlier. In regard to issues raised by Advaniji before the Election Commission yesterday an appropriate award has been given by the Election Commission. We feel pity that the right of a Member outside Parliamentary activities and right within is defined very clearly that only the proceedings of the Lok Sabha and the functions within the floor of the Assembly, the Rajya Sabha and the Lok Sabha is guided on the voting matter by the Whip and as far as President's election is concerned, since 1952, no party has issued whip but every party has the right to appeal to their party members to vote in a particular manner whether they support, oppose or abstain. Shri Das Munsi, speaking in Hindi, said that Advaniji had asked the members of the electoral college to vote according to their conscience. He has got the reply from Maharashtra first and then a loud voice of conscience came from Gujarat and the final voice of conscience will be heard by Advaniji on 21st July. I want that he hears and understands as to what is the voice of conscience. On the representation made to the Election Commission by the BJP on declaration of assets by presidential candidates, Shri Das Munsi said that he personally went to the Election Commission and asked for a copy of that representation but the Election Commission denied that they have received one. I have great respect for Shri Shekhawat and it shall continue even after he becomes ex-vice-president but I am sorry to state the way office of the vice-president has been denigrated and misused. Shri Shekhawat himself not only telephoned MPs but even called up the MLAs to vote for him and this has dishonoured the seat of the vice-president. If at all he wanted to do all this he should have done it honourably like Shri V.V. Giri who resigned from the seat of the vice-president. The way the high office of the vice-president has been misused is first in the history of Indian politics and is a cause of concern. To a question that when will the canvassing stop for presidential election, Shri Das Munsi said that till I go to vote, I have a right to appeal to any MPs I can and there is no rule like the Lok Sabha or Assembly polls which asks to stop campaigning by certain time.

1927. (18-7-2007) NEW DELHI : During the month of May 2007, the Ministry of Micro, Small and Medium Enterprises (MSME) continued to implement its various schemes, programmes, etc. to assist the promotion and growth of small enterprises. NSIC conducted 16 Intensive Campaigns and 11 Marketing Promotion Seminars at various places in the country. The National Institute of Micro, Small and Medium Enterprises (NIMSME), Hyderabad conducted 35 training programmes for 515 participants. The Indian Institute of Entrepreneurship (IIE), Guwahati conducted 18 training programmes for 932 participants. The National Institute for Entrepreneurship and Small Business Development (NIESBUD), NOIDA conducted 7 training programmes for 135 participants.

1928. (18-7-2007) NEW DELHI : The 'Unorganised Sector Workers Social Security Bill, 2007' is likely to be introduced in the forthcoming session of Parliament. This was stated by the Minister of State (Independent Charge) Labour and Employment Shri Oscar Fernandes while addressing the Parliamentary Consultative Committee attached to his Ministry here on Tuesday evening. Shri Fernandes said that the proposed legislation entails constitution of tripartite Social Security Advisory Boards at the national and state levels. He said that the proposed legislation also provides for formulation and notification of suitable welfare schemes for different sections of unorganized sector workers both by the Central and State Governments. These schemes would pertain to life and disability cover, health insurance and maternity benefits and old age protection. Shri Fernandes said that the proposed legislation has been drafted by the Ministry of Labour and Employment after deliberations at various levels. He said "In pursuance of the commitment made in the National Common Minimum Programme (for ensuring welfare and wellbeing of workers, particularly those in the unorganized sector) the Prime Minister took a meeting on 18.11.2005 in which the Committee of Secretaries (CoS) chaired by the Cabinet Secretary was directed to verify the numbers, estimate possible contribution of the Government of India, list out various issues relating to modalities of implementation and collate and evaluate various state level initiatives". Referring to various welfare schemes for beedi workers, Shri Fernandes said that under the Education Scheme Rs.78 crore have been provided in the current year's budget to meet the increasing demand for scholarships to the wards of beedi workers. He said that during last year scholarships amounting to Rs.40 crore were disbursed to 4.7 lakh students. Shri Fernandes also said that the Housing Scheme has been revised. It shall now be implemented through Welfare Commissioners of Labour Welfare Organisation. The Minister said that under the revised scheme, workers' contribution would be taken only after administrative approval and not at the time of submission of application, as was the practice earlier. He said that last year sanction was granted for construction of 18,808 houses. The Members appreciated the services being provided to beedi workers under various welfare schemes. They said that there are more beedi workers than the official estimate of around 50 lakh. Some Members wanted that a countrywide survey should be conducted to identify all beedi workers. It was suggested that multiple agencies should be engaged for their identification and identity cards should be issued to all as early as possible. The Director General, Labour Welfare informed the Members that the Welfare Commissioners have been directed not to insist on employer's letter for identification of beedi workers as was the practice earlier. Regarding the Unorganised Sector Workers Social Security Bill, the Members wanted that it should be more comprehensive. They said funding and benefits should be defined. One of the Members said that the Centre should provide 2% of GDP for unorganised sector workers. Shri Fernandes assured the Members that their suggestions would be actively considered. The Members of Parliament Shri Gurudas Dasgupta, Shri Rajendaran, Shri Bapu Hari Chaure, Shri Rajnarayan, Shri Dawa Narbula, Shri Narayan Singh Kesri and Shri Ashok Pradhan as well as the Secretary Labour & Employment Shrimati Sudha Pillai and senior officials of the Ministry participated in the meeting.

1929. (18-7-2007) NEW DELHI : For the benefit of passengers, the reserved tickets will also be issued from Post Offices in near future for which the modalities have already been finalised and agreement is likely to be signed shortly. This was stated by the Minister of Railways Shri Lalu Prasad while addressing the meeting of the Consultative Committee of Members of Parliament attached to the Ministry of Railways on the agenda "Marketing Strategies on Indian Railways' here last evening. He said that it will also be possible to buy reserved and unreserved tickets through ATMs to be installed by Public Sector Banks at 6,000 railway stations. The Minister said that Railways have increased the length of all trains upto 24 coaches and length of platforms is also being increased to accommodate 24 coaches. He said that, in addition, Railways have taken a number of initiatives to increase the freight loading which include construction of logistic park through Public Private Partnership (PPP), liberalization of container policy, wagon investment scheme, liberalization of the policy of siding construction and concession upto 40 per cent in empty flow direction. The Minister also informed the Members that Railways have taken several historic steps for the overall development of Indian Railways network in the near future that include construction of Dedicated Freight Corridor project on western and eastern sector routes with an estimated cost of Rs. 30,000 crore, opening of agricultural outlets at 7000 stations for helping the farmers to get reasonable price for their products, upgradation of 21 railway stations upto world class level through PPP. The Members brought to the notice of the Railway Minister some areas of concern, especially regarding passenger amenities where progress is yet to be made to the utmost satisfaction of passengers. The Minister assured the Members that Railways are committed to take all possible steps to make it consumer friendly. Members appreciated the efforts made by the Ministry of Railways for the excellent performance of the Indian Railways and also praised the Minister and his work force for taking measures, which have yielded remarkable results and have led to a 'turn around' in the Railways' financial position. The Members who attended the meeting included among others S/Shri Sartaj Singh Chhatwal, Girdhari Lal Bhargav, Dr. Sebastian Paul, Amitava Nandy, Anil Basu, Prabodh Panda, Devidas A. Pingale, Rabindra Rana, R.K.Dhawan, Motiur Rahman, S.K.Khabuddin Ahmed, Shri T.S.Bajwa,, Smt. Susmita Bauri, P.G.Narayanan, D.C.Srikantappa, Abdul Munnan Hossain and Nizamuddin. However, due to some unavoidable circumstances, the meeting could not be concluded and was adjourned for some other day, the date for which will be announced shortly.

1930. (18-7-2007) NEW DELHI : The Centre has cautioned the States that the availability of water is highly variable. Therefore, water has to be conserved through a judicious mix of major, medium and minor projects with due emphasis on traditional system of water harvesting. A comprehensive and integrated approach to planning is the need of the hour. The National Advisory Council on Recharge to Ground Water has taken several measures in connection with the management of ground water. Some of the success stories will be explained to the nation during the ground water congress that will be held in New Delhi on September 11, 2007. The surface water is not being utilised optimally and it is a great disadvantage. Facilities for storing ground water should be created by completing all the on going projects in a time bound manner and planning for new schemes. Storage sites provided by nature need to utilized fully and optimally

1931. (18-7-2007) NEW DELHI : The Prime Minister, Dr. Manmohan Singh today stressed the need to empower Public Enterprises by easing the bureaucratic and political hold of Government over them. Speaking on the occasion of the release of the book, "The Indian CEO-A Portrait of Excellence", he said, this requires reform of Government and the procedures we adopt to ensure Parliamentary accountability. The Prime Minister said that, "Parliamentary accountability should not degenerate into either ministerial or political interference in day-to-day management of enterprises, or bureaucratic stranglehold on managerial decision-making." Dr. Manmohan Singh said that he would like to see PSUs functioning in a more liberal environment. He further said that the public sector has some very talented and dedicated CEOs but we cannot rest content with a few success stories. "We need an army of world class managers who can turn our companies around and keep Indian enterprises on the road to high growth", he added. The Minister of Petroleum and Natural Gas, Shri Murli Deora, Principal Secretary to The Prime Minister, Shri T.K.A. Nair and the CEOs of the companies were also present on the occasion. Following is the text of the Prime Minister's address on the occasion: "I am delighted to release this book which is a product of valuable research. I compliment the research team, the Chief Executive Officers (CEOs) associated with the research and my Principal Secretary Mr. Nair, who took the initiative to launch this research programme. I also compliment the Public Enterprise Selection Board and Bharat Petroleum Ltd. for commissioning this study. I recall participating in a conference that was organized to discuss the results of this research work. As I had said at that time, I am a strong believer in the importance of individual leadership, but I do recognize that there are binding constraints imposed on even the most competent leaders. It is, therefore, not always easy to judge whether any given outcome is a product of the capabilities of the leader or of the inadequacies of the environment in which he or she must function. I therefore note with approval that this study contextualizes the role and performance of CEOs, especially of a public sector corporation, within the environment in which they have to perform. For public sector companies, this environment is defined as much by the Government as it is by the market. I am not surprised that this study comes to the conclusion that dealing with this external environment, dubbed as "boundary management", is the most important challenge facing public sector executives in India. I agree with an important conclusion of this study that the relationship between business and the "Government as regulator" needs to become "more transparent, more predictable, less uncertain and less time consuming".

1932. (18-7-2007) NEW DELHI : Recognizing the need to introduce innovative patterns of cultural funding in India, the National Culture Fund was set up as a trust under the Ministry of Culture in the year 1996 vide notification published in Gazette of India dated 28th November, 1996, with a purpose to augment governments efforts and to facilitate public-private partnership in the field of heritage conservation and promotion. National Culture Fund enables institutions and individuals to perform their rightful role in promoting and preserving India's rich cultural heritage. National Culture Fund constitutes an important departure from the implementation strategies of the Government, which hitherto was thought to be solely responsible for providing administrative and financial wherewithal for culture related endeavours in the country. NCF accepts private institutions and individuals as equal partners of the government in the management of the cultural heritage of India. It enables the government to mobilize extra budgetary resources by allowing direct contributions to the NCF account maintained outside the Consolidated Fund of India. All contributions to NCF are given 100% tax exemption under Section 80 G (2) of the Income Tax Act of 1961. The nature of funding has been made very flexible with the donor having an option to either execute the selected project directly wherein the donors can appoint and monitor the executive agencies to carry out the project work subject to the predefined technical/ aesthetic conditions laid down by the ASI. Alternatively, the donor can get the selected project executed through the ASI, which has the expertise to execute such projects. A Project Implementation Committee shall be set up with experts and representatives of the concerned institutions to monitor and implement the project. A Project Advisory Committee consisting of nominees of donors, NCF and representatives of other interest groups oversee the project. NCF facilitates all necessary clearances and permissions for the project. ASI shall specify the general terms about the activities permissible within the protected sites. The NCF is accountable to each donor in respect of funds donated. The funds can be donated either in Indian currency or any foreign convertible currency. A separate dedicated account for each project is opened by the NCF. The NCF is managed and administered by a council chaired by the Minister of Culture and an Executive Committee chaired by the Secretary, Ministry of Culture. Members of the NCF Council are from corporate houses, private foundations, experts in various art forms and academicians so as to increase non-governmental participation in the decision making process. Under the NCF it is possible for a donor to identify a project along with any specific location/aspect for funding and also an agency for the execution of the project.

1933. (18-7-2007) NEW DELHI : The total import of sensitive items for the period April-May 07 has been Rs.2606 crores as compared to Rs.2828 crores during the corresponding period last year thereby showing a decrease of 7.9%. The gross import of all commodities during same period of current year was Rs.148054 crores as compared to Rs.121305 crores during the same period of last year. Thus import of sensitive items constitute 2.3% and 1.8% of the gross imports during last year and current year respectively. Imports of edible oil, fruits & vegetables (including nuts), cotton & silk, products of SSI, spices, marble & Granite and milk & milk products have shown a decline at broad group level during the period. Imports of items viz. automobiles, rubber and Alcoholic beverages have shown increase during the period under reference. In the edible oil segment, the import has decreased from Rs.1601 crores last year to Rs.1381 crores for the corresponding period of this year. The import of both crude oil as well as refined oil have gone down by 13.6% and 16.4% respectively. The fall in edible oil import is mainly due to significant decrease in import of Soya-bean oil and its fractions (Crude), which has gone down by 63%. Imports of sensitive items from Indonesia, China P RP, Thailand, Germany, Japan, Cote D' Ivoire, Australia, United Kingdom etc. have gone up while those from Argentina, United States of America, Malaysia, Benin, Egypt A RP, Sri Lanka DSR, Brazil, Vietnam Soc Republic etc. have shown a decrease.

1934. (18-7-2007) NEW DELHI : The National Highways Authority of India (NHAI) today signed the Concession Agreement for four Projects to be executed in Tamil Nadu on Build, Operate and Transfer (BOT) basis under National Highways Development Project (NHDP) Phase III at a total cost of Rs. 2,318 Crores for four laning of 343 km. The Agreements were signed this afternoon by NHAI in the presence of Shri Pradeep Kumar, Chairman, NHAI with M/s Pondicherry Tindivanam Tollway Limited (an SPV formed by M/s Maytas-NCC Consortium) for Pondicherry-Tindivanam Section of NH-66, and M/s SU Toll Road Private Limited, M/s TD Toll Road Private Limited and M/s TK Toll Road Private Limited (SPVs formed by M/s Reliance Energy Limited) for Salem-Ulundurpet Section of NH-68, Trichy-Dindigul Section of NH-45 and Trichy-Karur Section of NH-67 respectively.

1935. (19-7-2007) NEW DELHI : Union Minister of Food Processing Industry Shri Subodh Kant Sahai has said that 30 Food Park are being established in the country. So that farmers could get remunerative prizes prices for there product. Chairing the Parliamentary Consultative Committee of his ministry on the subject of ' Strategic Interventions in the Food Processing Sector' he said that the Vision 2015 envisages inter-alia cluster based and demand drive farming, achieving integration of food processing infrastructure from farm to market, promoting a dynamic food processing industry. The Vision aims to increase the processing level from 6% to 20% Value addition from 20% to 35% and share in global trade from 1.6% to 3% by the year 2015. The Minister said that the priority areas identified for intervention and infrastructure development, modified integrated Food Zone/ Mega Food Park, modernization of, abattoirs setting up of National Meat Board, Irradiation Centre and Cold Chain, Value addition and preservation infrastructure. The Minister further said that the Ministry of Food Processing Industries under the scheme of modernization of abattoirs presently provides financial assistance upto 25% of the cost of Plant and Machineries/Technical Civil Works in general areas and 33.33% in difficult areas with a maximum of Rs. 4 crore. Against this, the cost of modernization of abattoirs is estimated to be Rs. 20 crore upwards. The Minister emphasized the need to setting up/Upgradation of Quality Control/ Food Testing Laboratories, the Centre/State Government Organizations, IITs and Universities are eligible for a grant in aid limited to the entire cost of capital equipments required for setting up/modernization of laboratories. The Minister also informed the members that the Ministry of Food Processing Industries is of the view that it is essential to provide infrastructure status to the specified investment in rural infrastructure under Mega Food Park scheme. The Minister said almost 2% of the urban population consists of street vendors, of which a significant portion consists of street food vendors belonging to the unorganized service sector of the economy providing large scale employment. The scheme of upgradation of quality of street food has been envisaged to give an identity to the downtrodden, street food vendors, provide them economic sustainability in life and improve the hygienic standards and quality of street food. Shri Sahai said that the Ministry of Food Processing Industries has taken up various steps under the scheme of upgradation of quality of street foods like assessment of the knowledge, attitude and practices of the street food vendors, grant of 25% towards the cost for safe and hygienically designed food cart, health checks, insurance, facilitating in micro-finance. The Minister also informed the members that after the approval of the Cabinet, we have now started assisting the Indian Wine Industry also setting up Modernization Scheme. The Members those who attended the meeting were S/ Shri Basngouda R. Patil, Shyama Charan Gupta, Mohammed Tahir Khan, M.P. Veerendra Kumar, Sujan Chakraborty, Vijay Kumar Rupani, C. Perumal, Bhagtwati Singh and Dr. Rdha Kant Nayak.

1936. (19-7-2007) NEW DELHI : Shri E.V.K.S. Elangovan, Minister of State for Textiles has said that the textile sector would attract an investment of Rs. 1,40,000 crore by the year 2010 at an annual growth rate of 8 per cent. The textile industry is the oldest which employs about 3.5 crore workers, contributing about 17 per cent in exports and 4 per cent in overall GDP. Shri Elangovan said this while releasing the book titled "Customs Classification of Textiles & Textile Articles under HSN-Explanatory Notes" written by Shri Ajay Kumar Gupta, an officer from the Indian Custom & Central Excise Service. Speaking on the occasion the Minister further said that the tariff classification of textiles still remained complex due to the fact that the present textile tariff classification has not been well explained. The aim of the book, now released, is to demystify the harmonized structure of classification with respect to textiles and textile articles. This book is an effort to synchronise the concepts of textiles within the existing harmonized system of classification with more illustrations and explanations, he said.

1937. (19-7-2007) NEW DELHI : The production of finished carbon steel has reached 12.088 million tonnes during the first quarter of this year recording an increase of 12.6 per cent. During the corresponding period of last year the total production of finish steel in the country was 10.734 million tonnes. Export of finished carbon steel has also shown an increase of 7.8 per cent.

1938. (19-7-2007) NEW DELHI : The Chairman of Scientific Advisory Council to Prime Minister Prof. C.N.R. Rao along with other members of the Council today called on the Union Rural Development Minister, Dr. Raghuvansh Prasad Singh, here today. The purpose of the meeting was to appraise the Rural Development Ministry about the Scientific Innovations in the field of Research and Development and its potential applications in the rural areas of the country. Prof. Rao was in favour of connecting the research and development work with the rural masses and setting up of a joint mechanism between the Scientist fraternity of the country and the M/o Rural Development. The members of the Council were of the view that now it is the time to work for the development of cost effective and viable technologies meant for the rural folks. The need for a central knowledge portal to find the apt areas of research and development was also felt during the meeting. The Rural Development Minister while agreeing with the views of the Council members apprised the members of the various programmes of the Ministry viz. the NREGA, Rural Housing, Rural Drinking Water Supply and Sanitation, rural Roads etc. and requested the Council to concentrate on the areas where services suitable for rural areas could be provided and that there should be concrete ideas in this regard. Moreover, the technologies developed should be in tune with the approach of the Ministry, he added. Earlier, Secretary, Rural Development, Dr. Subas Pani welcomed the members in the meeting. It was agreed that the next meeting of the Council member with the MRD will be held on 25th of this month. The members who participated in the meeting included Prof. Ashok Jhunjhunwala, Dr. K. Vijay Raghavan, Dr. Kiran Karnik, Dr. M.K. Bhan, Dr. N.K. Ganguly, Dr. Mangala Rai and Dr. T. Ramasami.

1939. (19-7-2007) NEW DELHI : A two day International Seminar and Exhibition on Naval Armament, 'NAVARMS-07', being co-organised by the Integrated Headquarters, MOD (Navy) and Confederation of Indian Industry (CII) was inaugurated by the Hon'ble Raksha Mantri Shri AK Antony on 19 Jul 07 at Hotel Intercontinental, New Delhi. Admiral Sureesh Mehta, Chief of the Naval Staff was the guest of honour during the inaugural session. Air Chief Marshal FH Major Chief of Air Staff, Lt Gen. Deepak Kapoor, Vice-chief of Army Staff, Secretary Defence Production Shri KP Singh, Shri Sunil Bharti Mittal, President CII and many senior dignitaries from the three services, DRDO, OFB, Industry and foreign delegates graced the occasion. During his welcome address, Shri Sunil Mittal called upon the industry to "rise to the occasion and grab the opportunity", which has come their way due to opening up of the defence industry for private participation. He emphasised that the need of the hour was to forge a mutually rewarding relationship and make noteworthy contribution towards the common goal of nation building. Vice Admiral Nirmal Verma, the Vice Chief of Naval Staff unfurled the theme of the seminar for evolving a closer synergy with the Industry in the field of Naval Armaments setting the tone for deliberations. In his key note address, the Chief of the Naval Staff Admiral Sureesh Mehta stressed the need for evolving a strong industrial base in the field of weapon/armament systems as the country could ill afford the astronomical cost of import. He brought out the huge strides made in the field of ship building and explained the vast potential that is waiting to be tapped in the armament field. He called upon the industry to participate not only in manufacturing of armaments but also to invest in R&D for the latest technological developments. The brochure for the NAVARMS-07 was released by the Hon'ble Raksha Mantri Shri AK Antony during the inaugural session. In his address, the Hon'ble Raksha Mantri brought out that the stupendous economic growth and the technological prowess seen in the last decade needs to be translated into a strong, technologically self reliant and sustainable defence sector as well. He called upon the private sector to enter in to the defence sphere with a long term commitment, not only adapting advance military technology but also develop their own. He exhorted the Indian private sector to combine their strengths and develop domain knowledge in defence technology to compete at international level. He complimented the Indian Navy and CII for the initiative and hoped that the deliberations would help in formulating a strategy for facilitating larger participation of private industry in the task of nation building through defence production in line with the theme of the seminar "Indigenous Armament-Opportunities and Challenges". After the inaugural session, the RM inaugurated the exhibition. Many Indian Industries, defence PSUs and prominent foreign manufacturers from USA, UK, Germany, Italy, Israel and France are participating in the exhibition.

1940. (19-7-2007) NEW DELHI : Indian agricultural scientists are working on ways to tackle the multi-pronged impact of climate change on agriculture. This includes weighing technological, agronomic and other options and evolving appropriate strategies. This came out during the discussions in the Parliamentary Consultative Committee meeting held here today to discuss 'Climate Change and Agriculture'. Steering the discussion, Agriculture Minister, Shri Sharad Pawar said: 'Irrespective of the outcome of the international negotiations on climatic change, agriculture has to become more competitive, efficient, profitable, and develop mechanisms to reduce its vulnerability. Indian farmers, scientists and policy makers have to address these issues in totality and develop strategies to increase our adaptive capacity. We have built capacity earlier to climatic extremes such as drought by establishing buffer food stocks, strengthening irrigation infrastructure, and developing agricultural insurance schemes. We now need to put more emphasis on anticipatory adaptation measures, especially 'no-regret' adaptation strategies that will allow attainment of sustainable development goals even if there is no climatic change or its magnitude is different from current projections.' The Minister emphasized the need to substantially increase capital investment in agriculture, which has been continuously going down in last few years. Investment in irrigation infrastructure, silos for food and feed, rural roads and power could enhance agriculture's resilience to climatic extremes. Vulnerability of coastal agricultural communities to increased frequency and intensity of cyclones can be reduced by investing in infrastructure that can protect them for short periods, the Minister said. The Minister further said that it would be very useful to establish early warning systems for environmental change. Such systems could help in determining the potential food insecure areas and communities given the type of risk and in providing assistance to policy planners in arranging relief. A trans-boundary pest monitoring system, if established, can forewarn about the likely resurgence and migration of pests associated with global warming. Enabling policies that encourage farm insurance can provide protection to the farmers from adverse effects on farm production due to natural calamities. Focussed agricultural research on development of more adapted varieties of crops, livestock and fish to future climate, and development of water and carbon conservation practices will also be useful, Shri Pawar stated. Agriculture Minister also informed that a high-powered Council chaired by the Prime Minister has recently been established to examine all issues related to climate change, including agriculture. In the Agriculture Ministry, ICAR has also been asked to organize consultation with other departments and experts towards evolving a strategy to deal with the likely impact of climate change on Indian agriculture. Shri Taslimuddin, Minister of State for Consumer Affairs, Food and Public Distribution and Dr. Akhilesh Prasad Singh, Minister of State also attended the meeting for Consumer Affairs, Food and Public Distribution. The members who attended the meeting include S/Shri A. Sai Prathap, Lalit Mohan Suklabaidya, Jai Parkash, P.C. Gaddigoudar, Hansraj Gangaram Ahir, Bhanu Pratap Singh Verma, Gauri Shankar Chaturbhuj Bisen, K. Francis George, M. Appadurai, Alok Kumar Mehata, Chandrapal Singh Yadav, Ranen Barman and Ms. Archana Nayak (Lok Sabha) Thennala G. Balakrishna Pillai, Pyarelal Khandelwal and Shri Sharad Joshi (Rajya Sabha).

1941. (19-7-2007) NEW DELHI : An integrated approach is required for development of Youth and Sports in India. This was stated by the Minister of Panchayati Raj, Youth Affairs & Sports and DoNER, Shri Mani Shankar Aiyar while addressing the Parliamentary Consultative Committee meeting attached to his Ministries on Wednesday evening. Shri Aiyar said that the National development is linked to the development of the youth in the country and this in turn is linked to better sports facilities. Out of 77 crore youth in India only 5 crore have access to sports facilities which puts a constraint on development of excellence in sports. Shri Mani Shankar Aiyar said that the sports policy 2002 put the responsibility of development of sports in the rural areas on the state, while the Union Ministry was to take care of the bigger sporting events. However, the Ministry has now got directions to draft a new sports policy which can encourage better integration and development of youth and sports. He said that the draft policy has been prepared and it will be published on the Ministry's website to invite comments so that the final policy can be arrived at. Shri Aiyar said that it is very important that the schools and Pathshalas have proper sports facilities to generate an interest of students in sports. He said that as of now only 43 per cent of Pathshalas have facilities for sports and in order to increase their number it is important that Panchayati Raj Sansthans should be actively involved in this exercise. The Minister said that there are about 2.5 lakh panchayats and about the same number of Nehru Yuvak Kendras and if the efforts of both are coordinated in the area of sports development, it can yield very good results. With a view to promoting community sports infrastructure at the grassroots level, the Union Government proposes to undertake the Panchayat Yuva Kendra aur Khel Abhiyan (PYKKA) in rural areas, which would cover all the village and block Panchayats in the country numbering around 250,000 over the Eleventh and Twelfth Five Year Plan periods. A similar programme is also envisaged for urban areas, the Nagar Palika Yuva Kendra aur Khel Abhiyan, which can be dovetailed with the Jawaharlal Nehru Urban Renewal Mission. There would be organized competition structure from the Panchayat level up to the national level. 700 million youth including adolescent have little or marginal access to sporting faculties. Of these, about 500 million rural youth including adolescent who are relatively even more deprived than their urban counterparts. Universalisation of sports cannot be achieved without adequate thrust on development of sports in rural areas. The Minister said that in the next ten years it is targetted that every panchayat should have sports facilities and this needs to be given national importance in order to come up with aspired results. Shri Aiyar said that new sports policy would be focusing on the following areas. As envisaged in the revised 20-point programme of 2006 the policy will focus on sports for all. The girls will be given sports facilities which either provide them exclusive facilities or exclusive time for practicising sports. Some special facilities are also being worked out for handicapped youth. He said that it is important that wide based sports facilities are provided so that there is a general health consciousness because this alone can lead to increased sports achievements. Shri Aiyar also said that a Sports Regulatory Authority is required which can decide on disputes between sports federations and other bodies through a democratic and transparent system. He emphasized the need for having special facilities in the Northeast region, which does not have the same sports facilities as other states. Shri Aiyar said that despite lack of facilities Northeast has given us some outstanding sports persons.

1942. (19-7-2007) NEW DELHI : Union Finance Minister, Shri P. Chidambaram has approved 17 Foreign Direct Investment proposals recommended by Foreign Investment Promotion Board (FIPB) in its meeting held on 13th July, 2007. The approval amounts to Rs. 589.8511 crores. The proposals relate to Ministries/

Departments, Chemicals & Petro chemicals, Civil Aviation, Commerce, Information & Broadcasting, Industrial Policy & Promotion, Posts, Telecommunications, Revenue and Economic Affairs. The major investment proposals pertain to the Ministry/Departments of Industrial Policy & Promotion, Information & Broadcasting, Revenue and Economic Affairs.

1943. (19-7-2007) NEW DELHI : Following is the text of the Defence Minister Shri A K Antony's address at International Seminar and Exhibition on Naval Armaments held here today. "I am happy to be amidst you to inaugurate this Seminar on naval armaments. Its timing is of particular relevance, in view of the ever increasing importance of maritime security, coupled with advances in armament technology and changing strategic calculus, it is imperative for us to have a lean and thin, yet a modern and well-equipped Navy. I am sure the Seminar will evolve a comprehensive strategy to deal with all the threats and challenges posed to us in this regard. A nation derives its power from a variety of factors-its geographical position, its economic strength, its administration or political system, its military and its people. While many strategists have defined and identified these parameters separately, they are closely interlinked. India is presently undergoing a major transformation and emerging as a formidable power-both in economic and political sense of the term. However, our emergence as an economic power and a major political player has placed onerous responsibilities on us. While we scale greater heights, our profile and strategy faces challenges on three fronts-the globalisation process in the new economic technological order, acquiring strategic-technological strengths and the vision of enhanced military prowess. Since the beginning of the 1990s, there has been a stupendous growth in the industrial and core sectors. Foreign firms are now increasingly looking at India as an attractive investment destination and for more cost-effective production. Global players are outsourcing work orders to Indian companies, benefiting from the high degree of skills and cost effectiveness prevalent in our country. Prior to the 1990s, the Government of India had placed the production of defence items in the reserve list, making it mandatory for production to be taken up only by the public sector. However, our effort now is to provide opportunities to industries in the private sector as well to participate actively in production of defence items. We want the private sector to come forward and become partners to PSUs in their endeavour to help the nation attain a high degree of self-reliance in defence preparedness. Our core strengths have reached a high level of development and we now need to focus on developing high technology areas. The global defence industry has undergone profound changes in recent years. The demand for military weapons and equipment, allocation of resources, national and international priorities of major states and several other factors have affected the defence industry in many ways. Our strategic planners are looking for newer strategies to ensure that our nation meets challenges effectively to sustain future requirements. A strong and healthy partnership between the public and private sector will be critical in maximising our defence capability and in creating a powerful domestic industrial base for the future. The

'Offset Clause 'in the defence procurement policy would definitely leverage India's position as a promoter of a vibrant and proactive defence Industry. Simultaneously, I would like the Armed Forces to ensure that all available infrastructure and resources are utilized judiciously and optimally. Though our self reliance drive has made some progress, much more needs to be done to minimise the gap between technology and our needs. The Indian Navy has been a catalyst in the development and building of warships. Today, India is one of the major warship design and manufacturing nations in the world and our indigenous warships have made their presence felt across the globe. The Indian Navy's vision of an indigenous and self reliant armament and weapon system provides a challenge and an opportunity for Indian Industry. Indigenous armament development is a major area of concern. The Industry must, as part of their evolution and national development, focus on research, development and production of armaments and weapon systems keeping in view the issues of quality, safety, reliability, and maintainability factors. A synergy needs to be built up between the Services, DRDO and Indian industry for putting in place an independent, competitive and market oriented research. I would like to see the private sector in India gearing up for a long term commitment and be far-sighted, not only in adopting advanced military technologies, but also developing their own. The private sector needs to combine its strengths and develop knowledge in defence technology to overcome shortcomings and help our nation to compete at international levels and not merely look at the domestic market I am sure NAVARMS 07 will be looking into the various aspects of the defence production and the needs, as well as the underlying concerns of the services. I wish the Indian Navy and CII all success. I hope that the deliberations would help us develop effective strategies towards achieving self-reliance in defence production."

1944. (19-7-2007) NEW DELHI : In view of the Presidential Election the Directorate General of Civil Aviation has directed all scheduled airlines operating in India to facilitate the air travel of officers and transport important election materials. They have been asked by the DGCA to ensure that all flights schedules are specifically adhered to and no flights are delayed. While the polling for the Presidential Election takes place today in New Delhi and the State Capitals, counting will take place on the 21st July 2007 at New Delhi only. Therefore the ballot boxes have to reach back New Delhi tomorrow. All the officers on duty will be returning by 'Executive Class'. The seats of these officers will be blocked in such a way that they are able to keep the polled ballot boxes adjacent to their seat as they will be carried as hand luggage in sealed condition and with due care so that the seal does not get damaged during transit. While the boxes will be screened through X-ray before being carried into the aircraft this shall be done with due care without damaging the seal. In some cases where the aircraft operated on the relevant route is of single configuration, the airlines have been asked to ensure that the seating provided to the officers is such that the poll ballot boxes can be brought in as cabin baggage without difficulty. As per the instructions of the Ministry of Civil Aviation, the Airports Authority of India, the Delhi International Airport Ltd., Indian Airlines Ltd., DGCA and BCAS have nominated one nodal officer each for coordinating with the Election Commission for the above purpose.

1945. (19-7-2007) NEW DELHI : Shri Kamal Nath, Union Minister of Commerce & Industry, has stated that the bilateral trade talks between India and Japan are more likely to be pragmatic and any negotiations between the two countries is likely to be more sustainable since both appreciate and understand each other's sensitivities better and have a larger perspective on issues of mutual interest. He stated this while welcoming Mr. Masahoru Kohno, Deputy Minister for Foreign Affairs, Government of Japan, here last evening. The two Ministers also reviewed several issues of bilateral importance as part of the India-Japan Strategic Dialogue on economic issues held in New Delhi. Both the Ministers discussed trade issues that are likely to dominate during the visit of Japanese Prime Minister to India in August 2007 when Shri Kamal Nath is expected to inaugurate the Indo-Japan Business Leaders Forum and release a joint statement emphasising the major role of the private sector in strategic economic engagement. Both sides are expected to nominate top CEOs for inclusion in the Business Leaders Forum. Discussions were also held on the progress of DMIC (Delhi-Mumbai Industrial Corridor) Project. DMIC project is conceptualised to take benefit of the high quality connectivity offered by Delhi-Mumbai Dedicated Rail Freight Corridor (DFC) by augmenting the required infrastructure. DMIC phase-I is synchronized to be completed by 2012 with DFC. DMIC project is proposed to be based on the approach of infrastructure development and connectivity (road, rail, port and air) rather than providing fiscal or financial incentives. Japan is fifth major investor in India with cumulative inflow of US $ 2.21 billion since 1991. Recently, many Japanese companies have shown interest in India particularly, Suzuki, Honda and Nissan. India needs many more such projects from Japanese businesses particularly in infrastructure sector.

1946. (19-7-2007) NEW DELHI : Train journey experience for passenger travelling between Mumbai and Goa has got more delightful with the two premium trains of Konkan Railway *i.e.* Mandovi Express and Konkankanya Express getting ISO 9001:2000 certificate recently and new On-Board Services introduced in these trains. Konkan Railway has made considerable efforts in providing quality service to passengers in these trains. The catering which includes a very sumptuous fare of South Indian delicacies, Chinese etc. in these trains is a huge hit with the passengers. In doing so, Konkan Railway has made an effort to make the train journey as pleasant and blissful as the joy of reaching the destination. Recently, Konkan Railway has also introduced On-Board Services in these two trains. This includes providing liquid soap/tissue paper in toilets in AC coaches, spray air freshers in AC coaches, periodical cleaning of toilets during the journey in all coaches of the trains, mopping and sweeping of all coaches, use of disinfectants in toilets of all coaches and providing good quality toilet soap to confirmed passengers in 1AC and 2AC coaches. The certificate, issued by QS Zurich AG, includes coaching maintenance (mechanical and electrical) along with Catering and Linen Service in these trains by Konkan Railway. The areas covered in ISO certification of coach maintenance are, top deck cleanliness, maintenance of passenger amenities in coaches and undergear safety equipment examination of the rakes. The agency inspected the trains over a period of seven months and checked the services being provided in these trains on international standard before awarding the certificate. Kokan Railway had also received ISO 9001:2000 certification for Ratnagiri and Madgaon railway station in the last two years.

1947. (19-7-2007) NEW DELHI : Indian Railways have carried 185.25 million tonnes of revenue earning freight traffic during the first quarter (*i.e.* April-June 2007) of the current financial year 2007-08. The freight carried shows an increase of 9.41 million tonnes over the freight traffic of 175.84 million tonnes actually carried during the corresponding period last year, reflecting an increase of 5.35 per cent. During the month of June 2007, the revenue earning freight traffic carried by Indian Railways was 60.46 million tonnes. There is an increase of 2.29 million tonnes over the freight traffic of 58.17 million tonnes actually carried by the Indian Railways during the same period last year, reflecting an increase of 3.94 per cent.

1948. (19-7-2007) NEW DELHI : Six envoys presented their credentials to the President of India, Dr. A.P.J. Abdul Kalam at a ceremony at Rashtrapati Bhavan here today. The envoys who presented their credentials were:-His Excellency Mr. Lawal M. Dutsin-Ma, the High Commissioner of Nigeria, His Excellency Mr. John W.H. Kijazi, the High Commissioner of Tanzania, His Excellency Mr. Ion de la Riva Guzman de Frutos, the Ambassador of Spain, His Excellency Mr. Wilfred Kenely, the High Commissioner of Malta, His Excellency Mr. Alem Tsehaye Woldemariam, the Ambassador of Eritrea and His Excellency Mr. Sayed Mehdi Nabizadeh, the Ambassador of Iran. The credential presentation ceremony was attended by the senior members of the missions, senior officials of the Ministry of External Affairs and Rashtrapati Bhavan.

1949. (20-7-2007) NEW DELHI : The Tourism and Culture Minister, Smt. Ambika Soni, released a book of poems 'Borough in the Mist' written by Sandeep Silas here today. The function was organized by the Poetry Club of India and attended by Chairman of the Sahitya Academy, Prof. Gopi Chand Narang, noted poet and art critic Keshav Malik and a large number of writers and scholars. Poet Sandeep Silas was born on 19th September 1960 at Agra. "Discover India by Rail" (Sterling Paperbacks, 2001), his first book, helps the tourist choose an itinerary for a holiday in India; travel and experience the beauty of the land. A Hindi translation of this book was brought out in 2004 titled "Rail Se Bharat Darshan". His next book to be published was "Know Your India" (Sterling Paperbacks, 2004). "Morrow's Face (Sterling Paperbacks, 2005) is his significant contribution to the world of poetry in English. Now we have from him "Borough in the Mist" another collection of poems in English.

1950. (20-7-2007) NEW DELHI : The Rural Development Minister, Dr. Raghuvansh Prasad Singh, has asked all the States to ensure the submission of monthly reports from all the districts on-line for efficient e-Governance applications. Presiding over a meeting of State Nodal Officers of the Ministry of Rural Development here today, he said that his Ministry will shortly stop receiving hard copy of reports. The Minister further said that reporting is an essential component of monitoring and vigilance and emphasised on the need for timely receipts of the progress reports of schemes which are already in place for implementation. The system of on-line reporting also serves the broader purpose of making information available to the public by putting the same on the web-site, he said. The Ministry of Rural Development has introduced a system of holding monthly meetings for monitoring of progress reports of the Rural Development (RD) Programmes. For this, the States/UTs were asked to nominate an officer each, called the Nodal Officer, to be responsible for coordinating all the Programmes of the Ministry in the respective State/UT. As a result, the reporting system has improved considerably and more than 400 districts have started furnishing on-line monthly progress reports regularly. The Ministry had already developed software for direct uploading of information from the district level.

1951. (20-7-2007) NEW DELHI : Press Information Bureau is organizing an Income Tax Return Receipt Camp at PIB Press Lounge to facilitate the receipt of IT returns of accredited media persons. The camp will be manned by the officials of Income Tax Department of CBDT and will operate from 11.00 a.m. to 5.00 p.m. on 23rd and 24th July. 2007. It is mandatory to quote a valid PAN on the return forms without which the returns would not be accepted.

1952. (20-7-2007) NEW DELHI : The area coverage of kharif crops as compared to 19th July last week has gone up considerably as per data compiled by Agriculture Ministry. Sugarcane is an exception The total coverage of kharif rice has gone up to 116.8 lakh ha as compared to 115.4 lakh hectare at this time last year, the weekly Crop Weather Watch Group meeting of the Ministry of Agriculture was informed here today. Transplanting of rice is in progress in almost all the States. Sowing is at its peak in Punjab. Total coarse cereals have covered an area of 144.1 lakh ha as compared to 136.7 lakh ha at this time last year. Cotton has been sown in 72.3 lakh ha as compared to 64.2 lakh ha last year. Out of this, 24.37 lakh hectare is under Bt cotton. Sugarcane coverage is reported to be 44.37 lakh hectare compared to 48.13 lakh ha last year, and jute 7.89 lakh hectare (last year 8.18 lakh ha.). The total coverage of oilseeds so far has been 121.6 lakh ha as compared to 117.4 lakh ha on July 19 last year. Soybean and groundnut have been sown in 6% higher area as compared to that in 2006.

1953. (20-7-2007) NEW DELHI : If the poor ailing people living in rural areas cannot go to a hospital, then the hospital should reach them. The Indian Railways were quick to realize it and the Lifeline Express, the world's first hospital-on-rails, was launched on July 16, 1991. The Lifeline Express-a partnership of the Indian

Railways and Impact India Foundation, has been serving the country for two decades against avoidable disablement. It is the first and most successful, of the worldwide network which now consists of nineteen autonomous Foundations. Impact was promoted by the United Nations and was sponsored by three UN Agencies-UNDP, UNICEF and WHO. The Indian Railways handed over five new state-of the-art coaches for the lifeline Express, to Impact India Foundation. The new coaches are designed and manufactured by Integral Coach Factory, Perambur. The hospital train is equipped with two operation theatres. The main operation theatre has three operating tables for conducting surgery for cataract, squints, micro surgery of the inner ear, correction of cleft lip and for deformed limbs. The second operation theatre is also well equipped with two operating tables and four recovery beds and also an ophthalmic testing room, laboratory, X-Ray etc., for other exigencies.

1954. (20-7-2007) NEW DELHI : Following is the text of the special public lecture delivered by the Finance Minister, Shri P. Chidambaram at the Rajiv Gandhi Centre for Contemporary Studies at the University of Mumbai in Mumbai today:-"I am happy and grateful to be invited to deliver the Sesquicentennial lecture at the University of Mumbai. My happiness is doubled because the lecture is being delivered at the Rajiv Gandhi Centre for Contemporary Studies at the University. The University of Mumbai ranks alongside the University of Calcutta and the University of Madras as India's first institutions of higher learning in the modern era. In this 150th year, we acknowledge and salute the University of Mumbai for its great contribution to the cause of higher education; for educating and qualifying hundreds of thousands of students to assume diverse responsibilities; and for the many volumes of research and publications that have enriched our body of knowledge. More than anything else, the University of Mumbai, along with some other institutions, is a symbol of the rich tapestry of life and work of the citizens of this premier city. Mumbai, already the commercial capital of India, is poised to play an even more important role when India emerges as the third largest economy in the world. It is my firm belief that this University will be central to the emergence of Mumbai as a global centre for finance and commerce. Many of you may be surprised that I have chosen to speak on the subject of 'financial literacy' to a select and learned audience at this University. Let me assure you that I do not doubt your literacy skills or your financial acumen. All in this audience, I am sure, can read and write, and perhaps in more than one language. Most of you may be able to read and understand the numbers in a balance sheet or a profit and loss account or a Directors' Report. I am also reasonably certain that you invest your money wisely and see it multiply. However, do these skills make one financially literate? Financial literacy has been described as the ability to make informed judgments; the ability to take effective action regarding the current and future use of money; and the ability to manage money. It is these skills that will enable an individual to save, borrow, invest and manage his or her financial affairs prudently. Most individuals, whom we regard as educated or wealthy, do not possess these skills. In fact, it is the wealthy who seek the assistance of financial advisers and money managers. If that be so, what can we say about those who are not very educated or not very wealthy? What can we say about those who have fixed salaries or uncertain incomes? They do not have the skills that would make them financially literate; nor do they have the means to seek sound financial advice. The poor level of financial literacy in India can be easily demonstrated by reference to a few facts. Only 60 per cent of urban households have a bank account and only 40 per cent of rural households have a bank account. One-half of India's farm households, *i.e.*, nearly 60 million out of 120 million, have not borrowed from any bank or financial institution. According to a recent survey by Invest India Dataworks, out of 321 million paid workers (the rest are not working or are unpaid or are children), nearly one-half, *i.e.*, 160 million do not have access to banking or any other formal financial service. Among those who earn and save, an overwhelming proportion keeps the money at home or in a bank: as a result, only 5.3 million of the 321 million paid workers invest in mutual funds and barely 4.3 million of these 321 million paid workers have invested in equities. NSDL has reported that it has only 7.4 million depository accounts. Though estimates vary widely India has an estimated 15-20 million investors in equities. Another indicator of low financial literacy would be the number of people in India who have any kind of insurance. The total number of life insurance policies as on 31.3.2007 was 22 crore and the total number of non-life insurance policies was about 5.75 crore Since an individual may have more than one policy, the actual number of insured persons would be far less than the number of policies. The chilling conclusion is that a very large part of the population has no insurance of any kind-life, home, health, fire, theft or natural calamity. While poverty is certainly a factor that inhibits the spread of financial literacy, there is no evidence that those who are not poor are financially literate. Further, poverty seems to breed financial illiteracy. For example, the poor are forced to borrow, and they do so from money lenders who charge them usurious rates of interest. It is the money lender who is financially literate for he knows the power of compounding, not the poor borrower. A NSSO survey of 2003 has revealed that the share of moneylenders in rural lending has, in fact, gone up between 1991 and 2003 even while the level of institutional credit has increased during the same period.

1955. (20-7-2007) NEW DELHI : The All-India Consumer Price Index for Agricultural and Rural Labourers (Base 1986-87 = 100) increased by four points each during June 2007 to stand at 399 points for Agricultural Labourers and 400 points for Rural Labourers. The rise and fall in index varied from state to state. In case of Agricultural Labourers 17 states reflected an increase in indices ranging between 1 to 8 points, in two states the indices went down by 2 to 5 points while in one state the index remained constant. In case of Rural Labourers, 16 states reflected an increase ranging between 1 to 7 points while in three states the indices fell by one to three points. The Indices remained constant in one state. Haryana experienced the highest increase of 8 points in respect of Agricultural Labourers while Andhra Pradesh and Haryana witnessed the highest increase of 7 points each for Rural Labourers. The rise has been mainly due to increase in the prices of Rice, Wheat Atta, Jowar, Groundnut Oil, Onions and Vegetables & Fruits. On the other hand, the indices in respect of Himachal Pradesh showed a maximum decrease of 5 and 3 points for Agricultural Labourers and Rural Labourers respectively mainly due to decrease in the prices of Wheat Atta, Gram Dal, Vegetables & Fruits and Sugar. Punjab with 429 points for Agricultural Labourers and 430 points for Rural Labourers figured at the top of the index table. Manipur with 353 points for Agricultural Labourers and 354 points for Rural Labourers remained at the bottom of the index.

1956. (20-7-2007) NEW DELHI : Shri Raj Nath Singh President of BJP today inaugurated National Legal Cell of BJP. He congratulated Ms. Pinky Anand, the first woman National Convenor of the Legal Cell and said that he has high hopes from the Legal Cell, particularly in this day and age when legal issues have very important role in the interplay of democracy. The inauguration function was presided by Sh BAL Apte, a Senior Advocate and Rajya Sabha Member of Parliament, Sh. Ramlalji, Gen. Secretary (org), Shri Ravi Shankar Parshad the spokesperson and M.P of BJP chaired the function. Present among others high ranking political leaders were Shri Shahnawaz Hussain M.P. from Bhagalpur, Shri Vijay Jolly MLA of Saket and President Delhi Study Group, Ms. Arti Mehra, the Mayor of Delhi. State Convenors and members of Legal Cells from Madhya Pradesh, Karnataka, Orissa, Chhatisgarh, Andhra Pradesh, Chandigarh, Delhi and other States were present in large numbers. Hon'ble President of the party Shri Rajnath Singh in his address to the legal cell highlighted the role of judiciary as the backbone of Democracy and suggested that the main aim of the legal cell should be to cater even to the poorest of poor. He suggested some issues like those of illegal infiltration and illegal conversion that should be raised by this BJP Cell. Rajnath Ji expressed pleasure and said that he had high hopes with the new convenor. Shri Bal Apte Ji in his address focused mainly on how all the citizens of the nation should strive to attain 'Rule of Law'. Shri Ravi Shankar Prasad too shared his valuable with us and highlighted the importance of PIL's. However he also spoke of the ills of PIL's and how from Public Interest Litigation, today an era of Private Interest Litigation has come. Delivering the welcome address, Ms. Pinky Anand National Convenor of BJP thanked Sh Rajnath Singh and his team for her appointment as National Convenor of the National Legal Cell. She said that she had been associated with BJP for the last several years since she was inducted as Joint Secretary, DUSU and thereafter first woman Secretary of DUSU. Since then she has been actively working with the party including the appointment of Arjun Munda the then Chief Minister of Jharkhand after the Supreme Court pre-poned the floor test in a petition filed by Ms. Pinky Anand for Mr. Munda. She was also responsible for the major victory for Meera Kanwaria Corporator which election dispute was contested in the Hon'ble Supreme Court and the election of Sunita was set aside. Several other cases were mentioned by her. Ms. Pinky Anand pointed out to her pet theme *i.e.* judiciary in aid of democracy. She said that time and again law and the course of justice had ensured the victory of the basic structure of the Constitution and upholding of the fundamental rights of the citizens. She referred to inter-alia to the Jharkhand case, Bihar Case and the famous Bommai case. In these times of coalition parties, she pointed out the importance of lawyers in various stages of politics; first being to advice lawyers to make law, upholding the Constitution and to ensure that constitutional functionaries acted within the scheme of the constitution. She assured the party that the legal cells would be strengthened right up to the grass root levels and would provide back up of BJP in all fields of law.

1957. (20-7-2007) NEW DELHI : Even as the Su-30 MKIs, F3 Tornadoes and Eurofighter Typhoons of the Indian Air Force (IAF) and the Royal Air Force (RAF), battle it out in the sky during-Indradhanush 2007, elsewhere discreetly and unseen at the 'Control and Reporting Centre' (CRC) of RAF Scampton, a team of 'fighter controllers' (FC) from both Air Forces remain closeted and deeply engrossed on computer screens, albeit keeping a close watch on the proceedings. Of a marked significance during the exercise is the role of FCs accompanying the IAF contingent. In an airspace that is normally bereft of any liberties, fighter pilots invariably depend on them for manoeuvring tactically when engaging enemy targets in the air. "It is a team work," informs Wing Commander Jaswinder Singh, a Master Fighter Controller (MFC) on the IAF side. FCs undertake the crucial job of airspace management by coordinating and controlling the conduct of missions while providing regular updates on target information. IAF FCs hone their 'controlling skills' while their winged colleagues manouevre in all the dimensions in air. Their exposure to the Airborne Warning and Control (AWAC) systems is expected to go a long way since the IAF, with its modernization plans of inducting new radars, aerostats and AWACs in place, is all set to enhance further its existing surveillance and control capabilities. Some of the MFCs had some prior exposure to the scenario during the last Indradhanush exercise held in India. They keenly observed the E3D Sentry's controlling prowess from the air during the current exercise also. "Since they have been at it for more than 20 years, we have a great deal to learn from their experience," echoes Squadron Leader Achin Pillai, an MFC. "The RAF controllers have been very forthcoming in sharing their experience and we are coping very well too," he further added on the quick assimilation, adaptation and professional acumen of the IAF FCs, a fact acknowledged by the RAF FCs too. The missions being undertaken in the current exercise mostly conform to the NATO/RAF methods of operations. The missions are vastly diverse and include the conventional 1vs1 to large force engagements, involving several aircraft of different types. This increases the challenge for the FCs and requires skills extraordinaire. And significantly, they also enhance flight safety.

1958. (20-7-2007) NEW DELHI : If ever the airmen on both sides-IAF and RAF, differed on tactics during the just-concluded 'Exercise Indradhanush 2007', at RAF Waddington, it never showed when the two sat together at the Mobile Catering Support Unit (MCSU) for their afternoon meals. While their respective aircraft received fuel at the tarmac for their next flight, five RAF and two IAF chefs were fuelling nourishment for the aircrew and the ground crew at the MCSU. More popular in the RAF as the 'field kitchen', the MCSU housed beneath three large canopied tents-a kitchen and two dining areas that remained the common meeting zone. Relishing the modest, yet appeasing fares were nearly 250 airmen from both the air forces during lunch, and about 60-70 RAF personnel, their dinner. Both, the visiting Chief of Air Staff from India, Air Chief Marshal FH Major and the RAF Commander-in-Chief Air Command, Air Chief Marshal Sir Clive Loader also had an opportunity to taste the mixed fare of English continental menu and a few Indian dish together, during their visit on the last day of the exercise. The five RAF chefs-Sergent Edwards, Corporals Fletcher, Alps and SACs Harrison and Kneller are all trained from RAF Houlton. But they had no clue to any of the Indian dishes that they cooked prior to the exercise. "Whatever little we tried (cooking) was picked up from some Indian recipe books," informed Kneller hoping that the visitors relished them. "The dal wasn't being sautéed with the essential ingredients, so we just tried to spice it up with whatever herbs that we could manage here" spoke AK Pandey, who together with BR Sharma are among the two IAF 'Non-Combatants' accompanying the "Rhinos" detachment from Pune. The MCSU consists of a superbly designed 'Operational Field Catering System' (OFCS) that has been in use in the RAF for over a year now. It consists of kerosene/electricity-operated hotplates, boilers, ovens, multipurpose cooking vessels and a brand-new savoury for serving. "They are not ideally suitable for cooking Indian favourites like rajma and other delicacies, since they are not like any of the pressure cooking devices that we use back home," opined Sharma. Some of the fares on the English menu included cornish pasty, sausage blyonnaise, pasta carbonara, vegetable moussaka, chilli con carnie, pizzas, nazi gorin-new names et al, for the taste buds of most Indians on the tour. Indian dals, chicken biryani, mutton rogan josh, tandoori chicken on the contrary, proved more familiar with the RAF, and popular too. The RAF personnel hugely relished the Indian fares served at the dinners hosted by the IAF. In addition, the Indian hospitality and warmth clearly bowled the 'exercise hosts'. But one individual who deserved and got the loudest round of applause from the Indians was Abdul Samad, a Bangladesh-born restaurateur at Lincoln whose sumptuous contracted Indian dinners hardly let any IAF personnel miss much of his home-cooked Indian meal during dinners.

1959. (20-7-2007) NEW DELHI : Accepting the World Health Organisation (WHO) Director General's Special Award for Tobacco Control, today, the Union Minister for Health & Family Welfare, Dr. Anbumani Ramadoss said while tobacco has been considered to be an important contributor to Indian economy, the economic contribution of tobacco is far less than the deleterious effects of tobacco on health, environmental and social aspects. The total economic cost of treating related diseases was estimated at almost Rs.308.33 million in 2002-03 and this was significantly less than the total tax receipts of the Government, from tobacco. Presenting the Award to Dr. Ramadoss, Dr. Samlee Plianbangchang, Regional Director, SEARO, WHO, said that the World Health Organisation deems it an honour to acknowledge, with deep appreciation, the outstanding contributions of the Hon'ble Minister for the steps taken to safeguard future generations from the devastating consequences of tobacco use. The function was also attended by Dr. S.J. Habayab, WHO Representative to India, Dr. Poonam Singh Khetrapal, Deputy Regional Director and Shri Naresh Dayal, Secretary (HFW). The following is the text of the Health Minister's speech: "I thank the World Health Organisation in recognizing our effort in Tobacco Control and conferring me with the Director General's Special Award. I take the opportunity of conveying my sincere appreciations to DG, WHO. Most of us are aware that tobacco is the foremost cause of preventable death and disease in the world today. Due to its intake, millions of persons suffer from mouth, throat and lung cancer, coronary artery and obstructive lung diseases etc., resulting in serious human and social costs. In the absence of any strategic shift and social change, India perhaps will have the fastest rate of rise in deaths attributable to tobacco in the first two decades of the 21st century. Many of these deaths would occur in the productive years of adult life, as a consequence of an addiction acquired in youth. The variety of forms of tobacco use is unique to India. Apart from the smoked forms (cigarettes, bidis and cigars), a plethora of smokeless forms of consumption exist and they account for about 35 percent of the total tobacco consumption, viz. gutka, khaini, zarda, mawa, mishri, paan masala etc. This has led to a very high incidence of oral cancer in the country.

1960. (20-7-2007) NEW DELHI : The Cabinet Committee on Economic Affairs today gave its approval for: (a) DCI to procure three new Trailer Suction Hopper Dredgers each with a capacity of 5000 cubic meters from M/s. IHC Holland Merwede BV, The Netherlands at a total expenditure of Rs.1087 crore; (b) DCI will be allowed to avail of external financing upto the extent of approximately Rs.730 crore. The loan would be sourced either from the domestic market or international market and in case DCI resorts to ECB funding, it would seek the necessary approval from the competent authority. (c) DCI to pay balance amount from its internal resources. At present, DCI has an installed dredging capacity of 79.85 million cubic metres. There are ambitious plans to increase the capacity of ports both by adding new berths/terminals and by increasing the draft to enable bigger vessels to call at Indian Major Ports. As per projections for 11th Plan, the estimated average maintenance and capital dredging demand in India is expected to be 82.30 million cubic metres and 133.09 million cubic metres respectively. Taking into account the present dredging capacity of DCI and other dredging companies in India, there is an average shortage of 78 million cubic metres dredging capacity. Therefore, there is an urgent need to augment DCI's dredging capacity to meet the dredging demand and ensure timely implementation of plans for augmentation of Port infrastructure in India.

1961. (20-7-2007) NEW DELHI : The Union Cabinet today gave its approval to the following proposals: i) Signing of the inter-governmental Agreement with Bhutan to implement the 1095 MW Punatsangchhu-I Hydropower Project in Bhutan, and 400 KV Double Circuit Transmission lines from Project site to Indo-Bhutan border and related works. ii) Funding for the Project to be at Rs.3514.82 crore on agreed terms and conditions by the two Governments, comprising Rs.1405.92 crore equivalent to 40% of the estimated cost to completion as grant and; Rs.2108.89 crore equivalent to 60% of the estimated cost to completion as loan. The loan shall carry an interest rate of 10% per annum and shall be repayable in 12 equated annual instalments, the first repayment commencing from one year after the mean date of commercial operation. iii) Additional budgetary support, over and above the estimated project cost of Rs.3514.81 crore, to cover the additional outflow on account of service tax (on actual basis). iv) To develop the project under the Clean Development Mechanism (CDM) to generate carbon credits. The Project will provide surplus power to India and thus augment power availability in the country. In addition, the project will contribute to our strategic objective of further integrating the economy of Bhutan with that of India. The Project is expected to be commissioned in 7 years from the date of commencement.

1962. (20-7-2007) NEW DELHI : The Union Cabinet today gave its approval for promulgation of the Ordinance under Article 123(1) of Constitution to give effect to the proposals for amending section 7 (1) of the Cigarettes and other Tobacco products (Prohibition of Advertisement and Regulation of Trade and Commerce, Production, Supply & Distribution) Act, 2003. The Union Cabinet also gave its approval for replacement of the same by introduction of a Bill in Parliament. It will enable the Government to make the depiction of the skull and cross bones in packaging of all tobacco products as optional.

1963. (20-7-2007) NEW DELHI : The Union Cabinet today gave its approval to the following proposals :-1. Selection of the Chairman by a Search Committee headed by the Cabinet Secretary and comprising Secretary, DORT&H, Secretary, Planning Commission, a CMD or MD of a financial institution and one of the directors of IIMs to be nominated by the Cabinet Secretary. The tenure of the Chairman to be fixed for at least three year which can be extended upto five years. Age in case of the Chairman to be relaxed upto 62 years if required for three-year tenure. 2. NHAI to have six full time members (against five at present)-one each for finance, administration, public private partnership (PPP), two Members (Project) and one Member (Technical). 3. Increase in the number of part-time Members by two (from 4 to 6), who would be from the non-Government sector, one from IITs / IIMs and the other from financial institutions. 4. Amendment in NHAI Act, 1988 5. Creation of the following 26 posts of CGMs over and above the existing 13 posts of CGMs : i) 15 posts of CGMs for project implementation and corridor management. ii) 11 posts of CGMs fo *i.e.* CGM(Finance) (2 posts), CGM(PQ), CGM(SR&D), CGM (Administration and HR), CGM (IT), CGM (LA), CGM (Legal), CGM (Safety), Financial Analyst (CGM level), Contract Management Specialist (CGM level). 6. Empowering the Authority to engage where required, outside experts with relaxation of age if needed) specifically the posts of financial analyst, transport economist, contract management specialist and legal expert. This decision will equip the Authority to manage the enhanced mandate and to handle the PPP projects effectively in future. It will meet the nation's need for the provision and maintenance of National Highways network to global standards and to meet user's expectations in the most time bound and cost effective e manner, with the strategic policy framework set by the Government of India and thus promote economic well being and quality of life of the people.

1964. (20-7-2007) NEW DELHI : The Union Cabinet today gave its approval for dispensing with controls over Gur and also gave its approval for amending the Sugarcane (Control) Order, 1966. The new amended Order will be called the Sugarcane (Control) Amendment Order, 2007. The amended Order will help sugarcane farmers to dispose of their cane and get higher cane price.

1965. (20-7-2007) NEW DELHI : Congress Spokesperson Shri Abhishek Singhvi said that the polling is over and the result is more or less known. Even the most severe critic, the most skeptical observer cannot run away from reality. There is in the air, history in the making, for the first time the lady from Jalgaon will be lighting the lamp in Raisina hills. But the larger question remains which the NDA must ask itself because the nation is asking the NDA and indeed the nonexistent Third Front. The question is, was it worth it all? Was it necessary to demean and denigrate a constitutional office in a manner in which it was done? Was it necessary to vitiate the atmosphere? Even more importantly, could the NDA have avoided it a self-inflicted wound? Could they have avoided a series of continuous non-truths, false-hoods, misleading innuendos and attempts to connect the non-connectables? This question that is being asked, will be asked, because the nation expected more from those who claim to be a responsible Opposition. Not only the nation expected more, the nation deserved more. If unity was the object of the NDA then it is a remarkable irony that at the end of a three-four week vicious false campaign they find the so-called unity in tatters. And if the NDA should not stay united, what hope is there for a so-called or a united Third Front. This so-called Third Front had a three-day life. It died a natural death in three days. It died a death before it was born. For all the labour pain it went through, it had only a stillborn to show. Well, the question remains and through you we ask the same question which the nation is asking that was all this necessary, either for a nonexistent, non-united Third Front. And equally important, was all this necessary for a Naturally Divided Alliance, the NDA. To a question that you say, was this necessary but Congress also indulged in vicious campaigning, Shri Singhvi said that we are saying this advisedly, correctly and we repeat it again and we said so before. The reason is simple, we did nothing except, as the ruling alliance, announced the candidate. Unprecedentedly, after the date of announcement, for two weeks the most vicious campaign ever remembered in India was unleashed. After more than two weeks naturally, reports published contemporaneously from Mr. Shekhawat's past were printed in magazines and newspapers, which were then referred to by the Congress. Now, if you expect that in a democratic election where the high standards have been maintained by the UPA, you should continue to turn the other cheek. Well, we admit that we are more palable than Gandhiji. To a question as to what is your advise to the NDA and its allies? Shri Singhvi said that we are the last persons to give advice, for two reasons. One, there are parties and NDA is one of them which never learns from their errors in the past. They never learn the errors of history. And secondly, we do not want to sully our hands by interfering in areas, which are best left to divided houses. But we are raising the question to highlight the question before the nation. To a question whether the Congress Party would opt for a non-political candidate for Vice-President and that Jayalalitha too voted in the Presidential election, Shri Singhvi said that answering your second question first, we never asked her, we never said yes, we never said no. She has originally given a reason and she has given another reason now. Really speaking, your question, which I think is a valid question, which as a question, normally one would endorse, has to be addressed, has to be answered by the lady herself. It is she alone who should explain the direct inconsistency but we don't mind, we don't object and we don't have anything to say. As far as the first question is concerned, as you are aware the appointment to a constitutional position is not only a serious, not only a sensitive but an important process which has to be done outside the glare of the Media, indeed outside the glare of many other parts of the civil society and when we know, we shall share it with you. We do not believe that it is possible to dichotomise the selection of a candidate into a political or a non-political binary formulations. We believe that there is a multitude of factors which have to be taken into account and they relate across the spectrum and those factors are not for discussion either before the press or in civil society. We cannot discuss that at the moment when the process is reaching a culmination. To a question that allegations have been made against Kerala PCC president, Shri Ramesh Chennithala, that he collected Rs. 10 crores, did he collect this for the Party or for personal purpose if the last is true is this the high moral standard that you preach, Shri Singhvi said that this is a question like, have you stopped beating your wife.

1966. (20-7-2007) NEW DELHI : Pension Fund Regulatory and Development Authority (PFRDA) had invited Expressions of Interest (EOI) from public sector entities for sponsoring Pension Funds for Government employees on 11th May 2007. To be eligible, the sponsors were required to have at least 5 years experience of fund management and average assets under management of not less than Rs. 10,000 crore. The last date for submission of EoI was 25th May 2007. In response, EoIs were received from seven public sector entities namely, Canara Bank, IDBI

Capital Market Services Limited, Life Insurance Corporation of India, State Bank of India, UTI Asset Management Company Private Limited, Securities Trading Corporation of India Limited and Punjab National Bank. Of these seven entities, four were found to be eligible. They were invited for issuance of Request for Proposal (RFP) for sponsoring Pension Funds under the NPS. The four entities to which the Request for Proposal (RFP) was issued on 11th June 2007 are IDBI Capital Market Services Limited, Life Insurance Corporation of India, State Bank of India and UTI Asset Management Company Private Limited. Proposals from all the four entities, including technical and commercial bids, were received in PFRDA by the deadline of 4th July 2007. A Committee was constituted by PFRDA and entrusted with the responsibility of evaluation of the proposals received from the eligible entities, and to short-list the three best value bidders in terms of requirements (technical & commercial) of RFP. Based on the overall evaluation, including technical and commercial parameters, the Committee found (i) State Bank of India, (ii) UTI Asset Management Company Private Limited and (iii) Life Insurance Corporation of India as the three best value bidders and recommended their appointment as sponsors of Pension Funds under the New Pension System. Report of the Committee is under consideration of the PFRDA. Meanwhile, the contract between PFRDA & NSDL is under finalisation and the work relating to CRA activities will commence as soon as NSDL obtains the approval of SEBI to undertake this work.

1967. (20-7-2007) NEW DELHI : Shri Kamal Nath, Union Minister of Commerce and Industry, has been named "FDI Personality of the Year 2007" for Asia as well as the worldwide winner by FDI magazine and Financial Times Business, which is published by the Financial Times Group in London. "This award is in recognition of your active efforts to attract foreign businesses to India, boost exports, and promote trade and investment-the results of which have been a substantial increase in FDI inflows to India and a rise in export volumes last year, contributing to the continued economic development of the country and adding to its attractiveness as an investment location", says the citation by the premier publication which reports on the issues and developments that corporate executives consider while making international investment decisions. "Each year, with our Personality of the Year awards, we recognize the political and business leaders around the world who have been the most proactive, dynamic and innovative in securing foreign investment and improving the business environments of their jurisdictions. Regional winners are selected for Asia, Africa, Europe, Latin America, the Middle East and North America; out of these candidates a global winner is chosen. In being named a Personality of the Year, you join the ranks of such previous winners as Mexican President Vincente Fox (2003), Brazilian President Luis Inacio Lula da Silva (2004), Mayor of Seoul Lee Myung-bak (2005) and Premier of Ontario Dalton McGuinty (2006)", the citation adds. Reacting to this honour, Shri Kamal Nath stated that India's exports have almost doubled from Rs.293367 crore in 2003-04 to Rs.563800 crore during 2006-07. India's exports grew at an average annual growth rate of about 25% during the past 3 years. The FDI equity inflows during the year 2003-04 stood at Rs.10237 crore and have risen to Rs.70630 crore during the year 2006-07, amounting to a cumulative growth of 700%. The percentage growth during 2004-05 was 44% over the previous year. During 2005-06 it grew by 72.29% while in 2006-07, the percentage growth is 183.56, Shri Kamal Nath added.

1968. (20-7-2007) NEW DELHI : Shri Kamal Nath, Union Minister of Commerce & Industry, has launched the e-filing of Patent & Trademark applications, at a function organised by the Department of Industrial Policy & Promotion (DIPP), here today. With the launch of e-filing facilities the Minister stated that applicants can file their patent and trademark applications from anywhere in the world at any time at their convenience through Internet. Payments can also be made through the Payment Gateway of authorised bankers, which would save time and money and the hassles involved in visiting and filing the applications in the offices. Dr. Ashwani Kumar, Minister of State for Industry and Dr. Ajay Dua, Secretary (DIPP), were also present on the occasion. Dwelling on the future initiatives, Shri Kamal Nath said the next step is making Indian Patent Office (IPO) an International Search Authority (ISA) and an International Preliminary Examining Authority (IPEA) under the Patent Cooperation Treaty. Application for this will be filed with the World Intellectual Property Organisation (WIPO) this month itself, he informed. Currently, there are only 12 such authorities. Recognition as ISA and IPEA will enhance the prestige of the IPO and may attract work from abroad. "India is also at an advanced stage of joining the Madrid Protocol on Trade Marks. The Bill for making the changes necessary in the Trade Mark law will be introduced in the forthcoming session of the Parliament. Madrid Protocol is a simple, facilitative and cost-effective system for registration of International Trademarks. India's membership of the Madrid Protocol will help Indian companies to register their trade marks in the member countries of the Protocol through a single application", the Minister further stated. Providing details of the programme, Shri Kamal Nath informed that a major programme of modernization of the infrastructure of Intellectual Property Offices of India costing Rs.153 crore was implemented during the 10th Five Year Plan. Computerization has been one of the key components of the modernization initiatives. As part of this, facilities have been created for e-filing of Patent and Trademark applications. There are only a dozen or so countries which have e-filing facilities at present and India now gets into this elite group consisting of countries like USA, Japan, South Korea, China and the European Patent Office. Shri Kamal Nath expressed hope that eventually the complete process of grant of patent or registration of trademarks will be on-line and the Indian Patent and Trade Mark Offices will function almost as paperless offices. This will be achieved in a time span of about two years. The modules for the e-filing and on-line processing have been developed by the National Informatics Centre. The payment gateway is currently provided by the State Bank of India. Speaking about the legal aspects, the Minister informed that all IP legislations have been amended to make them compatible with India's treaty obligations. Necessary safeguards have been built into the IP laws, in particular in the Patents law, for protection of public interest including public health. Along with the legislation, rules have also been amended to install a user-friendly system for processing of IP applications, Shri Nath added. The Minister quoted from the recent observations from WIPO: "the Indian Patent Office has been dramatically transformed in recent years. New building, an effective and well supportive new IT system and an enthusiastic and well qualified staff provide the essential base for a high quality examining office". India had embarked on introducing a world-class Intellectual Property (IP) regime from the beginning of this century. It first updated the IP legislations on patents, trade marks, designs, etc.; then revised the procedures for grant of various IP rights making them simple, transparent and user-friendly; and simultaneously updated the infrastructure. With the launching of the e-Filing facility the first phase of the modernisation drive comes to an end.

1969. (20-7-2007) NEW DELHI : The Railways have generated Rs.10896.61 crore of revenue earnings from freight traffic during the first quarter (*i.e.* April-June 2007) of the current financial year 2007-08 as compared to Rs. 9959.49 crore during the corresponding period last year, registering an increase of 9.41 per cent. Railways carried 185.25 million tonnes of freight traffic during April-June 2007 as compared to 175.84 million tonnes carried during the corresponding period last year, reflecting an increase of 5.35 per cent. The Net Tonne Kilo Metres (NTKM) went up from 116880 million during the months of April-June 2006 to 119870 million during April-June 2007, with an increase of 2.56 per cent. The earnings from freight traffic during the month of June 2007 was Rs. 3539.97 crore, compared to Rs. 3267.37 crore during the corresponding period last year showing an increase of 8.34 per cent. Railways carried 60.46 million tonnes (MTs) of freight traffic during the month of June 2007 as compared to 58.17 million tonnes of freight traffic during the corresponding period last year, registering an increase of 3.94 per cent. The Net Tonne Kilo Metres (NTKM) went up from 37746 million during the month of June 2006 to 38877 million during June 2007, showing an increase of 3.00 per cent. Of the total earnings during the month of June 2007, Rs. 1352.45 crore came from transportation of 26.22 million tonnes of coal, followed by Rs. 296.12 crore from 5.97 million tonnes of cement, Rs. 292.60 crore from 3.05 million tonnes of foodgrains, Rs. 250.31 crore from 2.85 million tonnes of petroleum oil and lubricant (POL), Rs. 244.29 crore from 3.62 million tonnes iron ore for exports, Rs. 176.40 crore from 2.97 million tonnes of fertilizers, Rs. 166.27 crore from 1.52 million tonnes of iron & steel for steel plants, Rs. 146.32 crore from 4.16 million tonnes of raw material for steel plants and Rs. 615.21 crore from 10.10 million tonnes of other goods.

1970. (20-7-2007) NEW DELHI : Farm commodity prices monitored by the Department of Consumer Affairs have generally remained steady or have shown mixed trend in different centres across the country in the week ending 13.7.2007.

Wheat prices remained steady at 11 centres. Lucknow, Ahmedabad, Jaipur and Bhubaneshwar saw an increase in wheat prices during the week. Wheat prices declined at Mumbai. Sugar prices remained steady across majority of the centres and increased at Ahmedabad, Mumbai and Thiruvananthapuram. Gram prices remained steady over the week across most of the centres; declined at Ahmedabad and increased at Agartala, Chennai and Hyderabad. Tur dal prices were also steady across majority of the centres; and increased at Mumbai, Kolkata and Bangalore. At Delhi, prices of tur dal and mustard oil remained steady over one week; those of wheat, atta, gram dal, sugar, salt, tea and milk remained steady over one month; and price of rice remained steady for over six months. Prices of groundnut oil, vanaspati, potato and onion increased during the week. As on 12.7.07, public sector agencies have contracted import of 10.38 lakh tonne pulses of which 2.27 lakh tonnes has already reached Indian ports. The imported pulses include urad, moong, dunpeas, masoor, chana, yellow peas and tur.

1971. (20-7-2007) NEW DELHI : The Minister of State for Commerce Shri Jairam Ramesh is visiting Dhaka on July 22, 2007 to be present at the launch of the India-Bangladesh Chamber of Commerce & Industry by Dr. Iajuddin Ahmed, President of Bangladesh. This Chamber is being launched by the Federation of Bangladesh Chambers of Commerce & Industry and the Federation of Indian Chamber of Commerce & Industry to provide a high-level forum for accelerating economic partnerships between the two countries. Dr. Mirza Azizul Islam, the Advisor for Finance, Planning and Commerce of the caretaker government will also be present at the inaugural ceremony. During the visit, Shri Jairam Ramesh will meet with prominent members of the business community and think-tanks and also have separate meetings with Dr. Mirza Azizul Islam and with Major General (Retd) M.A. Matin, the Adviser for Communications, Shipping, Civil Aviation & Tourism. Apart from several other issues pertaining to trade and investment relations between the two countries, the issue of trade balance is likely to figure in the discussions. India's exports to Bangladesh during Apr. 2006-Feb 2007, were $ 1.5 billion and imports from Bangladesh were $ 205 million. Bangladesh has expressed concern at this deficit and has also been pointing out what it feels are unfair non-tariff barriers to its exports to India. Shri Ramesh is also expected to take up proposals submitted by India for improving connectivity and access. The forthcoming visit of Shri Ramesh is coming soon after the visit of the External Affairs Minister Shri Pranab Mukherjee to Dhaka on February 19,2007 and the visit of the Foreign Secretary Shri Shiv Shankar Menon during June 25-26,2007 and thus demonstrates the seriousness of the Government of India to pursue closer economic engagement with Bangladesh. Shri Ramesh had last visited Dhaka in April 2006 to attend the first meeting of the SAFTA Ministerial Council. He subsequently inaugurated the first ever Bangladesh Single Country Fair in Agartala in March 2007. In the last year, the Minister of State for Commerce has also taken special interest in developing projects to upgrade infrastructure at land custom stations along the India-Bangladesh border in West Bengal, Assam, Tripura &

Meghalaya particularly at Petrapole in West Bengal through which about two-thirds of bilateral trade takes place.

1972. (21-7-2007) NEW DELHI : The following is the text of the Finance Minister's speech: "Twenty five years ago, National Bank for Agriculture and Rural Development (NABARD) was created as an apex institution to address the credit needs of agriculture and rural development and also to promote, develop and coordinate other non-credit elements to achieve integrated rural development. By any measure, that was an enormous mandate. Thankfully, NABARD inherited the credit functions of the Agriculture Credit Department of the Reserve Bank of India and the refinance functions of the erstwhile Agricultural Refinance and Development Corporation (ARDC) and has, during the last 25 years, built upon that legacy. NABARD, today, is a household word, especially in rural India. I can confidently say that most of the innovative financial products and services developed and mainstreamed over the last two decades can be either directly attributed to NABARD or have been positively influenced by NABARD. During the 25 year period, NABARD has gone through three phases. In the first phase from 1982-1991, food grain production rose from 129.52 million tonnes to 168.38 million tonnes and the credit flow to agriculture increased from Rs. 4,351 crore to Rs. 14,332 crore. NABARD's refinance support increased from Rs. 2,042 crore to Rs. 5,287 crore. In those early years, NABARD's refinance was intended to play a supporting role to Cooperative Banks and Regional Rural Banks. These institutions drew upon NABARD's expertise in project appraisal, preparation of model schemes, monitoring and evaluation, and human resource development. NABARD also pioneered the diversification of rural financing from agriculture to non-agricultural activities. Besides, it is during this period that farmers' clubs were started in rural areas for dissemination of information and spread of credit culture. The second phase was during the years 1992 to 2001. During this period, food grain production rose from 168.38 million tonnes to 212.85 million tonnes and credit flow to agriculture increased from Rs. 14,332 crore to Rs. 61,942 crore. NABARD's refinance support increased from Rs. 5,287 crore to Rs. 14,294 crore. Having established its core function of refinance, NABARD shifted its focus towards other developmental issues. The SHG-Bank Linkage mechanism was started by NABARD as a pilot to provide access to credit for self help groups of the poor. The movement was grounded patiently in training of bankers, nurturing the NGOs and empowering the poor. The rest is history. Today there are more than 27.87 lakh groups through which credit is provided to 4 crore rural poor. The 'watershed project' in Maharashtra pioneered in 1992 and the 'sustainable livelihood for tribals' project in Gujarat started in 1994 are two examples of innovative thinking and practice. Both have evolved into good and replicable programmes. In 1995-96, at the initiative of Dr. Manmohan Singh, then Finance Minister, NABARD was encouraged to open a new window called the Rural Infrastructure Development Fund (RIDF). Until 2006-07, NABARD has sanctioned more than Rs.60,000 crore to State Governments to invest in rural infrastructure. In many States, the phrase 'NABARD road' or

'NABARD school' has gained wide currency and the brand NABARD is instantly recognized by a cross-section of the people. In 1998, NABARD designed the Kisan Credit Card (KCC) and offered it to the banking system. Until May 2007, 6.7 crore credit cards have been issued by all the agencies taken together. The KCC is an extremely popular low cost product that delivers credit instantly to the farmer at reasonable rates of interest.

1973. (21-7-2007) NEW DELHI : Union Minister for Science and Technology and Earth Sciences Shri Kapil Sibal today inaugurated the Emerging Technologies Gallery at the National Science Centre in New Delhi. The new gallery " Emerging Technologies-A Look into the Future" showcases a range of sunrise technologies which promise to change human life in coming decades. These are mainly in the areas of Space, Information and Communication, Medicine and Biotechnology, Oceanography and Earth Sciences, Agriculture, Material Science, Nanotechnology, Energy and Transportation. On display are some attractive and interactive exhibits. These include a real endoscope that guides the visitor to view inside the stomach to diagnose diseases, a live telemedicine corner enabling tele-consult with expert doctors of Apollo Hospital in Chennai, a model of Tokomak (ITER), a joint international research and development project with India as a partner, which aims at demonstrating the scientific and technical feasibility of fusion power, a rotating virtual 3-D projection globe with supporting scientific information and content on Earth from Space, a virtual book about Gels and their uses to mankind and also a view of the interior of a Delhi Metro Rail coach. Addressing a large number of students who became the first group of visitors to the new gallery, Shri Kapil Sibal stressed the need for keeping alive the spirit of inquiry. Science, he said, is discovery of the unknown and spirit of inquiry, therefore, is a must. Terming the children as an 'Emerging Generation", he urged them not to be shy of using the words " Tell me Why". The Minister also lauded the efforts of the National Council of Science Museums and expressed hope that it will help generate excitement among students regarding various choices in Science and Technology. Also present on the occasion were Shri I K Mukherjee, Director General, National Council of Science Museums and Shri Shivprasad Khened, Director, National Science Centre, Delhi.

1974. (21-7-2007) NEW DELHI : Three teams of young innovators have been given the India Innovation Pioneers Challenge Awards for 2006-07. The Sparsha team consisting of Shri Rohit Singhal and Shri Soumyajit Dey of Indian Institute of Technology (IIT), Kharagpur bagged the first prize of Rs. 3 lakhs for their project called Sanyog, a vernacular iconic communication system in which the user selects icons as input and a complete sentence in the target language chosen by the user is generated. This technology enables disabled people, who are unable to speak, write or move, to communicate effectively in English and Indian regional languages. The Singularis team of Shri Ravi Saraogi and Shri Umesh Sachdev from Jaypee Institute of Information and Technology, Delhi got the second prize of Rs. 1 lakh for their project called MATS (Mobile Anti Theft Software), and innovative solution for curbing increasing cell phone theft across the world. The third prize of Rs. 50,000 went to Interface of Shri Tarun Janardhan Siripurapu from Indian Institute of Management (IIM), Kolkata for developing a computer interface that enables a blind person to use a computer. Giving away the awards at a function in New Delhi, Union Minister for Science and Technology and Earth Sciences, Shri Kapil Sibal called for the creation of innovation ecology in India. Urging the industry to join in the efforts of the government, he said we need to focus on building more incubators that will help the freshest of new ideas to see the light of day and become an economic reality. Congratulating the young innovators, the Minister expressed hope that such innovations would provide solutions that are accessible to those who are at the bottom of the pyramid. National Science & Technology Entrepreneurship Development Board (NSTEDB), DST, Intel and Indo-US Science and Technology Forum (IUSSTF) jointly organized the 'DST-Intel India Innovation Pioneers Challenge,' an innovative business plan competition for educational institutions, organizations and entrepreneurs across India with the objectives to create an entrepreneurial ecosystem in Indian academia & scientific enterprises through the Business Plan competitions. DST-Intel and IUSSTF have jointly invested of over Rs. 2.1 crore under the current entrepreneurial programmes. Shri Sibal also launched the India Innovation Pioneers Challenge 2007-08 to continue the journey embarked by DST, Intel and IUSSTF to boost the entrepreneurial spirit in India.

1975. (21-7-2007) NEW DELHI : The Union Minister of Shipping, Road Transport and Highways Thiru T.R. Baalu has said that the new Toll Policy has been finalized by the Government and the Toll Rules are under formulation. Speaking at the Conference of Chief Secretaries on 'Public-Private Partnership (PPP) in Infrastructure' organized by the Planning Commission here today, Thiru Baalu said that for toll collection, the Government has decided to shift to Electronic Toll Collection (ETC). Thiru Baalu chaired the Session on Highways at the Conference. Thiru Baalu said that for checking the cases of overloading, weigh-in motion bridges are being installed by the National Highways Authority of India (NHAI). The Minister disclosed that for real time traffic data collection, the Department of Road Transport and Highways is going to install 320 Automatic Traffic Counter-cum-Classifiers (ATCC) in the first stage at certain stretches of National Highways and finally, all the National Highways would be covered with ATCC. Thiru Baalu pointed out that the technology for user fee collection needs to be upgraded at the earliest in a time bound manner and the concepts like shadow tolling and congestion charging need to be examined for adoption in urban environment. Regulatory mechanism and speedy dispute resolution mechanism need to be formulated early, the Minister opined and said that non-compliance or default for the payment fee needs to be controlled through an effective enforcement mechanism. Referring to the issue of public-private partnership in infrastructure, the Minister said that lack of proper dissemination of project-related information and lack of adequate knowledge of local and geographical issues, generally a reason that very few global investors are aware of the project opportunities in India. Relatively, low size of projects and a lack of appropriate tie-ups with Indian partners also appear to be a major deterrent, he said. These issues require to be adequately addressed to encourage global investors, the Minister added. In order to address the concerns of private investors on loss of revenue due to absence of any control on access, the Minister said that we should give more emphasis on development of Expressways with control on access which would also provide the desired level of mobility for increased economic activity. Thiru Baalu informed that under the NHDP, the National Highways Authority of India (NHAI) has awarded 78 contracts aggregating to a length of around 4,500 kms at a cost of Rs.30,000 crores. So far, 16 projects aggregating to a length of 902 kms at a cost of Rs.5,242 crores have been completed, he said. During the financial year 2007-08, under the NHDP Phase-V (six-laning of National Highways), a length of 2,995 kms at a cost of Rs.18,988 crores are to be awarded on PPP basis. Similarly, under the NHDP Phase-III (four/six-laning of National Highways), 3,278 kms of roads at a cost of Rs.21,373 crores are to be awarded on PPP basis, the Minister added. Thiru Baalu also informed that in the Central sector, from the NHDP Phase-III onwards, implementation of road projects would be mainly through the PPP either on BOT (Toll) or on BOT (Annuity) and EPC in exceptional cases, *i.e.*, for strategic roads and roads in North-East especially. The Minister said that some of the State Governments such as Gujarat, Rajasthan, Madhya Pradesh, Maharashtra, Andhra Pradesh, Punjab, Kerala, Chhattisgarh and Tamil Nadu have also adopted the Public-Private Partnership approach for development of roads in their States. Earlier, the Secretary (Road Transport & Highways) Shri Vijay Singh made a presentation on the opportunities in the public-private partnership in the road sector.

1976. (21-7-2007) NEW DELHI : With an aim to document a pictorial account of the trials and tribulations of the Corps of Engineers, two Coffee Table Books namely 'Sappers' contribution in Nation Building' and 'Sappers in Disaster Mitigation' have been compiled under the patronage of the Engineers in Chief and Senior Colonel Commandant Corps of Engineers, Lt Gen. BS Dhaliwal. These compilations were formally released here today by the senior most sapper officer, erstwhile Engineer in Chief, Lt Gen. KN Dubey and junior most sapper officer, Lt Prabha Shankar Ojha. The function was attended by a large number of Engineer officers both retired and serving. The Corps of Engineers of the Indian Army is the key player in all rescue and relief activities having set a benchmark for service to the Nation. The sands of time bear testimony to the innumerable and vast array of indomitable tasks undertaken by the Sappers ranging from construction of dams, roads, jettys, infrastructure to helping in healing the scars of death and destruction in disasters such as the Orissa cyclone of 1999, Bhuj earthquake of 2001, Tsunami in 2003 and J&K earthquake of 2005. The Corps of Engineers have been omnipresent in the Nation's time of need true to their motto of 'SARVATRA'. The compilations commemorate the hallowed memory of 'The Brave Sapper' who laid down his life while bringing comfort and solace to our countrymen affected by calamities in addition to rendering dedicated and selfless service in Nation building.

1977. (21-7-2007) NEW DELHI : President APJ Abul Kalam said here today that I am indeed delighted to be here in the midst of the members of Rashtrapati Bhavan community with their families. May I thank the Officers, Staffs and their families particularly the children who have given full-fledged partnership for developing the Rashtrapati Bhavan during the last five years. Rashtrapati Bhavan has been nurtured continuously and progressively in many areas by the past ten distinguished Presidents, preceding me. I have had the privilege of the partnership of all of you during the period 2002-07 in continuing this process further. Rashtrapati Bhavan has given me many memorable events in which we have all worked together. It has been transformed into Peoples Bhavan, thanks to your efforts. Nearly one million people every year from all walks of life and all age groups such as farmers, sarpanches, police personnel, postmen, writers, educators, political leaders, judicial personalities, home makers, Indians living abroad, industrialists, teachers and students have enriched us with their presence. Invariably I have been getting lot of appreciation after their visit which has been due to the care and individual contribution from each one of you, be it the warm and courteous reception, catering, conducting around facilities, maintenance of the number of gardens, photography and transport. I have seen how the visitors get excited by the Children's Gallery, the exhibits in the Kitchen Museum, the display of paintings and sculptures in the Marble Hall, Herbal Garden, Spiritual Garden, Tactile Garden, Musical Fountain, the bio-diversity park, artificial lake, renovated paintings in the Asoka Hall and modernized reception. The foreign dignitaries have been quite impressed by the horse display, smartness in the parade and the music by our band. While in the present environment, the security personnel are providing us with constant vigil. I am glad that their facilities have been augmented for improving their working conditions. With the modern Multimedia studio established at Rashtrapati Bhavan, we have been able to reach far corners of the country and the world. In the health sector Rashtrapati Bhavan's clinic is connected to major hospitals like Research and Referral Hospital, All India Institute of Medical Sciences and CARE Hospital, Hyderabad. Employees and Family Members of Rashtrapati Bhavan above the age of 40 have been examined by the team of doctors and have been treated wherever necessary. They have also been followed up in the subsequent years including provision of counselling on lifestyle changes. Special screening has been done for children for early detection of hearing problems. The Clinic has been upgraded with latest technology equipment and has become a versatile medical centre in this region. I enjoyed meeting the staff members and families and greeting them on important festival days like Diwali, Rakhi, Holi, New Years Day and Id-ul-Fitr. During this period, I am happy that the housing environment, estate gardens have been improved, school has been given a technological upgradation and Gymnasiums have started functioning.

Rashtrapati Bhavan employees, families and their children participated with great enthusiasm in the special event of sports and other competition. I was very happy to see the Rashtrapati Bhavan School children participating in the Republic Day parade. We were happy to have the enthralling performances of leading and upcoming artists in music, dance and theatre from various parts of the country well attended by Rashtrapati Bhavan community and distinguished guests. During the five-year period, we have had one hundred and sixty nine tours covering all the States, Union Territories and sixteen foreign countries. These tours have been planned and implemented with high degree of military precision and has enabled my interaction with millions of people. With my personal association with you, I am sure all these facilities will be further nurtured and improved upon in years to come. I cherish my partnership with you in this beautiful environment of gardens, peacock, birds, animals nurtured by Rashtrapati Bhavan and above all the warmth, enthusiasm, cooperation, dedication and commitment shown by each one of you in every one of your activity during all these five years. My sincere thanks to all of you. I was thinking what I can ask you at this time. Each one of you grown-ups and children can plant one tree in Rashtrapati Bhavan. These trees will be named after each one of you. The Garden will be called Family Garden. Dr. Brahma Singh will give you a programme. I am sure you will give full support to plant atleast 10,000 saplings which will definitely improve the ecology of this place. Almighty will bless you. I am very proud of you. My best wishes to all of you in all your endeavours. May God bless you?

1978. (21-7-2007) NEW DELHI : The Vice President of India Shri Bhairon Singh Shekhawat met the President of India Dr. A.P.J. Abdul Kalam this evening. He has submitted his resignation from the post of Vice President of India.

1979. (22-7-2007) NEW DELHI : The Minister of State for Commerce, Shri Jairam Ramesh has stated that India has been reviewing the current restriction imposed on FDI from Bangladesh and there could be some positive news for Bangladeshi investors in the near future. Shri Ramesh was speaking at the launch of the India-Bangladesh Chamber of Commerce & Industry by Dr. Iajuddin Ahmed, President of Bangladesh in Dhaka today. "We have been reviewing these restrictions with a view to enabling FDI from Bangladesh into India on a case-to-case basis, subject to security clearance. I am hopeful that Bangladesh businessmen will receive some good news in this regard soon", he said. The Minister also touched upon the persistent Bangladeshi concern regarding a trade balance that is heavily in favour of India and opined that investments from India were a key to bridge the deficit. "Investments made by Indian companies in Bangladesh will help India to import more from Bangladesh", he said. The Minister also reiterated India's request for allowing transit routes to the North-East India and highlighted that apart from helping India, such routes would also provide Bangladesh with enormous trading opportunities with India's North-East and thus help Bangladesh to reduce its trade deficit with India even further. Shri

Ramesh also highlighted India's intention to undertake joint projects with Bangladesh and also suggested a possible agreement between the two countries on multi-modal transportation systems, including on container traffic, to facilitate joint projects. The Minister also requested Bangladesh to consider opening additional land customs stations to enable greater two-way trade. While commenting on the India-Bangladesh Chamber of Commerce & Industry (IBCCI), a joint effort of the Federation of Bangladesh Chambers of Commerce & Industry and the Federation of Indian Chamber of Commerce & Industry (FICCI), launched today, Shri Jairam Ramesh expressed the hope that the Chamber would soon emerge as a powerful force for sustained collaboration between our two economies and for deeper partnerships between our two societies. Following is the full text of Shri Jairam Ramesh's address at the launch of the IBCCI today at Dhaka : "His Excellency, Dr. Iajuddin Ahmed, Honourable President of the People's Republic of Bangladesh His Excellency, Dr. Mirza Azizul Islam, Mr. Mir Nasir Hossain, Mr. Abdul Matlub Ahmed, Ladies and Gentlemen, I am delighted to be back in Dhaka. I was here in April last year. Since then, I have been in touch with my friends in Bangladesh. In June 2006, I interacted with a Bangladesh business delegation in Kolkata. In March this year, I inaugurated the first-ever Bangladesh Single-Country Trade Fair in Agartala with a large number of enterprising businesswomen from Dhaka & Chittagong present. That day in Agartala was the historic occasion when Bangladesh outplayed India in the World Cup. That evening when we were at dinner, I found that my Bangladeshi friends were ecstatic on two counts:-on the performance of their own team; and on Sourav Ganguly's showing as well. This was yet another reminder to me how we are two countries separated by our commonalities. Today, we are launching India-Bangladesh Chamber of Commerce & Industry. Even though we have our distinctive identities, we are two countries who share the same author for their national anthems and who are bound together very intimately by geography, history, culture and language. I hope that this new Chamber will soon emerge as a powerful force for sustained collaboration between our two economies and for deeper partnerships between our two societies. Let me reiterate what should be obvious—that India is firmly committed to seeing and assisting in the emergence of an economically strong and prosperous Bangladesh.

1980. (23-7-2007) NEW DELHI : The President, Dr. A.P.J. Abdul Kalam will address the nation tomorrow over Doordarshan and All India Radio. The Address will be telecast over all channels of Doordarshan from 7 p.m. to 8 p.m. It will also be broadcast over all channels of All India Radio in English followed by Hindi from 7.30 p.m. onwards. In addition All India Radio will broadcast the regional language versions of the Address over their regional channels from 9.30 p.m. onwards.

1981. (23-7-2007) NEW DELHI : Government of India have announced the sale (re-issue) of " 7.55 percent Government Stock, 2010" under Market Stabilization Scheme for a notified amount of Rs. 2,000 crore (nominal). The Government Stock will be sold through price based auction using multiple price method. The auction will be conducted by the Reserve Bank of India, Mumbai Office, Fort, Mumbai on July 25, 2007 (Wednesday). Up to 5% of the amount notified for the sale of stock is reserved for allotment to eligible individuals and Institutions on non-competitive basis as per the Scheme for Non-Competitive Bidding Facility in the Auction of Government Securities. Bids in the prescribed form obtainable from the Regional Director, Reserve Bank of India, Mumbai Office (Public Debt Office), Fort, Mumbai-400 001 and RBI website www.rbi.org.in should be submitted to that Office on July 25, 2007. The NDS members should submit competitive as well as non-competitive bids in electronic format using Primary Market Operation (PMO) module of NDS. All bids should be submitted by 12.30 P.M. The result of the auction will be announced on July 25, 2007 and payment by successful bidders will be during banking hours on July 26, 2007 (Thursday).

1982. (23-7-2007) NEW DELHI : Smiling with joy, 6 national IRIS winners accepted certificates of excellence from the Union Minister for Science and Technology & Earth Sciences, Shri Kapil Sibal, when he rewarded them for their thought provoking innovations developed as projects for participation at Initiative for Research & Innovation in Science (IRIS). Declaring IRIS 2007 open from today, Shri Sibal urged students across the country to apply their theoretical knowledge to experiment and design innovations that could benefit the human race. A collaborative effort by Intel, Department of Science and Technology (DST) and Confederation of Indian Industry (CII), IRIS, India's biggest science fair was held at New Delhi in December 2006 to promote inventions and innovations amongst school children by encouraging a spirit of discovery in education. During the ceremony in New Delhi today, the national IRIS winners; Rishin Behl, Vaishnavi Vishwanathan, Tanay David Delima, Nikhil Khosla, Sarvesh Nevatia, and Rehan Netarwla who hail from different parts of the country spoke about their ideas and experiences in developing their innovative projects and participating at the World's largest Science Fair-Intel International Science & Engineering Fair (ISEF). Competing with more than 1500 students from 45+ countries, the Indian Contingent comprising of national IRIS winners bagged 8 awards among 14 scientific project categories at the international fair. While Rishin Behl won 5 awards for his project on Magnetic Lazer Siesmograph, Ram Raghunathan, Vaishnavi Viswanathan and the team of Tanay David Delima & Nikhil Khosla won one award each for their projects on FDIS: A Fast Frequency Distribution Based Interpolation Search Algorithm for Sorted Arrays, Termite Malady?-A Herbal Remedy and Prevention of vehicular tailgating accidents. Stressing the importance of innovation in today's world, Rahul Bedi, Director, Corporate Affairs, South Asia, Intel said that his company is inspired by the ground breaking projects of these young scientists. Tapping the fields of science & math, these students have proved that they are no less in conceptualizing original projects that can help global advancement. IRIS 2007, which would culminate in December 2007 with the announcement of national as well as subject category & special category winners, is inviting entries in 10 scientific categories from students in schools across the country. This year, participants in 3 categories are eligible for participation. The first category involves participation from students in 5th to 8th standard (under the age of 13 yrs), the second category involves 9th to 12th standard (under the age of 20 yrs) and third category involves College/ PG students (under the age of 35 yrs). IRIS is expected to touch over 20 lakh students in 25,000+ schools and institutes in India by 2010.

1983. (23-7-2007) NEW DELHI : The Central Board of Trustees of the Employees Provident Fund (EPF) has recommended to the government 8.5 percent rate of interest to be credited to the accounts of EPF members for 2006-07. The decision was taken at a special meeting of the Central Board of Trustees (CBT) presided over by the Minister of State (Independent Charge) for Labour and Employment, Shri Oscar Fernandes here today. The decision comes after the CBT accepted the Report of the Sub-Committee appointed to look into the accounts of Employees Provident Fund and said that the deficit of Rs. 449.90 crore would be met from the Interest Suspense Account. The expected interest income during 2006-07 would be Rs. 7372.67 crore while the liability at 8.5% interest rate would be Rs.7822.57 crore. Briefing mediapersons after the meeting Shri Fernandes said that according to the Report of the Sub-Committee, there was an accumulated balance of Rs. 347.78 crore in the Interest Suspense Account, Rs.185.69 crore in the Contingency Reserve Fund (CRF) also part of the Interest Suspense Account and Rs. 56.69 crore in the Special Reserve Fund (Total Rs.590.16 crore). After meeting the deficit of Rs. 449.90 crore, the EPFO would be left with a surplus of about Rs. 83 Crore while leaving aside Rs. 56.69 crore in the Special Reserve Fund. The meeting was attended by the representatives of the Employees, Employers and the Central and State governments.

1984. (23-7-2007) NEW DELHI : Finance Minister, Shri P. Chidambaram will inaugurate the All India Annual Conference of the Chief Commissioners & Director Generals of Customs and Central Excise, here tomorrow. The two day conference will commence with performance appraisal of the department in key areas such as revenue, trade facilitation, enforcement etc., followed by a session on the status of automation initiatives of CBEC. A separate session is being devoted for Integrity development in the department. The conclave will also deliberate on initiatives to fine-tune the tax administration, and the importance of buttressing it with rapid computerization. Other important issues such as measures to improve compliance levels in Indirect Taxation, Dispute Resolution, Goods and Service tax and Emerging Challenges before Customs will also be discussed. The conference will act as a catalyst for providing important contribution to strengthening of the Indirect Tax administration. It will also provide an opportunity to the Chief Commissioners and Director Generals to interact with each other, and discuss issues of general and common nature. The Minister of State for Finance (Revenue) Sh. S.S. Palanimanickam will preside over the valedictory function.

1985. (23-7-2007) NEW DELHI : There are 1 lakh village level Forest Management Committees (FMC) are involved in regeneration of 22 million hectares forests which is almost 29 per cent of the country's total forest area. This is the result of National Forest Policy which encourages people's formal involvement in protection, regeneration, development and management of India's degraded forests. Addressing the 11th meeting of the Consultative Committee of the Ministry of Environment and Forests, Thiru S. Regupathy, Minister of State for Environment and Forests further said that Joint Forest Management Committee (JFMC) has not only emerged as one of the most important programmes in the country, but also a role model for forest regeneration in many parts of the world. He said though JFM mainly lies within the domain of the States and Union Territories, centre continuously provides catalytic assistance through policy and funding support. JFMCs now enter into Memorandum of Understanding with respective States and ensure gender and social equity in this whole process. He added that during 10th Plan, the National afforestation plan has helped institutionalize JFM in more than 24,000 forest fringe villages. The 729 projects approved under the programme generated about 8 crore labour days. A presentation was made on Joint Forest Management before the Members of the Consultative Committee. It was stated that a big support of fund for this programme has come from National Afforestation Programme of the Ministry. There is a system of unique fund flow mechanism under which funds are directly available to the JFMCs through Forest Development Agency from the centre. At the Divisional level FDA is a federation of all JFMCs under Societies Registration Act under which the village level institution is represented by JFMC. At present there are 729 FDAs covering 24215 JFMCs managing an area of 9.2 lakh hectares. JFMCs also have power to work outside forest area. With the earnings they get from forest produce and other activities along with the funds from centre, they indulge in essential requirements like construction of school, hospital, panchayat ghars, community centres, tube-well etc. They have started Self Help Groups which help in micro finance. JFMC members take activities like cere-culture, cocoon gathering from forest for tusser silk, basket weaving, tendu leaves plates. NIFT-Calcutta and Ahmedabad helped some JFMCs to learn weaving. JFMCs has helped to increase productivity of marginal agricultural funds, improved and durable local water sources for irrigation and drinking water, poverty alleviation etc. JFM reservations of the States vary but they are mostly liberal. Income from non-timber goes to the local village community. They also get free brazing and firewood. All the Members appreciated the success of the JFM activities. They made constructive suggestions to have linkage with other Ministries like Textile, Rural Development, Village Industry, Tribal Affairs etc. who have funds for villages and tribal areas. They asked about basic, sufficient help being given to the community to collect forest produce, setting up of Cooperatives and removal of middleman, education to rural people to run their societies/JFM, plantation of trees of local species in their area, implementation of Rozgar Guarantee Yojana and providing security and insurance to JFM Members in disturbed areas. Shri Namo Narayan Meena, Minister of State for Environment and Forests informed that Rs. 1200 crore fund has been made available against requirement of Rs. 8000 crore for this programme. Under the 10th Five Year Plan 1.7 lakh forests fringe villages will be brought under JFM to provide livelihood, security and employment generation. Under 11th Plan 33% of area will be brought under forest cover against 24 per cent area of today. Secretary Ministry of Environment and Forests, Ms. Meena Gupta informed the Members that steps would be taken to encourage by giving incentive to the JFMs who perform very well. She informed about Indira Priyadarshini Award given to different institutes for planting activities. She also gave assurance that only useful trees will be planted in respective areas and post-care will be taken for long period. S/shri Mahaveer Bhagora, Dhan Singh Rawat, Ramjilal Suman Smt. Karuna Shukla from Lok Sabha and S/shri Ramdas Aggarwal, Thanga Tamil Salvan, Satyavrat Chaturvedi from Rajya Sabha attended the Meeting.

1986. (23-7-2007) NEW DELHI : The ceremony of assumption of office by Smt. Pratibha Devisingh Patil, the President-elect will be held on Wednesday, July 25, 2007, at 2.30 p.m. in the Central Hall of Parliament House, New Delhi. The Prime Minister, members of the Council of Ministers, Speaker of the Lok Sabha, Chief Justice of India, Deputy Chair person of the Rajya Sabha, Governors, Chief Ministers, Heads of Diplomatic Missions, Members of Parliament and principal Civil and Military Officers of the Government of India will assemble in the Central Hall for the ceremony. The President and the President-elect will arrive in the Central Hall in a ceremonial procession. After the President-elect takes the oath of office in the presence of the Chief Justice of India, a 21-gun salute will be fired. The President will then deliver an address. On the conclusion of the ceremony in Central Hall, the President will leave for the Rashtrapati Bhavan where an inter-services guard of honour will be given to her in the forecourt and courtesies will be extended to the outgoing President.

1987. (23-7-2007) NEW DELHI : A high level 15 member Indonesian Parliamentarian Delegation led by Mr. Abdul Hakam Naja, Vice Speaker of the Commissioner called on the Tourism and Culture Minister Smt. Ambika Soni here today. During their one hour meeting both sides discussed matters related to tourism and culture sector. The Tourism and Culture Minister told the visiting delegation about the steps taken by India to promote domestic as well as international tourism in the country. She said in the year 2006 more than 4.43 million tourists visited India and we are expecting 10 million foreign tourists into the country by 2010. She said the Government may allow visa on arrival facility once the upgradation and modernization of Delhi and Mumbai airports is complete. She said the move to give visa on arrival will also get facilitated with airlines giving advance passenger information to security agencies. Smt. Soni informed the Indonesian Parliamentarians that 100 % foreign direct investment is allowed in hotel sector in India and already 6.5 billion US $ is in the pipeline in hotel construction. The Minister invited the Indonesian investors to invest in the hotel industry in India. She said some of the areas of cooperation between the two countries which can be strengthened are human resource development in tourism sector, capacity building, participation in tourism marts and fairs, exchange of travel correspondents and writers and holding of exhibitions of art and culture in each other's country. She said both the countries can contribute significantly in promoting regional cooperation in Asia-Pacific region in the tourism sector. The Minister also recalled visit of Indian expert to assess the earthquake damaged Prambanan World Heritage Site and Tamansari Water Castle at Yogyakarta, Indonesia. The visiting delegation showed keen interest in the activities taking place in tourism and film sector in India and discussed the ways to further strengthen the cooperation in the sector between the two countries. India Tourism Office in Singapore looks after the Indonesian market. It participates in travel fairs and exhibitions held in Indonesia to showcase Indian tourism products to the consumers and travel trade of Indonesia. It is slated to participate in Indonesia Trade Fiesta 2007 from Ist August, 2007 at Jakarta and PATA Travel Mart at Bali in September, 2007. Six travel agents in 2005-06 and one travel writer was invited to India in 2006-07 under the hospitality scheme of the Ministry.

1988. (23-7-2007) NEW DELHI : 30 DRDAs in Orissa have been sanctioned grant-in-aid of Rs.34.23 crore as balance Payment of first instalment of Central Share of funds under Swarnjayanti Gram Swarojgar Yojana (SGSY) during the year 2007-2008 as per details given in the Annexure. The amount should be utilized on the Programme as per approved guidelines of SGSY. The funding pattern will be 75:25 by the Centre and the State. The State Government should release its share within one month of the date of release of the Central assistance. Under SGSY, assistance is given to the poor family living below the poverty line for taking up self-employment. It actively promotes group approach by organising the rural poor into Self-Help Groups.

1989. (23-7-2007) NEW DELHI : The Ministry of Rural Development has released grant-in-aid amounting to Rs.44.68 crore to 33 DRDAs in Maharashtra towards balance Payment of first instalment of Central Share of funds under Swarnjayanti Gram Swarojgar Yojana (SGSY) during the year 2007-2008 as per details given in the Annexure. The amount should be utilized on the Programme as per approved guidelines of SGSY. The funding pattern will be 75:25 by the Centre and the State. The State Government should release its share within one month of the date of release of the Central assistance. Under SGSY, assistance is given to the poor family living below the poverty line for taking up self-employment. It actively promotes group approach by organising the rural poor into Self-Help Groups.

1990. (23-7-2007) NEW DELHI : Prime Minister, Dr. Manmohan Singh has released a set of commemorative coins featuring Lokmanya Tilak on his 151st

Birth Anniversary here today. Following is the text of the PM's remarks on the occasion: "With his electrifying slogan, "Swaraj is my birth-right and I shall have it" Lokmanya Bal Gangadhar Tilak stirred the Indian people and breathed new life into our struggle of freedom. Born in 1856, just one year ahead of the First War of Indian Independence, Lokmanya Tilak grew up in an India that was frustrated and sullen, getting drawn into a whirlpool of despair and hopelessness after the failure of the 1857 revolt. While some people were losing hope, others began to believe that the British had now turned a new leaf and were beginning to do good. A viewpoint had gained currency that the people of India were not yet ready for freedom since they did not know how to govern themselves. Apologists for the Empire were arguing that improvements in colonial administration had begun to give Indians a "good government". It was in this environment of defeatism and cynicism, that Lokmanya Tilak stood up and said that the so-called "good government" was no substitute for "self-government". Indians wanted to regain their natural right to govern themselves. Swaraj, he therefore said, is our "birth-right". People did not have to "earn" their freedom, since every person is born with the right to be free. It had a great unifying impact on the Indian people belonging to different provinces, speaking a variety of languages and professing diverse faiths. I am very happy that our Government is today honouring Lokmanya Tilak with this set of commemorative coins to mark his birth anniversary. It is a great privilege for me to associate myself with this memorable occasion. Lokmanya Tilak belongs to the most revered pantheon of our freedom fighters. His impact on the people both inside and outside India was indeed mesmerizing. When the British authorities arrested him in 1908, a world-renowned personality like Lenin was so moved that he denounced it. His criticism of Lokmanya's imprisonment constituted a shattering condemnation of British Empire. Before Mahatma Gandhi spearheaded our struggle for independence, it was Lokmanya Tilak who was among its leading torchbearers. Tilak's clarion call came as a breath of fresh air for our people and a nation's straining at the leash of subjugation. It summoned from the depths of their hearts unprecedented energy and courage to stand up to the might of the British rule. Mahatma Gandhi described himself as Lokmanya's "strongest bulwark". Pandit Jawaharlal Nehru, then studying in London, described himself a "Tilakite".

1991. (23-7-2007) NEW DELHI : The total approximate earnings of Indian Railways on originating basis during the period 1st July-10th July 2007 were Rs. 1655.36 crore compared to Rs. 1496.53 crore during the same period last year, registering an increase of 10.61 per cent. The total goods earnings have gone up from Rs. 1017.30 crore during 1st July-10th July 2006 to Rs. 1107.62 crore during 1st July-10th July 2007, showing an increase of 8.88 per cent. The total passenger revenue earnings during the period 1-10 July 2007 were Rs. 480.59 crore compared to Rs. 429.91 crore during the same period last year, reflecting an increase of 11.79 per cent. The revenue earnings from other coaching amounted to Rs. 44.31 crore during this period compared to Rs. 38.93 crore during the same period last year, showing an increase of 13.82 per cent. The total sundry earnings have gone up from Rs. 10.39 crore during 1-10 June 2006 to Rs. 22.84 crore during 1-10 July 2007, showing an increase of 119.83 per cent. The total approximate number of passengers booked during the period 1-10 July 2007 were 185.76 million compared to 168.57 million during the same period last year, showing an increase of 10.20 per cent. In the suburban and non-suburban sectors, the number of passengers booked during 1-10 July 2007 were 104.82 million and 80.94 million compared to 92.81 million and 75.76 million during the same period last year, registering an increase of 12.94 per cent and 6.84 per cent respectively.

1992. (23-7-2007) NEW DELHI : The Ministry of Social Justice and Empowerment has released Rs. 7, 00 crore to the J & K Council for Rehabilitation of widows, orphans, handicapped and other Older Persons since the year 2004-05. The Ministry of Social Justice and Empowerment has been implementing the General Grant in aid Programme for providing financial assistance in the field of Social Defence. Under the Scheme, a number of programmes are being supported since its inception towards rehabilitation of children of prostitutes, Sex Workers' destitute children, widows, handicapped those who have been affected by the militancy or natural calamities. The Central assistance is being utilized to rehabilitate 8877 widows, orphans, handicapped and elderly persons in militancy-affected areas.

1993. (24-7-2007) NEW DELHI : The Empowered Group of Ministers (EGoM) on Ultra Mega Power Projects, in the course of its deliberations on the Sasan Ultra Mega Power Project, has concluded that the response to RfQ of Globeleq-Lanco Consortium was void ab initio. Hence, the EGoM has directed, that keeping in view the overall public interest and the terms and conditions of the bid documents, Sasan Power Limited shall examine the further course and submit its recommendations to the EGoM expeditiously.

1994. (24-7-2007) NEW DELHI: Bharatiya Janata Party condemns UPA government for its anti-people anti-farmer approach exhibited in management of wheat procurement and PDS. By its deliberate policy of allowing private companies to purchase directly from farmers, it has created artificial shortages in the market due to their hoarding large stocks of wheat. This has resulted in prices going up despite good production of wheat. The wheat production has increased to 74 million tonnes above 5 million tonnes more than last year. This should have actually reduced the prices had the market forces played on its own. The situation worsened due to lackluster performance of UPA government on procurement front. The procurement of wheat, which was 14 to 20 million tonnes every year during NDA regime from 1999 to 2004 has gone down to 9 and 11 million tonnes during UPA regime in 2006 and 2007 respectively. More curious is the fact that the total offtake through PDS of rice and wheat has also gone down in last two years. The offtake in 2005-06 and 2006-07 under TPDS has gone down to 181 and 175 lakh tonnes respectively from earlier offtake of 296 lakh tonnes in 2004-05. Actually, when the prices in the market go up the demand and offtake under TPDS should have increased. But this did not happen because both the quality and delivery deteriorated. The quality of imported wheat was so bad that even the poorest sections of the society did not purchased. This needs thorough probe and introspection. The bungling of the government of importing wheat this year at \$320-360 per MT by rejecting earlier tenders at \$263 has already come to fore, for which BJP has demanded a full fledged CBI inquiry and resignation of food minister Sh. Sharad Pawar. Another probe should go into the details of quality specifications at the time of imports last year and also probe the quality of the actual imports. It should also tell the nation whether all the imported wheat has been consumed or not. Bharatiya Janata Party charges the government of not only importing substandard wheat at much higher cost but also deliberately destroying the PDS by its anti-people policies.

1995. (24-7-2007) NEW DELHI : The Engineering Units of Central Public Sector Enterprises (CPSEs) achieved a turnover of Rs.1620.91 crore against a target of Rs.1478.61 crore during June 2007. The turnover of non-Engineering Units for the month was Rs.139.58 crore, while the turnover of Consultancy/ Contract Units was Rs.131.53 crore against a target of Rs.125.09 crore. The CPSEs that achieved or exceeded their targets were Andrew Yule & Company Ltd., Bharat Heavy Electricals Ltd., Bharat Heavy Plates & Vessels Ltd., Bharat Pumps & Compressors Ltd., Heavy Engineering Corporation, Cement Corporation of India, Hindustan Shipyard Ltd., Tyre Corporation of India Ltd., Engineering Projects (India) Ltd. and Braithwaite Burn & Jessop Construction Company Ltd.

1996. (24-7-2007) NEW DELHI : Reviewing the performance of Total Sanitation Campaign (TSC), in a meeting in New Delhi, the Minister of Rural Development, Dr. Raghuvansh Prasad Singh has asked the States to ensure implementation of sanctioned projects within the stipulated time-frame. He said that there is need for giving focused attention to the Campaign in case of poor performing States/ UTs of Meghalaya, Dadra & Nagar Haveli, Bihar, Manipur, Punjab, Assam, Pondicherry, Jharkhand, Rajasthan and Jammu & Kashmir where household sanitation coverage is much below the National average. Nirmal Gram Puraskar, a performance-linked incentive scheme has brought about a silent revolution in the rural areas of the country with the construction of 2.5 crore individual houselhold latrines in the last two and half years and this was possible because of involvement of local community through Panchayati Raj Institutions (PRIs) in many States, the Minister said. He, however, expressed concern over the pace of implementation of the programme in some States and emphasized the need for large-scale involvement of NGOs and Community-based organizations. The UN Millennium Goal aims for Total Sanitation Coverage by 2015. Government of India is implementing the programme with a view to provide Total Sanitation Coverage by the year 2012. The Government has sanctioned projects for Total Sanitation Coverage for 573 out of 593 districts of the country. The programme emphasizes on Community participation, which involves awareness generation, Information, Education & Communication (IEC) activities, financial incentives to the BPL people, revolving financial assistance to population above the poverty line and full Government support to sanitary requirements of the Communities. The Sanitation coverage as per 2001 Census was 21% of the rural households of the country, which has now gone up to 45%.

1997. (24-7-2007) NEW DELHI : Shri Shankersinh Vaghela, Minister of Textiles has raised the curtain for the forthcoming event of TEX Summit 2007 by formally launching the official website and brochures of the Summit, here today. Shri Vaghela, while briefing the media persons told that four working groups are being constituted for (1) Textile inputs (2) Human Resource Development (3) Policy framework and the role of the Government and (4) Market Development. The Minister further said that the two-day summit will discuss and come out solutions to the problems presently faced by the textile industry. However, the Minister observed that the textile sector which used to be called as sun-set sector has been converted into a sun-rise sector. He further said that the textile sector is the second largest employer after agriculture. In the year 2005-06 the growth rate was 20 per cent. However due to the rupee valuation in the current year the exporters faced problem. Even for overcoming this problem, he held meetings and after consultation with the Commerce and Finance Ministries, the Prime Minister has announced the duty draw back concession and thus made it a sun-rise sector.

1998. (24-7-2007) NEW DELHI : The Minister for Steel, Chemicals and Fertilisers Shri Ram Vilas Paswan has said that the Government wants to facilitate the Posco Steel Project in Orissa. He conveyed this to the Korean Ambassador to India Mr. Paek Young Sun when the envoy called on him here today. Welcoming the investment programme, the Minister said the Government has set up an Inter Ministerial Group headed by the Secretary, Ministry of Steel, to expedite the implementation of large steel projects. Shri Paswan said Korean companies like Hyundai, Dusan, Samsung and Posco have vast experience in heavy engineering and construction. They can participate in the expansion programme of SAIL and RINL. The Korean envoy said this is the single largest overseas investment proposal for India and sought the cooperation of the Minister in this regard. He also invited the Minister to visit Korea.

1999. (24-7-2007) NEW DELHI : Recognizing the urgent need for embarking upon a concerted effort to check doping in collaboration with the global anti doping community, the Government of India became one of the members of the Foundation Board of WADA, set up with the initiative of the International Olympic Committee and signed the Copenhagen Declaration on Anti Doping in December, 2004 after seeking the approval of the Cabinet in its meeting held on 15th December, 2004. Presently, the anti-doping programme in the country is being run under aegis of the Sports Authority of India (SAI) under the Central Sector

Plan Scheme of "Scheme of Dope Test" through an advanced Dope Control Centre with modern testing facility and having requisite ISO certification. However, in order to ensure the effective implementation of the guidelines/progrmmes as enshrined in the Copenhagen Declaration and further articulated in detail in the International Convention against Doping in Sport adopted by the General Conference of UNESCO, two institutions viz., National anti-Doping Agency (NADA) and National Dope Test Laboratory (NDTL) are being established/operationalised as independent bodies. National Anti-Doping Agency (NADA): NADA, established as an autonomous Society, shall act as an advisory body to the Government on policy formulation on anti-doping in sports and as a nodal agency for implementation of programmes relating to anti-doping in the country. The main activities of NADA shall pertain to Test Planning and Management and Education and Research in anti-doping. National Dope Test Laboratory (NDTL): The existing Dope Control Centre which is already under the process of getting WADA accreditation is preparing for the coming Commonwealth Youth Games 2008 in Pune and Commonwealth Games 2010 in New Delhi. This centre will be upgraded as National Dope Test Laboratory and it is proposed to enhance its present capacity of testing approximately from approximately 2000 samples a year to approximately 5000 samples a year by 2010. The existing scheme for Dope Test is under the process of revision to incorporate the newly created/proposed institutional framework as above. During the Xth Plan the scheme has been run through SAI with a budget outlay of Rs. 23.60 crores. Doping is the deliberate or inadvertent use by sportspersons of a substance or method banned by Medical Commission of International Olympic Committee/World Anti Doping Agency (WADA). In Pursuit of gold and glory, large number of sportspersons all over the world are tempted to and/or use performance enhancing substances in an effort to gain a competitive edge over others.

2000. (24-7-2007) NEW DELHI : Retail prices of essential commodities monitored by the Department of Consumer Affairs at four metropolitan cities have remained stable or shown mixed trend in the week ending 20.7.2007. Prices of rice, gram, tur, milk, potato and salt were steady while that of wheat, atta, groundnut oil and vanaspati marginally increased. In Delhi prices of rice, gram, potato and salt remained steady for over one month. Wheat prices increased by Rupee one per kg both at Delhi and Mumbai and atta price increased by 50 paise at Delhi. Sugar price decreased by Rupee one per kg at Delhi. Onion prices increased by Rupee one per kg at Delhi and declined by 50 paise at Mumbai. Mustard oil price declined by two Rupee per kg at Kolkata. Prices of vanaspati declined by Rs. two at Kolkata while there was an increase of Rupee one at Delhi and Rs. two at Chennai. Groundnut oil prices increased by Rs. two per kg at Delhi and Rupee one at Mumbai. Tea prices declined by Rupee one per kg at Delhi.

2001. (24-7-2007) NEW DELHI : More than seventy one lakh new telephone subscribers were added during the month of June 2007. This brings the total number of telephones in the country to more than 225.22 million. The total number of subscribers during June 2006 was 153.18 million *i.e.*, a growth of 47% during July 2006-June 2007. The GSM segment has shown an increase of 5.39 million during the month of June 2007, the CDMA segment of 1.95 million while the fixed segment has decreased by 0.18 million. The overall teledensity improved further to 19.86% in June 2007 as compared to 13.68% as on June 30, 2006. In the GSM segment, Tamilnadu telecom circle added more than 4.7 lakh subscribers during June 2007. In the CDMA segment, Andhra Pradesh telecom circle added 1.74 lakh subscribers during the period. Tamilnadu, Andhra Pradesh, Uttar Pradesh (E) and Uttar Pradesh (W) telecom circles have added more than 5 lakh subscribers each. The growth of broadband connections improved further and at the end of May 2007, about 2.43 million broadband connections were provided and coverage of broadband connectivity by public sector service providers has reached 1039 cities. Further, the total number of existing ISP licencees is 377. Under Bharat Nirman Programme, of the 66,822 villages remaining to be covered on November 2004, a total of 48125 Village Public Telephones (VPTs) have been provided. The remaining 18697 villages having more than 100 population and not lying in thick forest area etc. are to be covered by November 2007.

2002. (24-7-2007) NEW DELHI : Chargharia, a sleepy little village in West Tripura. Bwkhuk Chichha, is a Self Help Group of "eleven women" who have brought a sea change in this small hamlet 50 km from Agartala. The women mostly hail from the agri-labourers' community and tribal clan. The women are led by Sharbani Deb Barma and have a banana plantation, a fishery and a piggery project going. They also run a vermi compost project. All women members of SHG produce and merchandise tribal costumes of simple but intricate designs on their hand driven looms. Their income per month has increased up to a thousand rupees per head and the group has achieved gradation two as per the scheme-Sworojgari Yojana. The Group leader Sharbani Deb Barma has spared her courtyard for making the seed-bed following SRI method of paddy cultivation. She demonstrates to the other women the way to use 800 grams of seed in each hectare of land. Agriculture department is also extending a helping hand. For paddy cultivation and vermi compost projects assistance under the 'Technology Mission' has been sought. By way of agriculture or fisheries etc., the SHG is generating mandays too. Mrs. Deb Barma said that every member can deposit at least fifty rupees in the group's account per month and can earn a minimum of Rs. 500/-or even more. It is not only the income generation activity that they are involved in. The group has generated many more jobs too as Suraj Deb Barma said, "I have invested my wife's income in purchasing goats and chicken that has helped us to generate more money. Group members get loan on two percent interest from the collective fund". Shanti Deb Barma, mother of two little children has a dream-when the group becomes more stable, she would send her children to the city for better studies. Shova Deb Barma, second-in-command of the SHG is full of hope, to be dependent only on the SHG and its activities for livelihood. The Bwkhuk Chichha members are being involved in many other social activities too. They are now partners in adult literacy programme. The village is moving ahead with the success of total sanitation programme. The Bwkhuk Chichha members have involved themselves in motivating fellow families and the rural society. Chargharia has never missed any festival or fair to sell tribal costumes like Riya, Pachra and other handloom products. The group participated in SARAS held in New Delhi two years back and was very popular among the people living in the capital. With the help of these 11 ladies, the 2000-odd population of Chargharia is gradually developing and flourishing.

2003. (24-7-2007) NEW DELHI : The National Wage Boards for Working Journalists and Non-working Journalists of newspapers and news agencies will hold their first meetings at Kochi in Kerala on 2nd August 2007. The Meetings of the two Boards will be held at Kerala Guest House, Ernakulum, Kochi from 10.30 a.m. to 1.00 p.m. During the meetings the Boards will meet representatives of newspaper establishments, working journalists, non-journalist newspaper employees and other stakeholders interested in the fixation/ revision of rates of wages of working journalists, non-journalist newspaper employees. They can make representation in writing and can be handed over to the Chairman of the two Boards Dr. Justice K. Narayana Kurup. The written representation should state the rates of wages which, in the opinion of the person making the representation, would be reasonable, having regard to the capacity of the employer to pay the same, or to any other circumstance, whichever may seem relevant to the person making the representation. The Chairman of the two Boards Justice Kurup can also be contacted at telephone numbers 0484-2369163 or 09447091131. The two Wage Boards headed by Justice Kurup have been set up by the union Labour & Employment Ministry on 24th May 2007 for fixing or revising rates of wages of working journalists and newspaper employees and non-journalists newspapers employees in accordance with the provisions of the Working Journalists and Other Newspaper Employees (Conditions of service) and Miscellaneous Provisions Act, 1955. Both the Wage Boards have 10 members each. The Chairman Dr. Justice K. Narayana Kurup is a formal Judge of Kerala High Court and has also served as Acting Chief Justice of Madras High Court. Shri K.M. Sahni, former Labour and Employment Secretary, is the Member Secretary for both the Boards. The other independent members common to both the Boards are Shri B.P. Singh and Shri P.N. Prasanna Kumar. Shri Naresh Mohan (Indian Newspaper Society), Shri Gurinder Singh (All India Small and Medium Newspapers Federation), Shri Prataprai Tarachand Shah (Indian Language Newspaper Association) are representing employers on both the Wage Boards. Shri K. Vikram Rao (Indian Federation of Working Journalists), Shri Nand Kishore Trikha (National Union of Journalists (India) and Shri Suresh Akhouri (Indian Journalists Union) are representing the Working Journalists on the Wage Board for Working Journalists. Shri Madan Phadnis (All India Newspaper Employees Federation), Shri Uma Shankar Mishra (National Federation of Newspaper Employees) and Shri M.S.

Yadav (Press Trust of India) represent non-journalists on the Wage Boards for Non-Working Journalists.

2004. (24-7-2007) NEW DELHI : Grant-in-aid of Rs.18.24 lakh has been released by the Ministry of Rural Development to Kargil DRDA of Jammu & Kashmir towards payment of first instalment of Central share for the year 2007-2008 under DRDA Administration. The funding pattern under the scheme is 75:25 between Centre and the State. The utilization of funds is to be in accordance with the DRDA administration guidelines and the release of the second instalment during 2006-07 is subject to the fulfilment of all the conditions as per the DRDA Administration guidelines.

2005. (24-7-2007) NEW DELHI : An amount of Rs. 18.24 lakh has been released by the Ministry of Rural Development as grant-in-aid to Simdega DRDA of Jharkhand as payment of first instalment of Central Share for the year 2007-08 under DRDA Administration. The funding pattern under the scheme is 75:25 between Centre and the State. The utilization of funds is to be in accordance with the DRDA administration guidelines and the release of the second instalment during 2006-07 is subject to the fulfilment of all the conditions as per the DRDA Administration guidelines.

2006. (24-7-2007) NEW DELHI : The Election Commission has decided to hold bye election to fill up 2 (two) vacancies in the Lok Sabha, one is from 9-Jamshedpur Parliamentary Constituency (Jharkhand) arising out of the death of sitting member Sh. Sunil Kumar Mahto on 04.03.2007 and another is from 39-Ballia Parliamentary Constituency (Uttar Pradesh) arising out of the death of sitting member Sh. Chandra Shekhar on 08.07.2007. The Commission has also decided to hold bye elections to fill 1 (one) vacancy in the Legislative Assembly of Uttarakhand from 30-Dhumakot Assembly Constituency (A.C) arising out of the resignation of sitting member Sh.Tejpal Singh Rawat on 07-06-07 and also 3(three) vacancies in the Legislative Assembly of Uttar Pradesh from 20-Suar Tanda A.C on 23.05.2007, 25-Gunnaur A.C on 16.05.2007 and 296-Farrukhabad A.C on 11.06.2007 arising out of the resignation of sitting members namely Sh. Nawab Kazim Ali Khan, Sh.Mulayam Singh Yadav and Sh. Vijay Singh respectively.

2007. (24-7-2007) NEW DELHI : Till date more than 27,000 cards have been issued to the train passengers under the Scheme of Frequent Travellers (SOFT). With a view to reward the passengers who travel frequently by train, SOFT has been launched by Indian Railways Catering and Tourism Corporation (IRCTC) in collaboration with State Bank of India. To improve the patronization of higher classes, where occupancy level is relatively low as compared to that in Sleeper Class and 3-AC classes, this scheme was launched in February 2006 which is applicable to 1st AC, 2 AC and AC Chair Car classes. A passenger, who travels frequently by trains, has to get himself registered on payment of first year membership fee of Rs. 500/- after which a card is issued. The card has to be renewed every year on payment of an annual fee of Rs. 300/-. Passenger gets a complimentary train trip after certain numbers of reward points are accumulated.

2008. (25-7-2007) NEW DELHI : Department of Animal Husbandry, Dairying and Fisheries notified today an outbreak of Avian Influenza in Chingmeirong Village in East Imphal District of Manipur. The Central Rapid response Team of Ministry of Health and Family Welfare has been deputed to review and firm up preparedness measures. The 21 family members in a cluster of three houses and 9 veterinary staff who got exposed to the infected birds have been put under Oseltamivir chemoprophylaxis. Their health status is being monitored and all are healthy. No residents in neighbourhood are suffering from influenza like illness. The Central Rapid Response Team of this Ministry held discussions with State health and animal husbandry authorities, assessed the situation and a micro action plan was drawn up. For the active human surveillance 20 medical teams have been constituted, each team having one medical officer, 3 supervisory staff, 30 health workers. One health worker would cover 100 households doing house to house search for influenza like illness. Daily reports would be generated. A team of 20 doctors would monitor the health status of cullers who would be on oseltamivir chemoprophylaxis. Orientation training has been imparted to state medical Rapid Response Teams, hospital staff and field staff. An isolation ward has been set up in the Jawaharlal Nehru Hospital, Imphal to manage suspected human cases of Avian Influenza. Dedicated doctors, staff and ambulance have been identified. 5000 capsules of Oseltamivir, 2000 sets of personal protective equipments, 1000 sets of N-95 masks and 2 ventilators have been airlifted to Imphal. Adequate stocks of these items are available with Ministry of Health & Family Welfare. The situation is being closely monitored. As of now, there is no suspected human cases of Avian Influenza.

2009. (25-7-2007) NEW DELHI : Global Steel magnet Shri L.N. Mittal today called on the Minister for Steel, Chemicals and Fertilisers Shri Ram Vilas Paswan and sought the support of the Government for implementation of their mega steel projects in Jharkhand and Orissa. The Chairman of the Mittal Steels said, he will discuss with the Jharkhand Government issues like allotment of coal, iron ore mines and land. Expressing his commitment to the 12 million tonne steel plants in the two states, Shri Mittal said they would need the 600 million tonnes of iron ore in Jharkhand over 30 years and a similar amount in Orissa. Shri Paswan assured Shri Mittal of a level playing field in relation to the public sector companies. He said, India should be the second largest producer of steel in the world by 2015-16 and the government has fixed a target of 200 million tonnes capacity by 2020. That is why we would like both private and public sector players to set up additional capacities. On the question of allotment of iron ore mines, he said, the Group of Ministers has approved the mining policy and now it will go to the cabinet and then to parliament. Shri Paswan suggested that the Mittal Group should put in its applications as first as possible. Later talking to newsmen Shri

Paswan said, it is his belief that the Jharkhand government can provide six hundred million tonnes of iron ore from Chiria mines outside the disputed part which SAIL has been asking for. Shri Mittal apprised the Minister about the integration of Arcelor with Mittal Steels, and said the integration process is going on smoothly raising shareholder's value in the company. He also offered the benefits of their Research and Development capabilities to Indian companies including SAIL. The Secretary Steel, Shri R.S. Pandey and senior officials were present during the meeting.

2010. (25-7-2007) NEW DELHI : Russia has lifted the temporary ban on rice exports from India and some other countries imposed earlier this year. This has been achieved after vigorous efforts made by Shri Kamal Nath, Union Minister of Commerce & Industry who took up the issue with his counterpart H.E. Mr. G.O. Gref, Minister of Economic Development and Trade of Russia. This was further followed up by the discussions held during the visit of the Indian delegation led by Shri G.K. Pillai, Commerce Secretary to Moscow on 9-10 July 2007 for the Joint Study Group meeting. A decision has now been taken by the Federal Service for Veterinary and Phyto-Sanitary Supervision (FSVPS) of Russia to resume issuing Quarantine Certificates for import of rice from India to the Russian Federation. Temporary restrictions on import of rice into Russia from some countries including India were imposed by the Russian Government on the pretext that the exporters of rice to Russia were violating the Russian Sanitary-Epidemiological requirements, in particular, regarding pesticide residues. Russian team had visited several countries including India to inspect the testing facilities and the prevailing situations to ascertain the quality of exports of rice from various countries. The Russian team visited India in February 2007 and held deliberations with the officials of Department of Commerce, Department of Agriculture and Cooperation and APEDA. They had also visited the laboratory facilities for testing of export consignments, rice mills and National Accreditation Board for Testing and Calibration Laboratories (NABL).

2011. (25-7-2007) NEW DELHI : The Finance Minister has emphasized the need to accept returns on trust, and to devise less invasive measures to check tax evasion, using more data (AIR, BCTT, FIU & Data Mining) making the working of the Income Tax department non-discretionary and non-discriminatory. He was addressing the two-day Annual Conference of Chief Commissioners and Directors General of Income Tax on 17th July 2007. Taxpayer grievance was another area requiring focused attention and the number of taxpayer grievances need to be brought down from the current level, he added. Shri P. Chidambaram expressed confidence that during fiscal 2007-08, at the current GDP growth rate of 9%, a growth of 16.3% in direct tax collection would be achieved, if not exceeded. He said in the area of recovery of tax arrears, significant progress has been made in the last 4 years. For the first time in over 35 years, the cumulative tax arrears as on 31.3.2007 declined as compared to arrears at the beginning of the financial year. Agreeing with the need to augment and reorient its human resources, the Finance Minister desired that the department should have a Human Resources Management Directorate at the earliest with a legal wing to act as a repository of legal knowledge and develop in-house talent on advocacy skills so that the domain knowledge of the officers is utilized effectively in handling matters before Tribunals and Courts. Filing of e-TDS returns will be compulsory for certain category of taxpayers from 1.9.2007, while e-payment of taxes, currently available through 5 banks will be introduced at all the agency banks authorized to collect direct taxes with effect from 1.1.2008. In order to make the process of scrutiny less invasive, the department had moved towards the system of selection of cases for scrutiny through Computer Aided system. The officials stated that the department is also going through a comprehensive business process reengineering (BPR) exercise, involving examination of processes, procedures, human resources and technology needs of the department. Towards improving taxpayers services, the department launched the tax return Preparer Scheme and a pilot Refund Banker Scheme. As it has been observed that a large number of TDS returns did not contain the PAN of the deductees, it was agreed that all Commissioners would hold meetings with CEOs/ CFOs to emphasis the need of correctly quoting PAN of deductees in TDS returns. Shri Chidambaram pointed out that in the field of computerization every new measure throws up new challenges. Therefore, the Chief Commissioners should identify, with the help of consultants, problems and immediately intimate the DG (Systems) or CBDT through Video Conferencing. For this purpose, separate funds should be made available. In his valedictory address, the Minister of State Shri S.S. Palanimanickam appreciated the achievements of the department, particularly in the changed business environment, and expressed confidence that the department would be effectively able to meet future challenges.

2012. (25-7-2007) NEW DELHI : A one member Committee headed by Shri R.S.Ratraja Murti, Retired Member of Postal Service Board has been constituted by the Government to examine the Wage Structure, Service Conditions etc. of the Gramin Dak Sevaks in the Department of Posts. It has also been asked to examine the desirability and need to sanction any interim relief till the time of recommendations of the Committee are made and accepted by the Government. Under the terms of reference the Committee will also examine the system of extra departmental post offices, conditions of employment and recommend suitable changes considered if necessary. It has also been asked to examine the reasonableness of introducing a social security scheme for providing provident fund and retirement benefits to Gramin Dak Seveks. The Committee will also examine and suggest any change in methods of recruitment, minimum qualifications for employment as Gramin Dak Sevaks and conduct & disciplinary rules. The Committee has also been asked to review the facilities provided to the public at different classes of extra departmental post offices. The Department of Posts has 2.86 lakh Gramin Dak Sevaks who will come under the purview of the committee. The Committee will be assisted by Shri A.K.Sharma, a senior administrative grade officer who will act as its Secretary.

2013. (25-7-2007) NEW DELHI : President Pratibha Patil address to the nation my greetings to you all. I thank the Members of Parliament and State Legislatures for electing me to this high office. I am overwhelmed by the affection and regard shown to me by so many people across the length and breadth of the country during the past few weeks. I stand here today as the Republic's first servant, humbled by this experience. It will be my sincere endeavour to live up to the high expectations of all those who have chosen to elect me, and to serve the best interests of the people of India. I am fully aware of the great responsibility that has been placed on my humble shoulders. This year we celebrate the 150th anniversary of the First War of Indian Independence. As I stand before you, I draw inspiration from the courage and sacrifice of all those who led our nation to freedom. One of the unique features of our national movement, of our freedom struggle, was the equal participation of men and women. Among the many who led that battle against foreign rule were brave women like Rani Lakshmibai, Begum Hazrat Mahal and Kitturu Rani Chennamma. In a few days time we will be celebrating the 60th anniversary of our independence. I would like to remember with gratitude the great contribution to our freedom struggle made by leaders like Pandit Jawaharlal Nehru, Sardar Patel, Maulana Azad and Sarojini Naidu, who fought under the unique and path-breaking leadership of the father of our nation, Mahatma Gandhi. Therefore, I share the sense of pride of every Indian that the United Nations General Assembly has declared Gandhi Jayanti, the 2nd of October, as the International Day of Non-violence. We express our gratitude to the world community for this unique honour. Ours is an ancient civilization but a young nation. We look back with pride to the tremendous achievements made during the 60 years of our independence in all spheres of life. More than anything else we have demonstrated to the world that a developing country of over a billion people, each aspiring for a better quality of life, can live harmoniously and move forward within the framework of a secular democracy. As President I assure the people of India that in upholding the Constitution I will always be inspired by the stirring message of Dr. Babasaheb Ambedkar who, in his closing speech to the Constituent Assembly, emphasized the need to hold fast to the constitutional methods of achieving our social and economic objectives. Sixty years ago, speaking in these very premises, Pandit Jawaharlal Nehru had said, and I quote, "Freedom and power bring responsibility." He reminded us that this great responsibility, I quote "rests upon this Assembly, a sovereign body representing the sovereign people of India." Indira Gandhi as India's first and only woman Prime Minister, showed us that the upliftment of the underprivileged and alleviation of poverty must remain the foremost and sacred duty of those who hold public office. Today India stands at the threshold of a new era of progress. The nation is moving at historically unprecedented rates of growth. It should be our combined endeavour to sustain this growth and ensure that it is socially inclusive. We must ensure that every section of our society-particularly the weak and the disadvantaged-are equal partners in, and beneficiaries of, the development process. We must also ensure that every region of the country participates in and benefits from the process of economic growth. I am reminded of the words of the great seventeenth century, Marathi poet-saint, Sant Tukaram, who said: One who befriends the poor and the oppressed, Recognise him to be a Saint, for God is with him. Today, I commit myself to work for the well-being of all our citizens. To realize the full potential of our people, we must invest in their capabilities and empower them with modern education and comprehensive health care. We must banish malnutrition, social evils infant mortality and female foeticide. I wish to express my full commitment to the protection of child rights. We must wage a relentless campaign against poverty, ignorance and disease to seek a better future for our children. We must show wisdom and foresight in protecting our planet and our environment, for the good of all living species and future generations. I am deeply committed to the cause of education and would like to see every person, man and woman, boy and girl, be touched by the light of modern education. Empowerment of women is particularly important to me as I believe this leads to the empowerment of the nation. We must ensure that science and technology serve our needs better, and help us develop a scientific temper that will unleash the full potential of our people, of our farmers, our workers, our professionals and our entrepreneurs. The people of our country desire better governance, faster development and a life of peace and security. We must all stand united in the fight against such divisive and destructive tendencies as communalism, casteism, extremism and terrorism. The world has come to regard the success of social and economic development in India within the framework of a democracy as a symbol of hope for all humanity. As I think of the future of our great nation, and our duties and responsibilities in taking it forward, I am reminded of Gurudev Rabindranath Tagore's invocation about India awakening into that heaven of freedom where the mind is without fear and the head is held high. Let us all rededicate ourselves once again to our Constitutional ideals and work unitedly to build such an India. Jai Hind!

2014. (25-7-2007) NEW DELHI : Shri Arun Balakrishnan, C&MD of HPCL handed over a share certificate to Shri L N Mittal, founder and Chairman of Mittal Investments s.a.r.l(MI), here today in the presence of Shri Murli Deora, Minister of Petroleum and Natural Gas. M/S Mittal Group presented a cheque for Rs 500 crore as part of their equity contribution in the JV company M/s Guru Govind Singh Refinery Ltd. (GGSRL). This marks the formal participation of MI through its 100% subsidiary M/s Mittal Energy Investments Pte Ltd. as joint venture(JV) partner of HPCL in M/S GGSRL. GGSRL is setting up a 9 MMTPA Bathinda Refinery in Punjab. On this occasion, the Minister of State for Petroleum and Natural Gas Shri Dinsha Patel, Petroleum Secretary Shri M. S. Srinivasan were also present along with Chairman IOC, C&MD BPCL, C&MD EIL, senior officers of Petroleum Ministry, HPCL, Mittal Investments and other oil PSUs. Speaking to media persons, Shri Murli Deora said that the there are a lot of expectations from this partnership and called for adopting best practices followed by the Mittal group for expeditious implementation of this project. Re-iterating Government's commitment for speedy completion of this project, he said that the UPA Government under the leadership of Prime Minister Dr. Manmohan Singh and UPA Chairperson Smt. Sonia Gandhi has pushed for the completion of this prestigious project in full earnest. He added, " First, the deed of assurance was signed in August, 2005 by the Punjab Government providing tax incentives to improve financial strength of the project. Then we took the initiative to find a suitable partner with strong financial capability and global presence." He pointed out that HPCL and Mittal group had actually completed all the work for commercial agreement in February 2007. But due to Punjab elections, the formal agreement was signed after the election process was over. He also said that Punjab refinery at Bathinda was conceived more than a decade ago but the refinery did not make much progress. The Minister further said that this is the single largest investment, about Rs 19,000 crore, at any location in Punjab. The refinery will create a lot of job opportunities directly and indirectly in the region. There will be industrialization and development of support industries. Transport industry will also receive a boost and ancillary industries will come up. Shri Deora expressed hope that the Government of Punjab will provide full cooperation for successful and early completion of the project. During his interaction with media, Shri Mittal expressed his deep gratitude and appreciation to Shri Murli Deora, for enabling investment by Mittal group into the Punjab Refinery Project. He said, "At his initiative we entered into discussions with HPCL last year." Shri Mittal praised the Government for giving expeditious approval for the JV project He informed that they signed the JV agreement in March 2007 and by June 2007, the approval was granted. The speedy approval reinforces the seriousness of the Government to attract FDI. Later, the Chief Minister of Punjab Shri Prakash Singh Badal called on Shri Murli Deora and conveyed that the State Government will extend full support to the project. During their meeting the Minister of State for Petroleum and Natural Gas Shri Dinsha Patel, Petroleum Secretary Shri M. S. Srinivasan, Shri L N Mittal, founder and Chairman of Mittal Investments s.a.r.l(MI), Shri Arun Balakrishnan, C&MD, HPCL, senior officers of Petroleum Ministry, Government of Punjab, HPCL, Mittal Investment, etc. were present. The project is conceived as a world-class state of the art refinery incorporating the latest technologies enabling it to exceeding the current specifications available in the country. Configuration has been developed after extensive and intensive Linear Programming modelling, keeping the domestic and regional requirements in mind, the latest cost effective technologies available for generating required fuel specifications, and future changes.

2015. (25-7-2007) NEW DELHI : With a view to encourage e-ticket usage, Indian Railways have decided to reduce the e-ticket service charges from 1st July 2007. Minimum charge of Indian Railway Catering and Tourism Corporation (IRCTC) for e-tickets for Sleeper Class has been reduced from Rs. 15 to Rs 10 per ticket. Besides these minimum charges, the other additional charges per passenger will continue as at present. Service charges for issuing e-ticket for Rail

Travellers Service Agents (RTSA)/Travel Agents Association of India (TAAI)/ Indian Association of Tour Agents (IATA) members, Petrol Pumps, ATMs, Electronic Point of Sale (e-pos) and e-seva counters shall be reduced from Rs. 15/- to Rs 10/- per ticket for Sleeper/2S classes and from Rs. 25/- to Rs. 20/- per ticket for AC classes. IRCTC who has been authorized to expand e-ticketing facility to outside agencies, has appointed more than 8000 agents for booking e-tickets, which include RTSAs, RTAs, GSAs, members of IATA & TAAI, petrol pumps of Bharat Petroleum Corporation Limited, District Magistrate and Deputy Commissioners of State Governments, e-seva centres of Andhra Pradesh Government, Electronic Point of Sale (e-pos) through ICICI. For the benefit of passengers using e-ticketing facility, arrangements are also being made for issuing e-tickets through ATMs from various stations over Indian Railways. The reserved tickets will also be issued from Post Offices in near future for which the modalities have already been finalized and agreement is likely to be signed shortly.

2016. (25-7-2007) NEW DELHI : The Ministry of Rural Development has released balance payment of second instalment amounting to Rs.49.78 Lakh to the District Rural Development Agency for the implementation of Centrally sponsored scheme 'Drought Prone Areas Programme'(DPAP) under Haryali-III in Amravati District of Maharashtra during the year 2007-08. The grant is towards plan expenditure and its utilization is subject to the terms and conditions laid down in the guidelines for watershed development also to the conditions laid down from time to time. The Project Director is to ensure proper utilization of the funds by the Project Implementing Agencies (PIAs). The DRDA, should make the funds available to the PIA(s)/Gram Panchayats within 15 days of receiving it. The Ministry of Rural Development has initiated 'Hariyali' for empowering the village community through Panchayati Raj Institutions (PRIs) to undertake the area development progammes on watershed basis with financial and technical support from the Government. Under this initiative, all the on-going area development programmes, such as Integrated Wasteland Development Programmes (IWDP), Drought Prone Areas Programme (DPAP) and Desert Development Programme (DDP) are to be implemented through the PRIs. New projects under the aforesaid area development programmes are implemented under 'Hariyali Guidelines' from 1st April, 2003. Special emphasis is given to rain water harvesting and desilting of ponds under watershed projects. Under Hariyal programme of the Ministry, the efforts have resulted in bringing 87 lakh hectres of wasteland under green cover.

2017. (25-7-2007) NEW DELHI : The Ministry of Rural Development has sanctioned Rs. 19.29 crore to the State Government of Manipur towards first instalment of funds against the provisional allocation of Rs. 38.59 crore made for the Government of Manipur under the Centrally sponsored Accelerated Rural Water Supply Programme (Normal) of Rajiv Gandhi National Drinking Water Mission, during the year 2006-07. Up to 15 per cent of funds released under this sanction may be utilized for Operation & Maintenance and up to 5 per cent of funds may be spent for taking sustainability measures. States have been requested to delegate powers for management of Rural Water Supply Schemes through the Panchayati Raj Institutions (PRIs) as per the Constitution of India. As such Operation and Maintenance of the completed RWS Scheme should be transferred to the PRIs. No expenditure shall be incurred on taking water quality problems form the present release, as there is a separate allocation for the purpose. This release is being made for execution/completion of schemes to provide safe drinking water facilities to rural habitations and schools under the Centrally Sponsored ARWSP. Priorities set in ARWSP guidelines and through other instructions issued from time to time shall be followed for coverage of rural habitations and rural schools.

2018. (25-7-2007) NEW DELHI : The Ministry of Tourism of India has launched a new e-Commerce platform on its website www.incredibleindia.org. Launching the platform here today the Tourism and Culture Minister Smt. Ambika Soni said there is no doubt the web based enabled services tourism will strengthen the industry and empower the customers. She said it will facilitate customers to communicate directly with agencies, tour operators, hotels and Bed & Breakfast establishment 24 hours a day. She said it is indeed a matter of pleasure that many service providers, hotels, tour operators and Bed & Breakfast establishment have become registered members of the On line E Commerce Platform. She said amongst the niche tourism products, medical tourism should be brought on the E-Commerce Platform. The Minister said in India about one lakh fifty thousand patients arrived in 2004 from across the globe for medical treatment. The medical tourism market in India estimated at US$ 333 million in 2004 grew by about 25% and is predicted to become a US $ 2 billion-a-year business opportunity by 2012. Smt. Soni said while it is important for us to woo more tourists to this country through powerful global campaigns, it is equally important to continue focus on upgrading and improving the quality of infrastructure on ground. The Minister also gave certificates of merit to 22 renowned chefs on the occasion. The e-commerce platform has been developed jointly by Ministry of Tourism, and EVIIVO. The main objective of this platform to facilitate SME (Small and Medium Entrepreneur) to be on Global Network to promote/sale there produce online without any committed investment. www.incredibleindia.org and technology partner EVIIVO will now be offering online booking services for a range of accommodation businesses across India, enabling international visitors, currently representing 70% of the site traffic, and domestic visitors to use the new hotel and Bed & Breakfast establishment live availability search on the homepage and complete their transaction in USD or Indian Rupees. Ministry of Tourism through eviivo's technology will integrate third party consolidators and multiple partners so that it can offer a truly open platform for all service provider in the tourism industry. the Indian Bed & Breakfast sector. Small and medium-sized hotels, bed & breakfast and guesthouses that are currently approved under the new Government Scheme are being offered access to the eviivo frontdesk™ property management system to help them sell their rooms online through www.incredibleindia.org, their own website and a number of other commercial distribution channels. These businesses will have the opportunity to reach a worldwide and domestic audience and satisfy the demand for travellers interested in booking their trips online. Ministry of Tourism offering this opportunity to independent accommodation providers and tourism businesses in India, a powerful platform to sell their products online to a worldwide audience. This PPP will have a major impact in boosting the country's tourism industry and consumers will also benefit by having a wider choice of quality Indian accommodation, Tours on the internet." So far about 4000 accommodation units viz. hotels, guests houses, bed & breakfast unit have been partnered in the platform and expecting more in phased manner. Various State Governments like Madhya Pradesh, Assam, Rajasthan, Chattisgarh have shown interest to use thing platform to promote and sale there various tourism products. In order to encourage Public Private Partnership, the Ministry of Tourism join hands with various agencies, in its efforts to position India as most desirable tourist destination among the high end overseas travellers. BBC CNN, Experience India Society etc. partnering with Ministry of Tourism to promote Incredible India. During the current year BBC and CNN have produced a number of TV Commercials for Incredible India Campaign both in international and domestic markets. BBC World has produced 7 TV commercials of 10 second duration highlighting various themes viz (1) Camel Band (2) Raghurajpur Rural Village, Orissa (3) Floating Market on Dal Lake, Srinagar (4) Mask Dance, Hemis Monastery Ladakh (5) Orchid of North East (6) Mahabodhi Temple, Bodhgaya (7) Toy Train in Nilgiris. The philosophy behind these films are to portray unique facets of India and as such all these films ends with the line " Only In India". CNN has also produced 2 theme based commercial of 30 seconds highlighting Tea Tourism and Gourmet Tourism in India. Experience India Society has been actively involving itself in various promotional efforts of the Ministry of Tourism in India and overseas. During March 2007 in ITB-Berlin where India was Partner Country, the Experience India Society hosted a Gala Opening Dinner for a huge of gathering of over 4000 guests. The society also ran an authentic India Restaurant in Masse Berlin from 7-11 March, 2007 to promote Indian cuisine to global audience.

2019. (25-7-2007) NEW DELHI : Dr. Ashwani Kumar, Minister of State (Industry) who is currently on an official visit to Japan today met with Mr. N Ohasi, Chairman Mitsui and Co. and Co-chair of India Japan Business Cooperation Committee at Tokyo. He also met with Mr. Sakamoto, member of the Board of Marubeni, Corporation and discussed various initiatives to deepen Indo-Japanese economic engagement. The visit of Dr. Kumar to Japan is significant in view of PM Abe's visit to India next month and in view of the ambitious Delhi Mumbai Industrial Corridor and dedicated Rail Freight Corridor between India and Japan. Dr. Kumar informed, leaders of Japan Inc that the Delhi Mumbai Industrial Corridor and Delhi Mumbai Freight Corridors should be the flagship programme to cement a comprehensive strategic partnership between India and Japan, the importance of which has been repeatedly stressed by Dr. Manmohan Singh and PM Abe. Dr. Kumar informed the Japanese captains of Industry that the India remains focused on becoming a global hub for manufacturing activities given the various competitive advantages and high level human resource capabilities. Dr. Kumar stated that the need of the hour was to encourage more Japanese SME's to invest in India and also to de mystify the economic potentials of modern India and Japan. In separate hour long meetings with the two Japanese executives Dr. Kumar was assured that the Japanese government and the Industry perceived great opportunities arising from enhanced Indo-Japanese economic cooperation. Mr. Ohasi, Chairman of Mitsui said that he would be visiting India with PM Abe and a high level team from Mitsui will be visiting India between 25th to 28th August for extensive meetings to finalize plans for Mitsui major participation in different projects connected with the Delhi Mumbai Freight Corridor and the Delhi Mumbai Industrial Corridor. Mitsui is likely to invest in the locomotives space for the Freight Corridor project and would also seek suitable participation in the development of Indo Japan Business Conclave which is expected to invite an investment over US $ 2 billion. Mitsui would focus on the development of logistics and infrastructure at Greater Noida and Rajasthan. Dr. Kumar was informed that PM Abe's delegation would consist of 200 business leaders from Japan who are encouraged to explore major business opportunities in India. Mr. Sakamoto of Marubeni informed Dr. Kumar that Marubeni Corporation was actively exploring opportunities in Infrastructure including the Power sector apart from expanding significantly its trading operations in India. Marubeni has already constituted an internal study group to identify projects and Indian partners. Dr. Kumar is due to meet representatives of Japanese SME's and financial Institutions tomorrow.

2020. (25-7-2007) NEW DELHI : Avian Influenza has been reported in nearly 70 countries across four continents since the present wave commenced in 1997 in Hong Kong. It has exhibited a tendency to re-surface in outbreak countries having recurred in nearly 20 countries out of 25 countries affected in 2007 itself. It has been reported in countries neighbouring India viz. China, Pakistan, Myanmar, Bangladesh and Afghanistan. The North Eastern part of the country is particularly vulnerable because of continuing outbreaks in neighbouring countries. India reported an outbreak of Avian Influenza in 2006. Control and containment measures were carried out by the Government in the affected areas. The outbreak was successfully controlled. India declared freedom from Avian Influenza in August 2006. The country has remained under sustained surveillance with more than one lakh seventy thousand (1,70,000) samples having been tested in the country since February 2006 outbreak. No fresh outbreak was reported in the country after April 2006. Unusual mortality in poultry was reported from a small unit in East Imphal District of Manipur (Village Chingmeirong). 132 birds of the total flock died in a period of about six days from 7th July, 2007 onwards. The samples were forwarded to High Security Animal Disease Laboratory (HSADL), Bhopal and National Institute of Virology, Pune for testing. Samples are positive for Highly

Pathogenic Avian Influenza (HPAI) (H5) as per report of HSADL, Bhopal and (NIV), Pune as per specified regimen of tests. The disease appears to be very localized and limited presently to one unit in a State in the North Eastern part of the country. There is no other report of unusual mortality or sickness in the neighbouring area; the districts of East and West Imphal; the entire State of Manipur and any other place in the North-East. This is further supported by surveillance over a ten kilometer radius from the infected site including ducks, feeds and the source of birds of the farm which reported mortality. Pending test results and as a matter of abundant pre-caution, the remaining birds on the infected unit were killed. The unit was fully dis-infected and sanitized. The situation remained under constant review/assessment. Prophylactic cover was provided by the Ministry of Health to those exposed to infected poultry including family members and veterinary workforce. Initial supplies of personal protective equipment and oseltamivir etc. have been rushed to Manipur. Central team of Animal Husbandry and Public Health was also deputed to Manipur. In view of the positive results given by two laboratories viz. HSADL, Bhopal and NIV, Pune, India is required to notify the outbreak of HPAI to the global community through the Office International des Epizooties (OIE) (World Organization of Animal Health). Such notification is also required to initiate the control and containment operations for Avian Influenza. Accordingly, outbreak of Avian Influenza has been notified in Chingmeirong, East Imphal District on 25th July, 2007. Control and containment operations will now be initiated around the infected premises in Chingmeirong Village in Manipur. These comprise of killing of birds; disposal of birds and infected materials; quarantine and restrictions in the operational area; clean-up, dis-infection and sanitization followed by post-operation surveillance in and around Chingmeirong Village. Poultry will be culled in a radius of five kilometres and surveillance will be carried out in a further radius of five to ten kilometres. The country will follow the protocol laid down by OIE to regain freedom from Avian Influenza. The situation is under control particularly in view of the fact that the outbreak appears to be confined to one small poultry unit.

2021. (26-7-2007) NEW DELHI : The Prime Minister Dr. Manmohan Singh called on the President, Smt. Pratibha Patil at Rashtrapati Bhavan today. This was the first meeting since President Smt. Patil took the oath of office yesterday. The meeting lasted 20 minutes. The Prime Minister was accompanied by his wife Smt. Gursharan Kaur. The Prime Minister and his wife greeted the President on her assuming the office of the President of India. The two leaders discussed matters of national and international importance.

2022. (26-7-2007) NEW DELHI : The Minister for Rural Development, Dr. Raghuvansh Prasad Singh in a meeting today reviewed the three components of Area Development Programme, Integrated Wastelands Development Programme (IWDP), Drought Prone Area Programme (DPAP) and Desert Development Programme (DDP) with respect to the States of Punjab, Nagaland, Assam, Goa,

Haryana and Uttarakhand and asked the States to expedite the pace of implementation of all the programmes. He emphasized that projects which have been taken up must be implemented and completed on time and funds should be utilized in such a manner that targets in terms of physical achievements are ensured. He also informed that he is going to write to the Chief Ministers of those States where the implementation is not as per the desired pace. Dr. Singh has asked all the State Governments to undertake regular review meetings with the project implementation agencies. He further stressed the need for formation of local vigilance and monitoring committees. The details of the projects must be shared with all the people's representative and transparency, accountability and social audit must also be ensured in all the projects, he said. The Minister asked the States to improve the situation within three months and informed to review the projects again during the month of November in the current year. The Minister observed that implementation of the programmes in the States under review today has been found to be going on at a slow pace. In the State of Punjab, under IWDP, 17 projects have so far been sanctioned. For treatment of an area of 15,000 hectares of land, at a total cost of Rs.3490 lakhs, only Rs.10.37 crore has been released and only one project has been completed and the remaining schemes are under implementation. In Nagaland, 42 projects have been sanctioned, out of which seven have been completed, projects worth Rs.183 crore have been sanctioned, against which Rs.109 crore has been released. In the State of Assam, 149 IWDP projects have been sanctioned, against which only one project has been completed and others are pending. The area to be treated is 9.08 lakh hectares and the cost of the project sanctioned is Rs.535 crores, against which Rs.149 crores have so far been released. In Goa, 4 projects have been sanctioned at a total cost of Rs.7.75 crores to treat 12,000 hectares of land, out of which Rs.1.06 crore has been released. In Haryana, 26 projects have been sanctioned for treating 1.28 lakh hectares at a sanctioned cost of Rs.72 crore, against which Rs.28 crore has been released. In Uttarakhand, 51 projects have been sanctioned for treating 3.04 lakh hectares of land at an estimated cost of Rs.180 crore, out of which Rs.60 crore has been released.

2023. (26-7-2007) NEW DELHI : The Ministry of Information & Broadcasting has prohibited the transmission or retransmission of the advertisements of 'Lux Cozy Underwear' and 'Amul Macho Underwear' on all broadcasting platforms with immediate effect. All channels have also been directed to be more careful in future in selection of content of advertisements and to strictly adhere to the Advertisement Code prescribed under the Cable Television Networks (Regulation) Act, 1995 and Rules framed thereunder in order not to invite further action under the said Act and Rules. The advertisements of 'Lux Cozy Underwear' and 'Amul Macho Underwear', which are being telecast on several television channels, have been considered indecent, vulgar and suggestive and thus violative of Rule 7 (8) of the Advertising Code prescribed under the Cable Television Networks (Regulation) Act, 1995 and rules framed thereunder. The Ministry vide its advisory dated 26/27 April, 2007 in respect of indecent advertisement of Gen.-X undergarments had, inter alia, directed all the channels to be more careful in future in selection of content of advertisements and strictly adhere to the Advertising Code.

2024. (26-7-2007) NEW DELHI : The Cabinet Committee on Economic Affairs today gave its approval for removing the prohibition on investment of surplus funds by navratnas and Mini Rantnas only in Public Sector Mutual Funds subject to the following conditions: (i) Not more than 30% of the available surplus funds would be invested in equity mutual funds. (ii) The Boards of PSEs would decide the guidelines, procedures and management control systems for investment in MFs in consultation with their administrative Ministries. This decision will be reviewed after gaining experience for one year. The approval would provide Navratna and Mini Ratna PSEs with a level playing field with private sector entities who can invest in MFs and provide flexibility to the PSEs to choose schemes based on relative performance of the MFs.

2025. (26-7-2007) NEW DELHI : The Union Cabinet today gave its approval for introduction of a Bill in the coming Session of the Parliament for amendment of section 2(e) of the Payment of Gratuity Act, 1972 to insert the following definition of "employee" :- "" Employee" means any person (other than an apprentice) who is employed for wages, whether the terms of such employment are expressed or implied, in any kind of work, manual or otherwise, in or in connection with the work of a factory, mine, oilfield, plantation, port, railway company, shop or other establishment, to which this Act applies, but does not include any such person who holds a post under the Central Government or a State Government and is governed by any other Act or by any rules providing for payment of gratuity.' This will result in coverage of teachers in the educational institutions under the Payment of Gratuity Act, 1972.

2026. (26-7-2007) NEW DELHI : The Union Cabinet today gave its approval for introduction of Helicopter services in Nagaland. The amount of subsidy *i.e.* actual cost of operation of helicopter services minus recovery from passengers would be met on 75:25 basis *i.e.* 75% by Government of India (Ministry of Home Affairs) and 25% by the State Government of Nagaland. The overall ceiling of flying hours for the proposed helicopter service in Nagaland may be fixed at 40 hours per month. This decision would facilitate movement of people and officials of Nagaland within the State. Orders would be issued within one month.

2027. (26-7-2007) NEW DELHI : The Union Cabinet today gave its approval for signing of Agreement between India Egypt on Mutual Legal Assistance in Criminal Matters and also ratification of the Agreement. The Agreement aims at improving effective cooperation between India and Egypt in the matters of investigation, prosecution and suppression of crime through cooperation and mutual legal assistance in criminal matters.

2028. (26-7-2007) NEW DELHI : The competent authority has approved that the services of the following officers shall stand placed at the disposal of the President's Secretariat for appointment in the post mentioned against each, for a period co-terminus with the tenure of the President or until further orders, whichever is earlier: Shri Christy L. Fernandez, IAS (GJ, 1973), presently Secretary, Ministry of Tourism as Secretary to the President of India. Shri Barun Mitra, IAS (MT, 1987) presently Joint Secretary (in-situ) President's Secretariat, as Joint Secretary in relaxation of the tenure norms. Ms. Vijay Thakur Singh, IFS (1985), presently in the cadre, as Social Secretary. Shri Faiz Ahmed Kidwai, IAS (MP, 1996) presently in the cadre, as Deputy Secretary in the post to be created. Shri Vishal Chauhan, IAS (SK, 1998), presently in the cadre, as Deputy Secretary. Major Gen. K.J.S. Oberoi, IC-27321 General Officer Commanding, Delhi Area, as Military Secretary to the President.

2029. (26-7-2007) NEW DELHI : The Appointments Committee of the Cabinet has approved the following appointments: Shri Vijay Singh, IAS (MP, 1970) presently Secretary, Department of Road Transport and Highways, Ministry of Shipping, Road Transport and Highways as Defence Secretary in the vacancy of Shri Shekhar Dutt on his completing his tenure on 31st July, 2007. Shri Vijay Singh will be on tenure for a period of two years or until further orders, whichever is earlier. Shri Brahm Dutt, IAS (KN, 1973) presently Chairperson, National Authority for Chemical Weapons Convention, as Secretary, Department of Road Transport and Highways, Ministry of Shipping, Road Transport and Highways. Shri Pradeep Kumar, IAS (HY, 1972) presently Chairperson, National Highways Authority of India, Department of Road Transport and Highways, Ministry of Shipping, Road Transport and Highways as Secretary, Department of Disinvestment, Ministry of Finance. Smt. Sheela Bhide, IAS (AP, 1973) presently Special Secretary and Financial Adviser, Ministry of External Affairs as Chairperson, India Trade Promotion Organisation (ITPO), Department of Commerce, Ministry of Commerce and Industry. Smt. Bhide will have a tenure of three years as Chairperson, ITPO. Shri Ajay Shanker, IAS (UP, 1973) presently Principal Adviser, Planning Commission as Secretary, Department of Industrial Policy and Promotion, Ministry of Commerce and Industry. Shri J.S. Maini, IAS (PB, 1974) presently Additional Secretary and Financial Adviser, Department of Fertilizers, Ministry of Chemicals and Fertilizers as Chairperson, National Highways Authority of India, Department of Road Transport and Highways, Ministry of Shipping, Road Transport and Highways. Shri Badal K Das, IAS (MP, 1972) Secretary, Ministry of Culture shall hold the additional charge of the post of Secretary, Ministry of tourism, with immediate effect, for a period of three months or until further orders, whichever is earlier. Shri Falguni Rajkumar, IAS (KN, 1972), presently in cadre as Secretary, North Eastern Council Secretariat, Shillong, under the Ministry of Development of North Eastern Region.

2030. (26-7-2007) NEW DELHI : Dr. Dasari Narayana Rao Minister of State for Coal has emphasized that with steady increase in production of coal, proper accounting of coal production and dispatches assumes importance. Chairing a meeting of the Parliamentary Consultative Committee attached to his Ministry here today, Dr. Rao said that the coal production by Coal India subsidiaries has been steadily increasing. From 323 million tonnes in 2004-05, it has gone up to 362 million tonnes during 2006-07. He informed that a production of 383 million tonnes has been targeted during the current financial year by CIL. Referring to complexities in the coal production where both men and machines are involved, the Minister informed that Coal India has elaborate procedures for reporting of coal production, measurement of stocks and dispatches. Given the range of operations involved such measurement has both specific and volumetric components. In a presentation, the members were informed that coal production is to be reported in tonnes on shift and daily basis. Methods of measurement are spelt out for different technologies of production. Reported production should be checked on monthly basis and reconciled. In case of Under Ground (UG) mines stock is to be measured physically on monthly basis while in case of Open Cast (OC) mines stock is to be measured in situ on monthly basis. The members were informed that proper investigation by departmentally constituted committee is carried out to fix up responsibility for coal stock shortages. If shortage is more than 10,000 tonnes in a mine and 50,000 tonnes in a company, report of the departmental committee should be approved by concerned company board and sent to CIL with its recommendation and award of punishment for consideration of CIL Board. A (+/-) 5% variation between physical stock and book stock is considered as measurement tolerance due to instrumental error, error due to measurement of irregular volume and human error etc. Manager, Agent and General Manager are responsible for maintenance of stock shortage cases. Dr. Rao urged members to suggest ways to make coal distribution, transportation and measurement, more transparent and effective. Responding to the suggestions of the members, the Minister said that the Government has set time limits for production from captive coal blocks. The allottees are required to provide bank guarantees against adhering to the production schedule. Regarding safety in coal mining, Dr. Dasari Narayana Rao stressed that this issue is on his top priority. Coal is allocated to States for supply to small and tiny sector users.

2031. (26-7-2007) NEW DELHI : Lt Gen. Deepak Kapoor, PVSM, AVSM, SM, VSM, ADC, presently Vice Chief of Army Staff will be the next Chief of Army Staff. The present Chief of Army Staff Gen. JJ Singh, PVSM, AVSM, VSM, ADC retires from government service on September 30, 2007. Born in 1948, Lt Gen. Deepak Kapoor was commissioned into the Regiment of Artillery on June 11, 1967. During his long and distinguished service spanning over 40 years, he has worked in a variety of command, staff and instructional appointments. An alumnus of the Defence Services Staff College, Wellington, he has done the higher command and National Defence College courses. He is Masters in Business Administration, Political Science and Military Science. He had taken active part in the 1971 operations in Bangladesh. He served as Chief Operations Officer of the UN

Peacekeeping Mission deployed in Somalia during 1994-95. During his service as a Brigade Commander, deployed on the Line of Control in Jammu and Kashmir, Gen. Kapoor was awarded the Sena Medal (Devotion to Duty) in January 1998. He commanded one of the most prestigious Divisions of the Indian Army-the RAM Division as part of a Strike Corps, during OP PARAKRAM. He has been the Chief of Staff of 4 Corps in the North East, fighting insurgency in Assam and thereafter commanded 33 Corps, deployed on the India-China border. For his excellent command of the Corps, the General Officer was awarded Ati Vishisht Seva Medal in January 2006. On promotion as Army Commander, he commanded the Army Training Command at Shimla. Thereafter, he commanded the largest and the most sensitive command of the Indian Army, *i.e.* the Northern Command from 05 September 2005 to 31 December 2006. The General Officer was awarded Param Vishist Seva Medal in January 2007. Gen. Kapoor is married to Smt Kirti Kapoor and has a son and a daughter; both are married.

2032. (26-7-2007) NEW DELHI : The Comprehensive National Sports Policy 2007 aims at building on previous sports policies with a view to accomplishing the unfinished agenda and addressing the emerging challenges of India in the 21st century, most particularly the national goal of emerging as a global, yet inclusive, economic power in the near future. It aims at making the framework for sports in India more effective and inclusive with the full ownership and involvement of all stakeholders. The participant/athlete shall occupy centre-stage in the Comprehensive National Sports Policy, with all other stakeholders playing a promotional, supportive and convergent role.The Policy has three broad objectives: Sports for all, Excellence in sports and Contingent Constitutional, Legal and Institutional measures to operationalize the Policy.

2033. (26-7-2007) NEW DELHI : The Union Minister for Health & Family Welfare, Dr. Anbumani Ramadoss who is currently on a 7-days official visit to Australia addressing the 3rd Ministerial Conference on HIV/AIDS held at Sydney on 23rd July 2007 said that in India we have made a beginning by setting up a National Council on AIDS which is chaired by the Prime Minister himself and in the recently launched third phase of National AIDS Control Programmes our focus is on mainstreaming HIV/AIDS in different ministries, expanding coverage of workplace programmes in the organized and unorganized sectors, strengthening Public-Private Partnerships and mobilizing resources from the corporate sector to complement the national effort.

2034. (26-7-2007) NEW DELHI : Control and containment measures were initiated after confirmation of Avian Influenza by the Government of India. A high level meeting of concerned Departments, agencies and local representatives was chaired by the Chief Minister of Manipur (Shri O. Ibobi Singh) on 25th July, 2007 itself in order to determine the strategy for control and containment. The mobilization and deployment plan was determined by the Animal Husbandry Department. The infected and surveillance zones were identified. The Rapid Response Teams (RRTs) have been mobilized. Initially, 20 RRTs will start the operations. Culling was started on 26th July, 2007 after medical examination and briefing of the members of the RRTs by Health and Animal Husbandry officials. Poultry will be killed in a radius of 0 to 5 Kms. As per the initial details provided by the State Government, nearly 1,50,000 birds are likely to be killed in the operations. More than 75,000 of the poultry is backyard. About 128 small units of poultry are likely to be covered in the operations. The approximate population of ducks in the 5 kms. radius is 28,000. Culling will be undertaken in 8 villages surrounding the area of infection on the first day.

2035. (26-7-2007) NEW DELHI : In exercise of the powers conferred by clause (1) of article 224 of the Constitution of India, the President is pleased to appoint (i) Shri Thenammakkal Ismail Rawther Harun-ul-Rashid, (ii) Shri Valiyaparambil Kuttappan Mohanan and (iii) Shri Giri Venkitasubramani, to be Additional Judges of the Kerala High Court, in that order of seniority, for a period of two years with effect from the dates they assume charge of their respective offices.

2036. (26-7-2007) NEW DELHI : In exercise of the powers conferred by clause (1) of article 217 of the Constitution of India, the President is pleased to appoint (i) Shri Justice Shaileshkumar Ramanlal Brahmbhatt, (ii) Shrimati Justice Harsha Nathalal Devani, and (iii) Shri Justice Mukeshkumar Dahyalal Shah, Additional Judges of the Gujarat High Court, to be Judges of the Gujarat High Court, in that order of seniority, with effect from the dates they assume charge of their respective offices.

2037. (26-7-2007) NEW DELHI : Income tax offices throughout the country will remain open on 28th and 29th July, 2007 (Saturday & Sunday) to accept returns of income from taxpayers. The Department of Posts was authorised to receive returns of income in July, 2006 as one time measure in view of circumstances prevailing at that time and this scheme has been discontinued. For the benefits of tax payers in Delhi special arrangements have been made in Pragati Maidan for receiving the returns of income.

2038. (26-7-2007) NEW DELHI : An investment of about Rs.10,000/- crore is expected to flow into Railways' Container Operation sector in the next two years for wagons, logistics parks and Inland Container Depots (ICDs). This was stated by Shri K.C. Jena, Member Staff, Railway Board while speaking at a Conference on "Privatization of Container Transportation by Rail-Issues & Options" held here. Shri Jena who is also the National Chairman of the Chartered Institute of Logistics & Transport-India (CILT) said that the Rail Container policy announced by the Ministry of Railways requires the development of new ICDs and multi modal logistics parks, as the new container train entrants would need to have access to rail linked ICDs or develop their own ICDs within next three years. He said that overall the exercise is likely to make Logistics in India more effective to enable growth of physical trade and economy, and optimize the cost of supply chains and transactions. It will also facilitate moving towards a system of multimodalism based on co-existence of rail and road modes in the transport sector in our economy with a view to optimize fuel costs, control pollution, and minimize wasteful investment, he added. The Conference, which was attended by about 150 delegates from all over the country and abroad had a focused approach and was able to bring about consensus between the representatives of the container transport industries and the Government on the various issues. CILT is a worldwide organization of professional transportation, set up to promote the study of the art and science of transport in all its modes such as road, rail, shipping, civil aviation and pipelines.

2039. (26-7-2007) NEW DELHI : The draft Comprehensive Sports Policy 2007 has been put on the website of the Ministry of Youth Affairs & Sports (www.yas.nic.in). The Policy aims at building on previous sports policies with a view to accomplishing the unfinished agenda and addressing the emerging challenges of India in the 21st century, most particularly the national goal of emerging as a global, yet inclusive, economic power in the near future. It aims at making the framework for sports in India more effective and inclusive with the full ownership and involvement of all stakeholders. The participant/athlete shall occupy centre-stage in the Comprehensive National Sports Policy, with all other stakeholders playing a promotional, supportive and convergent role. The Policy has three broad objectives: Sports for all, Excellence in sports and Contingent Constitutional, Legal and Institutional measures to operationalize the Policy. Policy has been put on the website of the Ministry with the purpose of inviting comments and suggestions from the general public and other interested groups.

2040. (26-7-2007) NEW DELHI : The Ministry of Rural Development has sanctioned Rs. 18.67 lakh to the State Government of Himachal Pradesh towards first instalment of funds against the total allocation of Rs. 56.00 lakh under the Centrally sponsored Accelerated Rural Water Supply Programme-Desert Development Programme Areas of Rajiv Gandhi National Drinking Water Mission, during the year 2007-08. Up to 15 per cent of funds released under this sanction may be utilized for Operation & Maintenance and up to 5 per cent of funds may be spent for taking sustainability measures. States have been requested to delegate powers for management of Rural Water Supply Schemes through the Panchayati Raj Institutions (PRIs) as per the Constitution of India. As such Operation and Maintenance of the completed RWS Scheme should be transferred to the PRIs. No expenditure shall be incurred on taking water quality problems form the present release, as there is a separate allocation for the purpose. This release is being made for execution/completion of schemes to provide safe drinking water facilities to rural habitations and schools under the Centrally Sponsored ARWSP. Priorities set in ARWSP-DDP guidelines and through other instructions issued from time to time shall be followed for coverage of rural habitations and rural schools.

2041. (26-7-2007) NEW DELHI : Vice Admiral DK Dewan AVSM, takes over as Chief of Personnel at IHQ MoD (Navy) today. A Gunnery specialist, graduate of the Joint Staff course Paris and the Royal College of Defence Studies London, he is an alumnus of the National Defence Academy, Khadakwasla. The officer was promoted to Flag rank in Nov 03 and has held the appointments of Senior Directing Staff (Navy) at National Defence College and Flag Officer Commanding Maharastra Area (FOMA). The Flag Officer was promoted to the rank of Vice Admiral on 20 Mar 07 and was presently posted as Controller of Personnel Services (CPS) at IHQ MOD (Navy). The Flag Officer has had wide national and international exposure and has experience in various fields such as operations, international relations and defence planning. Having done his sea service in seven different ships, took up duties of Deputy Director Naval Plans at the Naval Headquarters and managed naval budget for four years. After promotion to Captain in 1994, he served as Captain LWT (East), Command Gunnery Officer (WNC), Naval Assistant to Chief of the Naval Staff and Senior Instructor (Navy) at National Defence Academy, Pune. In Dec 2002, he was appointed Principal Director Naval Plans at Naval Headquarters and was responsible for plans, foreign cooperation and budget.

2042. (26-7-2007) NEW DELHI : Ministry of Tourism, Government of India bags the Pacific Asia Travel Association (PATA) grand awards. The Pacific Asia Travel Association (PATA)'s Gold Awards recognise exceptional achievement in a variety of endeavours, bringing acclaim to the best the Asia Pacific's travel industry has to offer. The winning projects set industry standards for excellence and innovation, serving as examples for others to follow. In addition to the 24 Gold Awards, PATA also presents up to four Grand Awards for "best of show" entries in the following broad categories: Environment, Education & Training, Heritage & Culture and Marketing Campaign. The four "best-of-show" Grand Awards were bagged by the Ministry of Tourism, Government of India, in the Marketing category.

2043. (26-7-2007) NEW DELHI : The Minister for Social Justice and Empowerment, Smt. Meira Kumar chaired the meeting of the Consultative Committee to review the function of the National Handicapped Finance and Development Corporation (NHFDC) here today. During the meeting, the members of the Committee were apprised the progress made by the NHFDC. Smt. Meira Kumar said that the Ministry is committed to address the problems of the persons with disabilities. She further said that priority is being given to provide benefits to the persons with disabilities living in rural areas. She also informed that the centres for these persons have been established in 130 districts already. The members suggested that awareness programmes should be organized to aware about various benefit schemes to the persons with disabilities. The National Handicapped Finance and Development Corporation (NHFDC) was set up by the Ministry of Social Justice and Empowerment, Government of India, in January 1997. It is wholly owned by Government of India and has an authorized capital of Rs. 400 crore. The Corporation's Headquarters is at Faridabad (Haryana). NHFDC functions as an apex financial institution for channelising flow of funds to the persons with disabilities through the State Channelising Agencies (SCAs) nominated by the State Government(s) or through Non-Government Organizations (Under Micro Financing Scheme). NHFDC's main object is to promote development activities and self-employment ventures for the benefit of persons with disabilities and to extend loan to for upgradation of their skills and to peruse their professional/ technical education leading to vocational rehabilitation/self-employment.

2044. (27-7-2007) NEW DELHI : Union Minister for Science and Technology and Earth Sciences, Shri Kapil Sibal has said that an Early Warning System for Tsunami and Storm Surges will be commissioned soon. He was speaking on the occasion of the Foundation day function of the Ministry of Earth Sciences in New Delhi. Shri P. Chidambaram, Union Minister for Finance was the chief guest. Shri Sibal pointed out that scientific knowledge of oceans and earth systems were no more luxuries but are crucial and essential as Tsunami of 2004 brought to fore and expressed hope that Finance Minister would lend his support to establish the needed infrastructure across the depths of oceans and the heights of the Himalayas to capture the needed data to forewarn of such impending disasters. The Minister observed that in short period of a year of its inception, the Earth Sciences Ministry has caught the fancy of the people among others by pioneering the development of technology for Low Temperature Thermal Desalination of sea water, which has recently been demonstrated through the commissioning of a 1 million litre/day plant to supply water to Chennai and now there are grandiose plans to go on to a 10 million litre/day plant. The second attainment has been the planning and securing the international acceptance for the establishment of the third station at Antarctica and lastly the initiative to establish a 24 hour Weather Channel. Recalling former scientist-technocrat President Dr. Kalam's concept of Earth Systems Science as a dedicated, cohesive and seamless integration between researchers in multiple areas and in multiple organizations, Shri Sibal said that unlike research in strategic areas wherein the nations compete to maintain superiority over other nations, Earth Science is the ultimate realization of the mankind to cooperate and collaborate. Calling for the need to inspire, captivate and motivate school children, young university entrants and even fellow adults to pursue careers allied with earth sciences Shri Sibal said that an organized educational infrastructure that supports sustainability and scalability is required for the ocean and earth sciences. He said more educational programmes and courses that address cross disciplinary issues in earth sciences are needed.

2045. (27-7-2007) NEW DELHI : An amount of Rs. 122.03 crore has been sanctioned by the Ministry of Rural Development to the State Government of Rajasthan towards second installment under the Revised Sub Mission programme of Accelerated Rural Water Supply Programme (ARWSP)-(Quality) of Rajiv Gandhi National Drinking Water Mission (RGNDWM) during the year 2007-08. The first installment of Rs. 206.00 crore was released during the previous financial year. The grant included second installment of 45% share of Central share of Rs. 3.32 crore *i.e.* Rs. 1.50 crore released for 10 new projects sanctioned by the State with a capital outlay of Rs.4.52 crore. The Central share of Rs.120.53 crore is released for taking up 16 Major projects for providing safe drinking water(total outlay is Rs.2065.64 crore and against balance Central share of Rs.639.978 crore) including supply of domestic defluoridation filters in 1000 habitations @ Rs.800-00 per unit. States have been requested to delegate powers for management of Rural Water Supply Schemes through the Panchayati Raj Institutions (PRIs) as per the Constitution of India. As such Operation and Maintenance of the completed RWS Scheme should be transferred to the PRIs. All terms and conditions indicated in the revised Sub-Mission guidelines are to be strictly followed. Monthly and Quarterly progress report are to be sent urgently.

2046. (27-7-2007) NEW DELHI : The first country-wide war of independence was fought in 1857. Swatantrya Veer Savarkar termed it a First War of Independence. The BJP has decided to celebrate 150th anniversary of this First War of Independence throughout the country on a large scale. The BJP National President Shri Rajnath Singh has constituted a 1857 – WAR OF INDEPENDENCE PROGRAMME ORGANISING COMMITTEE under the convenership of General Secretary Shri Anant Kumar. The other members of the Committee are — Shri Kailash Joshi, Mukhtar Abbas Naqvi, Kalraj Mishra, Balbir Punj, Prabhat Jha, Vijaya Goel, Smt. Kiran Maheshwari, O. Rajagopal, Dharmendra Pradhan, Amit Thakar, Shyam Jaju and Prakash Javdekar. The objectives of this yearlong programme are respectful remembrance of our inspiring past, invocation of patriotism, pledge for freedom and democracy, oath of unity and solidarity and resolve for strong and prosperous India. The programme will continue from August 9, 2007 to May 10, 2008. There were three striking features of 1857 War of Independence. It was peoples' country wide collective struggle against British rule. It had large public participation. It had communal convergence as Hindus and the Muslims joined together to wage fight for the country. This is an opportunity to arouse new spirit in the country by remembering great war that was waged from Punjab to Bengal and from Nepal border to far off South. Unfortunately, the Congress-led UPA is not attaching due importance to this historical occasion. Had the UPA government so wished India, Pakistan and Bangladesh could have celebrated this anniversary of War of Independence jointly. But a government, that nurses ill feelings towards Veer Savarkar and other patriots, cannot be expected to act on such lines. That is why the BJP will take this theme of national pride emphatically to the people. In order to observe these programmes in each state and in each district, 1857-War of

Independence Programme Organizing Committees has been set up for which senior party functionaries of the state and districts has been co-opted as its conveners and co-conveners. Various programmes are being observed in other districts of the state keeping in view the main theme of the programme. Programmes like – Prabhat Pheris, Cycle Rallies, Torch Procession, Memorial Photo Exhibition. Essay and Speech competition in schools and colleges, Seminars, Rallies, Honouring of Freedom Fighters, Staging of Special Programmes on Freedom Memorials, Honouring of Veeranganas (Martyrs' wives), House to House distribution of message placards, Special conferences of youths & women, Jagruti Yatra etc. are being organized.

2047. (27-7-2007) NEW DELHI : The Executive Council and General Body of the Children's Film Society, India (CFSI) have been reconstituted. The tenure of the reconstituted Body shall be for a period of three years subject to the provisions of Rules 18, 33 and 34 of the CFSI Rules. Ms. Nafisa Ali continues to be the Chairperson of the Society. Ms. Rinki Bhattacharya has been appointed as the Vice-Chairperson.

2048. (27-7-2007) NEW DELHI : The Union Minister of Shipping, Road Transport and Highways, Thiru T. R. Baalu has sanctioned a sum of Rs. 86.70 Crore under the Central Road Fund Scheme for strengthening and improving various road stretches in the State of Haryana. As sum of Rs. 3643.15 lakh has been sanctioned for widening and strengthening along with reconstruction of concrete pavement in a section of Jhajjar to Kosli in Jhajjar district. In Rohtak district of the State, 4-laning and strengthening of sections of Old DHS road and Railway Road would in taken up in Sampla town at a cost of 1070.17 lakh and Rs. 118.10 lakh respectively. Similarly, another sum of Rs. 379.58 lakh has been sanctioned for widening and strengthening of a section covering Jhajjar Chowk to Railway Phatak in Sampla town in Rohtak district. Road improvement work has also been sanctioned for the section of Murthal-Sonipat-Kharkhoda-Sampla-Jhajjar-Dadri Road in Bhiwani district at a cost of Rs. 2106.28 lakh. In Mohendergarh district, widening and strengthening of sections of Mohindergarh-Dadri road would be taken up at a cost of Rs. 342.67 lakh. Thiru Baalu has also sanctioned a sum of Rs. 1009.45 lakh for widening and strengthening of scattered stretches of Tohana-Dharsul-Ratia-Rori road in Fatehabad district of the State.

2049. (27-7-2007) NEW DELHI : The prizes to the winners of the 41st Youth Parliament Competition, 2006-2007 for the schools under Directorate of Education, Government of NCT of Delhi and NDMC were given away today. The students of Government Sarvodaya Kanya Vidyalaya, Moti Nagar, bagged the first prize. The winning team also presented a short sitting of 'Youth Parliament". Smt. Suryakanta Patil, Hon'ble Minister of State for Rural Development & Parliamentary Affairs presided over the function and distributed the prizes to the winners. In her remarks, Smt. Patil said, our younger generation can play an important role in checking people's indifferent attitude towards democratic institutions. By taking interest in the working of our parliamentary democracy and by gathering knowledge about its procedures and conventions, they can sustain the democratic temper and processes of our nation. The 'youth Parliament Competitions' have helped the student community of our country to inculcate the habits of disciplined social behaviour, qualities of leadership, awareness of social problems and the democratic means of solving them. These 'Youth Parliament Competitions' have drawn praise from one and all who have witnessed them. The quality of the performances has only improved with each passing year. Secretary, Ministry of Parliamentary Affairs, Dr. Rekha Bhargava in her speech said, the primary objective of organizing the Youth Parliament Competitions is to educate the student community about the functioning of our parliamentary institutions and the rules of procedures of Parliament. The Youth Parliament Competition provides the students a platform to learn these parliamentary virtues and nuances, which are so necessary for a legislator to be successful. Trophy for the best educational district in the competition was awarded to the West-A Educational District, Directorate of Education, Government of NCT of Delhi and Trophy for standing first among new entrant schools was bagged by Government Girls Sr. Sec. School, No. 2, Najafgarh, New Delhi. Merit Trophies were awarded to eight schools for their meritorious performance in the competition. 31 schools took part in this year's competition. Ministry of Parliamentary Affairs have been organizing Youth Parliament Competitions in the schools under the Directorate of Education, Government of NCT of Delhi and NDMC every year since 1966. In 1978, Kendriya Vidyalayas situated in and around Delhi were incorporated in the competition along with Delhi schools. The Youth Parliament Scheme aims at promoting among the younger generation the spirit of self-discipline, tolerance of diverse opinion, righteous expression of views and other virtues of democratic way of life. It also acquaints the students with the practices and procedures of Parliament, techniques of discussion and debate and develops in them the qualities of leadership.

2050. (27-7-2007) NEW DELHI : The Minister of Rural Development, Dr. Raghuvansh Prasad Singh has expressed concern over the sturdy pace of implementation of SGSY projects in Bihar, Punjab, Tamil Nadu and Kerela and emphasized the need of proper utilization of funds and timely submission of reports in respect of special projects being implemented under Swarnajayanti Gram Swarozgar Yojana in these States. Presiding a review meeting of the status report on the SGSY Special Projects here today Dr. Singh advised the State functionaries for on-line submission of Quarterly Performance Reports. He also stressed upon the States to ensure completion of sanctioned projects within the stipulated time-frame and asked them to ensure better coordination between the different agencies like the DRDA, NGOs, Panchayats and Banks envolved in the implementation of SGSY projects in these States. Commenting on the shortcomings in the documentation of Audit report, utilization certificate non-availability of year wise details in the progress of Eight Special projects running in Bihar the Minister advised the State official to submit all the correct details by the end of August 2007. In case of the six projects of Punjab Dr. Singh expressed dissatisfaction on the slow pace and asked the officials to furnish the complete picture by the end of September this year.

2051. (27-7-2007) NEW DELHI : Shri Abhishek Singhvi said that we are happy that the rule of law has prevailed and that the Australian government has decided to release Dr. Haneef unconditionally and with honour. The Indian National Congress has always stood for fair, nondiscriminatory, transparent and judicious conduct in dealing with issues where emotion cannot be allowed to displace sobriety. Congress compliments and applauds the Government of India, headed by Prime Minister Dr. Manmohan Singh, in standing up for the cause of fair treatment of an innocent victim. The Congress party and the government of India made its point fully, unambiguously and categorically and yet within all acceptable norms of International relations. The contrast between this and the hysterical histrionics of the BJP cannot be more striking. Fortunately, Mr. Advani is in a small minority in this country who may sleep well even though an innocent victim may be hanged to death. Perhaps Mr. Advani thinks of a conscience only when he calls for a conscience vote. He has no qualms in referring to the act of the Prime Minister of this country as "appeasement of terrorism". Today's developments are a resounding political slap to such irresponsible and slanderous campaigns by the BJP against the Indian Prime Minister. For Mr. Advani and his party, everything is part of a political vote bank game and that is why they try to fool the Indian public by such provocative statements. Perhaps Mr. Advani's distorted definition of nationalism includes punishment of the innocent. Branding groups, religions or identities collectively and indiscriminately as terrorists reflects a fascist approach. The Congress party demands an immediate apology by Sh. Advani and by the BJP to the Prime Minister for their irresponsible utterances and actions. To a question as to what was party's contribution on the release of Dr. Haneef, Shri Singhvi said that from day one, it is the one entity which has spoken out totally and strongly, has been the UPA government, the Congress Party and several of the UPA constituents at several foras. You have to checkup the records, you have to check up your bytes, your denial will not change facts, they are on record and surely a Congress-led government is not going to make an official demand from a foreign country, which the main party of the Opposition opposes. Are you trying to suggest that? You should ask this question to the other parties in the Opposition. Which party! Those who are not in power in the government spoke up in the defence at that time. Ask that question first. To a question on the hanging decision of Md. Afzal, Shri Singhvi said that this party, once it states its stand does not change it like the weather everyday or every week or every month. The Congress Party stand on the Afzal issue has been declared in and out of Parliament from this podium and elsewhere. It remains the same, it's a constitutional process and everybody understands why to some extent the process has been additionally delayed because of constitutional changes at the very apex but ultimately, it is for that process to work itself out and not for us to fish in troubled waters. To a question on the situation in Goa, Shri Singhvi said that well, I think, although from a totally different angle, the answer would be the same. The constitutional process anticipates such events and provides further whether it is going to be ultimately resolved in the near future with a floor test or without a floor test or in other ways and means, these are all known and there is a constitutional process for it. It is regrettable that such instability arises but facts of life cannot be wished away. I think, we have to just wait for that process to work itself out. To a question as to what is Congress's Party view on Tariq Dar who was deported from Bangladesh? Shri Singhvi said that I am sorry that you have all your facts mixed up, all your premises are wrong. We have made a statement about Haneef from day one and not about any other name. So, you are gratuitously, deliberately bringing in name about which no statement was made. Secondly, the reason we have spoken about Haneef from day one is because, we always believed and several quarters in the world believed and today that stand has been vindicated that the supposed evidence on which he has been held appeared very tenuous. We are not the prosecuting authority, we are not the acquitting judge but people are entitled to hold their belief. Thirdly, despite that belief which was shared across the globe by several quarters, we did nothing which is contrary to accepting international norms, we conveyed our feelings for a fair, nondiscrimination treatment through official diplomatic channel and we mean the government of India naturally. Fourthly, you are connecting completely unconnectable, irrelevant examples. Ṭariq Dar and other names which you have taken have no connection. The Government of India is not used, perhaps as others are, to speaking out of turn on every international communal incident. We do not jump the gun and call diplomats and convey our feelings in every case. We do so, where there is a basis for belief that the true legal process will be delayed. That is what we did here. We did so openly, transparently and no other political party did so. This is a question which you ought to ask them rather then putting irrelevant questions to us but the important thing is that our stand has today been vindicated by forces over which we have no control. To a question whether Congress Party is in favour of a floor test or Governor rule in Goa, Shri Singhvi said that I think that would be precisely jumping the gun. This is something which a political party, from a national podium here, if it says anything either way would muddy the waters and create more confusion rather than solving. To a question that Congress government is in minority, Shri Singhvi said that we are going to make every legitimate, legal, proper effort to do what is necessary but certainly we are not going to share it with you so as to make sure no effort works or succeed.

2052. (27-7-2007) NEW DELHI : The area coverage of kharif crops as compared to 26th July last week has gone up considerably as per data compiled by Agriculture Ministry. Rice is an exception. The total coverage of kharif rice has gone up to 154 lakh ha as compared to 154.27 lakh hectare at this time last year, the weekly Crop Weather Watch Group meeting of the Ministry of Agriculture was informed here today. Transplanting of rice is in progress in almost all the States. In Assam, Chhattisgarh, Haryana, Maharashtra, Punjab and West Bengal, sowing is on peak. Total coarse cereals have covered an area of 172.77 lakh ha as compared to 154.23 lakh ha at this time last year. Cotton has been sown in 73.73 lakh ha as compared to 66.12 lakh ha last year. Out of this, 40.37 lakh hectare is under Bt cotton. Sugarcane coverage is reported to be 51.16 lakh hectare compared to 48.32 lakh ha last year, and jute 7.89 lakh hectare (last year 8.18 lakh ha.). The total coverage of oilseeds so far has been 137.42 lakh ha as compared to 129.13 lakh ha on July 26 last year. Soyabean has been sown in 6% and groundnut in 13% higher area as compared to that in 2006.

2053. (27-7-2007) NEW DELHI : Shri Shekhar Dutt, Defence Secretary has been appointed as Deputy National Security Advisor. He will hold this post in the National Security Council Secretariat for Strategic and Defence related subjects. Shri Dutt will be in the rank and pay of Secretary to the Government of India and will hold the post for a period of two years in the first instance or until further orders, whichever is earlier. Shri Dutt was appointed as Defence Secretary in July 2005. Prior to this appointment, he was Secretary Defence Production. He is an IAS officer of the 1969 batch of the Madhya Pradesh cadre. He has also served in the Army and for his role in the Western Sector during 1971 War; he was awarded Sena Medal for gallantry. In his long and distinguished career in the Indian Administrative service, Shri Dutt held several key posts, which include Director General Sports Authority of India and Principal Secretary in the Department of Tribal and Scheduled Caste Welfare and Principal Secretary, Departments of School Education, Sports & Youth Welfare both in the Government of Madhya Pradesh. Shri Dutt also held the appointment of Secretary, Department of Ayurveda, Yoga, Naturopathy, Unani, Siddha & Homeopathy in the Ministry of Health & Family Welfare. During his tenure in the Sports Authority of India, Shri Dutt played a pivotal role in the successful conduct of the First Afro-Asian Games in November 2003. As the Principal Secretary, Tribal Welfare Shri Dutt was instrumental in drawing up a number of schemes including special projects concerning area development, collection and marketing of minor forest produce and forest village development through joint forest management mechanism. In his capacity as Principal Secretary in the Departments of School Education, Sports & Youth Welfare, Shri Dutt was credited with the introduction of an innovative programme called Education Guarantee Scheme in which the community panchayats owned and administered the schools. The scheme helped in universalizing elementary education in Madhya Pradesh to a great extent.

2054. (27-7-2007) NEW DELHI : The Human Resource Development Minister and Chairman of National Implementation Committee Shri Arjun Singh has asked the states to organize commemorative events of the national importance at the grass root level to familiarize the youth with the values and ideals which emerged out of the freedom struggle. Addressing a meeting of the Chief Ministers and their representatives here today for commemoration of 150th anniversary of the first war of independence, 1857; 60th anniversary of Indian independence and other related events he said, the Central Government at the national level has identified a number of programmes to be taken up. However, to achieve popular participation in the commemoration progammes, it is very important that a series of programmes are organized at local and regional levels by the States. Shri Arjun Singh said that the National Implementation Committee has received some projects for financial assistance from States and feel that many of these could certainly be taken up by the States themselves. The Minister of Tourism and Culture Smt Ambika Soni in her welcome address briefed the meeting about the various functions to be organized on different occasions. She said the Chief Ministers' meeting was convened so that important role of states in taking out the message of freedom struggle to people can be underlined. The Home Minister Shri Shivraj V. Patil said, with the participation of all states the celebrations will be more meaningful and useful. The meeting discussed among other things constitution of state level committees for chalking out commemorative programmes. The Chairman, National Implementation Committee urged the States to constitute such committees at the earliest where no committee has been formed so far. The meeting also discussed the organization of events included in a calendar of events by the state governments in association with universities. The Calendar of Events was prepared by the Centre in consultation with Indian Council of Historical Research. Shri Arjun Singh, informed that calendar of events was only suggestive and not exhaustive. State governments could incorporate their programmes with special focus on events which happened in their respective states. Shri Arjun Singh assured that the suggestions made today will be taken into consideration for incorporation in the Calendar of Events.

2055. (27-7-2007) NEW DELHI : Rashtriya Ispat Nigam Limited (RINL), the corporate arm of Visakhapatnam Steel Plant, today signed a Memorandum Of Understanding with NTPC to form a Joint Venture Company for setting up of a 150 MW power plant in Visakhapatnam. The 50:50 Joint Venture will be christened as "NTPC-RINL Power Company Ltd.", the management control of which will be with NTPC and NTPC will also nominate the Chairman. The proposed joint venture will supply power to RINL, which is currently undertaking an expansion programme that will take its capacity to 6.3 million tonnes. The average power demand of RINL at 6.3 million tonnes stage is estimated to be 418 MW and the present generation of 226 MW meets its present requirement. The power generation from the proposed Gas Turbine Combined Cycle Power Project (GTCC) unit (JV with NTPC) will augment the power supply by 150 MW. The GTCC technology is environment friendly and more efficient in terms of power generation. The GTCC technology is the latest available for utilizing low calorific value lean gases and it envisages efficient utilization of large quantity of surplus gas available at the steel plant. NTPC is India's largest power utility with world-class technology and skills in design, engineering, construction, project management, operations and maintenance and renovation and modernization of power plants. It has a total installed capacity of 27,904 MW through 25 power stations. With 20% of all India's installed capacity NTPC contributes around 29% of the country's power generation. NTPC has an ambitious plan to become 75,000 MW plus Company by 2017. RINL is presently operating at 120% of the rated capacity with 3.6 million tonnes of liquid steel annually and is expected to touch 6.3 million tonnes by 2008 and 16 million tonnes by 2017-18. The MOU was signed by Shri P.K.Bishnoi, Chairman and Managing Director, RINL and Shri T.Sankaralingam, Chairman and Managing Director, NTPC Limited at Visakhapatnam.

2056. (27-7-2007) NEW DELHI : The Minister for Social Justice and Empowerment, Smt. Meira Kumar has requested the Minister of Information and Broadcasting to issue appropriate directions to the Press and Media agencies for using the Constitutionally accepted terms like Scheduled Castes, Scheduled Tribes, Other backward Classes while referring to the persons belonging to the aforementioned categories. She was of the view that the use of inappropriate terms, particularly, in the Government sponsored institutions would produce demagogy in the minds of persons belonging to the Schedule Castes, Scheduled Tribes and other Backward Classes. Further, this would weaken the social fabric of the Nation, besides, dampening the spirit of social justice and equity in the society. When the Indian Constitution mandates positive discrimination in the field of education, health, employment etc. specific instances of use of caste-based discrimination in Government Institutions have come to the notice of the Ministry. Expressing her serious concern over the discriminative approach being adopted in the Print and Electronic Media sources owned by the Government, Smt. Meira Kumar has sent a letter to Information and Broadcasting Ministry drawing their attention towards the usage of upper and lower castes in the media as she strongly felt that such usages perpetuates inequality in the society. The Ministry of Social Justice and Empowerment is mandated to work towards empowering the identified vulnerable sections of the society, like Scheduled Cases. The Ministry has been making sustainable efforts through its various policies and programmes for ensuring the fair treatment and a just share of the benefits of society for the marginalized groups.

2057. (27-7-2007) NEW DELHI : The total approximate earnings of Indian Railways on originating basis during the period 11th July-20th July 2007 were Rs. 1712.63 crore compared to Rs. 1547.79 crore during the same period last year, registering an increase of 10.65 per cent. The total goods earnings have gone up from Rs. 1066.66 crore during 11-20 July 2006 to Rs. 1163.74 crore during 11-20 July 2007, showing an increase of 9.10 per cent. The total passenger revenue earnings during the period 11-20 July 2007 were Rs. 491.27 crore compared to Rs. 433.69 crore during the same period last year, an increase of 13.36 per cent. The revenue earnings from other coaching amounted to Rs. 44.29 crore during this period compared to Rs. 36.51 crore during the same period last year, an increase of 21.31 per cent. The total sundry earnings have gone up from Rs. 11.23

crore during 11-20 July 2006 to Rs. 13.33 crore during 11-20 July 2007, showing an increase of 18.70 per cent. The total approximate number of passengers booked during the period 11-20 July 2007 were 189.94 million compared to 176.64 million during the same period last year, showing an increase of 7.53 per cent. In the suburban and non-suburban sectors, the number of passengers booked during 11-20 July 2007 were 110.12 million and 79.82 million compared to 102.36 million and 74.28 million during the same period last year, registering an increase of 7.58 per cent and 7.46 per cent respectively.

2058. (27-7-2007) NEW DELHI : The pace of control and containment measures against bird flu has been enhanced. As against 21 Rapid Response Teams (RRTs) yesterday, 32 RRTs have now been deployed. Twenty-two areas have been identified for culling and proper sanitization works in the culling zone. On 26th July 2007, the second day after the confirmation of outbreak of Avian Influenza, 9,472 poultry birds were culled; 7,159 eggs destroyed; and 450-kilogram poultry feed material disposed of. RRTs started the actual control and containment operations yesterday after requisite health check-up by medical teams and under coverage of Tamiflu tablet. All the members of RRTs were fully equipped with PPE (personal protection equipment) and control operations were carried out as per the guidelines issued by the Government of India in identified poultry units as well as backyard poultry. Eight areas/villages, 4 each in East and West Imphal districts, were covered on the second day. A Control Room has been set up at the Office of the Directorate of Veterinary and Animal Husbandry Services at Imphal with Telephone No. 0385-245 0224 and Fax No. 0385-245 4928.

2059. (27-7-2007) NEW DELHI : Dr. Ashwani Kumar Minister of State for Industry inaugurated the India Japan Fashion Show at Osaka last evening, as part of India Japan Friendship Year 2007 celebrations. The show sponsored by JETRO and the Embassy of India in Japan was intended to showcase Indian fabrics and textiles to increase India's share of global textile and clothing trade from the current level of 3.5% to 7%. In his inaugural address Dr. Kumar pointed out the that the National Manufacturing Competitiveness Commission (NMCC) has estimated that India's share in global clothing and textile trade can be increased from US $51 billion to US $ 110 billion by 2012. Remarking on the Fashion Show, he said that the event should be seen as an important initiative and deepen further the economic and cultural bonding between India and Japan. "Fashion represents the evolution of society and is also a manifestation of individual expression in which sense it is an art form", he said. The Minister expressed the hope that the event would raise the visibility of richness of India's fabrics in Japan, which received the first piece of Indian textiles in the early seventeenth century, which is still used as an ornamental screen for the Gion Rath Yatra-a key festival in Japan. The fashion event showcased Indian fabrics designed by Japanese fashion designer Ms. Hiroko Koshino and Manish Arora from India. Among those attending the event were Mr. Taro Nakayama, President Japan India Parliamentarians Friendship

League, Vice Governor and Mayor of OSAKA, Mr. Hiyashi, Chairman JETRO and H K Singh Indian Ambassador to Japan.

2060. (27-7-2007) NEW DELHI : The Minister of Women and Child Development Smt. Renuka Chowdhury has urged the SAARC Countries to adopt gender friendly lending system as economic empowerment of the women is vital for the overall development of the region. Access of the women to the economic resources enhance productivity not only of a particular household, but also provides better opportunities for education, health and social development. Inaugurating the SAARC Conference on Micro-Financing and Women Economic Empowerment here today, she said that rural women of India have shown that if given opportunities and access to income generating resources they can change the face of society. Underlining the importance of the economic empowerment of the women, Smt. Renuka Chowdhury said that the integration of the region's trade, investment and financial ties have altered the economic and social role of the women. The continued growth of service sector has also brought new opportunities for women to improve their economic and social status. Micro-finance has become important tool to enable women to seize these opportunities, she added. Urging the policy makers of the region to adopt gender friendly lending system, she said that women have emerged as most credible borrower. Micro-finance schemes have in many instances, demonstrated that the poor women are bankable and a valuable source for saving mobilization but the benefits and potential of micro-finance programme and schemes for women have not being uniformly realized in the countries of the region. She stressed that a diverse Micro-finance sector should be developed for women. Being organized by the Rashtriya Mahila Kosh under the aegis of Ministry of Women and Child Development, the Conference has on its agenda the issue of micro financing to the women in the region and diverse models of funding agencies to the self-help groups of women. It is being attended by the Government representatives, Micro-finance Institution, NGOs from Afghanistan, Bangladesh, Bhutan, Maldives, Nepal, Pakistan and Sri Lanka. The representatives from various International bodies are also participating in the Conference.

2061. (27-7-2007) NEW DELHI : The polling for the Vice Presidential Election, 2007 will take place on 10th of August 2007 (Friday) in Room No. 62, First Floor, Parliament House. Members of both the Houses of Parliament form the Electoral College for the said election. Following are the candidates who are contesting the election: 1. Mohd. Hamid Ansari 2. Dr. (Smt.) Najma A. Heptulla 3. Shri Rasheed Masood The polling will commence at 10.00 a.m. and close at 5. p.m. on that day. The counting of votes will commence at 6.00 p.m. on the same day and the results will be declared immediately thereafter. The polling arrangements in Parliament House are being made by the Returning Officer, Dr. Yogendra Narain, Secretary-General, Rajya Sabha.

2062. (27-7-2007) NEW DELHI : Alternative and Innovative Education (AIE) has been more effective in providing education to the older age group (11-14 years) never enrolled or dropout children, children who migrate seasonally with their families, street and other deprived urban children, working children and other vulnerable children in difficult circumstances. In 2005-06, over 30.78 lakh children benefited under AIE facilities of SSA. For 2006-2007, the total number of children targeted for coverage under AIE is 56.11 lakh.

2063. (28-7-2007) NEW DELHI : On 27th July, 2007, the 3rd day after confirmation of outbreak of Avian Influenza, the pace of control and containment measures was further intensified. On 27th July, 2007, 34 Rapid Response Teams (RRTs) (including of 2 teams sent in the afternoon as re-enforcement) were deployed for undertaking culling operation. A total of 22 villages/areas were covered on the 3rd day in the culling zone. Total number of poultry birds culled on 27th July 2007 was 25,094. Number of eggs destroyed was 3,277 and the quantity of poultry feed materials destroyed was 2,245 Kgs. On the 4th day of the operation *i.e.* 28th July, 2007, 28 villages/areas have been identified for culling and proper sanitization works in the culling zone. For this work, 30 RRTs have been deployed.

2064. (28-7-2007) NEW DELHI : The demand of the congress that Sh. L.K. Advani Leader of Opposition and former deputy Prime Minister should apologize seems not only curious but also comical because the congress has not given any response much less satisfactory response to the significant comment of Sh. Advani against the rather inappropriate observation of Dr. Manmohan Singh, the Prime Minister that he lost sleep when he saw parents of those who were arrested abroad in connection with their alleged implication in terror related incidents crying. It is our consistent stand that there should be no victimisation of innocent and law should be applied fairly but the larger issue is the highly selective way in which Dr. Manmohan Singh looses his sleep. Did the Prime Minister loose his sleep when so many innocent Indians were killed by terrorists violence and naked killings in the bomb blasts in Mumbai and Delhi and many other places. Was his sleep disturbed when the innocent pilgrims were killed by terrorists few days ago in Pahelgam in Kashmir or the attack on the critical Nuclear research centre in Srinagar. Does the Prime Minister ever realise that all this spurt in terror violence is because the government under his leadership has deliberately become soft on terror, which becomes increasingly evident from his persistence to take steps to reduce army deployment in Kashmir in spite of objection of the forces. This is vote bank politics at its worst.

2065. (28-7-2007) NEW DELHI : The Prime Minister, Dr. Manmohan Singh, has urged Air India to ensure world class service levels and to put greater focus and new management styles and better service quality in the years ahead. The Prime Minister was speaking on the occasion of arrival of new Boeing and Airbus Aircraft and launch of Freighter Aircraft Operations by Air India and Indian here today. Dr. Singh said that he was confident that Air India will once again regain its reputation of being one of the world's best airlines. Minister for Agriculture,

Shri Sharad Pawar, Minister of State for Civil Aviation, Shri Praful Patel, and Deputy Chairman, Planning Commission, Shri Montek Singh Ahluwalia were among those present on the occasion. Following is the text of the Prime Minister's speech at the occasion: "It gives me great pleasure to be here today to witness the arrival of new aircraft from Boeing and Airbus for addition to our fleet of the national carriers. I am also happy to launch the new freighter operations of our national carriers. These two happy developments have come at an opportune time, when the market for air travel and air cargo is expanding rapidly. This is a truly historic day for all those associated with Air India and Indian Airlines. I take pride in the fact that our Government has taken steps to bring to an end a long period of neglect of our national carriers. I compliment my colleague Shri Praful Patel and the present leadership of Air India and Indian Airlines for their important forward looking and innovative role. Over the last several decades, both Air India and Indian Airlines have rendered great service to our nation-both commercially and in providing logistic support for national efforts in diverse fields. There was a time when Air India was regarded as one of the world's best airlines. I am sure that Air India will once again regain that reputation. That should be our common ambition, that should be our common aim. In this, you have our support in full measure. Given our tradition of hospitality we in India should be at the forefront of growth of such service industries as civil aviation. I am also happy that with greater competition there is now increased pressure from market forces driving the process of change and improvement in civil aviation business as well. The aviation environment in our country has recorded a sea change over the last three to four years and I complement my colleague Praful Patel for this contribution to this happy outcome. The opening up of the skies has created new market opportunities for civil aviation business in our country. However, our national carriers were unable to take full advantage of the opportunities at hand for a variety of reasons. The shortage of aircraft was one such and our Government has taken decisive steps to address this particular problem. Within a short period of about one year we were able to place orders for 43 Airbus aircraft for Indian Airlines and 68 Boeing aircraft for Air India.

2066. (29-7-2007) NEW DELHI : Union Home Minister Sh. Shivraj Patil has strongly condemned today's blast in a bus in Srinagar in which five persons were killed. Sh.Patil has express is condolences to the bereaved families. Describing the attack as an act of frustration by terrorists, he said that the Government would continue to work for peace an normalcy in J&K.

2067. (30-7-2007) NEW DELHI : The 2-day (July 31-August 1) Secretary-level talks between India and Pakistan are scheduled to be held here from tomorrow. The Pakistani delegation would be led by Mr. Syed Asif Shah, Commerce Secretary while the Indian side would be led by Shri G.K. Pillai, Commerce Secretary. The other members of the Pakistani delegation include Mr. Aizaz Ahmed Choudhury, Director General (South Asia and SAARC) and Mr. Shahid Hussain Raja, Additional

Secretary. The agenda for the talks include trade in goods and services, important issues like tea exports from India, joint registration of basmati rice (GI), discussion on expanding bilateral trade, new items for trade such as cement etc. The bilateral trade between the two countries have grown at an impressive rate during the past 2 years. Pakistan exports to India have grown from US $ 94.97 million (2004-05) to US $ 323.19 million (2006-07). The Indian exports have grown from US $ 521.05 million (2004-05) to US $ 1003.22 million (2006-07).

2068. (30-7-2007) NEW DELHI : Government of India have announced the sale (re-issue) of "5.48 percent Government Stock, 2009" under Market Stabilization Scheme for a notified amount of Rs. 5,000 crore (nominal). The Government Stock will be sold through price based auction using multiple price method. The auction will be conducted by the Reserve Bank of India, Mumbai Office, Fort, Mumbai on August 1, 2007(Wednesday). Up to 5% of the amount notified for the sale of stock is reserved for allotment to eligible individuals and Institutions on non-competitive basis as per the Scheme for Non-Competitive Bidding Facility in the Auction of Government Securities. Bids in the prescribed form obtainable from the Regional Director, Reserve Bank of India, Mumbai Office (Public Debt Office), Fort, Mumbai-400 001 and RBI website www.rbi.org.in should be submitted to that Office on August 1, 2007. The NDS members should submit competitive as well as non-competitive bids in electronic format using Primary Market Operation (PMO) module of NDS. All bids should be submitted by 12.30 P.M. The result of the auction will be announced on August 1, 2007 and payment by successful bidders will be during banking hours on August 2, 2007 (Thursday). Department of Economic Affairs, Ministry of Finance New Delhi.

2069. (30-7-2007) NEW DELHI : The Minister of State for Defence Shri M M Pallam Raju has appealed the youth to join the National Cadet Corps (NCC) for inculcating discipline and patriotism. Addressing cadets at the NCC Special National Integration Camp at Leh, Ladakh yesterday, Shri Pallam Raju asked soldiers and ex-servicemen present there to motivate their children to join the NCC. He called upon the cadets to reap the benefit of modern technology for a bright career. The Minister reminded the cadets that they should aim for their goal, no matter how difficult the journey was. With determination, all obstacles on their way would be overcome, he added. Shri Pallam Raju later interacted with the cadets and praised their confidence and skills. The cadets presented a colourful cultural programme on the occasion. Over 160 boys and girls from various parts of the country are attending the camp, which will conclude.

2070. (30-7-2007) NEW DELHI : The Election Commission had announced on 24th July, 2007 the schedule for holding bye-elections to fill a number of casual vacancies in the Lok Sabha and State Legislative Assemblies including 39-Ballia Parliamentary Constituency, 20-Suar Tanda, 25-Gunnaur and 296-Farrukhabad Assembly Constituencies in Uttar Pradesh. In the meanwhile, the Chief Electoral

Officer, Uttar Pradesh, in view of the already existing flood situation in eastern U.P and likely water logging during the later half of the month of August in a considerable number of polling stations areas falling within Ballia Parliamentary Constituency, has requested the Commission to consider postponing the bye-election from 39-Ballia Lok Sabha constituency. The Commission having taken all aspects of the issue into consideration has decided to postpone the bye-election from 39-Ballia Parliamentary Constituency. A fresh schedule for the bye-election will be announced in due course. The Commission has also decided to change the date of poll, in respect of all the three Assembly Constituencies namely, 29-Suar Tanda, 25-Gunnaur and 296-Farrukhabad in Uttar Pradesh, from 29th August to 31st August, 2007. The date of counting of votes in all these three constituencies has been changed from 31st August, 2007, as announced earlier, to 3rd September, 2007 and the date before which the election shall be completed has been fixed on 5th September, 2007 in respect of all the three above referred assembly constituencies in Uttar Pradesh. As announced in the Press Note dated 24th July, 2007, the poll will take place in 9-Jamshedpur Parliamentary Constituency in Jharkhand and 30-Dhumakot Assembly Constituency in Uttarakhand on 29th August,2007. However, the date of counting for these two constituencies has been fixed on 2nd September, 2007 and the date before which these two bye-elections shall be completed has been fixed as 3rd September, 2007. Therefore, the Commission's press note no. ECI/PN/33/2007 dated 24th July, 2007 may be read as amended accordingly. Election Commission of India New Delhi.

2071. (30-7-2007) NEW DELHI : The farming community is one of the most vulnerable groups in the country. A whole season's effort can be put in jeopardy due to inclement weather conditions. In order to provide assistance to the farming community timely intervention is necessary. This can be possible only if information is available. The Department of Science & Technology has now developed the capability to monitor crop health in real time. Revealing this to the media in a Press Conference today Shri Kapil Sibal, Union Minister for Science & Technology and Earth Sciences said that this has been developed for Haryana and will be extended to the whole country in six months. Under this initiative the Department has built up a capacity to assess per hectare production in a village of wheat, mustard, gram, for the Rabi crops and for rice and cotton in the khariff crops. The estimates generated by the Department were tallied with crop cutting data for 6000 villages of Haryana. Validation showed that for ninety five percent of the villages per hectare production assessment at the village level were accurate. In built in this capacity was also a suite for real time monitoring of crop health. Weekly crop assessments were run for the Haryana Districts and it was possible to mark out areas which were under stress either due to heat conditions or due to lack of water. Daily/weekly/monthly rainfall, temperature and soil moisture data are being provided to the Haryana Government for trial. Government of Haryana will expand the dissemination of this information to the districts whereby these parameters can be monitored upto the village level. The Government of Haryana had posed a problem regarding sown area under different crops in the current khariff season. Cropped area data normally is available much later in the season when the land surveys are done. Under the current project this will be possible on a fortnightly basis and first estimates upto 19th July have been provided. The Department has delineated the areas under different crops for each of the districts. By middle of August, firm estimates of cropped area will be available and production estimates will be provided before harvesting. Shri Sibal that this initiative will provide the groundwork for making crop insurance more meaningful thereby extending the social safety net for the farming community. Currently it has not been possible to extend this because of lack of production data at the village level. Now with production data validated at the village level, an option is now open to the Government. This capability will not only monitor onset of drought in real time but also provide capability to assess crop damage due to onset of an extreme weather condition. Similar support can be provided to alternate insurance products such as weather insurance which depend on rainfall parameters. The Minister further added that this is only the beginning of the work for strengthening support to the farming communities. He said that as we progress, methodologies for assessment of crop diseases will also be built into the programme. In order to provide whole hearted support to the farmers and increase agriculture production, the Department will build this into a full fledged mission.

2072. (30-7-2007) NEW DELHI : Government of India, Department of Science & Technology (DST) has been considering the revision of research fellowships of Research Fellows and Research Associates from time to time. There are various practical considerations in deciding on the revision of fellowships which should take into account all possible scenarios and specially, availability of resources and the sustainability of increased fellowships. While attractive fellowships have to be instituted to attract promising candidates to take up research as a career, there is also a need to create an ambience required for pursuing research, which is a pre-requisite. The Exercise of revision of fellowships is conducted through an inter-agency and extensive consultative process. The Department, as a part of the consultative process, had discussions with all the S&T agencies including the Ministry of Human Resources Development (MHRD) and the University Grants Commission (UGC). The revision had taken into account the need for redesigning the research fellowships for meeting the needs of a competitive market environment for talent, and longer-term time horizon. It was also decided that both the Scientific Departments and the MHRD would harmonize the fellowship levels and effective dates for implementation. The following were the main recommendations apart from the revision of fellowships: The candidate who qualifies through NET examination or its equivalent for admission to do Ph.D. should get a fellowship amount of Rs 12000. All eligible candidates admitted in different disciplines to do Ph.D may be covered under a suitable fellowship programme in a phase-wise manner. Fellowships to candidates, other than those qualified in NET or equivalent examination, admitted to pursue Ph.D in the institutions, recognized by relevant

S&T agencies, would be covered by UGC norms. Based on these extensive deliberations, the Department of Science & Technology has proposed the enhancement in research fellowships.

2073. (30-7-2007) NEW DELHI : Following the outbreak of avian influenza in Manipur, 1,37,944 birds have been culled so far. This comprises 58,615 chicken and ducks culled on 29th July and 79,329 birds culled from 25 to 28 July. After 8,140 eggs were destroyed on 29th July, so far 20,249 eggs have been destroyed. So far 11,615 kg poultry feed has been destroyed which includes 5,773 kg destroyed on 29th July. Cleaning and disinfection of the State Government poultry farms at Mantripukhri and Porompat is in progress. Surveillance within a radius of 5-10 kms. is in progress. There are 79 villages (41 in East Imphal and 38 in West Imphal) in this area. There is no report of any abnormal mortality.

2074. (30-7-2007) HYDERABAD: The Communist Party of India (Marxist) and the Telugu Desam Party on Sunday demanded the resignation of Chief Minister Y.S. Rajasekhara Reddy for using 'brutal force' for 'suppression' of the Left struggle for land distribution to the poor, leading to the police firing at Mudigonda village in Khammam district on Saturday. The CPI(M), the CPI, the TDP and other parties organised a protest rally here to condemn the "indiscriminate police firing" and resolved to intensify their agitation. CPI(M) leader Sitaram Yechury, who participated in the rally, endorsed the State unit's demand. He said the Polit Bureau would meet on Monday to take stock of the situation. TDP president N. Chandrababu Naidu wanted Dr. Reddy to own moral responsibility and quit, though the CPI distanced itself from the demand saying it would dilute the land struggle.

2075. (30-7-2007) NEW DELHI : The Ministry of Rural Development has sanctioned Rs. 27.64 crore to the State Government of Kerala towards the balance of first instalment of funds against the provisional allocation of Rs. 82.93 crore under the Centrally sponsored Accelerated Rural Water Supply Programme (ARWSP) (Normal) of Rajiv Gandhi National Drinking Water Mission, during the year 2007-08. Up to 15 per cent of funds released under this sanction may be utilized for Operation & Maintenance and up to 5 per cent of funds may be spent for taking sustainability measures. States have been requested to delegate powers for management of Rural Water Supply Schemes through the Panchayati Raj Institutions (PRIs) as per the Constitution of India. As such Operation and Maintenance of the completed RWS Scheme should be transferred to the PRIs. No expenditure shall be incurred on taking water quality problems form the present release, as there is a separate allocation for the purpose. This release is being made for execution/completion of schemes to provide safe drinking water facilities to rural habitations and schools under the Centrally Sponsored ARWSP. Priorities set in ARWSP guidelines and through other instructions issued from time to time shall be followed for coverage of rural habitations and rural schools.

2076. (30-7-2007) NEW DELHI : The Minister of Railways Shri Lalu Prasad has said that Zonal Railways have to make urgent efforts to bring traffic from road to rail in important commodities and that there is a need to formulate different policies for carrying the raw material traffic and finished goods so that more traffic could be diverted from road to rail. Addressing the meeting of General Mangers of all zonal railways and production units, the Minister said that General Managers have been empowered to take all possible steps to popularize attractive schemes and incentives to get more and more traffic from road to rail. He urged them to continue vigorous efforts to meet the loading target of the current year especially in the field of Cement and Steel. He added that he has given directions to the Board to take urgent policy decision regarding commercial, operating and pricing matters so as to attract more and more traffic towards railway. The Minister further said that liberalization of container policy has created interest amongst private investors. He urged General Managers to help in creating rail connectivity to sidings so that the scheme could be implemented effectively. He also said that General Managers have to devote more attention to several schemes which have been launched to enhance rail capacity like rationalization of loco link, improvement in terminal facilities, computerization of guard's and driver's lobby, electrification of sidings etc. He also instructed General Managers to take adequate steps to provide safety and security to the railway passengers. He also called upon to take steps for stern action against corrupt contractors and all the officials conniving with such elements. He called upon the General Managers to continue with the tempo of the turnaround and carry their responsibilities with conviction and commitment. He complimented General Managers for their cooperation in bringing about turnaround in Railways. Speaking on the occasion, the Minister of State for Railways Shri R.Velu said that all the Zonal Railways should make all out efforts to achieve the internal loading target of 800 million tonnes of freight loading in 2007-08. He said that Railway Board has notified some attractive freight incentive schemes and General Managers should review the progress made in this regard. In addition, the Minister also pointed out some areas of concern, which require early action like cleanliness of trains & platforms, better passenger amenities and utilization of Special Railway Safety Fund. The Minister of State for Railways Shri Naranbhai J Rathwa has drawn the attention of General Managers towards improving the punctuality of trains. He said that efforts should continue to bring out improvement in the field of passenger amenities like supply of hygienic food and good quality bed-rolls, to utmost satisfaction of the passengers. He also emphasized the need for more result-oriented trainings for Railway officials to fulfil our dream of making Indian Railways the number one world-class railways. In his address, Chairman Railway Board, Shri J.P.Batra while appreciating the excellent performance by the Production units, said that Rail Coach Factory and Integral Coach factory should go for production of more Garib Rath type coaches. He also briefed in detail on all the steps and incentives being announced by the Railway Board for achieving the loading target for the financial year 2007-08.

2077. (30-7-2007) NEW DELHI : To a question that Opposition says that Congress has murdered democracy in Goa, Shri Singhvi said that we had pointed out that a constitutional process has to work itself out. Since the assembly is in session, that process must take place within and in the domain of the assembly. Please note three significant facts: 1) Ex-Congress MLA, Mrs. Victoria defied a party whip on the 24th July and on 24th itself a complaint was filed, not today, not yesterday but on 24th itself a disqualification 10th schedule complaint was filed. 2). Two MLAs of the MGP (Maharastrawadi Gomantak Party) on their own wrote a letter supposedly withdrawing support to the Congress Party, when by a general council meeting which was minuted. The main MGP political party had resolved to support the Congress Party. The MGP's resolution to support the Congress Party, which had been minuted, was never withdrawn. Yet, two MLAs on their own sought to withdraw from the Congress Party. On this also, after collecting all the papers including the minutes of the MGP general council meeting, fully supporting the Congress party. A second complaint was filed a couple of days ago. Both these complaints came to be decided on an interim urgent basis for the simple reason that the final hearing would have led to charges that the whole issue has been delayed. So, pending a final determination as the Speaker is fully entitled to, he passed an interim order on the clear unequivocal basis of the 10th Schedule and disqualifying three MLAs. Therefore, now that chapter or that stage of that chapter is over and whatever further assembly constitutional process or judicial process has to work itself out and will undoubly do so. But let me be very clear that the Congress Party or the ruling coalition did not start this destabilization process. The destabilization process was clearly a result of vested interests creating instability for their own, self-serving ends. The principle self-serving end was the land issues, issues of money, commerce relating to land since the regional plan had been proposed to be reviewed in the context of this destabilization tactics by parties and persons who did not get electoral mandate, by parties which wanted to enter through the back door. In a situation not of our making, we had to deal with the situation and in the face of explicit defiance of party whip and party's stand, a interim decision has been taken, permitted by the constitution, authorized by the constitution, mandated by the constitution, in affirmness with the constitution, of course the final decision can come later on as all procedures are open but today the government has a clear majority and the assembly has been adjourned sine die. To a question that there was difference between the MGP and the legislative party, Shri Singhvi said that you may be right. Obviously, these facts will have to be adjudicated by the sole designated authority under the 10th schedule and one of the issues which that constitutional designated authority will adjudicate will be the clear difference between the written minutes of the MGP extending support never withdrawn, subsisting and operating today as opposed to the suo-motu, unilateral letter written by two MLAs for willing to withdraw. That contradiction will have to be resolved but who is right and who is wrong, I cannot say it today. To a question on the incident of firing on farmers in Khammam District in Andhra

Pradesh, Shri Singhvi said that I must make relevant facts regarding Andhra Pradesh and Khammam clear to you. It is very important to note that unlike several other such incidents in different parts of the country, the state government of AP moved swiftly, sensitively and comprehensively. A) To take urgent disciplinary action against those who perceived to be errant policemen; b) For the care and concern of those injured or killed; c) The announcement and institute a judicial enquiry and d) Every effort made to calm the atmosphere down, not to have divisive politics, not to create provocative atmosphere given these circumstance, I think it is incumbent on all of us and it means all parties, all persons to work towards a healing touch for the time-being and the longer term issues can then be resolved in a calmer atmosphere. To a question that Shri Rajashekher Reddy created this crises and pacified it too, Shri Singhvi said that the Chief Minister of Andhra Pradesh and the Congress Party have never and do not believe as other parties may have done in different points of history, in creating crises and then trying to solve them. There is no question of that.

2078. (30-7-2007) NEW DELHI : A torch of Military World Games was lit at Leh yesterday with fanfare by Minister of State for Defence Shri MM Pallam Raju. The torch was handed over to the leader of EME Cycle Rally Team, which will carry it right up to Kanyakumari. The cycling expedition carrying the flame will cover a distance of 4249 kms in just 20 days. 'Bravo' the mascot of the Military World Games, is also accompanying this unique journey of Torch from Leh to Kanyakumari. Troops based at Leh, commanded by GOC, 14 Corps Lt Gen. PC Bhardwaj cheered the Mascot Bravo and members of Endurance Expedition as the flame was lit and carried away. The flame will reach New Delhi on 5th of next month. The torch will pass through Tangland-La, Charchu, Manali, Agra, Jhansi, Nagpur, Hyderabad, Kurnool, Hosur, etc. before reaching Kanyakumari. The event is part of series of events, which will be conducted as a precursor to the mega event, to be held in October this year. The Ceremony was organized to commemorate 75 days to the Military World Games. India is conducting the 4th CISM Military World Games in Hyderabad and Mumbai during 14-21 October this year. Nearly 100 countries are expected to participate in this mega event. Going by the size, this event is considered to be the biggest sporting event, next only to the Olympics. In Olympics almost 25% of the medal winners are from the armed forces from world over. These Champions will comprise the 6000 strong participants worldwide. India is conducting this event for the first time. Various activities are being conducted by different units of the Indian Armed Forces to publicise the Military World Games.

2079. (30-7-2007) NEW DELHI : The Prime Minister Dr. Manmohan Singh, spoke to the Chief Minister of Andhra Pradesh, Dr. Y.S. Rajasekhara Reddy and reviewed the situation arising out of the police firing in Khammam District. The Chief Minister informed the Prime Minister of the steps taken and of the decision to institute a judicial inquiry. The Prime Minister conveyed his heartfelt sympathy for the next of the kin of those who died in the firing. He enquired about the welfare of those injured. The Prime Minister expressed his regret at the unfortunate incident. The Prime Minister reiterated the Government's commitment to redistribute surplus land and fulfil its stated commitments to the rural poor, especially the landless. The Prime Minister will be visiting Hyderabad today to review the programmes with respect to agriculture, infrastructure and investment plans for the State.

2080. (30-7-2007) NEW DELHI : The Empowered Group of Ministers (EGoM) met today to consider the report submitted by the Board of Sasan Power Limited on the decisions of the EGoM taken in its last meeting. It was noted that Sasan Power Limited had received revised offers from the three remaining bidders *i.e.* M/s. Jaiprakash Associates, M/s. NTPC and M/s. Reliance Power Limited (formerly known as M/s. Reliance Energy Generation Ltd.), and that the revised bid of M/s. Reliance Power Limited quoting levellised tariff of Rs. 1.19616 per kilo watt hour was the lowest of the three bids. Accordingly, the EGoM has advised that the procurer should consider taking immediate action to issue the Letter of Intent to the lowest bidder. For this purpose, the EGoM has advised that the matter should be placed before the Board of Sasan Power Limited expeditiously for taking appropriate action.

2081. (30-7-2007) NEW DELHI : Several good practices have emerged in successful implementation of the mid day meal programme, including inter alia: Tamil Nadu: The State Government has been implementing a mid day meal programme-far beyond the programme for which Central Assistance is provided. It provides mid day meal to children in different age groups, namely 2-4 years, 5-9 years, 10-13 years and 14-15 years consequently covering children from the pre-school to higher secondary stage. The State Government has a well laid out feeding scale for children in the different age groups, which is further supplemented by 15 protein rich foods, omprising, boiled black gram, green gram, potatoes and eggs. Puducherry: Milk and sweet bread provided for breakfast before commencement of classes, and an evening snack provided before children return home. This is in addition to the mid day meal. Bihar: IN several schools of Bihar, children have been organised into a Bal Sansad. The Bal Sansad is actively associated in serving food. Karnataka: The Suvarna Chaitanya Arogya programme provides for regular health check of children. Health cards are prepared for all children and referral services are provided for children with serious ailments. Assistive devices are provided under SSA for children with hearing and visual impairments. In addition, the State has initiated a Swastha Plus kitchen garden in 20,000 primary school to enable children to grow vegetables which are used in the mid day meals. Karnataka has also instituted a roster system for the appointment of cooks: (a) a school with two cooks will have at least one cook belonging to the SC/ST group, (b) a school with three cooks will have one belonging to SC/ST and one to OBC, and (c) a school with four cooks will have at least one SC/ST, one OBC and one minority. Gujarat: Provision for micro-nutrients and de-worming tablets; Health check up takes places systematically. Chhattisgarh: In Koriya district of Chhattisgarh, the State Health Resource Centre (SHRC) have organised Mithanins (an intimate friend) to provide support to the mid day meal programme. Rajasthan: While in most schools, cooking is undertaken in the school itself by the cook appointed by the School Development and Management Committee (SDMC), the Government of Rajasthan has also associated the Annapurna Women Cooperative Society, to provide mid day meal in two Panchayats of each block. The meal is cooked in a centrally located school and distributed to different schools in the 16 Panchayat. Presently there are 463 Annapurna Women Cooperative Societies providing mid day meal to over 3 lakh children in 3500 schools.

2082. (30-7-2007) NEW DELHI : The President Smt. Pratibha Devisingh Patil has condoled the death of Shri Kazi Lhendup Dorjee. In a condolence message, the President said, "Shri Kazi Lhendup Dorjee was a distinguished statesman whose work as the first Chief Minister of Sikkim will always be remembered. In his passing away, the country has lost a personality who worked for the upliftment of the people of Sikkim especially the weak and the downtrodden. He had contributed to the development of Sikkim in a big way".

2083. (31-7-2007) NEW DELHI : Presiding over the review meetings organised by the Department of Land Resources in Ministry of Rural Development with 28 States from 10.7.2007 to 26.7.2007 to review the watershed programmes, Dr. Raghuvansh Prasad Singh, the Minister (RD) has expressed concern over the depleting water table in various parts of the country and the need to conserve and harvest the water. At present, 1742 projects under Integrated Wasteland Development Programme (IWDP) in 476 districts of 28 States, 19710 projects in 972 Blocks of 185 districts in 16 States under Drought Prone Area Development Programme (DPAP) and 13552 projects each covering an area of about 500 Ha. In 235 Blocks of 40 districts in 7 States are being implemented. Central assistance of Rs. 1115.00 crores was released during 2006-07 to the States. In 2007-08, an amount of Rs. 158.00 crores has been released as central assistance as on 26.07.2007. The Principal Secretaries/Secretaries in-charge of the watershed programmes form various States attended the review and informed about the status of these projects in the States. Under Integrated Wasteland Development Programme (IWDP), the pace of implementation in States like Andhra Pradesh, Rajasthan, Tamil Nadu, Karnataka, Madhya Pradesh, Uttar Pradesh, Chattisgarh and Nagaland has been satisfactory. Orissa has set up a watershed mission in the State for effective execution of the area development programmes in the State. Gujarat has also recently set up Gujarat State Watershed Management Agency (GSWMA) as an autonomous body to monitor and facilitate the watershed schemes in the State. Six Deputy Commissioners have been appointed in Maharashtra at the State Head Quarter to coordinate and monitor the watershed projects. The Minister (RD) expressed concern with the performance of the IWDP projects in the State of

Arunachal Pradesh, Bihar, Goa, Jharkhand, Kerala, Manipur and West Bengal. He directed that regular monthly reviews should be held by the concerned state authorities at the state and district level. Under Desert Development Programme (DDP), some states namely Haryana, Himachal Pradesh & Jammu & Kashmir have not been able to claim Central assistance in respect of projects sanctioned under Hariyali Guidelines from 2003-04 onwards and instructed all concerned officers to take special efforts to step-up the pace of implementation of the programmes in these states. In respect of Drought Prone Area Programme (DPAP), the States namely Bihar, Chhattisgarh, Jammu & Kashmir, Jharkhand, Uttaranchal, and West Bengal have also not been able to claim the Central assistance. The respective State representatives were advised to submit the claims with complete documents/information immediately in respect of projects where instalment is due so that the projects are completed within the stipulated period. Dr., Singh advised the concerned state representatives to complete the projects in a time bound manner so that the benefits of the programme reach the poor, small and marginal farmers as targeted under these schemes.

2084. (31-7-2007) NEW DELHI : The Indian Air Force frontline fighter aircraft would be taking part in a joint air display with the aircraft from the Air India's fleet at Mumbai on 09 Sep 07. The fly past is taking place as both Indian Air Force and Air India are celebrating their Platinum Jubilee this year. The frontline fighters of IAF such as SU-30s, MiG-29s, Jaguars and MiG-21 Bisons would be flying in close formation with representative aircraft from Air India's entire fleet. The fly past would be followed by an aerobatic display by IAF's Surya Kiran aerobatic team 'THE SKATS'. A solo aerobatic display by IAF SU-30 Air superiority fighter would also be taking place. The aircraft of the fly past and aerobatic display would be flying between Chowpaty and Nariman point at Mumbai. The essence of the entire effort, apart from a ceremonial public display is that, the flypast is likely to take place without any prior practices or rehearsals. This would also cause least disruption to the civil traffic. Recently when the Air India's Boeing 777 arrived at New Delhi for the first time from Seattle, USA they were ceremoniously escorted by IAF SU-30s on 28 Jul 07 at IGI Airport, New Delhi.

2085. (31-7-2007) NEW DELHI : The Directorate General of Lighthouses and Lightships has converted a large number of lights from petroleum vapour/dissolved acetylene gas/kerosene to the electric operation, thereby conserving the conventional fossil fuel. According to the Annual Report of the Ministry of Shipping, Road Transport & Highways, in the past incandescent electric lamps of 3000W and above were used for light source but now these lamps have been replaced with 150W to 400W metal halide lamps and 100W halogen lamps as per the requirement of a specific light. These lamps provide higher lumen than the earlier type of incandescent lamps and has helped to save on electric energy.

2086. (31-7-2007) NEW DELHI : The meeting of the Parliamentary Consultative Committee attached to the Ministry of Civil Aviation met at Mumbai today on the historic occasion of the first flight of the merged airline 'Air India'. Welcoming the Members, the Chairman of the Committee-the Minister for Civil Aviation, Shri Praful Patel highlighted the efforts of the Government to make the national carrier truly international by giving it strength and muscle in the form of a brand new fleet of the aircraft and giving it a competitive edge. The Minister added that all necessary steps are being taken so that the fleet acquisition and modernization process is firmly in place. Shri Patel spoke about the necessity of further fleet acquisition in view of the fact that by 2011 the entire existing fleets would have to be replaced. The fleet size would have gone down requiring further strengthening-the planning for which should begin now. He said that even if Air India grew at a conservative rate of 10%, the carrier would require a much bigger fleet size than what would be available to it. Speaking about why the merger was necessitated the Minister said that the Indian Airlines and Air India were being merged after a lot of consideration at different levels. The thinking for the necessity of the merger had been going on for the last 20 years or so, he added. After the opening up of skies, a stronger national carrier was even more necessary to face the competition of the other international carriers. He said that merger was also necessary for the national carrier to join one of the three existing airline alliances across the globe. None of them would have considered the national carriers on a stand-alone basis. The Members cutting across party line congratulated the Minister and the Ministry of Civil Aviation on the merger of the two national carriers, the successful fleet acquisition programme of the Government, the starting of non stop flight connecting India and America and the modernization and restructuring of all airports across the country. The Members highlighted on a number of crucial issues relating to the aviation sector like modernization of airport, security check at airport, other issues relating to security, bilateral, rationalization, creation of more infrastructure, creation of more facilities at the airports, congestion at airports, training schools for cabin crew, pilot training facilities for handicapped passengers, fog preparedness of airports and airlines, etc. and had detailed discussions on them. Members of Parliament who were present at the meeting were: S/Shri Madhu Goud Yashki, Sachin Pilot, Kunwar Jitin Prasad, Santosh Gangwar, Ratilal K. Verma, Ramswaroop Koli, Tarit Baran Topdar, A. Krishnaswamy, Sukhdev Singh Dhindsa, Smt. Sumitra Mahajan, Deepender Singh Hooda, Santosh Bagrodia, Tarlochan Singh, Dinesh Trivedi, Abdul Wahab Peevee, Dr. Farooq Abdullah, Sanjay Raut, Rajeev Shukla and Bashistha Narain Singh.

2087. (31-7-2007) NEW DELHI : Shri Vijay Singh has taken over as Defence Secretary. Born on July 13, 1948, Shri Singh obtained his Masters Degree in History from Delhi University and joined Indian Administrative Service in 1970. He was allotted Madhya Pradesh Cadre. Shri Singh worked in various capacities in Madhya Pradesh between 1971 and 1982 and held the post of District Magistrate of Gwalior and Bhopal. He served in the Government of India between 1982 and 1987 as Director and Coordinator for festival of India in USA, France, USSR and

Japan. He again served with the Madhya Pradesh Government between 1987 and 1996 as Commissioner Jabalpur Division, Indore Division and Home Secretary. He again returned to Government of India to serve as Financial Advisor, Ministry of Health and Family Welfare and Additional Secretary in the Ministries of Chemicals and Fertilizers and Information and Broadcasting from 1996 to 2004. Shri Singh was Chief Secretary Madhya Pradesh from October 2004 to January, 2006. He was Secretary, Department of Ayurveda, Yoga & Naturopathy, Unani, Siddha and Homoeopathy in the Ministry of Health & Family Welfare from February 2006 to July 2006. Prior to his appointment as Defence Secretary, Shri Singh held the charge of Secretary, Road Transport and Highways in the Ministry of Shipping, Road Transport and Highways. The outgoing Defence Secretary Shri Shekhar Dutt has been appointed as Deputy National Security Advisor for Strategic and Defence related subjects in the National Security Council Secretariat. Shri Dutt will be in the rank and pay of Secretary to the Government of India and will hold the post for a period of two years in the first instance or until further orders, whichever is earlier. Shri Dutt was appointed as Defence Secretary in July 2005. Prior to this appointment, he was Secretary Defence Production. He is an IAS officer of the 1969 batch of the Madhya Pradesh cadre. He has also served in the Army and for his role in the Western Sector during 1971 War; he was awarded Sena Medal for gallantry.

2088. (31-7-2007) NEW DELHI : Control and containment operations continued in and around the infected site in Manipur. 47294 birds (43176 chicken and 4118 ducks) were culled and disposed of on 30th July. Other infected materials such as eggs (1755) and feed/feed materials (2105 kg) were also disposed of. In all 1,85,231 birds had been killed in operations till 30th July 2007. The operations are continuing today. Culling and disposal will cover all 86 sectors in the 0 to 5 kms zone followed by mopping, clean up and disinfection. There is no report of any unusual mortality from East and West Imphal districts of Manipur or the country as a whole. Supplies of disinfectant and other materials required for control and containment have been rushed by Government of India to accelerate the pace of control and containment. Government of India has issued an advisory to the NE States to restrain from imposing any restriction on the Inter-State movement of poultry and poultry product and intensify surveillance especially vigilance on the border with the countries that have reported outbreak of avian influenza.

2089. (31-7-2007) NEW DELHI : Emphasizing the need for increased bilateral cooperation, India has suggested that Pakistan could identify products of export interest that could be looked at by India in terms of relevant import regime for these products to facilitate better understanding for Pakistan exporters and take steps to facilitate trade in those items. Addressing the Fourth Meeting on Economic and Commercial Cooperation between India and Pakistan under the Framework of Composite Dialogue here today, Shri G.K. Pillai, Commerce Secretary, has stated that while Pakistan can export cement to India, it would be commercially beneficial if the world's 3rd largest consumer Pakistan could buy tea from the world's largest producer, India, which is next door, he added. If tea is traded across our borders through the land route, it would reduce transaction costs and create economic advantages for the two countries, he further added. The Pakistani delegation was led by Mr. Syed Asif Shah, Commerce Secretary who also spoke on the occasion. Shri Rajeev Kher, Joint Secretary, Department of Commerce from Indian side and Mr. Shahid Malik, High Commissioner of Pakistan, Mr. Aizaz Ahmed Chaudhry, Director General (South Asia and SARC) and Mr. Shahid Hussain Raja, Additional Secretary, from Pakistan's side were the other members who were present at the talks. Shri Pillai observed that there is a need to recognise the sectoral overlap in product baskets and that is why proper diversification and development of exclusive and niche products on a sectoral value chain can help us achieve greater cooperation. Appreciating the efforts of Pakistan for ratifying SAFTA which signifies Pakistan's efforts in accepting India as a Most Favoured Nation, Shri Pillai said that our objective should be to make South Asia a region of free movement of people and goods. He further hoped that the Indo-Pak bilateral trade would touch US $ 10 billion by 2010. There is a need for both countries to improve the infrastructure at the designated border crossing points both on the rail and road networks so as to meet the needs of the business community, the Indian Commerce Secretary added. Providing details of the growth in bilateral trade between India and Pakistan, Shri Pillai informed that "our bilateral trade has grown phenomenally in the past few years. India's exports to Pakistan grew from US$ 521.05 million in 2004-2005 to US $ 1348.32 million in 2006-2007. Pakistan's exports to India grew from $ 94.97 million in 2004-2005 to $177.48 million in 2005-2006 and $ 323.19 million in 2006-2007, a compounded annual growth of more than 70%". Shri Pillai further observed that there is a strong case for us to see how we mainstream this diverted trade and reduce transaction costs to ultimately benefit the consumer on either side.

2090. (31-7-2007) NEW DELHI : Shri A.Raja, Minister of Communication and Information Technology has said that BSNL's vision should be to become the largest telecom service provider in South East Asia and to provide world class State-of-art telecom service and telecom infrastructure on demand at affordable prices to the country. The objective of BSNL should be to become leading Telecom Service Provider, build customer's confidence through quality and reliable service, including provision of Broadband on demand. Shri Raja was speaking at a function while inaugurating the Bharat Sanchar Bhawan here today. He said that while BSNL has been able to retain its landline base and has marginally increased from 32.40 million to 32.93 million, 28.42 million mobile connections and 10.20 lakh Broadband connections have been provided. During the financial year 2006-07 itself the mobile network has increased by over 95 lakh telephone connections and 3.90 lakh Broadband connections at a financial turnover of Rs.39,715 crore with profit of Rs.7,805 crore. All this was achieved when BSNL was competing with private operators who have deployed much younger and qualified work force. Technology is available to all operators but what makes the difference is the men behind these technologies. The aim of BSNL is to sustain as a market leader is highly at risk with a large work force in the above forty age bracket. This needs to be improved by systematic manpower planning, in both short terms, as well as long term. The current system of human resource management does not permit any preferential treatment or compensation to performers vis-a-vis non-performers. Appropriate motivational steps, linked with accountability at all levels, is the need of the hour, he said. Shri Shakeel Ahmad, Minister of State for Communication and Information Technology and Shri D.S.Mathur, Secretary, Department of Telecom also attended today's inaugural function. The new building has been constructed on a plot area of 2.27 acres and has a plinth area of 16314 sq.meters. This multistoried complex is equipped with Integrated Building Management System controls, excellent ambience, state of art conference halls, CMD's and Directors chambers and efficiently designed work spaces incorporating work station concepts.

2091. (31-7-2007) NEW DELHI : The Prime Minister, Dr. Manmohan Singh, has condoled the death of Shri Kazi Lhendup Dorjee Khang Serpa, the first Chief Minister of Sikkim. In a condolence message, the Prime Minister said : "I am deeply shocked and grieved to learn of the sad demise of Shri Kazi Lhendup Dorjee Khang Serpa, the first Chief Minister of Sikkim. He played a historic role as the architect of Sikkim's accession to the Indian Union and had the distinction of spearheading the State as its first Chief Minister from 1974 to 1979. The pride of place occupied by Sikkim as an important State of our country and its impressive progress in many spheres owe a lot to numerous policies initiated by him. In his unfortunate passing away the country in general and the State of Sikkim in particular has lost a veteran public figure whose many sided contributions to nation building endeared him to the people."

2092. (31-7-2007) NEW DELHI : The Minister for Rural Development, Dr. Raghuvansh Prasad Singh, has called upon the NGOs in creating mass awareness in rural areas for better implementation of Rural Development schemes across the country. Inaugurating the NGOs meet organized by CAPART (Council for Advancement of People's Action and Rural Technology) on Gramin Vikas Andolan and Nirmal Gram Abhiyan here today, Dr. Singh said there is lack of awareness among the masses in respect of various employment generation and infrastructure development schemes and this hinders effective implementation of development schemes. It is only the awareness and proper understanding of schemes, people's participation and observance of transparency at the ground level that can change the present scenario in rural areas, he added. He hoped that the NGOs working under CAPART-run campaigns, Gramin Vikas Andolan and Nirmal Gram Abhiyan, would play a key role in the successful implementation of programmes on sanitation and water conservation and its management so as to improve the delivery mechanism and bring in more transparency and awareness in rural areas. Ms. Santha Sheila

Nair, Secretary, Department of Drinking Water Supply in the M/o Rural Development, emphasized the need of maintaining water sustainability and tackling the issue of slipped back habitations. She said her department is promoting the use of low cost technologies in rural areas for better results. Earlier, the Director General, CAPART, Ms. V. Rao, welcomed the participants and said that CAPART is to act as facilitator of implementation of rural development schemes at the Panchayat level through its network of NGOs. The one-day NGOs meet on Gramin Vikas Andolan and Nirmal Gram Abhiyan is being attended by 165 NGOs from all over the country. Gramin Vikas Andolan is a campaign to create awareness in the rural areas about water conservation, sanitation and other programmes of the M/o Rural Development. It is under progress in 141 blocks across all States of the country. Nirmal Gram Abhiyan is a programme to sensitize the rural masses about the objectives of Total Sanitation Campaign. The programme is under implementation in 139 blocks of eight States viz, Chhattisgarh, Himachal Pradesh, Punjab, Arunachal Pradesh, Meghalaya, Nagaland, Rajasthan and Bihar. CAPART is funding, monitoring and implementing the campaign with cooperation from M/o Rural Development, NGOs and other stake holders.

2093. (31-7-2007) NEW DELHI : The annual precipitation including snowfall, which is the main source of water in the country, is estimated to be of the order of 4000 Billion Cubic Meters (BCM). The estimated precipitation during the monsoon season (June to September) is of the order of 3000 BCM. The average availability of water in the country is assessed at 1869 BCM, Out of which, the utilizable water resources are 1123 BCM (690 BCM of Surface water and 433 BCM of Replenishable ground water). A total storage capacity of 212.78 Billion Cum (BCM) has been created in the country through major and medium projects. The projects under construction will contribute to an additional 76.26 BCM, while the contribution expected from projects under consideration is 107.54 BCM. Central Water Commission is monitoring the storage position of 76 important reservoirs spread all over the country. The Total Storage capacity at Full Reservoir Level (FRL) in these reservoirs is 133.021 BCM. The total availability of water in the 76 major reservoirs was 109.77 BCM at the end of the monsoon of 2005 against 85.12 BCM at the end of the monsoon last year.

2094. (31-7-2007) NEW DELHI : Shri Subodh Kant Sahai Union Minister for food Processing has called upon for food Technology Revolution in the country. He was addressing an interactive meeting on 'Unleashing the potential of food Prossing Industry in West Bengal' Organized by Bengal National Chamber of Commerce & Industry in Kolkata yesterday evening. Outlining the vast possibility of the sector the Minister informed that a new bill 'food Authority of India' is coming in September-October 2007. The Minister pointed out that the food processing sector is a totally tax free and Subsidized sector. The need of the hour for this sector is investment and more investment. Sixty percent of the total population of India is dependent on Agriculture. However agriculture is not an attractive field for investment. The Minister stressed on the need of cluster wise demand wise, organized and Cooperative farming, Shri Sahai informed that 30 New Mega food park is to be built soon. The parks will have cold storage facilities, logistics and distribution centres. They will be linked to the markets to get better value for farmers. The Union Cabinet has already cleared this proposal and the food-processing Ministry will give Rs. 50 crore as grant for this. Shri Sahai stressed the need of demand driven farming which gives farmers the power to bargain. Union Minister of state for food processing informed that in India there are 15 climatic zones. Sixty percent of the world population is Indian. In the backdrop of globalization, retail marketing of processed food and food products coming and generating demands. Mr. Sahai pointed out all the big industrial houses are now coming to invest in this sector. The Minister praised the initiatives taken by the state government in the sector by creating a separate ministry on this. The meeting was also attend by Shri Sudhansu Gil M.P. and Shri Ravi; Inder Singh JT Secretary, food processing Ministry government of West Bengal.

2095. (31-7-2007) NEW DELHI : The Ministry of Overseas Indian Affairs (MOIA) and the International Organization for Migration (IOM) signed a Memorandum of Understanding (MOU) for the project "Regional Dialogue and Facilitating Managed and Legal Migration between Asia and the European Union". The MOU was signed by Shri Nirmal Singh, Secretary of MOIA and Shri Brunson McKinley, Director General of IOM in the presence of Shri Vayalar Ravi, the Minister for Overseas Indian Affairs in New Delhi today The Project is aimed at facilitating development of legal migration, enhancing regional cooperation on legal migration management, reducing irregular migration, enhancing placement capacity amongst recruiting agencies and dissemination of information relating to employment opportunities and procedures to intending emigrants. Specific activities would be undertaken under the project to enhance the capacity of MOIA to assess and respond to the manpower needs in the EU, to enhance cooperation between India and the EU countries in the field of migration management and to educate potential migrants about the opportunities in the EU, the migration procedures at both ends and the risks involved in deviating from these procedures. The EU Member States covered under the project are Germany, United Kingdom, Ireland, Spain and Italy. MOIA and IOM will jointly establish the PIU at New Delhi for the duration of the Project. The PIU will be staffed by a National Program Coordinator and a Program Assistant who will be selected by MOIA and seconded by IOM for working on the PIU. IOM shall bear the costs for establishing the PIU, including the salary of the National Program Coordinator and Program Assistant, costs for vehicle rents, office equipment and supplies and communications apart from specific activities to be implemented under the project. The MOIA will set up a Market Research Unit (MRU) to support the project activities. The objectives of the Asia-EU project are in harmony with the goals of MOIA in the matter of management of the migration of Indian workers for overseas employment and the project will result in capacity augmentation in India for reaping the demographic dividends of emerging employment opportunities in the EU countries. At present most skilled and semi-skilled workers from India migrate to the Gulf countries. This project will facilitate diversification of the migration process to a region where the future is likely to throw up major opportunities in the years to come. It will also help MOIA in developing key competencies for designing and administering planned overseas employment programmes to respond to the international labour market needs, which will immensely benefit Indian workers. The MOU with the IOM is a part of the ongoing efforts of MOIA for streamlining migration management and ensuring the protection of emigrants. The Ministry has initiated the process of comprehensively amending the Emigration Act, 1983. It has signed bilateral MOUs with the United Arab Emirates and Kuwait, has finalized an MOU with Malaysia and an additional protocol with Qatar and is pursuing similar MOUs with the other major labour receiving countries. The Ministry has taken several steps to liberalize the emigration system and make it emigrant-friendly. Now emigration check is not required if the worker's educational qualification is Class-X or above. Emigration check requirement has been dispensed with in respect of 174 countries recently. Further, the emigration process is being computerized throughout the country. Established in 1951, IOM is the leading inter-governmental organization in the field of migration and works closely with governmental, intergovernmental and non-governmental partners. With 120 member states, a further 19 states holding observer status and offices in over 100 countries, IOM is dedicated to promoting humane and orderly migration for the benefit of all. It does so by providing services and advice to governments and migrants. IOM works to help ensure the orderly and humane management of migration, to promote international cooperation on migration issues, to assist in the search for practical solutions to migration problems and to provide humanitarian assistance to migrants in need, including refugees and internally displaced people. IOM activities include the promotion of international migration law, policy debate and guidance, protection of migrants' rights, migration health and the gender dimension of migration. At present India is having "observer" status in the IOM.

2096. (31-7-2007) NEW DELHI : Government has appointed Shri Mahesh B. Lal as the Technical Member (P&NG) in the Appellate Tribunal for Electricity. He was administered the oath of office and secrecy by Shri Sushilkumar Shinde, Union Minister for Power. A product of IIT Kanpur and IIM Ahmedabad, Shri Lal has served as the CMD, Hindustan Petroleum Corporation Ltd. from June 2002 to March 2007. He was Director (Refineries) Bharat Petroleum Corporation Ltd. (May 1996 to June 2002), and Director (Operations), Madras Refineries Ltd. (March 1994 to May 1996) and OSD/Advisor (Refineries) in the Ministry of Petroleum & Natural Gas (June 1991 to March 1994). He was also Chairman, Scientific Advisory Committee on Hydrocarbons, Ministry of Petroluem & Natural Gas and Member, Board of Governors, Indian Institute of Management, Ahmedabad.

He has been awarded with life achievement award for contribution to refining sector from CHEMTECH Foundation and also conferred with honorary fellowship by Energy Institute, London, UK.

2097. (31-7-2007) NEW DELHI : The Government has prepared an Integrated Child Protection Scheme (ICPS), which will essentially create a strong backbone at State and districts levels to prevent and respond to any form of child protection failures. Under the scheme, all States and districts will have Child Protection Units with the budget of over Rs 2000 crores. This was disclosed by Smt.Renuka Chowdhury, Minister of women and Child Development while releasing Policy Framework for Children and AIDS' in India being brought out the Ministry of Health & Family Welfare, Ministry of Women and Child Development and NACO jointly here today. Highlighting the initiative, Smt. Renuka Chowdhury said to begin with ICPS is being implemented in five States-UP, MP, Meghalaya, Mizoram and Andhra Pradesh with a budget of Rs.90 crore. The Child Protection concept under the proposed scheme encompasses prevention, protection and rehabilitation aspects with a wide range of services like outreach services, short stay homes, counselling and legal aid, sponsorships, foster care programme, adoption services and childcare homes to be implemented at the State and District level. Smt. Renuka Chaowdhury said that the new scheme would improve existing child protection services and redressal mechanism, care system for children by implementing minimum standards of care in all forms. The structure proposed for the ICPS scheme would include a team of 25 persons in the State Unit and 10 Officers in the districts level unit. These Units shall be provided support through various other programmes like Child Line Scheme that will help in reporting and tracking the progress of each child in the concern district. She also disclosed that Ministry of Women and Child Development has set up working groups on the schemes related with health, education and welfare of the children with the representatives of concern ministries and experts from the outside. The Minister expressed the hope that new Child Protection structure would adequately support children and families for better health, education and protection of rights of children.

2098. (31-7-2007) NEW DELHI : The Tourism and Culture Minister Smt. Ambika Soni and the Chairman of National Knowledge Commission Shri Sam Pitroda discussed the recommendations of the National Knowledge Commission on Libraries when the latter called on the office of the Minister here recently. The Secretary, Culture Shri Badal K. Das was also present. During the meeting, the critical role of libraries in creating a knowledge society was underlined and it was felt that libraries in India need to make a paradigm shift from their present strategy of collection or acquisition of knowledge to a strategy of knowledge access. Shri Pitroda requested Minister to implement the recommendations of the Knowledge Commission specially regarding setting up of a Mission on Libraries and a National Library Commission. It was conveyed that the Government has already started the work on setting up of a Library Mission on priority basis later this year.

Smt. Ambika Soni said a draft project report on Library Mission has been prepared which will be finalized soon. A token provision has been made in Ministry's annual plan for the year 2007-08 for setting up of a Library Mission. On the proposal of setting up of a National Commission on Libraries, Smt. Ambika Soni said that the recommendation will be duly considered. The Minister said that so far as Libraries are concerned, her Ministry's stress is on better access, ambience and modernization of libraries. She said the Ministry has constituted a high powered committee for the upgradation and modernization of libraries. Smt. Ambika Soni said that a task force has been set-up by the Ministry of Culture to prepare a national census of all libraries. Raja Ram Mohan Rai Library Foundation, Kolkata is the nodal agency for the purpose.

2099. (31-7-2007) NEW DELHI : The Central Board of Direct Taxes has extended the last date of filing of income tax returns in the State of Bihar in view of the disruption caused by floods in the State. The due date of filing return of income is 31st July but tax payers in Bihar can file it by 16th August, 2007.

2100. (31-7-2007) NEW DELHI : Department of Posts and Indian Railways have signed an MOU here today to provide the facility to issue computerized rail tickets under the Passenger Reservation System of Railways, through the Post Offices. This cooperation between both the organizations is a win-win proposition for the people of India, as reserved railway tickets will now be available even in far flung and inaccessible tribal areas of the North-East through your friendly Post Office. This facility will initially be available in about 30 identified Post Offices throughout the country. This will be later extended to other Post Offices, where the Railways do not have a presence. The Post Offices will also be extending e-ticketing facilities to the public. With its huge network of more than 1,55,000, the Post Offices are best suited to provide this service to the people of India.This will go a long way in fulfilling the Department of Posts' commitment to provide customer friendly products to the public. The MOU was signed in the presence of the Minister of Railways, Shri Lalu Prasad Yadav, Minister of Communication and IT, Shri A.Raja, Minister of State for Communication and IT, Dr.Shakeel Ahmad, Minister of State for Railways, Shri Naranbhai J.Rathwa. The MOU was signed by Shri S.Samanth, Chief General Manager (Business Development) on behalf of the Department of Posts.

2101. (31-7-2007) NEW DELHI : Shri A.Raja, Minister of Communication and Information Technology has said that about one lakh Broadband enabled service centres will come up in the country by March 2008 at a total cost of Rs. 5400 crore. One centre will come up for every six villages with all e-governance services. Rs 1600 crore will be put up by central government and the rest by the private sector under the Public Private Partnership (PPP). The Minister was speaking at the e-India 2007 Conference which he inaugurated here today. The Minister said that for implementation of e-governance, government on its part is trying to provide basic infrastructure including internet, window Facilitation centre and last leg connectivity for implementation of e-governance, but participation of private sector and citizens is a key factor for providing totally transparent services to the public. The application of IT to government processes, e-governance in short, can have a profound impact-on the efficiency, responsiveness and accountability of government, thereby, on the quality of life and productivity of citizens, especially the poor, and ultimately, on the economic output and growth of the country as a whole, the Minister added. Shri Raja said that the Ministry of Communication and Information Technology has wide ranging activities from spreading of IT to masses to ensuring speedy IT led development. With Information and Communication (ICT) at its core, Department of Information Technology (DIT) has initiated the National e-Governance Plan (NeGP). It is an ambitious programme aimed at improving the quality, accessibility and effectiveness of government services to citizens and businesses with the help of information technology. It has enabled convenient and transparent access to the government and private services while providing equitable opportunities to all. It is also been used as an effective tool to drive administrative reforms within the government, and can change the perception of people about the government. In addition, it has created a national IT backbone for fast, reliable and efficient connectivity, data storage and access. The Indian economy is growing at a steady rate of 8-9 per cent. For this growth to be sustainable there is a need to increase efficacy of business processes especially those directly controlled by the government. NeGP in its current form consists of Mission Mode Projects (MMPs) and Functional components to be executed over a four-year period. Many states have started preparing Detailed Project Reports for implementation of these Mission Mode Projects. Many Ministries have initiated the process for designing Mission Mode Projects and are in the implementation phase currently. For implementing these MMPs, NeGP envisages putting in place a core infrastructure comprising State Wide Area Network (SWAN), Common Service Centres (CSCs) and State Data Centres (SDCs) which shall be used across MMPs for delivering desired services, he added. Shri Jainder Singh, Secretary, Department of Information Technology also spoke on the occasion. Shri M.P.Narayanan, President CDMS welcomed the gathering. The four day International Conference is organized by the Centre for Science, Development and Media Studies. Representatives of various Government Departments, UNDP etc. are participating in the Conference.

2102. (31-7-2007) NEW DELHI : The Ministry of Micro, Small & Medium Enterprises has formulated a new scheme to provide financial support to five select universities/colleges in every State to set up and run 1200 entrepreneurs clubs beginning 2006-07. Financial support will be provided to 50 select universities and training institutions for setting up of 100 enterprise incubators to host 1000 micro and small enterprises over 5 years beginning 2006-07. This scheme, to be worked out in detail, envisages selection of 50 universities and training institutions over 6 years throughout the country and providing them financial support as grant-in-aid to set up 100 business incubators to host about 1000 micro and small enterprises. Though, the extent of grant may vary based on the nature of the enterprises to be incubated, an average of Rs.5.00 lakh per enterprise seems reasonable. This will help in promoting new enterprises, specially in the fields of biotechnology, pharmaceuticals and similar new and innovative fields. An amount of Rs.1.13 crore has been earmarked in the BE of 2007-08, out of which Rs.0.23 crore has been set aside for SCs and STs.

2103. (31-7-2007) NEW DELHI : To add another landmark milestone in the achievements of Indian Railways, Indian Railways have taken another historic step to expand the reach of reserved tickets nearer to the doorsteps of passengers even in remote areas by allowing selling of reserved tickets through Post Offices. A Memorandum of Understating (MOU) in this regard was signed by Shri A.K. Goyal, Additional Member (Commercial), Railway Board and Shri S. Samant, Chief General Manager, Department of Posts (hereinafter referred to as "India Post") in the presence of the Minister of Railways Shri Lalu Prasad and the Minister of Communication & Information Technology Shri A.Raja here today. Also present on the occasion were Ministers of State for Railways Shri Naranbhai J. Rathwa & Shri R.Velu, Minister of State for Communications & IT, Dr. Shakeel Ahmad, Chairman Railway Board Shri J.P.Batra, Secretary, Department of Posts, Shri I.M.G.Khan, Railways Board Members and other senior officials from Department of Posts. Speaking on the occasion, the Minister of Railways Shri Lalu Prasad said that this is the joint endeavour of the Ministry of Railways and the Ministry of Communications and IT for the benefit of people especially those who are staying in remote areas to enable them to get reserved tickets from the nearby Post Offices. He also sought the cooperation of the Minister of Communication and IT for providing the facility of issuing unreserved tickets also at the post office so that Railway passengers from villages need not have to travel long distances and to stand in a long queue for obtaining the tickets. The Minister also said that in future the facility of issuing e-tickets will also be provided at mutually agreed locations where e-tickets will be issued from the Post Offices of India Post. Shri Lalu Prasad informed that the reserved tickets in the first phase will be available at 30 post offices. These are Phulbani (Orissa), Deoghar (Jharkhand), Auraiya (Uttar Pradesh), Anjaw (Arunachal Pradesh), Bishnupur (Manipur), Champhai (Mizoram), Mangaldoi (Assam), Jowai (Meghalaya), Senapati (Manipur), Udaipur (Tripura) Yingkiong, Daporijo, Bomdila & Along (Arunachal Pradesh), Doda (Jammu & Kashmir), Panchkula (Haryana), Poonch (J&K) Sundergarh (Orissa), Madras High Court (Tamil Nadu), Ahwa (Gujarat), Noida Sector 56 PO (Uttar Pradesh), Udyog Vihar PO, Gurgaon (Haryana), Dahisar, Mumbai (Maharashtra), Sriperambadur (Tamil Nadu), Pushkar (Rajasthan), DLF Gurgaon (Haryana), Dwarka Sector-6 (Delhi), Greater Noida Alpha (Uttar Pradesh), Indirapuram/ Shipra Sun city, Noida (Uttar Pradesh), Kavinagar, Ghaziabad (Uttar Pradesh). India Post will issue reserved railway tickets through the computerized Passenger

Reservation System (PRS) counters provided by Indian Railway at such Post Offices as are mutually agreed to by the Ministry of Railways and the India Post. These locations operated by India Post will be able to book all types of tickets including concession and Military vouchers like any other regular railway PRS centres etc. India Post will realize some service charges from the passengers in lieu of issue of tickets. These are Rs. 15/- for II class sleeper & II class sitting (2S), Rs. 20/- for III AC & AC Chair Car, Rs. 30/- for II AC, I AC & First Class and Rs. 10/- for cancellation charges (for all classes). Charges are inclusive of service tax. The PRS to be operated by India Post will be named as "India Post PRS Centre" and India Post would reserve railway ticket through the computerized PRS of Railways at such locations as are mutually agreed to by Ministry of Railways and the India Post. The Ministry of Railways will provide hardware, communication equipment and communication channels for which initial as well as recurring cost will be borne by the Ministry of Railways. The accommodation, lighting, other infrastructure arrangements and the staff for issuing the tickets will be provided by the India Post. The training of the staff of the India Post will be arranged by the Ministry of Railways at mutually agreed locations. The cost of training (excluding travelling, daily allowances etc. to be paid to the staff by India Post) will be borne by the Ministry of railways. The agreement will be valid for a period of five years and its progress will be reviewed annually. It will be renewed after expiry of the existing agreement on mutually agreed terms and conditions.

2104. (31-7-2007) NEW DELHI : The Fertiliser Advisory Forum meets in New Delhi tomorrow to discuss some of the key issues plaguing the sector. Representatives from state governments, Fertiliser Industry, Farmers and central governments departments will be attending the day long deliberations. On top of the agenda will be availability and distribution of fertilizer. Issues like fertilizer pricing, Nutrient Subsidy, alternative methodologies for delivery of fertilizer subsidy to farmers and usage of water-soluble fertilizers will be discussed. The Department of Fertilisers has taken a number of steps to ensure timely and adequate availability throughout the country after the first meeting of the Forum in March 2006. They include adoption of the New Pricing Scheme Stage-III for Urea, monitoring of fertiliser availability up to the district level, creation of a buffer stock up to 5 per cent of the seasonal demand in major fertilizer consuming states and payment of rail freight as per actual expenditure for transportation of urea. Rationalisation of road freight has also been carried out. The freight is being revised to account for increase in rail and road transport costs for Phosphatic and Potassic fertilisers. State governments have been advised to strengthen the State Institutional Agencies to coordinate with manufacturers and importers for streamlining fertiliser supplies. The Minister for Steel, Chemicals and Fertilisers Shri Ram Vilas Paswan will preside over the meeting while the Minister of State for Chemicals and Fertilisers Shri B.K.Handique will address the meeting.

2105. (31-7-2007) NEW DELHI : At the time of Independence, India was a stagnant economy, predominantly agrarian with little industrial development. The extremely narrow base of industrialization remained confined to a very few cities and produced mainly consumer goods like textiles and sugar. Intermediates like steel, cement, etc. were mostly imported. The artisan sector was left to languish and decay and was ill equipped to modernize. In the post-Independence period, the objectivse of India's development strategy has been to establish a socialistic pattern of society through economic growth with self-reliance, social justice and alleviation of poverty. These objectives were to be achieved within a democratic framework using the mechanism of a mixed economy where both public and private sectors co-exist. Accordingly, the industrial policy laid emphasis on achieving a high growth rate, national self-reliance, building up of indigenous capacity, encouraging village and small scale industry, a dream of our Rashtra Pita, Mahatma Gandhi, bringing about balanced regional development, prevention of concentration of economic power and reduction of income inequalities. The thrust on industrialization in India has helped in increasing substantially the share of industry in the Gross Domestic Product (GDP) from 15 per cent at the time of Independence to 29 per cent in recent years. Further, the growth rate of manufacturing sector which was around 6 per cent in the first two decade after Independence has increased to over 10 per cent in recent years. The composition of industry since Independence has also witnessed significant transformation, with share of consumer goods declining from 50 per cent to 20 per cent while the share of capital goods and basic good industries increasing from 4 per cent and 20 per cent to 24 per cent and 40 per cent respectively.

2106. (1-8-2007) NEW DELHI : A delegation led by Mr. Rosalio Rodriguez, Corporate Director of Bimbo Group of Mexico met Dr. Chandrapal, Secretary and other officers of the Ministry of Micro, Small and Medium Enterprises (MSME) here today. Bimbo group is a prominent baking company at global level manufacturing products like bread, pastries, cookies, cakes, chocolates etc. The delegation expressed keen interest in making investments in the bakery sector in India and discussed the collaboration possibilities with micro, small and medium enterprises engaged in bakery, bread making etc. in India. The Ministry of MSME had earlier signed Memorandum of Understanding on cooperation in the field of micro, small and medium enterprises with Secretariat of Economy of Mexico on 27.3.2006. Food processing sector has been identified as an area of priority attention for promoting trade and cooperation between the two countries under the MoU. The delegation would also be visiting Mumbai on 2nd and 3rd August, 2007 to see bakery units and study the retail and distribution channels of various bakery products.

2107. (1-8-2007) NEW DELHI : To a question on Shri Priyaranjan Das Munshi's comments on Sanjay Dutt's verdict, Shri Singhvi said that Mr. Munshi was expressing his personal opinion and there is absolutely nothing wrong in saying so. The Congress believes that ultimately it is the appellate process which has just begun and neither any political party not anyone else can jump that appellate process. It is for the person concerned to invoke it and use it and there is no doubt that he will also use the bail processes inherit in that appellate process. To a question as to how much chances are there for him, Shri Singhvi said that it would not be fair and right to express from a podium like this on a directly subjudice matter when a convict is appealing. If I were to express it would be infact a quite wrong and quite speculative and these are matters decided on the basis of hard-core, documentary, written evidence in a huge paper book which neither I have exercised nor you have seen. To a question on his bail prospects, Shri Singhvi said that I absolutely disagree with you that the Congress party has to have any stand in an individual matter of an individual conviction. To a question that his father and his sister is with the Congress Party, Shri Singhvi said that your expectations are wrong because you are connecting two unconnectables. The fact that his father and his sister are respected members of the party has no relation to an individual offence and decided on merits by a judge in which Mr. Dutt is exercising his appellate process. Neither does he need our comment nor is there any occasion for a political party to comment. To a question whether what happened in Goa was right? Shri Singhvi said that we absolutely believe that things have happened according to constitution but the answer to your question whether we believe it is right or wrong is decided ultimately by a court of law and not by us. Secondly, why we believe this is, for anybody who knows the sequence of events, you are aware that how the regional plan was created. You are aware how when the regional plan was distorted, protests came here in Delhi, action was taken to suspend what many believe was virtually a bartering away of the largest part of the state of Goa. It is clear that inspired by economics and commerce and not by ideology, people tried to create uncertainty and instability to protect land vested interests. Let me add, that there are two clear events in which the disqualification were based. One, that non-attendance, despite a whip, by one MLA. Anybody who knows the 10th Schedule knows that the defiance of a whip can lead to expulsion or defection or the stigma of 10th schedule. Secondly, the other incident relates to two other MLAs. In that case the written resolution minuted in the minute book shows that they have to support the party, the ruling party is the Congress party and the other is a coalition. Contrary to that without any change in those minutes, which is still continuing even today. The two members sought again to defy what was directive from the party which is equivalent to a binding direction and again vote contrary. Again, I think that is a matter under clause 4 of the 10th Schedule, which will be decided shortly. The third point is, does the Speaker have the power of granting interim order and the answer is clearly 'yes' in law.

2108. (1-8-2007) NEW DELHI : The 8th Bilateral Talks between the Home Secretaries of India and Bangladesh will be held here on 2-3 August, 2007. This is part of the bilateral institutional mechanism set up in 1994 to resolve security and border management issues. The Bangladesh delegation would be headed by

Mohd. Abdul Karim, Home Secretary, Government of Bangladesh and would include Director General, Bangladesh Rifles. The Indian side would be headed by the Union Home Secretary, Shri Madhukar Gupta and would include Director General, Border Security Force. The delegation is also likely to visit the National Police Academy at Hyderabad before it returns to Dhaka. The issues likely to be discussed include peaceful management of border, security-related issues, cross-border movements and enhanced police cooperation.

2109. (1-8-2007) NEW DELHI : The Ministry of Rural Development has sanctioned Rs. 61.90 crore to the Government of Rajasthan towards balance of first instalment of ARWSP-DDP funds against the provisional allocation of Rs.185.70 crore made under the Centrally sponsored Accelerated Rural Water Supply Programme-Drought Development Programme Areas of Rajiv Gandhi National Drinking Water Mission, during the year 2007-08. States have been requested to delegate powers for management of Rural Water Supply Schemes through the Panchayati Raj Institutions (PRIs) as per the Constitution of India. As such Operation and Maintenance of the completed RWS Scheme should be transferred to the PRIs. No expenditure shall be incurred on taking water quality problems form the present release, as there is a separate allocation for the purpose. This release is being made for execution/completion of schemes to provide safe drinking water facilities to rural habitations and schools under the Centrally Sponsored ARWSP-DDP Areas guidelines.

2110. (1-8-2007) NEW DELHI : The Ministry of Rural Development has sanctioned Rs. 6.00 lakh to the State Government of Mizoram as first instalment of funds for setting up of 3 District Water Testing Laboratories at Serchhip, Saiha and Kolasib districts in the State at the total approved cost of Rs.12.00 lakh @ Rs.4.00 lakh under the Centrally sponsored Accelerated Rural Water Supply Programme (Normal) of Rajiv Gandhi National Drinking Water Mission, during the year 2007-08. The release is subject to the terms and condition mentioned in the Technical Sanctions issued to State government from time to time. It is under Plan expenditure and should be used for the purpose specified. Diversion of funds is not allowed. The monthly/ quarterly reports are also required to be submitted along with the utilization certificate/ Audited expenditure to the Mission. States are delegated powers for management of Rural Water Supply Schemes through the Panchayati Raj Institutions (PRIs).

2111. (1-8-2007) NEW DELHI : The 2nd meeting of the Fertiliser Advisory Forum was held here today. The conference was attended by State Agriculture Ministers, Members of the Consultative Committee attached to the Ministry of Chemicals and Fertilisers, representatives of farmers and dealers from each State, CEOs of leading fertilizer companies and senior officials from various Departments/ Agencies of the Government of India as well as State Governments.

2112. (1-8-2007) NEW DELHI : Shri Brahm Dutt, a 1973-batch IAS officer of the Karnataka cadre, took over the charge as new Secretary, Road Transport and Highways in the Ministry of Shipping, Road Transport and Highways here today. Shri Brahm Dutt who till recently held the charge of the Chairman, National Authority, Chemicals Weapons Convention in the Cabinet Secretariat, took over from Shri Vijay Singh who has joined as Defence Secretary. Shri Dutt has vast experience in the Centre as he was Joint Secretary in the Ministry of Industry from 1994 to 1999 and later Special Secretary / Additional Secretary, in the Department of Personnel & Training, Government of India, from September 2005 to January 2007. He has also served as Commercial Counsellor and Financial Advisor at Embassy of India in Washington and also as CMD of Mysore Paper Mills, a public sector undertaking under the Government of Karnataka.

2113. (1-8-2007) NEW DELHI : 30 teams have been deployed for culling operations in 0-5 kms zone in the bird flu affected area of Manipur. As on 31st July 2007, 2.35 lakh birds have been culled including 50,000 birds culled on 31st July. So far, 22,938 eggs have been destroyed (including 934 eggs destroyed on 31st July) and 18,900 kg feed destroyed (including 5,180 kg destroyed on 31st July). Surveillance continued in 5-10 Kms zone. In addition, door to-door intensive surveillance in a radius of 5-10 Kms was in progress. There are 79 villages (41 in East Imphal and 38 in West Imphal) in the 5-10 Kms zone. Seven teams of veterinarians and other support staff were deployed for the surveillance work. There is no report of any abnormal mortality or sickness in Manipur or the country. Cleaning and dis-infection is also under progress in the 0-5 Kms zone. Upto 31st July Rs. 60 lakh have been paid as compensation, out of which Rs. 29.26 lakh in East Imphal district and Rs. 30.79 lakh in the West Imphal district. There is a good response from the public and NGOs since 29.7.2007 and the containment and control operations of avian influenza were accelerated due to this support. There are no reports of inter-district smuggling of poultry birds. The Rapid Response Teams and the district police of adjoining districts are tasked to control the same.

2114. (1-8-2007) NEW DELHI : Positive initiatives of the Government deserve due coverage and the media has a duty to carry these up to the people, says Minister of Information & Broadcasting and Parliamentary Affairs, Shri P. R. Dasmunsi. In his address after launching the booklet 'Taking the UPA Report Card to the Masses' Shri Dasmunsi said that media had every right to attack the Government whenever it feels that Government policies/programmes have any shortcomings at any level, but due credit needs to be given for good efforts of the Government. The effort of Lokmat group of newspapers in bringing out this book reflects a positive approach, he added. The Minister said that delivery system at the micro level is very important and the UPA Government is making concerted efforts in this direction. Shri Dasmunsi said that he plans to involve various other organisations around the country to carry out the UPA Report Card to the masses and assess the impact of the UPA Government's initiatives on the life of public at large. The Minister highlighted the positive developments in the economy over the last year in the areas of GDP, foodgrains, industrial growth, infrastructure development, forex reserves and lower fiscal deficit. Shri Suresh Pachauri, Minister of State for Parliamentary Affairs, in his remarks said that the responsibility undertaken by the Lokmat group is praise-worthy. They have come out with the impact of UPA policies at the grassroot level in Maharashtra. Compilation of information from the ground level reflects the sincere and laudable effort by the reporters of the Lokmat group.

2115. (1-8-2007) NEW DELHI : Under the Scheme of 'National Project for Repair, Renovation and Restoration of Water Bodies', the Ministry of Water Resources has approved 26 district projects of 15 States, namely Andhra Pradesh, Chattisgarh, Bihar, Jharkhand, Karnataka, Madhya Pradesh, Orissa, Rajasthan, Tamil Nadu, West Bengal, Himachal Pradesh, Jammu and Kashmir, Gujarat, Kerala and Maharashtra at a cost of Rs.299.9155 crores. Physical work in respect of 694 water bodies in 10 States have been confirmed to be completed by the State Governments by the end of May 2007.

2116. (1-8-2007) NEW DELHI : Shri Ajay Shankar (IAS: UP:1973) has taken over as the new Secretary for the Department of Industrial Policy & Promotion, under the Ministry of Commerce and Industry. Prior to his joining here, Shri Shankar has served in the Planning Commission and Ministry of Power, Government of India.

2117. (1-8-2007) NEW DELHI : India's exports during June, 2007 were valued at US $ 11867.11 million which was 14.05 % higher than the level of US $ 10405.07 million during June, 2006. In rupee terms, exports touched Rs.48386.49 crore, which was 0.97% higher than the value of exports during June, 2006. Cumulative value of exports for the period April-June, 2007 was US $ 34303.50 million (Rs.141330.65 Crore) as against US $ 29044.58 million (Rs.132164.90 Crore) during the same period last year. India's imports during June, 2007 were valued at US $ 19195.69 million representing an increase of 36.68 % over the level of imports valued at US $ 14044.43 million in June, 2006. In Rupee terms, imports increased by 21.00 %. Cumulative value of imports for the period April-June, 2007 was US$ 54908.83 million (Rs.226321.35 Crore) as against US$ 40885.73 million (Rs.185987.92 Crore) during the same period last year Oil imports during June, 2007 were valued at US $ 5664.99 million which was 9.85% higher than oil imports valued at US $ 5157.19 million in the corresponding period last year. Oil imports during April-June, 2007 were valued at US$ 14830.19 million which was 4.21% higher than the oil imports of US$ 14230.81 million in the corresponding period last year. Non-oil imports during June, 2007 were estimated at US $ 13530.70 million which was 52.25 % higher than growth on non oil imports of US$ 8887.25 million in June, 2006. Non-oil imports during April-June, 2007 were valued at US$ 40078.64 million which was 50.36% higher than the level of such imports valued at US$ 26654.92 million in April-June, 2006. The trade deficit for April-June, 2007 was estimated at US $ 20605.33 million which was higher than the deficit at US $ 11841.15 million during April-June, 2006.

2118. (1-8-2007) NEW DELHI : The Food Corporation of India, FCI, has been declared a public utility service under the Industrial Disputes Act, 1947 for six months with effect from July 31,2007. According to a notification issued by the Ministry of Labour and Employment in this regard, this has been done in public interest. The employees in this industry, as a result, would among other things be required to give notice to their employer six weeks in advance of proceeding on strike so that conciliatory proceedings could be started. During the conciliatory proceedings and seven days after their completion, the employees in this industry cannot go on strike.

2119. (1-8-2007) NEW DELHI : Shri Ramesh Chandra assumed the charge of the post of Chairman, Railway Board here yesterday *i.e.* 31st July 2007. He will also continue to look after the duties of Member Electrical, Railway Board. This follows the superannuation of outgoing Chairman, Railway Board, Shri J.P.Batra on 31st July 2007. An officer of 1968 batch of the Indian Railway Service of Electrical Engineers (IRSEE), Shri Chandra has been Member Electrical, Railway Board since 1st May 2005. Prior to this, he worked as General Manager, Southern Railway. During his 37 year long career, he served in various capacities including as Divisional Railway Manager, Mugalsarai, Chief Electrical Engineer, South Eastern Railway, Additional General Manager, Eastern Railway, Senior Deputy General Manager, South Central Railway and OSD, South East Central Railway. He is credited to have been associated with several important projects of Railway electrification including that between Delhi-Mathura-Agra-Jhansi-Bina-Bhopal-Itarsi-Bhusawal. He also contributed substantially while serving at RDSO, Lucknow. An Engineering graduate from Aligarh Muslim University and recipient of two Gold Medals, Shri Chandra was also awarded a Gold Medal by the Institution of Engineers, UP Centre in 1967. He was again conferred the eminent award by Institution of Engineers on the occasion of Engineers' Day on 15th September 2005. Shri Chandra has had several foreign assignments. He visited Japan, USA, Germany, UK, Switzerland and France in connection with various Training Programmes, Seminars, finalization of designs and test schedules.

2120. (2-8-2007) NEW DELHI : Government of India have announced the issue of "8.08 per cent Government Stock 2022" for an aggregate amount of Rs.2,969.411 crore (nominal), "8.26 per cent Government Stock 2027" for an aggregate amount of Rs.1,427.329 crore (nominal) and "8.32 per cent Government Stock 2032" for an aggregate amount of Rs.2,434.050 crore (nominal) to 11 nationalised banks on August 2, 2007. The Government Stocks are issued in lieu of outstanding amount of the following securities held by these nationalised banks. The Government stocks are issued at par.

2121. (2-8-2007) NEW DELHI : The Ministry of Railways has formulated various freight incentive schemes with the objective of increasing freight traffic as well as generating additional revenue for the Railways. There has been an encouraging response to the various such schemes from the customers. So far a total number of 326 proposals have been received by the Railways under these schemes out of which 244 proposals have been approved. This will generate additional earnings of Rs. 305.29 crore for the Railways during the current financial year. Under the Incentive Scheme for Traditional Empty Flow Direction, a total number of 48 proposals have been received by the Ministry of Railways, out of which 31 proposals have already been approved. This will give additional earnings of Rs. 38.58 crore during the current financial year. Under this scheme the freight discount upto 30 per cent has been permitted on traffic loaded in the notified traditional empty flow directions during both busy and lean seasons to generate additional business volume in the movement streams traditionally carrying predominantly empty wagons. The discount has been permitted even in less than block rake traffic also. Under the Long Term Special Incentive Scheme, a total number of 31 proposals have been approved out of total 78 proposals received so far. This will give additional earnings of Rs. 50.60 crore during the current financial year. Under this scheme, the Zonal Railways have been delegated the power to grant concession upto 20 per cent to the customers offering sizeable traffic. Railways will also generate additional earnings of Rs. 177.35 crore during the current year from the Incentive Scheme for Incremental Traffic. Out of a total number of 87 proposals, 72 proposals have already been approved under this scheme. The customer is eligible for discount upto 15 per cent for incremental earning in lean season under this scheme. A total number of 40 proposals have been received and approved under the Incentive Scheme for Freight Forwarders. To promote rail, road and warehousing integration and expansion of commodity basket for railways, composite freight rates have been offered to Freight Forwarders for loading in covered and BOXN wagons. This will give additional earnings of Rs. 10.82 crore during the current financial year. Under the Incentive Scheme for Two Leg, a total; number of 73 proposals, 70 proposals have already been approved. This will give additional earnings of Rs. 27.94 crore during the current financial year. Under this scheme, freight concession of 15 per cent in busy season and 20 per cent in lean season is granted to customer offering return traffic in covered wagon in Block Rakes. For aggregated cargo, Composite rate are being offered under this scheme. The Ministry of Railways has instructed all Zonal Railways to make all these scemes more popular to get more and more traffic from road to rail.

2122. (2-8-2007) NEW DELHI : The Government has approved captive mining for production of gas through coal gasification and liquefaction. The under ground coal gasification aims at extracting energy from coal seams which cannot be otherwise mined through conventional methods. The recent rise in international oil prices has led many countries to seek gainful use of such coal reserves for energy extraction. Underground coal gasification is a recognized clean coal technology while surface gasification of coal is a proven technology and both can be taken up as per requirements of the industry. Coal liquefaction aims at converting coal to liquid fuels, for which commercially proven technology is available. South Africa has been successfully producing gasoline and fuel oil from coal for quite some time. Coal reserves in India are amenable to coal gasification and liquefaction. The recognition of coal gasification and liquefaction as end uses would give a fillip to development of technologies by the public sector as well as the private sector. The notification would facilitate allocation of coal blocks for this purpose to interested parties.

2123. (2-8-2007) NEW DELHI : Shri Ashwani Kumar, Minister of State for Industry today inaugurated the Centennial celebrations of the Indian Merchants Chamber (IMC) at Johannesburg along with Dr. Mbeki, the President of South Africa. While addressing the opening session of the 2-day "India Calling" Conference organized on this eve, Shri Kumar highlighted the strong political and economic relations between the two countries and expressed optimism on the further growth of bilateral trade and investment relations. "Last year, when Prime Minister Manmohan Singh visited South Africa for the joint celebrations of the centenary of Satyagraha, he agreed with President Mbeki that our new target should be to treble the value of bilateral trade by 2010. I believe this is eminently achievable, provided our businesses exploit the tremendous potential that exists for fruitful collaboration in a number of areas such as infrastructure, IT, telecom, mining and energy, biotech & healthcare, media, sports & entertainment, all of which are the subject of individual sessions at this business conclave", he said. The trade between the two countries in 2005-6 was in the region of USD 4 billion. By the end of 2007 the two-way trade is expected to reach 6 billion dollar. The Minister also emphasized that both sides can benefit from the investment opportunities present in both countries. "We estimate that Indian companies are currently executing projects to the tune of over USD 2 billion in South Africa. These cover a broad range of sectors including automobiles, metallurgical industries, telecommunications, pharmaceuticals, processed foods, software development, minerals beneficiation, hospitality and financial services. But this is not a one-sided relationship. As the Indian economy grows annually at 8-9%, several South African companies have moved quickly to position themselves in the trillion dollar economy with a middle class of over 300 million. ACSA and Bidvest have won the contract for expansion and upgrade of Mumbai International Airport; SAB-Miller is now India's second largest brewer; Altech will soon start supplying set-top boxes in the Indian market and First Rand Bank has become the first African bank to establish a presence in India, joining financial services majors Old Mutual and Sanlam who have already been around for a while. Sasol, De Beers, BHP Biliton, Batemans and Tiger Brands are some of the other major South African companies which have set up presence in India", he said. Dr. Kumar is leading a 200 strong Indian delegation to this important event. The significance of the function is enhanced by the fact that Mahatma Gandhi was an honorary member of the Indian Merchants Chamber in 1931. That Chamber has a membership of over 5000 including a young entrepreneurs wing and ladies wing with 1600 women entrepreneurs. The Chamber represents more than 250 thousand businesses through its affiliates.

2124. (2-8-2007) NEW DELHI : Indian space programme turned a full circle when India's Polar Satellite Launch Vehicle (PSLV-C8) successfully launched AGILE, a satellite of the Italian Space Agency, in April 2007 under a commercial agreement. India has come a long way from using satellites of other nations to demonstrate the application of space technology for societal benefits in the 70's, using rockets of other space agencies to launch Indian experimental and, later, operational satellites to the present enviable status of building its own satellites and rockets to launch not only for Indian users but also of other countries. The 350 kg AGILE was precisely injected in the intended 550 km circular orbit, unequivocally demonstrating the maturity in this complex technology. Earlier, in January 2007, there was jubilation for another major landmark. The Space capsule Recovery Experiment (SRE-1) was launched by PSLV and later successfully recovered from the Bay of Bengal. This marked the beginning of a new era for the Indian space programme-that of not only providing a platform for the scientists to conduct experiments in the micro gravity environment of space and return the samples safely back to earth, but also, demonstrating India's capability in mastering critical technologies like aero-thermodynamics, recovery through deceleration and floatation system, navigation, guidance and control. All these technologies are important for re-recoverable and reusable launch vehicles as well as to undertake manned space missions.

2125. (2-8-2007) NEW DELHI : Reliance Industries plans to hire several thousands of ex-servicemen as it spreads wings in the retail sector. Having set up outlets in a number of cities, the Reliance Retail has offered jobs in plenty to the large pool of talented and qualified workforce emerging out of the forces. As its footprints expands across the country, the company has the capacity to employ all of around 60,000 uniformed men retiring every year, Colonel (Retired) S.P. Nanda, Vice-President, Reliance Industries, told a day-long seminar in New Delhi here today. A large number of jobs are also being constantly created by the group in specialized professions like drivers for cranes, bulldozers and earthmovers and heavy machinery operators. The Indian Veterans Network, a body of retired defence personnel from India and abroad, was launched on the occasion by the chief guest, former Information and Broadcasting Minister Brigadier (Retd.) K. P. Singh Deo,. An initiative of the Chandigarh-based Institute of Tourism and Future Management (ITFT-Group), the Network, to be registered as a society and consisting of retired officers of the three services, would provide a platform for reoccupation and welfare of their families. Addressing the delegates, Lt. General (Retd.) Ranjit Singh Dyal, ITFT Chairman and former Lt. Governor of Pondicherry and Andaman and Nicobar islands, said a global network conference of Indian Veterans would be held on the sidelines of the 3-day Bharatiya Pravasi Diwas celebrations in January next year. General Dyal said the conference would offer an opportunity to interact with about 8,000 ex-servicemen settled abroad, part of the 26 million Indian diaspora, and explore overseas job opportunities for retiring servicemen. Dr. Gulshan Sharma, Executive Director, ITFT, said the group runs a website Defence Welfare Call, www.defencewelfarecall.com to act as bridge between the Directorate General Resettlement (DGR) and the private industry. Major General Harwant Krishan, DGR, also spoke on the occasion.

2126. (2-8-2007) NEW DELHI : The Indian Steel Industry, is today acknowledged for its product quality. This is reflected by trends of rising exports and Indian companies mark in the global Mergers & Acquisitions market. From the fledgling one-million tonne capacity status at the time of Independence, India has now risen to be the 7th largest crude steel producer in the world and the largest producer of sponge iron. The steel industry now accounts for a capital base of Rs. 90,000 crore and contributes around 6 per cent of the Gross National Product, commanding a weight of 5.13 in the Index of Industrial Production and provides direct employment to more than 4 lakh people from being a negligible global presence. The first major change came during the first three Five Year Plans (1952-1970), when in line with the economic order of the day, the iron and steel industry was earmarked for state control. From the mid 50s to the early 70s, Government thus set up large integrated steel plants in the public sector at Bhilai, Durgapur, Rourkela and Bokaro. The large-scale capacity creation in the public sector during these years contributed to making India the 10th largest steel producer in the world as crude steel production grew markedly to nearly 15 million tonnes in the span of a decade from a mere 1 million tonnes in 1947. But the trend could not be sustained as from the late 70's onwards, economic slowdown adversely affected the pace of growth of the Indian steel industry. However, this phase was reversed, when in 1991-92, the country replaced economic controls by liberalization and deregulation in the context of globalization. The system therefore, underwent marked changes. For steel makers, opening up of the economy opened up new channels of procuring their inputs at competitive rates from overseas markets as also new markets for their products. It also led to greater access to information on global operations/techniques in manufacturing. This along with the pressures of a competitive global market increased the need to enhance efficiency levels so as to become internationally competitive. The steel consumer, was now able to choose items from an array of goods, be it indigenously manufactured or imported and this freedom to choose established the sovereignty of the consumer and made steel producers geared to provide a service level in tune with the needs of the consumers. With the opening up of economy in 1992, the country thus experienced rapid growth in steel making capacity.

2127. (2-8-2007) NEW DELHI : The Union Minister of State for Heavy Industries and Public Enterprises Smt. Kanti Singh has urged the Bihar Government to undertake the rescue and relief work on a war-footing in the flood ravaged districts of Bihar. In a letter addressed to the District Magistrate of Patna, she said Jamui Dharna Dam at Paliganj Block has been severely damaged due to heavy rains. As a result, several villages including Fatehpur, Nonia Chak, Gopipur, Gulal Chak, Sultanpur and Jamui have been partially submerged. The water passing through six channels of the dam has caused extensive damage to the standing crops. The people of this Naxalite-infested area are facing immense hardship. The Minister has also expressed her concern for the absence of the approach roads to various newly constructed culverts, which multiplied the plight of the people. The recent floods have disrupted traffic at many points on these roads, she added.

2128. (2-8-2007) NEW DELHI : The National Wage Boards for Working Journalists and Other Non-Journalist Employees of Newspapers headed by Dr. Justice K. Narayana Kurup met the representatives of Working Journalists, Newspaper employees at Kochi in Kerala today. The representatives of the Kerala Union of Working Journalists, Kerala Newspapers Employees, Federation and Kerala UNI Employees Union submitted their memorandum highlighting their demand of interim relief to the extent of 60 per cent and job security in print media. They called for the earlier submission of the report of the Wage Boards. The representatives also informed the Wage Boards that many newspapers/Journals have diversified into electronic media with the resources of the print media. Hence it would be important to bring electronic media workers also within the ambit of the Wage Boards. However, it was pointed that the electronic media does not come under the purview of the present Wage Boards. Shri K. M. Sahni, Member Secretary for both the Boards, Shri B.P. Singh and Shri P. N Prasanna Kumar, independent members common to both the Boards, Shri Naresh Mohan, Indian Newspaper Society, Shri Gurinder Singh, All India Small and Medium Newspapers Federation, Shri Prataprai Tarachand Shah, Indian Language Newspaper Association, Shri K. Vikram Rao, Indian Federation of Working Journalists, Shri Nand Kishore Trikha, National Union of Journalists, (India) and Shri Suresh Akhouri, Indian Journalists Union, Shri Madan Phadnis, All India Newspapers Employees Federation, Shri Uma Shankar Mishra National Federation of Newspapers Employees and Shri M S Yadav, Press Trust of India and senior officials of the Ministry of Labour & Employment attended the meeting.

2129. (2-8-2007) NEW DELHI : Sri Lankan Minister for Investment Promotion Shri Navin Dissanayake today expressed his country's keen interest on inviting Indian investments in several areas including Oil Exploration and refining, Information Technology and Apparel and Textile sectors. In his meeting with Shri Jairam Ramesh, Minister of State for Commerce here today, Shri Navin Dissanayake hoped that Indian companies would also help in the development of the infrastructure in the eastern province of Trincomalee, including the development of the proposed 1000 acre Special Economic Zone. Shri Jairam Ramesh informed the Sri Lankan

Minister of the ongoing projects of the Indian companies including the Lubricant Plant being set up by Indian Oil. "The Phase-I of the plant is likely to be commissioned by next month", Shri Ramesh said. Indian Oil is also looking at setting up a refinery as well as expanding its network of retail outlets in Sri Lanka. During the meeting, the Sri Lankan Minister also agreed on holding an Investment Expo in Sri Lanka in October-November this year, focusing exclusively on the Indian companies. Both Ministers agreed that the Expo should focus on two major sectors viz. Information Technology and Apparel & Textiles. Shri Ramesh informed that while National Association of Software & Service Companies (NASSCOM) could pilot India's participation on the IT side, the textile associations could engage on Apparel & Textile issues. The Minister promised to facilitate the active participation of Indian companies in the Expo. Both the Ministers also discussed the ongoing negotiations on the bilateral Comprehensive Economic Partnership Agreement (CEPA). Shri Jairam Ramesh impressed upon the Sri Lankan Minister the need to speed up the negotiations on the CEPA so that both sides could sign the agreement by October this year. "Both India and Sri Lanka can thrash out the differences and early conclusion of the CEPA would ensure the sustained interest of all the stake holders", Shri Ramesh said.

2130. (2-8-2007) NEW DELHI : The President has appointed Shri Rajendra B. Raghuvanshi as Additional Solicitor General of India in the High Court of Bombay at Mumbai. According to a notification issued here on August 1st 2007, Shri Raghuvanshi has been appointed with immediate effect for a period of two years. Shri Raghuvanshi has served as Assistant Government Pleader on behalf of Maharashtra State Government in various capacities. He has also functioned as Panel Counsel for Union of India in the Bombay High Court, Mumbai. Shri Raghuvanshi has been taking part at the activities of the Bar Council. He was elected unanimously as the Vice-Chairman of Bar Council of India in 2006. Prior to this in 2004 Shri Raghuvanshi was elected Member of Bar Council of India from Maharashtra and Goa. Earlier in 1988 he was elected as Chairman of Bar Council of Maharashtra and Goa. In 1990 Shri Raghuvanshi was elected as the youngest Vice-President of Western India Advocates Association, High Court, Mumbai. He has participated in several international conferences.

2131. (2-8-2007) NEW DELHI : Retail prices of essential commodities monitored by the Department of Consumer Affairs at four metropolitan cities have remained stable or shown mixed trend in the week ending 27.7.2007. Prices of wheat, rice, tur, mustard oil and milk were steady while that of gram dal, groundnut oil, vanaspati, sugar, tea, potato and salt marginally increased. Atta price declined by one Rupee per kg and gram dal price increased by Rupee one at Delhi. Groundnut oil price declined by Rupees two per kg at Chennai and increased by Rupee one at Delhi. Vanaspati price increased by Rupees two per kg at Kolkata. Sugar price increased by Rupee one per kg at Chennai. Tea prices increased by Rupees three per kg at Delhi and Rupees two per kg at Mumbai. Salt price increased by Rupee one per kg at Mumbai. At Delhi prices of rice and milk remained steady for six months; price of salt remained steady for one month and prices of wheat, tur, sugar, mustard oil and vanaspati remained steady for one week. Prices of gram, groundnut oil, tea loose and potato increased during the week. As on 24.7.2007 public sector agencies have contracted import of 10.38 lakh tonne pulses of which 2.30 lakh tonne has already reached Indian ports. The imported pulses include urad, moong, dunpeas, masoor, chickpeas, yellow peas and channa. As part of the measures taken by the Government to check rise in prices of edible oils, customs duty on crude palm oil including crude palmolien was reduced from 50% to 45 %; refined palm oil including RBD palmolien from 57.5% to 52.5%; soyabean oil from 45% to 40%; crude sunflower oil from 50% to 40% and refined sunflower oil from 60% to 50% effective from 17.7.2007.

2132. (2-8-2007) NEW DELHI : Central Water Commission is monitoring storage position of 78 important reservoirs spread all over the country, of which as many as 33 reservoirs have significant hydro-power benefits with installed capacity of more than 60 MW each. The combined live storage in these 78 reservoirs at the beginning of monsoon *i.e.* June 1,2007 was 25% of their designed capacity and stood at 57% of the designed capacity as on July 26,2007. The present storage is 135% of last year's storage and 181% of last 10 years average storage during the same period. Out of these 78 reservoirs, there are presently 8 reservoirs where this year's storage is 80% or less than the average of previous 10 years and in the remaining 70 reservoirs the storage is more than 80% of the average of previous 10 years. In order to derive the best possible benefits from the available water, Central Water Commission is keeping in touch with the Department of Agriculture and Cooperation and providing information of the weekly storage position to the Crop Weather Watch Group for evolving suitable crop strategies and also apprising the situation to various Departments and Ministries involved in Water Resources Planning.

2133. (2-8-2007) NEW DELHI : Culling of birds was completed in the 0-5 km zone on 1st August, 2007. Disposal of birds and infected materials was also completed in 0-5 km zone on the 1st August. 34 teams were deployed for continuing the culling operations in 0-5 km zone. All the sectors/villages have been covered. In all, 2,94,270 birds have been culled, 27,269 eggs destroyed and 23,490 kg feed destroyed. Mopping up operations commenced on 2nd August, 2007 in 0-5 km zone. Public has been informed through public address system by the District Administration. Surveillance in 5-10 km zone is in progress. Door-to-door surveillance in 79 villages/sectors is being undertaken through 7 teams. More than 500 households have been visited by these teams till 1st August, 2007 covering more than 60,000 poultry. There has been no report of any unusual mortality form the surveillance zone or in any other part of the State. Clean-up and dis-infection is under progress. Department of Animal Husbandry, Department of Health, Imphal Municipality and Deputy Commissioners of Imphal East and West will be involved in the process of clean-up and dis-infection.

2134. (2-8-2007) NEW DELHI : The Cabinet Committee on Economic Affairs today gave its approval for implementation of the scheme of Vocational Training Improvement project with World Bank assistance at a total cost of Rs.1581 crore on cost sharing basis {75%:25% between Centre and State Governments except for NE States and Sikkim the ratio will be 90:10.), out of which the share of the Central Government would be Rs.1231 crore. The States' share will be Rs.350 crore. The Project Development Objective is to improve the employment outcomes of graduates from vocational training system, by making the design and delivery of training more demand responsive. The Project has three components viz., (i) improving the Quality of Vocational Training, (ii) Promoting Systemic Reforms and Innovation, and (iii) Project Management, and Monitoring and Evaluation. 400 existing ITIs will be upgraded involving industry in all aspects of training from development of curriculum to trade testing. The approval aims at empowerment of ITIs, greater flexibility, reforms in administrative procedure, better linkages with work requirements and conducting training programmes in emerging areas apart from providing training to the trainers and undertaking other measures for sustainable development of vocational training in the country. This approach will bring significant improvement in internal and external efficiency of the ITIs including employment situation of the certificate holders.

2135. (2-8-2007) NEW DELHI : The Union Cabinet today gave its approval for acceptance and ratification of the International Convention against doping in Sport as adopted by the 33rd session of General Conference of UNESCO held in Paris on 19th October, 2005. Keeping in view the menace of doping in sports, this decision will result in rising global concern about its ill-effects; and India's commitment to anti-doping expressed through acceptance of Copenhagen Declaration in 2004. It will be implemented within a month by depositing the instruments of ratification / acceptance with Director General, UNESCO. Follow up action will be completed in six months.

2136. (2-8-2007) NEW DELHI : The election to the Office of the Vice President, to be held on 10th of this month, is the thirteenth. The earlier elections to this office were held in the years 1952, 1957 (both uncontested), 1962, 1967, 1969, 1974, 1979 (unopposed), 1984, 1987, 1992, 1997 and 2002. Under the provisions of Article 66(1) of Constitution of India, the Vice-President shall be elected by the members of an Electoral College consisting of Members of both the Houses of Parliament. The nominated members of both the Houses of Parliament (2 from Lok Sabha and 12 from Rajya Sabha) are also eligible to be included in the Electoral College along with the elected members of both the Houses of Parliament.

2137. (2-8-2007) NEW DELHI : The Union Cabinet today gave its approval for taking over the Rajiv Gandhi Centre for Biotechnology, Thiruvanthapuram, (RGCB) as an Autonomous Institute by the Central Government under the administrative control of Department of Biotechnology. RGCB would be the only Central Institute in the area of Biotechnology in the State of Kerala. The takeover of RGCB will have a major role in implementing relevant biotechnology projects both for the state and for the region as a whole.

2138. (3-8-2007) NEW DELHI : The Ministry of Corporate Affairs is all set to exploit the benefits of its ambitious e-Governance programme-MCA21, which is considered to have been successfully implemented by the Government of India as one of the Mission Mode Projects under the NeGP. For the first time a communication, using the Information and Communication Technology, has already been e-mailed to about 1.90 lakh Directors on companies whose e-mail IDs are available in the MCA21 database. Welcoming the Directors to the DIN database fold, the e-mail is addressed to the Directors requesting them to ensure filing of DIN Form-2 by them to the companies and the companies required to file Form DIN-3 with the Registry. "This is the beginning and we plan to continue to interact with our stakeholders on a continuing basis in future as well", said a Ministry official. Another communication, calling upon the companies to file Form DIN-3 (which contains the details of all the Directors/ Secretary/ Manager of a company) has been sent by e-mail to about one lakh companies. These are companies who have filed their Annual Returns and Balance Sheets on-line but have so far not filed Form DIN-3. Compliance management is under serious review. The Ministry has decided its priorities clearly and is keen to take up the issue of non-compliance of filing of statutory returns by the defaulting listed companies, public limited companies, Government companies and those with an authorised capital exceeding Rs. 1.00 crore in the first phase. "About 75% of the companies in this group are already compliant in filing the Annual Returns and the Balance Sheets. Our target is to take this to at least 90% compliance level in this group before the year end", said the Ministry sources. Steps are already underway to strike off the names of defunct companies and cleanse the Registries by initiating suo-motu action u/s 560 of the Act. The first phase of this initiative is targeted to be completed by October end. Separately, a major drive has been taken up to validate the database and carry out corrections wherever required so as to establish the integrity of the database on the corporate sector.

2139. (3-8-2007) NEW DELHI : A joint review of the agriculture sector of Karnataka on 3 August, 2007 at Bangalore by the Prime Minister, Dr. Manmohan Singh, Agriculture Minister, Shri Sharad Pawar, Chief Minister of Karantaka, Shri H.D. Kumaraswamy, Deputy Chairman, Planning Commission Dr. Montek Singh Ahluwalia identified the key thrust areas for the rejuvenation of the sector in the State to achieve the objectives set forth in the National Development Council Resolution of the 29th May 2007. While reaffirming the commitment of the State to achieve 4.5 per cent annual growth in agriculture sector in the State during the XI Five Year Plan period, the following was resolved: "Achieve additional production of 10 lakh tonnes of rice; 4 lakh tonnes of pulses; 5 lakh tonnes of maize and 9 lakh tonnes of oilseeds in the State under the National Food Security

Mission. Ensure expenditure above the baseline expenditure in agriculture and allied sectors and prepare District Agriculture Plans; aggregate them into a State Agriculture Plan in the next three months; and also formulate schemes/projects/ programmes along with the Detailed Project Reports for agriculture and allied sectors to avail of Additional Central Assistance under the new scheme of ACA. Efforts would be made to utilize the resources available from all existing schemes such as Backward Region Grant Fund, National Rural Employment Guarantee Programme and include livestock and fishing and be integrated with minor irrigation projects, rural development works and with the other schemes for water harvesting and conservation. Efforts would also be made to include schemes for beneficiaries of land reforms. Harness the potential of horticulture produce for export of grapes, pomegranate, lime etc. through cold chain facility and post harvest infrastructure at Bijapur and creation of similar facilities in other potential pockets in the State. Create infrastructure for better water availability especial focus on micro irrigation. Notify the Rules under the State APMC Amendment Act passed by the State Legislative recently in a time bound manner and initiate action to set up modern terminal market complexes in suitable areas; to achieve financial closure for Hassan and Channapatna and finalise selection of private entrepreneurs for Hubli and Bijapur terminal markets by March 2008.

2140. (3-8-2007) NEW DELHI : Prime Minister, Dr. Manmohan Singh has reviewed the Agricultural scenario in the State of Karnataka in Bangalore today. Following is the text of talking points on the occasion: "I am happy to be here in Karnataka to discuss with you a major area of shared concern-that of improving the condition of our farmers through improving agriculture. Karnataka is known across the country as a State, which has led in many development initiatives like land reforms, water shed management, democratic de-centralization to Panchayati Raj institutions, Yashaswini-your innovative health insurance scheme. You also led the country in engineering systems for water management and Sri Visvesvarayya has been an icon. It is rarely known that as early as in 1920, J.S. Chakravati, Diwan of Mysore, designed a scheme of Weather Insurance. It is a matter of satisfaction that you have come out with a new Karnataka Agriculture Policy in 2006 with five components of improving soil health, conservation of natural resources, timely deployment of credit and other inputs, integration of post-harvest technology with production and quicker dissemination and transfer of technology.

2141. (3-8-2007) NEW DELHI : A section of media has carried reports about coal availability crisis faced by NALCO. In this connection Ministry of Coal has clarified that Mahanadi Coalfields Limited (MCL) supplies coal to captive power plants of NALCO's, Angul Plant to the tune of 14000 tonnes per day on normative basis. However, due to adverse geo mining conditions in the linked mines as well as evacuation problem in Merry-go-round (MGR), there has been a shortfall in supply from the linked mine. The shortfall was being met from other mines of MCL using Indian Railways wagons. However, recently due to unavailability of

Indian Railway Wagons for supply of coal from other MCL mines in Talcher area, there has been lesser supply. A decision has now been taken in consultation with Railways, NALCO and coal companies to immediately provide coal from other coal companies/sources to ensure that there is no shortage of coal as against the linked quantity allocated to NALCO.

2142. (3-8-2007) NEW DELHI : Shri Sheelbhadra Banerjee, I.A.S. 1971 (A.P.) has taken over as Secretary, Ministry of Tourism. He replaces Shri Chirsty L.Fernandez who took over as Secretary to the President of India recently. Shri. S. Banerjee till now was serving as Director General (Acquisition) in Ministry of Defence.

2143. (3-8-2007) NEW DELHI : Dr. Raghuvansh Prasad Singh, Minister of Rural Development will be visiting the flood affected areas of Bihar on August 4th and 5th to take stock of the on-going relief measures. He has requested the State Government to intensify the relief measures to protect lives and properties and urged for large scale induction of ready food, polythene for shelter, medicines and boats, etc. to ensure people are not put to major hardship. Government of India has already provided Rs.53 crore under Calamity Relief Fund in March 2007. However, Rs.233 crore, the State share of CRF is yet to be released because of non-submission of utilization certificate by the State Government. The Minister has also asked the State Government to submit the utilization certificate to receive the entitled funds and intensify relief operation.

2144. (3-8-2007) NEW DELHI : The area coverage of kharif crops as compared to 2nd August last week has gone up considerably as per data compiled by Agriculture Ministry. Rice is an exception. The total coverage of kharif rice has gone up to 219.84 lakh ha as compared to 223.03 lakh hectare at this time last year, the weekly Crop Weather Watch Group meeting of the Ministry of Agriculture was informed here today. Transplanting of rice is in progress in almost all the States. In Assam, Bihar, Orissa, Chhattisgarh, Haryana, Maharashtra, Punjab and West Bengal, sowing is on peak. Total coarse cereals have covered an area of 182.71 lakh ha as compared to 168.86 lakh ha at this time last year. Cotton has been sown in 85.14 lakh ha as compared to 79.86 lakh ha last year. Out of this, 46.75 lakh hectare is under Bt cotton. Sugarcane coverage is reported to be 51.16 lakh hectare compared to 48.32 lakh ha last year, and jute 7.89 lakh hectare (last year 8.18 lakh ha.). The total coverage of oilseeds so far has been 149.38 lakh ha as compared to 141.83 lakh ha on August 2, last year. Soyabean has been sown in 6% and groundnut in 10% higher area as compared to that in 2006. Pulses cover an area of 95.19 lakh ha against 89.20 lakh ha during the last year.

2145. (3-8-2007) NEW DELHI : The Indian Textiles Industry has an overwhelming presence in the economic life of the country. Apart from providing one of the basic necessities of life, it also plays a pivotal role through its contribution to industrial output, employment generation and the export earnings of the country. The Textiles sector is the second largest provider of employment after agriculture. Thus, the growth and all round development of this industry has a direct bearing on the improvement of the economy of the nation. Currently, it contributes about 14 percent to industrial production, 4 percent to the GDP, and 16.63 percent to the country's export earnings. It provides direct employment to over 35 million people, which includes a substantial number of SC/ST and women. The industry is now accelerating at an annual growth rate of 9-10 percent and is expected to grow at a rate of 16 percent in value terms and will reach the level of US $ 115 billion by 2012. The clothing and apparel sub-sector are expected to grow at a rate of 16 percent in volume terms and 21 percent in value terms, and textiles exports are expected to grow at a rate of 22 percent in value terms, by 2012. The catalyst for this exponential growth is a buoyant domestic economy, substantial increase in cotton production, the conducive policy environment provided by the Government, and the expiration of the Multi Fibre Agreement on December 31, 2004.

2146. (3-8-2007) NEW DELHI : India's external trade has evolved and witnessed many a changes in its pace, nature and form ever since the country's Independence in 1947. In this evolutionary process, the Department of Commerce has played a key role in shaping the country's external trade policy in keeping with the ever-changing needs of the economy. Soon after Independence, the Government followed a policy of "progressive liberalisation" by relaxing import controls through expansion of the list of commodities under the Open General Licenses (OGL). However, foreign exchange crisis in 1956-57 put a quick end to this phase of liberalization. Comprehensive import controls were restored and maintained until 1966. Following devaluation of the Indian rupee in 1966, almost all liberalisation initiatives were reversed and import controls tightened. This regime was consolidated and strengthened in the subsequent years and remained more or less intact until the late 1970s and the early 1980's to fulfil the perceived need to protect domestic industry and promote self-sufficiency in the economy. The import substitution policy followed during the restrictive phase gave way to a new phase of trade reforms after mid 1980s aimed at easing trade restrictions to promote economic growth and competitiveness. First, the OGL list was steadily expanded to include capital goods and intermediate inputs. Secondly, the share of canalised imports was consciously reduced, extending the room for import of machinery and raw materials by private entrepreneurs. Thirdly, several export incentives were introduced including the Replenishment (REP) licenses, which could be freely traded on the market helping to relax constraints on imports and foreign exchange. The pace of change in India's external trade policy and practices gathered real momentum in the 1990's. A slew of reforms were launched which included drastic reduction of items on the OGL list. In July 1991 import licensing was done away on virtually all intermediate inputs and capital goods. A decade later on 1st April 2001, licenses / quantitative restrictions of remaining items were removed. Today, except for a handful of goods disallowed on environmental, health and safety grounds and a few others that are canalised such as fertiliser, cereals, edible oils and petroleum products, all goods can be imported without a license or other restrictions. Tariff reforms have also been addressed in a more systematic manner with across the board reduction in peak rates rather than selective exemptions. The peak rate of customs duty has been consistently brought down with the aim of converging it with the ASEAN levels.

2147. (3-8-2007) NEW DELHI : The Appointments Committee of the Cabinet has approved the extension of tenure of Dr. Sundeep Khanna, IAS of M.P. cadre, 1972 batch as Additional Secretary in the Ministry of Social Justice and Empowerment. He will hold this post till March 2008.

2148. (3-8-2007) NEW DELHI : The competent authority has approved the assignment of additional charge of the post of Chairperson, National Authority for Weapons Convention, Cabinet Secretariat to Dr. Renuka Viswanathan, IAS (K.N: 71) in addition to her own duties as Secretary (Coordination and Public Grievances) in the Cabinet Secretariat with immediate effect for a period of three months or until further orders, whichever is earlier.

2149. (3-8-2007) NEW DELHI : Nearly 74 percent of Indians live in villages of which 54 percent are engaged in the agricultural workforce. Women in particular, contribute significantly to agricultural production. In pursuance of the provisions in National Water Policy, 1987 and also 2002 farmers are to be involved progressively in various aspects of management of irrigation systems, particularly in water distribution and collection of water charges. Ministry of Water Resources, while issuing guidelines in April 1987, specifically emphasized upon the States to consider representation of women in the Water Users' Association (WUAs) at all levels. Many States have amended their Irrigation Acts or come out with specific Acts on the Participatory Irrigation management and some of them have made specific provisions of women's participation. The marginal representation of women, however is not adequate in view of the magnitude of the problem. Considering the importance of women in terms of their numerical strength and the significant contribution they make to the agricultural labour force, there is a need to encourage participation of more women in Water Users' Associations by bringing in a new culture among the water users.

2150. (3-8-2007) NEW DELHI : The competent authority has appointed Shri V. Vizia Saradhi, ED, HPCL to the post of Director (HR), Hindustan Petroleum Corporation Limited (HPCL) for a period of five years w.e.f. the date of assumption of charge of the post or till the date of his superannuation or until further orders, whichever event occurs earlier.

2151. (3-8-2007) NEW DELHI : The Eighth Home Secretary Level Bilateral Talks between India and Bangladesh were held in New Delhi on 2-3 August, 2007 in a warm, friendly, positive and constructive atmosphere. During the meeting, both sides approached all issues on the basis of mutual understanding and appreciation of each other's position and sensitivities, on the basis of reciprocity and mutual confidence. Both sides renewed their commitment to ensure that cooperation between the two countries is further widened, and to address issues of concern in a spirit of mutual understanding. Both sides noted the exchange of high level visits in the recent months which had given impetus and momentum to the diversified cooperation between the two countries and the commitment of the Governments to move the bilateral relationship forward. Both sides have expressed the hope that the current round of talks would provide a great opportunity to boost their historical relationship and would lead to enhanced and visible mutual cooperation in various aspects of security, border management and capacity building. Both sides strongly condemned terrorism and extremism and underlined the need to strengthen the existing bilateral arrangements by instituting new institutional mechanisms for enhanced cooperation and continuous and regular exchange of information to combat this menace. Both sides also agreed to revive the mechanism of the Joint Working Group (JWG) at the level of Joint Secretaries in the Ministries of Home Affairs and decided that the meetings could be held at regular intervals alternately in India and Bangladesh. Pursuant to the discussions in the last Home Secretary level talks in August 2006, Bangladesh side has nominated JS (Political) as the nodal point for dealing with matters related to trafficking in women and children. In this regard, it was noted that the Indian side had already nominated Joint Secretary (CS), Ministry of Home Affairs for this purpose.

2152. (3-8-2007) NEW DELHI : Safety is the prime concern of Indian Railways and considerable progress has been made in the execution of works sanctioned under Special Railway Safety Fund (SRSF). A non-lapsable SRSF of Rs. 17000 crore is operational since October 2001. Safety works worth Rs. 14,912 crore have already been completed upto 31.03.07 and another Rs. 1882 crore is targeted to be utilized in the financial year 2007-08. The Corporate Safety Plan for the period 2003-2013 lays down the objectives, targets and strategies which Indian Railways would be pursuing as financial schemes, involving huge investment of Rs. 31,835 crore including SRSF. The action plan indicates broad time frames for safety related works, rehabilitation and modernization of assets, induction of appropriate technologies to bring qualitative changes and reduced human dependence to prevent accidents. In physical terms almost 90 per cent to 100 per cent progress has been achieved against most of the critical items. The entire 16,538 kilometres of track targeted for renewal has been renewed up to 31.03.2007. Similarly rehabilitation of almost all of the 2370 identified bridges is targeted for completion by the end of next financial year. In addition, the renewal of signalling gears at 1359 places, complete station track circuiting works at 5397 locations would be completed by the end of 2007-08 where as renewal of 7698 wagons, 186 coaches and 93 locomotives would be completed by 31.08.2008.

2153. (3-8-2007) NEW DELHI : H.E. Lt. General Kayumba Nyamwasa, Ambassador of the Embassy of the Republic of Rwanda called on Dr. Chandrapal, Secretary, Micro, Small & Medium Enterprises here today. Dr. Chandrapal informed the Ambassador of the immense potential of the Micro, Small and Medium Enterprises Sector of India. He further stated that the Ministry of Micro, Small & Medium Enterprises propose to participate in the forthcoming fairs in Rwanda through various wings of the Ministry viz. National Small Industries Corporation, KVIC, Coir Board etc. The products to be displayed in the fair will come under one roof called "MSME India". Rwanda's MSMEs would get an opportunity to view the new trends and developments in the MSME Sector of India including trainers' training, capacity building and related areas, he added. The Ambassador of Rwanda assured Dr. Chandrapal to convey the proposal to his Government and take necessary steps in enhancing cooperation in the MSME Sector between the two countries.

2154. (3-8-2007) NEW DELHI : The Prime Minister, Dr. Manmohan Singh has requested states to urgently take steps for strengthening institutional arrangements in the tiger reserves and for priority recruitment of frontline staff of the Forest Department especially in sanctuaries. The Prime Minister in a letter to the state Chief Ministers, after a review of the implementation of the Tiger Task Force Report, said that a large number of frontline posts in the Department of Forests are lying vacant in several states. This may have happened on account of recruitment bans imposed at a time when State finances were under stress. He pointed out that situation had changed and urged the states to fill in the vacancies at the earliest. The Prime Minister has urged Chief Ministers to create a "development agency" in each tiger reserve for guidance in increasing local participation in tiger reserve management. These agencies would be under the Field Directors involving local Panchayats and professional wild life experts. Enabling provisions for constituting such an institutional mechanism have been provided in the Wildlife Protection Amendment Act, 2006 and related guidelines issued by the National Tiger Conservation Authority. The Prime Minister has also asked the states to consider major parks /tiger reserves as autonomous profit centres. He has suggested creation of a "development fund" in each tiger reserve, which would be made eligible for tourism gate receipts, assistance from governments, funds from Compensatory Aforestation Fund Management and Planning Authorities.

2155. (3-8-2007) NEW DELHI : The current meteorological conditions and interpretation of various numerical weather prediction models suggest a revival in monsoon activity over central and adjoining peninsular India, as a low pressure area is likely to form over northwest Bay of Bengal on 4th of August, 2007 along with a southward shift in monsoon trough. The low-pressure area is likely to become more marked and move slowly in a west-northwesterly direction. According to the Met department, the enhanced rainfall with isolated heavy to very heavy falls are likely over Orissa, north Andhra Pradesh and Chhattisgarh during 4th to

7th August. Subsequently, the enhanced rainfall belt is likely to shift to Madhya Pradesh, Maharashtra, Gujarat and south Rajasthan during August 8-11.Gujrat, Konkan & Goa and Madhya Maharashtra are also likely to receive extremely heavy rainfall (>25cm) particularly on 10th and 11th of August. The central and adjoining peninsular India may experience again another active spell of rainfall from 11th onwards in association with formation of a fresh low-pressure area over Northwest Bay of Bengal. However, the rainfall activity over northeastern states and northern plains is likely to be subdued till mid August 2007.

2156. (3-8-2007) NEW DELHI : The Solar Energy Centre is a technical focal point of the Ministry of New and Renewable Energy for the development and promotion of solar energy technologies. Talking to a group of journalists at the Centre, Dr. Bibek Bandopadhyay said that on this 200 acre campus we have buildings constructed on solar passive techniques to achieve energy efficiency and environmentally friendliness. We have incorporated more solar essential points which provides energy efficiency. It maximizes solar radiation during winter and avoids during summer. Centre has equipments, laboratories and other associated facilities for design development, testing and evaluation. We also have testing and standardization facilities, he added. The Centre provides assistance to Research Institutions, Academic Institutions and industries in the country in developing solar technology. The products developed by organizations are brought here for testing and standardization. The centre evaluate it and suggest ways for modifying it towards betterment. As a result of this, a more reliable and efficient product comes out. The solar thermal test facility is equipped for testing of solar thermal collectors, domestic solar water heating systems and solar cookers, both box type and concentrating type. The centre works closely with the Bureau of Indian Standard, which brought out Indian standards on solar flat-plate collectors at par with the International Standards. Giving details on solar photo-voltaic facility, it was informed that there are four other such centres in the world. They are ISPRA, Milan, Italy, TUV, Germany, Arizona University USA and Kyoto. The demand of solar cells which are called solar wafers and modules or solar panels is very high in the country. We import about 30 per cent solar cells. Telecom Ministry, Defence, Railways and ONGC are permanent users of this system. Referring to revolution in home light systems, Dr. Bandopadhyay said that LED, *i.e.* Light Emitting Diodes have been developed. Incandescent lights have been replaced by fluorescent lights. Recently, CFL bulbs with little modification in fluorescent system came in the market but this also does not have efficacy. So far LED was used in electronic equipments as indicators but with innovation of white LED, we will have LED light systems in the near future. They have longest life and they can work in hard environments. Fluorescent lights do not works in cold regions like Leh Ladakh and in vary hot regions like Rajasthan.

2157. (3-8-2007) NEW DELHI : Shri Pranab Mukherjee, Minister for External Affairs, led the Indian delegation to the 14th ASEAN Regional Forum (ARF) meeting in Manila yesterday. The ARF brings together the ten ASEAN countries, their ten Dialogue Partners such as India, China, the United States, EU and Russia, as well as seven other countries including the latest entrant Sri Lanka. The meeting, chaired by Philippines Foreign Minister, Secretary Romulo, discussed the regional and international security situation as well as the future programme and direction of ARF activities. In his intervention, Shri Mukherjee noted with satisfaction that ARF is helping consolidate efforts to address issues such as terrorism, trans-national organized crime, maritime security, natural disaster management, peacekeeping and energy security while continuing its basic task of promoting confidence building and mutual trust in the Asia-Pacific region. Condemning the killing of the South Korean hostages by the Taliban, he outlined India's perspective on developments in Afghanistan and pointed out that Indians engaged in humanitarian and reconstruction activity in Afghanistan too have fallen victim to the Taliban's violent and destructive agenda. He emphasised that all states should contribute with sincerity to Afghanistan's efforts to bring peace and development to all its regions. All states must also abide by the commitments that they have made in the Global Counter Terrorism Strategy, adopted by the UN General Assembly last September by consensus and to take practical measures to ensure that their territories are not used for terrorist installations or training camps or for the preparation or organisation of terrorist acts against other states or their citizens. Noting the progress of ARF activities in area of counter-terrorism, Shri Mukherjee announced that India shall be co-hosting in the coming year, along with Indonesia, the ARF Intersessional Meeting on Counter Terrorism and Transnational Crime. He offered India's help to ARF member states in building capacity to ensure the safety and security of sea lanes passing through the region. In this regard he announced that India would be designing and conducting a training module on maritime security specifically for the ARF Member States, with the themes of anti-piracy, search & rescue, offshore and port security, anti-smuggling and narcotics control and anti-poaching operation. In the same vein India would be conducting a regular training programme on UN Peacekeeping specifically for ARF Member States.

2158. (3-8-2007) NEW DELHI : Based on the recommendations of Foreign Investment Promotion Board (FIPB) in its meeting held on 27th July, 2007, Finance Minister, Shri P. Chidambaram has approved 17 proposals of Foreign Direct Investment amounting approximately to Rs. 575.83 crore. The proposals related to Ministries/Departments, namely, Chemicals & Petrochemicals, Commerce, Information & Broadcasting, Telecommunications and Economic Affairs.

2159. (3-8-2007) NEW DELHI : Mopping up operations was carried out on 2nd August, 2007. 27 teams were deployed for operations. The total number of birds culled so far has reached 3,31,606; number of eggs destroyed, 28,103; and feed destroyed, 25,242 kg. Surveillance in the radius of 5-10 km from the epicenter is in progress. Door-to-door surveillance is being undertaken through 7 teams.

Total of 783 households and nearly 1,27,000 poultry have been covered by door-to-door surveillance. In addition, general surveillance is being maintained which indicates no unusual mortality in the area of operation or any other part of the State. Compensation of more than Rs.70 lakh has been paid upto 2nd August, 2007. Work of cleaning and dis-infection is in progress. 16 RRTs assisted by labourers (58) and malaria workers of the Health Department (15) were engaged in the task of cleaning and dis-infection. Other RRTs were rested today. The labour and malaria workers were subjected to health check-up and given briefing in use of PPE kit and Tamiflu. Accommodation will be provided by the State Government to labour involved in clean up and dis-infection.

2160. (3-8-2007) NEW DELHI : Mopping up operations was carried out on 2nd August, 2007. 27 teams were deployed for operations. The total number of birds culled so far has reached 3,31,606; number of eggs destroyed, 28,103; and feed destroyed, 25,242 kg. Surveillance in the radius of 5-10 km from the epicenter is in progress. Door-to-door surveillance is being undertaken through 7 teams. Total of 783 households and nearly 1,27,000 poultry have been covered by door-to-door surveillance. In addition, general surveillance is being maintained which indicates no unusual mortality in the area of operation or any other part of the State. Compensation of more than Rs.70 lakh has been paid upto 2nd August, 2007. Work of cleaning and dis-infection is in progress. 16 RRTs assisted by labourers (58) and malaria workers of the Health Department (15) were engaged in the task of cleaning and dis-infection. Other RRTs were rested today. The labour and malaria workers were subjected to health check-up and given briefing in use of PPE kit and Tamiflu. Accommodation will be provided by the State Government to labour involved in clean up and dis-infection.

2161. (3-8-2007) NEW DELHI : Deptt of Animal Husbandry, Dairying and Fisheries notified an outbreak of avian influenza in Chingmeirong Village in East Imphal District of Manipur on 25.7.2007. The Central Rapid Response Team of Ministry of Health and F.W. deputed to Imphal is assisting the State Govt. The health status of the cullers are being monitored. Five cullers found medically unfit were withdrawn from the culling operations. They continued to be under quarantine and medical supervision. As of now, 172 cullers are under the cover of Tamiflu. In addition 37 supportive staff and 11 medical staff in the quarantine camp are also under Tamiflu. Their health status is also being monitored. The entire population of the infected zone [0-3 Kms] are under active surveillance on daily basis. For such purpose, the State Govt. has deployed health teams consisting of 597 health personnel. In this zone the surveillance teams could cover 44,475 houses [population of 2,32,233] on 1st August, 2007. They detected 130 fever/ ARI cases some of which are follow-up of earlier cases. These cases are being monitored. Surveillance activity has also been initiated with 83 health workers in the 3 to 10 Kms zone. 557 houses with a population of 2828 in Kangla, Takyel, Khurai, Kshertrigo have been covered. 7 cases of fever/ARI were detected and none of them had exposure to dead/ sick birds. Arrangements have been made in J.N. Hospital, Imphal for isolation and critical care. This is in addition to the critical care facilities available at Regional Institute of Medical Sciences, Imphal. Adequate supply of logistics [Tamiflu (10,000 caps), N-95 masks (1000) and personal protective gears (2000)] have been made available to the State Government. The situation is being closely monitored. As of now, there is no suspected human cases of Avian Influenza.

2162. (3-8-2007) NEW DELHI : The Central Government, today, notified the coming into force the English and Foreign Languages University Act, 2006 (No. 7 of 2007). Prof. Abhai Maurya of Department of Slavic Studies, University of Delhi has assumed the office of the first Vice-Chancellor of English and Foreign Languages University, Hyderabad w.e.f. August 03, 2007. The English and Foreign Languages University at Hyderabad would be the 24th Central University established by an Act of Parliament. With the coming into force of the English and Foreign Languages University Act, the country has now a dedicated Central University for promotion and development of English and Foreign Languages and their literature. Prof. Abhai Maurya, who comes from a peasant family in a village in Haryana, is a first generation learner. He has been a Professor of Russian Literature since 1988 and is the founder Head of the Department of Slavic Studies in the University of Delhi. He is the author of 12 books, both scholarly and creative, with more than 50 research papers to his credit. He has been awarded and facilitated internationally and has been actively associated with various bodies of UNESCO. One of such major awards is "A.S. Pushkin" Medal, the highest honour in the field of Russian literature and language. His novel Fall of a Hero (in English, 1998), Yugnayika (in Hindi, 2004) and Mukti-Path (in Hindi, 2006) have won a wide critical acclaim.

2163. (3-8-2007) NEW DELHI : Shri Ashwani Kumar, Minister of State for Industry has made a strong plea for the early finalization of a Preferential Trade Agreement (PTA) between India and South Africa to give a fresh boost to bilateral economic ties. Shri Kumar yesterday met Ms. Phumzile Mlambo-Ngcuka, Deputy President of South Africa on the margins of the India Calling Conference at Johannesburg and also held discussions with Mr. Mandisi Mpahlwa, Minister of Trade & Industry and with Dr. Essop Pahad, Minister in the President's Office. In these meetings, Shri Kumar urged for an early finalization of the PTA with South Africa. Mr. Mphlwa assured Shri Kumar that the agreement could be concluded soon, possibly before the expected visit of Prime Minister Dr. Manmohan Singh to South Africa in October this year. Considering the target to treble Indo-South African trade by 2010 to US $ 12 billion, the PTA between the two countries would be a major step forward. Dr. Pahad informed Shri Kumar that the India-South Africa CEOs Forum would meet in Mumbai on 16th August and that more and more South African companies are looking to participate in the development of infrastructure in India. Shri Kumar invited South African companies to invest in India and expressed the hope that Indian companies would also have an opportunity to participate in the development of infrastructure for the FIFA World Cup to be held in South Africa in 2010. Meanwhile in his address at the India Calling Conference at Johannesburg yesterday, Shri Kumar had underlined the crucial role that India and South Africa would play in defining the new global order as they addressed the challenges of economic growth and social justice within the context of heterogeneous societies and pluralistic, multiparty democracies. Describing India's ambitious plans to develop its infrastructure, he urged the assembled South African captains of trade and industry to become invest in India and to become partners in its economic growth. The India Calling Conference is being organized by the Mumbai-based Indian Merchants' Chamber (IMC) in partnership with Business Unity South Africa (BUSA), South Africa's apex trade and industry body. The Conference, significantly, coincides with the centenary celebrations of the IMC.

2164. (3-8-2007) NEW DELHI : Arctic Ocean and the surrounding regions are one of the most important areas that not only govern the earth's climate but have maintained the record of its past climatic history. The region is also an excellent indicator of future changes, because the signals or clues that signify climate change are so much stronger in the Arctic than elsewhere on the planet. The thermo-haline circulation that originates in the northern Atlantic and southern Arctic is the major force that drives not only the oceanic circulation but also regulate the global climate. Possible changes in this global circulation can pose a threat to Arctic region and thereby to the global climate, sea level, biodiversity etc. The region is also of special significance to the Indian subcontinent as studies have shown that there exists a tele-connection between the northern polar region and the intensity of Indian monsoon. However the exact mechanism by which this tele-connection functions is still not fully understood. India is a signatory to the Svalbard Treaty of 1920, which permits it to operate in the Svalbard archipelago, which is under the sovereign control of Norway. Many nations are already using the Ny-Ålesund research facilities operated by Norway at Spitsbergen island, while some have developed their own set up as well, including some Asian nations such as Japan, South Korea and China. In last few years initiatives were taken up by the Ministry of Earth Sciences, earlier known as Department of Ocean Development, to work out an Arctic Research Programme to complement our work in the Antarctica; so as to contribute to the global research by providing our expertise in the polar sciences. The National Centre for Antarctic and Ocean Research (NCAOR), Goa being the designated nodal agency for Polar research in India, held discussions with Norwegian Polar Research Institute (NPR), to develop a collaborative Arctic research programme.

2165. (3-8-2007) NEW DELHI : Ministry of Health & Family Welfare in its situational report dated 31st July, 2007 had mentioned that the Central Rapid Response Team is monitoring the health status of four persons with fever / acute upper respiratory tract infection who had contact with either dead or sick birds.

All of them are now afebrile. Their clinical samples have been tested at National Institute of Virology, Pune and National Institute of Communicable Diseases, Delhi and found negative for Avian Influenza virus by RT-PCR (Reverse Transcriptase Polymerase Chain Reaction).

2166. (3-8-2007) NEW DELHI : Union Minister for Science and Technology and earth Sciences Shri Kapil Sibal today launched the first Indian Arctic Expedition as he handed over the National Flag to Shri Rasik Ravindra, Director of the National Centre for Antarctic and Ocean Research (NCAOR), Goa who will lead a team consisting of Dr. S. M. Singh, Scientist from NCAOR, Dr. S. Shivaji, Dy. Director from CCMB, Hyderabad, Dr. C. G. Deshpande, Scientist from IITM, Pune and Dr. Dhruv Sen Singh, Lecturer, from University of Lucknow. At a formal sending off ceremony in New Delhi the Minister wished the team success in their planned scientific endeavours.

2167. (3-8-2007) NEW DELHI : Deptt of Animal Husbandry, Dairying and Fisheries notified an outbreak of Avian influenza in Chingmeirong Village in East Imphal District of Manipur on 25.7.2007. The Central Rapid Response Team of Ministry of Health and F.W. deputed to Imphal is assisting the State Govt. The health status of the cullers are being monitored. Four cullers found medically unfit were withdrawn from the culling operations. They continued to be under quarantine and medical supervision. As of now, 172 cullers are under the cover of Tamiflu. In addition 36 supportive staff and 11 medical staff in the quarantine camp are also under Tamiflu. Their health status is also being monitored. The entire population of the infected zone [0-3 Kms] are under active surveillance on daily basis. For such purpose, the State Govt. has deployed health teams consisting of 680 health personnel (20 medical officers, 60 supervisors and 600 workers). In this zone the surveillance teams cover 45,032 houses [population of 2,35,161] on daily basis. On 31st July they detected 126 fever/ ARI cases some of which are follow-up of earlier cases. They are being monitored. Surveillance activity has also been initiated in the 3 to 10 Kms zone. Doctors from the States of West Bengal, Tripura, Mizoram, Assam and Meghalaya are being provided hands on training at the site on containment operations. An officer from MOHFW visited the State from 29th to 31st July, 2007 and reviewed the operations and held discussions with the State health authorities. The isolation ward in J.N. Hospital, Imphal is ready to receive patients. Two ventilators have been installed to provide critical care. This is in addition to the critical care facilities available at Regional Institute of Medical Sciences, Imphal. Adequate supply of logistics [Tamiflu (10,000 caps), N-95 masks (1000) and personal protective gears (2000) have been made available to the State Government. The situation is being closely monitored. As of now, there is no suspected human cases of Avian Influenza. To know the situational report on a day-to-day basis, please log on to http://mohfw.nic.in/aviannew.htm.

2168. (5-8-2007) NEW DELHI : In a meeting with President Mbeki of South Africa at Johannesburg last Friday (August 3), Dr. Ashwani Kumar, Minister of

State for Industry extended the greetings of Prime Minister Dr. Manmohan Singh and UPA Chairperson, Smt. Sonia Gandhi. President Mbeki conveyed that he was very much looking forward to having discussions with Smt. Sonia Gandhi during her forthcoming visit to South Africa later this month and with the Prime Minister on his visit to South Africa in October for the next Summit of IBSA (India, Brazil and South Africa). Addressing the India Calling 2007 Conference organized by the Indian Merchants' Chamber in Johannesburg later in the afternoon, President Mbeki endorsed Dr. Kumar's perceptions about the need for inclusivist economic growth and the need for remedying the injustices of past centuries. Recalling the impact of Mahatma Gandhi's ideas on South Africa's freedom struggle, President Mbeki highlighted the special relationship between India and South Africa and said that India serves as an inspiring example to many South Africans. The emergence of Indian businesses as global players, he said, was an important development in addressing the fracture between the wealthy North and the marginalized South. President Mbeki urged the Indian business delegation to work with South African counterparts to address the challenges of poverty, inequality and skill development. Closer partnership between India and South Africa, he concluded, would not only benefit the two countries but was of a critical importance to billions of others and to the establishment of a new world order.

2169. (5-8-2007) NEW DELHI : Flying modern airplane require a high degree of physical and mental fitness to withstand the stresses that are placed on the aircrew. With the advent of more sophisticated high performance aircraft, the complexities facing the military aircrew have risen in geometrical progression. In the booming civil aviation sector long haul flights and their associated problems with relation to mental alertness are also an area of concern. It is therefore imperative that medical evaluation of pilots be conducted so that the combat potential of the Armed Forces and the flying potential of the Civil Aviation industry is not depleted and at the same time flight safety is not compromised. Towards achieving this objective, AFCME (Air Force Central Medical Establishment) one of the premier medical institutions of IAF, has rendered yeoman service and is now virtually the custodian of medical safety in aviation for the country as a whole. To further this goal and on the occasion of its Diamond Jubilee Celebrations, AFCME conducted a medical update on the "Current Trends in Aircrew Medical Evaluation" on 05 Aug 07. The update was inaugurated by the Air Chief Marshal FH Major PVSM, AVSM, SC, VM, ADC, Chief of the Air Staff and attended by a large number of eminent and renowned service and civil aviation delegates. The CAS in his inaugural address stressed on the need to integrate new capabilities, infuse innovations and to gear up medical evaluation in pursuit of enhanced flight safety, with no room for errors. The scientific sessions dealt with various aspects of clinical aviation medicine. Some of the significant areas like the changing scenario in diabetes mellitus and evaluation of aircrew with coronary artery disease were deliberated upon with the aim to put the pilot back into the cockpit as early as possible. Recently a new policy has been introduced for civil pilots suffering from diabetes mellitus, who were made permanently unfit for flying duties, to be cleared on medication compatible with flying. The Chief of the Air Staff also inaugurated a scientific exhibition portraying important medical products and equipment. AFCME has always strived hard to attain its objectives of maintaining flight safety by adopting correct practices of aircrew medical evaluation. In the last 60 years, AFCME has fulfilled the objective of being the most disciplined and professional medical evaluation centre.

2170. (6-8-2007) NEW DELHI : The Prime Minister, Dr. Manmohan Singh, chaired a meeting to discuss issues relating to conservation and development of the Yamuna River here today. It was decided to set up a high powered committee on Yamuna River Development with Lt. Governor of Delhi and Chief Minister of Delhi as Co-Chairpersons. The committee would have participation of all stakeholders and will commission studies on Yamuna river conservation and development. Pollution of the river being a major concern, it was noted that with execution of the sewerage and drainage plan prepared by the Delhi Jal Board, the water quality in Yamuna would improve significantly. Development of the river front, however, is an exercise which needs to be approached with due care, after proper studies on different aspects. The meeting was attended by Union Home Minister, Shri Shivraj Patil, Union Minister of Urban Development, Shri S. Jaipal Reddy, Lt. Governor of Delhi, Shri Tejender Khanna and Chief Minister of Delhi, Smt. Sheila Dikshit. Principal Secretary to Prime Minister, Shri T.K.A Nair, Cabinet Secretary, Shri K.M.Chandrasekhar and other senior officials were also present in the meeting.

2171. (6-8-2007) NEW DELHI : Government of India have announced the sale (re-issue) of " 5.48 percent Government Stock, 2009" under Market Stabilization Scheme for a notified amount of Rs. 4,000 crore (nominal). The Government Stock will be sold through price based auction using multiple price method. The auction will be conducted by the Reserve Bank of India, Mumbai Office, Fort, Mumbai on August 8, 2007 (Wednesday). Up to 5% of the amount notified for the sale of stock is reserved for allotment to eligible individuals and Institutions on non-competitive basis as per the Scheme for Non-Competitive Bidding Facility in the Auction of Government Securities. Bids in the prescribed form obtainable from the Regional Director, Reserve Bank of India, Mumbai Office (Public Debt Office), Fort, Mumbai-400 001 and RBI website www.rbi.org.in should be submitted to that Office on August 8, 2007. The NDS members should submit competitive as well as non-competitive bids in electronic format using Primary Market Operation (PMO) module of NDS. All bids should be submitted by 12.30 P.M. The result of the auction will be announced on August 8, 2007 and payment by successful bidders will be during banking hours on August 9, 2007 (Thursday).

2172. (6-8-2007) NEW DELHI : 25 Children of Bakarwals, a tribe which rears sheeps and goats for livelihood were felicitated by Army's Deputy Chief, Lt Gen

Susheel Gupta, here today. Based on their occupational needs, the bakarwals migrate from one region of J & K to another. As such their children generally do not receive any formal or structured education. Hence the Army is conducting them on North India tour to places of historical and industrial interests. Their visits include National Dairy at Karnal and JCT Mills, Jalandhar besides touring Jammu, Ambala, New Delhi and Agra. The children are in the age group of 13 to 16. In their interaction with Lt Gen Gupta, most of them stated that they had travelled by train for the first time in their lives. They were very happy to see various developmental activities such as the Metro rail and places of historical interests. They look forward to viewing Taj Mahal at Agra. Lt Gen Susheel Gupta advised the children to work for the national cause.

2173. (6-8-2007) NEW DELHI : In the new millennium, India has already crossed the one billion mark of population. The urban areas are struggling with the challenge to provide access to shelter and basic infrastructure services to the vast and ever-growing population. The Ministry of Housing & Urban Poverty Alleviation is the apex authority of the Government for formulation of housing policy and programmes relating thereto, review of the implementation of the plan schemes, collection and dissemination of data on housing, building materials/ techniques and for adopting general measures for reduction of building costs. In addition, it is entrusted with implementation and monitoring of the specific programmes of urban employment and urban poverty alleviation.

2174. (6-8-2007) NEW DELHI : Following is the text of the address of the President, Smt. Pratibha Devisingh Patil, at the National Academy of Agricultural Sciences at a special lecture on 'Agriculture Cannot Wait' : "I am very happy to be amidst you all today and it is immensely satisfying to note that to commemorate the 60th Anniversary of our Independence, the National Academy of Agricultural Sciences has organized a Special Lecture: 'Agriculture Cannot Wait'. It is fascinating to note that Pt. Nehru, the visionary thinker, had echoed the same thoughts more than half a century ago when he remarked, "Everything can wait, but not agriculture'. The theme of today's lecture is of special relevance globally, as we are poised at a critical juncture grappling with the formidable task of eradicating hunger and poverty from our planet. A nation is its people and our motherland is the abode of nearly one-sixth of all humanity. Securing a better life for our citizens where each one of us, can lead lives of dignity and fulfilment therefore merits undivided attention in our development strategy. A natural corollary to this is the attainment of the goal of food security for all. The need to catalyze agricultural growth through a result-oriented agricultural development strategy with the synergized endeavours of our policymakers, the farming community, farmers organisations, farming labour, agricultural scientists and agri-business enterprises is indeed the call of the moment. During the 60 years after Independence, we have made spectacular strides in the field of agriculture. The chronic spectre of famine, which was commonplace during colonial rule, has long been obliterated from our memories.

It is no mean achievement to be able to feed a population, which has crossed the one billion mark. I salute our farmers and congratulate our scientists who are responsible for this magnificent accomplishment and must add with all emphasis that the entire nation is proud of their dedicated work. We have amidst us, Dr. M.S. Swaminathan, a distinguished scientist who played a stellar role in ushering in the First Green Revolution. What is noteworthy of admiration is that he continues to be fired with the same zeal and spirit to pave the onward march of agriculture in our country. My special greetings also go to Dr. Jacques Diouf, Director General, Food and Agriculture Organization of the United Nations. The success story of the First Green Revolution has run its course. We cannot afford to rest on our laurels.

2175. (6-8-2007) NEW DELHI : Mopping, cleaning and dis-infection operations continued in Manipur over the weekend. 21 RRTs supported by 108 hired labourers and 15 persons from Malaria Wing of the Health Department were engaged in operations. The total number of birds culled so far has reached over 3,36,000; and feed destroyed, 25,242 kg. The work of clean up and dis-infection has been initiated in 28 sectors in the 0-5 km radious. The first round of door-to-door surveillance has been completed in the entire 5-10 kms zone covering all the 79 sectors and does not indicate any unusual mortality. There is also no report of unusual mortality in any other part of the state. Samples from Dibyoday Krishi Bigyan Kendra, Khowai under West Tripura District, Tripura and Vawmbuk Village, Saiha District are under test at High Security Animal Disease Laboratory (HSADL), Bhopal. Unusual mortality had been reported in Khowai resulting in death of about 500 out of 3000 birds over flock history of 38 days upto 2nd August, 2007. No mortality has been reported from the farm on 3rd August, 2007 onwards. Post-mortem is indicative of Infectious Bursal Disease. Unusual mortality of about 122 birds was also reported from Vawmbuk Village, Saiha District, Mizoram. However, no mortality has been reported from 3rd August, 2007 onwards. Symptom of poultry birds that have died is indicative of Fowl Pox. There is no other report of unusual mortality from any other part of the country.

2176. (6-8-2007) NEW DELHI : Under the Sampoorna Grameen Rozgar Yojana (SGRY) scheme, the Ministry of Rural Development has approved the release of 1030 MTs of wheat during the year 2007-08 to Baran District of Rajasthan State through Food Corporation of India depots in the State as per details given below: The release is towards plan expenditure and will be utilized for approved items of works subject to the conditions laid down in the SGRY Guidelines. The State Government must ensure timely payment of wages and timely and adequate supply of food grains. If the food grains are not available, wages should be paid in cash. Baran District has also been granted Rs.2.05 crore as first instalment, equal to 60% of the total allocation of Rs.3.43 crore by the Ministry of Rural Development as Central assistance for the implementation of the SGRY during the current financial year (2007-08). The expenditure on implementation of the programme with regard to cash component is to be shared on 75:25 basis between the Central and the State Government respectively.

2177. (6-8-2007) NEW DELHI : To a question that Congress party should stand by Sanjay Dutt, Congress Spokesperson Shri Abhishek Singhvi said that I think we are flogging an old horse. We have made our stand clear not once, not twice but thrice. Naturally, we may be concerned, we may be saddened but a political party cannot do anything in such circumstances where a law has to take its course. There is no reason whatsoever to doubt that justice will be done in a fair expeditious manner and I have nothing more to say to that. You have to ask other people, their view, their comments. I have made my view and my stand very clear. To a question about the plot to overthrow Chief Minister Smt. Shiela Dikshit and the Malhotra issue that has gripped the Delhi government, Shri Singhvi said that individual criminality has nothing whatsoever to do with a political party. Individual criminality is not something which a political party can or will take cognisance of. Let me emphatically and comprehensively state before you that these rumours and allegations of the so-called plot to overthrow the Delhi Government are nothing but the output of a febrile and fertile imagination which is obviously an idle and overactive mind. Let me make it clear that serious allegations of criminality involving land scams cannot be converted by this digressive method into a car number scam into a supposed plot to overthrow the Delhi Government. Please note that just before coming here we have also talked to the Chief Minister of Delhi and she has confirmed that nothing of the sort has either happened or that any of the MLAs think that it has happened. So, let us not go by rumour-mongering, let us clearly permit the police to do their job in a case of serious criminality. Of course I don't need to rely on the certificate of an alleged criminal like Mr. Malhotra who a few hours ago said that he has nothing to do with all these politicians and all other political figures. To a question about the nexus of political leaders with Mr. Malhotra, Shri Singhvi said that I deny it completely. There is not an iota of evidence of any kind to suggest that anybody in the Congress is associated with this so-called land scam. On the contrary something totally different has been brought in about car numbers and let me emphatically deny that any such thing is nothing but rumour-mongering and nothing but creating diversions and digressions. To a question that conspiracy case came from Congress office, Shri Singhvi said that it is in respect of that, that we have again specifically checked with the Chief Minister. The Chief Minister authorized us to say on our own basis of her investigations and that is absolutely incorrect and the MLAs do not believe so and there is no such plot and we deny it all-together. On the contrary these are tactics to divert attention from a fair and thorough investigations of what should be the main criminal elements, namely, the land dealings of this gentleman. To a question about the Supreme Court notice to Goa Speaker, Shri Singhvi said that court issues notice every day. Notice itself, as you know very well, is a notice to show cause which means that you must give reasons as to why the petition should not be dismissed. That is all that has happened. To a question that BJP has attacked the nuclear deal and demanded that the Indo-US agreement be debated first in the JPC and then Parliament should approve it, Shri Singhvi said that can I ask through you that the BJP also had at least a few years in power in the last 60 years. Under which provision of the constitution, under which provision of the constitution, under which provision of the law, under which provision of convention, practice did they, whenever they signed international treaty, put it to the JPC or Parliament. Is there any such convention in 60 years of Indian republic and I challenge the BJP to point out one such convention. Everybody in India knows that treaty making, agreement making is in the domain of the executive. Despite the absence of any obligation on the govt. the Prime Minister made a statement on the floor of the House. Now if the BJP cannot digest the fact that an incredible, unprecedented, historic agreement has been entered into which benefits India, which they could not get and if they are now trying to fish in troubled waters because of their frustration then they cannot distort the constitution to suit their frustration. They cannot distort the convention of India treaty making to suit their own frustration. If the BJP wants to start applying Rule 184 to every international treaty. I would have one simple advise for them, if and when they come to power after 20 years, let them make a rule that every treaty will be subject to Rule-184 (Calling of JPC) and they are welcome to do it and we are not going to do it.

2178. (6-8-2007) NEW DELHI : The Ministry of Rural Development in a letter had directed the States to make a precise assessment of the status of SGRY works started before March 31st of the current year and to compile full details of such works. The Ministry in its earlier communication has already made it clear for discontinuation of SGRY programmes and their merger with NREGA in the districts where NREGA is in operation. The Ministry has further informed that in case there are still incomplete SGRY works in any district, it is to be ensured that all incomplete SGRY works in NREGA phase II districts are positively closed with effect from 31.8.2007 and no further expenditure is incurred on them. The entire balance funds of SGRY as on 31st August, 07 must be transferred immediately to a separate account created for NREGA works at the district level. Those incomplete works which are permissible under NREGA can be taken as new project under NREGA, after following due process of selection of works as laid down in NREGA. Fresh sanctions for taking up completion of incomplete permissible works as new projects in NREGA shall be subject to permissibility of the project under NREGA and further subject to other terms and conditions indicated below:

2179. (6-8-2007) NEW DELHI : Bioreserves of the country have been allocated Rs. 2502.56 Lakhs during last five financial years as budgetary alloation. Rs. 284.45 Lakhs were allocated during 2001-2002, Rs. 402.676 Lakhs during 2002-03, Rs. 583.11 lakhs during 2003-2004, 578.674 lakhs during 2004-05 and Rs. 653.65 lakhs were allocated during 2005-06. A biosphere reserve is a unique concept which includes one or more protected areas and surrounding lands that are managed to combine both conservation and sustainable use of natural resources.

2180. (6-8-2007) NEW DELHI : A 15 member cycling expedition of Army's Corps of Electronics & Mechanical Engineers (EME) carrying the flame of World Military Games was flagged in by Lt Gen Arvind Mahajan, Director General of EME, here today. Shri Pallam Raju, Minister of State for Defence, flagged off the EME cycling expedition from Leh on 30 July 2007. It passed through very inhospitable terrain of Ladakh & Himachal Pradesh before arriving here today. It will now pass through Agra, Jhansi, Sagar, Hyderabad, Salem and Madurai before arriving at its destination-Kanyakumari, on 18 Aug 2007. The expedition aims at improving the record of 21 days as presently entered in Limca Book of Records for the journey from Leh to Kanyakumari. The cycling expedition is led by Lt Col Vishal Ahlawat. Lt Col Ahlawat was also the expedition leader of a mountaineering expedition in the recent past by the EME to Mount Leo Pargial. The cycling expedition was christened ASHWAMEGH as Ashwa (horse) signifies mechanical energy-a part of EME insignia. This expedition is also carrying the flame of the 4th Military World Games being held in India for the first time at Hyderabad from 14 to 21 October 2007. It is also showcasing Bravo, the mascot of Military World Games. Accordingly it has been rechristined Bravo-EME Endurance Challenge-Ashwamegh. The expedition will be covering a distance of 4249 Kms, through all kinds of terrain and weather conditions, including sub zero temperature at high altitude of Leh and the most challenging passes like Tanglang La (World second highest motorable pass at a height of 17,582 ft), Lachung La, Barlachala, Rohtang pass etc. The other objectives of the expedition are to showcase Army as a career full of adventure and excitement as also to attract the youth to join the Army, and to promote the importance of greening India by aforestation. As planned, the team is progressing well, and is cruising on its target of registering its name of the Corps in Limca Book of Records. The phenomenal progress made so far, speaks volumes of their grit, determination and the well planned out training carried out to ensure success of the laid down objectives. With a view to pay homage to the martyrs of the Nation, Lt Gen Arvind Mahajan, Director General of EME, along with the team laid wreath at Amar Jawan Jyoti, Indian Gate after the flagging in, here today.

2181. (6-8-2007) NEW DELHI : Deptt of Animal Husbandry, Dairying and Fisheries notified an outbreak of Avian influenza in Chingmeirong Village in East Imphal District of Manipur on 25.7.2007. The Central Rapid Response Team of Ministry of Health and F.W. deputed to Imphal is assisting the State Govt. The health statuses of the cullers are being monitored. Today, 338 cullers/supportive staff have been examined and they are under cover of Tamiflu. The population of the infected zone [0-3 Kms] is under active surveillance on daily basis. For such purpose, the State Govt. has deployed health teams consisting of 600 health personnel. In this zone the surveillance teams could cover 44,923 houses [population of 2,34,614] on 4th August,2007. They detected 51 fever/ ARI cases some of which are follow-up of earlier cases. One of them had history of having handled dead/sick birds. These cases are being monitored. Surveillance activity is also continuing with 158 health workers in the 3 to 10 Kms zone. 6,317 houses with a population of 35,206 in Ningthoubung, Top Naoriya, Ganga pat, Takyel mapal, Khabeisoi, Moirang Kampu, Kshetrigao, Malom, Tulihal, Kanto, Khurkhul, Maharabi, Pheidinga, Phumlou, Awangleikinthabi, Tingri, Serjam khunao, Loitang khunao area have been covered. 40 cases of fever/ARI were detected and 2 of them had history of having handled sick/dead birds. In the situational report of this Ministry dated 31st July, 2007 it had been mentioned that the Central Rapid Response Team is monitoring the health status of four persons with fever/ Acute Upper Respiratory Tract infection who had contact with either dead or sick birds. All of them are now afebrile. Their clinical samples have been tested at National Institute of Virology, Pune and National Institute of Communicable Diseases, Delhi and found negative for Avian Influenza virus by RT-PCR [Reverse Transcriptase Polymerase Chain Reaction]. Arrangements have been made in J.N. Hospital, Imphal for isolation and critical care. This is in addition to the critical care facilities available at Regional Institute of Medical Sciences, Imphal. Adequate supply of logistics [Tamiflu (15,000 caps), N-95 masks (1000) and personal protective gears (2000)] have been made available to the State Government. The situation is being closely monitored. As of now, there are no suspected human cases of Avian Influenza. To know the situational report on a day-to-day basis, please log on to http://mohfw.nic.in/aviannew.htm.

2182. (7-8-2007) NEW DELHI : The report of the testing of the samples from Dibyoday Krishi Bigyan Kendra, Khowai under West Tripura District, Tripura has been received from High Security Disease Laboratory (HSADL), Bhopal. The samples have tested negative for Avian Influenza (H5 and H7). The samples from Vawmbuk Village, Saiha District, Mizoram are under test at High Security Animal Disease Laboratory (HSADL), Bhopal.

2183. (7-8-2007) NEW DELHI : 53rd National Film Awards have been announced. As per the recommendations of the Juries, 'Kaalpurush-Memories in the Mist' (Bengali) (directed by Budhadeb Dasgupta) has been declared the Best Feature Film. The Award carries a Swarna Kamal and Rs 50,000 each for Producer and Director of the film. Best Popular Film providing wholesome entertainment is 'Rang De Basanti' (Hindi), (directed by Rakesh Omprakash Mehra). Nargis Dutt Award for the Best Feature Film on National Integration goes to 'Daivanamathil' (Malayalam), (directed by Jayaraj). Indira Gandhi Award for the Best First Film of a Director goes to a film 'Parineeta' (Hindi), (Directed by Vidhu Vinod Chopra). The Award for the best film on social issues goes to 'Iqbal' (Hindi), (Directed by Nagesh Mukunoor). The award for the Best Direction goes to Rahul Dholakia for the film 'Parzania'. Best Actor Award goes to Amitabh Bachchan for his performance in Hindi Film 'Black'. Sarika has been adjudged the best actress award in recognition of her performance in the film 'Parzania' directed by Rahul Dholakia. The Award for the Best Child Artist goes to Sai Kumar for his performance in Telugu film "Bommalata-A Bellyful of Dreams". The Award for the Best Male Playback Singer goes to Naresh Iyer in 'Rang De Basanti' and the Best Female Playback singer award to Shreya Ghoshal for her song in Paheli. The Best Non-Feature Film is "Riding Solo To The Top Of The World" (English), directed by Gaurav.A.Jani. Best Film Critic Award has gone to Baradwaj Rangan. 'Black' directed by Sanjay Leela Bhansali is the best feature film in Hindi.

2184. (7-8-2007) NEW DELHI : The External Commercial Borrowing (ECB) policy is constantly reviewed by the Government in consultation with Reserve Bank of India (RBI) to keep it in tune with the evolving macroeconomic situation, changing market conditions, sectoral requirements, the external sector and the lessons of experience.

2185. (7-8-2007) NEW DELHI : Films Division, Ministry of Information & Broadcasting, is organizing a festival of films commemorating 150th year of first war of independence. Titled 'Swatantrata Filmotsav' the festival will be on in Siri Fort Auditorium from August 11-14, 2007, and would showcase our long and spirited struggle for freedom. A total of 55 films, including 15 feature films and 40 documentaries would be screened during the four-day event. The films selected for screening include classics like 'Anand Math' (Directed by Hemen Gupta), 'Jhansi Ki Rani' (Directed by Sohrab Modi), 'Making of Mahatma' and 'Netaji Subhas Chandra Bose-A Forgotten Hero' (both Directed by Shyam Benegal), 'Train to Pakistan' (Directed by Pamela Rooks) and 'Sardar' (Directed by Ketan Mehta). The festival also has a film on unknown freedom fighters. The festival chronicles the history of the freedom movement meticulously. The very first revolt against the British, which was termed by oppressors as 'Mutiny' is visually presented as the inaugural film '1857-The Beginning' along with a magnum opus of yester years "Jhansi Ki Rani-A Brave Femal Warrior" by Sohrab Modi. The names, faces and events seen in the history books come alive through this film festival. One can have a clear idea about the freedom struggle of India, by watching the films to be screened at this festival. There are thought provoking documentaries, soul stirring feature films that will recreate the history in the minds of viewers.

2186. (7-8-2007) NEW DELHI : The Power Finance Corporation Ltd (PFC) has transferred Sasan Power Ltd. to the selected bidder namely, Reliance Power Ltd. on 7th August, 2007. Reliance Power Ltd. has quoted a levelised tariff of Rs.1.196/ Unit for Sasan UMPP, with 6 Units of 660 MW each. Sasan Power Ltd., under ownership of Reliance Power Ltd, will now be responsible for developing the Sasan Ultra Mega Power Project (6x660 MW) at Sasan, District Sidhi, M.P. along with associated captive coal mines. The Power Purchase Agreement, Escrow and Hypothecation Agreements were signed today. Transfer documents were formally exchanged in the presence of Union Minister of Power Shri Sushilkumar Shinde in a ceremony in New Delhi. The 'Letter of Intent' (LoI) for this Project was issued to M/s. Reliance Power Ltd. on 1st August, 2007. The Government has envisaged a capacity addition of 1,00,000 MW to meet its mission of 'Power For All by 2012'. Achievement of this target requires the development of large capacity projects at the national level to meet the requirements of a number of States. Recognizing the fact that economies of scale leading to cheaper power can be secured through development of large-size power projects using Super Critical Technology (having advantages of low consumption of coal and lower emissions), Ministry of Power, CEA and PFC are working together for development of 9 Ultra Mega Power Projects (UMPPs) through tariff-based competitive bidding out of which Mundra and Sasan UMPPs have now been transferred to successful bidders. These 9 UMPPs, each with a capacity of about 4000 MW, would also have scope for further expansion. These UMPPs will add about 36,000 MW within a span of 6-8 years and help in achievement of the targets for faster capacity addition. The fund requirement for the proposed 9 projects is estimated to be around Rs.1,60,000 crores. These projects would be awarded to developers on Build, Own, Operate (BOO) basis. The size of these projects being large, they will meet the power needs of a number of States through transmission of power on regional and national basis. In order to enhance investors' confidence, reduce risk perception and get good response to competitive bidding, Shell Companies have been set up as wholly-owned subsidiaries of PFC to facilitate tie-up of inputs, linkages, clearances and tie-ups including water, land and power selling arrangements, obtaining environmental clearance, etc. prior to award of these projects to successful bidders. Ministry of Power has been playing an important role as a facilitator to coordinate with Ministries concerned and State Governments for ensuring coal linkages, environment and forest clearances, financial closure, execution of PPAs and proper payment security mechanism with State Govt / State Utilities and monitoring the progress of Shell Companies with regard to pre-determined timelines.

2187. (7-8-2007) NEW DELHI : Steel Authority of India Ltd (SAIL) has decided to implement an Integrity Pact with bidders/vendors for all fresh purchases and contracts valued at Rs. 100 crores and above. Demonstrating its commitment towards enhancing transparency and accountability in its systems, SAIL has taken this significant step at a time when it is in the process of finalising expansion & modernisation projects that involve thousands of crores of rupees. The system will come into effect from August 16, 2007 and will ensure that both SAIL and bidders bear the onus of ensuring that tendering and award of contracts are done in a free and fair manner. The pact shall also be a contractual agreement between SAIL and vendors/purchasers committing both sides to adhere to certain prescribed ethical norms. The pact also has provisions for payment of damages and other retributive actions in case any of the prescribed norms are proven to be violated. Independent External Monitors (IEMs) will oversee the execution of the pact, which will help to increase transparency and provide a level playing field for both SAIL as well as bidders. In this regard, the Central Vigilance Commission has approved the appointment of Mr. P. Shankar, former Central Vigilance Commissioner, and Dr. P.L. Agarwal, former SAIL Chairman, as IEMs. The salient features of the pact have been vetted by the Additional Solicitor General of India.

2188. (7-8-2007) NEW DELHI : The Ministry of Rural Development has sanctioned the release of second instalment amounting to Rs.1.20 crore to the Zilla Panchayat, Chikmagalur Distt. of Karnataka for implementation of Centrally Sponsored Scheme "Drought Prone Areas Programme (DPAP) under "Hariyali Guidelines". The Ministry of Rural Development has initiated `Hariyali' for empowering the village community through Panchayati Raj Institutions (PRIs) to undertake the area development progammes on watershed basis with financial and technical support from the Government. Under this initiative, all the on-going area development programmes, such as Integrated Wasteland Development Programmes (IWDP), Drought Prone Areas Programme (DPAP) and Desert Development Programme (DDP) are to be implemented through the PRIs. New projects under the aforesaid area development programmes are implemented under `Hariyali Guidelines' from 1st April, 2003. Special emphasis is given to rain water harvesting and desilting of ponds under watershed projects. Under Hariyali programme of the Ministry, the efforts have resulted in bringing 87 lakh hectres of wasteland under green cover.

2189. (7-8-2007) NEW DELHI : The Union Government is providing high priority to the development and maintenance of roads in the North-Eastern Region. 28 National Highways of about 6,880 kms of total length are serving the North-Eastern Region. Though the density of National Highways in the North-Eastern Region is higher than the all-India average, road connectivity in the Region has remained inadequate due to under-development of roads of lower category. The potential of the region for the socio-economic development could not, therefore, be exploited fully. Many District Headquarter Towns lack even 2-lane road connectivity. Several backward and remote areas of the region could not be opened up to economic development because of lack of roads. The roads in the North-Eastern Region also acquire higher importance as railway facilities in the hilly areas is often not found feasible and cost-effective. The Union Ministry of Shipping, Road Transport & Highways has undertaken a number of programmes to improve existing roads as well as to construct new roads in all the States of the North Eastern India. These programmes are the biggest ever undertaken in this region, in addition to the yearly funds spent by the Centre on the maintenance and improvement of National Highways and other roads. These programmes are also in addition to substantial investment being made by Central Government on upgrading several State Roads through Ministry of Development of North Eastern Region and construction of rural roads under Pradhan Mantri Gram Sadak Yojna (PMGSY) by the Ministry of Rural Development.

2190. (7-8-2007) NEW DELHI : Ganga Action Plan Phase-I was the first attempt of Government to clean the river Ganga. The plan was formulated on the basis of a comprehensive survey of the Ganga basin carried out by the central Pollution Control Board (CPCB) in 1984. According to this survey, the total sewage generated from 25 class I towns in 1985 was estimated as 1340 millions litres per day (mld). Out of these pollution abatement works to 882 mld were taken up. To accomplish this task a total of 2061 projects of pollution abatement covering 25 towns in 3 states were sanctioned at a cost of Rs. 462 crores. 259 projects have been completed and rest of the projects which were delayed due to litigation have been taken care by the state government. Since GAP Phase-I did not cover the pollution load of Ganga fully, GAP Phase-II was approved from 1993 on wards. Out of a total of 271 sanctioned schemes, 87 schemes have been completed so far and the rest are in progress. The is being implemented in 16 towns covering 5 states. GAP Phases-II includes plans for Yamuna, Gomti, Damodar and Mahananda besides Ganga river.

2191. (7-8-2007) NEW DELHI : The legal agreements for World Bank assisted Himachal Pradesh State Roads Project were signed between Government of India and World Bank, here today. The agreements were signed by Shri Madhusudan Prasad, Joint Secretary, Department of Economic Affairs, Ministry of Finance on behalf of the Government of India, Ms. Isabel M. Guerrero, Country Director, World Bank on behalf of the World Bank and Shri Subhash Chander Negi, Principal Secretary, Public Works Department on behalf of the Government of Himachal Pradesh. The signing of the documents was done in the presence of Sh.P.Chidambaram, Union Finance Minister and Sh.Virbhadra Singh, Chief Minister of Himachal Pradesh. The objective of the proposed project is to reduce transport costs and to improve traffic flows on priority segments of the core road network of Himachal Pradesh. The total cost of the project is estimated at US$ 303.43 million with World Bank assistance of US$ 220 million. The balance amount of US$ 83.43 million would be met by the State Government.

2192. (7-8-2007) NEW DELHI : The Nation River Conservation Plan (NRCP) covers 34 rivers with works spread over 160 towns located in 20 states in the country. This plan do not cover Ganga, Yamuna, Gomti and Damodar rivers. They have been covered under Ganga Action Plans and Yamuna Action Plans. The total approved cost of NRCP is Rs. 4783 crores approximately. At present 622 of the 957 sanctioned schemes have been completed. A sewage treatment capacity of 1939 mld out of an approved capacity of 5377 mld has been created under this plan.

2193. (7-8-2007) ONGOLE: CPI State secretary, K Narayana has demanded the Government to cancel the lease of 565 acres of land given to a salt factory at Chinnaganjam village in Prakasam district and distribute the same among landless poor in 11 surrounding villages. Mr. Narayana visited Chinnaganjam village and inspected the lands given on lease to Anand Granites for establishing a salt factory. He later led 1000 people to Ongole where they staged a dharna seeking pattas for the land. They contended that the salt factory would pollute the drinking water sources. As Gundlakamma project and modernisation of Nagarjuna Sagar canals are on the anvil, they said these lands could be used for paddy cultivation. They threatened to launch mass hunger strike at Ongole from August 22 if the problem was not solved in the meantime. As the police did not allow Mr. Narayana and MLC Jalli Wilson to meet the Collector, they squatted on the road. The police later relented and allowed them to meet Collector K Devanand and submit a memorandum to him. Later speaking to newspersons, Mr. Narayana said the TDP Government had granted the lease to Anand Granites for setting up the salt factory at Chinnaganjam in 2000. When the local people launched agitation against the move, police opened fire killing two persons. As the Opposition leader in the Assembly then, Y S Rajasekhara Reddy visited the village and consoled the families. He later spoke for two hours in the Assembly demanding the TDP Government to cancel the lease and distribute the land among the poor. But after coming to power, Dr. Rajasekhara Reddy renewed the lease ignoring the pleas of the people. Mr. Narayana came down heavily on the Congress and TDP for saying something while in Opposition and doing the opposite after they come to power.

2194. (7-8-2007) NEW DELHI : Thirty two persons were injured when two engines and four coaches of Jodhpur-Howrah Express (2308Dn), which was on its way from Jodhpur to Howrah, derailed at Juhi yards, 8 kilometres form Kanpur station in Uttar Pradesh under Allahabad division of North Central Railway at about 12.25 PM today. All the 32 injured persons, out of which seven were grievously, were taken to Railway hospital and to civil hospitals at Hallot and Ursula in Kanpur. Accident Relief Train along with Railway medical team reached the accident spot immediately. General Manager, North Central Railway and DRM Allahabad Division have also reached at the accident site from Allahabad. The Jodhpur-Howrah Express with additional three coaches resumed its onward journey to Howrah. Railways have made on the spot payment of an ex-gratia of Rs. 5000/- for grievous injured persons and Rs. 500/- for those who received simple injuries in the derailment.. Shri R.K.Kardam, Commissioner Railway Safety, Northern Circle will conduct the enquiry into the accident. Normal traffic has been restored on this affected section.

2195. (7-8-2007) NEW DELHI : Shri Kamal Nath, Union Minister of Commerce and Industry and Ms. Doris Leuthard, Federal Councillor, Department of Economic Affairs of the Swiss Confederation, signed a Memorandum of Understanding on intellectual property, here today. After signing the MOU, Shri Kamal Nath stated that the MoU would benefit closer cooperation between the two countries in fostering the protection and promotion of intellectual property rights. The implementation of this memorandum will be jointly by the Office of the Controller General of Patents, Designs & Trade Marks, Department of Industrial Policy and Promotion under the Ministry of Commerce & Industry, Government of India and the Swiss Federal Institute of Intellectual Property.

2196. (7-8-2007) HYDERABAD: A CPI delegation on Monday submitted a memorandum to Home Minister K. Jana Reddy seeking the release of over 30 tribals, who were arrested by the police from the agency areas of Chintapalli Assembly constituency in Visakhapatnam district, on charges of supporting Maoists in their recent attacks. The delegation comprising, MLAs G. Demudu and Palla Venkat Reddy, told Mr. Reddy that 32 persons were lodged in Visakhapatnam and Rajahmundry Central Jails, after false cases booked against them. They were detained under non-bailable sections. They included a sarpanch of CPI, M. Narayana Rao. A press release of Mr. Demudu, who represents Chintapalli, said Mr. Reddy promised to issue directions for the release of the arrested persons.

2197. (7-8-2007) NEW DELHI : India has moved up two places in global ranking to 5th place in production of crude steel. An expert committee set up by the Ministry of Steel which went into the issue of under reporting of capacity and production data has revised the production figures for crude steel in calendar year 2006 to 49.45 million tonnes as against 44 million tonnes in the pre-revised data. Earlier India held the 7th rank among the global steel producers. The revised figures for crude steel production in 2006-07 is pegged at 50.71 million tonnes and that of finished steel at 51.90 million tonnes. It was perceived for quite some time that estimates of induction furnace and re-rolling sectors were on lower-side, owing mostly due to under-reporting of crude steel data by the electric induction furnace route of production. This in turn has affected production figures for semi-finished and re-rolling (long product) sectors. At the same time, flat steel products have faced the problem of double counting due to inclusion of standalone finished output as also its purchased finished steel input in total finished steel production.

2198. (7-8-2007) NEW DELHI : The Ministry of Tribal Affairs provided Rs. 15.90 crores as fellowship to more than 600 Tribal students during 2006-07 for taking up higher studies. The fellowship provided under Rajiv Gandhi National Fellowship Scheme for pursuing higher studies such as M.Phil and Ph.D at universities, institutions recognized by UGC. Each year more than 600 students are provided the fellowship for the maximum duration of five years. The scheme is implemented through UGC on behalf of the Ministry of Tribal Affairs. Financial assistance of Rs. 8000/- per month is provided for initial two years to Junior Research Fellow and Rs. 9000/- per month for remaining period of the fellowship. Beside this fellowship amount, contingency fund for humanities and social sciences is also provided at the rate of Rs. 10,000/- per annum for initial two years of the fellowship and Rs. 20,500/- per annum for remaining period of the research work. In the case of sciences the Contingency fund is provided Rs. 12,000/- per annum for initial two years and Rs. 25,000/- per annum for remaining tenure of the fellowship. The Government also provides assistance to the host institute for providing infrastructure. Amount of the departmental assistance is Rs. 3000/- per annum per student. An additional assistance of Rs. 1000/- per month is provided for escorts or reader assistance in cases of physically and visually handicapped candidates.

2199. (7-8-2007) NEW DELHI : Ministry of Tourism extends Central Financial Assistance to the State Governments/UTs for Product/Infrastructure Development of Destinations and Circuits. During the Xth Five Year Plan period a double-pronged strategy of upgrading the tourism infrastructure and vigorous marketing under the banner of 'Incredible India Campaign' was followed to position India as a global brand. During this period, Ministry of Tourism sanctioned 1160 projects amounting to Rs.2011.68 crore to various States and UTs. During 11th Five Year Plan (2007-2012) Ministry of Tourism propose to continue supporting creation of world class infrastructure in the country so that existing tourism products can be further improved and expanded to meet new market requirements and enhance the competitiveness of India as a tourist destination. In consultation with the State Governments and UTs the Ministry of Tourism have identified several tourist circuits and destinations for integrated development. During the first four months of the current financial year (2007-08) Ministry has sanctioned Central Financial Assistance for 27 Projects amounting to over Rs.70.00 crore. Some of the interesting projects are related to conservation and promotion of heritage destinations at Sanchi, Chettinath and Srirangam. Ministry have sanctioned projects for development and promotion of eco tourism at Dongargarh, Kodar (Chhattisgarh), Pathiramnal Bio Park (Kerala) and Bungus Valley (J&K). Kargil and Drass-Panikhar are being developed as tourist destinations. Financial assistance has been extended for development of Rural Tourism projects in the States of Gujarat, Jharkhand, J&K, Nagaland, Orissa, Uttar Pradesh and West Bengal. During the current year the Ministry is providing financial assistance for some mega projects for integrated development of circuits and destinations.

2200. (7-8-2007) NEW DELHI : The total import of sensitive items for the period April-June 07 has been Rs.4877 crores as compared to Rs.4371 crores during the corresponding period last year thereby showing an increase of 11.6%. The gross import of all commodities during same period of current year was Rs.226321 crores as compared to Rs.185988 crores during the same period of last year. Thus import of sensitive items constitute 2.4% and 2.2% of the gross imports during last year and current year respectively. Imports of fruits & vegetables (including nuts), products of SSI, spices, marble & Granite, Tea & Coffee and milk & milk products have shown a decline at broad group level during the period. Imports of items viz. edible oil, cotton & silk, automobiles, rubber and Alcoholic beverages have shown increase during the period under reference. In the edible oil segment, the import has increased from Rs.2407 crores last year to Rs.2802 crores for the corresponding period of this year. The import of both crude oil as well as refined oil have gone up by 15.7% and 30.9% respectively. The increase in edible oil import is mainly due to significant growth in import of Crude palm oil and its fractions, which has gone up by 28%. Imports of sensitive items from Indonesia, China P RP, Brazil, Germany, Japan, Thailand, Australia etc. have gone up while those from Argentina, United States of America, Cote D' Ivoire, Malaysia, Benin, Sri Lanka DSR, Egypt A RP etc. have shown a decrease.

2201. (8-8-2007) NEW DELHI : A meeting of the Secretaries of Water Resources of India and Bangladesh was held on August 7-8, 2007 to discuss pending issues between both the countries related to Water Resources Sector. The Indian delegation was led by Smt. Gauri Chatterji, Secretary, Ministry of Water Resources, Government of India. The Bangladesh delegation was led by Mr. Syed Mohammad Zobaer, Secretary, Ministry of Water Resources, Government of the People's Republic of Bangladesh. In pursuance of directions of 36th meeting of the Indo-Bangladesh Joint Rivers Commission (JRC), held in September, 2005 both sides discussed and exchanged the principles for sharing of waters of Teesta and other common rivers which would be put up before JRC for further consideration. It was agreed that further details would be worked out at Technical level headed by the Members, JRC of the two countries at the earliest for consideration in the next JRC meeting. Both sides also discussed other issues relating to River Bank Protection works, Lift Irrigation Schemes, Drinking Water Supply schemes on common border rivers and Dredging of river Ichamati in common reach. Both sides agreed to exchange the constructions details to execute these works in order to bring transparency and remove apprehensions from either side and recommended to Joint River Commission for consideration. Both sides expressed satisfaction on the outcome of the meeting. The leader of the Bangladesh delegation thanked the leader of the Indian delegation for the gracious hospitality accorded to him and his delegation members.

2202. (8-8-2007) NEW DELHI : The first Global Agro-Industries Forum (GAIF) will be organised in New Delhi from 8 to 11 April 2008. Union Minister of Agriculture, Consumer Affairs, Food & Public Distribution Shri Sharad Pawar and the Director General, Food and Agriculture Organisation of the United Nations (FAO), Dr. Jacques Diouf jointly made this announcement here today. The Indian government, FAO and the United Nations Industrial Development Organisation (UNIDO) are jointly organising the conference. Shri Pawar described the organisation of the conference as a timely initiative and expressed hope that the role of agro-industries in enhancing productivity and profitability in agriculture, employment generation and poverty alleviation, especially in developing countries would receive requisite attention. Dr. Diouf, who is presently on a three-day visit to India, stated that hosting this global event in New Delhi is a testimony to India's central place in the world agricultural scenario and that it will further strengthen FAO's and UNIDO's engagement with the country. A key challenge is to develop agro-industries and associated enterprises that are inclusive of smaller scale producers and processors and that also deliver better products at lower prices thus directly helping poor consumers. While high-income countries add, on average, US$180 of value by processing one tonne of agricultural products, developing countries generate only US$40 of value per tonne.

2203. (8-8-2007) NEW DELHI : Since Independence, technology has played a significant role in the development of India. In recent years, Information Communication Technology (ICT) has come to the forefront, as a key enabler of development. In order to harness the benefits of ICT, the Government of India set up the Department of Information Technology on October 15, 1999, from the erstwhile Department of Electronics. The advancement of Information Technology has made a profound impact on the economy. The total electronics productions of the IT industry have gone up from Rs. 173.0 crore in 1971-72 to an estimated figure of Rs. 245,600 crore in 2006-07 The total electronics hardware production has gone up from Rs. 173.0 crore during 1971-72 to Rs. 66,000 crore whereas the software production has gone up from almost nil in 1971-72 to an estimated amount of Rs. 179,600 crore in 2006-07. The software and services industry has emerged as one of the fastest growing sectors in the economy with a CAGR exceeding 48% in turnover and 52% in export over the last decade. The software and ITES exports from India grew from US$ 12.9 billion in the year 2003-04 to US$ 23.6 billion in 2005-06. It is estimated that total software and ITES exports from India exceed US$ 31.3 billion during the year 2006-07. Software and services exports are likely to beat forecasts and exceed 32 per cent in dollar terms during the year 2006-07. Export revenues from ITES-BPO are estimated to grow from US $ 6.3 billion in year 2005-06 to US $ 8.3 billion in year 2006-07, a year-on-year growth of over 31 percent was achieved. IT success story has highlighted India's attractiveness as preferred investment destination. Revenue from the domestic market is also expected to grow to about US $ 8.4 billion in 2006-07 as compared to US $ 6.7 billion in 2005-06 growths of about 25%. The total IT Software and Services employment expected to reach 1.6 million mark in 2006-07 (excluding employment in Hardware sector), as compared to 1.293 million in 2005-06 an anticipated growth of about 26%. The indirect employment attributed to the sector is about 3.0 million. Industry's Contribution to GDP has gone up from 4.8 percent in 2005-06 to 5.4 percent in 2006-07.

2204. (8-8-2007) NEW DELHI : Council for Advancement of Peoples Action and Rural Technology (CAPART) functions as an autonomous body under the aegis of Ministry of Rural Development with it's headquarter in Delhi. Established in 1986 CAPART guides and finances rural development projects which will result in sustainable development of the rural masses and improving their life styles. The mandate of council is to promote and facilitate rural action and use of appropriate technology for the benefit and betterment of the rural poor. Till March 31, 2007 it has assisted 25,510 projects and disbursed a sum of Rs. 956.53 crore involving 10,982 Voluntary organizations. Since its inception CAPART has assisted 25,510 projects and disbursed a sum of Rs. 956.53 crore involving 10,982 Voluntary Organizations. During the year 2006-07, 469 projects involving Rs. 67.51 crore have been sanctioned and Rs. 38.83 crore were released. CAPART during last two decades has been involved in capacity building of the voluntary sector and alleviation of the poverty in rural India with courage and commitment. It has restructure, re-oriented, re-positioned and re-defined its goal and future vision in meeting with contemporary rural situations.

2205. (8-8-2007) NEW DELHI : The Minister for Women and Child Development Smt. Renuka Chowdhury has said that her Ministry will prepare an action plan in consultation with the Indian Army for the welfare of the children of nomads who were affected by the Kargil war and other insurgency related incidents in the State of Jammu and Kashmir. The Minister assured all necessary support from the Ministry of Women and Child Development for providing basic services to the affected children in the State. 25 children, some of them accompanied by their guardians, from Kargil called on Smt. Chowdhury at her residence and interacted with the Minister over Breakfast. The group comprises of children of nomads whose families stay in the Drass region for about 4-5 months every year during the summer season and for the rest of the year they stay in lower hills and plains. Due to this reasons the children's education suffers as no schools are available in approximately 40 sq. km area where they reside in the summer. The Indian Army has set up static as well as mobile schools for these children and imparts education to them during their stay. These schools provide education from classes I to VIII and are affiliated and give education as per NCERT guidelines. The children who are on 14 days tour of the country, informed the Minister that they are very happy with their tour and would now visit Agra, Phagwara and some other cities of the country.

2206. (8-8-2007) NEW DELHI : Congress Spokesperson Smt Jayanti Natarajan said that the Monsoon Session of Parliament will begin on 10th August and there will be of course a new Chairman be elected by that time. During the monsoon session of Parliament we would call upon the Opposition to kindly play a constructive role, discuss many of the important issues that await discussion in Parliament in a constructive and cooperative manner. We would also call upon them to cooperate in the running of the House with the government and not allow the time of the House to be wasted so that this session of Parliament will have fruitful discussions and will shed and generate a great deal of light and no heat. To a question on Left's statement on nuclear agreement, Smt. Natarajan said that Prime Minister has very clearly spelt out the contents of the discussion and we are very confident that the government will under no circumstances face any kind of problem as envisaged by the Left or by anybody else and will always act in the best interest of the nation To a question on the implementation of the Sri Krishna report by the Maharashtra government, Smt Natarajan said that there is absolutely no worry about the Sri Krishna report implementation but regarding the actual implementation, and I think that this question will be best answered by the Maharashtra government. To a question whether Left's decision can destablise the UPA government ? Smt Natarajan said that there is absolutely no question of this government being destablised. This government will last its entire term and we are very much confident that the Prime Minister and the government will be able to convince the Left and that whatever steps have been taken, have been taken in the best interest of the nation and of the people of our country. To a question whether this treaty is negotiable or not? Smt Natarajan said that this is something which the PM already has spoken about and I would not like to add to it and whether it is negotiable or not is for the government that has to go into it. I will not be able to speak whether it is negotiable or not. To a question that Left and Opposition want all international treaties to be ratified by the Parliament, Smt. Natarajan said that this is a very complicated question with both national and international ramifications. For example, if a particular government enters into a treaty on behalf of the entire country and if a government that follows within a few months cancels that treaty, then it would lead to international ramifications. Therefore, this is a very serious matter and it is not a question of what Congress Party is going to say. This is a question which will have to be discussed very seriously by all the UPA allies and if the Left has made this demand, it will be discussed within the UPA and a view will be taken. To a question that judicial powers be given to all Commissions set-up for its implementation, Smt. Natarajan said that whatever powers that are given to the Commissions have been carefully considered by the government at the time when the Commission was set-up. If these powers need to be reviewed, I think they will be reviewed by the government, if necessary. All Commissions have a particular power and particular exercise of power. If greater powers are required these need to be reviewed on demand being made to the government and to the Parliament. To a question that Supreme Court continued the stay on the issue of reservation, Smt. Natarajan said that the matter is still open for argument and it is not over yet. And since the matter is subjudice, we will continue to present our argument to the court.

2207. (8-8-2007) NEW DELHI : Her Excellency Khunying Khaisri Sriaroon, Minister of Culture of Thailand called on the Tourism and Culture Minister Smt. Ambika Soni here today. During their half-an-hour meeting both the leaders underlined the importance of common heritage between the two countries and stressed the need to further strengthen the bilateral cultural ties. Both the leaders felt that there should be a timeframe for implementing the cultural exchange programme signed between the two countries recently. Smt. Ambika Soni said she wants more tourists from Thailand to come to India to experience the rich Indian cultural diversity. She conveyed to the visiting dignitary the steps being taken by the Government of India to promote Buddhist Circuit in India among South East Asian tourists. She said Lord Buddha's teachings are increasingly becoming more and more relevant in today's society. The Thai leader said her country is planning to open a Thai Cultural Centre in India and expressed hope that soon India will also open an Indian Cultural Centre in Thailand.

2208. (8-8-2007) NEW DELHI : Deptt of Animal Husbandry, Dairying and Fisheries notified an outbreak of avian influenza in Chingmeirong Village in East Imphal District of Manipur on 25.7.2007. The Central Rapid Response Team of Ministry of Health and F.W. deputed to Imphal is assisting the State Govt. The health status of the cullers are being monitored. Today, 359 cullers/supportive staff have been examined and they are under cover of Tamiflu. The population of the infected zone [0-3 Kms] are under active surveillance on daily basis. For such purpose, the State Govt. has deployed health teams consisting of 600 health personnel. In this zone the surveillance teams could cover 44,722 houses [population of 2,33,981] on 6th August, 2007. They detected 45 fever/ ARI cases some of which are follow-up of earlier cases. These cases are being monitored. Surveillance activity is also continuing with 152 health workers in the 3 to 10 Kms zone. 5,579 houses with a population of 31,536 in Khumbong, Naoriya, Pakhanglakpa, Topkhabi, Keibi, Langthabalphuramkhong, Mongsangei, Takkhokmakha, Nandeibam leikai, Okram leikai areas have been covered. 16 cases of fever/ARI were detected and none of them had history of having handled sick/dead birds. Arrangements have been made in J.N. Hospital, Imphal for isolation and critical care. This is in addition to the critical care facilities available at Regional Institute of Medical Sciences, Imphal. Adequate supply of logistics [Tamiflu (15,000 caps), N-95 masks (1000) and personal protective gears (2000)] have been made available to the State Government. The situation is being closely monitored. As of now, there is no suspected human cases of Avian Influenza.

2209. (8-8-2007) NEW DELHI : The Government has appointed Shri Kuldeep Goyal at present working as Director (Plg & NS) on Bharat Sanchar Nigam Ltd (BSNL) Board as Chairman and Managing Director on the Board of BSNL for a period of five years with effect from the date of assumption of charge or till his date of superannuation or until further orders, whichever event occurs earlier.

2210. (8-8-2007) NEW DELHI : The Board of Approval of the Special Economic Zones (SEZs) met here today to consider proposals for setting up of Special Economic Zones and also approve other miscellaneous requests pertaining to SEZs. In this meeting, 8 applications for setting up SEZs, including 3 proposals for conversion of in-principle approvals to formal approvals were considered. The Board recommended grant of 4 Formal approvals and 2 in-principle approvals.

2211. (8-8-2007) NEW DELHI : The Ministry of Environment and Forests invites nomination for Amrita Devi Bishnoi Wildlife Protection Award. It has been instituted for protecting wildlife which carries a cash award of Rs. One lakh apart from citation and medallion. This annual award is given to an individual/institution pertaining to rural communities for significant contribution in the field of wild life protection, which is recognized as having shown exemplary courage and valour or having done some exemplary work for the protection of wild life in the country. There is no age limit for the individuals.

2212. (8-8-2007) NEW DELHI : The Department of Posts will be releasing two stamps tomorrow August 9, 2007 to Commemorate the First War of Independence of 1857. The Department of Posts will be releasing two stamps of Rupee Five each. The stamps and the miniature sheet artistically depict the two pitched battles at Kanpur and Lucknow focusing on unknown soldiers. The First Day Cover depicts the dawn of the new nationalism symbolized by the rising sun; the guns whose greased cartridges provided the immediate catalyst. The First Day Cover also depicts a part of the constitution drafted by the sepoys. The two maxim cards depict war scenes, adopted from murals and tribal paintings from Madhya Pradesh.

2213. (8-8-2007) NEW DELHI : The Consultative Committee of the Members of Parliament on Power met today in New Delhi to discuss the capacity addition for the Eleventh Plan. Addressing the Members, the Chairman of the Committee and Union Power Minister, Shri Sushilkumar Shinde said that though electricity is a Concurrent subject the decline in the financial and operational health of State Electricity Boards and utilities has made the Centre play an important role not only in the generation segment but also in areas such as rural electrification which were hitherto in the exclusive domain of the States. He informed the Members that the Central Electricity Authority has assessed that a capacity addition of about 1,00,000 MW is required during the 10th and 11th Plan periods. Based on the 10th Plan actual capacity addition of 21,180 MW, a capacity addition of 78,000 MW comprising of 40,000 MW in Central sector, 28,000 MW in State sector and 10,000 MW in private sector has been proposed during the 11th Plan. The Minister said that out of 78,000 MW, project of 1,800 MW have been commissioned and projects of 51,000 MW (that is 65% of the proposed capacity) are already under construction and for the remaining projects it is expected that the ordering process would be completed by December 2007. Shri Shinde also pointed out that while many leading countries have several indigenous suppliers who individually have more than three and a half times capacity in comparison to the equipment manufacturer in India. He, therefore, emphasized the need to strengthen the domestic base of manufacturer to augment indigenous capability to deliver more power project equipment. Members, while expressing concern over the enhanced target for the 11th Plan, came out with several suggestions for implementing the capacity addition plan for achieving the goal of power for all by 2012. These included adequate planning, regular monitoring, less dependency on equipment manufacturer and coordinated efforts.

2214. (8-8-2007) NEW DELHI : Public Sector Undertakings under the Ministry of Steel will spend Rs. 230 crore on Corporate Social Responsibility during 2007-08. Out of this the major contributions are from Steel Authority of India Limited (Rs.100 crore), Rashtriya Ispat Nigam Limited (Rs.27 crore) and National Mineral Development Corporation (Rs.89 crore). Secretary Ministry of Steel Shri R.S.Pandey who reviewed the progress of the initiatives for implementation of the CSR activities at a meeting here urged the PSUs to ensure implementation of the planned programmes in a time bound manner. The Secretary said, administrative mechanism for CSR programmes should be strengthened and suitable officials be given administrative and financial powers to streamline implementation. PSUs whose top executives attended the review meeting included SAIL, RINL, NMDC, MECON, MOIL, MTC, KIOCL, HSCL, BRL and FSNL. Under the schemes, about 126 villages to be known as 'Model Steel Villages' will be provided with necessary amenities and constructive programmes to bring about all round improvement of the villages including promotion of steel use. Of these SAIL will be responsible for 79 villages, NMDC for 40, MOIL for two and RINL for five villages. Beginning with the peripheral areas around their respective plants, the

PSUs will gradually target the CSR activities to cover the areas populated by the SCs, STs and weaker sections of the society, so as to cover all the districts in the country within the next 2-3 years. It was also resolved that the PSUs will also be organizing around 150 health camps in about 100 districts in the country during the current fiscal year 2007-08. Such camps have already been organized successfully by Bokaro Steel Plant in Jharkhand and Bihar. In addition, the PSUs will also be providing assistance to National, State and reputed local organizations involved in the field of arts, culture, tourism, sports and other allied areas. For these the steel PSUs will be shortly drawing up a detailed action plan.

2215. (8-8-2007) NEW DELHI : Retail prices of essential commodities monitored by the Department of Consumer Affairs at four metropolitan cities have remained stable or shown mixed trend in the week ending 3.8.2007. Prices of wheat, rice, gram, sugar, vanaspati, and salt were steady over the week. Prices declined in the case of tea by Rs. 2 per kg at Delhi, potato by Rs. 1.50 per kg at Delhi, 50 paise each at Mumbai and Kolkata and onion by 50 paise per kg each at Delhi and Mumbai. Prices of atta increased Re. 1 per kg at Kolkatta, gram dal by Re 1 per kg and milk by Re. 1 per litre at Delhi, tur dal by Rs. 2 per kg at Mumbai and by Re. 1 at Kolkata, groundnut oil by Rs. 4 per kg and mustard oil by Rs. 2 per kg at Kolkata. At Delhi prices remained steady over the week and month, while there has been rise in prices over one year period. Prices of groundnut oil increased from Rs. 85 per kg to Rs. 107, tur from Rs. 33 per kg to Rs. 39, vanaspati from Rs. 50 per kg to Rs. 59 and milk from Rs. 16 per litre to Rs. 19. Prices of sugar declined from Rs. 21 per kg to Rs. 16 over the year. As on 31.7.2007 public sector agencies have contracted import of 10.40 lakh tonne pulses of which 2.43 lakh tonne has already reached Indian ports. The imported pulses include urad, moong, dunpeas, masoor, chickpeas, yellow peas and channa.

2216. (8-8-2007) NEW DELHI : The total approximate earnings of Indian Railways on originating basis during 1st April-31st July 2007 were Rs. 21787.89 crore compared to Rs. 19718.67 crore during the same period last year, registering an increase of 10.49 per cent. The total goods earnings have gone up from Rs. 13328.01 during 1st April-31st July 2006 to Rs. 14593.02 crore during 1st April-31st July 2007, showing an increase of 9.49 per cent. The total passenger revenue earnings during first four months of the financial year 2007-08 were Rs. 6331.14 crore compared to Rs. 5677.59 crore during the same period last year, registering an increase of 11.51 per cent. The revenue earnings from other coaching amounted to Rs. 611.88 crore during April-July 2007 compared to Rs. 521.12 crore during the same period last year, showing an increase of 17.42 per cent. The total sundry earnings have gone up from Rs. 191.95 crore during April-July 2006 to Rs. 251.85 crore during April-July 2007, registering an increase of 31.21 percent. The total approximate number of passengers booked during April-July 2007 were 2206.55 million compared to 2094.02 million during the same period last year, showing an increase of 5.37 per cent. In the suburban and non-suburban sectors, the number of passengers booked during April-July 2007 were 1196.67 million and 1009.88 million compared to 1138.52 million and 955.50 million during the same period last year, an increase of 5.11 per cent and 5.69 per cent respectively.

2217. (8-8-2007) NEW DELHI : The Prime Minister, Dr. Manmohan Singh, chaired a meeting to review issues pertaining to availability of funds for fertilizer subsidy. The Prime Minister directed the Union Finance Ministry and Fertilizer Ministry to ensure that adequate funds are available to meet the disbursal requirements for fertilizer subsidy. The Prime Minister said that while the existing subsidy system may have to be reviewed in the future, the Government was committed to the present system and will ensure that adequate funds are available to meet the requirements this year. The Prime Minister's Office will resolve matters in this regard. The meeting was attended by Agriculture Minister, Shri Sharad Pawar, Finance Minister, Shri P. Chidambaram, Fertilizer Minister, Shri Ram Vilas Paswan and Principal Secretary to the Prime Minister, Shri T.K.A.Nair.

2218. (8-8-2007) NEW DELHI : Grant-in-aid amounting to Rs. 12.22 crore has been released by the Ministry of Rural Development to Gujarat Water Supply & Sewerage Board, Gandhinagar during 2007-08 towards first instalment of ARWSP-DDP funds against provisional allocation of Rs.24.45 crore. The release is being made for execution/completion of schemes to provide safe drinking water facilities to rural habitations and schools under the Centrally Sponsored ARWSP-DDP Areas as per the priorities indicated in the Guidelines for implementation of Rural Water supply Programme under Rajiv Gandhi National Drinking Water Mission (RGNDWM). The terms and conditions for the release of ARWSP-DDP funds are included in the Guidelines for implementation of Rural Water supply Programme

2219. (8-8-2007) NEW DELHI : An amount of Rs. 2.01 crore has been released under Haryali III to the Ranga Reddy District of Andhra Pradesh during the year 2007-08 for the implementation of Centrally Sponsored Scheme of "Drought Prone Areas Programme (DPAP) under "Hariyali Guidelines". The Ministry of Rural Development has initiated `Hariyali' for empowering the village community through Panchayati Raj Institutions (PRIs) to undertake the area development progammes on watershed basis with financial and technical support from the Government. Under this initiative, all the on-going area development programmes, such as Integrated Wasteland Development Programmes (IWDP), Drought Prone Areas Programme (DPAP) and Desert Development Programme (DDP) are to be implemented through the PRIs. New projects under the aforesaid area development programmes are implemented under `Hariyali Guidelines' from 1st April, 2003. Special emphasis is given to rain water harvesting and desilting of ponds under watershed projects. Under Hariyali programme of the Ministry, the efforts have resulted in bringing 87 lakh hectres of wasteland under green cover.

2220. (8-8-2007) NEW DELHI : Shri Shyam Benegal one of the pioneers of new Indian Cinema has been selected for the prestigious Dadasaheb Phalke Award for 2005. 'The Award is given by the Government of India for outstanding contribution in the field of Indian Cinema. The award will be conferred on Shri Shyam Benegal by the Hon'ble President of India at a ceremony later this year. The award carries a cash prize of Rs.2,00,000/-, a Swarna Kamal and a shawl. Shri Shyam Benegal is considered one of the leading filmmakers in the country with his first feature film Ankur, which broke new grounds from the cinematic trends of the seventies. His films have been seen and acclaimed widely in India and at international film festivals for the past three decades. The core subjects of his films have been varied in nature but mainly centred around contemporary Indian experience. Problems of development, social and cultural change appear on many levels as a continuing thread in practically all his films. Apart from fiction features, he has made a number of documentaries on different subjects ranging from cultural anthropology and problems of industrialization, to music and so on. His work on television consists of several popular series based on international stories, short stories by well-known Indian writers and a mammoth 53 part series on the history of India based on Jawaharlal Nehru's book Discovery of India. He has also made an extra-mural educational series for rural children sponsored by UNICEF. Shyam Benegal taught mass-communication techniques between 1966 and 1973 and later took an active role in shaping film education as Chairman of the Film Television Institute of India during 1980-83 and 1989-92. He was part of the National Integration Council (1986-89) and the National Council of Art. The Government of India has conferred on him two of its most prestigious awards-Padma Shri (1976) and Padma Bhushan (1991). He has made 24 fiction features for the Cinema, several documentaries and TV series, Some of his other prominent films are Nishant, Manthan, Bhumika, Kondura, Junoon, Kalyug, Mandi, Trikal, Suraj Ka Satwan Ghoda, Mammo, Sardari Begum, Samar, The Making of the Mahatma, Zubeida and Netaji Subhash Chandra Bose. Shyam Benegal is presently a Member of Parliament, Rajya Sabha.

2221. (8-8-2007) NEW DELHI : All matters relating to 'Enemy Property' were being handled in the Department of Commerce by virtue of the subject under the business of the Department of Commerce. Government of India through a Presidential Notification dated 28th June 2007 has decided to transfer the subject to the Department of Internal Security, Ministry of Home Affairs. The change has been made keeping in view the advantage enjoyed by the Ministry of Home Affairs in having superior, closer and more sustained interface with the State Governments. This will facilitate the functioning of the Office of the Custodian of Enemy Property for India, located at Mumbai in liaising with the State Administration for effective implementation of the mandate given to him under the Enemy Property Act 1968.

2222. (8-8-2007) NEW DELHI : The Union Minister of Shipping, Road Transport and Highways, Thiru T. R. Baalu has approved the road improvement work in the State of Uttarakhand at a cost of Rs. 1419.45 lakh. The Minister has approved the proposal for construction of two-lane carriageway with improvement of geometrics from Km 176.0 to Km 182.35 of the National Highway-94 on Dharasu-Phoolchatti Section. The proposed stretch is single lane and its riding surface has a lot of cracks, undulation, sunken portion at several places and improper super elevation on curves. Since this stretch forms the part of the highways which leads to the pilgrimage place of Yamunotri Dham, there is heavy traffic during the 'Yatra season' starting from the month of April and continuing till the October end. Keeping in view the above, Thiru Baalu approved the proposal of widening and strengthening of the above stretch, which includes the provision of hill side cutting to make two lane road, slip clearance during the widening work, construction of Retaining wall, Breast Wall and Parapet and constructions of drains etc.

2223. (9-8-2007) NEW DELHI : Rajiv Gandhi Khel Ratna Award comprising cash award of Rs.5.00 lakh, a scroll of honour and a medal is given to one sportsperson in recognition of his/her spectacular and most outstanding performance in the field of sports. Arjuna Awards comprising a cash award of Rs.3.00 lakhs, statute and a scroll of honour are given to not more than 15 sportspersons in recognition of outstanding achievements at international level and for showing qualities of leadership, sportsmanship and sense of discipline. Dhyan Chand Awards for life-time achievement in sports and games comprising a cash award of Rs.3.00 lakhs, plaque and a scroll of honour are given to not more than 3 sportspersons in a particular year in recognition of their contribution to sports by their performance and continued contribution even after retirement from active sports career. Dronacharya Awards comprising cash award of Rs.3.00 lakh, a plaque and a scroll of honour are given to not more than 5 coaches for outstanding and meritorious work on a consistent basis to enable sportspersons to excel in international events. The Selection Committee constituted under the Chairmanship of Shri Kapil Dev to decide the Rajiv Gandhi Khel Ratna Award-2006, Arjuna Awards-2006 and Dhyan Chand Awards-2007 met on August 8, 2007 in Delhi and considered all the nominations received from the agencies authorized under the provisions of the respective schemes.

2224. (9-8-2007) NEW DELHI : The Minister of State for External Affairs, Shri Anand Sharma has said that Mahatma Gandhi's ideal of Satyagraha should be emulated by the world. It has not lost its relevance even today. Shri Sharma was speaking at a book release function here today. The book titled 'Gandhian Way-Peace, Nonviolence and Empowerment' edited by Shri Anand Sharma was released by the Prime Minister, Dr. Manmohan Singh in the presence of UPA chairperson Smt. Sonia Gandhi. Shri Sharma said the thought exchange of world leaders also found its place in the book. Referring to Satyagraha, Shri Sharma said that all the people of the world should revisit the essence of Satyagraha as it has not lost its purpose in the modern day world. He called Mahatma Gandhi a 'Yugpurush' and urged the world to eschew violence and emulate his ideals. The Defence Minister, Shri A.K. Antony and Smt. Tara Gandhi Bhattacharya from Gandhi Smriti were also present on the occasion.

2225. (9-8-2007) NEW DELHI : The Prime Minister, Dr. Manmohan Singh, launch a commemorative volume of "Gandhian Way-Peace, Nonviolence and Empowerment" here today. Following is the text of the Prime Minister's address at the occasion: "I am delighted that the International Conference on Peace, Non-Violence and Empowerment that we had organized under the inspiring leadership of Smt. Sonia Gandhi has generated this very impressive volume. I compliment all those associated with this valued effort. I hope this book will be used all over the world as a ready reference on the ideas and the ideals we associate with the name of Mahatma Gandhi. The theme of this conference was 'Gandhian Philosophy in the 21st Century.' It is a tribute to the continued and continuing relevance of Mahatma Gandhi's ideas and ideals, for our time and indeed for all time to come, that this Conference has attracted so much international attention. It is important for people as well as for the nations to recall the sacrifice and struggle of their national heroes. But then, Mahatma Gandhi was not just a national hero. His message had a global, universal relevance and continues to do so in our very troubled times. As long as we live in a world where there is injustice, where there is inequality, where there is violence, where there are greed and hatred, the message of Mahatma will ring true for all. Today is the 9th of August-the anniversary of the launch of the Quit India Movement. When Mahatma Gandhi gave that slogan, he was not giving a negative slogan of rejection of the world. He was giving a positive slogan of empowerment of our people. Mahatma Gandhi used Satyagraha as a means of arousing the latent energy of our people to fight for their freedom from a life of humiliation and seek a life of freedom and dignity. Gandhiji's heroic struggle and his philosophy based on truth and nonviolence inspired legendary freedom fighters and freedom movements worldwide. It was in South Africa that Gandhiji first experienced the regime of unjust discrimination which was sought to be enforced by the use of brute force. He exhorted the people not to surrender but to resist unitedly through peaceful civil disobedience. That is what led to the birth of Satyagraha, which over the years evolved into an effective revolutionary instrument of human empowerment. The commemoration of the centenary of the Satyagraha, therefore, in a befitting manner became our national duty. I am proud that the Indian National Congress, under the leadership of Smt. Sonia Gandhi, took the initiative to do so. The International Conference we organised brought together leaders of nations, freedom fighters, philosophers, social activists and civil society organizations from nearly every corner of the world. It provided a useful platform of interaction and an opportunity to discuss and debate the issues that were close to Gandhiji's heart, including peace and nonviolence, hunger and poverty, education and empowerment of the people. The Declaration adopted unanimously at the Conference reflected contemporary challenges confronting the world and reiterated the resolve of the world leaders to surmount them by invoking the Gandhian methods. I am very happy that one major demand of the Satyagraha Conference Declaration, to urge the United Nations to declare Mahatma Gandhi's date of birth (2nd October) as International Day of Non-Violence, has indeed met. To follow up the call of the Conference, India had tabled a Resolution in the United

Nations General Assembly, which received spontaneous support of an overwhelming majority of member countries. The decision was truly historic and universally welcomed. We are grateful to all those who supported us in this magnificent endeavour. This volume underscores once again that Mahatma Gandhi's message was not confined to his lifetime nor restricted to our people or only our region. It was and it is universal and all encompassing. He belongs to all humankind and the ideas and the values espoused by him will continue to inspire generations to come for a long time. This book is illuminated by the wisdom of world leaders who had honoured us by their presence in New Delhi. Their analytical and sincere observations will be read with keen interest by those who derive inspiration from the life and work of Mahatma Gandhi. May I take this opportunity to convey my very sincere appreciation of the leadership role played by the Congress President, Smt. Sonia Gandhi, in organizing this magnificent conference and in taking several initiatives to perpetuate the memory of Mahatma Gandhi for future generations. I also thank members of the Satyagraha Centenary Committee and all those associated with the New Delhi Conference and the publication of this volume. May your path be blessed."

2226. (9-8-2007) NEW DELHI : The Minister of State for Human Resource Development (HRD), Smt. D. Purandeswari stressed the need to strengthen the scheme of Community Polytechnics and Integrating Persons With Disabilities in the mainstream of Technical and Vocational Education and Polytechnic Education during XIth Plan, as these schemes give the real benefits to the people in the rural areas by way of attaining skills and getting self/ wage employment. Minister of State for HRD presided over a workshop to expand these two schemes during XIth Plan, on August 07, 2007. In the workshop, the Directors of Technical Education of the States and Union Territories and representatives of National Institute(s) of Technical Teachers Training and Research (NITTTRs) participated. At present, Community Polytechnic Scheme is being implemented from 669 All India Council for Technical Education (AICTE) approved polytechnics and the scheme of Integrating Persons With Disabilities in the mainstream of Technical and Vocational Education is being implemented through 50 (AICTE) approved polytechnics. The scheme of Community Polytechnics will be reviewed and revised for implementation during the XIth Plan. Secretary, Higher Education also highlighted the achievements of these schemes and appreciated the efforts made in their effective implementation. Besides expanding the schemes further to cover more polytechnics, the Secretary also opined that more number of polytechnics should be established as the ratio of Degree to Diploma students in the country is approximately 2:1, while it should ideally be 1:3. He informed that AICTE has already relaxed the infrastructure and other requirements for establishment of new polytechnics. He further stated that Public Private Partnership (PPP) may be encouraged to establish new polytechnics, specially in those Districts which do not have any polytechnic at present. The representatives of the State Governments also raised various issues concerning AICTE. These included delegation of powers to the State governments to accord approval for Diploma Level Institutions/ Programmes and effective consultation with the State Governments etc. Secretary (Higher Education) assured the States that AICTE shall consider these issues in their appropriate forums.

2227. (9-8-2007) NEW DELHI : Minister for Information and Broadcasting & Parliamentary Affairs, Shri Priya Ranjan Dasmunsi today released the DVDs 'Swarajnama' and 'Mahatma', brought out by Prasar Bharati. Based mainly on the material retrieved from Doordarshan archives, the two DVDs provide different facets of India's freedom struggle and the life of Mahatama Gandhi. The Minister presented the first copy of the DVD to Shri Girish Karnad. Speaking on the occasion, Shri Priya Ranjan Dasmunsi said that these DVDs would be of immense value for the youth, as they provide a deep insight into India's history of freedom movement. He praised Prasar Bharati's effort in bringing out these DVDs. The Minister said that Prasar Bharati has already launched a project of rendition of Gurudev Rabindranath Tagore's songs in Hindi and other Indian languages. He appealed for strengthening the public service broadcasting role of Pasar Bharati. 'Swarajnama' is directed by noted film personality Girish Karnad. Beginning with 1757, it recounts 190 years of India's freedom struggle, and is in a newscast format. 'Mahatama' has been directed by Brijendra Virehi. It remembers and focuses on the values that Mahatama loved and cherished. Noted Gandhian Smt. Nirmala Deshpande and Secretary, I&B, Smt. Asha Swarup were present on the occasion.

2228. (9-8-2007) NEW DELHI : A central team from the Ministry of Social Justice and Empowerment visited Gogmba and Kalol villages of Panchmahal district in Gujarat on 08.08.2007 to find out the truth behind the story of alleged confinement of an octogenarian by his son as told by a private TV Channel. Union Minister of Social Justice and Empowerment Smt. Meira Kumar rushed a team from her Ministry to the spot to take stock of the situation and to suggest measures. The news story has alleged that one Shri Jethabhai Makhwana, a resident of Gogumba village and also the village Sarpanch, has confined his father Shri Dudhabhai Khatubhai Makhwana for the last two years at his house. Expressing here deep concern for the octogenarian, Smt. Meira Kumar directed Shri Satyendra Prakash, Director, National Institute of Social Defence and officials of the District Disability Rehabilitation Centre, Nadian to visit Gogumba to render necessary help to the old man. The central team provided wheelchair and hearing aid to the old man who is in his mid eighties. He is frail and bedridden. The DDRC, Nadiad and Medial Officer of the nearby referral Hospital who had already examined Shri Dudhabhai have been directed for regular follow up. It was found that Shri Dudhabhai had been taken by his oldest daughter Smt. Kamlaben to her house in Kalol village in Panchmahal district. The other two daughters were also present in their sister's house. They informed that the story of confinement of their father by brother Jethabhai is false and was nothing but a conspiracy of Jethabhai's rivals of that village. The central team, accompanied by the officers of the State Social

Justice Department also met the Collector of Panchamahal who informed that though there were two contradictory reports in this regard, a cognizance note of the alleged confinement had been taken by the local police. He assured that the matter would be further investigated. Ministry of Social Justice and Empowerment, Government of India the nodal Ministry for the welfare of the older persons in India has already introduced a bill in the Parliament to ensure maintenance and welfare of the parents and senior citizens and to pre-empt any such incidence of harassment and deprivation to them.

2229. (9-8-2007) NEW DELHI : In India, agriculture is not a business carried out for profit, but a source of livelihood. Agriculture in India still engages about 60 per cent of the work force and contributes about a fifth of the GDP. A very large majority of the farmers/ cultivators belongs to the category of small and marginal holders. The number and proportion of such holdings have been growing over time and they depend on agriculture-based activities, to eke out their living. Therefore, what happens to small and marginal farmers has implications for the entire economy and people's livelihoods. Otherwise, they will only be losers in the process of globalization and liberalization. The viability of the small holdings is an important issue, and promoting agricultural diversification towards high value crops through an efficient marketing system is considered to be one of the means through which this can be achieved. Most agricultural commodity markets generally operate under the forces of demand and supply. However, with a view to protecting farmers' interest and to encourage them to increase production, the Government also fixes minimum support/ statutory prices for some crops and makes arrangements for their purchase by government agencies whenever their price falls below the support level. To achieve an efficient system of buying and selling of agricultural commodities, most of the State Governments and Union Territories have enacted legislations (APMC Act) to provide for regulation of agricultural produce markets. The basic objective of setting up of a network of physical markets has been to ensure reasonable gain to the farmers by creating environment in markets for fair play of supply and demand forces, regulate market practices and attain transparency in transactions. While in 1950, there were 286 regulated markets, today their number has reached 7600. Most of these regulated markets are wholesale markets. Besides, the country has 21,780 rural periodical markets, about 15% of which function under the ambit of regulation.

2230. (9-8-2007) NEW DELHI : Prof. Saifuddin Soz, Union Minister of Water Resources expressed the hope that India and Bangladesh would continue to tackle various problems in the water resources sector to better the lives of millions of people. After meeting the Bangladesh delegation today, he said that India and Bangladesh agreed to exchange the constructions details to execute river bank protection works in order to bring transparency and remove apprehensions from either side and recommended to Joint River Commission for consideration. A Bangladesh delegation led by Mr. Syed Mohammad Zobaer, Secretary of Water Resources of Bangladesh Government and comprising various other officers called on Prof. Saifuddin Soz, Union Minister of Water Resources here today. Smt. Gauri Chatterji, Secretary, Ministry of Water Resources, Government of India and other senior officers of the Ministry were also present. The Bangladesh delegation was in New Delhi for a two day meeting of the Secretaries of Water Resources of the Govt. of India and Govt. of Peoples Republic of Bangladesh to discuss pending issues between the two countries related to water resources sector. Earlier, 36th meeting of the Indo-Bangladesh Joint Rivers Commission (JRC), held in September, 2005 both sides discussed the issues relating to river bank protection works, lift irrigation schemes, dredging, drinking water supply schemes on common border rivers.

2231. (9-8-2007) NEW DELHI : The Ministry of New and Renewable Energy will celebrate Rajiv Gandhi Akshay Urja Diwas on 20th of this month. The main function will be organised at Hyderabad. Besides, other Districts and state capitals will also organize various programmes highlighting importance of new renewable energy sources. Renewable Energy Run, Rallies, Essay writing, Painting, Quiz competitions, Exhibitions will be organised all over country. At Hyderabad, National Half (21Km) Marathon for Men and Women will be organized through Sports Authority of Andhra Pradesh. The winners of the Marathon will get cash prize of Rs.50,000/- for each Men and Women. Three days Renewable Energy Exhibition from 20-22nd August, 2007 also will be organized. Administering of Renewable Energy pledge to over 10,000 school children will take place. Shri V.Subramanian, Secretary, Ministry of New and Renewable Energy said in Hyderabad today that new and renewable energy sources such as solar, biomass, wind and hydro will check environmental pollution and make energy needs for all sectors. He further said these sources are non-depleting and are available in most parts of the country throughout the year. Global warming and climate change are environmental hazards faced by all. In this situation, the Ministry tries to inculcate idea of using renewable energy through children so that the message reaches society at large. This is the reason, school children are invited to take pledge to use maximum renewable energy sources. Shri Subramanian further added that India had reached second position in Biogas development with installation of over 40.00 lakh Biogas plants and 4th position in Wind Energy development by achieving 7,300 MW power connecting to grids. Over 2 million sq. mt. solar collector area has also been achieved for Solar Hot Water, Solar Drier and other Solar thermal devices.

2232. (9-8-2007) NEW DELHI : The Government of India is targeting to achieve a growth rate of 4% in agriculture over the XIth Five Year Plan. Although agricultural production and growth are dictated by diverse factors such as credit and pricing policies, land reforms, etc., use and application of science and technology have significant role to play in enhancing the productivity and profitability of the sector. The two Ministries, Science & Technology (S&T) and Earth Sciences (ES), seek to contribute in realizing the challenging goal set by the Government for the agriculture sector. Accordingly, a brainstorming meeting was taken by the Minister Shri Kapil Sibal with over forty experts from the two Ministries to discuss about

"Reinvigorating Indian Agriculture through S&T". Briefing the media in New Delhi today Shri. Sibal said that the meeting resulted in a commitment to focus and strengthen those activities that could deliver visible and tenable outcomes in a period of about eighteen months for which a fast track approval system will be operationalised.

2233. (9-8-2007) NEW DELHI : India signed the Credit Agreement for the US$ 63 million Bihar Rural Livelihoods Project with the World Bank, here today. The Agreement was signed by Shri Madhusudan Prasad, Joint Secretary, Ministry of Finance on behalf of Government of India, Shri Navin Kumar, Principal Secretary, Department of Finance on behalf of the Government of Bihar and Ms. Isabel Guerrero, Country Director, India on behalf of the World Bank. The Bihar Rural Livelihoods Project, named "JEEVIKA" aims to improve rural livelihoods in Bihar through organizing institutions of the poor in 776 village Panchayats covering 4,000 villages in the districts of Nalanda, Gaya, Muzzafarpur, Madhubani, Khagaria, and Purnea. The project is expected to directly benefit about 2.9 million people belonging to 5,90,000 households. The project will help organize women from poor and disadvantaged households into vibrant and self managed institutions of the poor (self-help groups). These groups will be federated into village organization, which will receive project investments for various activities through a participatory micro-planning process. The village organizations in turn will be integrated as higher-level apex community-based organizations that will take up livelihood enhancement and income-generating activities, through developing partnerships and linkages with market institutions. The project will also partner with the public sector banking system and private microfinance institutions to enhance the flow of credit and insurance services to the poor, thereby reducing the burden of high cost debt that the poor in Bihar suffer from. The project will finance Community Investment Funds, designed to transfer financial and technical resources to the community organizations on a demand-driven basis through a participatory micro-planning process. The village organizations are expected to use this resource as a revolving fund to finance various economic and social activities through the self-help groups in the villages. International Development Agency (IDA) the World Bank's concessionary lending arm, is currently supporting five similar programmes in India with an outreach of about a million community groups and 10 million poor households across 60,000 villages in the states of Andhra Pradesh, Madhya Pradesh, Rajasthan, Chhattisgarh, and Tamil Nadu. These projects support the social and economic mobilization of the poor households into self-managed community organizations and facilitate development of linkages with the financial sector and the markets to enable the poor to become credit and investment worthy. The IDA credit has 35 years to maturity and a 10-year grace period.

2234. (9-8-2007) NEW DELHI : The National Commission for Enterprises in the Unorganised Sector (NCEUS) has advocated a "13 Point Action Programme" under four separate packages that should get "overriding and immediate priority", for the unorganized sector workers, in a report presented to the Prime Minister

Dr. Manmohan Singh yesterday. Addressing a press conference here today, Dr. Arjun Sengupta, Chairman, NCEUS said that the "Commission's Action Programme seeks to address core issues of social security and work conditions, through separate Bills." The Commission has recommended additional measures to make a difference to the lives of "77% of the Indian population who are currently earning less than Rs.20 a day", Dr. Sengupta informed. The first package of protective measures for unorganized workers includes National Minimum Social Security benefits like hospitalization benefit of Rs.15,000 per year; sickness allowance for 15 days @Rs.50/- per day and maternity benefit of Rs.1,000 to the worker/spouse. It further advocates life cover for all unorganized workers; old age pension of Rs.200 per month to all BPL workers above 60 and Provident Fund for all other registered workers. The scheme is to be implemented within a period of five years. The projected outlay to cover all agricultural workers is estimated at Rs.19,400 crore and non-agricultural at Rs.12,950 crore, Dr. Sengupta explained. The second package of measures for marginal and small farmers includes encouraging lending to small and marginal farmers by setting up a Credit Guarantee Fund in NABARD to provide cover against defaults on loans to this segment. Other actions for marginal and small farmers include accelerating land and water management programmes and setting up of Farmers' Debt Relief Commissions. The third package of measures for the Non-Agricultural Sector includes creating a National Fund for the Unorganised Sector (with an initial corpus of Rs.5000 crore funded by the Central Government, public sector banks etc.) Other actions for non-farm sector include improving credit flow to the sector, giving incentive to Self Help Groups and adopting a 'Growth Pole' model for cluster development. Finally, the fourth package of measures to expand Employment and improve Employability advocated strengthening self-employment programmes, expanding the National Rural Employment Programme to all districts and increasing employability through skill development, Dr. Sengupta added.

2235. (9-8-2007) NEW DELHI : Executive Director of Partners in Population and Development (PPD), Dhaka, Bangladesh, Mr. Harry S. Jooseery met the Union Minister for Health & Family Welfare, Dr. Anbumani Ramadoss today and apprised him of the new and emerging scenario, priorities and strategies in the areas of reproductive health, population and development. Secretary, Health & Family Welfare, Shri Naresh Dayal and senior officials from the Ministry were also present on the occasion. During the discussions, Shri Jooseery also extended an invitation to the Minister for the next Board meeting of PPD to be held in Islamabad, Pakistan. India is a Member of the Partners in Population and Development, an Inter-governmental alliance of developing countries established during the International Conference on Population and Development (ICPD) held in Cairo in 1994 and has a Permanent Observer status in the United Nations General Assembly. Current members are Bangladesh, Benin, China, Colombia, Egypt, the Gambia, India, Indonesia, Jordan, Kenya, Mali, Mexico, Morocco, Nigeria, Pakistan, Senegal, Thailand, Tunisia, Uganda, Yemen and Zimbabwe.

Annual membership fee of US $ 20,000 is paid to PPD regularly. China is the present Chairman of the Executive Board of the PPD. PPD holds it's Annual Board Meetings regularly and India hosted the 10th Annual Board Meeting at Agra during 21-23 November 2005. The 12th Annual Board Meeting was held in Beijing, China from 7-13 November 2006 in collaboration with the National Population and Family Planning Commission (NPFPC) of the Government of China. The next Board Meeting is to be held on 8th November 2007 in Islamabad, Pakistan. This meeting will be preceded by a 2-day International Workshop on Universal Access to Reproductive Health within the context of ICPD and Millennium Development Goals (MDGs).

2236. (9-8-2007) NEW DELHI : Ramsar Definition states, "Wetlands are areas of marsh, fen, peat land or water, whether natural or artificial, permanent or temporary, with water that is static or flowing, fresh, brackish or salt, including areas of marine water the depth of which at low tide does not exceed six meters." Wetlands are life support system, winter resorts for variety of birds for shelter and feeding, effective in flood control, waste water treatment etc.

2237. (9-8-2007) NEW DELHI : The Government is finalizing the National Tribal Policy to safeguard interest of tribals and to bring them into mainstream. The proposed policy would suggest measures for rehabilitation and resettlement of the tribals and ensure that tribals affected with developmental activities become partners in the growth. This was disclosed by the Minister for Tribal Affairs, Shri P.R. Kyndiah addressing the celebration of World Indigenous peoples' Day organized by Indian Confederation of Indigenous and tribal peoples, here today. Highlighting the various measures taken by the Government for the welfare of tribal people, Shri Kyndiah said that the Government is working on various schemes for the empowerment of tribals and to reduce gap in human development index of the tribal population and the general population so that they could bring them at part by 2020. He said wherever displacement of tribals is made in the interest of the nation, they should be taken into confidence and compensated with land. If large-scale displacement is involved, then the project should be reconsider to minimize the displacement, the Minister added. Shri Kyndiah also informed that Government has finalise rules for the implementation of the Scheduled Tribes and Other Traditional Forest Dwellers (Recognition of Forest Rights Act). With the implementation of the act, traditional forest dwellers and Scheduled Tribes would become owner of their land and would have access to the forest resources.

2238. (9-8-2007) NEW DELHI : The Ministry of Railways has allowed nine more banks to install Automated Teller Machines (ATMs) at railway stations in all Zonal Railways. These banks together will set up ATMs at 440 locations, making the total ATM locations 1833 across the countries. Out of these, more than 1200 locations will have e-ticketing facilities through Internet kiosks installed alongside the ATMs. These nine banks are; Bank of Rajasthan, Bank of India, Indian Overseas Bank, ICICI Bank, UTI Bank, UCO Bank, HDFC Bank, Syndicate Bank and J&K Bank. Out of 440 locations, ATMs will be set up at 75 stations in Western Railway, at 65 stations in Central Railway, 63 in Northern Railway, 54 in Southern Railway, 53 in North Western Railway, 24 in West Central Railway, 21 in South Central Railway, 20 in Eastern Railway, 15 in South Eastern Railway, 12 in South Western Railway, 11 in North Central Railway, 6 each East Central & South East Central Railways and 5 each in East Coast, North Eastern & Northeast Frontier Railways. With a view to improve the disbursal of railway tickets, a large number of ATMs are being installed at various railway stations. Last year, the Ministry of Railways had entered into an agreement with State Bank of India for installation of ATMs at 682 railway stations across the country followed by allowing six more banks to install ATMs at 711 locations. These banks are; Canara Bank, Punjab National Bank, Indian Bank, Dena Bank, Union Bank of India and Bank of Baroda. The Ministry of Railways has asked all these banks to complete the installation of all ATMs by 31st March 2008.

2239. (9-8-2007) NEW DELHI : The Ministry of Rural Development has released an amount of Rs. 29.76 crore to the State Government of Uttarakhand towards balance of first instalment of funds against the provisional allocation of Rs. 89.30 crore made for the Government of Uttarakhand under Accelerated Rural Water Supply Programme (Normal) of Rajiv Gandhi National Drinking Water Mission, during the year 2007-08. Up to 15 per cent of funds released under this sanction may be utilized for Operation & Maintenance and up to 5 per cent of funds may be spent for taking sustainability measures. States have been requested to delegate powers for management of Rural Water Supply Schemes through the Panchayati Raj Institutions (PRIs) as per the Constitution of India. As such Operation and Maintenance of the completed RWS Scheme should be transferred to the PRIs. No expenditure shall be incurred on taking water quality problems form the present release, as there is a separate allocation for the purpose. This release is being made for execution/completion of schemes to provide safe drinking water facilities to rural habitations and schools under the Centrally Sponsored ARWSP. Priorities set in ARWSP guidelines and through other instructions issued from time to time shall be followed for coverage of rural habitations and rural schools.

2240. (9-8-2007) NEW DELHI : An amount of Rs. 74.12 lakh as balance Central share has been released by the Ministry of Rural Development for planning and development of watershed projects for implementation of Centrally Sponsored Scheme 'Desert Development Programme (DDP)' in Kargil district of Jammu & Kashmir during 2007-08. An amount of Rs. 273.97 lakh has already been released out of the due amount of Rs.348.10 lakh. The grant is towards plan expenditure and its utilization is subject to the terms and conditions laid down in the guidelines for watershed development issued from time to time. For empowering the village community through Panchayati Raj Institutions (PRIs) to undertake the area development progammes on watershed basis with financial and technical support from the Government, the Ministry of Rural Development has initiated 'Hariyali'.

Under this initiative, all the on-going area development programmes, such as Integrated Wasteland Development Programmes (IWDP), Drought Prone Areas Programme (DPAP) and Desert Development Programme (DDP) are to be implemented through the PRIs. Approval for Six Laning of existing Four lane National Highways of selected 4 sub-projects under NHDP Phase-V.

2241. (9-8-2007) NEW DELHI : The Union Cabinet today gave its approval for placement of the contract with M/s Arianespace (of Europe) for the launching of GSAT-8/INSAT-4G at a price not exceeding US$ 67.5 million (Rs. 297 Crores @ 1 US$ = Rs.44), along with an option for on additional launch and also waiver of the Bank Guarantee requirements. This will facilitate the timely launch of GSAT-8/INSAT-4G in 2008-09 timeframe. GSAT-8/INSAT-4G will provide 18 high power Ku-band (DTH quality) transponders to the INSAT System along with the second Geo Stationary augmentation payload for the GPS and GEO Augmented navigation (GAGAN). This will facilitate a number of services in the field of navigation, telecommunications, TV broadcasting and distribution, Ku-band VSAT, broadband services, digital video broadcast, rural areas communications and distance education.

2242. (9-8-2007) NEW DELHI : The Union Cabinet today gave its approval for opening of Indian Missions / Post in Reykjavik (Iceland), Guatemala City, Niamey (Niger), Bamako (Mali) and Guangzhou (China) and also for creation of one Consulate General and four Ambassadors in the Grade of Joint Secretary. This decision will help in order to safeguard and promote India's strategic, economic and political interests in the respective regions. The opening of the Missions and creation of the posts is likely to be undertaken during 2007-08.

2243. (10-8-2007) NEW DELHI : The Independence Day celebrations on 15th August are synonymous with the unfurling of the national flag by the Prime Minister on the Red Fort, in Delhi in the morning. As we celebrate the 61st Independence Day, we take a look at the ceremony at the Red Fort down the years. Pandit Jawaharlal Nehru, the first Prime Minister of independent India, unfurled the national flag for the first time on the Red Fort on August 16, 1947. Since then the hoisting of the tricolour atop the Red Fort has become a symbol of Indian independence and our pride. Figuratively speaking, Pandit Nehru hoisted the flag atop the Red Fort 17 times since 1947, the maximum number of times by any Indian Prime Minister during the sixty-one years of our independence. His daughter Indira Gandhi comes a close second, unfurling the tricolour 16 times. Next in the line, Shri Atal Behari Vajpayee has hoisted flag atop the Red Fort six times, followed by Rajiv Gandhi and PV Narasimha Rao-five each, Lal Bahadur Shastri in 1964 and '65, Morarji Desai in 1977 and '78, Charan Singh in 1979, Shri VP Singh-1990, Shri HD Deve Gowda-1996 and Shri Inder Kumar Gujral-1997. Interestingly, Gulzari Lal Nanda, in his two brief tenures as interim Prime Minister, never hoisted the flag, besides Chandra Shekhar. The present Prime Minister Dr.

Manmohan Singh will be hoisting the national flag atop the Red Fort for the 4th time on August 15, 2007. We are releasing herewith photographs of the 12 different Prime Ministers who have unfurled the National Flag from the Ramparts of the Red Fort.

2244. (10-8-2007) NEW DELHI : The Indian Diaspora constitutes a significant economic, social and cultural force in the world. Overseas Indians estimated at over twenty five million are spread across 110 countries. Their industry, enterprise, economic strength, education and professional skills are widely recognized. The creation of the Ministry of Overseas Indian Affairs (MOIA) acknowledges the fact that the welfare of overseas Indians needs mainstream attention. The heterogeneous Indian Diaspora spread across eight major regions of the world is a product of different waves of migration over hundreds of years and have distinct expectations from the home country. The focus of the Ministry therefore is to establish an institutional framework to benefit from networks with and among Overseas Indians based on three value propositions. Through multi-skilled market driven entities spawned by MOIA and with knowledge partners from the private sector. States will be stakeholder partners as OI supported initiatives have to be anchored in the States and MOIA will stay small, facilitate activity on the ground and drive policy changes.

2245. (10-8-2007) NEW DELHI : The Prime Minister Dr. Manmohan Singh will unfurl the National Flag on the ramparts of the Red Fort on 15th of this month to celebrate the 61st Independence Day. After unfurling the Tricolor, Dr. Manmohan Singh will address the Nation. On arrival at Lahore Gate of Red Fort, the Prime Minister will be received by the Defence Minister Shri AK Antony and the Minister of State for Defence Shri M M Pallam Raju, Minister of State for Defence Production Rao Inderjit Singh and Defence Secretary Shri Vijay Singh. The Defence Secretary will introduce General Officer Commanding, Delhi Area, Major General KJS Oberoi to the Prime Minister. The GOC Delhi Area will then conduct the Prime Minister to the Saluting Base where a combined inter-services and police guard will present general salute to the Prime Minister. Thereafter, Dr. Manmohan Singh will inspect the guard of honour. The Guard of Honour contingent for the Prime Minister will consist of five officers and 96 men drawn from Army, Navy, Air Force and Delhi Police. This year, the Air Force being the coordinating agency, the Guard of Honour will be commanded by Wg Cdr Y M Nadkarni. The Army Contingent by Major Ravi Kumar Maney, Sena Medal, Naval Contingent by Lt. Cdr R Jai Kumar, Air Force Contingent by Sq. Ldr. Kamran Nazeer and the Police Contingent will be commanded by Shri M I Haider, ACP. Delhi Police Contingent has been participating in the Independence Day Parade ever since India became independent and has a distinct place among the other contingents because of its smartly dressed Jawans with a height between 5' 11" to 6' 4".